The Treasury of
AMERICAN POETRY

The Treasury of AMERICAN POETRY

Selected and with an Introduction by

NANCY SULLIVAN

DOUBLEDAY & COMPANY, INC.
Garden City, New York

Library of Congress Cataloging in Publication Data
Main entry under title:
Treasury of American poetry.
1. American poetry. I. Sullivan, Nancy.
PS584.T7 811′.008 77-92232
ISBN: 0-385-12033-X

Printed in the United States of America

ACKNOWLEDGMENTS

GRATEFUL acknowledgment is made for permission to include excerpts from the following copyrighted publications:

"Recipe for an Ocean in the absence of the Sea," "On Arrival," and "209 Canal" from *Findings*, by Richard Howard, copyright © 1964, 1968, 1969, 1970, 1971 by Richard Howard. "209 Canal" appeared originally in *Poetry*. Reprinted by permission of Atheneum Publishers.

"Salami" from *They Feed They Lion*, by Philip Levine, copyright © 1968, 1969, 1970, 1971, 1972 by Philip Levine. Reprinted by permission of Atheneum Publishers.

"Manos Karastefanís" from *Divine Commedies*, by James Merrill, copyright © 1976 by James Merrill and appeared originally in *Atlantic Monthly*. Reprinted by permission of Atheneum Publishers.

"The Mad Scene" from *Nights and Days*, by James Merrill, copyright © 1966 and appeared originally in *Poetry*. Reprinted by permission of Atheneum Publishers.

"The Grand Canyon" from *Water Street*, by James Merrill, copyright © 1960, 1961, 1962 by James Merrill. Reprinted by permission of Atheneum Publishers.

"Last Words" from *The Firescreen*, by James Merrill, copyright © 1964, 1966, 1967, 1968, 1969 by James Merrill and appeared originally in *Atlantic Monthly*. Reprinted by permission of Atheneum Publishers.

"King Midas" and "The Hand" from *Selected Poems*, by Howard Moss, copyright © 1960, 1971 by Howard Moss. "The Hand" appeared originally in *The New Yorker*, and "King Midas" in Howard Moss's *A Winter Come, A Summer Gone*. Reprinted by permission of Atheneum Publishers.

"The Woman at the Washington Zoo" from *The Woman at the Washington Zoo*, by Randall Jarrell, copyright © 1960 by Randall Jarrell. Reprinted by permission of Atheneum Publishers.

"Keeping Things Whole" from *Reasons For Moving*, by Mark Strand, copyright © 1968 by Mark Strand. Reprinted by permission of Atheneum Publishers.

"Biography," "Ka 'Ba," "Poem for Half-White College Students," from *Black Magic Poetry 1961–1967*, by LeRoi Jones, copyright © 1969 by LeRoi Jones. Reprinted by permission of The Bobbs-Merrill Company, Inc., and The Sterling Lord Agency, Inc.

"Judy-One," "Mixed Sketches," "Change Is Not Always Progress," from *We Walk the Way of the New World*, by Don L. Lee, copyright © 1970 by Don L. Lee (Haki R. Madhubuti). Reprinted by permission of Broadside Press.

"A Different Image," "Roses and Revolution," from *Cities Burning*, by Dudley Randall, copyright © 1968 by Dudley Randall. Reprinted by permission of Broadside Press.

"The Profile on the Pillow," from *Black Poetry*, by Dudley Randall, copyright © 1969 by Dudley Randall. Reprinted by permission of Broadside Press.

"Nikki-Rosa," from *Black Judgement*, by Nikki Giovanni, copyright © 1970 by Nikki Giovanni. Reprinted by permission of Broadside Press.

"Kidnap Poem," from *Re:Creation*, by Nikki Giovanni, copyright © 1970 by Nikki Giovanni. Reprinted by permission of Broadside Press.

"Riot," "An Aspect of Love, Alive in the Ice and Fire," from *Riot*, by Gwendolyn Brooks, copyright © 1969 by Gwendolyn Brooks. Reprinted by permission of Broadside Press.

"Hard Rock Returns to Prison from the Hospital for the Criminal Insane," "Haiku," from *Poems from Prison*, by Etheridge Knight, copyright © 1968 by Etheridge Knight. Reprinted by permission of Broadside Press.

"Howl" (Parts I and II), "A Supermarket in California," from *Howl &*

Other Poems, by Allen Ginsberg, copyright © 1956, 1959 by Allen Ginsberg. Reprinted by permission of City Lights Books.

"A Prophecy," from *The Fall of America*, by Allen Ginsberg, copyright © 1972 by Allen Ginsberg. Reprinted by permission of City Lights Books.

"Skin Diving in the Virgins" and "Letter from an Island," first appearing in *The New Yorker*, and "Roethke Plain," excerpted from *Skin Diving in the Virgins*, by John Malcolm Brinnin, copyright 1943, 1944, 1949, 1950, 1951, 1952, 1953, copyright © 1956, 1958, 1960, 1962, 1963, 1970 by John Malcolm Brinnin. Reprinted by permission of Delacorte Press/Seymour Lawrence.

"My Papa's Waltz," copyright 1942 by Hearst Magazines, Inc.; "Elegy for Jane," copyright 1950 by Theodore Roethke; "The Waking," copyright 1953 by Theodore Roethke; "In a Dark Time," copyright © 1960 by Beatrice Roethke, Administratrix of the Estate of Theodore Roethke; "Frau Bauman, Frau Schmidt & Frau Schwartze," copyright 1952 by Theodore Roethke; "I Knew a Woman," copyright 1954 by Theodore Roethke; "Cuttings," copyright 1948 by Theodore Roethke; "Cuttings (later)," copyright 1948 by Theodore Roethke; "In Evening Air," copyright © 1960 by Beatrice Roethke, Administratrix of the Estate of Theodore Roethke; "Wish for a Young Wife," copyright © 1963 by Beatrice Roethke, Administratrix of the Estate of Theodore Roethke; all from *The Collected Poems of Theodore Roethke*. Reprinted by permission of Doubleday & Company, Inc.

"The Light Woman's Song," "Rhyme for the Child as a Wet Dog," copyright © 1969 by Quest; "Just," copyright © 1973 by Judith Johnson Sherwin, from *Impossible Buildings*, by Judith Johnson Sherwin. Reprinted by permission of Doubleday & Company, Inc.

"The Night a Sailor Came to Me in a Dream," copyright © 1968 by Diane Wakoski; "The Father of My Country," copyright © 1967 by Diane Wakoski; "An Apology," from *Inside the Blood Factory*, copyright © 1962, 1968 by Diane Wakoski. Reprinted by permission of Doubleday & Company, Inc.

"Enough," copyright © 1972 by Esquire, Inc.; "Two Shapes," copyright © 1975 by the Pembroke Magazine, from *The Past Now*, by Arthur Gregor. Reprinted by permission of Doubleday & Company, Inc.

"The Mind Is an Ancient Famous Capital," "I Am a Book I Neither Wrote Nor Read," from *Summer Knowledge*, by Delmore Schwartz, copyright © 1959 by Delmore Schwartz. Reprinted by permission of Doubleday & Company, Inc.

"We Become New," copyright © 1973 by Marge Piercy; "The Spring Offensive of the Snail," originally published in *The Liberated Guardian* and later appearing in *To Be of Use*, copyright © 1969, 1971, 1973 by

Marge Piercy, from *To Be of Use,* by Marge Piercy. Reprinted by permission of Doubleday & Company, Inc.

"History," copyright © 1971 by Commonweal Publishing Company, Inc., and "Lyric," copyright © 1970 by Arthur Gregor, from *Arthur Gregor: Selected Poems.* Reprinted by permission of Doubleday & Company, Inc.

"Walking Past Paul Blackburn's Apartment on 7th Street," from *Virtuoso Literature for Two and Four Hands,* by Diane Wakoski, copyright © 1974 by Lakes and Prairies. Reprinted by permission of Doubleday & Company, Inc.

"The Shade-Seller," copyright © 1965 by Commonweal Publishing Company, Inc.; "The Matadors," "When the Five Prominent Poets," copyright © 1974 by Josephine Jacobsen, from *The Shade-Seller,* by Josephine Jacobsen. Reprinted by permission of Doubleday & Company, Inc.

"Shore," "Country Villa," "Amsterdam," from *Chartres and Prose Poems,* by Jean Garrigue. Reprinted by permission of The Eakins Press Foundation.

"The Marshes," "For the Market," from *Givers and Takers 1,* by Jane Mayhall. Reprinted by permission of The Eakins Press Foundation.

"The Human Animal," from *Givers and Takers 2,* by Jane Mayhall. Reprinted by permission of The Eakins Press Foundation.

"First Fig," "Recuerdo," Sonnet XCIX "Love is not all: it is not meat nor drink," Sonnet XLV "Euclid alone has looked on Beauty bare," Sonnet XLII "What lips my lips have kissed, and where, and why," Sonnet XIX "And you as well must die, beloved dust," Sonnet XI "I shall forget you presently, my dear," from *Collected Poems,* by Edna St. Vincent Millay, published by Harper & Row, copyright 1921, 1922, 1923, 1931, 1948, 1950, 1951, © 1958 by Edna St. Vincent Millay and Norma Millay Ellis. Reprinted by permission of Norma Millay Ellis.

#14 "Life, friends is boring. We must not say so."; #94 "Ill lay he long, upon this last return"; #100 "How this woman came by the courage, how she got"; #104 "Welcome, grinned Henry, welcome, fifty-one!"; #172 "Your face broods from my table, Suicide."; #262 "You couldn't bear to grow old, but we grow old."; #299 "The Irish have the thickest ankles in the world"; from *The Dream Songs,* by John Berryman, copyright © 1959, 1962, 1963, 1964, 1966, 1967, 1968, 1969 by John Berryman. Reprinted by permission of Farrar, Straus & Giroux, Inc.

"The Armadillo," "House Guest" from *The Complete Poems,* by Elizabeth Bishop, copyright © 1957, 1968 by Elizabeth Bishop. These poems originally appeared in *The New Yorker.* Reprinted by permission of Farrar, Straus & Giroux, Inc.

"The Death of the Ball Turret Gunner," "90 North," "Losses" from *The Complete Poems*, by Randall Jarrell, copyright 1941, 1945, 1948 by Mrs. Randall Jarrell; copyright renewed 1969, 1972, 1975 by Mrs. Randall Jarrell. Reprinted by permission of Farrar, Straus & Giroux, Inc.

"Sailing Home from Rapallo," "Skunk Hour," "The Public Garden," "Night Sweat," "History," "Reading Myself" from *Selected Poems*, by Robert Lowell, copyright 1944, 1946, 1947, 1950, 1951, © 1956, 1959, 1960, 1961, 1962, 1963, 1964, 1965, 1966, 1967, 1968, 1969, 1970, 1973, 1976 by Robert Lowell; copyright renewed 1972, 1974, 1975 by Robert Lowell. Reprinted by permission of Farrar, Straus & Giroux, Inc.

"He said," "Anaesthesia," "April" from *Ordinary Things* by Jean Valentine, copyright © 1972, 1973, 1974 by Jean Valentine. "Pilgrims," from *Pilgrims* by Jean Valentine, copyright © 1965, 1966, 1967, 1968, 1969 by Jean Valentine. Reprinted by permission of Farrar, Straus & Giroux, Inc.

"From Creature to Ghost," by Pauline Hanson. Reprinted by permission of Folder Editions.—Daisy Aldan

"Telling It," "Eclipses," "His Necessary Darkness," "To My Body," from *Telling It*, by Nancy Sullivan, copyright © 1975 by Nancy Sullivan. Reprinted by permission of David R. Godine Publisher.

"The Brain Cells," "White Apples," "The Raisin," first appearing in *The New Yorker*, "The Town of Hill," from *The Town of Hill*, by Donald Hall, copyright © 1975 by Donald Hall. Reprinted by permission of David R. Godine Publisher.

"Chicago," "Fog," "The Harbor," "I Am the People, the Mob," from *Chicago Poems*, by Carl Sandburg, copyright 1916 by Holt, Rinehart and Winston, Inc.; copyright 1944 by Carl Sandburg. Reprinted by permission of Harcourt Brace Jovanovich, Inc.

"Cool Tombs," from *Cornhuskers*, by Carl Sandburg, copyright 1918 by Holt, Rinehart and Winston, Inc.; copyright © 1956 by Carl Sandburg. Reprinted by permission of Harcourt Brace Jovanovich, Inc.

"The Quaker Graveyard in Nantucket," from *Lord Weary's Castle*, copyright 1946, © 1974 by Robert Lowell. Reprinted by permission of Harcourt Brace Jovanovich, Inc.

"my father moved through dooms of love," "anyone lived in a pretty how town," "as freedom is a breakfastfood," copyright 1940 by E. E. Cummings; copyright © 1968 by Marion Morehouse Cummings. Reprinted from *Complete Poems 1913–1962*, by E. E. Cummings, by permission of Harcourt Brace Jovanovich, Inc.

"Spring is like a perhaps hand," copyright 1925 by E. E. Cummings. Reprinted from *Complete Poems 1913–1962*, by E. E. Cummings, by permission of Harcourt Brace Jovanovich, Inc.

"i thank you God for most this amazing," copyright 1947 by E. E. Cummings; copyright © 1975 by Nancy T. Andrews. Reprinted from *Complete Poems 1913–1962*, by E. E. Cummings, by permission of Harcourt Brace Jovanovich, Inc.

"i carry your heart," copyright 1952 by E. E. Cummings. Reprinted from *Complete Poems 1913–1962*, by E. E. Cummings, by permission of Harcourt Brace Jovanovich, Inc.

"a man who had fallen among the thieves," "next to of course god america i," copyright 1926 by Horace Liveright; copyright 1954 by E. E. Cummings. Reprinted from *Complete Poems 1913–1962*, by E. E. Cummings, by permission of Harcourt Brace Jovanovich, Inc.

"pity this busy monster," copyright 1944 by E. E. Cummings; copyright © 1972 by Nancy T. Andrews. Reprinted from *Complete Poems 1913–1962*, by E. E. Cummings, by permission of Harcourt Brace Jovanovich, Inc.

"Buffalo Bill's," "the Cambridge ladies," copyright 1923, 1951 by E. E. Cummings. Reprinted from *Complete Poems 1913–1962*, by E. E. Cummings, by permission of Harcourt Brace Jovanovich, Inc.

"Love Calls Us to the Things of This World," from *Things of This World*, copyright © 1956 by Richard Wilbur. Reprinted by permission of Harcourt Brace Jovanovich, Inc.

"Juggler," first appearing in *The New Yorker*, copyright 1949 by Richard Wilbur. Reprinted from *Ceremony and Other Poems*, by Richard Wilbur, by permission of Harcourt Brace Jovanovich, Inc.

"Museum Piece," from *Ceremony and Other Poems*, by Richard Wilbur, copyright 1948, 1949, 1950 by Richard Wilbur. Reprinted by permission of Harcourt Brace Jovanovich, Inc.

"The Love Song of J. Alfred Prufrock," "Gerontion," "The Waste Land," "Journey of the Magi," "Little Gidding," from *Collected Poems 1909–1962*, by T. S. Eliot, copyright 1936 by Harcourt Brace Jovanovich, Inc.; copyright © 1963, 1964 by T. S. Eliot. Reprinted by permission of the publisher and Faber and Faber Limited.

"Yet Do I Marvel," "A Brown Girl Dead," "(Epitaphs) for a Lady I Know," from *On These I Stand*, by Countee Cullen, copyright 1925 by Harper & Row, Publishers, Inc.; renewed 1953 by Ida M. Cullen. Reprinted by permission of Harper & Row, Publishers, Inc.

"We Real Cool," "The Bean Eaters," copyright © 1959 by Gwendolyn Brooks; "Sadie and Maud," copyright 1945 by Gwendolyn Brooks Blakely, from *The World of Gwendolyn Brooks* (1971), by Gwendolyn Brooks. Reprinted by permission of Harper & Row, Publishers, Inc.

"Cut," "Lady Lazarus," "Edge," from *Ariel*, by Sylvia Plath, copyright © 1963 by Ted Hughes. Reprinted by permission of Harper & Row, Publishers, Inc., and Ms. Olwyn Hughes.

"After Love," "A Family Man," "At the End of the Affair," from *The Nightmare Factory*, by Maxine Kumin, copyright © 1970 by Maxine Kumin. Reprinted by permission of Harper & Row, Publishers, Inc.

"After Experience Taught Me . . . ," copyright © 1964 by W. D. Snodgrass; "Lobsters in the Window," copyright © 1963 by W. D. Snodgrass, originally appearing in *The New Yorker*, both from *After Experience* (1968), by W. D. Snodgrass. Reprinted by permission of Harper & Row, Publishers, Inc.

Poems #67, 80, 108, 165, 173, 214, 249, 280, 288, 303, 318, 465, 516, 697, 712, 844, 970, 986, 1052, 1129, 1263, 1659, from *The Poems of Emily Dickinson*, edited by Thomas H. Johnson (Cambridge, Mass.: The Belknap Press of Harvard University Press), copyright 1951, © 1955 by the President and Fellows of Harvard College. Reprinted by permission of the publishers and the Trustees of Amherst College.

"The Woman Who Loved to Cook," from *Half-Lives*, by Erica Jong, copyright © 1971, 1972, 1973 by Erica Mann Jong. Reprinted by permission of Holt, Rinehart and Winston, Publishers.

"Provide, Provide," "The Silken Tent," "Home Burial," "Dust of Snow," "Mending Wall," "After Apple Picking," "The Oven Bird," "Birches," "The Road Not Taken," "Tree at My Window," "Fire and Ice," "Stopping by Woods on a Snowy Evening," "Acquainted with the Night," "To Earthward," "Desert Places," "Design," "Neither Out Far Nor in Deep," "Nothing Gold Can Stay," from *The Poetry of Robert Frost*, edited by Edward Connery Lathem, copyright 1916, 1923, 1928, 1930, 1939, © 1969 by Holt, Rinehart and Winston; copyright 1936, 1942, 1944, 1951, © 1956, 1958 by Robert Frost; copyright © 1964, 1967, 1970 by Lesley Frost Ballantine. Reprinted by permission of Holt, Rinehart and Winston, Publishers.

"Walt Whitman," "Being Somebody," "Who," "Through You," by Edwin Honig. Reprinted by permission of the author.

"Night in the Forest," "The Bear," "The Correspondence School Instructor Says Goodbye to His Poetry Students," from *Body Rags*, by Galway Kinnell, copyright © 1967 by Galway Kinnell. Reprinted by permission of Houghton Mifflin Company.

"Ringing the Bells," "Her Kind," from *To Bedlam and Part Way Back*, by Anne Sexton, copyright © 1960 by Anne Sexton. Reprinted by permission of Houghton Mifflin Company.

"The Truth the Dead Know," from *All My Pretty Ones,* by Anne Sexton, copyright © 1961 by Anne Sexton. Reprinted by permission of Houghton Mifflin Company.

"Wanting to Die," from *Live or Die,* by Anne Sexton, copyright © 1966 by Anne Sexton. Reprinted by permission of Houghton Mifflin Company.

"Ars Poetica," "You Also, Gaius Valerius Catullus," "The End of the World," from *Collected Poems, 1917–1952,* by Archibald MacLeish, copyright 1952 by Archibald MacLeish. Reprinted by permission of Houghton Mifflin Company.

"Merchant Marine," from *To All Appearances,* by Josephine Miles. Copyright © 1946 by Josephine Miles. Reprinted by permission of the University of Illinois Press.

"Poetry Concert," "Grandfather," "Nightmare Begins Responsibility," from *Nightmare Begins Responsibility,* by Michael S. Harper. Reprinted by permission of the University of Illinois Press.

"Reason," "Belief," from *Poems 1930–1960,* by Josephine Miles, copyright © 1960 by Indiana University Press. Reprinted by permission of the publisher.

"Poem to My Sister, Ethel Ennis, Who Sang 'The Star-Spangled Banner' at the Second Inauguration of Richard Milhous Nixon, January 20, 1973," "Getting Down to Get Over," "Queen Anne's Lace," by June Jordan. Reprinted by permission of the author.

"Tributes to Henry Ford," by Richard Kostelanetz, from *Visual Language,* published by Assembling Press, copyright © 1968, 1970 by Richard Kostelanetz. Reprinted by permission of the author.

#341, #970, #113, copyright 1929 by Martha Dickinson Bianchi, copyright © 1957 by Mary L. Hampson; #1333, copyright 1914, 1942 by Martha Dickinson Bianchi, from *The Complete Poems of Emily Dickinson,* edited by Thomas H. Johnson. Reprinted by permission of Little, Brown and Company.

"The Turtle," copyright 1940 by Ogden Nash; "The Terrible People," copyright 1933, © 1955 by Ogden Nash, from *Verses from 1929 On,* by Ogden Nash. Reprinted by permission of Little, Brown and Company.

"The Anatomy of Happiness," from *The Face Is Familiar,* by Ogden Nash, copyright 1938 by Ogden Nash. Reprinted by permission of Little, Brown and Company.

"The Illumination," copyright © 1970 by Stanley Kunitz; "After the Last Dynasty," copyright © 1962 by Stanley Kunitz, from *The Testing Tree: Poems,* by Stanley Kunitz. Reprinted by permission of Little, Brown and Company.

"From *The Bridge:* 'Proem: To Brooklyn Bridge,'" "Black Tambourine," "Garden Abstract," "Voyages" I–VI, "Repose of Rivers," "At Melville's Tomb," "To Emily Dickinson," "Chaplinesque," from *The Complete Poems and Selected Letters and Prose of Hart Crane,* edited by Brom Weber, copyright 1933, © 1966 by Liveright Publishing Corporation. Reprinted by permission of Liveright Publishing Corporation.

"The Sheaves," "New England," from *Collected Poems,* by E. A. Robinson, copyright 1925 by Edwin Arlington Robinson; renewed 1953 by Ruth Nivison and Barbara R. Holt. Reprinted by permission of Macmillan Publishing Co., Inc.

"Eros Turannos," from *Collected Poems,* by E. A. Robinson, copyright 1916 by Edwin Arlington Robinson; renewed 1944 by Ruth Nivison. Reprinted by permission of Macmillan Publishing Co., Inc.

"Mr. Flood's Party," from *Collected Poems,* by E. A. Robinson, copyright 1921 by Edwin Arlington Robinson, renewed 1949 by Ruth Nivison. Reprinted by permission of Macmillan Publishing Co., Inc.

"Poetry," "A Grave," copyright 1935 by Marianne Moore, renewed 1963 by Marianne Moore and T. S. Eliot; "Spenser's Ireland," copyright 1941 by Marianne Moore, renewed 1969 by Marianne Moore; all from *Collected Poems,* by Marianne Moore. Reprinted by permission of Macmillan Publishing Co., Inc., and Faber and Faber Limited.

"Off to Patagonia," copyright © 1972, 1973, 1974, 1975, 1976 by Theodore Weiss, originally appearing in *Antaeus;* "As You Like It," copyright © 1972 by Theodore Weiss, originally published in *Encounter,* from *Fireweeds,* by Theodore Weiss. Reprinted by permission of Macmillan Publishing Co., Inc.

"Yes, But . . . ," from *The World Before Us,* by Theodore Weiss, copyright © 1970 by Theodore Weiss. Reprinted by permission of Macmillan Publishing Co., Inc.

"The Fire at Alexandria," copyright © 1959 by Theodore Weiss, originally published in *Poetry;* "Barracks Apt. 14," copyright © 1957 by Theodore Weiss; "An Egyptian Passage," copyright © 1957 by Theodore Weiss, originally published in *The Kenyon Review;* all from *Outlanders,* by Theodore Weiss. Reprinted by permission of Macmillan Publishing Co., Inc.

"Abraham Lincoln Walks at Midnight," "The Congo," copyright 1914 by Macmillan Publishing Co., Inc.; renewed 1942 by Elizabeth C. Lindsay; "General William Booth Enters into Heaven," copyright 1913 by Macmillan Publishing Co., Inc., from *Collected Poems,* by Vachel Lindsay. Reprinted by permission of Macmillan Publishing Co., Inc.

"Simon Legree–A Negro Sermon," from *Chinese Nightingale,* by Vachel Lindsay, copyright 1917 by Macmillan Publishing Co., Inc., renewed 1945 by Elizabeth C. Lindsay. Reprinted by permission of Macmillan Publishing Co., Inc.

"The Lost Children," from *The Lost World*, by Randall Jarrell. Copyright © 1965 by Randall Jarrell. Reprinted by permission of Macmillan Publishing Co., Inc.

"Bleecker Street," copyright 1947, 1953, © 1959, 1960, 1962, 1963, 1964, 1966, 1967 by Jean Garrigue; "Epitaph for My Cat," copyright © 1964 by Jean Garrigue, from *New and Selected Poems*, by Jean Garrigue. Reprinted by permission of Macmillan Publishing Co., Inc.

"Movie Actors Scribbling Letters Very Fast in Crucial Scenes," "Song for 'Buvez Les Vins du Postillon," from *Studies for an Actress and Other Poems*, by Jean Garrigue. Copyright © 1968, 1969, 1970, 1971, 1972, 1973 by the Estate of Jean Garrigue. Reprinted by permission of Macmillan Publishing Co., Inc.

"A Circle, a Square, a Triangle and a Ripple of Water," copyright © 1962, 1967, 1968, 1969, 1972, 1973 by Jane Cooper; "Waiting," copyright © 1973 by Jane Cooper, from *Maps & Windows*, by Jane Cooper. Reprinted by permission of Macmillan Publishing Co., Inc.

"The Hill," "Fiddler Jones," "Petit, the Poet," from *Spoon River Anthology*, by Edgar Lee Masters, copyright 1914, 1915 by Edgar Lee Masters; "Marx the Sign Painter," "Unknown Soldiers," from *The New Spoon River*, copyright 1924 by Edgar Lee Masters, renewed 1968 by The Macmillan Company. Reprinted by permission of Mrs. Ellen C. Masters.

"Marriage," from *The Happy Birthday of Death*, by Gregory Corso, copyright © 1960 by New Directions Publishing Corporation. Reprinted by permission of the publisher.

"Constantly risking absurdity and death," "The pennycandystore beyond the El," "Frightened by the sound of my own voice," "In Goya's greatest scenes we seem to see," from *A Coney Island of the Mind*, by Lawrence Ferlinghetti, copyright © 1958 by Lawrence Ferlinghetti. Reprinted by permission of New Directions Publishing Corporation.

"O Taste and See," "The Ache of Marriage," from *O Taste and See*, by Denise Levertov, copyright © 1964 by Denise Levertov Goodman. Reprinted by permission of New Directions Publishing Corporation.

"Mad Song," from *Relearning the Alphabet*, by Denise Levertov, copyright © 1970 by Denise Levertov Goodman. Reprinted by permission of New Directions Publishing Corporation.

"Salutation," "A Pact," "The River-Merchant's Wife: a Letter," "In a Station of the Metro," "Portrait d'une Femme," "A Virginal," "Hugh Selwyn Mauberley" I–XII, "Envoi," from *Personae*, by Ezra Pound, copyright 1926 by Ezra Pound. Reprinted by permission of New Directions Publishing Corporation.

"Canto III," from *The Cantos,* by Ezra Pound, copyright 1934 by Ezra Pound. Reprinted by permission of New Directions Publishing Corporation.

"Florida," "Woman," from *Amulet,* by Carl Rakosi, copyright © 1967 by Callman Rawley. Reprinted by permission of New Directions Publishing Corporation.

"In a Warm Bath," from *Ere-Voice,* by Carl Rakosi, copyright © 1971 by Callman Rawley. Reprinted by permission of New Directions Publishing Corporation.

"Meeting the Mountains," from *Regarding Wave,* by Gary Snyder, copyright © 1970 by Gary Snyder. Reprinted by permission of New Directions Publishing Corporation.

"The Bath," from *Turtle Island,* by Gary Snyder, copyright © 1974 by Gary Snyder. Reprinted by permission of New Directions Publishing Corporation.

"The Young Housewife," "Proletarian Portrait," "Flowers by the Sea," "Nantucket," "Young Sycamore," "The Widow's Lament in Springtime," "Tract," "Danse Russe," "Queen-Anne's-Lace," "Spring and All" (By the road . . .), "The Red Wheelbarrow," "This Is Just to Say," "Between Walls," "To a Poor Old Woman," "On Gay Wallpaper," "Smell!" from *Collected Earlier Poems,* by William Carlos Williams, copyright 1938 by New Directions Publishing Corporation. Reprinted by permission of the publisher.

"The Horse Show," "The Dance," "A Sort of Song," from *Collected Later Poems,* by William Carlos Williams, copyright 1944, 1949 by William Carlos Williams. Reprinted by permission of New Directions Publishing Corporation.

"Paterson, Book I," from *Paterson,* by William Carlos Williams, copyright 1946 by William Carlos Williams. Reprinted by permission of New Directions Publishing Corporation.

"Song for a Dancer," "Lute Music," "Further Advantages of Learning," "Fifty," "Only Years," from *Collected Shorter Poems,* by Kenneth Rexroth, copyright 1944, © 1956 by New Directions Publishing Corporation; copyright 1949, 1952, © 1966 by Kenneth Rexroth. Reprinted by permission of New Directions Publishing Corporation.

"Oread," "Heat," "Stars Wheel in Purple," "Helen," "The Mysteries Remain," from *Selected Poems,* by H. D. (Hilda Doolittle), copyright 1925, 1953, © 1957 by Norman Holmes Pearson. Reprinted by permission of New Directions Publishing Corporation.

"Viable," "Cut the Grass," "The Confirmers," "Clarity," from *Collected Poems, 1951–1971,* by A. R. Ammons, copyright © 1972 by A. R. Ammons. Reprinted by permission of W. W. Norton & Company, Inc.

"Peeling Onions," "Attention," "Living in Sin," "Two Songs," "Reforming the Crystal," "Dialogue," "The Ninth Symphony of Beethoven Understood at Last as a Sexual Message," from *Poems, Selected and New, 1950–1974*, by Adrienne Rich, copyright © 1975, 1973, 1971, 1969, 1966 by W. W. Norton & Company, Inc.; copyright © 1967, 1963, 1962, 1961, 1960, 1959, 1958, 1957, 1956, 1955, 1954, 1953, 1952, 1951 by Adrienne Rich. Reprinted by permission of W. W. Norton & Company, Inc.

"The Fury of Aerial Bombardment," "The Groundhog," from *Collected Poems 1930–1976*, by Richard Eberhart, copyright © 1960, 1976 by Richard Eberhart. Reprinted by permission of Oxford University Press, Inc., and Chattos & Windus, Ltd.

"Hatteras Calling," "Herman Melville," "The Wedding," from *Collected Poems, Second Edition*, by Conrad Aiken, copyright © 1970 by Conrad Aiken. Reprinted by permission of Oxford University Press, Inc.

"And change with hurried hand has swept these scenes," "Under the mountain, as when first I knew," "Thin little leaves of wood fern, ribbed and toothed," "An upper chamber in a darkened house," "Here, where the red man swept the leaves away," from *The Complete Poems of Frederick Goddard Tuckerman*, edited with an introduction by N. Scott Momaday, copyright © 1965 by Oxford University Press, Inc. Reprinted by permission of the publisher.

"Nails," "The House on Buder Street," from *Nails*, by Gary Gildner, copyright © 1975 by Gary Gildner. Reprinted by permission of the University of Pittsburgh Press.

"Meditation Six," "Meditation Eight," "Huswifery," "Upon a Spider Catching a Fly," from *The Poetical Works of Edward Taylor*, edited by Thomas H. Johnson, copyright Rockland, 1939; Princeton University Press, 1943. Reprinted by permission of Princeton University Press.

"Bearded Oaks," copyright 1942; renewed 1970 by Robert Penn Warren; "Original Sin, A Short Story," copyright 1942 by Robert Penn Warren, from *Selected Poems 1923–1975*, by Robert Penn Warren. Reprinted by permission of Random House, Inc.

"April Inventory," copyright © 1957 by W. D. Snodgrass; "The Campus on the Hill," copyright © 1958 by W. D. Snodgrass; "The Operation," copyright © 1959 by W. D. Snodgrass, from *Heart's Needle*, by W. D. Snodgrass. Reprinted by permission of Alfred A. Knopf, Inc.

"Wholesome," "His Plans for Old Age," from *Hazard the Painter*, by William Meredith, copyright © 1973 by William Meredith. Reprinted by permission of Alfred A. Knopf, Inc.

"Winter Verse for His Sister," copyright © 1967 by William Meredith, first appearing in *The New Yorker*, from *Earth Walk: New and Selected*

Poems, by William Meredith. Reprinted by permission of Alfred A. Knopf, Inc.

"The Open Sea," from *The Open Sea and Other Poems*, by William Meredith, copyright 1953 by William Meredith. Reprinted by permission of Alfred A. Knopf, Inc.

"Good Times," "For deLawd," from *Good Times*, by Lucille Clifton, copyright © 1969 by Lucille Clifton. Reprinted by permission of Random House, Inc.

"Cezanne," copyright 1946 by Random House, Inc.; "Susie Asado," Act III, Scene 2, from *Four Saints in Three Acts*, copyright 1934 and renewed 1962 by Alice B. Toklas, from *Selected Writings of Gertrude Stein*. Reprinted by permission of Random House, Inc.

"Cross," "The Negro Speaks of Rivers," from *Selected Poems*, by Langston Hughes, copyright 1926 by Alfred A. Knopf, Inc., and renewed 1954 by Langston Hughes. Reprinted by permission of Alfred A. Knopf, Inc.

"The Colossus," from *The Colossus and Other Poems*, by Sylvia Plath, copyright © 1961 by Sylvia Plath. Reprinted by permission of Alfred A. Knopf, Inc., and Olwyn Hughes.

"Peter Quince at the Clavier," "Sunday Morning," copyright 1923 and renewed 1951 by Wallace Stevens; "Men Made Out of Words," copyright 1947 by Wallace Stevens; "Anecdote of the Jar," "The Emperor of Ice Cream," copyright 1923 and renewed 1951 by Wallace Stevens; "The Idea of Order at Key West," copyright 1936 and renewed 1964 by Holly Stevens; "No Possum, No Sop, No Taters," copyright 1947 by Wallace Stevens; "Not Ideas About the Thing but the Thing Itself," copyright 1954 by Wallace Stevens; "The Glass of Water," copyright 1942 by Wallace Stevens and renewed 1970 by Holly Stevens; "Thirteen Ways of Looking at a Blackbird," "A High-Toned Old Christian Woman," copyright 1923 and renewed 1951 by Wallace Stevens; "Of Modern Poetry," copyright 1942 by Wallace Stevens and renewed 1970 by Holly Stevens, from *The Collected Poems of Wallace Stevens*. Reprinted by permission of Alfred A. Knopf, Inc.

"Bells for John Whiteside's Daughter," "Here Lies a Lady," copyright 1924 by Alfred A. Knopf, Inc., and renewed 1952 by John Crowe Ransom; "Piazza Piece," "Blue Girls," "Janet Waking," "The Equilibrists," "Survey of Literature," copyright 1927 by Alfred A. Knopf, Inc., and renewed 1955 by John Crowe Ransom, from *Selected Poems, Third Edition, Revised and Enlarged*, by John Crowe Ransom. Reprinted by permission of the publisher.

"So Beautiful Is the Tree of Night," from *Across Countries of Anywhere*, by Pauline Hanson, copyright © 1957 by Pauline Hanson. Reprinted by permission of Alfred A. Knopf, Inc.

"Meditations in an Emergency," copyright 1954 by Maureen Granville-Smith, Administratrix of the Estate of Frank O'Hara; "An Abortion," copyright © 1969 by Maureen Granville-Smith, Administratrix of the Estate of Frank O'Hara; "Homosexuality," copyright © 1970 by Maureen Granville-Smith, Administratrix of the Estate of Frank O'Hara, from *The Collected Poems of Frank O'Hara*, edited by Donald Allen. Reprinted by permission of Alfred A. Knopf, Inc.

"Hurt Hawks," copyright 1928 and renewed 1956 by Robinson Jeffers; "Shine, Perishing Republic," copyright 1925 and renewed 1953 by Robinson Jeffers, from *The Selected Poetry of Robinson Jeffers*. Reprinted by permission of Random House, Inc.

"But I Am Growing Old and Indolent," from *The Beginning and the End and Other Poems*, by Robinson Jeffers, copyright © 1963 by Garth Jeffers and Donnan Jeffers. Reprinted by permission of Random House, Inc.

"Miniver Cheevy," from *The Town Down the River*, by Edwin A. Robinson, copyright 1907 by Charles Scribner's Sons. Reprinted by permission of the publisher.

"Richard Cory," "Charles Carville's Eyes," "Reuben Bright," "George Crabbe," "Credo," from *The Children of the Night*, by E. A. Robinson. Reprinted by permission of Charles Scribner's Sons.

"The Language," "The Window," from *Words*, by Robert Creeley, copyright © 1964 by Robert Creeley. Reprinted by permission of Charles Scribner's Sons and Calder and Boyars Ltd.

"The Warning," from *For Love*, by Robert Creeley, copyright © 1962 by Robert Creeley. Reprinted by permission of Charles Scribner's Sons and Calder and Boyars Ltd.

"The Man Who Married Magdalene," from *Poets of Today II, Good News of Death and Other Poems*, by Louis Simpson, copyright © 1955 by Louis Simpson. Reprinted by permission of Charles Scribner's Sons.

"Things to Do Around a Lookout," "Mid-August at Sourdough Mountain Lookout," by Gary Snyder. Reprinted by permission of the author.

"Ode to the Confederate Dead," from *Poems*, by Allen Tate, copyright © 1960, 1965 by Allen Tate. Reprinted by permission of The Swallow Press, Inc., Chicago.

"London Pavement Artist," "Green Frog at Roadstead," from *Violence and Glory: Poems 1962–1968*, by James Schevill, copyright © 1969 by James Schevill. Reprinted by permission of The Swallow Press, Inc., Chicago.

"Freud, Dying in London," "Huck Finn at Ninety," from *The Buddhist Car and Other Characters*, by James Schevill, copyright © 1973 by James Schevill. Reprinted by permission of The Swallow Press, Inc., Chicago.

printed by permission of Vanderbilt University Press. "Not Seeing Is Believing," reprinted by permission of Paul Petrie.

"Fear of Death," first appearing in *The New Yorker*, from *Self-Portrait in a Convex Mirror*, by John Ashbery, copyright © 1974 by John Ashbery. Reprinted by permission of The Viking Press.

"Rent" and "Childhood in Jacksonville, Florida," first published in *Aphra*, and "Praise," first published in *Transatlantic Review*, all by Jane Cooper. Reprinted by permission of the author.

"Tenderness, ache on me, and lay your neck," from *The Zodiac*, by James Dickey, copyright © 1976 by James Dickey. Reprinted by permission of Doubleday & Company, Inc.

"The Runner," by Gary Gildner. Reprinted by permission of the author.

"On the Night in Question," "After the Second Operation," "The Serious Merriment of Women," and "Daily the Ocean Between Us," by Patricia Goedicke. Reprinted by permission of the author.

"Grandfather," by Michael S. Harper, was first published in the *Ohio Review*. Reprinted by permission of the author.

"It Is the Season," by Josephine Jacobsen, was originally published in *Yankee* and reprinted in *Best Poems of 1975*; "Rainy Night at the Writers' Colony" was originally published in *The New Boston Review* and reprinted as a Folger Poetry Series Broadsheet, 1975–76. Reprinted by permission of the author.

"City Sparrow," by Jane Mayhall. Reprinted by permission of the author.

"Fugue," "The Western Approaches," "Speculation" from *The Western Approaches* (University of Chicago Press), copyright © 1976 by Howard Nemerov. Reprinted by permission of the author.

"Power," by Adrienne Rich, copyright © 1975 by Adrienne Rich. Reprinted by permission of the author.

"A Screamer Discusses Methods of Screaming," by James Schevill; first published in *Antaeus*. Reprinted by permission of the author.

For N. A. J. P.

INTRODUCTION

The title of this anthology suggests the thrust of its contents: The treasures inside are the definition of a country characterized by diversity, power, stability, and strife. Because of the complexity of American life and of America's heritage, it is easier to explain what American poetry is not than to explain what it is. There is, however, no denying that the myriad events and personalities which produced this country provoked and shaped a poetic heritage which can only be defined as a national treasure. Not every poem in this anthology is a jewel in the literal sense, but each one, verbal emerald as well as verbal opal, has its intrinsic quality and character. Collectively they shape a unique and haphazard crown for a monarchless country.

Both Ralph Waldo Emerson and Wallace Stevens dub the poet as an *emperor*. This is not an easy role in a country always more given to peddlers of ice cream than to verbal drummers. How then did American poetry come into itself? And what *is* American poetry?

In the beginning there was only the water on which the little boats sailed slowly toward what would so much later be the United States. Most vessels had decidedly English crews and passengers, bringing with them a language, mores, and idiosyncrasies which would in good time affect every aspect of world culture. What they found when they got here were Indians and hardship. Not that those Indians did not have their own cultural heritage, but it was far distant from the one which would establish itself and finally diminish the Indian on his own terrain. Regrettably, until quite recently American literature had little to do with Indians, even though one stalked through a poem or novel every now and then.

On those first boats only a very few books occupied precious cargo space. Might even one of them have been a book of poetry? Unlikely, unless you considered the Bible "literature," which most of the Colonists did not. More realistically, the few crates of books probably contained volumes on practical or religious subjects. Most of the first settlers were people without much interest in literature, people interested in hacking out a new life in the cruel wilderness of the New World, and this world was a far cry from the Europe they had left, and was light-years removed from modern Europe. Very few Englishmen could read and few who made the trip here had much notion about where they were going or what the place would look like. The New World was not a subject that interested English landscape painters as keenly as it did artists on the Continent. Most immigrants to Colonial America visualized the country in their imaginations: a vague, terrifying, misleading, inhospitable, and inaccessible place. They were right. What a miracle that anyone ever ventured to settle here at all!

The second miracle was that Anne Bradstreet was among those early settlers. Born before Shakespeare died, she was to enjoy an honor she would never know about: she was America's first poet of any merit, despite being a woman.

Anne Bradstreet wrote like the English gentlewoman she was. Although perhaps better off than some and certainly better educated than most women in the Colonies, she was a transplanted English subject writing English poetry in a foreign and puzzling land. But she had an eye for the homely detail, the unique situation. When she writes about the burning of her house, the experience takes on the poignant universality of such a disaster anywhere *but* with the undeniable detail if not language that classifies it as American. Any immigrant who followed her could identify with the particular sadness of losing treasured souvenirs of a vanished homeland. It was a sexless tragedy couched in domestic language, an example of individualism in an early Colonial New England where individualism was almost completely masculine. There were no Roman matrons in Massachusetts wielding the power behind their emperor squires. More than likely, they were wielding axes or spinning cloth, not tales or odes.

For years poets in this country have been accused of writing against the grain of American life, of emphasizing the alienation from rather than the affection for this country which nurtured even if it did not nourish them. America's poets have been both traditionalists and revolutionaries, but even the most revolutionary of them has been deeply influenced by the very traditions they sought to escape. In a country founded on the amazing notion of religious and ethnic variety, a diversity of poetry was inevitable, a diversity characterized at first by a mutual wariness and awkwardness beneath its religious zeal. As American poetry escalated so did its aims and its subject matter. The poets got used to the country and vice versa.

In 1855 the idealistic Walt Whitman in his Preface to *Leaves of Grass* could say, "The United States themselves are essentially the greatest poem" and though whistling in a poetic dark he could dream: "The proof of a poet is that his country absorbs him as affectionately as he has absorbed it." It was not that easy for him or for the poets who jogged and waddled after him. Some thirty years later, a more mellow and realistic Whitman would admit that he had not sprung newborn from the head of an American Zeus and that his roots too were in a past he had once rejected. Whitman, the poet of the Now, admitted, although not very modestly, that "he could not have written *Leaves of Grass* had not Homer, Aeschylus, Sophocles, Dante and Shakespeare preceded and nourished him." He finally realized that there was room on the ranch of American poetry for more variety and whimsicality—much as he prided himself on possessing a large slice of the latter—than he had thought. Even the antithetical Poe was given acreage.

But at every point, Whitman's blessing and encouragement were bestowed not only on himself but on poets who were his contemporaries and, more importantly, on the poets yet to come. Sounding more than a little like Muhammad Ali, Whitman carped, "Of all nations the United States with veins full of poetical stuff most needs poets and will doubtless have the greatest and use them the greatest."

Whitman's contemporary and mentor, Ralph Waldo Emerson, shared his exalted views about the poet's proper place in American society. Emerson saw the poet as an "emperor in his own right" and America as "a poem in our eyes; its ample geography dazzles the imagination and it will not wait long for metres." Emerson was ready to greet the first American poet, the genius he had not yet encountered: "The poet has a new thought; he has a whole new experience to unfold; he will tell us how it was with him, and all men will be the richer in his fortune. For the experience of each new age requires a new confession, and the world seems always waiting for its poet." Emerson's essay "The Poet" complained that America as yet had no poet of genius: he had not then discovered Whitman. Perhaps had he known about Emily Dickinson, he might have thought the same. At any event, in Whitman America had its first modern poet.

Only sixteen poets precede Whitman in this anthology, some of them notable and popular: Bryant, Emerson, Longfellow, Whittier, and Poe, for example, but none of these viewed in the hindsight of the present moment seems as powerful as Whitman or as durable. Whitman discovered America, and the poets who followed discovered him.

In bucking the powerful current of a European tradition, particularly an English tradition, American poetry began to make its own waves. Whitman was chief oarsman. He wrote in the American grain and about the American grain; he wrote about Brooklyn and Long Island and about the Midwest and Far West. He never looked back with longing at a London he had never seen or at a Europe he had never revered. Others followed—some obviously, some secretly. And a singular poet, Emily Dickinson, wrote out of a situation so universal that it was beyond nationality: "I'm Nobody! Who are you? / Are you—Nobody—too?" American poetry had become itself: muscular, delicate, free, and controlled.

In 1939 Robert Frost described his impressions of poetic construction: "The figure a poem makes. It begins in delight and ends in wisdom. The figure is the same as for love." Frost, alternately admired or dismissed as a modern-day New England sage, realized that poetry evolved out of the country of the heart and spirit without regard to the nationality stamped on the poet's passport. But his idiom was unmistakably American and male. The tweed of his poems was woven on a loom of beautiful compromises which resulted in a poetry we call "unmistakably American," even though his first recognition and publication occurred in England. So it continues. To write against the grain of American life is to write in its grain, since the American experience has always involved controversy and diversity.

Amid the diversity of taste are certain undeniable giants whose abundant presence in such an anthology is guaranteed, indeed demanded: Bradstreet, Emerson, Whitman, Dickinson, Robinson, Frost, Eliot, Stevens, Williams, Lowell. But what then of the less well known, ultra contemporary, or neglected poets? How, within the limitations of space and funds for permission rights, can the anthologist choose between Karl Shapiro and Carl Rakosi, for example? None of my decisions were easy ones.

My choices of contemporary poets have been influenced by a number of factors; the quality of their poems, however, has been the dominant one. It would be foolish to suggest that my own idiosyncrasies and taste have not influenced some of these decisions, but the more important truth is that every poet in this anthology, in my opinion, deserves the few or many pages he or she inhabits. For many

I wish there had been more space, and for certain poets, omitted for one reason or another, at least some space.

I also attempted to select poems, particularly in the latter half of the book, that reflect something of the changing styles, content, and concerns of twentieth-century poetry in the United States. The fascinating technological and scientific changes in the modern world, recognized and absorbed into his poems so long ago by Whitman, became in modern America an essential factor for the poet to assimilate. Hart Crane's "The Bridge" and William Carlos Williams' "Paterson" are but two obvious examples of twentieth-century poetry grappling with contemporary life. Not that poets always liked everything they discovered in this urbanized, technological world. Some of them bucked the system with all of its ramifications, but in so doing continued to write in the American grain by writing against it. Allen Ginsberg's "Howl," for instance, jolted the country into a new although bitter awareness of itself and its destiny.

Awareness on various levels has earmarked recent American poetry: political and cultural, personal and regional, sexual and racial. The vitality of poetry by contemporary black poets has been extraordinary, as has the new wave of poetry by women writing out of and about their experiences as women. There have always been women poets, but never, with the exception of Emily Dickinson, have they written with more knowledge of themselves or with more integrity and power.

A definition of American poetry is, hopefully, what you will find in the following pages: a wealth of poems by a variety of American poets both male and female, both black and white. Together they represent a cultural and poetic treasury, one which encompasses all of America's diversity, energy, and wisdom.

With a shaky belief in a theory that holds that this country is most accurately represented in poetry by poets who write in American English and by those most fully influenced by the American experience whether they liked it or not, I have reluctantly omitted poems written by the early American Indians, by Hispanics, and by other vital ethnic groups. This decision was partially the result of space limitations. Any anthology, no matter how comprehensive, is ultimately limited. Let this anthology be judged not on what is *not* in it but on what *is*, and may those who read it derive joy and strength from its pages.

NANCY SULLIVAN

CONTENTS

Introduction xxi

ANNE BRADSTREET, 1612–1672

To My Dear and Loving Husband 1
In Reference to Her Children, 23 June 1659 1
The Flesh and the Spirit 4
Deliverance from a Fit of Fainting 7
Some Verses upon the Burning of Our House, July 10th, 1666 7
The Prologue 9
The Author to Her Book 11

EDWARD TAYLOR, 1645?–1729

Huswifery 12
6. Meditation. Canticles 2:1. I am . . . the Lily of the Valleys 13
8. Meditation. John 6:51. I Am the Living Bread 13
11. Meditation. Isaiah 25:6. A Feast of Fat Things 15
Upon a Spider Catching a Fly 16

PHILIP FRENEAU, 1752–1832

The Wild Honey Suckle 18
On a Honey Bee 19
To a Caty-did 20
The Hurricane 22
To Sir Toby 23
On the Emigration to America and Peopling the Western Country 25

Literary Importation 27
The American Soldier 28
A Warning to America 29
To a Noisy Politician 30
Tobacco 30
The Indian Convert 31
The Indian Burying Ground 32

PHILLIS WHEATLEY (Phillis Peters), 1753?–1784

To the University of Cambridge in New England 34
To the King's Most Excellent Majesty 35
To a Lady on the Death of Her Husband 35
On Being Brought from Africa to America 36
An Hymn to the Morning 37
On Virtue 38

JOEL BARLOW, 1754–1812

The Hasty Pudding 39

ROYALL TYLER, 1757–1826

Gambling 50
A Love Song 52

WILLIAM CULLEN BRYANT, 1794–1878

Thanatopsis 53
The Yellow Violet 55
Inscription for the Entrance to a Wood 56
To a Waterfowl 57
A Forest Hymn 58
A Meditation on Rhode Island Coal 62
To the Fringed Gentian 65
The Prairies 65
The Poet 69
To Cole, the Painter, Departing for Europe 70
"Oh Fairest of the Rural Maids" 71
The Tides 72
The Death of Lincoln 73

RALPH WALDO EMERSON, 1803–1882

Concord Hymn 74
Brahma 74
The Rhodora 75
Each and All 76
The Problem 77
Woodnotes 79
The Snowstorm 80
Days 81
Hamatreya 81
  Earth Song 82
Experience 83
Forbearance 84
Compensation 84
The Past 85
Ode Inscribed to W. H. Channing 86
Give All to Love 89
Terminus 90
Good-bye 92

HENRY WADSWORTH LONGFELLOW, 1807–1882

Hymn to the Night 93
A Psalm of Life 94
My Lost Youth 95
Divina Commedia 98
Chaucer 100
Milton 101
Keats 101
In the Churchyard at Cambridge 102
The Jewish Cemetery at Newport 103
Mezzo Cammin 105
Nature 105
Snow-flakes 106
The Fire of Drift-wood 106
Seaweed 108
The Cross of Snow 110
The Tide Rises, the Tide Falls 110
Aftermath 111

JOHN GREENLEAF WHITTIER, 1807–1892

Telling the Bees 112
Ichabod 114
Maud Muller 115
Snow-bound 119
Proem 139

OLIVER WENDELL HOLMES, 1809–1894

Old Ironsides 141
My Aunt 142
The Deacon's Masterpiece or, The Wonderful "One-Hoss Shay" 143

EDGAR ALLAN POE, 1809–1849

Dreams 147
A Dream Within a Dream 148
Sonnet—To Science 149
To Helen 149
The City in the Sea 150
The Sleeper 151
The Haunted Palace 153
Dreamland 155
The Raven 156
To One in Paradise 160
The Bells 161
Ulalume—A Ballad 164
Eldorado 167
Annabel Lee 168
Israfel 169

JONES VERY, 1813–1880

Today 171
The Hand and Foot 172
The Eagles 172
The Garden 173
On Visiting the Graves of Hawthorne and Thoreau 173
Thy Brother's Blood 174
The Dead 174

The Slave 175
The Fugitive Slaves 175
On the Completion of the Pacific Telegraph 176

HENRY DAVID THOREAU, 1817–1862

What's the Railroad to Me? 177
Light-winged Smoke, Icarian Bird 177
Woof of the Sun, Ethereal Gauze 178
I Am a Parcel of Vain Strivings Tied 178

JAMES RUSSELL LOWELL, 1819–1891

from *A Fable for Critics:* 180
Emerson 182
Bryant 183
Hawthorne 185
Cooper 186
Poe 187
Irving 188
Lowell 188
Auspex 189
The First Snowfall 190

HERMAN MELVILLE, 1819–1891

The Maldive Shark 192
The Portent 192
The March into Virginia 193
Malvern Hill 194
The Berg 195
In the Prison Pen 196
"Formerly a Slave" 197
The Martyr 198
Old Age in His Ailing 199

WALT WHITMAN, 1819–1892

Song of Myself 200
Out of the Cradle Endlessly Rocking 257
I Sit and Look Out 263
When Lilacs Last in the Dooryard Bloomed 263

O Captain! My Captain! 272
Good-bye My Fancy! 273
Joy, Shipmate, Joy! 273
To a Locomotive in Winter 274
A Noiseless Patient Spider 275
Facing West from California's Shores 275
On the Beach at Night Alone 276
When I Heard the Learn'd Astronomer 276
The Dalliance of the Eagles 277
Cavalry Crossing a Ford 277
A Sight in Camp in the Daybreak Gray and Dim 278
The Wound-dresser 278
Vigil Strange I Kept on the Field One Night 281
Crossing Brooklyn Ferry 282
As I Ebb'd with the Ocean of Life 288
There Was a Child Went Forth 290

A Sampler of Hymns, Spirituals and Songs:

We Raise de Wheat 293
Black Soldier's Civil War Chant 293
Raise a "Rucus" To-night 294
from a Slave Marriage Ceremony 295
I Thank God I'm Free at Las' 295
Crucifixion 296
Joshua Fit de Battle of Jericho 297
Deep River 297
The Star-Spangled Banner 298
Battle Hymn of the Republic 299
America the Beautiful 299

FREDERICK GODDARD TUCKERMAN, 1821–1873

And Change with Hurried Hand Has Swept These Scenes 301
Under the Mountain, as When First I Knew 301
Thin Little Leaves of Wood Fern, Ribbed and Toothed 302
An Upper Chamber in a Darkened House 302
Here, Where the Red Man Swept the Leaves Away 303

HENRY TIMROD, 1828–1867

Ode 304
Charleston 305

EMILY DICKINSON, 1830–1886

49 I never lost as much but twice, 307
67 Success is counted sweetest 307
80 Our lives are Swiss— 308
92 My friend must be a Bird— 308
108 Surgeons must be very careful 308
165 A *Wounded* Deer—leaps highest— 309
173 A fuzzy fellow, without feet, 309
185 "Faith" is a fine invention 310
214 I taste a liquor never brewed— 310
241 I like a look of Agony, 311
249 Wild Nights—Wild Nights! 311
254 "Hope" is the thing with feathers— 312
280 I felt a Funeral, in my Brain, 312
288 I'm Nobody! Who are you? 313
301 I reason, Earth is short— 313
303 The Soul selects her own Society— 314
318 I'll tell you how the Sun rose— 314
341 After great pain, a formal feeling comes— 315
441 This is my letter to the World 315
465 I heard a Fly buzz—when I died— 316
516 Beauty—be not caused—It Is— 316
697 I could bring You Jewels—had I a mind to— 317
712 Because I could not stop for Death— 317
844 Spring is the Period 318
970 Color—Caste—Denomination— 318
986 A narrow Fellow in the Grass 319
1052 I never saw a Moor— 320
1129 Tell all the Truth but tell it slant— 320
1263 There is no Frigate like a Book 321
1274 The Bone that has no Marrow, 321
1333 A little Madness in the Spring 322
1659 Fame is a fickle food 322

EDGAR LEE MASTERS, 1868–1950

from *Spoon River Anthology:*
The Hill 323
Fiddler Jones 324
Petit, the Poet 325
from *The New Spoon River:*
Marx the Sign Painter 326
Unknown Soldiers 326

EDWIN ARLINGTON ROBINSON, 1869–1935

Richard Cory 327
Miniver Cheevy 328
Reuben Bright 329
George Crabbe 329
Credo 330
Mr. Flood's Party 330
Eros Turannos 332
Charles Carville's Eyes 334
The Sheaves 334
The Miller's Wife 335
New England 336

STEPHEN CRANE, 1871–1900

A God in Wrath 337
In the Desert 337
Many Workmen 338
Behold, the Grave 338
Black Riders Came from the Sea 339
A Man Said to the Universe 339
Many Red Devils 339
War Is Kind 340

ROBERT FROST, 1874–1963

The Road Not Taken 341
Mending Wall 342
After Apple Picking 343
Birches 344
Home Burial 346

Dust of Snow 349
The Silken Tent 350
To Earthward 350
Design 351
Neither Out Far nor In Deep 352
The Oven Bird 353
Tree at My Window 353
Stopping by Woods on a Snowy Evening 354
Acquainted with the Night 354
Desert Places 355
Provide, Provide 356
Fire and Ice 357
Nothing Gold Can Stay 357

GERTRUDE STEIN, 1874–1946

Susie Asado 358
Cézanne 358
from *Four Saints in Three Acts:* "Pigeons on the grass alas" 359

CARL SANDBURG, 1878–1967

Fog 360
Cool Tombs 360
The Harbor 361
Chicago 362
I Am the People, the Mob 363

VACHEL LINDSAY, 1879–1931

Simon Legree—A Negro Sermon 364
General William Booth Enters into Heaven 366
The Congo 368
Abraham Lincoln Walks at Midnight 372

WALLACE STEVENS, 1879–1955

The Emperor of Ice Cream 374
The Idea of Order at Key West 374
Peter Quince at the Clavier 376
Sunday Morning 378

Anecdote of the Jar 382
No Possum, No Sop, No Taters 382
Not Ideas About the Thing but the Thing Itself 383
The Glass of Water 384
Thirteen Ways of Looking at a Blackbird 385
A High-Toned Old Christian Woman 387
Men Made Out of Words 388
Of Modern Poetry 389

WILLIAM CARLOS WILLIAMS, 1883–1963

Tract 390
The Red Wheelbarrow 392
The Young Housewife 392
Proletarian Portrait 393
Flowers by the Sea 393
Nantucket 394
Young Sycamore 394
Queen-Anne's-Lace 395
The Widow's Lament in Springtime 396
The Horse Show 397
Danse Russe 398
Spring and All 399
To a Poor Old Woman 400
This Is Just to Say 400
Between Walls 401
The Dance 401
On Gay Wallpaper 402
Smell! 403
A Sort of a Song 403
from Book I, *Paterson* 404

EZRA POUND, 1885–1972

Salutation 406
A Pact 406
The River-Merchant's Wife: A Letter 407
In a Station of the Metro 408
Portrait d'une Femme 408
A Virginal 409

Hugh Selwyn Mauberley 409
Canto III 417

H.D. (Hilda Doolittle), 1886–1961

Oread 419
Heat 419
Star Wheel in Purple 420
Helen 420
The Mysteries Remain 421

ROBINSON JEFFERS, 1887–1962

Hurt Hawks 422
Shine, Perishing Republic 423
But I Am Growing Old and Indolent 424

MARIANNE MOORE, 1887–1972

Poetry 425
A Grave 426
Spenser's Ireland 427

T. S. ELIOT, 1888–1965

The Love Song of J. Alfred Prufrock 430
Gerontion 434
The Waste Land 436
Journey of the Magi 448
Little Gidding 449

JOHN CROWE RANSOM, 1888–1974

Bells for John Whiteside's Daughter 457
Piazza Piece 458
Here Lies a Lady 458
Blue Girls 459
Janet Waking 459
Survey of Literature 460
The Equilibrists 462

CONRAD AIKEN, 1889–1973

Hatteras Calling 464

Herman Melville 465
The Wedding 466

CLAUDE McKAY, 1890–1948

America 468
The Harlem Dancer 468
The White City 469

ARCHIBALD MacLEISH, 1892–

You Also, Gaius Valerius Catullus 470
Ars Poetica 471
The End of the World 472

EDNA ST. VINCENT MILLAY, 1892–1950

Recuerdo 473
Love Is Not All: It Is Not Meat nor Drink 474
Euclid Alone Has Looked on Beauty Bare 474
What Lips My Lips Have Kissed, and Where, and Why 475
And You As Well Must Die, Belovèd Dust 475
I Shall Forget You Presently, My Dear 476
First Fig 476

E. E. CUMMINGS, 1894–1962

my father moved through dooms of love 477
Spring is like a perhaps hand 479
i thank You God for most this amazing 480
i carry your heart with me(i carry it in 480
a man who had fallen among thieves 481
"next to of course god america i 482
anyone lived in a pretty how town 482
pity this busy monster,manunkind, 483
Buffalo Bill's 484
the Cambridge ladies who live in furnished souls 485
as freedom is a breakfastfood 485

HART CRANE, 1899–1932

Black Tambourine 487
from *The Bridge:* Proem: To Brooklyn Bridge 487

Voyages 489
At Melville's Tomb 494
To Emily Dickinson 495

ALLEN TATE, 1899–

Ode to the Confederate Dead 496

LANGSTON HUGHES, 1902–1967

Cross 499
The Negro Speaks of Rivers 500

OGDEN NASH, 1902–1971

The Turtle 501
The Terrible People 501
The Anatomy of Happiness 502

COUNTEE CULLEN, 1903–1946

Yet Do I Marvel 504
For a Lady I Know 504
A Brown Girl Dead 505

CARL RAKOSI, 1903–

Woman 506
Florida 507
In a Warm Bath 507

RICHARD EBERHART, 1904–

The Fury of Aerial Bombardment 509
The Groundhog 510

STANLEY KUNITZ, 1905–

The Illumination 512
After the Last Dynasty 513

KENNETH REXROTH, 1905–

Song for a Dancer 515
Lute Music 516
Further Advantages of Learning 517

Fifty 517
Only Years 518

ROBERT PENN WARREN, 1905–

Bearded Oaks 519
Original Sin: A Short Story 520

THEODORE ROETHKE, 1908–1963

Frau Bauman, Frau Schmidt, and Frau Schwartze 522
Cuttings 523
Cuttings (later) 523
In Evening Air 524
Elegy for Jane 525
My Papa's Waltz 526
Wish for a Young Wife 526
The Waking 527
I Knew a Woman 528
In a Dark Time 529

JOSEPHINE JACOBSEN, 1908–

The Shade-seller 530
The Matadors 531
When the Five Prominent Poets 532
Rainy Night at the Writers' Colony 532
It Is the Season 533

ELIZABETH BISHOP, 1911–

House Guest 535
The Armadillo 537

JOSEPHINE MILES, 1911–

Reason 539
Belief 539
Merchant Marine 540

JEAN GARRIGUE, 1912–1972

Bleecker Street 541
Epitaph for My Cat 542

Shore 542
Amsterdam 543
Country Villa 544
Movie Actors Scribbling Letters Very Fast in Crucial Scenes 545
Song for "Buvez les Vins du Postillon"—Advt. 545

DELMORE SCHWARTZ, 1913–1966

The Mind Is an Ancient and Famous Capital 546
"The Heavy Bear Who Goes with Me" 547
I Am a Book I Neither Wrote nor Read 548

JOHN BERRYMAN, 1914–1972

from *The Dream Songs:* 549
14—Life, friends, is boring. We must not say so. 549
94—Ill lay he long, upon this last return, 549
100—How this woman came by the courage, how she got 550
104—Welcome, grinned Henry, welcome, fifty-one! 551
172—Your face broods from my table, Suicide. 551
262—You couldn't bear to grow old, but we grow old. 552
299—The Irish have the thickest ankles in the world 552

RANDALL JARRELL, 1914–1965

Losses 554
The Death of the Ball Turret Gunner 555
90 North 555
The Woman at the Washington Zoo 556
The Lost Children 557

DUDLEY RANDALL, 1914–

The Profile on the Pillow 560
A Different Image 560
Roses and Revolutions 561

JOHN MALCOLM BRINNIN, 1916–

Skin Diving in the Virgins 562

Letter from an Island 563
Roethke Plain 565

THEODORE WEISS, 1916–

The Fire at Alexandria 569
An Egyptian Passage 570
"Yes, But . . ." 572
Barracks Apt. 14 573
Off to Patagonia 575
As You Like It 576

GWENDOLYN BROOKS, 1917–

Sadie and Maud 578
The Bean Eaters 579
We Real Cool 579
Riot 580
An Aspect of Love Alive in the Ice and Fire 581

PAULINE HANSON, 1917–

So Beautiful Is the Tree of Night 582
And I Am Old to Know 583
From Creature to Ghost 583

ROBERT LOWELL, 1917–1977

Sailing Home from Rapallo 585
The Quaker Graveyard in Nantucket 586
Skunk Hour 590
The Public Garden 592
Night-Sweat 593
History 594
Reading Myself 594

LAWRENCE FERLINGHETTI, 1919?–

Constantly Risking Absurdity 595
The Pennycandystore Beyond the El 596
Frightened 597
In Goya's Greatest Scenes We Seem to See 597

EDWIN HONIG, 1919–

Through You 599
Who 599
Being Somebody 601
Walt Whitman 604

WILLIAM MEREDITH, 1919–

Winter Verse for His Sister 606
The Open Sea 607
Wholesome 607
His Plans for Old Age 608

MAY SWENSON, 1919–

The Shape of Death 610
Landing on the Moon 611
Fire Island 613

REED WHITTEMORE, 1919–

The Departure 614
Clamming 615
Thinking of Tents 616

HOWARD NEMEROV, 1920–

Fugue 617
The Western Approaches 618
Speculation 619

JAMES SCHEVILL, 1920–

London Pavement Artist 620
Green Frog at Roadstead, Wisconsin 620
Freud: Dying in London, He Recalls the Smoke of His Cigar Beginning to Sing 621
Huck Finn at Ninety, Dying in a Chicago Boarding House Room 623
A Screamer Discusses Methods of Screaming 624

JANE MAYHALL, 1921–

City Sparrow 625
The Human Animal 625

The Marshes 626
For the Market 627

RICHARD WILBUR, 1921–

Love Calls Us to the Things of This World 628
Juggler 629
Museum Piece 630

HOWARD MOSS, 1922–

King Midas 631
The Hand 632

JAMES DICKEY, 1923–

The Heaven of Animals 633
Adultery 634
The Sheep Child 635
from *The Zodiac*, X "Tenderness, ache on me, and lay your neck" 637

ARTHUR GREGOR, 1923–

History 639
Lyric 639
Two Shapes 640
Enough 641

DENISE LEVERTOV, 1923–

O Taste and See 642
Mad Song 642
The Ache of Marriage 643

LOUIS SIMPSON, 1923–

American Poetry 644
The Man Who Married Magdalene 644
To the Western World 645
A Story About Chicken Soup 646
My Father in the Night Commanding No 647

JANE COOPER, 1924–

A Circle, A Square, A Triangle and A Ripple of Water 649

Waiting 649
Rent 650
Childhood in Jacksonville, Florida 651
Praise 652

MAXINE KUMIN, 1925–

After Love 653
A Family Man 654
At the End of the Affair 654

A. R. AMMONS, 1926–

The Confirmers 656
Clarity 657
Cut the Grass 657
Viable 658

ROBERT CREELEY, 1926–

The Warning 659
The Language 659
The Window 660

ALLEN GINSBERG, 1926–

from *Howl*, parts I & II 662
A Supermarket in California 670
A Prophecy 671

JAMES MERRILL, 1926–

The Mad Scene 672
The Grand Canyon 672
Manos Karastefanís 673
Last Words 674

FRANK O'HARA, 1926–1966

Homosexuality 675
An Abortion 676
Meditations in an Emergency 676

W. D. SNODGRASS, 1926–

The Operation 679

April Inventory 680
The Campus on the Hill 682
"After Experience Taught Me . . ." 683
Lobsters in the Window 684

JOHN ASHBERY, 1927–

White Roses 686
The Tennis Court Oath 687
Thoughts of a Young Girl 688
Fear of Death 689

GALWAY KINNELL, 1927–

Night in the Forest 690
The Bear 691
The Correspondence School Instructor Says Goodbye to His Poetry Students 694

PAUL PETRIE, 1927–

The Dream 696
The Phases of Darkness 697
Not Seeing Is Believing 698
The Old Pro's Lament 699

JAMES WRIGHT, 1927–

Complaint 701
A Poem About Breasts 701
Speak 702

DONALD HALL, 1928–

White Apples 704
The Town of Hill 704
The Raisin 705
The Brain Cells 707

PHILIP LEVINE, 1928–

Animals Are Passing from Our Lives 708
Salami 709
On the Edge 711
To a Child Trapped in a Barber Shop 712

ANNE SEXTON, 1928–1974

Ringing the Bells 713
Her Kind 714
The Truth the Dead Know 714
Wanting to Die 715

RICHARD HOWARD, 1929–

209 Canal 717
Natural History 717
Recipe for an Ocean in the Absence of the Sea 719
On Arrival 720

ADRIENNE RICH, 1929–

Living in Sin 721
Attention 722
Peeling Onions 722
Two Songs 723
Dialogue 724
The Ninth Symphony of Beethoven Understood at Last as a Sexual Message 725
Re-forming the Crystal 726
Power 727

NANCY SULLIVAN, 1929–

Telling It 728
Eclipses 729
To My Body 731
His Necessary Darkness 732

GREGORY CORSO, 1930–

Marriage 733

GARY SNYDER, 1930–

Things to Do Around a Lookout 737
The Bath 738
Meeting the Mountains 740
Mid-August at Sourdough Mountain Lookout 741

PATRICIA GOEDICKE, 1931–

On the Night in Question 742
After the Second Operation 743
The Serious Merriment of Women 744
Daily the Ocean Between Us 745

SYLVIA PLATH, 1932–1963

The Colossus 747
Cut 748
Lady Lazarus 749
Edge 752

ETHERIDGE KNIGHT, 1933–

Hard Rock Returns to Prison from the Hospital for the Criminal Insane 754
Haiku 755

IMAMU AMIRI BARAKA (LeRoi Jones), 1934–

Biography 757
Poem for Half-White College Students 758
Ka 'Ba 759

MARK STRAND, 1934–

Keeping Things Whole 760
Eating Poetry 761

JEAN VALENTINE, 1934–

Pilgrims 762
April 763
He said, 763
Anaesthesia 764

LUCILLE CLIFTON, 1936–

For deLawd 765
Good Times 765

JUNE JORDAN, 1936–

Poem to My Sister, Ethel Ennis, Who Sang "The Star-Spangled Banner" at the Second Inauguration of Richard Milhous Nixon, January 20, 1973 767

Getting Down to Get Over 769
Queen Anne's Lace 779

MARGE PIERCY, 1936–

We Become New 780
Apron Strings 781
The Spring Offensive of the Snail 781

JUDITH JOHNSON SHERWIN, 1936–

Rhyme for the Child as a Wet Dog 784
The Light Woman's Song 785
Just 785

DIANE WAKOSKI, 1937–

The Night a Sailor Came to Me in a Dream 786
The Father of My Country 787
An Apology 791
Walking Past Paul Blackburn's Apt. on 7th St. 792

GARY GILDNER, 1938–

Nails 794
The House on Buder Street 796
The Runner 798

MICHAEL S. HARPER, 1938–

Poetry Concert 800
Grandfather 800
Nightmare Begins Responsibility 802

RICHARD KOSTELANETZ, 1940–

Concentric 803
Tribute to Henry Ford 804

ERICA JONG, 1942–

The Woman Who Loved to Cook 805

HAKI R. MADHUBUTI (Don L. Lee), 1942–

Judy-One 807

Mixed Sketches 807
Change Is Not Always Progress 809

NIKKI GIOVANNI, 1943–

Nikki-Rosa 810
Kidnap Poem 811

Author Index 813
Index of Titles 815
Index of First Lines 824

ANNE BRADSTREET
(1612–1672)

To My Dear and Loving Husband

If ever two were one, then surely we.
If ever man were loved by wife, then thee;
If ever wife was happy in a man,
Compare with me, ye women, if you can.
I prize thy love more than whole mines of gold
Or all the riches that the East doth hold.
My love is such that rivers cannot quench,
Nor ought but love from thee, give recompense.
Thy love is such I can no way repay,
The heavens reward thee manifold, I pray.
Then while we live, in love let's so persevere
That when we live no more, we may live ever.

In Reference to Her Children,
23 June 1659

I had eight birds hatched in one nest,
Four cocks there were, and hens the rest.
I nursed them up with pain and care,
Nor cost, nor labour did I spare,
Till at the last they felt their wing,
Mounted the trees, and learned to sing;
Chief of the brood then took his flight
To regions far and left me quite.
My mournful chirps I after send,
Till he return, or I do end:
Leave not thy nest, thy dam and sire,
Fly back and sing amidst this choir.

My second bird did take her flight,
And with her mate flew out of sight;
Southward they both their course did bend,
And seasons twain they there did spend,
Till after blown by southern gales,
They norward steered with filled sails.
A prettier bird was no where seen,
Along the beach among the treen.
I have a third of colour white,
On whom I placed no small delight;
Coupled with mate loving and true,
Hath also bid her dam adieu;
And where Aurora first appears,
She now hath perched to spend her years.
One to the academy flew
To chat among that learned crew;
Ambition moves still in his breast
That he might chant above the rest,
Striving for more than to do well,
That nightingales he might excel.
My fifth, whose down is yet scarce gone,
Is 'mongst the shrubs and bushes flown,
And as his wings increase in strength,
On higher boughs he'll perch at length.
My other three still with me nest,
Until they're grown, then as the rest,
Or here or there they'll take their flight,
As is ordained, so shall they light.
If birds could weep, then would my tears
Let others know what are my fears
Lest this my brood some harm should catch,
And be surprised for want of watch,
Whilst pecking corn and void of care,
They fall un'wares in fowler's snare,
Or whilst on trees they sit and sing,
Some untoward boy at them do fling,
Or whilst allured with bell and glass,
The net be spread, and caught, alas.
Or lest by lime-twigs they be foiled,
Or by some greedy hawks be spoiled.
O would my young, ye saw my breast,
And knew what thoughts there sadly rest,

Great was my pain when I you bred,
Great was my care when I you fed,
Long did I keep you soft and warm,
And with my wings kept off all harm,
My cares are more and fears than ever,
My throbs such now as 'fore were never.
Alas, my birds, you wisdom want,
Of perils you are ignorant;
Oft times in grass, on trees, in flight,
Sore accidents on you may light.
O to your safety have an eye,
So happy may you live and die.
Meanwhile my days in tunes I'll spend,
Till my weak lays with me shall end.
In shady woods I'll sit and sing,
And things that past to mind I'll bring.
Once young and pleasant, as are you,
But former toys (no joys) adieu.
My age I will not once lament,
But sing, my time so near is spent.
And from the top bough take my flight
Into a country beyond sight,
Where old ones instantly grow young,
And there with seraphims set song;
No seasons cold, nor storms they see;
But spring lasts to eternity.
When each of you shall in your nest
Among your young ones take your rest,
In chirping language, oft them tell,
You had a dam that loved you well,
That did what could be done for young,
And nursed you up till you were strong,
And 'fore she once would let you fly,
She showed you joy and misery;
Taught what was good, and what was ill,
What would save life, and what would kill.
Thus gone, amongst you I may live,
And dead, yet speak, and counsel give:
Farewell, my birds, farewell adieu,
I happy am, if well with you.

The Flesh and the Spirit

In secret place where once I stood
Close by the banks of Lacrim flood,
I heard two sisters reason on
Things that are past and things to come;
One flesh was called, who had her eye
On worldly wealth and vanity;
The other Spirit, who did rear
Her thoughts unto a higher sphere:
Sister, quoth Flesh, what liv'st thou on,
Nothing but meditation?
Doth contemplation feed thee so
Regardlessly to let earth go?
Can speculation satisfy
Notion without reality?
Dost dream of things beyond the moon,
And dost thou hope to dwell there soon?
Hast treasures there laid up in store
That all in th' world thou count'st but poor?
Art fancy sick, or turned a sot
To catch at shadows which are not?
Come, come, I'll show unto thy sense,
Industry hath its recompense.
What canst desire, but thou may'st see
True substance in variety?
Dost honour like? Acquire the same,
As some to their immortal fame,
And trophies to thy name erect
Which wearing time shall ne'er deject.
For riches doth thou long full sore?
Behold enough of precious store.
Earth hath more silver, pearls, and gold,
Than eyes can see or hands can hold.
Affect's thou pleasure? Take thy fill,
Earth hath enough of what you will.

Then let not go, what thou may'st find
For things unknown, only in mind.
Spir. Be still thou unregenerate part,
Disturb no more my settled heart,
For I have vowed (and so will do)
Thee as a foe still to pursue.
And combat with thee will and must,
Until I see thee laid in th' dust.
Sisters we are, yea, twins we be,
Yet deadly feud 'twixt thee and me;
For from one father are we not,
Thou by old Adam wast begot,
But my arise is from above,
Whence my dear Father I do love.
Thou speak'st me fair, but hat'st me sore,
Thy flatt'ring shows I'll trust no more.
How oft thy slave, hast thou me made,
When I believed what thou hast said,
And never had more cause of woe
Than when I did what thou bad'st do.
I'll stop mine ears at these thy charms,
And count them for my deadly harms.
Thy sinful pleasures I do hate,
Thy riches are to me no bait,
Thine honours do, nor will I love;
For my ambition lies above.
My greatest honour it shall be
When I am victor over thee,
And triumph shall with laurel head,
When thou my captive shalt be led,
How I do live, thou need'st not scoff,
For I have meat thou know'st not of;
The hidden manna I do eat,
The word of life it is my meat.
My thoughts do yield me more content
Than can thy hours in pleasure spent.
Nor are they shadows which I catch,
Nor fancies vain at which I snatch,
But reach at things that are so high,
Beyond thy dull capacity;

Eternal substance I do see,
With which enriched I would be.
Mine eye doth pierce the heavens and see
What is invisible to thee.
My garments are not silk nor gold,
Nor such like trash which earth doth hold,
But royal robes I shall have on,
More glorious than the glist'ring sun;
My crown not diamonds, pearls, and gold,
But such as angels' heads enfold.
The city where I hope to dwell,
There's none on earth can parallel;
The stately walls both high and strong,
Are made of precious jasper stone;
The gates of pearl, both rich and clear,
And angels are for porters there;
The streets thereof transparent gold,
Such as no eye did e'er behold;
A crystal river there doth run,
Which doth proceed from the Lamb's throne.
Of life, there are the waters sure,
Which shall remain forever pure,
Nor sun, nor moon, they have no need,
For glory doth from God proceed.
No candle there, nor yet torchlight,
For there shall be no darksome night.
From sickness and infirmity
For evermore they shall be free;
Nor withering age shall e'er come there,
But beauty shall be bright and clear;
This city pure is not for thee,
For things unclean there shall not be.
If I of heaven may have my fill,
Take thou the world and all that will.

Deliverance from a Fit of Fainting

Worthy art Thou, O Lord, of praise,
But ah! It's not in me.
My sinking heart I pray Thee raise
So shall I give it Thee.

My life as spider's webb's cut off,
Thus fainting have I said,
And living man no more shall see
But be in silence laid.

My feeble spirit Thou didst revive,
My doubting Thou didst chide,
And though as dead mad'st me alive,
I here a while might 'bide.

Why should I live but to Thy praise?
My life is hid with Thee.
O Lord, no longer be my days
Than I may fruitful be.

Some Verses upon the Burning of Our House, July 10th, 1666

In silent night when rest I took
For sorrow near I did not look
I wakened was with thund'ring noise
And piteous shrieks of dreadful voice.
That fearful sound of "Fire!" and "Fire!"
Let no man know is my desire.
I, starting up, the light did spy,
And to my God my heart did cry
To strengthen me in my distress
And not to leave me succorless.
Then, coming out, beheld a space
The flame consume my dwelling place.
And when I could no longer look,
I blest His name that gave and took,

That laid my goods now in the dust.
Yea, so it was, and so 'twas just.
It was His own, it was not mine,
Far be it that I should repine:
He might of all justly bereft
But yet sufficient for us left.
When by the ruins oft I past
My sorrowing eyes aside did cast,
And here and there the places spy
Where oft I sat and long did lie:
Here stood that trunk, and there that chest,
There lay that store I counted best.
My pleasant things in ashes lie,
And them behold no more shall I.
Under thy roof no guest shall sit,
Nor at thy table eat a bit.
No pleasant tale shall e'er be told,
Nor things recounted done of old.
No candle e'er shall shine in thee,
Nor bridegroom's voice e'er heard shall be.
In silence ever shall thou lie,
Adieu, Adieu, all's vanity.
Then straight I 'gin my heart to chide,
And did thy wealth on earth abide?
Didst fix thy hope on mold'ring dust?
The arm of flesh didst make thy trust?
Raise up thy thoughts above the sky
That dunghill mists away may fly.
Thou hast an house on high erect,
Framed by that mighty Architect,
With glory richly furnished,
Stands permanent though this be fled.
It's purchased and paid for too
By Him who hath enough to do.
A price so vast as is unknown
Yet by His gift is made thine own;
There's wealth enough, I need no more,
Farewell, my pelf, farewell my store.
The world no longer let me love,
My hope and treasure lies above.

The Prologue

1

To sing of wars, of captains, and of kings,
Of cities founded, commonwealths begun,
For my mean pen are too superior things:
Or how they all, or each their dates have run
Let poets and historians set these forth,
My obscure lines shall not so dim their worth.

2

But when my wond'ring eyes and envious heart
Great Bartas' sugared lines do but read o'er,
Fool I do grudge the Muses did not part
'Twixt him and me that overfluent store;
A Bartas can do what a Bartas will
But simple I according to my skill.

3

From schoolboy's tongue no rhet'ric we expect,
Nor yet a sweet consort from broken strings,
Nor perfect beauty where's a main defect:
My foolish, broken, blemished Muse so sings,
And this to mend, alas, no art is able,
'Cause nature made it so irreparable.

4

Nor can I, like that fluent sweet tongued Greek,
Who lisped at first, in future times speak plain.
By art he gladly found what he did seek,
A full requital of his striving pain.
Art can do much, but this maxim's most sure:
A weak or wounded brain admits no cure.

5

I am obnoxious to each carping tongue
Who says my hand a needle better fits,
A poet's pen all scorn I should thus wrong;
For such despite they cast on female wits:
If what I do prove well, it won't advance,
They'll say it's stol'n, or else it was by chance.

6

But sure the antique Greeks were far more mild
Else of our sex, why feigned they those nine
And poesy made Calliope's own child;
So 'mongst the rest they placed the arts divine:
But this weak knot they will full soon untie,
The Greeks did nought, but play the fools and lie.

7

Let Greeks be Greeks, and women what they are
Men have precedency and still excel,
It is but vain unjustly to wage war;
Men can do best, and women know it well.
Preeminence in all and each is yours;
Yet grant some small acknowledgement of ours.

8

And oh ye high flown quills that soar the skies,
And ever with your prey still catch your praise,
If e'er you deign these lowly lines your eyes,
Give thyme or parsley wreath, I ask no bays;
This mean and unrefined ore of mine
Will make your glist'ring gold but more to shine.

The Author to Her Book

Thou ill-formed offspring of my feeble brain,
Who after birth didst by my side remain,
Till snatched from thence by friends, less wise than true,
Who thee abroad, exposed to public view,
Made thee in rags, halting to th' press to trudge,
Where errors were not lessened (all may judge).
At thy return my blushing was not small,
My rambling brat (in print) should mother call,
I cast thee by as one unfit for light,
Thy visage was so irksome in my sight;
Yet being mine own, at length affection would
Thy blemishes amend, if so I could:
I washed thy face, but more defects I saw,
And rubbing off a spot still made a flaw.
I stretched thy joints to make thee even feet,
Yet still thou run'st more hobbling than is meet;
In better dress to trim thee was my mind,
But nought save homespun cloth i' th' house I find.
In this array 'mongst vulgars may'st thou roam.
In critic's hands beware thou dost not come,
And take thy way where yet thou art not known;
If for thy father asked, say thou hadst none;
And for thy mother, she alas is poor,
Which caused her thus to send thee out of door.

EDWARD TAYLOR
(1645?–1729)

Huswifery

Make me, O Lord, thy Spining Wheele compleate.
    Thy Holy Worde my Distaff make for mee.
Make mine Affections thy Swift Flyers neate
    And make my Soule thy holy Spoole to bee.
    My Conversation make to be thy Reele
    And reele the yarn thereon spun of thy Wheele.

Make me thy Loome then, knit therein this Twine:
    And make thy Holy Spirit, Lord, winde quills:
Then weave the Web thyselfe. The yarn is fine.
    Thine Ordinances make my Fulling Mills.
    Then dy the same in Heavenly Colours Choice,
    All pinkt with Varnisht Flowers of Paradise.

Then cloath therewith mine Understanding, Will,
    Affections, Judgment, Conscience, Memory
My Words, and Actions, that their shine may fill
    My wayes with glory and thee glorify.
    Then mine apparell shall display before yee
    That I am Cloathd in Holy robes for glory.

6. Meditation. Canticles 2:1. I Am . . . the Lily of the Valleys.

Am I thy Gold? Or Purse, Lord, for thy Wealth;
    Whether in mine, or mint refinde for thee?
Ime counted so, but count me o're thyselfe,
    Lest gold washt face, and brass in Heart I bee.
    I Feare my Touchstone touches when I try
    Mee, and my Counted Gold too overly.

Am I new minted by thy Stamp indeed?
    Mine Eyes are dim; I cannot clearly see.
Be thou my Spectacles that I may read
    Thine Image, and Inscription stampt on mee.
    If thy bright Image do upon me stand
    I am a Golden Angell in thy hand.

Lord, make my Soule thy Plate: thine Image bright
    Within the Circle of the same enfoile.
And on its brims in golden Letters write
    Thy Superscription in an Holy style.
    Then I shall be thy Money, thou my Hord:
    Let me thy Angell bee, bee thou my Lord.

8. Meditation. John 6:51. I Am the Living Bread.

I kening through Astronomy Divine
    The Worlds bright Battlement, wherein I spy
A Golden Path my Pensill cannot line,
    From that bright Throne unto my Threshold ly.
    And while my puzzled thoughts about it pore
    I finde the Bread of Life in't at my doore.

When that this Bird of Paradise put in
    This Wicker Cage (my Corps) to tweedle praise
Had peckt the Fruite forbad: and so did fling
    Away its Food; and lost its golden dayes;
    It fell into Celestiall Famine sore:
    And never could attain a morsell more.

Alas! alas! Poore Bird, what wilt thou doe?
    The Creatures field no food for Souls e're gave.
And if thou knock at Angells dores they show
    An Empty Barrell: they no soul bread have.
    Alas! Poore Bird, the Worlds White Loafe is done.
    And cannot yield thee here the smallest Crumb.

In this sad state, Gods Tender Bowells run
    Out streams of Grace: And he to end all strife
The Purest Wheate in Heaven, his deare-dear Son
    Grinds, and kneads up into this Bread of Life.
    Which Bread of Life from Heaven down came and stands
    Disht on thy Table up by Angells Hands.

Did God mould up this Bread in Heaven, and bake,
    Which from his Table came, and to thine goeth?
Doth he bespeake thee thus, This Soule Bread take.
    Come Eate thy fill of this thy Gods White Loafe?
    Its Food too fine for Angells, yet come, take
    And Eate thy fill. Its Heavens Sugar Cake.

What Grace is this knead in this Loafe? This thing
    Souls are but petty things it to admire.
Yee Angells, help: This fill would to the brim
    Heav'ns whelm'd-down Chrystall meele Bowle, yea and
        higher.
    This Bread of Life dropt in thy mouth, doth Cry.
    Eate, Eate me, Soul, and thou shalt never dy.

11. Meditation. Isaiah 25:6. A Feast of Fat Things.

A Deity of Love Incorporate
    My Lord, lies in thy Flesh, in Dishes stable
Ten thousand times more rich than golden Plate
    In golden Services upon thy Table,
    To feast thy People with. What Feast is this!
    Where richest Love lies Cookt in e'ry Dish?

A Feast, a Feast, a Feast of Spiced Wine
    Of Wines upon the Lees, refined well
Of Fat things full of Marrow, things Divine
    Of Heavens blest Cookery which doth excell.
    The Smell of Lebanon, and Carmell sweet
    Are Earthly damps unto this Heavenly reech.

This Shew-Bread Table all of Gold with white
    Fine Table Linen of Pure Love, 's ore spred
And Courses in Smaragdine Chargers bright
    Of Choicest Dainties Paradise e're bred.
    Where in each Grace like Dainty Sippits lie
    Oh! brave Embroderies of sweetest joy!

Oh! what a Feast is here? This Table might
    Make brightest Angells blush to sit before.
Then pain my Soule! Why wantst thou appitite?
    Oh! blush to thinke thou hunger dost no more.
    There never was a feast more rich than this:
    The Guests that Come hereto shall swim in bliss.

Upon a Spider Catching a Fly

Thou sorrow, venom elf;
  Is this thy play,
To spin a web out of thyself
  To catch a fly?
    For why?

I saw a pettish wasp
  Fall foul therein:
Whom yet thy whorl pins did
      not hasp
  Lest he should fling
    His sting

But as afraid, remote
  Didst stand hereat,
And with thy little fingers
      stroke
  And gently tap
    His back.

Thus gently him didst treat
  Lest he should pet,
And in a froppish, aspish heat
  Should greatly fret
    Thy net.

Whereas the silly fly,
  Caught by its leg,
Thou by the throat tookst
      hastily,
  And 'hind the head
    Bite dead.

This goes to pot, that not
Nature doth call.
Strive not above what
strength hath got,
Lest in the brawl
Thou fall.

This fray seems thus to us:
Hell's spider gets
His entrails spun to whipcords
thus,
And wove to nets,
And sets.

To tangle Adam's race
In's stratagems
To their destructions, spoiled,
made base
By venom things,
Damned sins.

But mighty, gracious Lord,
Communicate
Thy grace to break the cord;
afford
Us glory's gate
And state

We'll nightingale sing like,
When perched on high
In glory's cage, thy glory,
bright:
Yea, thankfully,
For joy.

PHILIP FRENEAU
(1752–1832)

The Wild Honey Suckle

Fair flower, that dost so comely grow,
Hid in this silent, dull retreat,
Untouched thy honied blossoms blow,
Unseen thy little branches greet:
    No roving foot shall crush thee here,
    No busy hand provoke a tear.

By Nature's self in white arrayed,
She bade thee shun the vulgar eye,
And planted here the guardian shade,
And sent soft waters murmuring by;
    Thus quietly thy summer goes,
    Thy days declining to repose.

Smit with those charms, that must decay,
I grieve to see your future doom;
They died—nor were those flowers more gay,
The flowers that did in Eden bloom;
    Unpitying frosts, and Autumn's power
    Shall leave no vestige of this flower.

From morning suns and evening dews
At first thy little being came:
If nothing once, you nothing lose,
For when you die you are the same;
    The space between, is but an hour,
    The frail duration of a flower.

On a Honey Bee

Drinking from a Glass of Wine and Drowned Therein

Thou, born to sip the lake or spring,
Or quaff the waters of the stream,
Why hither come on vagrant wing?—
Does Bacchus tempting seem—
Did he, for you, this glass prepare?—
Will I admit you to a share?

Did storms harass or foes perplex,
Did wasps or king-birds bring dismay—
Did wars distress, or labours vex,
Or did you miss your way?—
A better seat you could not take
Than on the margin of this lake.

Welcome!—I hail you to my glass:
All welcome, here, you find;
Here, let the cloud of trouble pass,
Here, be all care resigned.—
This fluid never fails to please,
And drown the griefs of men or bees.

What forced you here, we cannot know,
And you will scarcely tell—
But cheery we would have you go
And bid a glad farewell:
On lighter wings we bid you fly,
Your dart will now all foes defy.

Yet take not, oh! too deep a drink,
And in this ocean die;
Here bigger bees than you might sink,
Even bees full six feet high.
Like Pharaoh, then, you would be said
To perish in a sea of red.

Do as you please, your will is mine;
Enjoy it without fear—
And your grave will be this glass of wine,
Your epitaph—a tear—
Go, take your seat in Charon's boat,
We'll tell the hive, you died afloat.

To
A *Caty-did*

In a branch of a willow hid
Sings the evening Caty-did:
From the lofty locust bough
Feeding on a drop of dew,
In her suit of green array'd
Hear her singing in the shade
Caty-did, Caty-did, Caty-did!

While upon a leaf you tread,
Or repose your little head,
On your sheet of shadows laid,
All the day you nothing said:
Half the night your cheery tongue
Revell'd out its little song,
Nothing else but Caty-did.

From your lodgings on the leaf
Did you utter joy or grief—?
Did you only mean to say,
I have had my summer's day,
And am passing, soon, away
To the grave of Caty-did;—
Poor, unhappy Caty-did!

But you would have utter'd more
Had you known of nature's power—
From the world when you retreat,
And a leaf's your winding sheet,

Long before your spirit fled,
Who can tell but nature said,
Live again, my Caty-did!
  Live, and chatter Caty-did.

  Tell me, what did Caty do?
Did she mean to trouble you?—
Why was Caty not forbid
To trouble little Caty-did?—
Wrong, indeed at you to fling,
Hurting no one while you sing
  Caty-did! Caty-did! Caty-did!

  Why continue to complain?
Caty tells me, she again
Will not give you plague or pain:—
Caty says you may be hid
Caty will not go to bed
While you sing us Caty-did.
  Caty-did! Caty-did! Caty-did!

  But, while singing, you forgot
To tell us what did Caty *not:*
Caty-did not think of cold,
Flocks retiring to the fold,
Winter, with his wrinkles old,
Winter, that yourself foretold
  When you gave us Caty-did.

  Stay securely in your nest;
Caty now, will do her best,
All she can, to make you blest;
But, you want no human aid—
Nature, when she form'd you, said,

"Independent you are made,
My dear little Caty-did:
Soon yourself must disappear
With the verdure of the year,"—
And to go, we know not where,
  With your song of Caty-did.

The Hurricane

Happy the man who, safe on shore,
  Now trims, at home, his evening fire;
Unmov'd, he hears the tempests roar,
  That on the tufted groves expire:
Alas! on us they doubly fall,
Our feeble barque must bear them all.

Now to their haunts the birds retreat,
  The squirrel seeks his hollow tree,
Wolves in their shaded caverns meet,
  All, all are blest but wretched we—
Foredoomed a stranger to repose,
No rest the unsettled ocean knows.

While o'er the dark abyss we roam,
  Perhaps, with last departing gleam,
We saw the sun descend in gloom,
  No more to see his morning beam;
But buried low, by far too deep,
On coral beds, unpitied, sleep!

But what a strange, uncoasted strand
  Is that, where fate permits no day—
No charts have we to mark that land,
  No compass to direct that way—
What Pilot shall explore that realm,
What new Columbus take the helm!

While death and darkness both surround,
  And tempests rage with lawless power,
Of friendship's voice I hear no sound,
  No comfort in this dreadful hour—
What friendship can in tempests be,
  What comfort on this raging sea?

The barque, accustomed to obey,
  No more the trembling pilots guide:
Alone she gropes her trackless way,
  While mountains burst on either side—
Thus, skill and science both must fall;
And ruin is the lot of all.

To Sir Toby

A Sugar Planter in the interior parts of Jamaica, near the City of San Jago de la Vega, (Spanish Town) 1784

The motions of his spirit are black as night,
And his affections dark as Erebus.—SHAKESPEARE.

  If there exists a hell—the case is clear—
Sir Toby's slaves enjoy that portion here:
Here are no blazing brimstone lakes, 'tis true;
But kindled Rum too often burns as blue,
In which some fiend, whom nature must detest,
Steeps Toby's brand and marks poor Cudjoe's breast.
  Here whips on whips excite perpetual fears,
And mingled howlings vibrate on my ears:
Here nature's plagues abound, to fret and teaze,
Snakes, scorpions, despots, lizards, centipedes—
No art, no care escapes the busy lash;
All have their dues—and all are paid in cash—
The eternal driver keeps a steady eye
On a black herd, who would his vengeance fly,
But chained, imprisoned, on a burning soil,
For the mean avarice of a tyrant, toil!
The lengthy cart-whip guards this monster's reign—
And cracks, like pistols, from the fields of cane.
  Ye powers! who formed these wretched tribes, relate,
What had they done, to merit such a fate!
Why were they brought from Eboe's sultry waste,
To see that plenty which they must not taste—

Food, which they cannot buy, and dare not steal;
Yams and potatoes—many a scanty meal!—
  One, with a gibbet wakes his negro's fears,
One to the windmill nails him by the ears;
One keeps his slave in darkened dens, unfed,
One puts the wretch in pickle ere he's dead:
This, from a tree suspends him by the thumbs,
That, from his table grudges even the crumbs!
  O'er yond' rough hills a tribe of females go,
Each with her gourd, her infant, and her hoe;
Scorched by a sun that has no mercy here,
Driven by a devil, whom men call overseer—
In chains, twelve wretches to their labours haste;
Twice twelve I saw, with iron collars graced!—
  Are such the fruits that spring from vast domains?
Is wealth, thus got, Sir Toby, worth your pains!—
Who would your wealth on terms, like these, possess,
Where all we see is pregnant with distress—
Angola's natives scourged by ruffian hands,
And toil's hard product shipp'd to foreign lands.
  Talk not of blossoms and your endless spring;
What joy, what smile, can scenes of misery bring?—
Though Nature, here, has every blessing spread,
Poor is the labourer—and how meanly fed!—
  Here Stygian paintings light and shade renew,
Pictures of hell, that Virgil's pencil drew:
Here, surly Charons make their annual trip,
And ghosts arrive in every Guinea ship,
To find what beasts these western isles afford,
Plutonian scourges, and despotic lords:—
  Here, they, of stuff determined to be free,
Must climb the rude cliffs of the Liguanee;
Beyond the clouds, in skulking haste repair,
And hardly safe from brother traitors there.

On the *Emigration to America* and Peopling the Western Country

To western woods, and lonely plains,
Palemon from the crowd departs,
Where Nature's wildest genius reigns,
To tame the soil, and plant the arts—
What wonders there shall freedom show,
What mighty States successive grow!

From Europe's proud, despotic shores
Hither the stranger takes his way,
And in our new found world explores
A happier soil, a milder sway,
Where no proud despot holds him down,
No slaves insult him with a crown.

What charming scenes attract the eye,
On wild Ohio's savage stream!
There Nature reigns, whose works outvie
The boldest pattern art can frame;
There ages past have rolled away,
And forests bloomed but to decay.

From these fair plains, these rural seats,
So long concealed, so lately known,
The unsocial Indian far retreats,
To make some other clime his own,
When other streams, less pleasing flow,
And darker forests round him grow.

Great Sire of floods! whose varied wave
Through climes and countries takes its way,
To whom creating Nature gave
Ten thousand streams to swell thy sway!
No longer shall they useless prove,
Nor idly through the forests rove;

Nor longer shall your princely flood
From distant lakes be swelled in vain,
Nor longer through a darksome wood
Advance, unnoticed, to the main,
Far other ends, the heavens decree—
And commerce plans new freights for thee.

While virtue warms the generous breast,
There heaven-born freedom shall reside,
Nor shall the voice of war molest,
Nor Europe's all-aspiring pride—
There Reason shall new laws devise,
And order from confusion rise.

Forsaking kings and regal state,
With all their pomp and fancied bliss,
The traveller owns, convinced though late,
No realm so free, so blest as this—
The east is half to slaves consigned,
Where kings and priests enchain the mind.

O come the time, and haste the day,
When man shall man no longer crush,
When Reason shall enforce her sway,
Nor these fair regions raise our blush,
Where still the *African* complains,
And mourns his yet unbroken chains.

Far brighter scenes a future age,
The muse predicts, these States will hail,
Whose genius may the world engage,
Whose deeds may over death prevail,
And happier systems bring to view,
Than all the eastern sages knew.

Literary Importation

However we wrangled with Britain awhile
We think of her now in a different stile,
And many fine things we receive from her isle;
Among all the rest,
Some demon possessed
Our dealers in knowledge and sellers of sense
To have a good *bishop* imported from thence.

The words of *Sam Chandler* were thought to be vain,
When he argued so often and proved it *so plain*
"That Satan must flourish till bishops should reign:"
Though he went to the wall
With his project and all,
Another bold Sammy, in bishop's array,
Has got something more than his pains for his pay.

It seems we had spirit to humble a throne,
Have genius for science inferior to none,
But hardly encourage a plant of our own:
If a college be planned,
'Tis all at a stand
'Till in Europe we send at a shameful expense,
To send us a book-worm to teach us some sense.

Can we never be thought to have learning or grace
Unless it be brought from that horrible place
Where tyranny reigns with her impudent face;
And popes and pretenders,
And sly faith-defenders
Have ever been hostile to reason and wit,
Enslaving a world that shall conquer them yet.

'Tis folly to fret at the picture I draw:
And I say what was said by a *Doctor Magraw*,
"If they give us their Bishops, they'll give us their law."
How that will agree
With such people as we,
Let us leave to the learned to reflect on awhile,
And say what they think in a handsomer stile.

The American Soldier
(A Picture from the Life)

To serve with love,
And shed your blood,
Approved may be above,
And here below
(Examples shew)
'Tis dangerous to be good.

LORD OXFORD.

Deep in a vale, a stranger now to arms,
Too poor to shine in courts, too proud to beg,
He, who once warred on Saratoga's plains,
Sits musing o'er his scars, and wooden leg.

Remembering still the toil of former days,
To *other* hands he sees his earnings paid;—
They share the due reward—*he* feeds on praise,
Lost in the abyss of want, misfortune's shade.

Far, far from domes where splendid tapers glare,
'Tis his from dear bought peace no wealth to win,
Removed alike from courtly cringing 'squires,
The great-man's *Levee,* and the proud man's grin.

Sold are those arms which once on Britons blazed,
When, flushed with conquest, to the charge they came,
That power repelled, and *Freedom's* fabrick raised,
She leaves her soldier—*famine* and a *name!*

A Warning to America

Removed from Europe's feuds, a hateful scene
(Thank heaven, such wastes of ocean roll between)
Where tyrant kings in bloody schemes combine,
And each forbodes in tears, *Man is no longer mine!*
Glad we recall the DAY that bade us first
Spurn at their power, and shun their wars accurst;
Pitted and gaffed no more for England's glory
Nor made the tag-rag-bobtail of their story.

Something still wrong in every system lurks,
Something imperfect haunts all human works—
Wars must be hatched, unthinking men to fleece,
Or we, *this day,* had been in perfect peace,
With double bolts our Janus' temple shut,
Nor terror reigned through each back-woods-man's hut,
No rattling drums assailed the peasant's ear
Nor Indian yells disturbed our sad frontier,
Nor *gallant chiefs,* 'gainst Indian hosts combined
Scaped from the trap—*to leave their tails behind.*

Peace to all feuds!—and come the happier day
When Reason's sun shall light us on our way;
When erring man shall all his RIGHTS retrieve,
No despots rule him, and no priests deceive,
Till then, Columbia!—watch each stretch of power,
Nor sleep too soundly at the midnight hour,
By flattery won, and lulled by soothing strains,
Silenus took his nap—and waked in chains—
In a soft dream of smooth delusion led
Unthinking Gallia bowed her drooping head
To tyrants' yokes—and met such bruises there,
As now must take three ages to repair;
Then keep the paths of dear bought freedom clear,
Nor slavish systems grant admittance here.

To a *Noisy Politician*

Since *Shylock's* book has walk'd the circles *here*,
What numerous blessings to our country flow!
Whales on our shores have run aground,
Sturgeons are in our rivers found;
Nay, ships have on the Delaware sail'd,
A sight most new!
Wheat has been sown, harvests have grown,
And *Shylock* held strange dialogues with *Sue*.

On coaches, now, gay coats of arms are wore
By *some*, who hardly had a coat before:
Silk gowns instead of homespun, now, are seen,
And, sir, 'tis true ('twixt me and you)
That some have grown prodigious fat,
That were prodigious lean!

Tobacco

(Supposed to be Written by a Young Beginner)

This *Indian weed*, that once did grow
On fair *Virginia's* fertile plain,
From whence it came—again may go,
To please some happier swain:
Of all the plants that Nature yields
This, least beloved, shall shun my fields.

In evil hour I first essayed
To chew this vile forbidden leaf,
When, half ashamed, and half afraid,
I touched, and tasted—to my grief:
Ah me! the more I was forbid,
The more I wished to take a *quid*.

But when I smoaked, in thought profound,
And raised the spiral circle high,
My heart grew sick, my head turned round—
And what can all this mean, (said I)—
Tobacco surely was designed
To poison, and destroy mankind.

Unhappy they, whom choice, or fate
Inclines to prize this bitter weed;
Perpetual source of female hate;
On which no beast—but man will feed;
That sinks my heart, and turns my head,
And sends me, reeling, home to bed!

The Indian Convert

An Indian, who lived at *Muskingum,* remote,
Was teased by a parson to join his dear flock,
To throw off his blanket and put on a coat,
And of grace and religion to lay in a stock.

The Indian long slighted an offer so fair,
Preferring to preaching his fishing and fowling;
A *sermon* to him was a heart full of care,
And singing but little superior to howling.

At last by persuasion and constant harassing
Our Indian was brought to consent to be *good;*
He saw that the malice of *Satan* was pressing,
And the *means* to repel him not yet understood.

Of heaven, one day, when the parson was speaking,
And painting the beautiful things of the place,
The *convert,* who something substantial was seeking,
Rose up, and confessed he had doubts in the case.—

Said he, *Master Minister*, this place that you talk of,
Of things for the stomach, pray what has it got;
Has it liquors in plenty?—if so I'll soon walk off
And put myself down in the heavenly spot.

You fool (said the preacher) no liquors are there!
The place I'm describing is most like our meeting,
Good people, all singing, with preaching and prayer;
They live upon these without eating or drinking.

But the doors are all locked against folks that are wicked:
And you, I am fearful, will never get there:—
A life of REPENTANCE must purchase the ticket,
And few of you, Indians, can buy it, I fear.

Farewell (said the Indian) I'm none of your mess;
On victuals, so airy, I faintish should feel,
I cannot consent to be lodged in a place
Where there's nothing to eat and but little to steal.

The Indian Burying Ground

In spite of all the learned have said,
  I still my old opinion keep;
The posture, that we give the dead,
  Points out the soul's eternal sleep.

Not so the ancients of these lands—
  The Indian, when from life released,
Again is seated with his friends,
  And shares again the joyous feast.

His imaged birds, and painted bowl,
  And venison, for a journey dressed,
Bespeak the nature of the soul,
  Activity, that knows no rest.

His bow, for action ready bent,
  And arrows, with a head of stone,
Can only mean that life is spent,
  And not the old ideas gone.

Thou, stranger, that shalt come this way,
  No fraud upon the dead commit—
Observe the swelling turf, and say
  They do not lie, but here they sit.

Here still a lofty rock remains,
  On which the curious eye may trace
(Now wasted, half, by wearing rains)
  The fancies of a ruder race.

Here still an aged elm aspires,
  Beneath whose far-projecting shade
(And which the shepherd still admires)
  The children of the forest played!

There oft a restless Indian queen
  (Pale Shebah, with her braided hair)
And many a barbarous form is seen
  To chide the man that lingers there.

By midnight moons, o'er moistening dews;
  In habit for the chase arrayed,
The hunter still the deer pursues,
  The hunter and the deer, a shade!

And long shall timorous fancy see
  The painted chief, and pointed spear,
And Reason's self shall bow the knee
  To shadows and delusions here.

PHILLIS WHEATLEY (Phillis Peters)
(1753?–1784)

To the University of Cambridge in New England

While an intrinsic ardor prompts to write,
The muses promise to assist my pen;
'Twas not long since I left my native shore
The land of errors, and *Egyptian* gloom:
Father of mercy, 'twas thy gracious hand
Brought me in safety from those dark abodes.
  Students, to you 'tis giv'n to scan the heights
Above, to traverse the ethereal space,
And mark the systems of revolving worlds.
Still more, ye sons of science, ye receive
The blissful news by messengers from heav'n
How *Jesus'* blood for your redemption flows.
See Him with hands outstretched upon the cross;
Immense compassion in His bosom glows;
He hears revilers, nor resents their scorn;
What matchless mercy in the Son of God!
When the whole human race by sin had fall'n,
He deign'd to die that they might rise again,
And share with Him in the sublimest skies,
Life without death, and glory without end.
  Improve your privileges while they stay,
Ye pupils, and each hour redeem, that bears
Or good or bad report of you to heav'n.
Let sin, that baneful evil to the soul,
By you be shunned, nor once remit your guard;
Suppress the deadly serpent in its egg.

Ye blooming plants of human race divine,
An *Ethiop* tells you 'tis your greatest foe;
Its transient sweetness turns to endless pain,
And in immense perdition sinks the soul.

To the King's Most Excellent Majesty

Your subjects hope, dread Sire——
The crown upon your brows may flourish long,
And that your arm may in your God be strong!
O, may your sceptre num'rous nations sway,
And all with love and readiness obey!
  But how shall we the *British* King reward?
Rule thou in peace, our father, and our lord!
Midst the remembrance of thy favors past,
The meanest peasants most admire the last.
May *George*, beloved by all the nations round,
Live with heav'n's choicest constant blessings crown'd!
Great God, direct, and guard him from on high,
And from his head let ev'ry evil fly!
And may each clime with equal gladness see
A monarch's smile can set his subjects free!

To a Lady on the Death of Her Husband

Grim monarch! see, deprived of vital breath
A young physician in the dust of death!
Dost thou go on incessant to destroy?
The grief to double and lay waste the joy?
Enough thou never yet wast known to say,
Tho' millions die the vassals of thy sway:
Nor youth, nor science, nor the ties of love,
Nor aught on earth thy flinty heart can move.
The friend, the spouse, from his dire dart to save,
In vain we ask the sovereign of the grave.

Fair mourner, there see thy lov'd *Leonard* laid,
And o'er him spread the deep impervious shade;
Clos'd are his eyes and heavy fetters keep
His senses bound in never-waking sleep,
Till time shall cease, till many a starry world,
Shall fall from heav'n, in dire confusion hurl'd;
Till Nature in her final wreck shall lie,
Till Her last groan shall rend the azure sky;
Not till then his active soul shall claim,
His body, a divine immortal frame.
  But, see the softly stealing tears apace,
Pursue each other down the mourner's face;
But cease thy tears, bid ev'ry sigh depart,
And cast the load of anguish from thine heart;
From the cold shell of his great soul arise,
And look beyond, thou native of the skies;
There fix thy view where fleeter than the wind
Thy *Leonard* mounts, and leaves the earth behind.

Thyself prepare to pass the vale of night,
To join forever on the hills of light;
To thine embrace, his joyful spirit moves,
To thee, the partner of his earthly loves;
He welcomes thee to pleasures more refin'd
And better suited to th' immortal mind.

On Being Brought from Africa to America

'Twas mercy brought me from my *Pagan* land,
Taught my benighted soul to understand
That there's a God, that there's a *Saviour* too;
Once I redemption neither sought nor knew,
Some view our sable race with scornful eye,
"Their color is a diabolic die."
Remember, *Christians, Negroes,* black as *Cain,*
May be refined, and join th' angelic train.

An Hymn to the Morning

Attend my lays, ye ever honour'd nine,
Assist my labours, and my strains refine;
In smoothest numbers pour the notes along,
For bright *Aurora* now demands my song.
  Aurora hail, and all the thousand dyes,
Which deck thy progress through the vaulted skies;
The morn awakes, and wide extends her rays,
On ev'ry leaf the gentle zephyr plays;
Harmonious lays the feather'd race resume,
Dart the bright eye, and shake the painted plume.
  Ye shady groves, your verdant gloom display
To shield your poet from the burning day:
Calliope awake the sacred lyre,
While thy fair sisters fan the pleasing fire:
The bow'rs, the gales, the variegated skies
In all their pleasures in my bosom rise.
  See in the east th' illustrious king of day!
His rising radiance drives the shades away—
But oh! I feel his fervid beams too strong,
And scarce begun, concludes th' abortive song.

On Virtue

O Thou bright jewel in my aim I strive
To comprehend thee. Thine own words declare
Wisdom is higher than a fool can reach.
I cease to wonder, and no more attempt
Thine height t' explore, or fathom thy profound,
But, O, my soul, sink not into despair,
Virtue is near thee, and with gentle hand
Would now embrace thee, hovers o'er thine head.
Fain would the heav'n-born soul with her converse,
Then seek, then court her for her promis'd bliss,
  Auspicious queen, thine heav'nly pinions spread,
And lead celestial *Chastity* along;
Lo! now her sacred retinue descends,
Array'd in glory from the orbs above.
Attend me, *Virtue*, thro' my youthful years!
O leave me not to the false joys of time!
But guide my steps to endless life and bliss.
Greatness, or *Goodness*, say what I shall call thee,
To give an higher appellation still,
Teach me a better strain, a nobler lay,
O thou, enthron'd with Cherubs in the realms of day.

JOEL BARLOW
(1754–1812)

The Hasty Pudding

A POEM IN THREE CANTOS

Written at Chambery, in Savoy, January 1793

Omne tulit punctum qui miscuit utile dulci.
He makes a good breakfast who mixes pudding with molasses.

Preface

A simplicity in diet, whether it be considered with reference to the happiness of individuals or the prosperity of a nation, is of more consequence than we are apt to imagine. In recommending so important an object to the rational part of mankind, I wish it were in my power to do it in such a manner as would be likely to gain their attention. I am sensible that it is one of those subjects in which example has infinitely more power than the most convincing arguments or the highest charms of poetry. Goldsmith's *Deserted Village*, though possessing these two advantages in a greater degree than any other work of the kind, has not prevented villages in England from being deserted. The apparent interest of the rich individuals, who form the taste as well as the laws in that country, has been against him; and with that interest it has been vain to contend.

The vicious habits which in this little piece I endeavor to combat, seem to me not so difficult to cure. No class of people has any *interest* in supporting them; unless it be the interest which certain families may feel in vying with each other in sumptuous entertainments. There may indeed be some instances of depraved appetites, which no arguments will conquer; but these must be rare. There are very few persons but what would always prefer a plain dish for themselves, and would prefer it likewise for their guests, if there were no risk of reputation in the case. This difficulty can only be removed by example; and the example should proceed from those whose situation enables them to take the lead in forming the manners of a nation. Persons of this description in America, I should hope, are neither above nor below the influence of truth and reason, when conveyed in language suited to the subject.

Whether the manner I have chosen to address my arguments to them be such as to promise any success is what I cannot decide. But I certainly had hopes of doing some good, or I should not have taken the pains of putting so many rimes together. The example of domestic virtues has doubtless a great effect. I only wish to rank *simplicity of diet* among the virtues. In that case I should hope it will be cherished and more esteemed by others than it is at present.

The Author

Canto I

Ye Alps audacious, through the heavens that rise,
To cramp the day and hide me from the skies;
Ye Gallic flags, that o'er their heights unfurled,
Bear death to kings, and freedom to the world,
I sing not you. A softer theme I choose,
A virgin theme, unconscious of the muse,
But fruitful, rich, well suited to inspire
The purest frenzy of poetic fire.

Despise it not, ye bards to terror steeled,
Who hurl your thunders round the epic field;
Nor ye who strain your midnight throats to sing
Joys that the vineyard and the stillhouse bring;
Or on some distant fair your notes employ,
And speak of raptures that you ne'er enjoy.
I sing the sweets I know, the charms I feel,
My morning incense, and my evening meal,
The sweets of Hasty Pudding. Come, dear bowl,
Glide o'er my palate, and inspire my soul.
The milk beside thee, smoking from the kine,
Its substance mingled, married in with thine,
Shall cool and temper thy superior heat,
And save the pains of blowing while I eat.

Oh! could the smooth, the emblematic song
Flow like thy genial juices o'er my tongue,
Could those mild morsels in my numbers chime,
And, as they roll in substance, roll in rime,

No more thy awkward unpoetic name
Should shun the muse, or prejudice thy fame;
But rising grateful to the accustomed ear,
All bards should catch it, and all realms revere!
    Assist me first with pious toil to trace
Through wrecks of time thy lineage and thy race;
Declare what lovely squaw, in days of yore,
(Ere great Columbus sought thy native shore)
First gave thee to the world; her works of fame
Have lived indeed, but lived without a name.
Some tawny Ceres, goddess of her days,
First learned with stones to crack the well-dried maize,
Through the rough sieve to shake the golden shower,
In boiling water stir the yellow flour:
The yellow flour, bestrewed and stirred with haste,
Swells in the flood and thickens to a paste,
Then puffs and wallops, rises to the brim,
Drinks the dry knobs that on the surface swim;
The knobs at last the busy ladle breaks,
And the whole mass its true consistence takes.
    Could but her sacred name, unknown so long,
Rise, like her labors, to the son of song,
To her, to them, I'd consecrate my lays,
And blow her pudding with the breath of praise.
If 'twas Oella, whom I sang before,
I here ascribe her one great virtue more.
Not through the rich Peruvian realms alone
The fame of Sol's sweet daughter should be known,
But o'er the world's wide climes should live secure,
Far as his rays extend, as long as they endure.
    Dear Hasty Pudding, what unpromised joy
Expands my heart, to meet thee in Savoy!
Doomed o'er the world through devious paths to roam,
Each clime my country, and each house my home,
My soul is soothed, my cares have found an end,
I greet my long-lost, unforgotten friend.
    For thee through Paris, that corrupted town,
How long in vain I wandered up and down,
Where shameless Bacchus, with his drenching hoard,
Cold from his cave usurps the morning board.

London is lost in smoke and steeped in tea;
No Yankee there can lisp the name of thee;
The uncouth word, a libel on the town,
Would call a proclamation from the crown.
For climes oblique, that fear the sun's full rays,
Chilled in their fogs, exclude the generous maize;
A grain whose rich luxuriant growth requires
Short gentle showers, and bright ethereal fires.
    But here, though distant from our native shore,
With mutual glee we meet and laugh once more.
The same! I know thee by that yellow face,
That strong complexion of true Indian race,
Which time can never change, nor soil impair,
Nor Alpine snows, nor Turkey's morbid air;
For endless years, through every mild domain,
Where grows the maize, there thou art sure to reign.
    But man, more fickle, the bold incense claims,
In different realms to give thee different names.
Thee the soft nations round the warm Levant
polanta call, the French of course *polenta;*
Ev'n in thy native regions, how I blush
To hear the Pennsylvanians call thee *mush!*
On Hudson's banks, while men of Belgic spawn
Insult and eat thee by the name *suppawn.*
All spurious appellations, void of truth;
I've better known thee from my earliest youth,
Thy name is *Hasty Pudding!* thus our sires
Were wont to greet thee fuming from their fires;
And while they argued in thy just defence
With logic clear, they thus explained the sense:
"In *haste* the boiling cauldron, o'er the blaze,
Receives and cooks the ready-powdered maize;
In *haste* 'tis served, and then in equal *haste,*
With cooling milk, we make the sweet repast.
No carving to be done, no knife to grate
The tender ear, and wound the stony plate;
But the smooth spoon, just fitted to the lip,
And taught with art the yielding mass to dip,
By frequent journeys to the bowl well stored,
Performs the hasty honors of the board."

Such is thy name, significant and clear,
A name, a sound to every Yankee dear,
But most to me, whose heart and palate chaste
Preserve my pure hereditary taste.
    There are who strive to stamp with disrepute
The luscious food, because it feeds the brute;
In tropes of high-strained wit, while gaudy prigs
Compare thy nursling, man, to pampered pigs;
With sovereign scorn I treat the vulgar jest,
Nor fear to share thy bounties with the beast.
What though the generous cow gives me to quaff
The milk nutritious; am I then a calf?
Or can the genius of the noisy swine,
Though nursed on pudding, thence lay claim to mine?
Sure the sweet song, I fashion to thy praise,
Runs more melodious than the notes they raise.
    My song resounding in its grateful glee,
No merit claims; I praise myself in thee.
My father loved thee through his length of days;
For thee his fields were shaded o'er with maize;
From thee what health, what vigor he possessed,
Ten sturdy freemen from his loins attest;
Thy constellation ruled my natal morn,
And all my bones were made of Indian corn.
Delicious grain! whatever form it take,
To roast or boil, to smother or to bake,
In every dish 'tis welcome still to me,
But most, my Hasty Pudding, most in thee.
    Let the green succotash with thee contend,
Let beans and corn their sweetest juices blend,
Let butter drench them in its yellow tide,
And a long slice of bacon grace their side;
Not all the plate, how famed soe'er it be,
Can please my palate like a bowl of thee.
    Some talk of hoe-cake, fair Virginia's pride,
Rich johnny-cake this mouth has often tried;
Both please me well, their virtues much the same;
Alike their fabric, as allied their fame,
Except in dear New England, where the last
Receives a dash of pumpkin in the paste,
To give it sweetness and improve the taste.

But place them all before me, smoking hot,
The big round dumpling rolling from the pot;
The pudding of the bag, whose quivering breast,
With suet lined, leads on the Yankee feast;
The charlotte brown, within whose crusty sides
A belly soft the pulpy apple hides;
The yellow bread, whose face like amber glows,
And all of Indian that the bakepan knows—
You tempt me not—my favorite greets my eyes,
To that loved bowl my spoon by instinct flies.

Canto II

To mix the food by vicious rules of art,
To kill the stomach and to sink the heart,
To make mankind to social virtue sour,
Cram o'er each dish, and be what they devour;
For this the kitchen muse first framed her book,
Commanding sweat to stream from every cook;
Children no more their antic gambols tried,
And friends to physic wandered why they died.
Not so the Yankee—his abundant feast,
With simples furnished, and with plainness dressed,
A numerous offspring gathers round the board,
And cheers alike the servant and the lord;
Whose well-bought hunger prompts the joyous taste,
And health attends them from the short repast.
While the full pail rewards the milkmaid's toil,
The mother sees the morning cauldron boil;
To stir the pudding next demands their care,
To spread the table and the bowls prepare;
To feed the children, as their portions cool,
And comb their heads, and send them off to school.
Yet may the simplest dish some rules impart,
For nature scorns not all the aids of art.
Ev'n Hasty Pudding, purest of all food,
May still be bad, indifferent, or good,
As sage experience the short process guides,
Or want of skill, or want of care presides.
Whoe'er would form it on the surest plan,
To rear the child and long sustain the man;

To shield the morals while it mends the size,
And all the powers of every food supplies,
Attend the lessons that the muse shall bring.
Suspend your spoons, and listen while I sing.

But since, O man! thy life and health demand
Not food alone, but labor from thy hand,
First in the field, beneath the sun's strong rays,
Ask of thy mother earth the needful maize;
She loves the race that courts her yielding soil,
And gives her bounties to the sons of toil.

When now the ox, obedient to thy call,
Repays the loan that filled the winter stall,
Pursue his traces o'er the furrowed plain,
And plant in measured hills the golden grain.
But when the tender germ begins to shoot,
And the green spire declares the sprouting root,
Then guard your nursling from each greedy foe,
The insidious worm, the all-devouring crow.
A little ashes, sprinkled round the spire,
Soon steeped in rain, will bid the worm retire;
The feathered robber with his hungry maw
Swift flies the field before your man of straw,
A frightful image, such as schoolboys bring
When met to burn the Pope or hang the King.

Thrice in the season, through each verdant row
Wield the strong plowshare and the faithful hoe;
The faithful hoe, a double task that takes,
To till the summer corn, and roast the winter cakes.

Slow springs the blade, while checked by chilling rains,
Ere yet the sun the seat of Cancer gains;
But when his fiercest fires emblaze the land,
Then start the juices, then the roots expand;
Then, like a column of Corinthian mold,
The stalk struts upward, and the leaves unfold;
The busy branches all the ridges fill,
Entwine their arms, and kiss from hill to hill.
Here cease to vex them, all your cares are done;
Leave the last labors to the parent sun;
Beneath his genial smiles the well-dressed field,
When autumn calls, a plenteous crop shall yield.

Now the strong foliage bears the standards high,
And shoots the tall top-gallants to the sky;
The suckling ears their silky fringes bend,
And pregnant grown, their swelling coats distend;
The loaded stalk, while still the burden grows,
O'erhangs the space that runs between the rows;
High as a hop-field waves the silent grove,
A safe retreat for little thefts of love,
When the pledged roasting-ears invite the maid,
To meet her swain beneath the new-formed shade;
His generous hand unloads the cumbrous hill,
And the green spoils her ready basket fill;
Small compensation for the two-fold bliss,
The promised wedding and the present kiss.

Slight depredations these; but now the moon
Calls from his hollow tree the sly raccoon;
And while by night he bears his prize away,
The bolder squirrel labors through the day.
Both thieves alike, but provident of time,
A virtue rare, that almost hides their crime.
Then let them steal the little stores they can,
And fill their granaries from the toils of man;
We've one advantage where they take no part,
With all their wiles they ne'er have found the art
To boil the Hasty Pudding; here we shine
Superior far to tenants of the pine;
This envied boon to man shall still belong,
Unshared by them in substance or in song.

At last the closing season browns the plain,
And ripe October gathers in the grain;
Deep loaded carts the spacious corn-house fill,
The sack distended marches to the mill;
The laboring mill beneath the burden groans,
And showers the future pudding from the stones;
Till the glad housewife greets the powdered gold,
And the new crop exterminates the old.

Canto III

The days grow short; but though the falling sun
To the glad swain proclaims his day's work done,

Night's pleasing shades his various task prolong,
And yield new subjects to my various song.
For now, the corn-house filled, the harvest home,
The invited neighbors to the *husking* come;
A frolic scene, where work, and mirth, and play,
Unite their charms, to chase the hours away.
Where the huge heap lies centered in the hall,
The lamp suspended from the cheerful wall,
Brown corn-fed nymphs, and strong hard-handed beaux,
Alternate ranged, extend in circling rows,
Assume their seats, the solid mass attack;
The dry husks rustle, and the corncobs crack;
The song, the laugh, alternate notes resound,
And the sweet cider trips in silence round.
The laws of husking every wight can tell;
And sure no laws he ever keeps so well:
For each red ear a general kiss he gains,
With each smut ear he smuts the luckless swains;
But when to some sweet maid a prize is cast,
Red as her lips, and taper as her waist,
She walks the round, and culls one favored beau,
Who leaps, the luscious tribute to bestow.
Various the sport, as are the wits and brains
Of well-pleased lasses and contending swains;
Till the vast mound of corn is swept away,
And he that gets the last ear wins the day.
Meanwhile the housewife urges all her care,
The well-earned feast to hasten and prepare.
The sifted meal already waits her hand,
The milk is strained, the bowls in order stand,
The fire flames high; and, as a pool (that takes
The headlong stream that o'er the milldam breaks)
Foams, roars, and rages with incessant toils,
So the vexed cauldron rages, roars, and boils.
First with clean salt she seasons well the food,
Then strews the flour, and thickens all the flood.
Long o'er the simmering fire she lets it stand;
To stir it well demands a stronger hand;
The husband takes his turn; and round and round
The ladle flies; at last the toil is crowned;

When to the board the thronging huskers pour,
And take their seats as at the corn before.
I leave them to their feast. There still belong
More copious matters to my faithful song.
For rules there are, though ne'er unfolded yet,
Nice rules and wise, how pudding should be ate.
Some with molasses line the luscious treat,
And mix, like bards, the useful with the sweet.
A wholesome dish, and well deserving praise,
A great resource in those bleak wintry days,
When the chilled earth lies buried deep in snow,
And raging Boreas drives the shivering cow.
Blessed cow! thy praise shall still my notes employ,
Great source of health, the only source of joy;
Mother of Egypt's God—but sure, for me,
Were I to leave my God, I'd worship thee.
How oft thy teats these pious hands have pressed!
How oft thy bounties proved my only feast!
How oft I've fed thee with my favorite grain!
And roared, like thee, to find thy children slain!
Ye swains who know her various worth to prize,
Ah! house her well from winter's angry skies.
Potatoes, pumpkins, should her sadness cheer,
Corn from your crib, and mashes from your beer;
When spring returns she'll well acquaint the loan,
And nurse at once your infants and her own.
Milk then with pudding I should always choose;
To this in future I confine my muse,
Till she in haste some further hints unfold,
Well for the young, nor useless to the old.
First in your bowl the milk abundant take,
Then drop with care along the silver lake
Your flakes of pudding; these at first will hide
Their little bulk beneath the swelling tide;
But when their growing mass no more can sink,
When the soft island looms above the brink,
Then check your hand; you've got the portion's due,
So taught our sires, and what they taught is true.
There is a choice in spoons. Though small appear
The nice distinction, yet to me 'tis clear.

The deep-bowled Gallic spoon, contrived to scoop
In ample draughts the thin diluted soup,
Performs not well in those substantial things,
Whose mass adhesive to the metal clings;
Where the strong labial muscles must embrace,
The gentle curve, and sweep the hollow space.
With ease to enter and discharge the freight,
A bowl less concave but still more dilate,
Becomes the pudding best. The shape, the size,
A secret rests unknown to vulgar eyes.
Experienced feeders can alone impart
A rule so much above the lore of art.
These tuneful lips that thousand spoons have tried,
With just precision could the point decide,
Though not in song; the muse but poorly shines
In cones, and cubes, and geometric lines;
Yet the true form, as near as she can tell,
Is that small section of a goose-egg shell,
Which in two equal portions shall divide
The distance from the center to the side.
    Fear not to slaver; 'tis no deadly sin.
Like the free Frenchman, from your joyous chin
Suspend the ready napkin; or, like me,
Poise with one hand your bowl upon your knee;
Just in the zenith your wise head project,
Your full spoon, rising in a line direct,
Bold as a bucket, heeds no drops that fall,
The wide-mouthed bowl will surely catch them all.

ROYALL TYLER
(1757–1826)

Gambling

Of every vice pursued by those
In folly's by-paths rambling,
There's none so bad in its dread close,
As the vile vice of gambling.
It taints our morals, wastes our time
And fills us with vexation.
Destroys our wealth and youthful prime,
And mars our reputation.
Yet I'll aver, with my own eyes,
And I am not called stupid,
I caught sweet Fanny by surprise
A gambling with young Cupid!
Beneath the silent moon's soft beams
In fragrant flowery arbor,
That noted gambling house it seems,
Where players love to harbor.
The cunning god and simple fair,
Sat down to play at leisure
And staked such sums as might impair
A mighty monarch's treasure.
And first they played for locks of hair
And Fanny won the game.
Then cheeks and lips & skin so fair
Her luck was all the same.
Vex'd by the maid to be outdone
Then Cupid made a high bet,
Stak'd all his smiles—a mighty sum
With dimples for a by-bet.

But still she won, & Cupid crost
Made dreadful sad grimaces,
Not only his own smiles he lost,
But all his mother's graces.
Proud Fanny's air and looks and eyes
Of victory gave token,
Her winnings seemed a noble prize,
A bank not to be broken.
Beware sweet girl and go no more
To midnight arbors rambling,
But think how soon you may deplore,
The dreadful end of gambling.
Sly Cupid has but played the knave,
And let you come off winner;
This is the way all gamblers have,
With every new beginner.
Some sharper soon will with you sport,
By Cupid's malice sent hence,
Win all your winnings and leave naught,
But sorrow and repentance.

A Love Song

By the fierce flames of Love I'm in a sad taking,
I'm singed like a pig that is hung up for bacon,
My stomach is scorched like an over-done mutton-chop,
That for want of gravy wont afford a single drop.
    Love, love, love is like a dizziness,
    Wont let a poor man go about his business.

My great toes and little toes are burnt to a cinder,
As a hot burning-glass burns a dish-cloth to tinder,
As cheese by a hot salamander is roasted,
By beauty that's red-hot, like a cheese am I toasted.
    Love, love, love is like a dizziness,
    Wont let a poor man go about his business.

Attend all young lovers, who after ladies dandle,
I'm singed like a duck's foot over a candle,
By this that and t'other, I'm treated uncivil,
Like a gizzard I'm peppered, and then made a devil.
    Love, love, love is like a dizziness,
    Wont let a poor man go about his business.

WILLIAM CULLEN BRYANT
(1794–1878)

Thanatopsis

To him who in the love of Nature holds
Communion with her visible forms, she speaks
A various language; for his gayer hours
She has a voice of gladness, and a smile
And eloquence of beauty, and she glides
Into his darker musings, with a mild
And healing sympathy, that steals away
Their sharpness, ere he is aware. When thoughts
Of the last bitter hour come like a blight
Over thy spirit, and sad images
Of the stern agony, and shroud, and pall,
And breathless darkness, and the narrow house,
Make thee to shudder, and grow sick at heart;—
Go forth, under the open sky, and list
To Nature's teachings, while from all around—
Earth and her waters, and the depths of air—
Comes a still voice.—

Yet a few days, and thee
The all-beholding sun shall see no more
In all his course; nor yet in the cold ground,
Where thy pale form was laid, with many tears,
Nor in the embrace of ocean, shall exist
Thy image. Earth, that nourished thee, shall claim
Thy growth, to be resolved to earth again,
And, lost each human trace, surrendering up
Thine individual being, shalt thou go
To mix for ever with the elements,
To be a brother to the insensible rock

And to the sluggish clod, which the rude swain
Turns with his share, and treads upon. The oak
Shall send his roots abroad, and pierce thy mould.

Yet not to thine eternal resting-place
Shalt thou retire alone, nor couldst thou wish
Couch more magnificent. Thou shalt lie down
With patriarchs of the infant world—with kings,
The powerful of the earth—the wise, the good,
Fair forms, and hoary seers of ages past,
All in one mighty sepulchre. The hills
Rock-ribbed and ancient as the sun,—the vales
Stretching in pensive quietness between;
The venerable woods—rivers that move
In majesty, and the complaining brooks
That make the meadows green; and, poured round all,
Old Ocean's gray and melancholy waste,—
Are but the solemn decorations all
Of the great tomb of man. The golden sun,
The planets, all the infinite host of heaven,
Are shining on the sad abodes of death,
Through the still lapse of ages. All that tread
The globe are but a handful to the tribes
That slumber in its bosom.—Take the wings
Of morning, pierce the Barcan wilderness,
Or lose thyself in the continuous woods
Where rolls the Oregon, and hears no sound,
Save his own dashings—yet the dead are there:
And millions in those solitudes, since first
The flight of years began, have laid them down
In their last sleep—the dead reign there alone.
So shalt thou rest, and what if thou withdraw
In silence from the living, and no friend
Take note of thy departure? All that breathe
Will share thy destiny. The gay will laugh
When thou art gone, the solemn brood of care
Plod on, and each one as before will chase
His favorite phantom; yet all these shall leave
Their mirth and their employments, and shall come
And make their bed with thee. As the long train
Of ages glides away, the sons of men,
The youth in life's fresh spring, and he who goes

In the full strength of years, matron and maid,
The speechless babe, and the gray-headed man—
Shall one by one be gathered to thy side,
By those, who in their turn shall follow them.

So live, that when thy summons comes to join
The innumerable caravan, which moves
To that mysterious realm, where each shall take
His chamber in the silent halls of death,
Thou go not, like the quarry-slave at night,
Scourged to his dungeon, but, sustained and soothed
By an unfaltering trust, approach thy grave,
Like one who wraps the drapery of his couch
About him, and lies down to pleasant dreams.

The Yellow Violet

When beechen buds begin to swell,
  And woods the blue-bird's warble know,
The yellow violet's modest bell
  Peeps from the last year's leaves below.

Ere russet fields their green resume,
  Sweet flower, I love, in forest bare,
To meet thee, when thy faint perfume
  Alone is in the virgin air.

Of all her train, the hands of Spring
  First plant thee in the watery mould,
And I have seen thee blossoming
  Beside the snow-bank's edges cold.

Thy parent sun, who bade thee view
  Pale skies, and chilling moisture sip,
Has bathed thee in his own bright hue,
  And streaked with jet thy glowing lip.

Yet slight thy form, and low thy seat,
  And earthward bent thy gentle eye,
Unapt the passing view to meet,
  When loftier flowers are flaunting nigh.

Oft, in the sunless April day,
  Thy early smile has stayed my walk;
But midst the gorgeous blooms of May,
  I passed thee on thy humble stalk.

So they, who climb to wealth, forget
  The friends in darker fortunes tried.
I copied them—but I regret
  That I should ape the ways of pride.

And when again the genial hour
  Awakes the painted tribes of light,
I'll not o'erlook the modest flower
  That made the woods of April bright.

Inscription for the Entrance to a Wood

Stranger, if thou hast learned a truth which needs
No school of long experience, that the world
Is full of guilt and misery, and hast seen
Enough of all its sorrows, crimes, and cares,
To tire thee of it, enter this wild wood
And view the haunts of Nature. The calm shade
Shall bring a kindred calm, and the sweet breeze
That makes the green leaves dance, shall waft a balm
To thy sick heart. Thou wilt find nothing here
Of all that pained thee in the haunts of men,
And made thee loathe thy life. The primal curse
Fell, it is true, upon the unsinning earth,
But not in vengeance. God hath yoked to guilt
Her pale tormentor, misery. Hence, these shades
Are still the abodes of gladness; the thick roof
Of green and stirring branches is alive

And musical with birds, that sing and sport
In wantonness of spirit; while below
The squirrel, with raised paws and form erect,
Chirps merrily. Throngs of insects in the shade
Try their thin wings and dance in the warm beam
That waked them into life. Even the green trees
Partake the deep contentment; as they bend
To the soft winds, the sun from the blue sky
Looks in and sheds a blessing on the scene.
Scarce less the cleft-born wild-flower seems to enjoy
Existence than the wingèd plunderer
That sucks its sweets. The mossy rocks themselves,
And the old and ponderous trunks of prostrate trees
That lead from knoll to knoll a causey rude
Or bridge the sunken brook, and their dark roots,
With all their earth upon them, twisting high,
Breathe fixed tranquillity. The rivulet
Sends forth glad sounds, and tripping o'er its bed
Of pebbly sands, or leaping down the rocks,
Seems, with continuous laughter, to rejoice
In its own being. Softly tread the marge,
Lest from her midway perch thou scare the wren
That dips her bill in water. The cool wind,
That stirs the stream in play, shall come to thee,
Like one that loves thee nor will let thee pass
Ungreeted, and shall give its light embrace.

To a Waterfowl

Whither, midst falling dew,
  While glow the heavens with the last steps of day,
Far, through their rosy depths, dost thou pursue
  Thy solitary way?

  Vainly the fowler's eye
Might mark thy distant flight to do thee wrong,
As, darkly painted on the crimson sky,
  Thy figure floats along.

Seek'st thou the plashy brink
Of weedy lake, or marge of river wide,
Or where the rocking billows rise and sink
On the chafed ocean-side?

There is a Power whose care
Teaches thy way along that pathless coast—
The desert and illimitable air—
Lone wandering, but not lost.

All day thy wings have fanned,
At that far height, the cold, thin atmosphere,
Yet stoop not, weary, to the welcome land,
Though the dark night is near.

And soon that toil shall end;
Soon shalt thou find a summer home, and rest,
And scream among thy fellows; reeds shall bend,
Soon, o'er thy sheltered nest.

Thou'rt gone, the abyss of heaven
Hath swallowed up thy form; yet, on my heart
Deeply has sunk the lesson thou hast given,
And shall not soon depart.

He who, from zone to zone,
Guides through the boundless sky thy certain flight,
In the long way that I must tread alone,
Will lead my steps aright.

A Forest Hymn

The groves were God's first temples. Ere man learned
To hew the shaft, and lay the architrave,
And spread the roof above them—ere he framed
The lofty vault, to gather and roll back
The sound of anthems; in the darkling wood,
Amid the cool and silence, he knelt down,

And offered to the Mightiest solemn thanks
And supplication. For his simple heart
Might not resist the sacred influence
Which, from the stilly twilight of the place,
And from the gray old trunks that high in heaven
Mingled their mossy boughs, and from the sound
Of the invisible breath that swayed at once
All their green tops, stole over him, and bowed
His spirit with the thought of boundless power
And inaccessible majesty. Ah, why
Should we, in the world's riper years, neglect
God's ancient sanctuaries, and adore
Only among the crowd, and under roofs
That our frail hands have raised? Let me, at least,
Here, in the shadow of this aged wood,
Offer one hymn—thrice happy, if it find
Acceptance in His ear.

Father, thy hand
Hath reared these venerable columns, thou
Didst weave this verdant roof. Thou didst look down
Upon the naked earth, and, forthwith, rose
All these fair ranks of trees. They, in thy sun,
Budded, and shook their green leaves in thy breeze,
And shot toward heaven. The century-living crow
Whose birth was in their tops, grew old and died
Among their branches, till, at last, they stood,
As now they stand, massy, and tall, and dark,
Fit shrine for humble worshipper to hold
Communion with his Maker. These dim vaults,
These winding aisles, of human pomp or pride
Report not. No fantastic carvings show
The boast of our vain race to change the form
Of thy fair works. But thou art here—thou fill'st
The solitude. Thou art in the soft winds
That run along the summit of these trees
In music; thou art in the cooler breath
That from the inmost darkness of the place
Comes, scarcely felt; the barky trunks, the ground,
The fresh moist ground, are all instinct with thee.
Here is continual worship;—Nature, here,

In the tranquillity that thou dost love,
Enjoys thy presence. Noiselessly, around,
From perch to perch, the solitary bird
Passes; and yon clear spring, that, midst its herbs,
Wells softly forth and wandering steeps the roots
Of half the mighty forest, tells no tale
Of all the good it does. Thou has not left
Thyself without a witness, in the shades,
Of thy perfections. Grandeur, strength, and grace
Are here to speak of thee. This mighty oak—
By whose immovable stem I stand and seem
Almost annihilated—not a prince,
In all that proud old world beyond the deep,
E'er wore his crown as loftily as he
Wears the green coronal of leaves with which
Thy hand has graced him. Nestled at his root
Is beauty, such as blooms not in the glare
Of the broad sun. That delicate forest flower,
With scented breath and look so like a smile,
Seems, as it issues from the shapeless mould,
An emanation of the indwelling Life,
A visible token of the upholding Love,
That are the soul of this great universe.

My heart is awed within me when I think
Of the great miracle that still goes on,
In silence, round me—the perpetual work
Of thy creation, finished, yet renewed
Forever. Written on thy works I read
The lesson of thy own eternity.
Lo! all grow old and die—but see again,
How on the faltering footsteps of decay
Youth presses—ever gay and beautiful youth
In all its beautiful forms. These lofty trees
Wave not less proudly that their ancestors
Moulder beneath them. Oh, there is not lost
One of earth's charms: upon her bosom yet,
After the flight of untold centuries,
The freshness of her far beginning lies
And yet shall lie. Life mocks the idle hate
Of his arch-enemy Death—yea, seats himself

Upon the tyrant's throne—the sepulchre,
And of the triumphs of his ghastly foe
Makes his own nourishment. For he came forth
From thine own bosom, and shall have no end.

There have been holy men who hid themselves
Deep in the woody wilderness, and gave
Their lives to thought and prayer, till they outlived
The generation born with them, nor seemed
Less aged than the hoary trees and rocks
Around them;—and there have been holy men
Who deemed it were not well to pass life thus.
But let me often to these solitudes
Retire, and in thy presence reassure
My feeble virtue. Here its enemies,
The passions, at thy plainer footsteps shrink
And tremble and are still. O God! when thou
Dost scare the world with tempests, set on fire
The heavens with falling thunderbolts, or fill,
With all the waters of the firmament,
The swift dark whirlwind that uproots the woods
And drowns the villages; when, at thy call,
Uprises the great deep and throws himself
Upon the continent, and overwhelms
Its cities—who forgets not, at the sight
Of these tremendous tokens of thy power,
His pride, and lays his strifes and follies by?
Oh, from these sterner aspects of thy face
Spare me and mine, nor let us need the wrath
Of the mad unchained elements to teach
Who rules them. Be it ours to meditate,
In these calm shades, thy milder majesty,
And to the beautiful order of thy works
Learn to conform the order of our lives.

A Meditation on Rhode Island Coal

Decolor, obscurus, vilis, non ille repexam
Cesariem regum, non candida virginis ornat
Colla, nec insigni splendet per cingula morsu
Sed nova si nigri videas miracula saxi,
Tunc superat pulchros cultus et quicquid Eois
Indus litoribus rubra scrutatur in alga.

CLAUDIAN.

I sat beside the glowing grate, fresh heaped
 With Newport coal, and as the flame grew bright
—The many-colored flame—and played and leaped,
 I thought of rainbows, and the northern light,
Moore's Lalla Rookh, the Treasury Report,
And other brilliant matters of the sort.

And last I thought of that fair isle which sent
 The mineral fuel; on a summer day
I saw it once, with heat and travel spent,
 And scratched by dwarf-oaks in the hollow way.
Now dragged through sand, now jolted over stone—
A rugged road through rugged Tiverton.

And hotter grew the air, and hollower grew
 The deep-worn path, and horror-struck, I thought,
Where will this dreary passage lead me to?
 This long dull road, so narrow, deep, and hot?
I looked to see it dive in earth outright;
I looked—but saw a far more welcome sight.

Like a soft mist upon the evening shore,
 At once a lovely isle before me lay,
Smooth, and with tender verdure covered o'er,
 As if just risen from its calm inland bay;
Sloped each way gently to the grassy edge,
And the small waves that dallied with the sedge.

The barley was just reaped; the heavy sheaves
  Lay on the stubble-field; the tall maize stood
Dark in its summer growth, and shook its leaves,
  And bright the sunlight played on the young wood—
For fifty years ago, the old men say,
The Briton hewed their ancient groves away.

I saw where fountains freshened the green land,
  And where the pleasant road, from door to door,
With rows of cherry-trees on either hand,
  Went wandering all that fertile region o'er—
Rogue's Island once—but when the rogues were dead,
Rhode Island was the name it took instead.

Beautiful island! then it only seemed
  A lovely stranger; it has grown a friend.
I gazed on its smooth slopes, but never dreamed
  How soon that green and quiet isle would send
The treasures of its womb across the sea,
To warm a poet's room and boil his tea.

Dark anthracite! that reddenest on my hearth,
  Thou in those island mines didst slumber long;
But now thou art come forth to move the earth,
  And put to shame the men that mean thee wrong:
Thou shalt be coals of fire to those that hate thee,
And warm the shins of all that underrate thee.

Yea, they did wrong thee foully—they who mocked
  Thy honest face, and said thou wouldst not burn;
Of hewing thee to chimney-pieces talked,
  And grew profane, and swore, in bitter scorn,
That men might to thy inner caves retire,
And there, unsinged, abide the day of fire.

Yet is thy greatness nigh. I pause to state,
  That I too have seen greatness—even I—
Shook hands with Adams, stared at La Fayette,
  When, barehead, in the hot noon of July,
He would not let the umbrella be held o'er him,
For which three cheers burst from the mob before him.

And I have seen—not many months ago—
  An eastern Governor in chapeau bras
And military coat, a glorious show!
  Ride forth to visit the reviews, and ah!
How oft he smiled and bowed to Jonathan!
How many hands were shook and votes were won!

'Twas a Great Governor; thou too shalt be
  Great in thy turn, and wide shall spread thy fame
And swiftly; furthest Maine shall hear of thee,
  And cold New Brunswick gladden at thy name;
And, faintly through its sleets, the weeping isle
That sends the Boston folks their cod shall smile.

For thou shalt forge vast railways, and shalt heat
  The hissing rivers into steam, and drive
Huge masses from thy mines, on iron feet,
  Walking their steady way, as if alive,
Northward, till everlasting ice besets thee,
And South as far as the grim Spaniard lets thee.

Thou shalt make mighty engines swim the sea,
  Like its own monsters—boats that for a guinea
Will take a man to Havre—and shalt be
  The moving soul of many a spinning-jenny,
And ply thy shuttles, till a bard can wear
As good a suit of broadcloth as the mayor.

Then we will laugh at winter when we hear
  The grim old churl about our dwellings rave:
Thou, from that "ruler of the inverted year,"
  Shalt pluck the knotty sceptre Cowper gave,
And pull him from his sledge, and drag him in,
And melt the icicles from off his chin.

To the Fringed Gentian

Thou blossom bright with autumn dew,
And colored with the heaven's own blue,
That openest when the quiet light
Succeeds the keen and frosty night.

Thou comest not when violets lean
O'er wandering brooks and springs unseen,
Or columbines, in purple dressed,
Nod o'er the ground-bird's hidden nest.

Thou waitest late and com'st alone,
When woods are bare and birds are flown,
And frosts and shortening days portend
The aged year is near his end.

Then doth thy sweet and quiet eye
Look through its fringes to the sky,
Blue—blue—as if that sky let fall
A flower from its cerulean wall.

I would that thus, when I shall see
The hour of death draw near to me,
Hope, blossoming within my heart,
May look to heaven as I depart.

The Prairies

These are the gardens of the Desert, these
The unshorn fields, boundless and beautiful,
For which the speech of England has no name—
The Prairies. I behold them for the first,
And my heart swells, while the dilated sight

Takes in the encircling vastness. Lo! they stretch,
In airy undulations, far away,
As if the ocean, in his gentlest swell,
Stood still, with all his rounded billows fixed,
And motionless forever.—Motionless?—
No—they are all unchained again. The clouds
Sweep over with their shadows, and, beneath,
The surface rolls and fluctuates to the eye;
Dark hollows seem to glide along and chase
The sunny ridges. Breezes of the South!
Who toss the golden and the flame-like flowers.
And pass the prairie-hawk that, poised on high,
Flaps his broad wings, yet moves not—ye have played
Among the palms of Mexico and vines
Of Texas, and have crisped the limpid brooks
That from the fountains of Sonora glide
Into the calm Pacific—have ye fanned
A nobler or a lovelier scene than this?
Man hath no power in all this glorious work:
The hand that built the firmament hath heaved
And smoothed these verdant swells, and sown their slopes
With herbage, planted them with island groves,
And hedged them round with forests. Fitting floor
For this magnificent temple of the sky—
With flowers whose glory and whose multitude
Rival the constellations! The great heavens
Seem to stoop down upon the scene in love,—
A nearer vault, and of a tenderer blue,
Than that which bends above our eastern hills.

As o'er the verdant waste I guide my steed,
Among the high rank grass that sweeps his sides
The hollow beating of his footstep seems
A sacrilegious sound. I think of those
Upon whose rest he tramples. Are they here—
The dead of other days?—and did the dust
Of these fair solitudes once stir with life
And burn with passion? Let the mighty mounds
That overlook the rivers, or that rise
In the dim forest crowded with old oaks,
Answer. A race, that long has passed away,

Built them;—a disciplined and populous race
Heaped, with long toil, the earth, while yet the Greek
Was hewing the Pentelicus to forms
Of symmetry, and rearing on its rock
The glittering Parthenon. These ample fields
Nourished their harvests, here their herds were fed,
When haply by their stalls the bison lowed,
And bowed his manèd shoulder to the yoke.
All day this desert murmured with their toils,
Till twilight blushed, and lovers walked, and wooed
In a forgotten language, and old tunes,
From instruments of unremembered form,
Gave the soft winds a voice. The red man came—
The roaming hunter tribes, warlike and fierce,
And the mound-builders vanished from the earth.
The solitude of centuries untold
Has settled where they dwelt. The prairie-wolf
Hunts in their meadows, and his fresh-dug den
Yawns by my path. The gopher mines the ground
Where stood their swarming cities. All is gone;
All—save the piles of earth that hold their bones,
The platforms where they worshipped unknown gods,
The barriers which they builded from the soil
To keep the foe at bay—till o'er the walls
The wild beleaguerers broke, and, one by one,
The strongholds of the plain were forced, and heaped
With corpses. The brown vultures of the wood
Flocked to those vast uncovered sepulchres,
And sat unscared and silent at their feast.
Haply some solitary fugitive,
Lurking in marsh and forest, till the sense
Of desolation and of fear became
Bitterer than death, yielded himself to die.
Man's better nature triumphed then. Kind words
Welcomed and soothed him; the rude conquerors
Seated the captive with their chiefs; he chose
A bride among their maidens, and at length
Seemed to forget—yet ne'er forgot—the wife
Of his first love, and her sweet little ones,
Butchered, amid their shrieks, with all his race.

Thus change the forms of being. Thus arise
Races of living things, glorious in strength,
And perish, as the quickening breath of God
Fills them, or is withdrawn. The red man, too,
Has left the blooming wilds he ranged so long,
And, nearer to the Rocky Mountains, sought
A wilder hunting-ground. The beaver builds
No longer by these streams, but far away,
On waters whose blue surface ne'er gave back
The white man's face—among Missouri's springs,
And pools whose issues swell the Oregon—
He rears his little Venice. In these plains
The bison feeds no more. Twice twenty leagues
Beyond remotest smoke of hunter's camp,
Roams the majestic brute, in herds that shake
The earth with thundering steps—yet here I meet
His ancient footprints stamped beside the pool.

Still this great solitude is quick with life.
Myriads of insects, gaudy as the flowers
They flutter over, gentle quadrupeds,
And birds, that scarce have learned the fear of man,
Are here, and sliding reptiles of the ground,
Startlingly beautiful. The graceful deer
Bounds to the wood at my approach. The bee,
A more adventurous colonist than man,
With whom he came across the eastern deep,
Fills the savannas with his murmurings,
And hides his sweets, as in the golden age,
Within the hollow oak. I listen long
To his domestic hum, and think I hear
The sound of that advancing multitude
Which soon shall fill these deserts. From the ground
Comes up the laugh of children, the soft voice
Of maidens, and the sweet and solemn hymn
Of Sabbath worshippers. The low of herds
Blends with the rustling of the heavy grain
Over the dark brown furrows. All at once
A fresher wind sweeps by, and breaks my dream,
And I am in the wilderness alone.

The Poet

Thou, who wouldst wear the name
  Of poet mid thy brethren of mankind,
And clothe in words of flame
  Thoughts that shall live within the general mind!
Deem not the framing of a deathless lay
The pastime of a drowsy summer day.

But gather all thy powers,
  And wreak them on the verse that thou dost weave,
And in thy lonely hours,
  At silent morning or at wakeful eve,
While the warm current tingles through thy veins,
Set forth the burning words in fluent strains.

No smooth array of phrase,
  Artfully sought and ordered though it be,
Which the cold rhymer lays
  Upon his page with languid industry,
Can wake the listless pulse to livelier speed,
Or fill with sudden tears the eyes that read.

The secret wouldst thou know
  To touch the heart or fire the blood at will?
Let thine own eyes o'erflow;
  Let thy lips quiver with the passionate thrill;
Seize the great thought, ere yet its power be past,
And bind, in words, the fleet emotion fast.

Then, should thy verse appear
  Halting and harsh, and all unaptly wrought,
Touch the crude line with fear,
  Save in the moment of impassioned thought;
Then summon back the original glow, and mend
The strain with rapture that with fire was penned.

Yet let no empty gust
  Of passion find an utterance in thy lay,
A blast that whirls the dust
  Along the howling street and dies away;
But feelings of calm power and mighty sweep,
Like currents journeying through the windless deep.

Seek'st thou, in living lays,
  To limn the beauty of the earth and sky?
Before thine inner gaze
  Let all that beauty in clear vision lie;
Look on it with exceeding love, and write
The words inspired by wonder and delight.

Of tempests wouldst thou sing,
  Or tell of battles—make thyself a part
Of the great tumult; cling
  To the tossed wreck with terror in thy heart;
Scale, with the assaulting host, the rampart's height,
And strike and struggle in the thickest fight.

So shalt thou frame a lay
  That haply may endure from age to age,
And they who read shall say:
  "What witchery hangs upon this poet's page!
What art is his the written spells to find
That sway from mood to mood the willing mind!"

To Cole, the Painter, Departing for Europe

Thine eyes shall see the light of distant skies;
  Yet, Cole! thy heart shall bear to Europe's strand
  A living image of our own bright land,
Such as upon thy glorious canvas lies;
Lone lakes—savannas where the bison roves—
  Rocks rich with summer garlands—solemn streams—
  Skies, where the desert eagle wheels and screams—
Spring bloom and autumn blaze of boundless groves.

Fair scenes shall greet thee where thou goest—fair,
But different—everywhere the trace of men,
Paths, homes, graves, ruins, from the lowest glen
To where life shrinks from the fierce Alpine air.
Gaze on them, till the tears shall dim thy sight,
But keep that earlier, wilder image bright.

"Oh Fairest of the Rural Maids"

Oh fairest of the rural maids!
Thy birth was in the forest shades;
Green boughs, and glimpses of the sky,
Were all that met thine infant eye.

Thy sports, thy wanderings, when a child,
Were ever in the sylvan wild;
And all the beauty of the place
Is in thy heart and on thy face.

The twilight of the trees and rocks
Is in the light shade of thy locks;
Thy step is as the wind, that weaves
Its playful way among the leaves.

Thine eyes are springs, in whose serene
And silent waters heaven is seen;
Their lashes are the herbs that look
On their young figures in the brook.

The forest depths, by foot unpressed,
Are not more sinless than thy breast;
The holy peace, that fills the air
Of those calm solitudes, is there.

The Tides

The moon is at her full, and, riding high,
    Floods the calm fields with light;
The airs that hover in the summer-sky
    Are all asleep to-night.

There comes no voice from the great woodlands round
    That murmured all the day;
Beneath the shadow of their boughs the ground
    Is not more still than they.

But ever heaves and moans the restless Deep;
    His rising tides I hear,
Afar I see the glimmering billows leap;
    I see them breaking near.

Each wave springs upward, climbing toward the fair
    Pure light that sits on high—
Springs eagerly, and faintly sinks, to where
    The mother-waters lie.

Upward again it swells; the moonbeams show
    Again its glimmering crest;
Again it feels the fatal weight below,
    And sinks, but not to rest.

Again and yet again; until the Deep
    Recalls his brood of waves;
And, with a sullen moan, abashed, they creep
    Back to his inner caves.

Brief respite! they shall rush from that recess
    With noise and tumult soon,
And fling themselves, with unavailing stress,
    Up toward the placid moon.

O restless Sea, that, in thy prison here,
Dost struggle and complain;
Through the slow centuries yearning to be near
To that fair orb in vain;

The glorious source of light and heat must warm
Thy billows from on high,
And change them to the cloudy trains that form
The curtain of the sky.

Then only may they leave the waste of brine
In which they welter here,
And rise above the hills of earth, and shine
In a serener sphere.

The Death of Lincoln

Oh, slow to smite and swift to spare,
Gentle and merciful and just!
Who, in the fear of God, didst bear
The sword of power, a nation's trust!

In sorrow by thy bier we stand,
Amid the awe that hushes all,
And speak the anguish of a land
That shook with horror at thy fall.

Thy task is done; the bound are free:
We bear thee to an honored grave,
Whose proudest monument shall be
The broken fetters of the slave.

Pure was thy life: its bloody close
Hath placed thee with the sons of light,
Among the noble host of those
Who perished in the cause of Right.

RALPH WALDO EMERSON
(1803–1882)

Concord Hymn

Sung at the completion of the Battle Monument, July 4, 1837

By the rude bridge that arched the flood,
  Their flag to April's breeze unfurled,
Here once the embattled farmers stood
  And fired the shot heard round the world.

The foe long since in silence slept;
  Alike the conqueror silent sleeps;
And Time the ruined bridge has swept
  Down the dark stream which seaward creeps.

On this green bank, by this soft stream,
  We set today a votive stone;
That memory may their deed redeem,
  When, like our sires, our sons are gone.

Spirit, that made those heroes dare,
  To die, and leave their children free,
Bid Time and Nature gently spare
  The shaft we raise to them and thee.

Brahma

If the red slayer think he slays,
  Or if the slain think he is slain,
They know not well the subtle ways
  I keep, and pass, and turn again.

Far or forgot to me is near;
  Shadow and sunlight are the same;
The vanquished gods to me appear;
  And one to me are shame and fame.

They reckon ill who leave me out;
  When me they fly, I am the wings;
I am the doubter and the doubt,
  And I the hymn the Brahmin sings.

The strong gods pine for my abode,
  And pine in vain the sacred Seven;
But thou, meek lover of the good!
  Find me, and turn thy back on heaven.

The Rhodora

On Being Asked, Whence is the Flower?

In May, when sea winds pierced our solitudes,
I found the fresh rhodora in the woods,
Spreading its leafless blooms in a damp nook,
To please the desert and the sluggish brook.
The purple petals, fallen in the pool,
Made the black water with their beauty gay;
Here might the redbird come his plumes to cool,
And court the flower that cheapens his array.
Rhodora! if the sages ask thee why
This charm is wasted on the earth and sky,
Tell them, dear, that if eyes were made for seeing,
Then Beauty is its own excuse for being:
Why thou wert there, O rival of the rose!
I never thought to ask, I never knew:
But, in my simple ignorance, suppose
The selfsame Power that brought me there brought you.

Each and All

Little thinks, in the field, yon red-cloaked clown
Of thee from the hilltop looking down;
The heifer that lows in the upland farm,
Far-heard, lows not thine ear to charm;
The sexton, tolling his bell at noon,
Deems not that great Napoleon
Stops his horse, and lists with delight,
Whilst his files sweep round yon Alpine height;
Nor knowest thou what argument
Thy life to thy neighbor's creed has lent.
All are needed by each one;
Nothing is fair or good alone.
I thought the sparrow's note from heaven,
Singing at dawn on the alder bough;
I brought him home, in his nest, at even;
He sings the song, but it cheers not now,
For I did not bring home the river and sky;—
He sang to my ear,—they sang to my eye.
The delicate shells lay on the shore;
The bubbles of the latest wave
Fresh pearls to their enamel gave,
And the bellowing of the savage sea
Greeted their safe escape to me.
I wiped away the weeds and foam,
I fetched my sea-born treasures home;
But the poor, unsightly, noisome things
Had left their beauty on the shore
With the sun and the sand and the wild uproar.
The lover watched his graceful maid,
As 'mid the virgin train she strayed,
Nor knew her beauty's best attire
Was woven still by the snow-white choir.
At last she came to his hermitage,
Like the bird from the woodlands to the cage;—

The gay enchantment was undone,
A gentle wife, but fairy none.
Then I said, "I covet truth;
Beauty is unripe childhood's cheat;
I leave it behind with the games of youth."—
As I spoke, beneath my feet
The ground pine curled its pretty wreath,
Running over the club moss burs;
I inhaled the violet's breath;
Around me stood the oaks and firs;
Pine cones and acorns lay on the ground;
Over me soared the eternal sky,
Full of light and of deity;
Again I say, again I heard,
The rolling river, the morning bird;—
Beauty through my senses stole;
I yielded myself to the perfect whole.

The Problem

I like a church; I like a cowl;
I love a prophet of the soul;
And on my heart monastic aisles
Fall like sweet strains, or pensive smiles;
Yet not for all his faith can see
Would I that cowlèd churchman be.

Why should the vest on him allure,
Which I could not on me endure?

Not from a vain or shallow thought
His awful Jove young Phidias brought;
Never from lips of cunning fell
The thrilling Delphic oracle;
Out from the heart of nature rolled
The burdens of the Bible old;
The litanies of nations came,
Like the volcano's tongue of flame,

Up from the burning core below,—
The canticles of love and woe:
The hand that rounded Peter's dome
And groined the aisles of Christian Rome
Wrought in a sad sincerity;
Himself from God he could not free;
He builded better than he knew;—
The conscious stone to beauty grew.

Knowst thou what wove yon wood bird's nest
Of leaves, and feathers from her breast?
Or how the fish outbuilt her shell,
Painting with morn each annual cell?
Or how the sacred pine tree adds
To her old leaves new myriads?
Such and so grew these holy piles,
Whilst love and terror laid the tiles.
Earth proudly wears the Parthenon,
As the best gem upon her zone,
And Morning opes with haste her lids
To gaze upon the Pyramids;
O'er England's abbeys bends the sky,
As on its friends, with kindred eye;
For out of Thought's interior sphere
These wonders rose to upper air;
And Nature gladly gave them place,
Adopted them into her race,
And granted them an equal date
With Andes and with Ararat.

These temples grew as grows the grass;
Art might obey, but not surpass.
The passive Master lent his hand
To the vast soul that o'er him planned;
And the same power that reared the shrine
Bestrode the tribes that knelt within.
Ever the fiery Pentecost
Girds with one flame the countless host,
Trances the heart through chanting choirs,
And through the priest the mind inspires.

The word unto the prophet spoken
Was writ on tables yet unbroken;
The word by seers or sibyls told,
In groves of oak, or fanes of gold,
Still floats upon the morning wind,
Still whispers to the willing mind.
One accent of the Holy Ghost
The heedless world hath never lost.
I know what say the fathers wise,—
The Book itself before me lies,
Old *Chrysostom*, best Augustine,
And he who blent both in his line,
The younger *Golden Lips* or mines,
Taylor, the Shakespeare of divines.
His words are music in my ear.
I see his cowlèd portrait dear;
And yet, for all his faith could see,
I would not the good bishop be.

Woodnotes

In unplowed Maine he sought the lumberers' gang
Where from a hundred lakes young rivers sprang;
He trode the unplanted forest floor, whereon
The all-seeing sun for ages hath not shone;
Where feeds the moose, and walks the surly bear,
And up the tall mast runs the woodpecker.
He saw beneath dim aisles, in odorous beds,
The slight Linnaea hang its twin-born heads,
And blessed the monument of the man of flowers,
Which breathes his sweet frame through the northern bowers.
He heard, when in the grove, at intervals,
With sudden roar the aged pine tree falls,—
One crash, the death hymn of the perfect tree,
Declares the close of its green century.
Low lies the plant to whose creation went
Sweet influence from every element;

Whose living towers the years conspired to build,
Whose giddy top the morning loved to gild.
Through these green tents, by eldest Nature dressed,
He roamed, content alike with man and beast.
Where darkness found him he lay glad at night;
There the red morning touched him with its light.
Three moons his great heart him a hermit made,
So long he roved at will the boundless shade.
The timid it concerns to ask their way,
And fear what foe in caves and swamps can stray,
To make no step until the event is known,
And ills to come as evils past bemoan.
Not so the wise; no coward watch he keeps
To spy what danger on his pathway creeps;
Go where he will, the wise man is at home,
His hearth the earth,—his hall the azure dome;
Where his clear spirit leads him, there's his road
By God's own light illumined and foreshadowed.

The Snowstorm

Announced by all the trumpets of the sky,
Arrives the snow, and, driving o'er the fields,
Seems nowhere to alight: the whited air
Hides hills and woods, the river, and the heaven,
And veils the farmhouse at the garden's end.
The sled and traveler stopped, the courier's feet
Delayed, all friends shut out, the housemates sit
Around the radiant fireplace, enclosed
In a tumultuous privacy of storm.

Come see the north wind's masonry.
Out of an unseen quarry evermore
Furnished with tile, the fierce artificer
Curves his white bastions with projected roof
Round every windward stake, or tree, or door.
Speeding, the myriad-handed, his wild work
So fanciful, so savage, nought cares he
For number or proportion. Mockingly,

On coop or kennel he hangs Parian wreaths;
A swanlike form invests the hidden thorn;
Fills up the farmer's lane from wall to wall,
Mauger the farmer's sighs; and at the gate
A tapering turret overtops the work.
And when his hours are numbered, and the world
Is all his own, retiring, as he were not,
Leaves, when the sun appears, astonished Art
To mimic in slow structures, stone by stone,
Built in an age, the mad wind's night work,
The frolic architecture of the snow.

Days

Daughters of Time, the hypocritic Days,
Muffled and dumb like barefoot dervishes,
And marching single in an endless file,
Bring diadems and fagots in their hands.
To each they offer gifts after his will,
Bread, kingdoms, stars, and sky that holds them all.
I, in my pleached garden, watched the pomp,
Forgot my morning wishes, hastily
Took a few herbs and apples, and the Day
Turned and departed silent. I, too late,
Under her solemn fillet saw the scorn.

Hamatreya

Bulkeley, Hunt, Willard, Hosmer, Meriam, Flint,
Possessed the land which rendered to their toil
Hay, corn, roots, hemp, flax, apples, wool and wood.
Each of these landlords walked amidst his farm,
Saying, "'Tis mine, my children's and my name's.
How sweet the west wind sounds in my own trees!
How graceful climb those shadows on my hill!
I fancy these pure waters and the flags

Know me, as does my dog: we sympathize;
And, I affirm, my actions smack of the soil."
Where are these men? Asleep beneath their grounds:
And strangers, fond as they, their furrows plow.
Earth laughs in flowers, to see her boastful boys
Earth-proud, proud of the earth which is not theirs;
Who steer the plow, but cannot steer their feet
Clear of the grave.
They added ridge to valley, brook to pond,
And sighed for all that bounded their domain;
"This suits me for a pasture; that's my park;
We must have clay, lime, gravel, granite ledge,
And misty lowland, where to go for peat.
The land is well,—lies fairly to the south.
'Tis good, when you have crossed the sea and back,
To find the sitfast acres where you left them."
Ah! the hot owner sees not Death, who adds
Him to his land, a lump of mold the more.
Hear what the Earth says:—

Earth Song

"Mine and yours;
Mine, not yours.
Earth endures;
Stars abide—
Shine down in the old sea;
Old are the shores;
But where are old men?
I who have seen much,
Such have I never seen.

"The lawyer's deed
Ran sure,
In tail,
To them, and to their heirs
Who shall succeed,
Without fail,
Forevermore.

"Here is the land,
Shaggy with wood,
With its old valley,
Mound and flood.
But the heritors?—
Fled like the flood's foam.
The lawyer, and the laws,
And the kingdom,
Clean swept herefrom.

"They called me theirs,
Who so controlled me;
Yet every one
Wished to stay, and is gone.
How am I theirs,
If they cannot hold me,
But I hold them?"

When I heard the Earth song
I was no longer brave;
My avarice cooled
Like lust in the chill of the grave.

Experience

The lords of life, the lords of life,—
I saw them pass
In their own guise,
Like and unlike,
Portly and grim,—
Use and surprise,
Surface and dream,
Succession swift, and spectral wrong,
Temperament without a tongue,
And the inventor of the game
Omnipresent without name;—
Some to see, some to be guessed,
They marched from east to west:

Little man, least of all,
Among the legs of his guardians tall,
Walked about with puzzled look.
Him by the hand dear Nature took,
Dearest Nature, strong and kind,
Whispered, "Darling, never mind!
Tomorrow they will wear another face,
The founder thou; these are thy race!"

Forbearance

Hast thou named all the birds without a gun?
Loved the wood rose, and left it on its stalk?
At rich men's tables eaten bread and pulse?
Unarmed, faced danger with a heart of trust?
And loved so well a high behavior,
In man or maid, that thou from speech refrained,
Nobility more nobly to repay?
O, be my friend, and teach me to be thine!

Compensation

Why should I keep holiday
  When other men have none?
Why but because, when these are gay,
  I sit and mourn alone?

And why, when mirth unseals all tongues,
  Should mine alone be dumb?
Ah! late I spoke to silent throngs,
  And now their hour is come.

The Past

The debt is paid,
The verdict said,
The Furies laid,
The plague is stayed,
All fortunes made;
Turn the key and bolt the door,
Sweet is death forevermore.
Nor haughty hope, nor swart chagrin,
Nor murdering hate, can enter in.
All is now secure and fast;
Not the gods can shake the past;
Flies-to the adamantine door
Bolted down forevermore.
None can re-enter there—
No thief so politic,
No Satan with a royal trick
Steal in by window, chink, or hole,
To bind or unbind, add what lacked,
Insert a leaf, or forge a name,
New-face or finish what is packed,
Alter or mend eternal fact.

Ode Inscribed to W. H. Channing

Though loath to grieve
The evil time's sole patriot,
I cannot leave
My honeyed thought
For the priest's cant,
Or statesman's rant.

If I refuse
My study for their politic,
Which at the best is trick,
The angry Muse
Puts confusion in my brain.

But who is he that prates
Of the culture of mankind,
Of better arts and life?
Go, blindworm, go,
Behold the famous States
Harrying Mexico
With rifle and with knife!

Or who, with accent bolder
Dare praise the freedom-loving mountaineer?
I found by thee, O rushing Contoocook!
And in thy valleys, Agiochook!
The jackals of the Negro-holder.

The God who made New Hampshire
Taunted the lofty land
With little men;—
Small bat and wren
House in the oak:—
If earth-fire cleave
The upheaved land, and bury the folk,

The southern crocodile would grieve.
Virtue palters; Right is hence;
Freedom praised, but hid;
Funeral eloquence
Rattles the coffin lid.

What boots thy zeal,
O glowing friend,
That would indignant rend
The northland from the south?
Wherefore? to what good end?
Boston Bay and Bunker Hill
Would serve things still;—
Things are of the snake.

The horseman serves the horse,
The neatherd serves the neat,
The merchant serves the purse,
The eater serves his meat;
'Tis the day of the chattel,
Web to weave, and corn to grind;
Things are in the saddle,
And ride mankind.

There are two laws discrete,
Not reconciled,—
Law for man, and law for thing;
The last builds town and fleet,
But it runs wild,
And doth the man unking.

'Tis fit the forest fall,
The steep be graded,
The mountain tunneled,
The sand shaded,
The orchard planted,
The glebe tilled,
The prairie granted
The steamer built.

Let man serve law for man;
Live for friendship, live for love,
For truth's and harmony's behoof;
The state may follow how it can,
As Olympus follows Jove.

Yet do not I implore
The wrinkled shopman to my sounding woods,
Nor did the unwilling senator
Ask votes of thrushes in the solitudes.
Everyone to his chosen work—
Foolish hands may mix and mar;
Wise and sure the issues are.
Round they roll till dark is light,
Sex to sex, and even to odd;—
The overgod
Who marries Right to Might,
Who peoples, unpeoples,—
He who exterminates
Races by stronger races,
Black by white faces,—
Knows to bring honey
Out of the lion;
Grafts gentlest scion
On pirate and Turk.

The Cossack eats Poland,
Like stolen fruit;
Her last noble is ruined,
Her last poet mute;
Straight, into double band
The victors divide;
Half for freedom strike and stand;—
The astonished Muse finds thousands at her side.

Give All to Love

Give all to love;
Obey thy heart;
Friends, kindred, days,
Estate, good fame,
Plans, credit, and the Muse,—
Nothing refuse.

'Tis a brave master;
Let it have scope:
Follow it utterly,
Hope beyond hope:
High and more high
It dives into noon,
With wing unspent,
Untold intent;
But it is god,
Knows its own path
And the outlets of the sky.

It was never for the mean;
It requireth courage stout.
Souls above doubt,
Valor unbending,
It will reward,—
They shall return
More than they were,
And ever ascending.

Leave all for love;
Yet, hear me, yet,
One word more thy heart behoved,
One pulse more of firm endeavor,—
Keep thee today,
Tomorrow, forever,
Free as an Arab
Of thy beloved.

Cling with life to the maid;
But when the surprise,
First vague shadow of surmise
Flits across her bosom young,
Of a joy apart from thee,
Free be she, fancy free;
Nor thou detain her vesture's hem,
Nor the palest rose she flung
From her summer diadem.

Though thou loved her as thyself,
As a self of purer clay,
Though her parting dims the day,
Stealing grace from all alive;
Heartily know,
When half gods go,
The gods arrive.

Terminus

It is time to be old,
To take in sail:—
The god of bounds,
Who sets to seas a shore,
Come to me in his fatal rounds,
And said: "No more!
No farther shoot
Thy broad ambitious branches, and thy root.
Fancy departs: no more invent;
Contract thy firmament
To compass of a tent.
There's not enough for this and that,
Make thy option which of two;
Economize the failing river,
Not the less revere the Giver,
Leave the many and hold the few.

Timely wise accept the terms,
Soften the fall with wary foot;
A little while
Still plan and smile,
And,—fault of novel germs,—
Mature the unfallen fruit.
Curse, if thou wilt, thy sires,
Bad husbands of their fires,
Who, when they gave thee breath,
Failed to bequeath
The needful sinew stark as once,
The baresark marrow to thy bones,
But left a legacy of ebbing veins,
Inconstant heat and nerveless reins,—
Amid the Muses, left thee deaf and dumb,
Amid the gladiators, halt and numb."

As the bird trims her to the gale,
I trim myself to the storm of time,
I man the rudder, reef the sail,
Obey the voice at eve obeyed at prime:
"Lowly faithful, banish fear,
Right onward drive unharmed;
The port, well worth the cruise, is near,
And every wave is charmed."

Good-bye

Good-bye, proud world! I'm going home:
Thou art not my friend, and I'm not thine.
Long through thy weary crowds I roam;
A river ark on the ocean brine,
Long I've been tossed like the driven foam;
But now, proud world! I'm going home.

Good-bye to Flattery's fawning face;
To Grandeur with his wise grimace;
To upstart Wealth's averted eye;
So supple Office, low and high;
To crowded halls, to court and street;
To frozen hearts and hasting feet;
To those who go, and those who come;
Good-bye, proud world! I'm going home.

I am going to my own hearthstone,
Bosomed in yon green hills alone,—
A secret nook in a pleasant land,
Whose groves the frolic fairies planned;
Where arches green, the livelong day,
Echo the blackbird's roundelay,
And vulgar feet have never trod
A spot that is sacred to thought and God.

O, when I am safe in my sylvan home
I tread on the pride of Greece and Rome;
And when I am stretched beneath the pines,
Where the evening star so holy shines,
I laugh at the lore and the pride of man,
At the sophist schools, and the learned clan;
For what are they all, in their high conceit
When man in the bush with God may meet?

HENRY WADSWORTH LONGFELLOW
(1807–1882)

Hymn to the Night

I heard the trailing garments of the Night
   Sweep through her marble halls!
I saw her sable skirts all fringed with light
   From the celestial walls!

I felt her presence, by its spell of might,
   Stoop o'er me from above;
The calm, majestic presence of the Night,
   As of the one I love.

I heard the sounds of sorrow and delight,
   The manifold, soft chimes,
That fill the haunted chambers of the Night,
   Like some old poet's rhymes.

From the cool cisterns of the midnight air
   My spirit drank repose;
The fountain of perpetual peace flows there,—
   From those deep cisterns flows.

O holy Night! from thee I learn to bear
   What man has borne before!
Thou layest thy finger on the lips of Care,
   And they complain no more.

Peace! Peace! Orestes-like I breathe this prayer!
   Descend with broad-winged flight,
The welcome, the thrice-prayed for, the most fair,
   The best-beloved Night!

A *Psalm of Life*

WHAT THE HEART OF THE YOUNG MAN SAID TO THE PSALMIST

Tell me not, in mournful numbers,
  Life is but an empty dream!—
For the soul is dead that slumbers,
  And things are not what they seem.

Life is real! Life is earnest!
  And the grave is not its goal;
Dust thou art, to dust returnest,
  Was not spoken of the soul.

Not enjoyment, and not sorrow,
  Is our destined end or way;
But to act, that each to-morrow
  Find us farther than to-day.

Art is long, and Time is fleeting,
  And our hearts, though stout and brave,
Still, like muffled drums, are beating
  Funeral marches to the grave.

In the world's broad field of battle,
  In the bivouac of Life,
Be not like dumb, driven cattle!
  Be a hero in the strife!

Trust no Future, howe'er pleasant!
  Let the dead Past bury its dead!
Act,—act in the living Present!
  Heart within, and God o'erhead!

Lives of great men all remind us
  We can make our lives sublime,
And, departing, leave behind us
  Footprints on the sands of time;

Footprints, that perhaps another,
  Sailing o'er life's solemn main,
A forlorn and shipwrecked brother,
  Seeing, shall take heart again.

Let us, then, be up and doing,
  With a heart for any fate;
Still achieving, still pursuing,
  Learn to labor and to wait.

My Lost Youth

Often I think of the beautiful town
  That is seated by the sea;
Often in thought go up and down
The pleasant streets of that dear old town,
  And my youth comes back to me.
    And a verse of a Lapland song
    Is haunting my memory still:
    "A boy's will is the wind's will,
And the thoughts of youth are long, long thoughts."

I can see the shadowy lines of its trees,
  And catch, in sudden gleams,
The sheen of the far-surrounding seas,
And islands that were the Hesperides
  Of all my boyish dreams.
    And the burden of that old song,
    It murmurs and whispers still:
    "A boy's will is the wind's will,
And the thoughts of youth are long, long thoughts."

I remember the black wharves and the slips,
  And the sea-tides tossing free;
And Spanish sailors with bearded lips,
And the beauty and mystery of the ships,
  And the magic of the sea.

And the voice of that wayward song
Is singing and saying still:
"A boy's will is the wind's will,
And the thoughts of youth are long, long thoughts."

I remember the bulwarks by the shore,
And the fort upon the hill;
The sunrise gun, with its hollow roar,
The drum-beat repeated o'er and o'er,
And the bugle wild and shrill.
And the music of that old song
Throbs in my memory still:
"A boy's will is the wind's will,
And the thoughts of youth are long, long thoughts."

I remember the sea-fight far away,
How it thundered o'er the tide!
And the dead captains, as they lay
In their graves, o'erlooking the tranquil bay
Where they in battle died.
And the sound of that mournful song
Goes through me with a thrill:
"A boy's will is the wind's will,
And the thoughts of youth are long, long thoughts."

I can see the breezy dome of groves,
The shadows of Deering's Woods;
And the friendships old and the early loves
Come back with a Sabbath sound, as of doves
In quiet neighborhoods.
And the verse of that sweet old song,
It flutters and murmurs still:
"A boy's will is the wind's will,
And the thoughts of youth are long, long thoughts."

I remember the gleams and glooms that dart
Across the school-boy's brain;
The song and the silence in the heart,
That in part are prophecies, and in part
Are longings wild and vain.

And the voice of that fitful song
Sings on, and is never still:
"A boy's will is the wind's will,
And the thoughts of youth are long, long thoughts."

There are things of which I may not speak;
There are dreams that cannot die;
There are thoughts that make the strong heart weak,
And bring a pallor into the cheek,
And a mist before the eye.
And the words of that fatal song
Come over me like a chill:
"A boy's will is the wind's will,
And the thoughts of youth are long, long thoughts."

Strange to me now are the forms I meet
When I visit the dear old town;
But the native air is pure and sweet,
And the trees that o'ershadow each well-known street,
As they balance up and down,
Are singing the beautiful song,
Are sighing and whispering still:
"A boy's will is the wind's will,
And the thoughts of youth are long, long thoughts."

And Deering's Woods are fresh and fair,
And with joy that is almost pain
My heart goes back to wander there,
And among the dreams of the days that were,
I find my lost youth again.
And the strange and beautiful song,
The groves are repeating it still:
"A boy's will is the wind's will,
And the thoughts of youth are long, long thoughts."

Divina Commedia

I

Oft have I seen at some cathedral door
  A laborer, pausing in the dust and heat,
  Lay down his burden, and with reverent feet
  Enter, and cross himself, and on the floor
Kneel to repeat his paternoster o'er;
  Far off the noises of the world retreat;
  The loud vociferations of the street
  Become an undistinguishable roar.
So, as I enter here from day to day,
  And leave my burden at this minster gate,
  Kneeling in prayer, and not ashamed to pray,
The tumult of the time disconsolate
  To inarticulate murmurs dies away,
  While the eternal ages watch and wait.

II

How strange the sculptures that adorn these towers!
  This crowd of statues, in whose folded sleeves
  Birds build their nests; while canopied with leaves
  Parvis and portal bloom like trellised bowers,
And the vast minster seems a cross of flowers!
  But fiends and dragons on the gargoyled eaves
  Watch the dead Christ between the living thieves,
  And, underneath, the traitor Judas lowers!
Ah! from what agonies of heart and brain,
  What exultations trampling on despair,
  What tenderness, what tears, what hate of wrong,
What passionate outcry of a soul in pain,
  Uprose this poem of the earth and air,
  This mediæval miracle of song!

III

I enter, and I see thee in the gloom
Of the long aisles, O poet saturnine!
And strive to make my steps keep pace with thine.
The air is filled with some unknown perfume;
The congregation of the dead make room
For thee to pass; the votive tapers shine;
Like rooks that haunt Ravenna's groves of pine
The hovering echoes fly from tomb to tomb.
From the confessionals I hear arise
Rehearsals of forgotten tragedies,
And lamentations from the crypts below;
And then a voice celestial that begins
With the pathetic words, "Although your sins
As scarlet be," and ends with "as the snow."

IV

With snow-white veil and garments as of flame,
She stands before thee, who so long-ago
Filled thy young heart with passion and the woe
From which thy song and all its splendors came;
And while with stern rebuke she speaks thy name,
The ice about thy heart melts as the snow
On mountain heights, and in swift overflow
Comes gushing from thy lips in sobs of shame.
Thou makest full confession; and a gleam,
As of the dawn on some dark forest cast,
Seems on thy lifted forehead to increase;
Lethe and Eunoë—the remembered dream
And the forgotten sorrow—bring at last
That perfect pardon which is perfect peace.

V

I lift mine eyes, and all the windows blaze
With forms of Saints and holy men who died,
Here martyred and hereafter glorified;
And the great Rose upon its leaves displays
Christ's Triumph, and the angelic roundelays,
With splendor upon splendor multiplied;
And Beatrice again at Dante's side
No more rebukes, but smiles her words of praise.

And then the organ sounds, and unseen choirs
  Sing the old Latin hymns of peace and love
  And benedictions of the Holy Ghost;
And the melodious bells among the spires
  O'er all the house-tops and through heaven above
  Proclaim the elevation of the Host!

VI

O star of morning and of liberty!
  O bringer of the light, whose splendor shines
  Above the darkness of the Apennines,
  Forerunner of the day that is to be!
The voices of the city and the sea,
  The voices of the mountains and the pines,
  Repeat thy song, till the familiar lines
  Are footpaths for the thought of Italy!
Thy flame is blown abroad from all the heights,
  Through all the nations, and a sound is heard,
  As of a mighty wind, and men devout,
Strangers of Rome, and the new proselytes,
  In their own language hear thy wondrous word,
  And many are amazed and many doubt.

Chaucer

An old man in a lodge within a park;
  The chamber walls depicted all around
  With portraitures of huntsman, hawk, and hound,
  And the hurt deer. He listeneth to the lark,
Whose song comes with the sunshine through the dark
  Of painted glass in leaden lattice bound;
  He listeneth and he laugheth at the sound,
  Then writeth in a book like any clerk.

He is the poet of the dawn, who wrote
The Canterbury Tales, and his old age
Made beautiful with song; and as I read
I hear the crowing cock, I hear the note
Of lark and linnet, and from every page
Rise odors of ploughed field or flowery mead.

Milton

I pace the sounding sea-beach and behold
How the voluminous billows roll and run,
Upheaving and subsiding, while the sun
Shines through their sheeted emerald far unrolled,
And the ninth wave, slow gathering fold by fold
All its loose-flowing garments into one,
Plunges upon the shore, and floods the dun
Pale reach of sands, and changes them to gold.
So in majestic cadence rise and fall
The mighty undulations of thy song,
O sightless bard, England's Mæonides!
And ever and anon, high over all
Uplifted, a ninth wave superb and strong,
Floods all the soul with its melodious seas.

Keats

The young Endymion sleeps Endymion's sleep;
The shepherd-boy whose tale was left half told!
The solemn grove uplifts its shield of gold
To the red rising moon, and loud and deep
The nightingale is singing from the steep;
It is midsummer, but the air is cold;
Can it be death? Alas, beside the fold
A shepherd's pipe lies shattered near his sheep.

Lo! in the moonlight gleams a marble white,
  On which I read: "Here lieth one whose name
  Was writ in water." And was this the meed
Of his sweet singing? Rather let me write:
  "The smoking flax before it burst to flame
  Was quenched by death, and broken the bruised reed."

In the Churchyard at Cambridge

In the village churchyard she lies,
Dust is in her beautiful eyes,
    No more she breathes, nor feels, nor stirs;
At her feet and at her head
Lies a slave to attend the dead,
    But their dust is white as hers.

Was she, a lady of high degree,
So much in love with the vanity
    And foolish pomp of this world of ours?
Or was it Christian charity,
And lowliness and humility,
    The richest and rarest of all dowers?

Who shall tell us? No one speaks;
No color shoots into those cheeks,
    Either of anger or of pride,
At the rude question we have asked;
Nor will the mystery be unmasked
    By those who are sleeping at her side.

Hereafter?—And you think to look
On the terrible pages of that Book
    To find her failings, faults and errors?
Ah, you will then have other cares,
In your own shortcomings and despairs,
    In your own secret sins and terrors!

The Jewish Cemetery at Newport

How strange it seems! These Hebrews in their graves,
  Close by the street of this fair seaport town,
Silent beside the never-silent waves,
  At rest in all this moving up and down!

The trees are white with dust, that o'er their sleep
  Wave their broad curtains in the south-wind's breath,
While underneath these leafy tents they keep
  The long, mysterious Exodus of Death.

And these sepulchral stones, so old and brown,
  That pave with level flags their burial-place,
Seem like the tablets of the Law, thrown down
  And broken by Moses at the mountain's base.

The very names recorded here are strange,
  Of foreign accent, and of different climes;
Alvares and Rivera interchange
  With Abraham and Jacob of old times.

"Blessed be God, for he created Death!"
  The mourners said, "and Death is rest and peace;"
Then added, in the certainty of faith,
  "And giveth Life that nevermore shall cease."

Closed are the portals of their Synagogue,
  No Psalms of David now the silence break,
No Rabbi reads the ancient Decalogue
  In the grand dialect the Prophets spake.

Gone are the living, but the dead remain,
  And not neglected; for a hand unseen,
Scattering its bounty, like a summer rain,
  Still keeps their graves and their remembrance green.

How came they here? What burst of Christian hate,
  What persecution, merciless and blind,
Drove o'er the sea—that desert desolate—
  These Ishmaels and Hagars of mankind?

They lived in narrow streets and lanes obscure,
  Ghetto and Judenstrass, in mirk and mire;
Taught in the school of patience to endure
  The life of anguish and the death of fire.

All their lives long, with the unleavened bread
  And bitter herbs of exile and its fears,
The wasting famine of the heart they fed,
  And slaked its thirst with marah of their tears.

Anathema maranatha! was the cry
  That rang from town to town, from street to street:
At every gate the accursed Mordecai
  Was mocked and jeered, and spurned by Christian feet.

Pride and humiliation hand in hand
  Walked with them through the world where'er they went;
Trampled and beaten were they as the sand,
  And yet unshaken as the continent.

For in the background figures vague and vast
  Of patriarchs and of prophets rose sublime,
And all the great traditions of the Past
  They saw reflected in the coming time.

And thus forever with reverted look
  The mystic volume of the world they read,
Spelling it backward, like a Hebrew book,
  Till life became a Legend of the Dead.

But ah! what once has been shall be no more!
  The groaning earth in travail and in pain
Brings forth its races, but does not restore,
  And the dead nations never rise again.

Mezzo Cammin

Written at Boppard on the Rhine, August 25, 1842,
just before leaving for home

Half of my life is gone, and I have let
  The years slip from me and have not fulfilled
  The aspiration of my youth, to build
  Some tower of song with lofty parapet.
Not indolence, nor pleasure, nor the fret
  Of restless passions that would not be stilled,
  But sorrow, and a care that almost killed,
  Kept me from what I may accomplish yet;
Though, half-way up the hill, I see the Past
  Lying beneath me with its sounds and sights,—
  A city in the twilight dim and vast,
With smoking roofs, soft bells, and gleaming lights,—
  And hear above me on the autumnal blast
  The cataract of Death far thundering from the heights.

Nature

As a fond mother, when the day is o'er,
  Leads by the hand her little child to bed,
  Half willing, half reluctant to be led,
  And leave his broken playthings on the floor,
Still gazing at them through the open door,
  Nor wholly reassured and comforted
  By promises of others in their stead,
  Which, though more splendid, may not please him more;
So nature deals with us, and takes away
  Our playthings one by one, and by the hand
  Leads us to rest so gently, that we go
Scarce knowing if we wish to go or stay,
  Being too full of sleep to understand
  How far the unknown transcends the what we know.

Snow-flakes

Out of the bosom of the Air,
  Out of the cloud-folds of her garments shaken,
Over the woodlands brown and bare,
  Over the harvest-fields forsaken,
    Silent, and soft, and slow
    Descends the snow.

Even as our cloudy fancies take
  Suddenly shape in some divine expression,
Even as the troubled heart doth make
  In the white countenance confession,
    The troubled sky reveals
    The grief it feels.

This is the poem of the air,
  Slowly in silent syllables recorded;
This is the secret of despair,
  Long in its cloudy bosom hoarded,
    Now whispered and revealed
    To wood and field.

The Fire of Drift-wood

Devereaux Farm, Near Marblehead

We sat within the farm-house old,
  Whose windows, looking o'er the bay,
Gave to the sea-breeze damp and cold
  An easy entrance, night and day.

Not far away we saw the port,
  The strange, old-fashioned, silent town,
The lighthouse, the dismantled fort,
  The wooden houses, quaint and brown.

We sat and talked until the night,
  Descending, filled the little room;
Our faces faded from the sight,
  Our voices only broke the gloom.

We spake of many a vanished scene,
  Of what we once had thought and said,
Of what had been, and might have been,
  And who was changed, and who was dead;

And all that fills the hearts of friends,
  When first they feel, with secret pain,
Their lives thenceforth have separate ends,
  And never can be one again;

The first slight swerving of the heart,
  That words are powerless to express,
And leave it still unsaid in part,
  Or say it in too great excess.

The very tones in which we spake
  Had something strange, I could but mark;
The leaves of memory seemed to make
  A mournful rustling in the dark.

Oft died the words upon our lips,
  As suddenly, from out the fire
Built of the wreck of stranded ships,
  The flames would leap and then expire.

And, as their splendor flashed and failed,
  We thought of wrecks upon the main,
Of ships dismasted, that were hailed
  And sent no answer back again.

The windows, rattling in their frames,
  The ocean, roaring up the beach,
The gusty blast, the bickering flames,
  All mingled vaguely in our speech;

Until they made themselves a part
    Of fancies floating through the brain,
The long-lost ventures of the heart,
    That send no answers back again.

O flames that glowed! O hearts that yearned!
    They were indeed too much akin,
The drift-wood fire without that burned,
    The thoughts that burned and glowed within.

Seaweed

When descends on the Atlantic
        The gigantic
Storm-wind of the equinox,
Landward in his wrath he scourges
        The toiling surges,
Laden with seaweed from the rocks:

From Bermuda's reefs; from edges
        Of sunken ledges,
In some far-off, bright Azore;
From Bahama, and the dashing,
        Silver-flashing
Surges of San Salvador;

From the tumbling surf, that buries
        The Orkneyan skerries,
Answering the hoarse Hebrides;
And from wrecks of ships, and drifting
        Spars, uplifting
On the desolate, rainy seas;—

Ever drifting, drifting, drifting
    On the shifting
Currents of the restless main;
Till in sheltered coves, and reaches
    Of sandy beaches,
All have found repose again.

So when storms of wild emotion
    Strike the ocean
Of the poet's soul, erelong
From each cave and rocky fastness,
    In its vastness,
Floats some fragment of a song:

From the far-off isles enchanted,
    Heaven has planted
With the golden fruit of Truth;
From the flashing surf, whose vision
    Gleams Elysian
In the tropic clime of Youth;

From the strong Will, and the Endeavor
    That forever
Wrestle with the tides of Fate;
From the wreck of Hopes far-scattered,
    Tempest-shattered,
Floating waste and desolate;—

Ever drifting, drifting, drifting
    On the shifting
Currents of the restless heart;
Till at length in books recorded,
    They, like hoarded
Household words, no more depart.

The Cross of Snow

In the long, sleepless watches of the night,
  A gentle face—the face of one long dead—
  Looks at me from the wall, where round its head
  The night-lamp casts a halo of pale light.
Here in this room she died; and soul more white
  Never through martyrdom of fire was led
  To its repose; nor can in books be read
  The legend of a life more benedight.
There is a mountain in the distant West
  That, sun-defying, in its deep ravines
  Display a cross of snow upon its side.
Such is the cross I wear upon my breast
  These eighteen years, through all the changing scenes
  And seasons, changeless since the day she died.

The Tide Rises, the Tide Falls

The tide rises, the tide falls,
The twilight darkens, the curlew calls;
Along the sea-sands damp and brown
The traveller hastens toward the town,
    And the tide rises, the tide falls.

Darkness settles on roofs and walls,
But the sea, the sea in the darkness calls;
The little waves, with their soft, white hands,
Efface the footprints in the sands,
    And the tide rises, the tide falls.

The morning breaks; the steeds in their stalls
Stamp and neigh, as the hostler calls;
The day returns, but nevermore
Returns the traveller to the shore,
    And the tide rises, the tide falls.

Aftermath

When the summer fields are mown,
When the birds are fledged and flown,
  And the dry leaves strew the path;
With the falling of the snow,
With the cawing of the crow,
Once again the fields we mow
  And gather in the aftermath.

Not the sweet, new grass with flowers
Is this harvesting of ours;
  Not the upland clover bloom;
But the rowen mixed with weeds,
Tangled tufts from marsh and meads,
Where the poppy drops its seeds
  In the silence and the gloom.

JOHN GREENLEAF WHITTIER
(1807–1892)

Telling the Bees

Here is the place; right over the hill
  Runs the path I took;
You can see the gap in the old wall still,
  And the stepping-stones in the shallow brook.

There is the house, with the gate red-barred,
  And the poplars tall;
And the barn's brown length, and the cattle-yard,
  And the white horns tossing above the wall.

There are the beehives ranged in the sun;
  And down by the brink
Of the brook are her poor flowers, weed-o'errun,
  Pansy and daffodil, rose and pink.

A year has gone, as the tortoise goes,
  Heavy and slow;
And the same rose blows, and the same sun glows,
  And the same brook sings of a year ago.

There's the same sweet clover-smell in the breeze;
  And the June sun warm
Tangles his wings of fire in the trees,
  Setting, as then, over Fernside farm.

I mind me how with a lover's care
  From my Sunday coat
I brushed off the burrs, and smoothed my hair,
  And cooled at the brookside my brow and throat.

Since we parted, a month had passed,—
  To love, a year;
Down through the beeches I looked at last
  On the little red gate and the well-sweep near.

I can see it all now,—the slantwise rain
  Of light through the leaves,
The sundown's blaze on her window-pane,
  The bloom of her roses under the eaves.

Just the same as a month before,—
  The house and the trees,
The barn's brown gable, the vine by the door,—
  Nothing changed but the hives of bees.

Before them, under the garden wall,
  Forward and back,
Went drearily singing the chore-girl small,
  Draping each hive with a shred of black.

Trembling, I listened: the summer sun
  Had the chill of snow;
For I knew she was telling the bees of one
  Gone on the journey we all must go!

Then I said to myself, "My Mary weeps
  For the dead to-day:
Haply her blind old grandsire sleeps
  The fret and the pain of his age away."

But her dog whined low; on the doorway sill,
  With his cane to his chin,
The old man sat; and the chore-girl still
  Sung to the bees stealing out and in.

And the song she was singing ever since
  In my ear sounds on:—
"Stay at home, pretty bees, fly not hence!
  Mistress Mary is dead and gone!"

Ichabod

So fallen! so lost! the light withdrawn
  Which once he wore!
The glory from his gray hairs gone
  Forevermore!

Revile him not, the Tempter hath
  A snare for all;
And pitying tears, not scorn and wrath,
  Befit his fall!

Oh, dumb be passion's stormy rage,
  When he who might
Have lighted up and led his age,
  Falls back in night.

Scorn! would the angels laugh, to mark
  A bright soul driven,
Fiend-goaded, down the endless dark,
  From hope and heaven!

Let not the land once proud of him
  Insult him now,
Nor brand with deeper shame his dim,
  Dishonored brow.

But let its humbled sons, instead,
  From sea to lake,
A long lament, as for the dead,
  In sadness make.

Of all we loved and honored, naught
  Save power remains:
A fallen angel's pride of thought,
  Still strong in chains.

All else is gone; from those great eyes
  The soul has fled:
When faith is lost, when honor dies,
  The man is dead!

Then, pay the reverence of old days
  To his dead fame;
Walk backward, with averted gaze,
  And hide the shame!

Maud Muller

Maud Muller on a summer's day
Raked the meadow sweet with hay.

Beneath her torn hat glowed the wealth
Of simple beauty and rustic health.

Singing, she wrought, and her merry glee
The mock-bird echoed from his tree.

But when she glanced to the far-off town,
White from its hill-slope looking down,

The sweet song died, and a vague unrest
And a nameless longing filled her breast,—

A wish that she hardly dared to own,
For something better than she had known.

The Judge rode slowly down the lane,
Smoothing his horse's chestnut mane.

He drew his bridle in the shade
Of the apple-trees, to greet the maid,

And asked a draught from the spring that flowed
Through the meadow across the road.

She stooped where the cool spring bubbled up,
And filled for him her small tin cup,

And blushed as she gave it, looking down
On her feet so bare, and her tattered gown.

"Thanks!" said the Judge; "a sweeter draught
From a fairer hand was never quaffed."

He spoke of the grass and flowers and trees,
Of the singing birds and the humming bees;

Then talked of the haying, and wondered whether
The cloud in the west would bring foul weather.

And Maud forgot her brier-torn gown,
And her graceful ankles bare and brown;

And listened, while a pleased surprise
Looked from her long-lashed hazel eyes.

At last, like one who for delay
Seeks a vain excuse, he rode away.

Maud Muller looked and sighed: "Ah me!
That I the Judge's bride might be!

"He would dress me up in silks so fine,
And praise and toast me at his wine.

"My father should wear a broadcloth coat,
My brother should sail a painted boat.

"I'd dress my mother so grand and gay,
And the baby should have a new toy each day.

"And I'd feed the hungry and clothe the poor,
And all should bless me who left our door."

The Judge looked back as he climbed the hill,
And saw Maud Muller standing still.

"A form more fair, a face more sweet,
Ne'er hath it been my lot to meet.

"And her modest answer and graceful air
Show her wise and good as she is fair.

"Would she were mine, and I to-day,
Like her, a harvester of hay;

"No doubtful balance of rights and wrongs,
Nor weary lawyers with endless tongues,

"But low of cattle and song of birds,
And health and quiet and loving words."

But he thought of his sisters, proud and cold,
And his mother, vain of her rank and gold.

So, closing his heart, the Judge rode on,
And Maud was left in the field alone.

But the lawyers smiled that afternoon,
When he hummed in court an old love-tune;

And the young girl mused beside the well
Till the rain on the unraked clover fell.

He wedded a wife of richest dower,
Who lived for fashion, as he for power.

Yet oft, in his marble hearth's bright glow,
He watched a picture come and go;

And sweet Maud Muller's hazel eyes
Looked out in their innocent surprise.

Oft, when the wine in his glass was red,
He longed for the wayside well instead;

And closed his eyes on his garnished rooms
To dream of meadows and clover-blooms.

And the proud man sighed, with a secret pain,
"Ah, that I were free again!

"Free as when I rode that day,
Where the barefoot maiden raked her hay."

She wedded a man unlearned and poor,
And many children played round her door.

But care and sorrow, and childbirth pain,
Left their traces on heart and brain.

And oft, when the summer sun shone hot
On the new-mown hay in the meadow lot,

And she heard the little spring brook fall
Over the roadside, through the wall,

In the shade of the apple-tree again
She saw a rider draw his rein;

And, gazing down with timid grace,
She felt his pleased eyes read her face.

Sometimes her narrow kitchen walls
Stretched away into stately halls;

The weary wheel to a spinnet turned,
The tallow candle an astral burned,

And for him who sat by the chimney lug,
Dozing and grumbling o'er pipe and mug,

A manly form at her side she saw,
And joy was duty and love was law.

Then she took up her burden of life again
Saying only, "It might have been."

Alas for maiden, alas for Judge,
For rich repiner and household drudge!

God pity them both! and pity us all,
Who vainly the dreams of youth recall.

For of all sad words of tongue or pen,
The saddest are these: "It might have been!"

Ah, well! for us all some sweet hope lies
Deeply buried from human eyes;

And, in the hereafter, angels may
Roll the stone from its grave away!

Snow-bound

A Winter Idyl

To the Memory of the Household It Describes
THIS POEM IS DEDICATED BY THE AUTHOR

As the Spirits of Darkness be stronger in the dark, so Good Spirits, which be Angels of Light, are augmented not only by the Divine light of the Sun, but also by our common Wood Fire: and as the Celestial Fire drives away dark spirits, so also this our Fire of Wood doth the same.

—COR. AGRIPPA, *Occult Philosophy*, Book I. ch. v.

Announced by all the trumpets of the sky,
Arrives the snow, and, driving o'er the fields,
Seems nowhere to alight: the whited air
Hides hills and woods, the river and the heaven,
And veils the farm-house at the garden's end.
The sled and traveller stopped, the courier's feet
Delayed, all friends shut out, the housemates sit
Around the radiant fireplace, enclosed
In a tumultuous privacy of storm.

EMERSON. The Snow Storm.

The sun that brief December day
Rose cheerless over hills of gray,
And, darkly circled, gave at noon
A sadder light than waning moon.

Slow tracing down the thickening sky
Its mute and ominous prophecy,
A portent seeming less than threat,
It sank from sight before it set.
A chill no coat, however stout,
Of homespun stuff could quite shut out,
A hard, dull bitterness of cold,
That checked, mid-vein, the circling race
Of life-blood in the sharpened face,
The coming of the snow-storm told.
The wind blew east; we heard the roar
Of Ocean on his wintry shore,
And felt the strong pulse throbbing there
Beat with low rhythm our inland air.

Meanwhile we did our nightly chores,—
Brought in the wood from out of doors,
Littered the stalls, and from the mows
Raked down the herd's-grass for the cows:
Heard the horse whinnying for his corn;
And, sharply clashing horn on horn,
Impatient down the stanchion rows
The cattle shake their walnut bows;
While, peering from his early perch
Upon the scaffold's pole of birch,
The cock his crested helmet bent
And down his querulous challenge sent.
Unwarmed by any sunset light
The gray day darkened into night,
A night made hoary with the swarm
And whirl-dance of the blinding storm,
As zigzag, wavering to and fro,
Crossed and recrossed the wingëd snow:
And ere the early bedtime came
The white drift piled the window-frame,
And through the glass the clothes-line posts
Looked in like tall and sheeted ghosts.

So all night long the storm roared on:
The morning broke without a sun;

In tiny spherule traced with lines
Of Nature's geometric signs,
In starry flake, and pellicle,
All day the hoary meteor fell;
And, when the second morning shone,
We looked upon a world unknown,
On nothing we could call our own.
Around the glistening wonder bent
The blue walls of the firmament,
No cloud above, no earth below,—
A universe of sky and snow!
The old familiar sights of ours
Took marvellous shapes; strange domes and towers
Rose up where sty or corn-crib stood,
Or garden-wall, or belt of wood;
A smooth white mound the brush-pile showed,
A fenceless drift what once was road;
The bridle-post an old man sat
With loose-flung coat and high cocked hat;
The well-curb had a Chinese roof;
And even the long sweep, high aloof,
In its slant splendor, seemed to tell
Of Pisa's leaning miracle.

A prompt, decisive man, no breath
Our father wasted: "Boys, a path!"
Well pleased, (for when did farmer boy
Count such a summons less than joy?)
Our buskins on our feet we drew;
With mittened hands, and caps drawn low,
To guard our necks and ears from snow,
We cut the solid whiteness through.
And, where the drift was deepest, made
A tunnel walled and overlaid
With dazzling crystal: we had read
Of rare Aladdin's wondrous cave,
And to our own his name we gave,
With many a wish the luck were ours
To test his lamp's supernal powers.
We reached the barn with merry din,
And roused the prisoned brutes within.

The old horse thrust his long head out,
And grave with wonder gazed about;
The cock his lusty greeting said,
And forth his speckled harem led;
The oxen lashed their tails, and hooked,
And mild reproach of hunger looked;
The hornëd patriarch of the sheep,
Like Egypt's Amun roused from sleep,
Shook his sage head with gesture mute,
And emphasized with stamp of foot.

All day the gusty north-wind bore
The loosening drift its breath before;
Low circling round its southern zone,
The sun through dazzling snow-mist shone.
No church-bell lent its Christian tone
To the savage air, no social smoke
Curled over woods of snow-hung oak.
A solitude made more intense
By dreary-voicëd elements,
The shrieking of the mindless wind,
The moaning tree-boughs swaying blind,
And on the glass the unmeaning beat
Of ghostly finger-tips of sleet.
Beyond the circle of our hearth
No welcome sound of toil or mirth
Unbound the spell, and testified
Of human life and thought outside.
We minded that the sharpest ear
The buried brooklet could not hear,
The music of whose liquid lip
Had been to us companionship,
And, in our lonely life, had grown
To have an almost human tone.

As night drew on, and, from the crest
Of wooded knolls that ridged the west,
The sun, a snow-blown traveller, sank
From sight beneath the smothering bank,
We piled, with care, our nightly stack
Of wood against the chimney-back,—

The oaken log, green, huge, and thick,
And on its top the stout back-stick;
The knotty forestick laid apart,
And filled between with curious art
The ragged brush; then, hovering near,
We watched the first red blaze appear,
Heard the sharp crackle, caught the gleam
On whitewashed wall and sagging beam,
Until the old, rude-furnished room
Burst, flower-like, into rosy bloom;
While radiant with a mimic flame
Outside the sparkling drift became,
And through the bare-boughed lilac-tree
Our own warm hearth seemed blazing free,
The crane and pendent trammels showed,
The Turks' heads on the andirons glowed;
While childish fancy, prompt to tell
The meaning of the miracle,
Whispered the old rhyme: "*Under the tree,*
When fire outdoors burns merrily,
To here the witches are making tea."

The moon above the eastern wood
Shone at its full; the hill-range stood
Transfigured in the silver flood,
Its blown snows flashing cold and keen,
Dead white, save where some sharp ravine
Took shadow, or the sombre green
Of hemlocks turned to pitchy black
Against the whiteness at their back.
For such a world and such a night
Most fitting that unwarming light,
Which only seemed where'er it fell
To make the coldness visible.

Shut in from all the world without,
We sat the clean-winged hearth about,
Content to let the north-wind roar
In baffled rage at pane and door,
While the red logs before us beat
The frost-line back with tropic heat;

And ever, when a louder blast
Shook beam and rafter as it passed,
The merrier up its roaring draught
The great throat of the chimney laughed;
The house-dog on his paws outspread
Laid to the fire his drowsy head,
The cat's dark silhouette on the wall
A couchant tiger's seemed to fall;
And, for the winter fireside meet,
Between the andirons' straddling feet,
The mug of cider simmered slow,
The apples sputtered in a row,
And, close at hand, the basket stood
With nuts from brown October's wood.

What matter how the night behaved?
What matter how the north-wind raved?
Blow high, blow low, not all its snow
Could quench our hearth-fire's ruddy glow.
O Time and Change!—with hair as gray
As was my sire's that winter day,
How strange it seems, with so much gone
Of life and love, to still live on!
Ah, brother! only I and thou
Are left of all that circle now,—
The dear home faces whereupon
That fitful firelight paled and shone.
Henceforward, listen as we will,
The voices of that hearth are still;
Look where we may, the wide earth o'er,
Those lighted faces smile no more.
We tread the paths their feet have worn,
  We sit beneath their orchard trees,
  We hear, like them, the hum of bees
And rustle of the bladed corn;
We turn the pages that they read,
  Their written words we linger o'er,
But in the sun they cast no shade,
No voice is heard, no sign is made,
  No step is on the conscious floor!

Yet Love will dream, and Faith will trust,
(Since He who knows our need is just,)
That somehow, somewhere, meet we must.
Alas for him who never sees
The stars shine through his cypress-trees!
Who, hopeless, lays his dead away,
Nor looks to see the breaking day
Across the mournful marbles play!
Who hath not learned, in hours of faith,
  The truth to flesh and sense unknown,
That Life is ever lord of Death,
  And Love can never lose its own!

We sped the time with stories old,
Wrought puzzles out, and riddles told,
Or stammered from our school-book lore
"The Chief of Gambia's golden shore."
How often since, when all the land
Was clay in Slavery's shaping hand,
As if a far-blown trumpet stirred
The languorous sin-sick air, I heard:
"*Does not the voice of reason cry,*
  Claim the first right which Nature gave,
From the red scourge of bondage fly,
  Nor deign to live a burdened slave!"
Our father rode again his ride
On Memphremagog's wooded side;
Sat down again to moose and samp
In trapper's hut and Indian camp;
Lived o'er the old idyllic ease
Beneath St. François' hemlock-trees;
Again for him the moonlight shone
On Norman cap and bodiced zone;
Again he heard the violin play
Which led the village dance away.
And mingled in its merry whirl
The grandam and the laughing girl.
Or, nearer home, our steps he led
Where Salisbury's level marshes spread
  Mile-wide as flies the laden bee;

Where merry mowers, hale and strong,
Swept, scythe on scythe, their swaths along
  The low green prairies of the sea.
We shared the fishing off Boar's Head,
  And round the rocky Isles of Shoals
  The hake-broil on the drift-wood coals;
The chowder on the sand-beach made,
Dipped by the hungry, steaming hot,
With spoons of clam-shell from the pot.
We heard the tales of witchcraft old,
And dream and sign and marvel told
To sleepy listeners as they lay
Stretched idly on the salted hay,
Adrift along the winding shores,
When favoring breezes deigned to blow
The square sail of the gundelow
And idle lay the useless oars.

Our mother, while she turned her wheel
Or run the new-knit stocking-heel,
Told how the Indian hordes came down
At midnight on Cocheco town,
And how her own great-uncle bore
His cruel scalp-mark to fourscore.
Recalling, in her fitting phrase,
  So rich and picturesque and free,
  (The common unrhymed poetry
Of simple life and country ways,)
The story of her early days,—
She made us welcome to her home;
Old hearths grew wide to give us room;
We stole with her a frightened look
At the gray wizard's conjuring-book,
The fame whereof went far and wide
Through all the simple country side;
We heard the hawks at twilight play,
The boat-horn on Piscataqua,
The loon's weird laughter far away;
We fished her little trout-brook, knew
What flowers in wood and meadow grew,

What sunny hillsides autumn-brown
She climbed to shake the ripe nuts down,
Saw where in sheltered cove and bay
The ducks' black squadron anchored lay,
And heard the wild-geese calling loud
Beneath the gray November cloud.

Then, haply, with a look more grave,
And soberer tone, some tale she gave
From painful Sewel's ancient tome,
Beloved in every Quaker home,
Of faith fire-winged by martyrdom,
Or Chalkley's Journal, old and quaint,—
Gentlest of skippers, rare sea-saint!—
Who, when the dreary calms prevailed,
And water-butt and bread-cask failed,
And cruel, hungry eyes pursued
His portly presence mad for food,
With dark hints muttered under breath
Of casting lots for life or death,
Offered, if Heaven withheld supplies,
To be himself the sacrifice.
Then, suddenly, as if to save
The good man from his living grave,
A ripple on the water grew,
A school of porpoise flashed in view.
"Take, eat," he said, "and be content;
These fishes in my stead are sent
By Him who gave the tangled ram
To spare the child of Abraham."

Our uncle, innocent of books,
Was rich in lore of fields and brooks,
The ancient teachers never dumb
Of Nature's unhoused lyceum.
In moons and tides and weather wise,
He read the clouds as prophecies,
And foul or fair could well divine,
By many an occult hint and sign,
Holding the cunning-warded keys
To all the woodcraft mysteries;

Himself to Nature's heart so near
That all her voices in his ear
Of beast or bird had meanings clear,
Like Appollonius of old,
Who knew the tales the sparrows told,
Or Hermes, who interpreted
What the sage cranes of Nilus said;
A simple, guileless, childlike man,
Content to live where life began;
Strong only on his native grounds,
The little world of sights and sounds
Whose girdle was the parish bounds,
Whereof his fondly partial pride
The common features magnified,
As Surrey hills to mountains grew
In White of Selborne's loving view,—
He told how teal and loon he shot,
And how the eagle's eggs he got,
The feats on pond and river done,
The prodigies of rod and gun;
Till, warming with the tales he told,
Forgotten was the outside cold,
The bitter wind unheeded blew,
From ripening corn the pigeons flew,
The partridge drummed i' the wood, the mink
Went fishing down the river-brink.
In fields with bean or clover gay,
The woodchuck, like a hermit gray,
  Peered from the doorway of his cell;
The muskrat plied the mason's trade,
And tier by tier his mud-walls laid;
And from the shagbark overhead
  The grizzled squirrel dropped his shell.

Next, the dear aunt, whose smile of cheer
And voice in dreams I see and hear,—
The sweetest woman ever Fate
Perverse denied a household mate,
Who, lonely, homeless, not the less
Found peace in love's unselfishness,

And welcome wheresoe'er she went,
A calm and gracious element,
Whose presence seemed the sweet income
And womanly atmosphere of home,—
Called up her girlhood memories,
The huskings and the apple-bees,
The sleigh-rides and the summer sails,
Weaving through all the poor details
And homespun warp of circumstance
A golden woof-thread of romance.
For well she kept her genial mood
And simple faith of maidenhood;
Before her still a cloud-land lay,
The mirage loomed across her way;
The morning dew, that dries so soon
With others, glistened at her noon;
Through years of toil and soil and care,
From glossy tress to thin gray hair,
All unprofaned she held apart
The virgin fancies of the heart.
Be shame to him of woman born
Who hath for such but thought of scorn.

There, too, our elder sister plied
Her evening task the stand beside;
A full, rich nature, free to trust,
Truthful and almost sternly just,
Impulsive, earnest, prompt to act,
And make her generous thought a fact,
Keeping with many a light disguise
The secret of self-sacrifice.
O heart sore-tried! thou hast the best
That Heaven itself could give thee,—rest,
Rest from all bitter thoughts and things!
  How many a poor one's blessing went
  With thee beneath the low green tent
Whose curtain never outward swings!

As one who held herself a part
Of all she saw, and let her heart
  Against the household bosom lean,

Upon the motley-braided mat
Our youngest and our dearest sat,
Lifting her large, sweet, asking eyes,
  Now bathed in the unfading green
And holy peace of Paradise.
Oh, looking from some heavenly hill,
  Or from the shade of saintly palms,
  Or silver reach of river calms,
Do those large eyes behold me still?
With me one little year ago:—
The chill weight of the winter snow
  For months upon her grave has lain;
And now, when summer south-winds blow
  And brier and harebell bloom again,
I tread the pleasant paths we trod,
I see the violet-sprinkled sod
Whereon she leaned, too frail and weak
The hillside flowers she loved to seek,
Yet following me where'er I went
With dark eyes full of love's content.
The birds are glad; the brier-rose fills
The air with sweetness; all the hills
Stretch green to June's unclouded sky;
But still I wait with ear and eye
For something gone which should be nigh,
A loss in all familiar things,
In flower that blooms, and bird that sings.
And yet, dear heart! remembering thee,
  Am I not richer than of old?
Safe in thy immortality,
  What change can reach the wealth I hold?
  What chance can mar the pearl and gold
Thy love hath left in trust with me?
And while in life's late afternoon,
  Where cool and long the shadows grow,
I walk to meet the night that soon
  Shall shape and shadow overflow,
I cannot feel that thou art far,
Since near at need the angels are;

And when the sunset gates unbar,
  Shall I not see thee waiting stand,
And, white against the evening star,
  The welcome of thy beckoning hand?

Brisk wielder of the birch and rule,
The master of the district school
Held at the fire his favored place,
Its warm glow lit a laughing face
Fresh-hued and fair, where scarce appeared
The uncertain prophecy of beard.
He teased the mitten-blinded cat,
Played cross-pins on my uncle's hat,
Sang songs, and told us what befalls
In classic Dartmouth's college halls.
Born the wild Northern hills among,
From whence his yeoman father wrung
By patient toil subsistence scant,
Not competence and yet not want,
He early gained the power to pay
His cheerful, self-reliant way;
Could doff at ease his scholar's gown
To peddle wares from town to town;
Or through the long vacation's reach
In lonely lowland districts teach,
Where all the droll experience found
At stranger hearths in boarding round,
The moonlit skater's keen delight,
The sleigh-drive through the frosty night,
The rustic party, with its rough
Accompaniment of blind-man's-buff,
And whirling-plate, and forfeits paid,
His winter task a pastime made.
Happy the snow-locked homes wherein
He tuned his merry violin,
Or played the athlete in the barn,
Or held the good dame's winding-yarn,
Or mirth-provoking versions told
Of classic legends rare and old,
Wherein the scenes of Greece and Rome
Had all the commonplace of home,

And little seemed at best the odds
'Twixt Yankee pedlers and old gods;
Where Pindus-born Arachthus took
The guise of any grist-mill brook,
And dread Olympus at his will
Became a huckleberry hill.

A careless boy that night he seemed;
   But at his desk he had the look
And air of one who wisely schemed,
   And hostage from the future took
   In trainëd thought and lore of book.
Large-brained, clear-eyed, of such as he
Shall Freedom's young apostles be,
Who, following in War's bloody trail,
Shall every lingering wrong assail;
All chains from limb and spirit strike,
Uplift the black and white alike;
Scatter before their swift advance
The darkness and the ignorance,
The pride, the lust, the squalid sloth,
Which nurtured Treason's monstrous growth,
Made murder pastime, and the hell
Of prison-torture possible;
The cruel lie of caste refute,
Old forms remould, and substitute
For Slavery's lash the freeman's will,
For blind routine, wise-handed skill;
A school-house plant on every hill,
Stretching in radiate nerve-lines thence
The quick wires of intelligence;
Till North and South together brought
Shall own the same electric thought,
In peace a common flag salute,
And, side by side in labor's free
And unresentful rivalry,
Harvest the fields wherein they fought.

Another guest that winter night
Flashed back from lustrous eyes the light.

Unmarked by time, and yet not young,
The honeyed music of her tongue
And words of meekness scarcely told
A nature passionate and bold,
Strong, self-concentred, spurning guide,
Its milder features dwarfed beside
Her unbent will's majestic pride.
She sat among us, at the best,
A not unfeared, half-welcome guest,
Rebuking with her cultured phrase
Our homeliness of words and ways.
A certain pard-like, treacherous grace
Swayed the lithe limbs and drooped the lash,
Lent the white teeth their dazzling flash;
And under low brows, black with night,
Rayed out at times a dangerous light;
The sharp heat-lightnings of her face
Presaging ill to him whom Fate
Condemned to share her love or hate.
A woman tropical, intense
In thought and act, in soul and sense,
She blended in a like degree
The vixen and the devotee,
Revealing with each freak or feint
　The temper of Petruchio's Kate,
The raptures of Siena's saint.
Her tapering hand and rounded wrist
Had facile power to form a fist;
The warm, dark languish of her eyes
Was never safe from wrath's surprise.
Brows saintly calm and lips devout
Knew every change of scowl and pout;
And the sweet voice had notes more high
And shrill for social battle-cry.

Since then what old cathedral town
Has missed her pilgrim staff and gown,
What convent-gate has held its lock
Against the challenge of her knock!
Through Smyrna's plague-hushed thoroughfares,
Up sea-set Malta's rocky stairs,

Gray olive slopes of hills that hem
Thy tombs and shrines, Jerusalem,
Or startling on her desert throne
The crazy Queen of Lebanon
With claims fantastic as her own,
Her tireless feet have held their way;
And still, unrestful, bowed, and gray,
She watches under Eastern skies,
  With hope each day renewed and fresh,
  The Lord's quick coming in the flesh,
Whereof she dreams and prophesies!

Where'er her troubled path may be,
  The Lord's sweet pity with her go!
The outward wayward life we see,
  The hidden springs we may not know.
Nor is it given us to discern
  What threads the fatal sisters spun,
  Through what ancestral years has run
The sorrow with the woman born,
What forged her cruel chain of moods,
What set her feet in solitudes,
  And held the love within her mute,
What mingled madness in the blood,
  A life-long discord and annoy,
  Water of tears with oil of joy,
And hid within the folded bud
  Perversities of flower and fruit.
It is not ours to separate
The tangled skein of will and fate,
To show what metes and bounds should stand
Upon the soul's debatable land,
And between choice and Providence
Divide the circle of events;
But He who knows our frame is just,
Merciful and compassionate,
And full of sweet assurances
And hope for all the language is,
That He remembereth we are dust!

At last the great logs, crumbling low,
Sent out a dull and duller glow,
The bull's-eye watch that hung in view,
Ticking its weary circuit through,
Pointed with mutely warning sign
Its black hand to the hour of nine.
That sign the pleasant circle broke:
My uncle ceased his pipe to smoke,
Knocked from its bowl the refuse gray,
And laid it tenderly away;
Then roused himself to safely cover
The dull red brands with ashes over.
And while, with care, our mother laid
The work aside, her steps she stayed
One moment, seeking to express
Her grateful sense of happiness
For food and shelter, warmth and health,
And love's contentment more than wealth,
With simple wishes (not the weak,
Vain prayers which no fulfilment seek,
But such as warm the generous heart,
O'er-prompt to do with Heaven its part)
That none might lack, that bitter night,
For bread and clothing, warmth and light.

Within our beds awhile we heard
The wind that round the gables roared,
With now and then a ruder shock,
Which made our very bedsteads rock.
We heard the loosened clapboards tost,
The board-nails snapping in the frost;
And on us, through the unplastered wall,
Felt the light sifted snow-flakes fall.
But sleep stole on, as sleep will do
When hearts are light and life is new;
Faint and more faint the murmurs grew,
Till in the summer-land of dreams
They softened to the sound of streams,
Low stir of leaves, and dip of oars,
And lapsing waves on quiet shores.

Next morn we wakened with the shout
Of merry voices high and clear;
And saw the teamsters drawing near
To break the drifted highways out.
Down the long hillside treading slow
We saw the half-buried oxen go,
Shaking the snow from heads uptost,
Their straining nostrils white with frost.
Before our door the straggling train
Drew up, an added team to gain.
The elders threshed their hands a-cold,
  Passed, with the cider-mug, their jokes
  From lip to lip; the younger folks
Down the loose snow-banks, wrestling, rolled,
Then toiled again the cavalcade
  O'er windy hill, through clogged ravine,
  And woodland paths that wound between
Low drooping pine-boughs winter-weighed.
From every barn a team afoot,
At every house a new recruit,
Where, drawn by Nature's subtlest law,
Haply the watchful young men saw
Sweet doorway pictures of the curls
And curious eyes of merry girls,
Lifting their hands in mock defence
Against the snow-ball's compliments,
And reading in each missive tost
The charm with Eden never lost.

We heard once more the sleigh-bells' sound;
  And, following where the teamsters led,
The wise old Doctor went his round,
Just pausing at our door to say,
In the brief autocratic way
Of one who, prompt at Duty's call,
Was free to urge her claim on all,
  That some poor neighbor sick abed
At night our mother's aid would need.
For, one in generous thought and deed,
  What mattered in the sufferer's sight
  The Quaker matron's inward light,

The Doctor's mail of Calvin's creed?
All hearts confess the saints elect
  Who, twain in faith, in love agree,
And melt not in an acid sect
  The Christian pearl of charity!

So days went on: a week had passed
Since the great world was heard from last.
The Almanac we studied o'er,
Read and reread our little store
Of books and pamphlets, scarce a score;
One harmless novel, mostly hid
From younger eyes, a book forbid,
And poetry, (or good or bad,
A single book was all we had,)
Where Ellwood's meek, drab-skirted Muse,
  A stranger to the heathen Nine,
  Sang, with a somewhat nasal whine,
The wars of David and the Jews.
At last the floundering carrier bore
The village paper to our door.
Lo! broadening outward as we read,
To warmer zones the horizon spread
In panoramic length unrolled
We saw the marvels that it told.
Before us passed the painted Creeks,
  And daft McGregor on his raids
  In Costa Rica's everglades.
And up Taygetos winding slow
Rode Ypsilanti's Mainote Greeks,
A Turk's head at each saddle-bow!
Welcome to us its week-old news,
Its corner for the rustic Muse,
  Its monthly gauge of snow and rain,
Its record, mingling in a breath
The wedding bell and dirge of death:
Jest, anecdote, and love-lorn tale,
The latest culprit sent to jail;
Its hue and cry of stolen and lost,
Its vendue sales and goods at cost,
  And traffic calling loud for gain.

We felt the stir of hall and street,
The pulse of life that round us beat;
The chill embargo of the snow
Was melted in the genial glow;
Wide swung again our ice-locked door,
And all the world was ours once more!

Clasp, Angel of the backward look
  And folded wings of ashen gray
  And voice of echoes far away,
The brazen covers of thy book;
The weird palimpsest old and vast,
Wherein thou hid'st the spectral past;
Where, closely mingling, pale and glow
The characters of joy and woe;
The monographs of outlived years,
Or smile-illumed or dim with tears,
  Green hills of life that slope to death,
And haunts of home, whose vistaed trees
Shade off to mournful cypresses
  With the white amaranths underneath.
Even while I look, I can but heed
  The restless sands' incessant fall,
Importunate hours that hours succeed,
Each clamorous with its own sharp need,
  And duty keeping pace with all.
Shut down and clasp the heavy lids;
I hear again the voice that bids
The dreamer leave his dream midway
For larger hopes and graver fears:
Life greatens in these later years,
The century's aloe flowers to-day!

Yet, haply, in some lull of life,
Some Truce of God which breaks its strife,
The worldling's eyes shall gather dew,
  Dreaming in throngful city ways
Of winter joys his boyhood knew;
And dear and early friends—the few
Who yet remain—shall pause to view

These Flemish pictures of old days;
Sit with me by the homestead hearth,
And stretch the hands of memory forth
To warm them at the wood-fire's blaze!
And thanks untraced to lips unknown
Shall greet me like the odors blown
From unseen meadows newly mown,
Or lilies floating in some pond,
Wood-fringed, the wayside gaze beyond;
The traveller owns the grateful sense
Of sweetness near, he knows not whence,
And, pausing, takes with forehead bare
The benediction of the air.

Proem

I love the old melodious lays
Which softly melt the ages through,
The songs of Spenser's golden days,
Arcadian Sidney's silvery phrase,
Sprinkling our noon of time with freshest morning dew.

Yet, vainly in my quiet hours
To breathe their marvellous notes I try;
I feel them, as the leaves and flowers
In silence feel the dewy showers,
And drink with glad, still lips the blessing of the sky.

The rigor of a frozen clime,
The harshness of an untaught ear,
The jarring words of one whose rhyme
Beat often Labor's hurried time,
Or Duty's rugged march through storm and strife, are here.

Of mystic beauty, dreamy grace,
No rounded art the lack supplies;
Unskilled the subtle lines to trace,
Or softer shades of Nature's face,
I view her common forms with unanointed eyes.

Nor mine the seer-like power to show
The secrets of the heart and mind;
To drop the plummet-line below
Our common world of joy and woe,
A more intense despair or brighter hope to find.

Yet here at least an earnest sense
Of human right and weal is shown;
A hate of tyranny intense,
And hearty in its vehemence,
As if my brother's pain and sorrow were my own.

O Freedom! if to me belong
Nor mighty Milton's gift divine,
Nor Marvell's wit and graceful song.
Still with a love as deep and strong
As theirs, I lay, like them, my best gifts on thy shrine.

OLIVER WENDELL HOLMES
(1809–1894)

Old Ironsides

Ay, tear her tattered ensign down!
  Long has it waved on high,
And many an eye has danced to see
  That banner in the sky;
Beneath it rung the battle shout,
  And burst the cannon's roar;—
The meteor of the ocean air
  Shall sweep the clouds no more.

Her deck, once red with heroes' blood,
  Where knelt the vanquished foe,
When winds were hurrying o'er the flood,
  And waves were white below,
No more shall feel the victor's tread,
  Or know the conquered knee;—
The harpies of the shore shall pluck
  The eagle of the sea!

Oh, better that her shattered hulk
  Should sink beneath the wave;
Her thunders shook the mighty deep,
  And there should be her grave;
Nail to the mast her holy flag,
  Set every threadbare sail,
And give her to the god of storms,
  The lightning and the gale!

My Aunt

My aunt! my dear unmarried aunt!
  Long years have o'er her flown;
Yet still she strains the aching clasp
  That binds her virgin zone;
I know it hurts her,—though she looks
  As cheerful as she can;
Her waist is ampler than her life,
  For life is but a span.

My aunt! my poor deluded aunt!
  Her hair is almost gray;
Why will she train that winter curl
  In such a spring-like way?
How can she lay her glasses down,
  And say she reads as well,
When through a double convex lens
  She just makes out to spell?

Her father—grandpapa! forgive
  This erring lip its smiles—
Vowed she should make the finest girl
  Within a hundred miles;
He sent her to a stylish school;
  'T was in her thirteenth June;
And with her, as the rules required,
  "Two towels and a spoon."

They braced my aunt against a board,
  To make her straight and tall;
They laced her up, they starved her down,
  To make her light and small;
They pinched her feet, they singed her hair,
  They screwed it up with pins;—
Oh, never mortal suffered more
  In penance for her sins.

So, when my precious aunt was done,
  My grandsire brought her back;
(By daylight, lest some rabid youth
  Might follow on the track;)
"Ah!" said my grandsire, as he shook
  Some powder in his pan,
"What could this lovely creature do
  Against a desperate man!"

Alas! nor chariot, nor barouche,
  Nor bandit cavalcade,
Tore from the trembling father's arms
  His all-accomplished maid.
For her how happy had it been!
  And Heaven had spared to me
To see one sad, ungathered rose
  On my ancestral tree.

The Deacon's Masterpiece

or, The Wonderful "One-Hoss Shay"

A Logical Story

Have you heard of the wonderful one-hoss shay,
That was built in such a logical way
It ran a hundred years to a day,
And then, of a sudden, it—ah, but stay,
I'll tell you what happened without delay,
Scaring the parson into fits,
Frightening people out of their wits,—
Have you ever heard of that, I say?

Seventeen hundred and fifty-five.
Georgius Secundus was then alive,—
Snuffy old drone from the German hive.
That was the year when Lisbon-town
Saw the earth open and gulp her down,

And Braddock's army was done so brown,
Left without a scalp to its crown.
It was on the terrible Earthquake-day
That the Deacon finished the one-hoss shay.

Now in building of chaises, I tell you what,
There is always *somewhere* a weakest spot,—
In hub, tire, felloe, in spring or thill,
In panel, or crossbar, or floor, or sill,
In screw, bolt, thoroughbrace,—lurking still,
Find it somewhere you must and will,—
Above or below, or within or without,—
And that's the reason, beyond a doubt,
That a chaise *breaks down*, but doesn't *wear out*.

But the Deacon swore (as Deacons do,
With an "I dew vum," or an "I tell *yeou*")
He would build one shay to beat the taown
'N' the keounty 'n' all the kentry raoun';
It should be so built that it *couldn'* break daown:
"Fur," said the Deacon, "'t's mighty plain
Thut the weakes' place mus' stan' the strain;
'N' the way t' fix it, uz I maintain,
        Is only jest
T' make that place uz strong uz the rest."

So the Deacon inquired of the village folk
Where he could find the strongest oak,
That couldn't be split nor bent nor broke,—
That was for spokes and floor and sills;
He sent for lancewood to make the thills;
The crossbars were ash, from the straightest trees,
The panels of white-wood, that cuts like cheese,
But lasts like iron for things like these;
The hubs of logs from the "Settler's ellum,"—
Last of its timber,—they couldn't sell 'em,
Never an axe had seen their chips,
And the wedges flew from between their lips,
Their blunt ends frizzled like celery-tips;
Step and prop-iron, bolt and screw,
Spring, tire, axle, and linchpin too,
Steel of the finest, bright and blue;

Thoroughbrace bison-skin, thick and wide;
Boot, top, dasher, from tough old hide
Found in the pit when the tanner died.
That was the way he "put her through."
"There!" said the Deacon, "naow she'll dew!"

Do! I tell you, I rather guess
She was a wonder, and nothing less!
Colts grew horses, beards turned gray,
Deacon and deaconess dropped away,
Children and grandchildren—where were they?
But there stood the stout old one-hoss shay
As fresh as on Lisbon-earthquake-day!

Eighteen hundred;—it came and found
The Deacon's masterpiece strong and sound.
Eighteen hundred increased by ten;—
"Hahnsum kerridge" they called it then.
Eighteen hundred and twenty came;—
Running as usual; much the same.
Thirty and forty at last arrive,
And then come fifty, and fifty-five.

Little of all we value here
Wakes on the morn of its hundredth year
Without both feeling and looking queer.
In fact, there's nothing that keeps its youth,
So far as I know, but a tree and truth.
(This is a moral that runs at large;
Take it.—You're welcome.—No extra charge.)

First of November,—the Earthquake-day,—
There are traces of age in the one-hoss shay,
A general flavor of mild decay,
But nothing local, as one may say.
There couldn't be,—for the Deacon's art
Had made it so like in every part
That there wasn't a chance for one to start.
For the wheels were just as strong as the thills,
And the floor was just as strong as the sills,

And the panels just as strong as the floor,
And the whipple-tree neither less nor more,
And the back crossbar as strong as the fore,
And spring and axle and hub *encore.*
And yet, *as a whole,* it is past a doubt
In another hour it will be *worn out!*

First of November, 'Fifty-five!
This morning the parson takes a drive.
Now, small boys, get out of the way!
Here comes the wonderful one-hoss shay,
Drawn by a rat-tailed, ewe-necked bay.
"Huddup!" said the parson.—Off went they.
The parson was working his Sunday's text,—
Had got to *fifthly,* and stopped perplexed
At what the—Moses—was coming next.
All at once the horse stood still,
Close by the meet'n'-house on the hill.
First a shiver, and then a thrill,
Then something decidedly like a spill,—
And the parson was sitting upon a rock,
At half past nine by the meet'n'-house clock,—
Just the hour of the Earthquake shock!
What do you think the parson found,
When he got up and stared around?
The poor old chaise in a heap or mound,
As if it had been to the mill and ground!
You see, of course, if you're not a dunce,
How it went to pieces all at once,—
All at once, and nothing first,—
Just as bubbles do when they burst.

End of the wonderful one-hoss shay.
Logic is logic. That's all I say.

EDGAR ALLAN POE
(1809–1849)

Dreams

Oh! that my young life were a lasting dream!
My spirit not awak'ning till the beam
Of an eternity should bring the morrow.
Yes! though that long dream were of hopeless sorrow,
'Twere better than the cold reality
Of waking life, to him whose heart must be,
And hath been still, upon the lovely earth,
A chaos of deep passion, from his birth.
But should it be—that dream eternally
Continuing—as dreams have been to me
In my young boyhood—should it thus be given,
'Twere folly still to hope for higher heaven.
For I have reveled, when the sun was bright
I' the summer sky, in dreams of living light
And loveliness,—have left my very heart
In climes of mine imagining, apart
From mine own home, with beings that have been
Of mine own thought—what more could I have seen?
'Twas once—and only once—and the wild hour
From my remembrance shall not pass—some pow'r
Or spell had bound me—'twas the chilly wind
Came o'er me in the night, and left behind
Its image on my spirit—or the moon
Shone on my slumbers in her lofty noon
Too coldly—or the stars—howe'er it was,
That dream was on that night wind—let it pass.
I *have been* happy, though but in a dream.
I have been happy—and I love the theme:

Dreams! in their vivid coloring of life,
As in that fleeting, shadowy, misty strife
Of semblance with reality which brings
To the delirious eye, more lovely things
Of paradise and love—and all our own!
Than young hope in his sunniest hour hath known.

A Dream Within a Dream

Take this kiss upon the brow!
And, in parting from you now,
Thus much let me avow:
You are not wrong, who deem
That my days have been a dream;
Yet if hope has flown away
In a night, or in a day,
In a vision, or in none,
Is it therefore the less *gone?*
All that we see or seem
Is but a dream within a dream.

I stand amid the roar
Of a surf-tormented shore,
And I hold within my hand
Grains of the golden sand—
How few! yet how they creep
Through my fingers to the deep,
While I weep—while I weep!
O God! can I not grasp
Them with a tighter clasp?
O God! can I not save
One from the pitiless wave?
Is *all* that we see or seem
But a dream within a dream?

Sonnet—To Science

Science! true daughter of old Time thou art!
  Who alterest all things with thy peering eyes.
Why preyest thou thus upon the poet's heart,
  Vulture, whose wings are dull realities?
How should he love thee? or how deem thee wise,
  Who wouldst not leave him in his wandering
To seek for treasure in the jeweled skies,
  Albeit he soared with an undaunted wing?
Hast thou not dragged Diana from her car,
  And driven the hamadryad from the wood
To seek a shelter in some happier star?
  Hast thou not torn the naiad from her flood,
The elfin from the green grass, and from me
The summer dream beneath the tamarind tree?

To Helen

Helen, thy beauty is to me
  Like those Nicéan barks of yore,
That gently, o'er a perfumed sea,
  The weary, way-worn wanderer bore
  To his own native shore.

On desperate seas long wont to roam,
  Thy hyacinth hair, thy classic face,
Thy naiad airs have brought me home
  To the glory that was Greece
And the grandeur that was Rome.

Lo! in yon brilliant window niche
  How statuelike I see thee stand,
  The agate lamp within thy hand!
Ah, Psyche, from the regions which
  Are holy land!

The City in the Sea

Lo! Death has reared himself a throne
In a strange city lying alone
Far down within the dim West,
Where the good and the bad and the worst and the best
Have gone to their eternal rest.
There shrines and palaces and towers
(Time-eaten towers that tremble not!)
Resemble nothing that is ours.
Around, by lifting winds forgot,
Resignedly beneath the sky
The melancholy waters lie.

No rays from the holy heaven come down
On the long nighttime of that town;
But light from out the lurid sea
Streams up the turrets silently—
Gleams up the pinnacles far and free—
Up domes—up spires—up kingly halls—

Up fanes—up Babylon-like walls—
Up shadowy long-forgotten bowers
Of sculptured ivy and stone flowers—
Up many and many a marvelous shrine
Whose wreathèd friezes intertwine
The viol, the violet, and the vine.

Resignedly beneath the sky
The melancholy waters lie.
So blend the turrets and shadows there
That all seem pendulous in air,
While from a proud tower in the town
Death looks gigantically down.

There open fanes and gaping graves
Yawn level with the luminous waves;
But not the riches there that lie
In each idol's diamond eye—
Not the gaily jeweled dead
Tempt the waters from their bed;
For no ripples curl, alas!
Along that wilderness of glass—
No swellings tell that winds may be
Upon some far-off happier sea—
No heavings hint that winds have been
On seas less hideously serene.

But lo, a stir is in the air!
The wave—there is a movement there!
As if the towers had thrust aside,
In slightly sinking, the dull tide—
As if their tops had feebly given
A void within the filmy heaven.
The waves have now a redder glow—
The hours are breathing faint and low—
And when, amid no earthly moans,
Down, down that town shall settle hence,
Hell, rising from a thousand thrones,
Shall do it reverence.

The Sleeper

At midnight, in the month of June,
I stand beneath the mystic moon.
An opiate vapor, dewy, dim,
Exhales from out her golden rim,
And softly dripping, drop by drop,
Upon the quiet mountaintop,
Steals drowsily and musically
Into the universal valley.
The rosemary nods upon the grave;
The lily lolls upon the wave;

Wrapping the fog about its breast,
The ruin molders into rest;
Looking like Lethe, see! the lake
A conscious slumber seems to take,
And would not, for the world, awake.
All Beauty sleeps!—and lo! where lies
Irene, with her Destinies!

Oh, lady bright! can it be right—
This window open to the night?
The wanton airs, from the treetop,
Laughingly through the lattice drop—
The bodiless airs, a wizard rout,
Flit through thy chamber in and out,
And wave the curtain canopy
So fitfully—so fearfully—
Above the closed and fringèd lid
'Neath which thy slumb'ring soul lies hid,
That, o'er the floor and down the wall,
Like ghosts the shadows rise and fall!
Oh, lady dear, hast thou no fear?
Why and what art thou dreaming here?
Sure thou art come o'er far-off seas,
A wonder to these garden trees!
Strange is thy pallor! strange thy dress!
Strange, above all, thy length of tress,
And this all solemn silentness!

The lady sleeps! Oh, may her sleep,
Which is enduring, so be deep!
Heaven have her in its sacred keep!
This chamber changed for one more holy,
This bed for one more melancholy,
I pray to God that she may lie
Forever with unopened eye,
While the pale sheeted ghosts go by!

My love, she sleeps! Oh, may her sleep,
As it is lasting, so be deep!
Soft may the worms about her creep!

Far in the forest, dim and old,
For her may some tall vault unfold—
Some vault that oft hath flung its black
And wingèd panels fluttering back,
Triumphant, o'er the crested palls
Of her grand family funerals—
Some sepulcher, remote, alone,
Against whose portal she hath thrown,
In childhood, many an idle stone—
Some tomb from out whose sounding door
She ne'er shall force an echo more,
Thrilling to think, poor child of sin!
It was the dead who groaned within.

The Haunted Palace

In the greenest of our valleys
  By good angels tenanted,
Once a fair and stately palace—
  Radiant palace—reared its head.
In the monarch Thought's dominion,
  It stood there!
Never seraph spread a pinion
  Over fabric half so fair!

Banners yellow, glorious, golden,
  On its roof did float and flow
(This—all this—was in the olden
  Time long ago),
And every gentle air that dallied,
  In that sweet day,
Along the ramparts plumed and pallid,
  A wingèd odor went away.

Wanderers in that happy valley,
  Through two luminous windows, saw
Spirits moving musically,
  To a lute's well-tunèd law,

Round about a throne where, sitting,
  Porphyrogene!
In state his glory well befitting,
  The ruler of the realm was seen.

And all with pearl and ruby glowing
  Was the fair palace door,
Through which came flowing, flowing, flowing,
  And sparkling evermore,
A troop of Echoes, whose sweet duty
  Was but to sing,
In voices of surpassing beauty,
  The wit and wisdom of their king.

But evil things, in robes of sorrow,
  Assailed the monarch's high estate.
(Ah, let us mourn!—for never morrow
  Shall dawn upon him, desolate!)
And round about his home the glory
  That blushed and bloomed,
Is but a dim-remembered story
  Of the old time entombed.

And travelers, now, within that valley,
  Through the red-litten windows see
Vast forms that move fantastically
  To a discordant melody,
While, like a ghastly rapid river,
  Through the pale door
A hideous throng rush out forever,
  And laugh—but smile no more.

Dreamland

By a route obscure and lonely,
Haunted by ill angels only,
Where an eidolon, named Night,
On a black throne reigns upright,
I have reached these lands but newly
From an ultimate dim Thule—
From a wild weird clime that lieth, sublime,
Out of space—out of time.

Bottomless vales and boundless floods,
And chasms, and caves, and titan woods,
With forms that no man can discover
For the tears that drip all over;
Mountains toppling evermore
Into seas without a shore;
Seas that restlessly aspire,
Surging, unto skies of fire;
Lakes that endlessly outspread
Their lone waters, lone and dead,—
Their still waters, still and chilly
With the snows of the lolling lily.

By the lakes that thus outspread
Their lone waters, lone and dead,—
Their sad waters, sad and chilly
With the snows of the lolling lily,—
By the mountains—near the river
Murmuring lowly, murmuring ever,—
By the gray woods,—by the swamp
Where the toad and the newt encamp,—
By the dismal tarns and pools
Where dwell the ghouls,—
By each spot the most unholy—
In each nook most melancholy,—

There the traveler meets, aghast,
Sheeted memories of the past—
Shrouded forms that start and sigh
As they pass the wanderer by—
White-robed forms of friends long given,
In agony, to the earth—and heaven.

For the heart whose woes are legion
'Tis a peaceful, soothing region—
For the spirit that walks in shadow
'Tis—oh, 'tis an Eldorado!
But the traveler, traveling through it,
May not—dare not openly view it;
Never its mysteries are exposed
To the weak human eye unclosed;
So wills its king, who hath forbid
The uplifting of the fringèd lid;
And thus the sad soul that here passes
Beholds it but through darkened glasses.

By a route obscure and lonely,
Haunted by ill angels only,
Where an eidolon, named Night,
On a black throne reigns upright,
I have wandered home but newly
From this ultimate dim Thule.

The Raven

One upon a midnight dreary, while I pondered, weak and weary,
Over many a quaint and curious volume of forgotten lore—
While I nodded, nearly napping, suddenly there came a tapping,
As of someone gently rapping, rapping at my chamber door.
"'Tis some visitor," I muttered, "tapping at my chamber door—
Only this and nothing more."

Ah, distinctly I remember it was in the bleak December;
And each separate dying ember wrought its ghost upon the floor.
Eagerly I wished the morrow;—vainly I had sought to borrow
From my books surcease of sorrow—sorrow for the lost Lenore—
For the rare and radiant maiden whom the angels name Lenore—
Nameless *here* forevermore.

And the silken, sad, uncertain rustling of each purple curtain
Thrilled me—filled me with fantastic terrors never felt before;
So that now, to still the beating of my heart, I stood repeating,
"'Tis some visitor entreating entrance at my chamber door—
Some late visitor entreating entrance at my chamber door;—
This it is and nothing more."

Presently my soul grew stronger; hesitating then no longer,
"Sir," said I, "or madam, truly your forgiveness I implore;
But the fact is I was napping, and so gently you came rapping,
And so faintly you came tapping, tapping at my chamber door,
That I scarce was sure I heard you"—here I opened wide the door;—
Darkness there and nothing more.

Deep into that darkness peering, long I stood there wondering, fearing,
Doubting, dreaming dreams no mortal ever dared to dream before;
But the silence was unbroken, and the stillness gave no token,
And the only word there spoken was the whispered word, "Lenore?"
This I whispered, and an echo murmured back the word, "Lenore!"
Merely this and nothing more.

Back into the chamber turning, all my soul within me burning,
Soon again I heard a tapping somewhat louder than before.
"Surely," said I, "surely that is something at my window lattice;
Let me see, then, what thereat is, and this mystery explore—
Let my heart be still a moment and this mystery explore;—
'Tis the wind and nothing more!"

Open here I flung the shutter, when, with many a flirt and flutter,
In there stepped a stately Raven of the saintly days of yore;
Not the least obeisance made he; not a minute stopped or stayed he;

But, with mien of lord or lady, perched above my chamber door—
Perched upon a bust of Pallas just above my chamber door—
    Perched, and sat, and nothing more.

Then this ebony bird beguiling my sad fancy into smiling,
By the grave and stern decorum of the countenance it wore,
"Though thy crest be shorn and shaven, thou," I said, "art sure no
  craven,
Ghastly grim and ancient Raven wandering from the nightly shore—
Tell me what thy lordly name is on the night's Plutonian shore!"
    Quoth the Raven, "Nevermore."

Much I marveled this ungainly fowl to hear discourse so plainly,
Though its answer little meaning—little relevancy bore;
For we cannot help agreeing that no living human being
Ever yet was blessed with seeing bird above his chamber door—
Bird or beast upon the sculptured bust above his chamber door,
    With such name as "Nevermore."

But the Raven, sitting lonely on the placid bust, spoke only
That one word, as if his soul in that one word he did outpour.
Nothing farther then he uttered—not a feather then he fluttered—
Till I scarcely more than muttered, "Other friends have flown
  before—
On the morrow *he* will leave me, as my hopes have flown before."
    Then the bird said, "Nevermore."

Startled at the stillness broken by reply so aptly spoken,
"Doubtless," said I, "what it utters is its only stock and store
Caught from some unhappy master whom unmerciful disaster
Followed fast and followed faster till his songs one burden bore—
Till the dirges of his hope that melancholy burden bore
    Of 'Never—nevermore'."

But the Raven still beguiling my sad fancy into smiling,
Straight I wheeled a cushioned seat in front of bird and bust and
  door;
Then, upon the velvet sinking, I betook myself to linking
Fancy unto fancy, thinking what this ominous bird of yore—
What this grim, ungainly, ghastly, gaunt, and ominous bird of yore
    Meant in croaking "Nevermore."

This I sat engaged in guessing, but no syllable expressing
To the fowl whose fiery eyes now burned into my bosom's core;
This and more I sat divining, with my head at ease reclining
On the cushion's velvet lining that the lamplight gloated o'er,
But whose velvet-violet lining with the lamplight gloating o'er,
    She shall press, ah, nevermore!

Then, methought, the air grew denser, perfumed from an unseen censer
Swung by seraphim whose footfalls tinkled on the tufted floor.
"Wretch," I cried, "thy God hath lent thee—by these angels he hath sent thee
Respite—respite and nepenthe from thy memories of Lenore;
Quaff, oh, quaff this kind nepenthe and forget this lost Lenore!"
    Quoth the Raven, "Nevermore."

"Prophet!" said I, "thing of evil!—prophet still, if bird or devil!—
Whether Tempter sent, or whether tempest tossed thee here ashore,
Desolate yet all undaunted, on this desert land enchanted—
On this home by horror haunted—tell me truly, I implore—
Is there—*is* there balm in Gilead?—tell me—tell me, I implore!"
    Quoth the Raven, "Nevermore."

"Prophet!" said I, "thing of evil—prophet still, if bird or devil!
By that heaven that bends above us—by that God we both adore—
Tell this soul with sorrow laden if, within the distant Aidenn,
It shall clasp a sainted maiden whom the angels name Lenore—
Clasp a rare and radiant maiden whom the angels name Lenore."
    Quoth the Raven, "Nevermore."

"Be that word our sign of parting, bird or fiend!" I shrieked, upstarting—
"Get thee back into the tempest and the night's Plutonian shore!
Leave no black plume as a token of that lie thy soul hath spoken!
Leave my loneliness unbroken!—quit the bust above my door!
Take thy beak from out my heart, and take thy form from off my door!"
    Quoth the Raven, "Nevermore."

And the Raven, never flitting, still is sitting, *still* is sitting
On the pallid bust of Pallas just above my chamber door;
And his eyes have all the seeming of a demon's that is dreaming,
And the lamplight o'er him streaming throws his shadow on the floor;
And my soul from out that shadow that lies floating on the floor
Shall be lifted—nevermore!

To One in Paradise

Thou wast that all to me, love,
For which my soul did pine—
A green isle in the sea, love,
A fountain and a shrine,
All wreathed with fairy fruits and flowers,
And all the flowers were mine.

Ah, dream too bright to last!
Ah, starry hope! that didst arise
But to be overcast!
A voice from out the future cries,
"On! on!"—but o'er the past
(Dim gulf!) my spirit hovering lies
Mute, motionless, aghast!

For, alas! alas! with me
The light of life is o'er!
No more—no more—no more—
(Such language holds the solemn sea
To the sands upon the shore)
Shall bloom the thunder-blasted tree,
Or the stricken eagle soar!

And all my days are trances,
And all my nightly dreams
Are where thy gray eye glances,
And where thy footstep gleams—
In what ethereal dances,
By what eternal streams.

The Bells

I

Hear the sledges with the bells—
Silver bells!
What a world of merriment their melody foretells!
How they tinkle, tinkle, tinkle,
In the icy air of night!
While the stars that oversprinkle
All the heavens, seem to twinkle
With a crystalline delight;
Keeping time, time, time,
In a sort of runic rhyme,
To the tintinnabulation that so musically wells
From the bells, bells, bells, bells,
Bells, bells, bells—
From the jingling and the tinkling of the bells.

II

Hear the mellow wedding bells—
Golden bells!
What a world of happiness their harmony foretells!
Through the balmy air of night
How they ring out their delight!—
From the molten-golden notes,
And all in tune,
What a liquid ditty floats
To the turtledove that listens, while she gloats
On the moon!
Oh, from out the sounding cells,
What a gush of euphony voluminously wells!
How it swells!
How it dwells
On the future!—how it tells
Of the rapture that impels
To the swinging and the ringing
Of the bells, bells, bells—

Of the bells, bells, bells, bells,
Bells, bells, bells—
To the rhyming and the chiming of the bells!

III

Hear the loud alarum bells—
Brazen bells!
What a tale of terror, now, their turbulency tells!
In the startled ear of night
How they scream out their affright!
Too much horrified to speak,
They can only shriek, shriek,
Out of tune,
In a clamorous appealing to the mercy of the fire,
In a mad expostulation with the deaf and frantic fire,
Leaping higher, higher, higher,
With a desperate desire,
And a resolute endeavor
Now—now to sit, or never,
By the side of the pale-faced moon.
Oh, the bells, bells, bells!
What a tale their terror tells
Of despair!
How they clang, and clash, and roar!
What a horror they outpour
On the bosom of the palpitating air!
Yet the ear, it fully knows
By the twanging
And the clanging,
How the danger ebbs and flows;
Yet the ear distinctly tells,
In the jangling
And wrangling,
How the danger sinks and swells,
By the sinking or the swelling in the anger of the bells—
Of the bells,—

IV

Hear the tolling of the bells—
Iron bells!
What a world of solemn thought their monody compels!

In the silence of the night,
How we shiver with affright
At the melancholy menace of their tone!
For every sound that floats
From the rust within their throats
Is a groan.
And the people—ah, the people—
They that dwell up in the steeple,
All alone,
And who tolling, tolling, tolling,
In that muffled monotone,
Feel a glory in so rolling
On the human heart a stone—
They are neither man nor woman—
They are neither brute nor human—
They are ghouls:—
And their king it is who tolls:—
And he rolls, rolls, rolls,
Rolls
A paean from the bells!
And his merry bosom swells
With the paean of the bells!
And he dances, and he yells;
Keeping time, time, time,
In a sort of runic rhyme,
To the paean of the bells—
Of the bells—
Keeping time, time, time,
In a sort of runic rhyme,
To the throbbing of the bells—
Of the bells, bells, bells—
To the sobbing of the bells;
Keeping time, time, time,
As he knells, knells, knells,
In a happy runic rhyme,
To the rolling of the bells—
Of the bells, bells, bells:—
To the tolling of the bells—
Of the bells, bells, bells, bells,
Bells, bells, bells—
To the moaning and the groaning of the bells.

Ulalume—A Ballad

The skies they were ashen and sober;
    The leaves they were crispèd and sere—
    The leaves they were withering and sere:
It was night, in the lonesome October
    Of my most immemorial year:
It was hard by the dim lake of Auber,
    In the misty mid-region of Weir—
It was down by the dank tarn of Auber,
    In the ghoul-haunted woodland of Weir.

Here once, through an alley titanic,
    Of cypress, I roamed with my soul—
    Of cypress with Psyche, my soul
These were days when my heart was volcanic
    As the scoriac rivers that roll—
    As the lavas that restlessly roll
Their sulphurous currents down Yaanek
    In the ultimate climes of the Pole—
That groan as they roll down Mount Yaanek
    In the realms of the boreal Pole.

Our talk had been serious and sober,
    But our thoughts they were palsied and sere—
    Our memories were treacherous and sere;
For we knew not the month was October,
    And we marked not the night of the year
    (Ah, night of all nights in the year!)—
We noted not the dim lake of Auber
    (Though once we had journeyed down here)—
We remembered not the dank tarn of Auber,
    Nor the ghoul-haunted woodland of Weir.

And now, as the night was senescent
    And star dials pointed to morn—
    As the star dials hinted of morn—

At the end of our path a liquescent
And nebulous luster was born,
Out of which a miraculous crescent
Arose with a duplicate horn—
Astarte's bediamonded crescent
Distinct with its duplicate horn.

And I said: "She is warmer than Dian;
She rolls through an ether of sighs—
She revels in a region of sighs.
She has seen that the tears are not dry on
These cheeks, where the worm never dies,
And has come past the stars of the Lion,
To point us the path to the skies—
To the Lethean peace of the skies—
Come up, in despite of the Lion,
To shine on us with her bright eyes—
Come up through the lair of the Lion,
With love in her luminous eyes."

But Psyche, uplifting her finger,
Said: "Sadly this star I mistrust—
Her pallor I strangely mistrust:
Ah, hasten!—ah, let us not linger.
Ah, fly!—let us fly!—for we must."
In terror she spoke, letting sink her
Wings till they trailed in the dust—
In agony sobbed, letting sink her
Plumes till they trailed in the dust—
Till they sorrowfully trailed in the dust.

I replied: "This is nothing but dreaming:
Let us on by this tremulous light!
Let us bathe in this crystalline light!
Its sibylic splendor is beaming
With hope and in beauty tonight:—
See!—it flickers up the sky through the night!
Ah, we safely may trust to its gleaming,
And be sure it will lead us aright—
We surely may trust to a gleaming,
That cannot but guide us aright,
Since it flickers up to heaven through the night."

Thus I pacified Psyche and kissed her,
    And tempted her out of her gloom—
    And conquered her scruples and gloom;
And we passed to the end of the vista,
    But were stopped by the door of a tomb—
    By the door of a legended tomb;
And I said: "What is written, sweet sister,
    On the door of this legended tomb?"
    She replied: "Ulalume—Ulalume!—
    'Tis the vault of thy lost Ulalume!"

Then my heart it grew ashen and sober
    As the leaves that were crispèd and sere—
    As the leaves that were withering and sere;
And I said: "It was surely October
    On *this* very night of last year
    That I journeyed—I journeyed down here!—
    That I brought a dread burden down here—
    On this night of all nights in the year,
    Ah, what demon hath tempted me here?
Well I know, now, this dim lake of Auber—
    This misty mid-region of Weir—
Well I know, now, this dank tarn of Auber,
    This ghoul-haunted woodland of Weir."

Said we, then—the two, then: "Ah, can it
    Have been that the woodlandish ghouls—
    The pitiful, the merciful ghouls—
To bar up our way and to ban it
    From the secret that lies in these wolds—
    From the thing that lies hidden in these wolds—
Have drawn up the specter of a planet
    From the limbo of lunary souls—
This sinful scintillant planet
    From the hell of the planetary souls?"

Eldorado

Gaily bedight,
A gallant knight,
In sunshine and in shadow,
Had journeyed long,
Singing a song,
In search of Eldorado.

But he grew old—
This knight so bold—
And o'er his heart a shadow
Fell as he found
No spot of ground
That looked like Eldorado.

And, as his strength
Failed him at length,
He met a pilgrim shadow—
"Shadow," said he,
"Where can it be—
This land of Eldorado?"

"Over the mountains
Of the moon,
Down the valley of the shadow,
Ride, boldly ride,"
The shade replied,—
"If you seek for Eldorado!"

Annabel Lee

It was many and many a year ago,
    In a kingdom by the sea,
That a maiden there lived whom you may know
    By the name of Annabel Lee;—
And this maiden she lived with no other thought
    Than to love and be loved by me.

She was a child and *I* was a child,
    In this kingdom by the sea,
But we loved with a love that was more than love—
    I and my Annabel Lee—
With a love that the wingèd seraphs of heaven
    Coveted her and me.

And this was the reason that, long ago,
    In this kingdom by the sea,
A wind blew out of a cloud by night
    Chilling my Annabel Lee;
So that her highborn kinsmen came
    And bore her away from me,
To shut her up in a sepulcher
    In this kingdom by the sea.

The angels, not half so happy in heaven,
    Went envying her and me:—
Yes! that was the reason (as all men know,
    In this kingdom by the sea)
That the wind came out of the cloud, chilling
    And killing my Annabel Lee.

But our love it was stronger by far than the love
    Of those who were older than we—
    Of many far wiser than we—
And neither the angels in heaven above

Nor the demons down under the sea,
Can ever dissever my soul from the soul
Of the beautiful Annabel Lee:—

For the moon never beams without bringing me dreams
Of the beautiful Annabel Lee;
And the stars never rise but I see the bright eyes
Of the beautiful Annabel Lee;
And so, all the nighttide, I lie down by the side
Of my darling, my darling, my life and my bride,
In her sepulcher there by the sea—
In her tomb by the side of the sea.

Israfel

In Heaven a spirit doth dwell
"Whose heart-strings are a lute";
None sing so wildly well
As the angel Israfel,
And the giddy stars (so legends tell),
Ceasing their hymns, attend the spell
Of his voice, all mute.

Tottering above
In her highest noon,
The enamoured moon
Blushes with love,
While, to listen, the red levin
(With the rapid Pleiads, even,
Which were seven,)
Pauses in Heaven.

And they say (the starry choir
And the other listening things)
That Israfeli's fire
Is owing to that lyre
By which he sits and sings—
The trembling living wire
Of those unusual strings.

But the skies that angel trod,
    Where deep thoughts are a duty,
Where Love's a grown-up God,
    Where the Houri glances are
Imbued with all the beauty
    Which we worship in a star.

Therefore, thou art not wrong,
    Israfeli, who despisest
An unimpassioned song;
To thee the laurels belong,
    Best bard, because the wisest!
Merrily live, and long!

The ecstasies above
    With thy burning measures suit—
Thy grief, thy joy, thy hate, thy love,
    With the fervour of thy lute—
    Well may the stars be mute!

Yes, Heaven is thine; but this
    Is a world of sweets and sours;
    Our flowers are merely—flowers,
And the shadow of thy perfect bliss
    Is the sunshine of ours.

If I could dwell
Where Israfel
    Hath dwelt, and he where I,
He might not sing so wildly well
    A mortal melody,
While a bolder note than this might swell
    From my lyre within the sky.

JONES VERY
(1813–1880)

Today

I live but in the present,—where art thou?
Hast thou a home in some past, future year?
I call to thee from every leafy bough,
But thou art far away and canst not hear.

Each flower lifts up its red or yellow head,
And nods to thee as thou art passing by:
Hurry not on, but stay thine anxious tread,
And thou shalt live with me, for there am I.

The stream that murmurs by thee,—heed its voice,
Nor stop thine ear; 'tis I that bid it flow;
And thou with its glad waters shalt rejoice,
And of the life I live within them know.

And hill, and grove, and flowers, and running stream,
When thou dost live with them shall look more fair;
And thou awake as from a cheating dream,
The life today with me and mine to share.

The Hand and Foot

The hand and foot that stir not, they shall find
Sooner than all the rightful place to go:
Now in their motion free as roving wind,
Though first no snail so limited and slow;
I mark them full of labor all the day,
Each active motion made in perfect rest;
They cannot from their path mistaken stray,
Though 't is not theirs, yet in it they are blest;
The bird has not their hidden track found out,
The cunning fox though full of art he be;
It is the way unseen, the certain route,
Where ever bound, yet thou art ever free;
The path of Him, whose perfect law of love
Bids spheres and atoms in just order move.

The Eagles

The eagles gather on the place of death
So thick the ground is spotted with their wings,
The air is tainted with the noisome breath
The wind from off the field of slaughter brings;
Alas! no mourners weep them for the slain,
But all unburied lies the naked soul;
The whitening bones of thousands strew the plain,
Yet none can now the pestilence control;
The eagles gathering on the carcass feed,
In every heart behold their half-formed prey;
The battened wills beneath their talons bleed,
Their iron beaks without remorse must slay;
Till by the sun no more the place is seen,
Where they who worshipped idol gods have been.

The Garden

I saw the spot where our first parents dwelt;
And yet it wore to me no face of change,
For while amid its fields and groves I felt
As if I had not sinned, nor thought it strange;
My eye seemed but a part of every sight,
My ear heard music in each sound that rose,
Each sense forever found a new delight,
Such as the spirit's vision only knows;
Each act some new and ever-varying joy
Did by my father's love for me prepare;
To dress the spot my ever fresh employ,
And in the glorious whole with Him to share;
No more without the flaming gate to stray,
No more for sin's dark stain the debt of death to pay.

On Visiting the Graves of Hawthorne and Thoreau

Beneath these shades, beside yon winding stream,
Lies Hawthorne's manly form, the mortal part!
The soul, that loved to meditate and dream,
Might linger here unwilling to depart,
But that a higher life has called away
To fairer scenes, to nobler work and thought.
Why should the spirit then on earth delay,
That has a glimpse of such bright regions caught!
And near another, Nature's child, doth rest,—
Thoreau, who loved each woodland path to tread;
So gently sleeping on his mother's breast!
Living, though numbered with the numerous dead.
We mourn! But hope will whisper in the heart,
We meet again! and meet no more to part.

Thy Brother's Blood

I have no brother. They who meet me now
Offer a hand with their own wills defiled,
And, while they wear a smooth, unwrinkled brow,
Know not that Truth can never be beguiled.
Go wash the hand that still betrays thy guilt;—
Before the Spirit's gaze what stain can hide?
Abel's red blood upon the earth is spilt,
And by thy tongue it cannot be denied.
I hear not with the ear,—the heart doth tell
Its secret deeds to me untold before;
Go, all its hidden plunder quickly sell,
Then shalt thou cleanse thee from thy brother's gore,
Then will I take thy gift;—that bloody stain
Shall not be seen upon thy hand again.

The Dead

I see them,—crowd on crowd they walk the earth,
Dry leafless trees no autumn wind laid bare;
And in their nakedness find cause for mirth,
And all unclad would winter's rudeness dare;
No sap doth through their clattering branches flow,
Whence springing leaves and blossoms bright appear;
Their hearts the living God have ceased to know
Who gives the spring-time to th' expectant year.
They mimic life, as if from Him to steal
His glow of health to paint the livid cheek;
They borrow words for thoughts they cannot feel,
That with a seeming heart their tongue may speak;
And in their show of life more dead they live
Than those that to the earth with many tears they give.

The Slave

I saw him forging link by link his chain,
Yet while he felt its strength he thought him free,
And sighed for those borne o'er the barren main
To bondage that to his would freedom be;
Yet on he walked with eyes far-gazing still
On wrongs that from his own dark bosom flowed,
And while he thought to do his master's will
He but the more his disobedience showed;
I heard a wild rose by the stony wall,
Whose fragrance reached me in the passing gale,
A lesson give—it gave alike to all—
And I repeat the moral of its tale,
"That from the spot where deep its dark roots grew
Bloomed forth the fragrant rose that all delight to view."

The Fugitive Slaves

Ye sorrowing people! who from bondage fly,
And cruel laws that men against you make,—
Think not that none there are who hear your cry
And for yourselves and children thought will take.
Though now bowed down with sorrow and with fear,
Lift up your heads! for you are not alone;
Some Christian hearts are left your flight to cheer,
Some human hearts not wholly turned to stone;
God to His angels shall give strictest charge,
And in their hands they'll bear you safe from harm,
Where in a freer land you'll roam at large,
Nor dread pursuit, nor start at each alarm;
Till in His time you shall return again,
No more to feel man's wrath or dread his chain.

On the Completion of the Pacific Telegraph

Swift to the western bounds of this wide land,
Swifter than light, the Electric Message flies;
The continent is in a moment spanned,
And furthest West to furthest East replies.
While War asunder drives the nearest States,
And doth to them all intercourse deny;
Since new bonds of Union still creates,
And the most distant brings forever nigh!
I hail this omen for our Country's cause;
For it the stars do in their courses fight!
In vain men strive against the eternal laws
Of Peace, and Liberty, and social Right,
Rebel again the light, and hope to stay
The dawn on earth of Freedom's perfect day.

HENRY DAVID THOREAU
(1817–1862)

What's the Railroad to Me

What's the railroad to me?
I never go to see
Where it ends.
It fills a few hollows,
And makes banks for the swallows,
It sets the sand a-blowing,
And the blackberries a-growing.

Light-winged Smoke, Icarian Bird

Light-winged Smoke, Icarian bird,
Melting thy pinions in thy upward flight,
Lark without song, and messenger of dawn,
Circling above the hamlets as thy nest;
Or else, departing dream, and shadowy form
Of midnight vision, gathering up thy skirts;
By night star-veiling, and by day
Darkening the light and blotting out the sun;
Go thou my incense upward from this hearth,
And ask the gods to pardon this clear flame.

Woof of the Sun, Ethereal Gauze

Woof of the sun, ethereal gauze,
Woven of Nature's richest stuffs,
Visible heat, air-water, and dry sea,
Last conquest of the eye;
Toil of the day displayed, sun-dust,
Aerial surf upon the shores of earth,
Ethereal estuary, frith of light,
Breakers of air, billows of heat,
Fine summer spray on inland seas;
Bird of the sun, transparent-winged
Owlet of noon, soft-pinioned,
From heath or stubble rising without song;
Establish thy serenity o'er the fields.

I Am a Parcel of Vain Strivings Tied

I am a parcel of vain strivings tied
    By a chance bond together,
  Dangling this way and that, their links
    Were made so loose and wide,
        Methinks,
      For milder weather.

A bunch of violets without their roots,
    And sorrel intermixed,
  Encircled by a wisp of straw
    Once coiled about their shoots,
        The law
      By which I'm fixed.

A nosegay which Time clutched from out
Those fair Elysian fields,
With weeds and broken stems, in haste,
Doth make the rabble rout
That waste
The day he yields.

And here I bloom for a short hour unseen,
Drinking my juices up,
With no root in the land
To keep my branches green,
But stand
In a bare cup.

Some tender buds were left upon my stem
In mimicry of life,
But ah! the children will not know,
Till time has withered them,
The woe
With which they're rife.

But now I see I was not plucked for naught,
And after in life's vase
Of glass set while I might survive,
But by a kind hand brought
Alive
To a strange place.

That stock thus thinned will soon redeem its hours,
And by another year,
Such as God knows, with freer air,
More fruits and fairer flowers
Will bear,
While I droop here.

JAMES RUSSELL LOWELL
(1819–1891)

from *A Fable for Critics*

Reader! walk up at once (it will soon be too late),
and buy at a perfectly ruinous rate

A FABLE FOR CRITICS:

OR, BETTER,

(I LIKE, AS A THING THAT THE READER'S FIRST FANCY MAY STRIKE,
AN OLD-FASHIONED TITLE-PAGE,
SUCH AS PRESENTS A TABULAR VIEW OF THE VOLUME'S CONTENTS),

A GLANCE AT A FEW OF OUR LITERARY PROGENIES

(MRS. MALAPROP'S WORD)

FROM THE TUB OF DIOGENES;

A VOCAL AND MUSICAL MEDLEY,

THAT IS,

A SERIES OF JOKES

By A Wonderful Quiz,

WHO ACCOMPANIES HIMSELF WITH A RUB-A-DUB-DUB, FULL OF SPIRIT AND GRACE, ON THE TOP OF THE TUB.

Set forth in October, the 31st day,
In the year '48, G. P. Putnam, Broadway.

It being the commonest mode of procedure, I premise a few candid remarks

TO THE READER:—

This trifle, begun to please only myself and my own private fancy, was laid on the shelf. But some friends, who had seen it, induced me, by dint of saying they liked it, to put it in print. That is, having come to that very conclusion, I asked their advice when 'twould make no confusion. For though (in the gentlest of ways) they had hinted it was scarce worth the while, I should doubtless have printed it.

I began it, intending a Fable, a frail, slender thing, rhyme-ywinged, with a sting in its tail. But, by addings and alterings not previously planned, digressions chance-hatched, like birds' eggs in the sand, and dawdlings to suit every whimsey's demand (always freeing the bird which I held in my hand, for the two perched, perhaps out of reach, in the tree),—it grew by degrees to the size which you see. I was like the old woman that carried the calf, and my neighbors, like hers, no doubt, wonder and laugh; and when, my strained arms with their grown burthen full, I call it my Fable, they call it a bull.

Having scrawled at full gallop (as far as that goes) in a style that is neither good verse nor bad prose, and being a person whom nobody knows, some people will say I am rather more free with my readers than it is becoming to be, that I seem to expect them to wait on my leisure in following wherever I wander at pleasure, that, in short, I take more than a young author's lawful ease, and laugh in a queer way so like Mephistopheles, that the public will doubt, as they grope through my rhythm, if in truth I am making fun *of* them or *with* them.

So the excellent Public is hereby assured that the sale of my book is already secured. For there is not a poet throughout the whole land but will purchase a copy or two out of hand, in the fond expectation of being amused in it, by seeing his betters cut up and abused in it. Now, I find, by a pretty exact calculation, there are something like ten thousand bards in the nation, of that special variety whom the Review and Magazine critics call *lofty* and *true*, and about thirty thousand (*this* tribe is increasing) of the kinds who are termed *full of promise* and *pleasing*. The Public will see by a glance at this schedule, that they cannot expect me to be over-sedulous about courting *them*, since it seems I have got enough fuel made sure of for boiling my pot.

As for such of our poets as find not their names mentioned once in my pages, with praises or blames, let them send in their cards, without further delay, to my friend G. P. Putnam, Esquire, in Broadway, where a list will be kept with the strictest regard to the day and the hour of receiving the card. Then, taking them up as I chance to have time (that is, if their names can be twisted in rhyme), I will honestly give each his proper position, at the rate of one author to each new edition. Thus a PREMIUM is offered sufficiently high (as the magazines say when they tell their best lie) to induce bards to club their resources and buy the balance of every edition, until they have all of them fairly been run through the mill.

One word to such readers (judicious and wise) as read books with something behind the mere eyes, of whom in the country, perhaps, there are two, including myself, gentle reader, and you. All the characters sketched in this slight *jeu d'esprit,* though it may be, they seem, here and there, rather free, and drawn from a somewhat too cynical standpoint, are *meant* to be faithful, for that is the grand point, and none but an owl would feel sore at a rub from a jester who tells you, without any subterfuge, that he sits in Diogenes' tub.

[EMERSON]

"There comes Emerson first, whose rich words, every one,
Are like gold nails in temples to hang trophies on,
Whose prose is grand verse, while his verse, the Lord knows,
Is some of it pr—— No, 'tis not even prose;
I'm speaking of metres; some poems have welled
From those rare depths of soul that have ne'er been excelled;
They're not epics, but that doesn't matter a pin,
In creating, the only hard thing's to begin;
A grass-blade's no easier to make than an oak;
If you've once found the way, you've achieved the grand stroke;
In the worst of his poems are mines of rich matter,
But thrown in a heap with a crash and a clatter;
Now it is not one thing nor another alone
Makes a poem, but rather the general tone,
The something pervading, uniting the whole,
The before unconceived, unconceivable soul,
So that just in removing this trifle or that, you
Take away, as it were, a chief limb of the statue;
Roots, wood, bark, and leaves singly perfect may be,
But, clapt hodge-podge together, they don't make a tree.

"But, to come back to Emerson (whom, by the way,
I believe we left waiting),—his is, we may say,
A Greek head on right Yankee shoulders, whose range
Has Olympus for one pole, for t' other the Exchange;
He seems, to my thinking (although I'm afraid
The comparison must, long ere this, have been made),

A Plotinus-Montaigne, where the Egyptian's gold mist
And the Gascon's shrewd wit cheek-by-jowl coexist;
All admire, and yet scarcely six converts he's got
To I don't (nor they either) exactly know what;
For though he builds glorious temples, 't is odd
He leaves never a doorway to get in a god.
'T is refreshing to old-fashioned people like me
To meet such a primitive Pagan as he,
In whose mind all creation is duly respected
As parts of himself—just a little projected;
And who's willing to worship the stars and the sun,
A convert to—nothing but Emerson.
So perfect a balance there is in his head,
That he talks of things sometimes as if they were dead;
Life, nature, love, God, and affairs of that sort,
He looks at as merely ideas; in short,
As if they were fossils stuck round in a cabinet,
Of such vast extent that our earth's a mere dab in it;
Composed just as he is inclined to conjecture her,
Namely, one part pure earth, ninety-nine parts pure lecturer;
You are filled with delight at his clear demonstration,
Each figure, word, gesture, just fits the occasion,
With the quiet precision of science he'll sort 'em,
But you can't help suspecting the whole a *post mortem*.

. . .

"He has imitators in scores, who omit
No part of the man but his wisdom and wit,—
Who go carefully o'er the sky-blue of his brain,
And when he has skimmed it once, skim it again;
If at all they resemble him, you may be sure it is
Because their shoals mirror his mists and obscurities,
As a mud-puddle seems deep as heaven for a minute,
While a cloud that floats o'er is reflected within it.

. . .

[Bryant]

"There is Bryant, as quiet, as cool, and as dignified,
As a smooth, silent iceberg, that never is ignified,
Save when by reflection 't is kindled o' nights
With a semblance of flame by the chill Northern Lights.

He may rank (Griswold says so) first bard of your nation
(There's no doubt that he stands in supreme ice-olation),
Your topmost Parnassus he may set his heel on,
But no warm applauses come, peal following peal on,—
He's too smooth and too polished to hang any zeal on:
Unqualified merits, I'll grant, if you choose, he has 'em,
But he lacks the one merit of kindling enthusiasm;
If he stir you at all, it is just, on my soul,
Like being stirred up with the very North Pole.

"He is very nice reading in summer, but *inter*
Nos, we don't want *extra* freezing in winter;
Take him up in the depth of July, my advice is,
When you feel an Egyptian devotion to ices."
But, deduct all you can, there's enough that's right good in him,
He has a true soul for field, river, and wood in him:
And his heart, in the midst of brick walls, or where'er it is,
Glows, softens, and thrills with the tenderest charities—
To you mortals that delve in this trade-ridden planet?
No, to old Berkshire's hills, with their limestone and granite.
If you're one who *in loco* (add *foco* here) *desipis*,
You will get of his outermost heart (as I guess) a piece;
But you'd get deeper down if you came as a precipice,
And would break the last seal of its inwardest fountain,
If you only could palm yourself off for a mountain.
Mr. Quivis, or somebody quite as discerning,
Some scholar who's hourly expecting his learning,
Calls B. the American Wordsworth; but Wordsworth
May be rated at more than your whole tuneful herd's worth.
No, don't be absurd, he's an excellent Bryant;
But, my friends, you'll endanger the life of your client,
By attempting to stretch him up into a giant:
If you choose to compare him, I think there are two per-
sons fit for a parallel—Thompson and Cowper;
I don't mean exactly,—there's something of each,
There's T.'s love of nature, C.'s penchant to preach;
Just mix up their minds so that C.'s spice of craziness
Shall balance and neutralize T.'s turn for laziness,
And it gives you a brain cool, quite frictionless, quiet,
Whose internal police nips the buds of all riot,—

A brain like a permanent strait-jacket put on
The heart that strives vainly to burst off a button,—
A brain which, without being slow or mechanic,
Does more than a larger less drilled, more volcanic;
He's a Cowper condensed, with no craziness bitten,
And the advantage that Wordsworth before him had written.

"But, my dear little bardlings, don't prick up your ears
Nor suppose I would rank you and Bryant as peers;
If I call him an iceberg, I don't mean to say
There is nothing in that which is grand in its way;
He is almost the one of your poets that knows
How much grace, strength, and dignity lie in Repose;
If he sometimes fall short, he is too wise to mar
His thought's modest fulness by going too far;
'T would be well if your authors should all make a trial
Of what virtue there is in severe self-denial,
And measure their writings by Hesiod's staff,
Which teaches that all has less value than half.

. . .

[Hawthorne]

"There is Hawthorne, with genius so shrinking and rare
That you hardly at first see the strength that is there;
A frame so robust, with a nature so sweet,
So earnest, so graceful, so lithe and so fleet,
Is worth a descent from Olympus to meet;
'T is as if a rough oak that for ages had stood,
With his gnarled bony branches like ribs of the wood,
Should bloom, after cycles of struggle and scathe,
With a single anemone trembly and rathe;
His strength is so tender, his wildness so meek,
That a suitable parallel sets one to seek,—
He's a John Bunyan Fouqué, a Puritan Tieck;
When Nature was shaping him, clay was not granted
For making so full-sized a man as she wanted,
So, to fill out her model, a little she spared
From some finer-grained stuff for a woman prepared,
And she could not have hit a more excellent plan
For making him fully and perfectly man.

. . .

[Cooper]

"Here's Cooper, who's written six volumes to show
He's as good as a lord: well, let's grant that he's so;
If a person prefer that description of praise,
Why, a coronet's certainly cheaper than bays;
But he need take no pains to convince us he's not
(As his enemies say) the American Scott.
Choose any twelve men, and let C. read aloud
That one of his novels of which he's most proud,
And I'd lay any bet that, without ever quitting
Their box, they'd be all, to a man, for acquitting.
He has drawn you one character, though, that is new,
One wildflower he's plucked that is wet with the dew
Of this fresh Western world, and, the thing not to mince,
He has done naught but copy it ill ever since;
His Indians, with proper respect be it said,
Are just Natty Bumppo, daubed over with red,
And his very Long Toms are the same useful Nat,
Rigged up in duck pants and a sou'wester hat
(Though once in a Coffin, a good chance was found
To have slipped the old fellow away underground).
All his other men-figures are clothes upon sticks,
The *dernière chemise* of a man in a fix
(As a captain besieged, when his garrison's small,
Sets up caps upon poles to be seen o'er the wall);
And the women he draws from one model don't vary,
All sappy as maples and flat as a prairie.
When a character's wanted, he goes to the task
As a cooper would do in composing a cask;
He picks out the staves, of their qualities heedful,
Just hoops them together as tight as is needful,
And, if the best fortune should crown the attempt, he
Has made at the most something wooden and empty.

"Don't suppose I would underrate Cooper's abilities;
If I thought you'd do that, I should feel very ill at ease;
The men who have given to *one* character life
And objective existence are not very rife;
You may number them all, both prose-writers and singers,
Without overrunning the bounds of your fingers,
And Natty won't go to oblivion quicker
Than Adams the parson or Primrose the vicar.

"There is one thing in Cooper I like, too, and that is
That on manners he lectures his countrymen gratis;
Not precisely so either, because, for a rarity,
He is paid for his tickets in unpopularity.
Now he may overcharge his American pictures,
But you'll grant there's a good deal of truth in his strictures;
And I honor the man who is willing to sink
Half his present repute for the freedom to think,
And, when he has thought, be his cause strong or weak,
Will risk t' other half for the freedom to speak,
Caring naught for what vengeance the mob has in store,
Let that mob be the upper ten thousand or lower.

. . .

[Poe]

"There comes Poe, with his raven, like Barnaby Rudge,
Three fifths of him genius and two fifths sheer fudge,
Who talks like a book of iambs and pentameters,
In a way to make people of common sense damn metres,
Who has written some things quite the best of their kind,
But the heart somehow seems all squeezed out by the mind,
Who— But hey-day! What's this? Messieurs Mathews and Poe,
You mustn't fling mud-balls at Longfellow so,
Does it make a man worse that his character's such
As to make his friends love him (as you think) too much?
Why, there is not a bard at this moment alive
More willing than he that his fellows should thrive;
While you are abusing him thus, even now
He would help either one of you out of a slough;
You may say that he's smooth and all that till you're hoarse,
But remember that elegance also is force;
After polishing granite as much as you will,
The heart keeps its tough old persistency still;
Deduct all you can, *that* still keeps you at bay;
Why, he'll live till men weary of Collins and Gray.
I'm not over-fond of Greek metres in English,
To me rhyme's a gain, so it be not too jinglish,
And your modern hexameter verses are no more
Like Greek ones than sleek Mr. Pope is like Homer;
As the roar of the sea to the coo of a pigeon is,
So, compared to your moderns, sounds old Melesigenes;

I may be too partial, the reason, perhaps, o't is
That I've heard the old blind man recite his own rhapsodies,
And my ear with that music impregnate may be,
Like the poor exiled shell with the soul of the sea,
Or as one can't bear Strauss when his nature is cloven
To its deeps within deeps by the stroke of Beethoven;
But, set that aside, and 't is truth that I speak,
Had Theocritus written in English, not Greek,
I believe that his exquisite sense would scarce change a line
In that rare, tender, virgin-like pastoral Evangeline.
That's not ancient nor modern, its place is apart
Where time has no sway, in the realm of pure Art,
'T is a shrine of retreat from Earth's hubbub and strife
As quiet and chaste as the author's own life.

. . .

[IRVING]

"What! Irving? thrice welcome, warm heart and fine brain,
You bring back the happiest spirit from Spain,
And the gravest sweet humor, that ever were there
Since Cervantes met death in his gentle despair:
Nay, don't be embarrassed, nor look so beseeching,
I sha'n't run directly against my own preaching,
And, having just laughed at their Raphaels and Dantes,
Go to setting you up beside matchless Cervantes;
But allow me to speak what I honestly feel,—
To a true poet-heart add the fun of Dick Steele,
Throw in all of Addison, *minus* the chill,
With the whole of that partnership's stock and good-will,
Mix well, and while stirring, hum o'er, as a spell,
The fine *old* English Gentleman, simmer it well,
Sweeten just to your own private liking, then strain,
That only the finest and clearest remain,
Let it stand out of doors till a soul it receives
From the warm lazy sun loitering down through green leaves,
And you'll find a choice nature, not wholly deserving
A name either English or Yankee,—just Irving.

. . .

[LOWELL]

"There is Lowell, who's striving Parnassus to climb
With a whole bale of *isms* tied together with rhyme,

He might get on alone, spite of brambles and boulders,
But he can't with that bundle he has on his shoulders,
The top of the hill he will ne'er come nigh reaching
Till he learns the distinction 'twixt singing and preaching;
His lyre has some chords that would ring pretty well,
But he'd rather by half make a drum of the shell,
And rattle away till he's old as Methusalem,
At the head of a march to the last new Jerusalem.

. . .

Auspex

My heart, I cannot still it,
Nest that had song-birds in it;
And when the last shall go,
The dreary days, to fill it,
Instead of lark or linnet,
Shall whirl dead leaves and snow.

Had they been swallows only,
Without the passion stronger
That skyward longs and sings,—
Woe's me, I shall be lonely
When I can feel no longer
The impatience of their wings!

A moment, sweet delusion,
Like birds the brown leaves hover;
But it will not be long
Before their wild confusion
Fall wavering down to cover
The poet and his song.

The First Snowfall

The snow had begun in the gloaming,
  And busily all the night
Had been heaping field and highway
  With a silence deep and white.

Every pine and fir and hemlock
  Wore ermine too dear for an earl,
And the poorest twig on the elm-tree
  Was ridged inch deep with pearl.

From sheds new-roofed with Carrara
  Came Chanticleer's muffled crow,
The stiff rails were softened to swan's-down,
  And still fluttered down the snow.

I stood and watched by the window
  The noiseless work of the sky,
And the sudden flurries of snow-birds,
  Like brown leaves whirling by.

I thought of a mound in sweet Auburn
  Where a little headstone stood;
How the flakes were folding it gently,
  As did robins the babes in the wood.

Up spoke our own little Mabel,
  Saying, "Father, who makes it snow?"
And I told of the good All-father
  Who cares for us here below.

Again I looked at the snow-fall,
  And thought of the leaden sky
That arched o'er our first great sorrow,
  When that mound was heaped so high.

I remembered the gradual patience
  That fell from that cloud-like snow,
Flake by flake, healing and hiding
  The scar of our deep-plunged woe.

And again to the child I whispered,
  "The snow that husheth all,
Darling, the merciful Father
  Alone can make it fall!"

Then, with eyes that saw not, I kissed her;
  And she, kissing back, could not know
That *my* kiss was given to her sister,
  Folded close under deepening snow.

HERMAN MELVILLE

(1819–1891)

The Maldive Shark

About the Shark, phlegmatical one,
Pale sot of the Maldive sea,
The sleek little pilot-fish, azure and slim,
How alert in attendance be.
From his saw-pit of mouth, from his charnel of maw
They have nothing of harm to dread,
But liquidly glide on his ghastly flank
Or before his Gorgonian head;
Or lurk in the port of serrated teeth
In white triple tiers of glittering gates,
And there find a haven when peril's abroad,
An asylum in jaws of the Fates!
They are friends; and friendly they guide him to prey,
Yet never partake of the treat—
Eyes and brains to the dotard lethargic and dull,
Pale ravener of horrible meat.

The Portent

Hanging from the beam,
  Slowly swaying (such the law),
Gaunt the shadow on your green,
  Shenandoah!
The cut is on the crown
  (Lo, John Brown),
And the stabs shall heal no more.

Hidden in the cap
  Is the anguish none can draw;
So your future veils its face,
  Shenandoah!
But the streaming beard is shown
  (Weird John Brown),
The meteor of the war.

The March into Virginia

ENDING IN THE FIRST MANASSAS

(July 1861)

Did all the lets and bars appear
  To every just or larger end,
Whence should come the trust and cheer?
  Youth must its ignorant impulse lend—
Age finds place in the rear.
  All wars are boyish, and are fought by boys,
The champions and enthusiasts of the state:
  Turbid ardors and vain joys
    Not barrenly abate—
Stimulants to the power mature,
  Preparatives of fate.

Who here forecasteth the event?
What heart but spurns at precedent
And warnings of the wise,
Contemned foreclosures of surprise?
The banners play, the bugles call,
The air is blue and prodigal.
  No berrying party, pleasure-wooed,
No picnic party in the May,
Ever went less loth than they
  Into that leafy neighborhood.
In Bacchic glee they file toward Fate,
Moloch's uninitiate;
Expectancy, and glad surmise
Of battle's unknown mysteries.

All they feel is this: 'tis glory,
A rapture sharp, though transitory,
Yet lasting in belaureled story.
So they gayly go to fight,
Chatting left and laughing right.

But some who this blithe mood present,
  As on in lightsome files they fare,
Shall die experienced ere three days be spent—
  Perish, enlightened by the vollied glare;
Or shame survive, and, like to adamant,
  Thy after shock, Manassas, share.

Malvern Hill

(July 1862)

Ye elms that wave on Malvern Hill
  In prime of morn and May,
Recall ye how McClellan's men
    Here stood at bay?
While deep within yon forest dim
  Our rigid comrades lay—
Some with the cartridge in their mouth,
Others with fixed arms lifted South—
    Invoking so
The cypress glades? Ah wilds of woe!

The spires of Richmond, late beheld
  Through rifts in musket-haze,
Were closed from view in clouds of dust
    On leaf-walled ways,
Where streamed our wagons in caravan;
  And the Seven Nights and Days
Of march and fast, retreat and fight,
Pinched our grimed faces to ghastly plight—
    Does the elm wood
Recall the haggard beards of blood?

The battle-smoked flag, with stars eclipsed,
  We followed (it never fell!)—
In silence husbanded our strength—
  Received their yell;
Till on this slope we patient turned
  With cannon ordered well;
Reverse we proved was not defeat;
But ah, the sod what thousands meet!—
      Does Malvern Wood
Bethink itself, and muse and brood?

We elms of Malvern Hill
  Remember every thing;
But sap the twig will fill:
Wag the world how it will,
  Leaves must be green in Spring.

The Berg
(A DREAM)

I saw a ship of martial build
(Her standards set, her brave apparel on)
Directed as by madness mere
Against a stolid iceberg steer,
Nor budge it, though the infatuate ship went down.
The impact made huge ice-cubes fall
Sullen, in tons that crashed the deck;
But that one avalanche was all—
No other movement save the foundering wreck.

Along the spurs of ridges pale,
Not any slenderest shaft and frail,
A prism over glass-green gorges lone,
Toppled; or lace of traceries fine,
Nor pendant drops in grot or mine
Were jarred, when the stunned ship went down.
Nor sole the gulls in cloud that wheeled
Circling one snow-flanked peak afar,
But nearer fowl the floes that skimmed
And crystal beaches, felt no jar.

No thrill transmitted stirred the lock
Of jack-straw needle-ice at base;
Towers undermined by waves—the block
Atilt impending—kept their place.
Seals, dozing sleek on sliddery ledges
Slipt never, when by loftier edges
Through very inertia overthrown,
The impetuous ship in bafflement went down.

Hard Berg (methought), so cold, so vast,
With mortal damps self-overcast;
Exhaling still thy dankish breath—
Adrift dissolving, bound for death;
Though lumpish thou, a lumbering one—
A lumbering lubbard loitering slow,
Impingers rue thee and go down,
Sounding thy precipice below,
Nor stir the slimy slug that sprawls
Along thy dead indifference of walls.

In the Prison Pen

(1864)

Listless he eyes the palisades
  And sentries in the glare;
'Tis barren as a pelican-beach—
  But his world is ended there.

Nothing to do; and vacant hands
  Bring on the idiot-pain;
He tries to think—to recollect,
  But the blur is on his brain.

Around him swarm the plaining ghosts
  Like those on Virgil's shore—
A wilderness of faces dim,
  And pale ones gashed and hoar.

A smiting sun. No shed, no tree;
  He totters to his lair—
A den that sick hands dug in earth
  Ere famine wasted there,

Or, dropping in his place, he swoons,
  Walled in by throngs that press,
Till forth from the throngs they bear him dead—
  Dead in his meagreness.

"Formerly a Slave"

AN IDEALIZED PORTRAIT, BY E. VEDDER, IN THE SPRING EXHIBITION OF THE NATIONAL ACADEMY, 1865

The sufferance of her race is shown,
  And restrospect of life,
Which now too late deliverance dawns upon;
  Yet is she not at strife.

Her children's children they shall know
  The good withheld from her;
And so her reverie takes prophetic cheer—
  In spirit she sees the stir

Far down the depth of thousand years,
  And marks the revel shine;
Her dusky face is lit with sober light,
  Sibylline, yet benign.

The Martyr

INDICATIVE OF THE PASSION OF THE PEOPLE ON THE 15TH OF APRIL 1865

Good Friday was the day
  Of the prodigy and crime,
When they killed him in his pity,
  When they killed him in his prime
Of clemency and calm—
    When with yearning he was filled
    To redeem the evil-willed,
And, though conqueror, be kind;
  But they killed him in his kindness,
  In their madness and their blindness,
And they killed him from behind.

There is sobbing of the strong,
  And a pall upon the land;
But the People in their weeping
        Bare the iron hand:
Beware the People weeping
  When they bare the iron hand.

He lieth in his blood—
  The father in his face;
They have killed him, the Forgiver—
  The Avenger takes his place,
The Avenger wisely stern,
    Who in righteousness shall do
    What the heavens call him to,
And the parricides remand;
  For they killed him in his kindness,
  In their madness and their blindness,
And his blood is on their hand.

There is sobbing of the strong,
  And a pall upon the land;
But the People in their weeping
          Bare the iron hand:
Beware the People weeping
  When they bare the iron hand.

Old Age in His Ailing

Old Age in his ailing
At youth will be railing
It scorns youth's regaling
Pooh-pooh it does, silly dream;
But me, the fool, save
From waxing so grave
As, reduced to skimmed milk, to slander the cream.

WALT WHITMAN
(1819–1892)

Song of Myself

1

I celebrate myself, and sing myself,
And what I assume you shall assume,
For every atom belonging to me as good belongs to you.
I loaf and invite my soul,
I lean and loaf at my ease observing a spear of summer grass.
My tongue, every atom of my blood, formed from this soil, this air,
Born here of parents born here from parents the same, and their parents the same,
I, now thirty-seven years old in perfect health begin,
Hoping to cease not till death.
Creeds and schools in abeyance,
Retiring back awhile sufficed at what they are, but never forgotten,
I harbor for good or bad, I permit to speak at every hazard,
Nature without check with original energy.

2

Houses and rooms are full of perfumes, the shelves are crowded with perfumes,
I breathe the fragrance myself and know it and like it,
The distillation would intoxicate me also, but I shall not let it.

The atmosphere is not a perfume, it has no taste of the distillation, it is odorless,
It is for my mouth forever, I am in love with it,

I will go to the bank by the wood and become undisguised and naked,
I am mad for it to be in contact with me.

The smoke of my own breath,
Echoes, ripples, buzzed whispers, love root, silk thread, crotch and vine,
My respiration and inspiration, the beating of my heart, the passing of blood and air through my lungs,
The sniff of green leaves and dry leaves, and of the shore and dark-colored sea rocks, and of hay in the barn,
The sound of the belched words of my voice loosed to the eddies of the wind,
A few light kisses, a few embraces, a reaching around of arms,
The play of shine and shade on the trees as the supple boughs wag,
The delight alone or in the rush of the streets, or along the fields and hillsides,
The feeling of health, the full-noon trill, the song of me rising from bed and meeting the sun.

Have you reckoned a thousand acres much? have you reckoned the earth much?
Have you practiced so long to learn to read?
Have you felt so proud to get at the meaning of poems?

Stop this day and night with me and you shall possess the origin of all poems,
You shall possess the good of the earth and sun (there are millions of suns left),
You shall no longer take things at second or third hand, nor look through the eyes of the dead, nor feed on the specters in books,
You shall not look through my eyes either, nor take things from me,
You shall listen to all sides and filter them from yourself.

3

I have heard what the talkers were talking, the talk of the beginning and the end,
But I do not talk of the beginning or the end.

There was never any more inception than there is now,
Nor any more youth or age than there is now,
And will never be any more perfection than there is now,
Nor any more heaven or hell than there is now.

Urge and urge and urge,
Always the procreant urge of the world.
Out of the dimness opposite equals advance, always substance and increase, always sex,
Always a knit of identity, always distinction, always a breed of life.

To elaborate is no avail, learned and unlearned feel that it is so.

Sure as the most certain sure, plumb in the uprights, well entretied, braced in the beams,
Stout as a horse, affectionate, haughty, electrical,
I and this mystery here we stand.

Clear and sweet is my soul, and clear and sweet is all that is not my soul.

Lack one lacks both, and the unseen is proved by the seen,
Till that becomes unseen and receives proof in its turn.

Showing the best and dividing it from the worst age vexes age,
Knowing the perfect fitness and equanimity of things, while they discuss I am silent, and go bathe and admire myself.

Welcome is every organ and attribute of me, and of any man hearty and clean,
Not an inch nor a particle of an inch is vile, and none shall be less familiar than the rest.

I am satisfied—I see, dance, laugh, sing;
As the hugging and loving bedfellow sleeps at my side through the night, and withdraws at the peep of the day with stealthy tread,
Leaving me baskets covered with white towels swelling the house with their plenty,
Shall I postpone my acceptation and realization and scream at my eyes,
That they turn from gazing after and down the road,
And forthwith cipher and show me to a cent,
Exactly the value of one and exactly the value of two, and which is ahead?

4

Trippers and askers surround me,
People I meet, the effect upon me of my early life or the ward and city I live in, or the nation,
The latest dates, discoveries, inventions, societies, authors old and new,
My dinner, dress, associates, looks, compliments, dues,
The real or fancied indifference of some man or woman I love,
The sickness of one of my folks or of myself, or ill-doing or loss or lack of money, or depressions or exaltations,
Battles, the horrors of fratricidal war, the fever of doubtful news, the fitful events;
These come to me days and nights and go from me again,
But they are not the Me myself.
Apart from the pulling and hauling stands what I am,
Stands amused, complacent, compassionating, idle, unitary,
Looks down, is erect, or bends an arm on an impalpable certain rest,
Looking with side-curved head curious what will come next,
Both in and out of the game and watching and wondering at it.
Backward I see in my own days where I sweated through fog with linguists and contenders,
I have no mockings or arguments, I witness and wait.

5

I believe in you my soul, the other I am must not abase itself to you,
And you must not be abased to the other.
Loaf with me on the grass, loose the stop from your throat,
Not words, not music or rhyme I want, not custom or lecture, not even the best,
Only the lull I like, the hum of your valvèd voice.
I mind how once we lay such a transparent summer morning,
How you settled your head athwart my hips, and gently turned over upon me,
And parted the shirt from my bosom bone, and plunged your tongue to my bare-stripped heart,
And reached till you felt my beard, and reached till you held my feet.
Swiftly arose and spread around me the peace and knowledge that pass all the argument of the earth,
And I know that the hand of God is the promise of my own,
And I know that the spirit of God is the brother of my own,
And that all the men ever born are also my brothers, and the women my sisters and lovers,
And that a kelson of the creation is love,
And limitless are leaves stiff or drooping in the fields,
And brown ants in the little wells beneath them,
And mossy scabs of the worm fence, heaped stones, elder, mullein and pokeweed.

6

A child said *What is the grass?* fetching it to me with full hands,
How could I answer the child? I do not know what it is any more than he.
I guess it must be the flag of my disposition, out of hopeful green stuff woven.
Or I guess it is the handkerchief of the Lord,
A scented gift and remembrancer designedly dropped,
Bearing the owner's name someway in the corners, that we may see and remark, and say *Whose?*

Or I guess the grass is itself a child, the produced babe of
the vegetation.

Or I guess it is a uniform hieroglyphic,
And it means, Sprouting alike in broad zones and narrow
zones,
Growing among black folks as among white,
Canuck, Tuckahoe, Congressman, Cuff, I give them the
same, I receive them the same.

And now it seems to me the beautiful uncut hair of graves.
Tenderly will I use you curling grass,
It may be you transpire from the breasts of young men,
It may be if I had known them I would have loved them,
It may be you are from old people, or from offspring taken
soon out of their mothers' laps,
And here you are the mothers' laps.
This grass is very dark to be from the white heads of old
mothers,
Darker than the colorless beards of old men,
Dark to come from under the faint red roof of mouths.
O I perceive after all so many uttering tongues,
And I perceive they do not come from the roofs of mouths
for nothing.
I wish I could translate the hints about the dead young men
and women,
And the hints about old men and mothers, and the offspring
taken soon out of their laps.
What do you think has become of the young and old men?
And what do you think has become of the women and
children?
They are alive and well somewhere,
The smallest sprout shows there is really no death,
And if ever there was it led forward life, and does not wait
at the end to arrest it,
And ceased the moment life appeared.
All goes onward and outward, nothing collapses,
And to die is different from what anyone supposed, and
luckier.

7

Has anyone supposed it lucky to be born?
I hasten to inform him or her it is just as lucky to die, and I know it.
I pass death with the dying and birth with the new-washed babe, and am not contained between my hat and boots,
And peruse manifold objects, no two alike and everyone good,
The earth good and the stars good, and their adjuncts all good.
I am not an earth nor an adjunct of an earth,
I am the mate and companion of people, all just as immortal and fathomless as myself,
(They do not know how immortal, but I know.)
Every kind for itself and its own, for me mine male and female,
For me those that have been boys and that love women,
For me the man that is proud and feels how it stings to be slighted,
For me the sweetheart and the old maid, for me mothers and the mothers of mothers,
For me lips that have smiled, eyes that have shed tears,
For me children and the begetters of children.
Undrape! you are not guilty to me, nor stale nor discarded,
I see through the broadcloth and gingham whether or no,
And am around, tenacious, acquisitive, tireless, and cannot be shaken away.

8

The little one sleeps in its cradle,
I lift the gauze and look a long time, and silently brush away flies with my hand.
The youngster and the red-faced girl turn aside up the bushy hill,
I peeringly view them from the top.
The suicide sprawls on the bloody floor of the bedroom,
I witness the corpse with its dabbled hair, I note where the the pistol has fallen.

The blab of the pave, tires of carts, sluff of boot soles, talk of the promenaders,
The heavy omnibus, the driver with his interrogating thumb, the clank of the shod horses on the granite floor,
The snow sleighs, clinking, shouted jokes, pelts of snowballs,
The hurrahs for popular favorites, the fury of roused mobs,
The flap of the curtained litter, a sick man inside borne to the hospital,
The meeting of enemies, the sudden oath, the blows and fall,
The excited crowd, the policeman with his star quickly working his passage to the center of the crowd,
The impassive stones that receive and return so many echoes,
What groans of overfed or half-starved who fall sunstruck or in fits,
What exclamations of women taken suddenly who hurry home and give birth to babes,
What living and buried speech is always vibrating here, what howls restrained by decorum,
Arrests of criminals, slights, adulterous offers made, acceptances, rejections with convex lips,
I mind them or the show or resonance of them—I come and I depart.

9

The big doors of the country barn stand open and ready,
The dried grass of the harvest time loads the slow-drawn wagon,
The clear light plays on the brown gray and green intertinged,
The armfuls are packed to the sagging mow.
I am there, I help, I came stretched atop of the load,
I felt its soft jolts, one leg reclined on the other,
I jump from the crossbeams and seize the clover and timothy,
And roll head over heels and tangle my hair full of wisps.

10

Alone far in the wilds and mountains I hunt,
Wandering amazed at my own lightness and glee,
In the late afternoon choosing a safe spot to pass the night,
Kindling a fire and broiling the fresh-killed game,
Falling asleep on the gathered leaves with my dog and gun by my side.

The Yankee clipper is under her sky sails, she cuts the sparkle and scud,
My eyes settle the land, I bend at her prow or shout joyously from the deck.
The boatmen and clam-diggers arose early and stopped for me,
I tucked my trouser ends in my boots and went and had a good time;
You should have been with us that day round the chowder kettle.

I saw the marriage of the trapper in the open air in the far west, the bride was a red girl,
Her father and his friends sat near cross-legged and dumbly smoking, they had moccasins to their feet and large thick blankets hanging from their shoulders,
On a bank lounged the trapper, he was dressed mostly in skins, his luxuriant beard and curls protected his neck, he held his bride by the hand,
She had long eyelashes, her head was bare, her coarse straight locks descended upon her voluptuous limbs and reached to her feet.

The runaway slave came to my house and stopped outside,
I heard his motions crackling the twigs of the woodpile,
Through the swung half-door of the kitchen I saw him limpsy and weak,
And went where he sat on a log and led him in and assured him,

And brought water and filled a tub for his sweated body and bruised feet,
And gave him a room that entered from my own, and gave him some coarse clean clothes,
And remember perfectly well his revolving eyes and his awkwardness,
And remember putting plasters on the galls of his neck and ankles;
He stayed with me a week before he was recuperated and passed north,
I had him sit next me at table, my firelock leaned in the corner.

11

Twenty-eight young men bathe by the shore,
Twenty-eight young men and all so friendly;
Twenty-eight years of womanly life and all so lonesome.
She owns the fine house by the rise of the bank,
She hides handsome and richly dressed aft the blinds of the window.
Which of the young men does she like the best?
Ah, the homeliest of them is beautiful to her.
Where are you off to, lady? for I see you,
You splash in the water there, yet stay stock still in your room.
Dancing and laughing along the beach came the twenty-ninth bather,
The rest did not see her, but she saw them and loved them.
The beards of the young men glistened with wet, it ran from their long hair,
Little streams passed all over their bodies.
An unseen hand also passed over their bodies,
It descended tremblingly from their temples and ribs.

The young men float on their backs, their white bellies bulge to the sun, they do not ask who seizes fast to them,
They do not know who puffs and declines with pendant and bending arch,
They do not think whom they souse with spray.

12

The butcher boy puts off his killing clothes, or sharpens his knife at the stall in the market,
I loiter enjoying his repartee and his shuffle and breakdown.
Blacksmiths with grimed and hairy chests environ the anvil,
Each has his main sledge, they are all out, there is a great heat in the fire.
From the cinder-strewed threshold I follow their movements,
The lithe sheer of their waists plays even with their massive arms,
Overhand the hammers swing, overhand so slow, overhand so sure,
They do not hasten, each man hits in his place.

13

The Negro holds firmly the reins of his four horses, the block swags underneath on its tied-over chain.
The Negro that drives the long dray of the stoneyard, steady and tall he stands poised on one leg on the stringpiece,
His blue shirt exposes his ample neck and breast and loosens over his hip band,
His glance is calm and commanding, he tosses the slouch of his hat away from his forehead,
The sun falls on his crispy hair and mustache, falls on the black of his polished and perfect limbs.
I behold the picturesque giant and love him, and I do not stop there,
I go with the team also.

In me the caresser of life wherever moving, backward as well as forward sluing,
To niches aside and junior bending, not a person or object missing,
Absorbing all to myself and for this song.

Oxen that rattle the yoke and chain or halt in the leafy shade, what is that you express in your eyes?

It seems to me more than all the print I have read in my
life.

My tread scares the wood drake and wood duck on my
distant and day-long ramble,
They rise together, they slowly circle around.

I believe in those winged purposes,
And acknowledge red, yellow, white, playing within me.
And consider green and violet and the tufted crown intentional,
And do not call the tortoise unworthy because she is not
something else,
And the jay in the woods never studied the gamut, yet trills
pretty well to me,
And the look of the bay mare shames silliness out of me.

14

The wild gander leads his flock through the cool night,
Ya-honk he says, and sounds it down to me like an invitation,
The pert may suppose it meaningless, but I listening close,
Find its purpose and place up there toward the wintry sky.

The sharp-hoofed moose of the north, the cat on the house
sill, the chickadee, the prairie dog,
The litter of the grunting sow as they tug at her teats,
The brood of the turkey hen and she with her half-spread
wings,
I see in them and myself the same old law.

The press of my foot to the earth springs a hundred affections,
They scorn the best I can do to relate them.

I am enamored of growing outdoors,
Of men that live among cattle or taste of the ocean or
woods,
Of the builders and steerers of ships and the wielders of axes
and mauls, and the drivers of horses,
I can eat and sleep with them week in and week out.

What is commonest, cheapest, nearest, easiest, is Me,
Me going in for my chances, spending for vast returns,
Adorning myself to bestow myself on the first that will take
me,
Not asking the sky to come down to my good will,
Scattering it freely forever.

15

The pure contralto sings in the organ loft,
The carpenter dresses his plank, the tongue of his foreplane
whistles its wild ascending lisp,
The married and unmarried children ride home to their
Thanksgiving dinner,
The pilot seizes the kingpin, he heaves down with a strong
arm,
The mate stands braced in the whaleboat, lance and
harpoon are ready,
The duck shooter walks by silent and cautious stretches,
The deacons are ordained with crossed hands at the altar,
The spinning girl retreats and advances to the hum of the
big wheel,
The farmer stops by the bars as he walks on a First-day loaf
and looks at the oats and rye,
The lunatic is carried at last to the asylum a confirmed case,
(He will never sleep any more as he did in the cot in his
mother's bedroom);
The jour printer with gray head and gaunt jaws works at his
case,
He turns his quid of tobacco while his eyes blur with the
manuscript;
The malformed limbs are tied to the surgeon's table,
What is removed drops horribly in a pail;
The quadroon girl is sold at the auction stand, the drunkard
nods by the barroom stove,
The machinist rolls up his sleeves, the policeman travels his
beat, the gatekeeper marks who pass.
The young fellow drives the express wagon (I love him,
though I do not know him);
The half-breed straps on his light boots to compete in the
race,

The western turkey-shooting draws old and young, some lean on their rifles, some sit on logs,
Out from the crowd steps the marksman, takes his position, levels his piece;
The groups of newly come immigrants cover the wharf or levee,
As the wooly-pates hoe in the sugar field, the overseer views them from his saddle,
The bugle calls in the ballroom, the gentlemen run for their partners, the dancers bow to each other,
The youth lies awake in the cedar-roofed garret and harks to the musical rain,
The Wolverine sets traps on the creek that helps fill the Huron,
The squaw wrapped in her yellow-hemmed cloth is offering moccasins and bead bags for sale,
The connoisseur peers along the exhibition gallery with half-shut eyes bent sideways,
As the deck hands make fast the steamboat the plank is thrown for the shore-going passengers,
The young sister holds out the skein while the elder sister winds it off in a ball, and stops now and then for the knots,
The one-year wife is recovering and happy having a week ago borne her first child.
The clean-haired Yankee girl works with her sewing machine or in the factory or mill,
The paving man leans on his two-handed rammer, the reporter's lead flies swiftly over the notebook, the sign painter is lettering with blue and gold,
The canal boy trots on the towpath, the bookkeeper counts at his desk, the shoemaker waxes his thread,
The conductor beats time for the band and all the performers follow him,
The child is baptized, the convert is making his first professions,
The regatta is spread on the bay, the race is begun (how the white sails sparkle!);
The drover watching his drove sings out to them that would stray,

The peddler sweats with his pack on his back (the purchaser higgling about the odd cent);
The bride unrumples her white dress, the minute hand of the clock moves slowly,
The opium eater reclines with rigid head and just-opened lips,
The prostitute draggles her shawl, her bonnet bobs on her tipsy and pimpled neck,
The crowd laugh at her blackguard oaths, the men jeer and wink to each other,
(Miserable! I do not laugh at your oaths nor jeer you);
The President holding a Cabinet council is surrounded by the great Secretaries,
On the piazza walk three matrons stately and friendly with twined arms,
The crew of the fish smack pack repeated layers of halibut in the hold,
The Missourian crosses the plains toting his wares and his cattle,
As the fare collector goes through the train he gives notice by the jingling of loose change,
The floormen are laying the floor, the tinners are tinning the roof, the masons are calling for mortar,
In single file each shouldering his hod pass onward the laborers;
Seasons pursuing each other the indescribable crowd is gathered, it is the fourth of Seventh-month (what salutes of cannon and small arms!);
Seasons pursuing each other the plower plows, the mower mows, and the winter grain falls in the ground;
Off on the lakes the pike fisher watches and waits by the hole in the frozen surface,
The stumps stand thick round the clearing, the squatter strikes deep with his ax,
Flatboatmen make fast towards dusk near the cottonwood or pecan trees,
Coon seekers go through the regions of the Red River or through those drained by the Tennessee, or through those of the Arkansas,

Torches shine in the dark that hangs on the Chattahoochee or Altamahaw,
Patriarchs sit at supper with sons and grandsons and great-grandsons around them,
In walls of adobe, in canvas tents, rest hunters and trappers after their day's sport,
The city sleeps and the country sleeps,
The living sleep for their time, the dead sleep for their time,
The old husband sleeps by his wife and the young husband sleeps by his wife;
And these tend inward to me, and I tend outward to them,
And such as it is to be of these more or less I am,
And of these one and all I weave the song of myself.

16

I am of old and young, of the foolish as much as the wise,
Regardless of others, ever regardful of others,
Maternal as well as paternal, a child as well as a man,
Stuffed with the stuff that is coarse and stuffed with the stuff that is fine,
One of the Nation of many nations, the smallest the same and the largest the same,
A Southerner soon as a Northerner, a planter nonchalant and hospitable down by the Oconee I live,
A Yankee bound my own way ready for trade, my joints the limberest joints on earth and the sternest joints on earth,
A Kentuckian walking the vale of the Elkhorn in my deer-skin leggings, a Louisianian or Georgian,
A boatman over lakes or bays or along coasts, a Hoosier, a Badger, Buckeye;
At home on Canadian snowshoes or up in the bush, or with fishermen off Newfoundland,
At home in the fleet of iceboats, sailing with the rest and tacking,
At home on the hills of Vermont or in the woods of Maine, or the Texan ranch,
Comrade of Californians, comrade of Free Northwesterners, (loving their big proportions),

Comrade of raftsmen and coalmen, comrade of all who shake hands and welcome to drink and meat,
A learner with the simplest, a teacher of the thoughtfulest,
A novice beginning yet experient of myriads of seasons,
Of every hue and caste am I, of every rank and religion,
A farmer, mechanic, artist, gentleman, sailor, Quaker,
Prisoner, fancy man, rowdy, lawyer, physician, priest.

I resist anything better than my own diversity,
Breathe the air but leave plenty after me,
And am not stuck up, and am in my place.

(The moth and the fish eggs are in their place,
The bright suns I see and the dark suns I cannot see are in their place,
The palpable is in its place and the impalpable is in its place.)

17

These are really the thoughts of all men in all ages and lands, they are not original with me,
If they are not yours as much as mine they are nothing, or next to nothing,
If they are not the riddle and the untying of the riddle they are nothing,
If they are not just as close as they are distant they are nothing
This is the grass that grows wherever the land is and the water is,
This is the common air that bathes the globe.

18

With music strong I come, with my cornets and my drums,
I play not marches for accepted victors only, I play marches for conquered and slain persons.
Have you heard that it was good to gain the day?
I also say it is good to fall, battles are lost in the same spirit in which they are won.
I beat and pound for the dead,

I blow through my embouchures my loudest and gayest for them.
Vivas to those who have failed!
And to those whose war vessels sank in the sea!
And to those themselves who sank in the sea!
And to all generals that lost engagements, and all overcome heroes!
And the numberless unknown heroes equal to the greatest heroes known!

19

This is the meal equally set, this the meat for natural hunger,
It is for the wicked just the same as the righteous, I make appointments with all,
I will not have a single person slighted or left away,
The kept woman, sponger, thief, are hereby invited,
The heavy-lipped slave is invited, the venerealee is invited;
There shall be no difference between them and the rest.
This is the press of a bashful hand, this the float and odor of hair,
This the touch of my lips to yours, this the murmur of yearning,
This the far-off depth and height reflecting my own face,
This the thoughtful merge of myself, and the outlet again.
Do you guess I have some intricate purpose?
Well I have, for the Fourth-month showers have, and the mica on the side of a rock has.
Do you take it I would astonish?
Does the daylight astonish? does the early redstart twittering through the woods?
Do I astonish more than they?
This hour I tell things in confidence,
I might not tell everybody, but I will tell you.

20

Who goes there? hankering, gross, mystical, nude;
How is it I extract strength from the beef I eat?
What is a man anyhow? what am I? what are you?
All I mark as my own you shall offset it with your own,
Else it, were time lost listening to me.

I do not snivel that snivel the world over,
That months are vacuums and the ground but wallow and filth.
Whimpering and truckling fold with powders for invalids, conformity goes to the fourth-removed,
I wear my hat as I please indoors or out.
Why should I pray? why should I venerate and be ceremonious?
Having pried through the strata, analyzed to a hair, counseled with doctors and calculated close,
I find no sweeter fat than sticks to my own bones.
In all people I see myself, none more and not one a barley-corn less,
And the good or bad I say of myself I say of them.
I know I am solid and sound,
To me the converging objects of the universe perpetually flow,
All are written to me, and I must get what the writing means.
I know I am deathless,
I know this orbit of mine cannot be swept by a carpenter's compass,
I know I shall not pass like a child's carlacue cut with a burnt stick at night.
I know I am august,
I do not trouble my spirit to vindicate itself or be understood,
I see that the elementary laws never apologize,
(I reckon I behave no prouder than the level I plant my house by, after all.)
I exist as I am, that is enough,
If no other in the world be aware I sit content,
And if each and all be aware I sit content.
One world is aware and by far the largest to me, and that is myself,
And whether I come to my own today or in ten thousand or ten million years,
I can cheerfully take it now, or with equal cheerfulness I can wait.
My foothold is tenoned and mortised in granite,
I laugh at what you call dissolution,
And I know the amplitude of time.

21

I am the poet of the Body and I am the poet of the Soul,
The pleasures of heaven are with me and the pains of hell
are with me,
The first I graft and increase upon myself, the latter I trans-
late into a new tongue.
I am the poet of the woman the same as the man,
And I say it is as great to be a woman as to be a man,
And I say there is nothing greater than the mother of men.
I chant the chant of dilation or pride,
We have had ducking and deprecating about enough,
I show that size is only development.
Have you outstripped the rest? are you the President?
It is a trifle, they will more than arrive there every one, and
still pass on.
I am he that walks with the tender and growing night,
I call to the earth and sea half-held by the night.
Press close bare-bosomed night—press close magnetic nour-
ishing night!
Night of south winds—night of the large few stars!
Still nodding night—mad naked summer night.
Smile O voluptuous cool-breathed earth!
Earth of the slumbering and liquid trees!
Earth of departed sunset—earth of the mountains misty-
topped!
Earth of the vitreous pour of the full moon just tinged with
blue!
Earth of shine and dark mottling the tide of the river!
Earth of the limpid gray of clouds brighter and clearer for
my sake!
Far-swooping elbowed earth—rich apple-blossomed earth!
Smile, for your lover comes.
Prodigal, you have given me love—therefore I to you give
love!
O unspeakable passionate love.

22

You sea! I resign myself to you also—I guess what you mean,
I behold from the beach your crooked inviting fingers,
I believe you refuse to go back without feeling of me,

We must have a turn together, I undress, hurry me out of sight of the land,
Cushion me soft, rock me in billowy drowse,
Dash me with amorous wet, I can repay you.
Sea of stretched ground swells,
Sea breathing broad and convulsive breaths,
Sea of the brine of life and of unshoveled yet always-ready graves,
Howler and scooper of storms, capricious and dainty sea,
I am integral with you, I too am of one phase and of all phases.
Partaker of influx and efflux I, extoller of hate and conciliation,
Extoller of armies and those that sleep in each other's arms,
I am he attesting sympathy,
(Shall I make my list of things in the house and skip the house that supports them?)
I am not the poet of goodness only, I do not decline to be the poet of wickedness also.
What blurt is this about virtue and about vice?
Evil propels me and reform of evil propels me, I stand indifferent,
My gait is no faultfinder's or rejector's gait;
I moisten the roots of all that has grown.
Did you fear some scrofula out of the unflagging pregnancy?
Did you guess the celestial laws are yet to be worked over and rectified?
I find one side a balance and the antipodal side a balance,
Soft doctrine as steady help as stable doctrine,
Thoughts and deeds of the present our rouse and early start.
This minute that comes to me over the past decillions,
There is no better than it and now.
What behaved well in the past or behaves well today is not such a wonder,
The wonder is always and always how there can be a mean man or an infidel.

23

Endless unfolding of words of ages!
And mine a word of the modern, the word En Masse.
A word of the faith that never balks,

Here or henceforward it is all the same to me, I accept Time
absolutely.
It alone is without flaw, it alone rounds and completes all,
That mystic baffling wonder alone completes all.
I accept Reality and dare not question it,
Materialism first and last imbuing.
Hurrah for positive science! long live exact demonstration!
Fetch stonecrop mixed with cedar and branches of lilac,
This is the lexicographer, this the chemist, this made a
grammar of the old cartouches,
These mariners put the ship through dangerous unknown
seas,
This is the geologist, this works with the scalpel, and this is
a mathematician.
Gentlemen, to you the first honors always!
Your facts are useful, and yet they are not my dwelling,
I but enter by them to an area of my dwelling.
Less the reminders of properties told my words,
And more the reminders they of life untold, and of free-
dom and extrication,
And make short account of neuters and geldings, and favor
men and women fully equipped.
And beat the gong of revolt, and stop with fugitives and
them that plot and conspire.

24

Walt Whitman, a cosmos, of Manhattan the son,
Turbulent, fleshy, sensual, eating, drinking and breeding,
No sentimentalist, no stander above men and women or
apart from them,
No more modest than immodest.
Unscrew the locks from the doors!
Unscrew the doors themselves from their jambs!
Whoever degrades another degrades me,
And whatever is done or said returns at last to me.
Through me the afflatus surging and surging, through me
the current and index.
I speak the password primeval, I give the sign of democracy,
By God! I will accept nothing which all cannot have their
counterpart of on the same terms.
Through me many long dumb voices,

Voices of the interminable generations of prisoners and slaves.
Voices of the diseased and despairing and of thieves and dwarfs,
Voices of cycles of preparation and accretion,
And of the threads that connect the stars, and of wombs and of the father stuff,
And of the rights of them the others are down upon,
Of the deformed, trivial, flat, foolish, despised,
Fog in the air, beetles rolling balls of dung.
Through me forbidden voices,
Voices of sexes and lusts, voices veiled and I remove the veil,
Voices indecent by me clarified and transfigured.
I do not press my fingers across my mouth,
I keep as delicate around the bowels as around the head and heart,
Copulation is no more rank to me than death is.
I believe in the flesh and the appetites,
Seeing, hearing, feeling, are miracles, and each part and tag of me is a miracle.
Divine am I inside and out, and I make holy whatever I touch or am touched from,
The scent of these armpits aroma finer than prayer,
This head more than churches, bibles, and all the creeds.
If I worship one thing more than another it shall be the spread of my own body, or any part of it,
Translucent mold of me it shall be you!
Shaded ledges and rests it shall be you!
Firm masculine colter it shall be you!
Whatever goes to the tilth of me it shall be you!
You my rich blood! your milky stream pale strippings of my life!
Breast that presses against other breasts it shall be you!
My brain it shall be your occult convolutions!
Root of washed sweet flag! timorous pond snipe! nest of guarded duplicate eggs! it shall be you!
Mixed tussled hay of head, beard, brawn, it shall be you!
Trickling sap of maple, fiber of manly wheat, it shall be you!
Sun so generous it shall be you!

Vapors lighting and shading my face it shall be you!
You sweaty brooks and dews it shall be you!
Winds whose soft-tickling genitals rub against me it shall be you!
Broad muscular fields, branches of live oak, loving lounger in my winding paths, it shall be you!
Hands I have taken, face I have kissed, mortal I have ever touched, it shall be you.
I dote on myself, there is that lot of me and all so luscious,
Each moment and whatever happens thrills me with joy,
I cannot tell how my ankles bend, nor whence the cause of my faintest wish,
Nor the cause of the friendship I emit, nor the cause of the friendship I take again.
That I walk up my stoop, I pause to consider if it really be,
A morning glory at my window satisfies me more than the metaphysics of books.
To behold the daybreak!
The little light fades the immense and diaphanous shadows,
The air tastes good to my palate.
Hefts of the moving world at innocent gambols silently rising, freshly exuding,
Scooting obliquely high and low.
Something I cannot see puts upward libidinous prongs,
Seas of bright juice suffuse heaven.
The earth by the sky stayed with, the daily close of their junction,
The heaved challenge from the east that moment over my head,
The mocking taunt, See then whether you shall be master!

25

Dazzling and tremendous how quick the sunrise would kill me,
If I could not now and always send sunrise out of me.
We also ascend dazzling and tremendous as the sun,
We found our own O my soul in the calm and cool of the daybreak.
My voice goes after what my eyes cannot reach,
With the twirl of my tongue I encompass worlds and volumes of worlds.

Speech is the twin of my vision, it is unequal to measure itself,
It provokes me forever, it says sarcastically,
Walt you contain enough, why don't you let it out then?
Come now I will not be tantalized, you conceive too much of articulation,
Do you not know O speech how the buds beneath you are folded?
Waiting in gloom, protected by frost,
The dirt receding before my prophetical screams,
I underlying causes to balance them at last,
My knowledge my live parts, it keeping tally with the meaning of all things,
Happiness (which whoever hears me let him or her set out in search of this day).
My final merit I refuse you, I refuse putting from me what I really am,
Encompass worlds, but never try to encompass me,
I crowd your sleekest and best by simply looking toward you.
Writing and talk do not prove me,
I carry the plenum of proof and everything else in my face,
With the hush of my lips I wholly confound the skeptic.

26

Now I will do nothing but listen,
To accrue what I hear into this song, to let sounds contribute toward it.
I hear bravuras of birds, bustle of growing wheat, gossip of flames, clack of sticks cooking my meals,
I hear the sound I love, the sound of the human voice,
I hear all sounds running together, combined, fused or following,
Sounds of the city and sounds out of the city, sounds of the day and night,
Talkative young ones to those that like them, the loud laugh of work people at their meals,
The angry base of disjointed friendship, the faint tones of the sick,
The judge with hands tight to the desk, his pallid lips pronouncing a death sentence,

The heave'e'yo of stevedores unloading ships by the wharves, the refrain of the anchor lifters,
The ring of alarm bells, the cry of fire, the whirr of swift-streaking engines and hose carts with premonitory tinkles and colored lights,
The steam whistle, the solid roll of the train of approaching cars,
The slow march played at the head of the association marching two and two,
(They go to guard some corpse, the flag tops are draped with black muslin.)
I hear the violoncello ('tis the young man's heart's complaint),
I hear the keyed cornet, it glides quickly in through my ears,
It shakes mad-sweet pangs through my belly and breast.
I hear the chorus, it is a grand opera,
Ah this indeed is music—this suits me.
A tenor large and fresh as the creation fills me,
The orbic flex of his mouth is pouring and filling me full.
I hear the trained soprano (what work with hers is this?)
The orchestra whirls me wider than Uranus flies,
It wrenches such ardors from me I did not know I possessed them,
It sails me, I dab with bare feet, they are licked by the indolent waves,
I am cut by bitter and angry hail, I lose my breath,
Steeped amid honeyed morphine, my windpipe throttled in fakes of death,
At length let up again to feel the puzzle of puzzles,
And that we call Being.

27

To be in any form, what is that?
(Round and round we go, all of us, and ever come back thither),
If nothing lay more developed the quahog in its callous shell were enough.
Mine is no callous shell,
I have instant conductors all over me whether I pass or stop,
They seize every object and lead it harmlessly through me.

I merely stir, press, feel with my fingers, and am happy,
To touch my person to someone else's is about as much as I can stand.

28

Is this then a touch? quivering me to a new identity,
Flames and ether making a rush for my veins,
Treacherous tip of me reaching and crowding to help them,
My flesh and blood playing out lightning to strike what is hardly different from myself,
On all sides prurient provokers stiffening my limbs,
Straining the udder of my heart for its withheld drip,
Behaving licentious toward me, taking no denial,
Depriving me of my best as for a purpose,
Unbuttoning my clothes, holding me by the bare waist,
Deluding my confusion with the calm of the sunlight and pasture fields,
Immodestly sliding the fellow senses away,
They bribed to swap off with touch and go and graze at the edges of me,
No consideration, no regard for my draining strength or my anger,
Fetching the rest of the herd around to enjoy them awhile,
Then all uniting to stand on a headland and worry me.
The sentries desert every other part of me,
They have left me helpless to a red marauder,
They all come to the headland to witness and assist against me.

I am given up by traitors,
I talk wildly, I have lost my wits, I and nobody else am the greatest traitor,
I went myself first to the headland, my own hands carried me there.
You villain touch! what are you doing? my breath is tight in its throat,
Unclench your floodgates, you are too much for me.

29

Blind loving wrestling touch, sheathed hooded sharp-toothed touch!

Did it make you ache so, leaving me?
Parting tracked by arriving, perpetual payment of perpetual
loan,
Rich showering rain, and recompense richer afterward.
Sprouts take and accumulate, stand by the curb prolific and
vital,
Landscapes projected masculine, full-sized and golden.

30

All truths wait in all things,
They neither hasten their own delivery nor resist it,
They do not need the obstetric forceps of the surgeon,
The insignificant is as big to me as any,
(What is less or more than a touch?)
Logic and sermons never convince,
The damp of the night drives deeper into my soul.
(Only what proves itself to every man and woman is so,
Only what nobody denies is so.)
A minute and a drop of me settle my brain,
I believe the soggy clods shall become lovers and lamps,
And a compend of compends is the meat of a man or
woman,
And a summit and flower there is the feeling they have for
each other,
And they are to branch boundlessly out of that lesson until
it becomes omnific,
And until one and all shall delight us, and we them.

31

I believe a leaf of grass is no less than the journeywork of
the stars,
And the pismire is equally perfect, and a grain of sand, and
the egg of the wren,
And the tree toad is a chef-d'oeuvre for the highest,
And the running blackberry would adorn the parlors of
heaven,
And the narrowest hinge in my hand puts to scorn all machinery,
And the cow crunching with depressed head surpasses any
statue,

And a mouse is miracle enough to stagger sextillions of infidels.
I find I incorporate gneiss, coal, long-threaded moss, fruits, grains, esculent roots,
And am stuccoed with quadrupeds and birds all over,
And have distanced what is behind me for good reasons,
But call anything back again when I desire it.
In vain the speeding or shyness,
In vain the plutonic rocks send their old heat against my approach,
In vain the mastodon retreats beneath its own powdered bones,
In vain objects stand leagues off and assume manifold shapes,
In vain the ocean settling in hollows and the great monsters lying low,
In vain the buzzard houses herself with the sky,
In vain the snake slides through the creepers and logs,
In vain the elk takes to the inner passes of the woods,
In vain the razor-billed auk sails far north to Labrador,
I follow quickly, I ascend to the nest in the fissure of the cliff.

32

I think I could turn and live with animals, they are so placid and self-contained,
I stand and look at them long and long.
They do not sweat and whine about their condition,
They do not lie awake in the dark and weep for their sins,
They do not make me sick discussing their duty to God,
Not one is dissatisfied, not one is demented with the mania of owning things,
Not one kneels to another, nor to his kind that lived thousands of years ago,
Not one is respectable or unhappy over the whole earth.
So they show their relations to me and I accept them,
They bring me tokens of myself, they evince them plainly in their possession.

I wonder where they get those tokens,
Did I pass that way huge times ago and negligently drop them?
Myself moving forward then and now and forever,
Gathering and showing more always and with velocity,
Infinite and omnigenous, and the like of these among them,
Not too exclusive toward the reachers of my remembrancers,
Picking out here one that I love, and now go with him on brotherly terms.
A gigantic beauty of a stallion, fresh and responsive to my caresses,
Head high in the forehead, wide between the ears,
Limbs glossy and supple, tail dusting the ground,
Eyes full of sparkling wickedness, ears finely cut, flexibly moving.
His nostrils dilate as my heels embrace him,
His well-built limbs tremble with pleasure as we race around and return.
I but use you a minute, then I resign you, stallion,
Why do I need your paces when I myself outgallop them?
Even as I stand or sit passing faster than you.

33

Space and Time! now I see it is true, what I guessed at,
What I guessed when I loafed on the grass,
What I guessed while I lay alone in my bed,
And again as I walked the beach under the paling stars of the morning.
My ties and ballasts leave me, my elbows rest in sea gaps,
I skirt sierras, my palms cover continents,
I am afoot with my vision.
By the city's quadrangular houses—in log huts, camping with lumbermen,
Along the ruts of the turnpike, along the dry gulch and rivulet bed,
Weeding my onion patch or hoeing rows of carrots and parsnips, crossing savannas, trailing in forests,
Prospecting, gold digging, girdling the trees of a new purchase,
Scorched ankle-deep by the hot sand, hauling my boat down the shallow river,

Where the panther walks to and fro on a limb overhead, where the buck turns furiously at the hunter,
Where the rattlesnake suns his flabby length on a rock, where the otter is feeding on fish,
Where the alligator in his tough pimples sleeps by the bayou,
Where the black bear is searching for roots or honey, where the beaver pats the mud with his paddle-shaped tail;
Over the growing sugar, over the yellow-flowered cotton plant, over the rice in its low moist field,
Over the sharp-peaked farmhouse, with its scalloped scum and slender shoots from the gutters,
Over the western persimmon, over the long-leaved corn, over the delicate blue-flower flax,
Over the white and brown buckwheat, a hummer and buzzer there with the rest,
Over the dusky green of the rye as it ripples and shades in the breeze;
Scaling mountains, pulling myself cautiously up, holding on by low scragged limbs,
Walking the path worn in the grass and beat through the leaves of the brush,
Where the quail is whistling betwixt the woods and the wheat lot,
Where the bat flies in the Seventh-month eve, where the great goldbug drops through the dark,
Where the brook puts out of the roots of the old tree and flows to the meadow,
Where cattle stand and shake away flies with the tremulous shuddering of their hides,
Where the cheesecloth hangs in the kitchen, where andirons straddle the hearth slab, where cobwebs fall in festoons from the rafters;
Where trip hammers crash, where the press is whirling its cylinders,
Where the human heart beats with terrible throes under its ribs,
Where the pear-shaped balloon is floating aloft (floating in it myself and looking composedly down),

Where the life car is drawn on the slip noose, where the heat hatches pale-green eggs in the dented sand,
Where the she-whale swims with her calf and never forsakes it,
Where the steamship trails hindways its long pennant of smoke,
Where the fin of the shark cuts like a black chip out of the water,
Where the half-burned brig is riding on unknown currents,
Where shells grow to her slimy deck, where the dead are corrupting below;
Where the dense-starred flag is borne at the head of the regiments,
Approaching Manhattan up by the long-stretching island,
Under Niagara, the cataract falling like a veil over my countenance,
Upon a doorstep, upon the horse block of hardwood outside,
Upon the race course, or enjoying picnics or jigs or a good game of baseball,
At he-festivals, with blackguard gibes, ironical license, bull dances, drinking, laughter,
At the cider mill tasting the sweets of the brown mash, sucking the juice through a straw,
At apple peelings wanting kisses for all the red fruit I find,
At musters, beach parties, friendly bees, huskings, house raisings;
Where the mockingbird sounds his delicious gurgles, cackles, screams, weeps,
Where the hayrick stands in the barnyard, where the dry stalks are scattered, where the brood cow waits in the hovel,
Where the bull advances to do his masculine work, where the stud to the mare, where the cock is treading the hen,
Where the heifers browse, where geese nip their food with short jerks,
Where sundown shadows lengthen over the limitless and lonesome prairie,

Where herds of buffalo make a crawling spread of the square miles far and near,
Where the hummingbird shimmers, where the neck of the long-lived swan is curving and winding,
Where the laughing gull scoots by the shore, where she laughs her near-human laugh,
Where beehives range on a gray bench in the garden half hid by the high weeds,
Where band-necked partridges roost in a ring on the ground with their heads out,
Where burial coaches enter the arched gates of a cemetery,
Where winter wolves bark amid wastes of snow and icicled trees,
Where the yellow-crowned heron comes to the edge of the marsh at night and feeds upon small crabs,
Where the splash of swimmers and divers cools the warm noon,
Where the katydid works her chromatic reed on the walnut tree over the well,
Through patches of citrons and cucumbers with silver-wired leaves,
Through the salt lick or orange glade, or under conical firs,
Through the gymnasium, through the curtained saloon, through the office or public hall;
Pleased with the native and pleased with the foreign, pleased with the new and old,
Pleased with the homely woman as well as the handsome,
Pleased with the Quakeress as she puts off her bonnet and talks melodiously,
Pleased with the tune of the choir of the whitewashed church,
Pleased with the earnest words of the sweating Methodist preacher, impressed seriously at the camp meeting;
Looking in at the shop windows of Broadway the whole forenoon, flatting the flesh of my nose on the thick plate glass,
Wandering the same afternoon with my face turned up to the clouds, or down a lane or along the beach,

My right and left arms round the sides of two friends, and
I in the middle;
Coming home with the silent and dark-cheeked bush boy,
(behind me he rides at the drape of the day),
Far from the settlements studying the print of animals' feet,
or the moccasin print,
By the cot in the hospital reaching lemonade to a feverish
patient,
Nigh the coffined corpse when all is still, examining with a
candle;
Voyaging to every port to dicker and adventure,
Hurrying with the modern crowd as eager and fickle as any,
Hot toward one I hate, ready in my madness to knife him,
Solitary at midnight in my back yard, my thoughts gone
from me a long while,
Walking the old hills of Judea with the beautiful gentle
God by my side,
Speeding through space, speeding through heaven and the
stars,
Speeding amid the seven satellites and the broad ring, and
the diameter of eighty thousand miles,
Speeding with tailed meteors, throwing fireballs like the rest,
Carrying the crescent child that carries its own full mother
in its belly,
Storming, enjoying, planning, loving, cautioning,
Backing and filling, appearing and disappearing,
I tread day and night such roads.
I visit the orchards of spheres and look at the product,
And look at quintillions ripened and look at quintillions
green.
I fly those flights of a fluid and swallowing soul,
My course runs below the soundings of plummets.
I help myself to material and immaterial,
No guard can shut me off, no law prevent me.
I anchor my ship for a little while only,
My messengers continually cruise away or bring their re-
turns to me.
I go hunting polar furs and the seal, leaping chasms with a
pike-pointed staff, clinging to topples of
brittle and blue.

I ascend to the foretruck,
I take my place late at night in the crow's nest,
We sail the arctic sea, it is plenty light enough,
Through the clear atmosphere I stretch around on the wonderful beauty,
The enormous masses of ice pass me and I pass them, the scenery is plain in all directions,
The white-topped mountains show in the distance, I fling out my fancies toward them,
We are approaching some great battlefield in which we are soon to be engaged,
We pass the colossal outposts of the encampment, we pass with still feet and caution,
Or we are entering by the suburbs some vast and ruined city,
The blocks and fallen architecture more than all the living cities of the globe.
I am a free companion, I bivouac by invading watchfires,
I turn the bridegroom out of bed and stay with the bride myself,
I tighten her all night to my thighs and lips.
My voice is the wife's voice, the screech by the rail of the stairs,
They fetch my man's body up dripping and drowned.
I understand the large hearts of heroes,
The courage of present times and all times,
How the skipper saw the crowded and rudderless wreck of the steamship, and Death chasing it up and down the storm,
How he knuckled tight and gave not back an inch, and was faithful of days and faithful of nights,
And chalked in large letters on a board, *Be of good cheer, we will not desert you;*
How he followed with them and tacked with them three days and would not give it up,
How he saved the drifting company at last,
How the lank loose-gowned women looked when boated from the side of their prepared graves,
How the silent old-faced infants and the lifted sick, and the sharp-lipped unshaven men;
All this I swallow, it tastes good, I like it well, it becomes mine,
I am the man, I suffered, I was there.

The disdain and calmness of martyrs,
The mother of old, condemned for a witch, burnt with dry wood, her children gazing on,
The hounded slave that flags in the race, leans by the fence, blowing, covered with sweat,
The twinges that sting like needles his legs and neck, the murderous buckshot and the bullets,
All these I feel or am.

I am the hounded slave, I wince at the bite of the dogs,
Hell and despair are upon me, crack and again crack the marksmen,
I clutch the rails of the fence, my gored ribs, thinned with the ooze of my skin,
I fall on the weeds and stones,
The riders spur their unwilling horses, haul close,
Taunt my dizzy ears and beat me violently over the head with whipstocks.

Agonies are one of my changes of garments.
I do not ask the wounded person how he feels, I myself become the wounded person,
My hurts turn livid upon me as I lean on a cane and observe.

I am the mashed fireman with breastbone broken,
Tumbling walls buried me in their debris,
Heat and smoke I inspired, I heard the yelling shouts of my comrades,
I heard the distant click of their picks and shovels,
They have cleared the beams away, they tenderly lift me forth.

I lie in the night air in my red shirt, the pervading hush is for my sake,
Painless after all I lie exhausted but not so unhappy,
White and beautiful are the faces around me, the heads are bared of their fire caps,
The kneeling crowd fades with the light of the torches.

Distant and dead resuscitate.
They show as the dial or move as the hands of me, I am the clock myself.

I am an old artillerist, I tell of my fort's bombardment,
I am there again.

Again the long roll of the drummers,
Again the attacking cannon, mortars,
Again to my listening ears the cannon responsive.

I take part, I see and hear the whole,
The cries, curses, roar, the plaudits for well-aimed shots,
The ambulanza slowly passing trailing its red drip,
Workmen searching after damages, making indispensable repairs,
The fall of grenades through the rent roof, the fan-shaped explosion,
The whizz of limbs, heads, stone, wood, iron, high in the air.

Again gurgles the mouth of my dying general, he furiously waves with his hand,
He gasps through the clot *Mind not me—mind—the entrenchments.*

34

Now I tell what I knew in Texas in my early youth,
(I tell not the fall of Alamo,
Not one escaped to tell the fall of Alamo,
The hundred and fifty are dumb yet at Alamo,)
'Tis the tale of the murder in cold blood of four hundred and twelve young men.

Retreating they had formed in a hollow square with their baggage for breastworks,
Nine hundred lives out of the surrounding enemy's, nine times their number, was the price they took in advance,
Their colonel was wounded and their ammunition gone,
They treated for an honorable capitulation, received writing and seal, gave up their arms and marched back prisoners of war.

They were the glory of the race of rangers,
Matchless with horse, rifle, song, supper, courtship,

Large, turbulent, generous, handsome, proud, and affectionate,
Bearded, sunburnt, dressed in the free costume of hunters,
Not a single one over thirty years of age.

The second First-day morning they were brought out in squads and massacred, it was beautiful early summer,
The work commenced about five o'clock and was over by eight.

None obeyed the command to kneel,
Some made a mad and helpless rush, some stood stark and straight,
A few fell at once, shot in the temple or heart, the living and dead lay together,
The maimed and mangled dug in the dirt, the newcomers saw them there,
Some half-killed attempted to crawl away,
These were dispatched with bayonets or battered with the blunts of muskets.
A youth not seventeen years old seized his assassin till two more came to release him,
The three were all torn and covered with the boy's blood.

At eleven o'clock began the burning of the bodies;
That is the tale of the murder of the four hundred and twelve young men.

35

Would you hear of an old-time sea fight?
Would you learn who won by the light of the moon and stars?
List to the yarn, as my grandmother's father the sailor told it to me.

Our foe was no skulk in his ship I tell you (said he),
His was the surly English pluck, and there is no tougher or truer, and never was, and never will be;
Along the lowered eve he came horribly raking us.

We closed with him, the yards entangled, the cannon touched,
My captain lashed fast with his own hands.

We had received some eighteen-pound shots under the water,
On our lower gun deck two large pieces had burst at the first fire, killing all around and blowing up overhead.

Fighting at sundown, fighting at dark,
Ten o'clock at night, the full moon well up, our leaks on the gain, and five feet of water reported
The master-at-arms loosing the prisoners confined in the afterhold to give them a chance for themselves.

The transit to and from the magazine is now stopped by the sentinels,
They see so many strange faces they do not know whom to trust.

Our frigate takes fire,
The other asks if we demand quarter?
If our colors are struck and the fighting done?

Now I laugh content, for I hear the voice of my little captain,
We have not struck, he composedly cries, *we have just begun our part of the fighting.*

Only three guns are in use,
One is directed by the captain himself against the enemy's mainmast,
Two well served with grape and canister silence his musketry and clear his decks.

The tops alone second the fire of this little battery, especially the maintop,
They hold out bravely during the whole of the action.

Not a moment's cease,
The leaks gain fast on the pumps, the fire eats toward the powder magazine.
One of the pumps has been shot away, it is generally thought we are sinking.
Serene stands the little captain,
He is not hurried, his voice is neither high nor low,
His eyes give more light to us than our battle lanterns.

Toward twelve there in the beams of the moon they surrender to us.

36

Stretched and still lies the midnight,
Two great hulls motionless on the breast of the darkness,
Our vessel riddled and slowly sinking, preparations to pass to the one we have conquered,
The captain on the quarterdeck coldly giving his orders through a countenance white as a sheet,
Nearby the corpse of the child that served in the cabin,
The dead face of an old salt with long white hair and carefully curled whiskers,
The flames spite of all that can be done flickering aloft and below,
The husky voices of the two or three officers yet fit for duty,
Formless stacks of bodies and bodies by themselves, dabs of flesh upon the masts and spars,
Cut of cordage, dangle of rigging, slight shock of the soothe of waves,
Black and impassive guns, litter of powder parcels, strong scent,
A few large stars overhead, silent and mournful shining,
Delicate sniffs of sea breeze, smells of sedgy grass and fields by the shore, death messages given in charge to survivors,
The hiss of the surgeon's knife, the gnawing teeth of his saw,
Wheeze, cluck, swash of falling blood, short wild scream, and long, dull, tapering groan,
These so, these irretrievable.

37

You laggards there on guard! look to your arms!
In at the conquered doors they crowd! I am possessed!
Embody all presences outlawed or suffering,
See myself in prison shaped like another man.
And feel the dull unintermitted pain,
For me the keepers of convicts shoulder their carbines and keep watch.
It is I let out in the morning and barred at night.

Not a mutineer walks handcuffed to jail but I am handcuffed to him and walk by his side,
(I am less the jolly one there, and more the silent one with sweat on my twitching lips,)

Not a youngster is taken for larceny but I go up too, and am tried and sentenced.

Not a cholera patient lies at the last gasp but I also lie at the last gasp,
My face is ash-colored, my sinews gnarl, away from me people retreat.

Askers embody themselves in me and I am embodied in them,
I project my hat, sit shamefaced, and beg.

38

Enough! enough! enough!
Somehow I have been stunned. Stand back!
Give me a little time beyond my cuffed head, slumbers, dreams, gaping,
I discover myself on the verge of a usual mistake.
That I could forget the mockers and insults!
That I could forget the trickling tears and the blows of the bludgeons and hammers!
That I could look with a separate look on my own crucifixion and bloody crowning!

I remember now,
I resume the overstaid fraction,
The grave of rock multiplies what has been confided to it, or to any graves,
Corpses rise, gashes heal, fastenings roll from me.

I troop forth replenished with supreme power, one of an average unending procession,
Inland and seacoast we go, and pass all boundary lines,
Our swift ordinances on their way over the whole earth,
The blossoms we wear in our hats the growth of thousands of years.

Elèves, I salute you! come forward!
Continue your annotations, continue your questionings.

39

The friendly and flowing savage, who is he?
Is he waiting for civilization, or past it and mastering it?

Is he some Southwesterner raised outdoors? is he Canadian?
Is he from the Mississippi country? Iowa, Oregon, California?
The mountains? prairie life, bush life? or sailor from the sea?
Wherever he goes men and women accept and desire him,
They desire he should like them, touch them, speak to them, stay with them.

Behavior lawless as snowflakes, words simple as grass, uncombed head, laughter, and naïveté,
Slow-stepping feet, common features, common modes and emanations,
They descend in new forms from the tips of his fingers,
They are wafted with the odor of his body or breath, they fly out of the glance of his eyes.

40

Flaunt of the sunshine I need not your bask—lie over!
You light surfaces only, I force surfaces and depths also.

Earth! you seem to look for something at my hands,
Say, old topknot, what do you want?
Man or woman, I might tell how I like you, but cannot,
And might tell what it is in me and what it is in you, but cannot,
And might tell that pining I have, that pulse of my nights and days.

Behold, I do not give lectures or a little charity,
When I give I give myself.

You there, impotent, loose in the knees,
Open your scarfed chops till I blow grit within you,
Spread your palms and lift the flaps of your pockets,
I am not to be denied, I compel, I have stores plenty and to spare,
And anything I have I bestow.

I do not ask who you are, that is not important to me,
You can do nothing and be nothing but what I will infold you.

To cotton-field drudge or cleaner of privies I lean,
On his right cheek I put the family kiss,
And in my soul I swear I never will deny him.

On women fit for conception I start bigger and nimbler babes,
(This day I am jetting the stuff of far more arrogant republics.)

To anyone dying, thither I speed and twist the knob of the door,
Turn the bedclothes toward the foot of the bed,
Let the physician and the priest go home.

I seize the descending man and raise him with resistless will,
O despairer, here is my neck,
By God, you shall not go down! hang your whole weight upon me.

I dilate you with tremendous breath, I buoy you up,
Every room of the house do I fill with an armed force,
Lovers of me, bafflers of graves.

Sleep—I and they keep guard all night,
Not doubt, not disease shall dare to lay finger upon you,
I have embraced you, and henceforth possess you to myself,
And when you rise in the morning you will find what I tell you is so.

41

I am he bringing help for the sick as they pant on their backs,
And for strong upright men I bring yet more needed help.

I heard what was said of the universe,
Heard it and heard it of several thousand years;
It is middling well as far as it goes—but is that all?

Magnifying and applying come I,
Outbidding at the start the old cautious hucksters,
Taking myself the exact dimensions of Jehovah,
Lithographing Cronos, Zeus his son, and Hercules his grandson,
Buying drafts of Osiris, Isis Belus, Brahma, Buddha,
In my portfolio placing Manito loose, Allah on a leaf, the crucifix engraved,
With Odin and the hideous-faced Mexitli and every idol and image,
Taking them all for what they are worth and not a cent more,
Admitting they were alive and did the work of their days,
(They bore mites as for unfledged birds who have now to rise and fly and sing for themselves,)
Accepting the rough deific sketches to fill out better in myself, bestowing them freely on each man and woman I see,
Discovering as much or more in a framer framing a house,
Putting higher claims for him there with his rolled-up sleeves driving the mallet and chisel,

Not objecting to special revelations, considering a curl of smoke or a hair on the back of my hand just as curious as any revelation,
Lads ahold of fire engines and hook-and-ladder ropes no less to me than the gods of the antique wars,
Minding their voices peal through the crash of destruction,
Their brawny limbs passing safe over charred laths, their white foreheads whole and unhurt out of the flames;
By the mechanic's wife with her babe at her nipple interceding for every person born,
Three scythes at harvest whizzing in a row from three lusty angels with shirts bagged out at their waists,
The snag-toothed hostler with red hair redeeming sins past and to come,
Selling all he possesses, traveling on foot to fee lawyers for his brother and sit by him while he is tried for forgery;
What was strewn in the amplest strewing the square rod about me, and not filling the square rod then,
The bull and the bug never worshiped half enough,
Dung and dirt more admirable than was dreamed,
The supernatural of no account, myself waiting my time to be one of the supremes,
The day getting ready for me when I shall do as much good as the best, and be as prodigious;
But my life lumps! becoming already a creator,
Putting myself here and now to the ambushed womb of the shadows.

42

A call in the midst of the crowd,
My own voice, orotund sweeping and final.

Come my children,
Come my boys and girls, my women, household and intimates,
Now the performer launches his nerve, he has passed his prelude on the reeds within.

Easily written loose-fingered chords—I feel the thrum of your climax and close.

My head slues round on my neck,
Music rolls, but not from the organ,
Folks are around me, but they are no household of mine.

Ever the hard unsunk ground,
Ever the eaters and drinkers, ever the upward and downward sun, ever the air and the ceaseless tides,
Ever myself and my neighbors, refreshing, wicked, real,
Ever the old inexplicable query, ever that thorned thumb, that breath of itches and thirsts,
Ever the vexer's *hoot! hoot!* till we find where the sly one hides and bring him forth,
Ever love, ever the sobbing liquid of life,
Ever the bandage under the chin, ever the trestles of death.

Here and there with dimes on the eyes walking,
To feed the greed of the belly the brains liberally spooning,
Tickets buying, taking, selling, but into the feast never once going,
Many sweating, plowing, thrashing, and then the chaff for payment receiving,
A few idly owning, and they the wheat continually claiming.

This is the city and I am one of the citizens,
Whatever interests the rest interests me, politics, wars, markets, newspapers, schools,
The mayor and councils, banks, tariffs, steamships, factories, stocks, stores, real estate and personal estate.

The little plentiful manikins skipping around in collars and tailed coats,
I am aware who they are (they are positively not worms or fleas),
I acknowledge the duplicates of myself, the weakest and shallowest is deathless with me,
What I do and say the same waits for them,

Every thought that flounders in me the same flounders in
them.

I know perfectly well my own egotism,
Know my omnivorous lines and must not write any less,
And would fetch you whoever you are flush with myself.

Not words of routine this song of mine,
But abruptly to question, to leap beyond yet nearer bring;
This printed and bound book—but the printer and the
printing-office boy?
The well-taken photographs—but your wife or friend close
and solid in your arms?
The black ship mailed with iron, her mighty guns in her
turrets—but the pluck of the captain and
engineers?
In the houses the dishes and fare and furniture—but the
host and hostess, and the look out of their
eyes?
The sky up there—yet here or next door, or across the way?
The saints and sages in history—but you yourself?
Sermons, creeds, theology—but the fathomless human brain,
And what is reason? and what is love? and what is life?

43

I do not despise you priests, all time, the world over,
My faith is the greatest of faiths and the least of faiths,
Enclosing worship ancient and modern and all between an-
cient and modern,
Believing I shall come again upon the earth after five thou-
sand years,
Waiting responses from oracles, honoring the gods, saluting
the sun,
Making a fetish of the first rock or stump, powowing with
sticks in the circle of obis,
Helping the lama or brahman as he trims the lamps of the
idols,
Dancing yet through the streets in a phallic procession, rapt
and austere in the woods a gymnosophist,
Drinking mead from the skullcap, to shastas and Vedas ad-
mirant, minding the Koran,

Walking the teokallis, spotted with gore from the stone and knife, beating the serpent-skin drum,
Accepting the Gospels, accepting him that was crucified, knowing assuredly that he is divine,
To the Mass kneeling or the puritan's prayer rising, or sitting patiently in a pew,
Ranting and frothing in my insane crisis, or waiting dead-like till my spirit arouses me,
Looking forth on pavement and land, or outside of pavement and land,
Belonging to the winders of the circuit of circuits.

One of that centripetal and centrifugal gang I turn and talk like a man leaving charges before a journey.

Downhearted doubters dull and excluded,
Frivolous, sullen, moping, angry, affected, disheartened, atheistical,
I know every one of you, I know the sea of torment, doubt, despair and unbelief.

How the flukes splash!
How they contort rapid as lightning, with spasms and spouts of blood!

Be at peace bloody flukes of doubters and sullen mopers,
I take my place among you as much as among any,
The past is the push of you, me, all, precisely the same,
And what is yet untried and afterward is for you, me, all precisely the same.

I do not know what is untried and afterward,
But I know it will in its turn prove sufficient, and cannot fail.

Each who passes is considered, each who stops is considered, not a single one can it fail.

It cannot fail the young man who died and was buried,
Nor the young woman who died and was put by his side,

Nor the little child that peeped in at the door, and then drew back and was never seen again,
Nor the old man who has lived without purpose, and feels it with bitterness worse than gall,
Nor him in the poorhouse tubercled by rum and the bad disorder,
Nor the numberless slaughtered and wrecked, nor the brutish koboo called the ordure of humanity,
Nor the sacs merely floating with open mouths for food to slip in,
Nor anything in the earth, or down in the oldest graves of the earth,
Nor anything in the myriads of spheres, nor the myriads of myriads that inhabit them,
Nor the present, nor the least wisp that is known.

44

It is time to explain myself—let us stand up.
What is known I strip away,
I launch all men and women forward with me into the Unknown.
The clock indicates the moment—but what does eternity indicate?
We have thus far exhausted trillions of winters and summers,
There are trillions ahead, and trillions ahead of them.
Births have brought us richness and variety,
And other births will bring us richness and variety.
I do not call one greater and one smaller,
That which fills its period and place is equal to any.

Were mankind murderous or jealous upon you, my brother, my sister?
I am sorry for you, they are not murderous or jealous upon me,
All has been gentle with me, I keep no account with lamentation,
(What have I to do with lamentation?)

I am an acme of things accomplished, and I am encloser of things to be.

My feet strike an apex of the apices of the stairs,
On every step bunches of ages, and larger bunches between the steps,
All below duly traveled, and still I mount and mount.
Rise after rise bow the phantoms behind me,
Afar down I see the huge first Nothing, I know I was even there,
I waited unseen and always, and slept through the lethargic mist,
And took my time, and took no hurt from the fetid carbon.

Long I was hugged close—long and long.
Immense have been the preparations for me,
Faithful and friendly the arms that have helped me.

Cycles ferried my cradle, rowing and rowing like cheerful boatmen,
For room to me stars kept aside in their own rings,
They sent influences to look after what was to hold me.
Before I was born out of my mother generations guided me,
My embryo has never been torpid, nothing could overlay it.

For it the nebula cohered to an orb,
The long slow strata piled to rest it on,
Vast vegetables gave it sustenance,
Monstrous sauroids transported it in their mouths and deposited it with care.
All forces have been steadily employed to complete and delight me,
Now on this spot I stand with my robust soul.

45

O span of youth! ever-pushed elasticity.
O manhood, balanced, florid and full.

My lovers suffocate me,
Crowding my lips, thick in the pores of my skin.
Jostling me through streets and public halls, coming naked to me at night,
Crying by day *Ahoy!* from the rocks of the river, swinging and chirping over my head,

Calling my name from flower beds, vines, tangled underbrush,
Lighting on every moment of my life,
Bussing my body with soft balsamic busses,
Noiselessly passing handfuls out of their hearts and giving them to be mine.

Old age superbly rising! O welcome, ineffable grace of dying days!

Every condition promulges not only itself, it promulges what grows after and out of itself,
And the dark hush promulges as much as any.

I open my scuttle at night and see the far-sprinkled systems,
And all I see multiplied as high as I can cipher edge but the rim of the farther systems.
Wider and wider they spread, expanding, always expanding,
Outward and outward and forever outward.
My sun has his sun and round him obediently wheels,
He joins with his partners a group of superior circuit,
And greater sets follow, making specks of the greatest inside them.

There is no stoppage and never can be stoppage,
If I, you, and the worlds, and all beneath or upon their surfaces, were this moment reduced back to a pallid float, it would not avail in the long run,
We should surely bring up again where we now stand,
And surely go as much farther, and then farther and farther.

A few quadrillions of eras, a few octillions of cubic leagues, do not hazard the span or make it impatient,
They are but parts, anything is but a part.

See ever so far, there is limitless space outside of that,
Count ever so much, there is limitless time around that.
My rendezvous is appointed, it is certain,

The Lord will be there and wait till I come on perfect terms,
The great Camerado, the lover true for whom I pine will be there.

46

I know I have the best of time and space, and was never measured and never will be measured.
I tramp a perpetual journey (come listen all!),
My signs are a rainproof coat, good shoes, and a staff cut from the woods,
No friend of mine takes his ease in my chair,
I have no chair, no church, no philosophy,
I lead no man to a dinner table, library, exchange,
But each man and each woman of you I lead upon a knoll,
My left hand hooking you round the waist,
My right hand pointing to landscapes of continents and the public road.
Not I, not anyone else can travel that road for you,
You must travel it for yourself.
It is not far, it is within reach,
Perhaps you have been on it since you were born and did not know,
Perhaps it is everywhere on water and on land.
Shoulder your duds, dear son, and I will mine, and let us hasten forth,
Wonderful cities and free nations we shall fetch as we go.
If you tire, give me both burdens, and rest the chuff of your hand on my hip,
And in due time you shall repay the same service to me,
For after we start we never lie by again.
This day before dawn I ascended a hill and looked at the crowded heaven,
And I said to my spirit *When we become the enfolders of those orbs, and the pleasure and knowledge of everything in them, shall we be filled and satisfied then?*
And my spirit said *No, we but level that lift to pass and continue beyond.*
You are also asking me questions and I hear you,
I answer that I cannot answer, you must find out for yourself.

Sit awhile, dear son,
Here are biscuits to eat and here is milk to drink,
But as soon as you sleep and renew yourself in sweet clothes, I kiss you with a good-by kiss and open the gate for your egress hence.
Long enough have you dreamed contemptible dreams,
Now I wash the gum from your eyes,
You must habit yourself to the dazzle of the light and of every moment of your life.
Long have you timidly waded holding a plank by the shore,
Now I will you to be a bold swimmer,
To jump off in the midst of the sea, rise again, nod to me, shout, and laughingly dash with your hair.

47

I am the teacher of athletes,
He that by me spreads a wider breast than my own proves the width of my own,
He most honors my style who learns under it to destroy the teacher.
The boy I love, the same becomes a man not through derived power, but in his own right,
Wicked rather than virtuous out of conformity or fear,
Fond of his sweetheart, relishing well his steak,
Unrequited love or a slight cutting him worse than sharp steel cuts,
First-rate to ride, to fight, to hit the bull's-eye, to sail a skiff, to sing a song or play on the banjo,
Preferring scars and the beard and faces pitted with smallpox over all latherers,
And those well-tanned to those that keep out of the sun.
I teach straying from me, yet who can stray from me?
I follow you whoever you are from the present hour,
My words itch at your ears till you understand them.
I do not say these things for a dollar or to fill up the time while I wait for a boat,
(It is you talking just as much as myself, I act as the tongue of you,
Tied in your mouth, in mine it begins to be loosened.)
I swear I will never again mention love or death inside a house,

And I swear I will never translate myself at all, only to him
or her who privately stays with me in the
open air.
If you would understand me go to the heights or water
shore,
The nearest gnat is an explanation, and a drop or motion of
waves a key,
The maul, the oar, the handsaw, second my words.
No shuttered room or school can commune with me,
But roughs and little children better than they.
The young mechanic is closest to me, he knows me well,
The woodman that takes his ax and jug with him shall take
me with him all day,
The farm boy plowing in the field feels good at the sound of
my voice,
In vessels that sail my words sail, I go with fishermen and
seamen and love them.
The soldier camped or upon the march is mine,
On the night ere the pending battle many seek me, and I do
not fail them,
On that solemn night (it may be their last) those that know
me seek me.
My face rubs to the hunter's face when he lies down alone
in his blanket,
The driver thinking of me does not mind the jolt of his
wagon,
The young mother and old mother comprehend me,
The girl and the wife rest the needle a moment and forget
where they are,
They and all would resume what I have told them.

48

I have said that the soul is not more than the body,
And I have said that the body is not more than the soul,
And nothing, not God, is greater to one than one's self is,
And whoever walks a furlong without sympathy walks to his
own funeral dressed in his shroud,
And I or you pocketless of a dime may purchase the pick of
the earth,
And to glance with an eye or show a bean in its pod con-
founds the learning of all times,

And there is no trade or employment but the young man following it may become a hero,
And there is no object so soft but it makes a hub for the wheeled universe,
And I say to any man or woman, Let your soul stand cool and composed before a million universes.

And I say to mankind, Be not curious about God,
For I who am curious about each am not curious about God.
(No array of terms can say how much I am at peace about God and about death.)
I hear and behold God in every object, yet understand God not in the least,
Nor do I understand who there can be more wonderful than myself.
Why should I wish to see God better than this day?
I see something of God each hour of the twenty-four, and each moment then,
In the faces of men and women I see God, and in my own face in the glass,
I find letters from God dropped in the street, and every one is signed by God's name,
And I leave them where they are, for I know that wheresoe'er I go
Others will punctually come forever and ever.

49

And as to you Death, and you bitter hug of mortality, it is idle to try to alarm me.
To his work without flinching the accoucheur comes,
I see the elder hand pressing receiving supporting,
I recline by the sills of the exquisite flexible doors,
And mark the outlet, and mark the relief and escape.
And as to you Corpse I think you are good manure, but that does not offend me,
I smell the white roses sweet-scented and growing.
I reach to the leafy lips, I reach to the polished breasts of melons.

And as to you Life I reckon you are the leavings of many deaths,
(No doubt I have died myself ten thousand times before.)
I hear you whispering there O stars of heaven,
O suns—O grass of graves—O perpetual transfers and promotions,
If you do not say anything how can I say anything?
Of the turbid pool that lies in the autumn forest,
Of the moon that descends the steeps of the soughing twilight,
Toss, sparkles of day and dusk—toss on the black stems that decay in the muck,
Toss to the moaning gibberish of the dry limbs.
I ascend from the moon, I ascend from the night,
I perceive that the ghastly glimmer is noonday sunbeams reflected,
And debouch to the steady and central from the offspring great or small.

50

There is that in me—I do not know what it is—but I know it is in me.
Wrenched and sweaty—calm and cool then my body becomes,
I sleep—I sleep long.
I do not know it—it is without name—it is a word unsaid,
It is not in any dictionary, utterance, symbol.
Something it swings on more than the earth I swing on,
To it the creation is the friend whose embracing awakes me.
Perhaps I might tell more. Outlines! I plead for my brothers and sisters.
Do you see O my brothers and sisters?
It is not chaos or death—it is form, union, plan—it is eternal life—it is Happiness.

51

The past and present wilt—I have filled them, emptied them,
And proceed to fill my next fold of the future.
Listener up there! what have you to confide to me?
Look in my face while I snuff the sidle of evening,

(Talk honestly, no one else hears you, and I stay only a minute longer.)
Do I contradict myself?
Very well then I contradict myself,
(I am large, I contain multitudes.)
I concentrate toward them that are nigh, I wait on the door slab.
Who has done his day's work? who will soonest be through with his supper?
Who wishes to walk with me?
Will you speak before I am gone? will you prove already too late?

52

The spotted hawk swoops by and accuses me, he complains of my gab and my loitering.
I too am not a bit tamed, I too am untranslatable,
I sound my barbaric yawp over the roofs of the world.

The last scud of day holds back for me,
It flings my likeness after the rest and true as any on the shadowed wilds,
It coaxes me to the vapor and the dusk.

I depart as air, I shake my white locks at the runaway sun,
I effuse my flesh in eddies, and drift it in lacy jags.

I bequeath myself to the dirt to grow from the grass I love,
If you want me again look for me under your boot soles.

You will hardly know who I am or what I mean,
But I shall be good health to you nevertheless,
And filter and fiber your blood.

Failing to fetch me at first keep encouraged,
Missing me one place search another,
I stop somewhere waiting for you.

Out of the Cradle Endlessly Rocking

Out of the cradle endlessly rocking,
Out of the mockingbird's throat, the musical shuttle,
Out of the Ninth-month midnight,
Over the sterile sands and the fields beyond, where the child leaving his bed wandered alone, bareheaded, barefoot,
Down from the showered halo,
Up from the mystic play of shadows twining and twisting as if they were alive,
Out from the patches of briers and blackberries,
From the memories of the bird that chanted to me,
From your memories sad brother, from the fitful risings and fallings I heard,
From under that yellow half-moon late-risen and swollen as if with tears,
From those beginning notes of yearning and love there in the mist,
From the thousand responses of my heart never to cease,
From the myriad thence-aroused words,
From the word stronger and more delicious than any,
From such as now they start the scene revisiting,
As a flock, twittering, rising, or overhead passing,
Borne hither, ere all eludes me, hurriedly,
A man, yet by these tears a little boy again,
Throwing myself on the sand, confronting the waves,
I, chanter of pains and joys, uniter of here and hereafter,
Taking all hints to use them, but swiftly leaping beyond them,
A reminiscence sing.

Once Paumanok,
When the lilac scent was in the air and Fifth-month grass was growing,
Up this seashore in some briers,
Two feathered guests from Alabama, two together,

And their nest, and four light-green eggs spotted with brown,
And every day the he-bird to and fro near at hand,
And every day the she-bird crouched on her nest, silent, with bright eyes,
And every day I, a curious boy, never too close, never disturbing them,
Cautiously peering, absorbing, translating.

Shine! shine! shine!
Pour down your warmth, great sun!
While we bask, we two together.
Two together!
Winds blow south, or winds blow north,
Day come white, or night come black,
Home, or rivers and mountains from home,
Singing all time, minding no time,
While we two keep together.

Till of a sudden,
Maybe killed, unknown to her mate,
One forenoon the she-bird crouched not on the nest,
Nor returned that afternoon, nor the next,
Nor ever appeared, again.
And thenceforward all summer in the sound of the sea,
And at night under the full of the moon in calmer weather,
Over the hoarse surging of the sea,
Or flitting from brier to brier by day,
I saw, I heard at intervals the remaining one, the he-bird,
The solitary guest from Alabama.

Blow! blow! blow!
Blow up sea winds along Paumanok's shore;
I wait and I wait till you blow my mate to me.

Yes, when the stars glistened,
All night long on the prong of a moss-scalloped stake,
Down almost amid the slapping waves,
Sat the lone singer wonderful causing tears.
He called on his mate,
He poured forth the meanings which I of all men know.

Yes my brother I know,
The rest might not, but I have treasured every note,
For more than once dimly down to the beach gliding,
Silent, avoiding the moonbeams, blending myself with the shadows,
Recalling now the obscure shapes, the echoes, the sounds and sights after their sorts,
The white arms out in the breakers tirelessly tossing,
I, with bare feet, a child, the wind wafting my hair,
Listened long and long.
Listened to keep, to sing, now translating the notes,
Following you my brother.

Soothe! soothe! soothe!
Close on its wave soothes the wave behind,
And again another behind embracing and lapping, every one close,
But my love soothes not me, not me.
Low hangs the moon, it rose late,
It is lagging—O I think it is heavy with love, with love.
O madly the sea pushes upon the land,
With love, with love.
O night! do I not see my love fluttering out among the breakers?
What is that little black thing I see there in the white?

Loud! loud! loud!
Loud I call to you, my love!
High and clear I shoot my voice over the waves,
Surely you must know who is here, is here,
You must know who I am, my love.
Low-hanging moon!
What is that dusky spot in your brown yellow?
O it is the shape, the shape of my mate!
O moon do not keep her from me any longer.
Land! land! O land!
Whichever way I turn, O I think you could give me my mate back again if you only would,
For I am almost sure I see her dimly whichever way I look.
O rising stars!

Perhaps the one I want so much will rise, will rise with some of you.
O throat! O trembling throat!
Sound clearer through the atmosphere!
Pierce the woods, the earth,
Somewhere listening to catch you must be the one I want.

Shake out carols.
Solitary here, the night's carols!
Carols of lonesome love! death's carols!
Carols under that lagging, yellow, waning moon!
O under the moon where she droops almost down into the sea!
O reckless despairing carols.
But soft! sink low!
Soft! let me just murmur,
And do you wait a moment you husky-noised sea,
For somewhere I believe I heard my mate responding to me,
So faint, I must be still, be still to listen,
But not altogether still, for then she might not come immediately to me.

Hither my love!
Here I am! here!
With this just-sustained note I announce myself to you,
This gentle call is for you my love, for you.
Do not be decoyed elsewhere,
That is the whistle of the wind, it is not my voice,
That is the fluttering, the fluttering of the spray,
Those are the shadows of leaves.

O darkness! O in vain!
O I am very sick and sorrowful.
O brown halo in the sky near the moon, drooping upon the sea!
O troubled reflection in the sea!
O throat! O throbbing heart!
And I singing uselessly, uselessly all the night.
O past! O happy life! O songs of joy!
In the air, in the woods, over fields,

Loved! loved! loved! loved! loved!
But my mate no more, no more with me!
We two together no more.

The aria sinking,
All else continuing, the stars shining,
The winds blowing, the notes of the bird continuous echoing,
With angry moans the fierce old mother incessantly moaning,
On the sands of Paumanok's shore gray and rustling,
The yellow half-moon enlarged, sagging down, drooping, the face of the sea almost touching,
The boy ecstatic, with his bare feet the waves, with his hair the atmosphere dallying,
The love in the heart long pent, now loose, now at last tumultuously bursting,
The aria's meaning, the ears, the soul, swiftly depositing,
The strange tears down the cheeks coursing,
The colloquy there, the trio, each uttering,
The undertone, the savage old mother incessantly crying,
To the boy's soul's questions sullenly timing, some drowned secret hissing,
To the outsetting bard.

Demon or bird! (said the boy's soul).
Is it indeed toward your mate you sing? or is it really to me?
For I, that was a child, my tongue's use sleeping, now I have heard you,
Now in a moment I know what I am for, I awake,
And already a thousand singers, a thousand songs, clearer, louder and more sorrowful than yours,
A thousand warbling echoes have started to life within me, never to die.

O you singer solitary, singing by yourself, projecting me,
O solitary me listening, never more shall I cease perpetuating you,
Never more shall I escape, never more the reverberations,
Never more the cries of unsatisfied love be absent from me,

Never again leave me to be the peaceful child I was before
what there in the night,
By the sea under the yellow and sagging moon,
The messenger there aroused, the fire, the sweet hell within,
The unknown want, the destiny of me.

O give me the clue! (it lurks in the night here somewhere),
O if I am to have so much, let me have more!
A word then (for I will conquer it),
The word final, superior to all,
Subtle, sent up—what is it?—I listen;
Are you whispering it, and have been all the time, you sea
waves?
Is that it from your liquid rims and wet sands?
Whereto answering, the sea,
Delaying not, hurrying not,
Whispered me through the night, and very plainly before
daybreak,
Lisped to me the low and delicious word death,
And again death, death, death, death,
Hissing melodious, neither like the bird nor like my aroused
child's heart,
But edging near as privately for me rustling at my feet,
Creeping thence steadily up to my ears and laving me soft
all over,
Death, death, death, death, death.

Which I do not forget,
But fuse the song of my dusky demon and brother,
That he sang to me in the moonlight on Paumanok's gray
beach,
With the thousand responsive songs at random,
My own songs awaked from that hour,
And with them the key, the word up from the waves,
The word of the sweetest song and all songs,
That strong and delicious word which, creeping to my feet,
(Or like some old crone rocking the cradle, swathed in sweet
garments, bending aside),
The sea whispered me.

I Sit and Look Out

I sit and look out upon all the sorrows of the world, and
upon all oppression and shame,
I hear secret convulsive sobs from young men at anguish
with themselves, remorseful after deeds done,
I see in low life the mother misused by her children, dying,
neglected, gaunt, desperate,
I see the wife misused by her husband, I see the treacherous
seducer of young women,
I mark the ranklings of jealousy and unrequited love attempted to be hid, I see these sights on the earth,
I see the workings of battle, pestilence, tyranny, I see
martyrs and prisoners,
I observe a famine at sea, I observe the sailors casting lots
who shall be killed to preserve the lives of the rest,
I observe the slights and degradations cast by arrogant persons upon laborers, the poor, and upon Negroes, and
the like;
All these—all the meanness and agony without end I sitting
look out upon,
See, hear, and am silent.

When Lilacs Last in the Dooryard Bloomed

1

When lilacs last in the dooryard bloomed,
And the great star early drooped in the western sky in the
night,
I mourned, and yet shall mourn with ever-returning spring.

Ever-returning spring, trinity sure to me you bring,
Lilac blooming perennial and drooping star in the west,
And thought of him I love.

2

O powerful western fallen star!
O shades of night—O moody, tearful night!
O great star disappeared—O the black murk that hides the star!
O cruel hands that hold me powerless—O helpless soul of me!
O harsh surrounding cloud that will not free my soul.

3

In the dooryard fronting an old farmhouse near the white-washed palings,
Stands the lilac bush tall-growing with heart-shaped leaves of rich green,
With many a pointed blossom rising delicate, with the perfume strong I love,
With every leaf a miracle—and from this bush in the dooryard,
With delicate-colored blossoms and heart-shaped leaves of rich green,
A sprig with its flower I break.

4

In the swamp in secluded recesses,
A shy and hidden bird is warbling a song.

Solitary the thrush,
The hermit withdrawn to himself, avoiding the settlements,
Sings by himself a song.

Song of the bleeding throat,
Death's outlet song of life (for well dear brother I know,
If thou wast not granted to sing thou wouldst surely die).

5

Over the breast of the spring, the land, amid cities,
Amid lanes and through old woods, where lately the violets peeped from the ground, spotting the gray debris,

Amid the grass in the fields each side of the lanes, passing the endless grass,
Passing the yellow-speared wheat, every grain from its shroud in the dark-brown fields uprisen,
Passing the apple-tree blows of white and pink in the orchards,
Carrying a corpse to where it shall rest in the grave,
Night and day journeys a coffin.

6

Coffin that passes through lanes and streets,
Through day and night with the great cloud darkening the land,
With the pomp of the inlooped flags with the cities draped in black,
With the show of the States themselves as of crape-veiled women standing,
With processions long and winding and the flambeaus of the night,
With the countless torches lit, with the silent sea of faces and the unbared heads,
With the waiting depot, the arriving coffin, and the somber faces,
With dirges through the night, with the thousand voices rising strong and solemn,
With all the mournful voices of the dirges poured around the coffin,
The dim-lit churches and the shuddering organs—where amid these you journey,
With the tolling tolling bells' perpetual clang,
Here, coffin that slowly passes,
I give you my sprig of lilac.

7

(Nor for you, for one alone,
Blossoms and branches green to coffins all I bring,
For fresh as the morning, thus would I chant a song for you O sane and sacred death.
All over bouquets of roses,
O death, I cover you over with roses and early lilies,
But mostly and now the lilac that blooms the first,

Copious I break, I break the sprigs from the bushes,
With loaded arms I come, pouring for you,
For you and the coffins all of you O death.)

8

O western orb sailing the heaven,
Now I know what you must have meant as a month since I walked,
As I walked in silence the transparent shadowy night,
As I saw you had something to tell as you bent to me night after night,
As you drooped from the sky low down as if to my side (while the other stars all looked on),
As we wandered together the solemn night (for something I know not what kept me from sleep),
As the night advanced, and I saw on the rim of the west how full you were of woe,
As I stood on the rising ground in the breeze in the cool transparent night,
As I watched where you passed and was lost in the netherward black of the night,
As my soul in its trouble dissatisfied sank, as where you sad orb,
Concluded, dropped in the night, and was gone.

9

Sing on there in the swamp,
O singer bashful and tender, I hear your notes, I hear your call,
I hear, I come presently, I understand you,
But a moment I linger, for the lustrous star has detained me,
The star my departing comrade holds and detains me.

10

O how shall I warble myself for the dead one there I loved?
And how shall I deck my song for the large sweet soul that has gone?
And what shall my perfume be for the grave of him I love?
Sea winds blown from east and west,

Blown from the Eastern sea and blown from the Western sea, till there on the prairies meeting,
These and with these and the breath of my chant,
I'll perfume the grave of him I love.

11

O what shall I hang on the chamber walls?
And what shall the pictures be that I hang on the walls,
To adorn the burial house of him I love?
Pictures of growing spring and farms and homes,
With the Fourth-month eve at sundown, and the gray smoke lucid and bright,
With floods of the yellow gold of the gorgeous, indolent, sinking sun, burning, expanding the air
With the fresh sweet herbage underfoot, and the pale green leaves of the trees prolific,
In the distance the flowing glaze, the breast of the river, with a wind dapple here and there,
With ranging hills on the banks, with many a line against the sky, and shadows,
And the city at hand with dwellings so dense, and stacks of chimneys,
And all the scenes of life and the workshops, and the workmen homeward returning.

12

Lo, body and soul—this land,
My own Manhattan with spires, and the sparkling and hurrying tides, and the ships,
The varied and ample land, the South and the North in the light, Ohio's shores and flashing Missouri,
And ever the far-spreading prairies covered with grass and corn.
Lo, the most excellent sun so calm and haughty,
The violet and purple morn with just-felt breezes,
The gentle soft-born measureless light,
The miracle spreading bathing all, the fulfilled noon,
The coming eve delicious, the welcome night and the stars,
Over my cities shining all, enveloping man and land.

13

Sing on, sing on you gray-brown bird,
Sing from the swamps, the recesses, pour your chant from the bushes,
Limitless out of the dusk, out of the cedars and pines.
Sing on dearest brother, warble your reedy song,
Loud human song, with voice of uttermost woe.
O liquid and free and tender!
O wild and loose to my soul—O wondrous singer!
You only I hear—yet the star holds me (but will soon depart),
Yet the lilac with mastering odor holds me.

14

Now while I sat in the day and looked forth,
In the close of the day with its light and the fields of spring, and the farmers preparing their crops,
In the large unconscious scenery of my land with its lakes and forests,
In the heavenly aerial beauty (after the perturbed winds and the storms),
Under the arching heavens of the afternoon swift passing, and the voices of children and women,
The many-moving sea tides, and I saw the ships how they sailed,
And the summer approaching with richness, and the fields all busy with labor,
And the infinite separate houses, how they all went on, each with its meals and minutia of daily usages,
And the streets how their throbbings throbbed, and the cities pent—lo, then and there,
Falling upon them all and among them all, enveloping me with the rest,
Appeared the cloud, appeared the long black trail,
And I knew death, its thought, and the sacred knowledge of death.

Then with the knowledge of death as walking one side of me,
And the thought of death close-walking the other side of me,

And I in the middle as with companions, and as holding the
hands of companions,
I fled forth to the hiding receiving night that talks not,
Down to the shores of the water the path by the swamp in
the dimness,
To the solemn shadowy cedars and ghostly pines so still.
And the singer so shy to the rest received me,
The gray-brown bird I know received us comrades three,
And he sang the carol of death, and a verse for him I love.
From deep secluded recesses
From the fragrant cedars and the ghostly pines so still,
Came the carol of the bird.
And the charm of the carol rapt me,
As I held as if by their hands my comrades in the night,
And the voice of my spirit tallied the song of the bird.

Come lovely and soothing death,
Undulate round the world, serenely arriving, arriving,
In the day, in the night, to all, to each,
Sooner or later delicate death.
Praised be the fathomless universe,
For life and joy, and for objects and knowledge curious,
And for love, sweet love—but praise! praise! praise!
For the sure-enwinding arms of cool-enfolding death.
Dark mother always gliding near with soft feet,
Have none chanted for thee a chant of fullest welcome?
Then I chant it for thee, I glorify thee above all,
I bring thee a song that when thou must indeed come, come
unfalteringly.
Approach strong deliveress,
When it is so, when thou hast taken them I joyously sing
the dead,
Lost in the loving floating ocean of thee,
Laved in the flood of thy bliss O death.
From me to thee glad serenades,
Dances for thee I propose saluting thee, adornments and
feastings for thee,
And the sights of the open landscape and the high-spread
sky are fitting,
And life and the fields, and the huge and thoughtful night.

The night in silence under many a star,
The ocean shore and the husky whispering wave whose voice I know,
And the soul turning to thee O vast and well-veiled death,
And the body gratefully nestling close to thee.
Over the treetops I float thee a song,
Over the rising and sinking waves, over the myriad fields and the prairies wide,
Over the dense-packed cities all and the teeming wharves and ways,
I float this carol with joy, with joy to thee O death.

15

To the tally of my soul,
Loud and strong kept up the gray-brown bird,
With pure deliberate notes spreading filling the night.
Loud in the pines and cedars dim,
Clear in the freshness moist and the swamp perfume,
And I with my comrades there in the night.
While my sight that was bound in my eyes unclosed,
As to long panoramas of visions.
And I saw askant the armies,
I saw as in noiseless dreams hundreds of battle flags,
Borne through the smoke of the battles and pierced with missiles I saw them,
And carried hither and yon through the smoke, and torn and bloody,
And at last but a few shreds left on the staffs (and all in silence),
And the staffs all splintered and broken.
I saw battle corpses, myriads of them,
And the white skeletons of young men, I saw them,
I saw the debris and debris of all the slain soldiers of the war,
But I saw they were not as was thought,
They themselves were fully at rest, they suffered not,
The living remained and suffered, the mother suffered,
And the wife and the child and the musing comrade suffered,
And the armies that remained suffered.

16

Passing the visions, passing the night,
Passing, unloosing the hold of my comrades' hands,
Passing the song of the hermit bird and the tallying song of my soul,
Victorious song, death's outlet song, yet varying ever-altering song,
As low and wailing, yet clear the notes, rising and falling, flooding the night,
Sadly sinking and fainting, as warning and warning, and yet again bursting with joy,
Covering the earth and filling the spread of the heaven,
As that powerful psalm in the night I heard from recesses,
Passing, I leave thee lilac with heart-shaped leaves,
I leave thee there in the dooryard, blooming, returning with spring.
I cease from my song for thee,
From my gaze on thee in the west, fronting the west, communing with thee,
O comrade lustrous with silver face in the night.

Yet each to keep and all, retrievements out of the night,
The song, the wondrous chant of the gray-brown bird,
And the tallying chant, the echo aroused in my soul,
With the lustrous and drooping star with the countenance full of woe,
With the holders holding my hand nearing the call of the bird,
Comrades mine and I in the midst, and their memory ever to keep, for the dead I loved so well,
For the sweetest, wisest soul of all my days and lands—and this for his dear sake,
Lilac and star and bird twined with the chant of my soul,
There in the fragrant pines and the cedars dusk and dim.

O Captain! My Captain!

O Captain! my Captain! our fearful trip is done,
The ship has weathered every rack, the prize we sought is won,
The port is near, the bells I hear, the people all exulting,
While follow eyes the steady keel, the vessel grim and daring;
    But O heart! heart! heart!
        O the bleeding drops of red,
            Where on the deck my Captain lies,
                Fallen cold and dead.

O Captain! my Captain! rise up and hear the bells;
Rise up—for you the flag is flung—for you the bugle trills,
For you bouquets and ribboned wreaths—for you the shores acrowding,
For you they call, the swaying mass, their eager faces turning;
    Here Captain! dear father!
        The arm beneath your head!
            It is some dream that on the deck,
                You've fallen cold and dead.

My Captain does not answer, his lips are pale and still,
My father does not feel my arm, he has no pulse nor will,
The ship is anchored safe and sound, its voyage closed and done,
From fearful trip the victor ship comes in with object won:
    Exult O shores, and ring O bells!
        But I with mournful tread,
            Walk the deck my Captain lies,
                Fallen cold and dead.

Good-bye My Fancy!

Good-bye my Fancy!
Farewell dear mate, dear love!
I'm going away, I know not where,
Or to what fortune, or whether I may ever see you again,
So Good-bye my Fancy.

Now for my last—let me look back a moment;
The slower fainter ticking of the clock is in me,
Exit, nightfall, and soon the heart-thud stopping.
Long have we lived, joyed, caressed together;
Delightful!—now separation—Good-bye my Fancy.

Yet let me not be too hasty,
Long indeed have we lived, slept, filtered, become really
blended into one;
Then if we die together (yes, we'll remain one),
If we go anywhere we'll go together to meet what happens,
Maybe we'll be better off and blither, and learn something,
Maybe it is yourself now really ushering me to the true
songs, (who knows?),
Maybe it is you the mortal knob really undoing, turning—so
now finally,
Good-bye—and hail! my Fancy.

Joy, Shipmate, Joy!

Joy, shipmate, joy!
(Pleased to my soul at death I cry.)
Our life is closed, our life begins,
The long, long anchorage we leave,
The ship is clear at last, she leaps!
She swiftly courses from the shore.
Joy, shipmate, joy!

To a Locomotive in Winter

Thee for my recitative,
Thee in the driving storm even as now, the snow, the winter-day declining,
Thee in thy panoply, thy measur'd dual throbbing and thy beat convulsive,
Thy black cylindric body, golden brass and silvery steel,
Thy ponderous side-bars, parallel and connecting rods, gyrating, shuttling at thy sides,
Thy metrical, now swelling pant and roar, now tapering in the distance,
Thy great protruding head-light fix'd in front,
Thy long, pale, floating vapor-pennants, tinged with delicate purple,
The dense and murky clouds out-belching from thy smoke-stack,
Thy knitted frame, thy springs and valves, the tremulous twinkle of thy wheels,
Thy train of cars behind, obedient, merrily following,
Through gale or calm, now swift, now slack, yet steadily careering;
Type of the modern—emblem of motion and power—pulse of the continent,
For once come serve the Muse and merge in verse, even as here I see thee,
With storm and buffeting gusts of wind and falling snow,
By day thy warning ringing bell to sound its notes,
By night thy silent signal lamps to swing.

Fierce-throated beauty!
Roll through my chant with all thy lawless music, thy swinging lamps at night,
Thy madly-whistled laughter, echoing, rumbling like an earthquake, rousing all,
Law of thyself complete, thine own track firmly holding,
(No sweetness debonair of tearful harp or glib piano thine,)
Thy trills of shrieks by rocks and hills return'd,
Launch'd o'er the prairies wide, across the lakes,
To the free skies unpent and glad and strong.

A Noiseless Patient Spider

A noiseless patient spider,
I mark'd where on a little promontory it stood isolated,
Mark'd how to explore the vacant vast surrounding,
It launch'd forth filament, filament, filament, out of itself,
Ever unreeling them, ever tirelessly speeding them.

And you O my soul where you stand,
Surrounded, detached, in measureless oceans of space,
Ceaselessly musing, venturing, throwing, seeking the spheres to connect them,
Till the bridge you will need be form'd, till the ductile anchor hold,
Till the gossamer thread you fling catch somewhere, O my soul.

Facing West from California's Shores

Facing west from California's shores,
Inquiring, tireless, seeking what is yet unfound,
I, a child, very old, over waves, towards the house of maternity, the land of migrations, look afar,
Look off the shores of my Western sea, the circle almost circled;
For starting westward from Hindustan, from the vales of Kashmere,
From Asia, from the north, from the God, the sage, and the hero,
From the south, from the flowery peninsulas and the spice islands,
Long having wander'd since, round the earth having wander'd,
Now I face home again, very pleas'd and joyous,
(But where is what I started for so long ago?
And why is it yet unfound?)

On the Beach at Night Alone

On the beach at night alone,
As the old mother sways her to and fro singing her husky song,
As I watch the bright stars shining, I think a thought of the clef of the universes and of the future.

A vast similitude interlocks all,
All spheres, grown, ungrown, small, large, suns, moons, planets,
All distances of place however wide,
All distances of time, all inanimate forms,
All souls, all living bodies though they be ever so different, or in different worlds,
All gaseous, watery, vegetable, mineral processes, the fishes, the brutes,
All nations, colors, barbarisms, civilizations, languages,
All identities that have existed or may exist on this globe, or any globe,
All lives and deaths, all of the past, present, future,
This vast similitude spans them, and always has spann'd,
And shall forever span them and compactly hold and enclose them.

When I Heard the Learn'd Astronomer

When I heard the learn'd astronomer,
When the proofs, the figures, were ranged in columns before me,
When I was shown the charts and diagrams, to add, divide, and measure them,
When I sitting heard the astronomer where he lectured with much applause in the lecture-room,
How soon unaccountable I became tired and sick,
Till rising and gliding out I wander'd off by myself,
In the mystical moist night-air, and from time to time,
Look'd up in perfect silence at the stars.

The Dalliance of the Eagles

Skirting the river road, (my forenoon walk, my rest,)
Skyward in air a sudden muffled sound, the dalliance of the eagles,
The rushing amorous contact high in space together,
The clinching interlocking claws, a living, fierce, gyrating wheel,
Four beating wings, two beaks, a swirling mass tight grappling,
In tumbling turning clustering loops, straight downward falling,
Till o'er the river pois'd, the twain yet one, a moment's lull,
A motionless still balance in the air, then parting, talons loosing,
Upward again on slow-firm pinions slanting, their separate diverse flight,
She hers, he his, pursuing.

Cavalry Crossing a Ford

A line in long array where they wind betwixt green islands,
They take a serpentine course, their arms flash in the sun—hark to the musical clank,
Behind the silvery river, in it the splashing horses loitering stop to drink,
Behold the brown-faced men, each group, each person a picture, the negligent rest on the saddles,
Some emerge on the opposite bank, others are just entering the ford—while,
Scarlet and blue and snowy white,
The guidon flags flutter gayly in the wind.

A Sight in Camp in the Daybreak Gray and Dim

A sight in camp in the daybreak gray and dim,
As from my tent I emerge so early sleepless,
As slow I walk in the cool fresh air the path near by the hospital tent,
Three forms I see on stretchers lying, brought out there untended lying,
Over each the blanket spread, ample brownish woolen blanket,
Gray and heavy blanket, folding, covering all.

Curious I halt and silent stand,
Then with light fingers I from the face of the nearest the first just lift the blanket;
Who are you elderly man so gaunt and grim, with well-gray'd hair, and flesh all sunken about the eyes?
Who are you my dear comrade?

Then to the second I step—and who are you my child and darling?
Who are you sweet boy with cheeks yet blooming?

Then to the third—a face nor child nor old, very calm, as of beautiful yellow-white ivory;
Young man I think I know you—I think this face is the face of the Christ himself,
Dead and divine and brother of all, and here again he lies.

The Wound-dresser

1

An old man bending I come among new faces,
Years looking backward resuming in answer to children,
Come tell us old man, as from young men and maidens that love me,
(Arous'd and angry, I'd thought to beat the alarum, and urge relentless war,

But soon my fingers fail'd me, my face droop'd and I resign'd myself,
To sit by the wounded and soothe them, or silently watch the dead;)
Years hence of these scenes, of these furious passions, these chances,
Of unsurpass'd heroes, (was one side so brave? the other was equally brave;)
Now be witness again, paint the mightiest armies of earth,
Of those armies so rapid so wondrous what saw you to tell us?
What stays with you latest and deepest? of curious panics,
Of hard-fought engagements or sieges tremendous what deepest remains?

2

O maidens and young men I love and that love me,
What you ask of my days those the strangest and sudden your talking recalls,
Soldier alert I arrive after a long march cover'd with sweat and dust,
In the nick of time I come, plunge in the fight, loudly shout in the rush of successful charge,
Enter the captur'd works—yet lo, like a swift-running river they fade,
Pass and are gone they fade—I dwell not on soldiers' perils or soldiers' joys,
(Both I remember well—many the hardships, few the joys, yet I was content.)

But in silence, in dreams' projections,
While the world of gain and appearance and mirth goes on,
So soon what is over forgotten, and waves wash the imprints off the sand,
With hinged knees returning I enter the doors, (while for you up there,
Whoever you are, follow without noise and be of strong heart.)

Bearing the bandages, water and sponge,
Straight and swift to my wounded I go,
Where they lie on the ground after the battle brought in,
Where their priceless blood reddens the grass the ground,
Or to the rows of the hospital tent, or under the roof'd hospital,
To the long rows of cots up and down each side I return,
To each and all one after another I draw near, not one do I miss,

An attendant follows holding a tray, he carries a refuse pail,
Soon to be fill'd with clotted rags and blood, emptied, and fill'd
again.

I onward go, I stop,
With hinged knees and steady hand to dress wounds,
I am firm with each, the pangs are sharp yet unavoidable,
One turns to me his appealing eyes—poor boy! I never knew you,
Yet I think I could not refuse this moment to die for you, if that
would save you.

3

On, on I go, (open doors of time! open hospital doors!)
The crush'd head I dress, (poor crazed hand tear not the bandage
away,)
The neck of the cavalry-man with the bullet through and through
I examine,
Hard the breathing rattles, quite glazed already the eye, yet life
struggles hard,
(Come sweet death! be persuaded O beautiful death!
In mercy come quickly.)
From the stump of the arm, the amputated hand,
I undo the clotted lint, remove the slough, wash off the matter
and blood,
Back on his pillow the soldier bends with curv'd neck and side-falling
head,
His eyes are closed, his face is pale, he dares not look on the
bloody stump,
And has not yet look'd on it.

I dress a wound in the side, deep, deep,
But a day or two more, for see the frame all wasted and sinking,
And the yellow-blue countenance see.

I dress the perforated shoulder, the foot with the bullet-wound,
Cleanse the one with a gnawing and putrid gangrene, so sickening,
so offensive,
While the attendant stands behind aside me holding the tray and
pail.

I am faithful, I do not give out,
The fractur'd thigh, the knee, the wound in the abdomen,
These and more I dress with impassive hand, (yet deep in my breast
a fire, a burning flame.)

4

Thus in silence in dreams' projections,
Returning, resuming, I thread my way through the hospitals,
The hurt and wounded I pacify with soothing hand,
I sit by the restless all the dark night, some are so young,
Some suffer so much, I recall the experience sweet and sad,
(Many a soldier's loving arms about this neck have cross'd and
rested,
Many a soldier's kiss dwells on these bearded lips.)

Vigil Strange I Kept on the Field One Night

Vigil strange I kept on the field one night;
When you my son and my comrade dropped at my side that day,
One look I but gave which your dear eyes returned with a look I
shall never forget,
One touch of your hand to mine O boy, reached up as you lay on
the ground,
Then onward I sped in the battle, the even-contested battle,
Till late in the night relieved to the place at last again I made my
way,
Found you in death so cold dear comrade, found your body son of
responding kisses (never again on earth responding),
Bared your face in the starlight, curious the scene, cool blew the mod-
erate night wind,
Long there and then in vigil I stood, dimly around me the battle-
field spreading.
Vigil wondrous and vigil sweet there in the fragrant silent night,
But not a tear fell, not even a long-drawn sigh, long, long I gazed,
Then on the earth partially reclining sat by your side leaning my
chin in my hands,
Passing sweet hours, immortal and mystic hours with you dearest
comrade—not a tear, not a word,

Vigil of silence, love and death, vigil for you my son and my soldier,
As onward silently stars aloft, eastward new ones upward stole,
Vigil final for you brave boy (I could not save you, swift was your death
I faithfully loved you and cared for you living, I think we shall surely meet again),
Till at latest lingering of the night, indeed just as the dawn appeared,
My comrade I wrapped in his blanket, enveloped well his form,
Folded the blanket well, tucking it carefully over head and carefully under feet,
And there and then and bathed by the rising sun, my son in his grave, in his rude-dug grave I deposited,
Ending my vigil strange with that, vigil of night and battlefield dim,
Vigil for boy of responding kisses (never again on earth responding),
Vigil for comrade swiftly slain, vigil I never forget, how as day brightened,
I rose from the chill ground and folded my soldier well in his blanket,
And buried him where he fell.

Crossing Brooklyn Ferry

1

Flood-tide below me! I see you face to face!
Clouds of the west—sun there half an hour high—I see you also face to face.
Crowds of men and women attired in the usual costumes, how curious you are to me!
On the ferry-boats the hundreds and hundreds that cross, returning home, are more curious to me than you suppose,
And you that shall cross from shore to shore years hence are more to me, and more in my meditations, than you might suppose.

2

The impalpable sustenance of me from all things at all hours of the day,
The simple, compact, well-join'd scheme, myself disintegrated, every one disintegrated yet part of the scheme,
The similitudes of the past and those of the future,

The glories strung like beads on my smallest sights and hearings, on the walk in the street and the passage over the river,
The current rushing so swiftly and swimming with me far away,
The others that are to follow me, the ties between me and them,
The certainty of others, the life, love, sight, hearing of others.

Others will enter the gates of the ferry and cross from shore to shore,
Others will watch the run of the flood-tide,
Others will see the shipping of Manhattan north and west, and the heights of Brooklyn to the south and east,
Others will see the islands large and small;
Fifty years hence, others will see them as they cross, the sun half an hour high,
A hundred years hence, or ever so many hundred years hence, others will see them,
Will enjoy the sunset, the pouring-in of the flood-tide, the falling-back to the sea of the ebb-tide.

3

It avails not, time nor place—distance avails not,
I am with you, you men and women of a generation, or ever so many generations hence,
Just as you feel when you look on the river and sky, so I felt,
Just as any of you is one of a living crowd, I was one of a crowd,
Just as you are refresh'd by the gladness of the river and the bright flow, I was refresh'd,
Just as you stand and lean on the rail, yet hurry with the swift current, I stood yet was hurried,
Just as you look on the numberless masts of ships and the thick-stemm'd pipes of steamboats, I look'd.

I too many and many a time cross'd the river of old,
Watched the Twelfth-month sea-gulls, saw them high in the air floating with motionless wings, oscillating their bodies,
Saw how the glistening yellow lit up parts of their bodies and left the rest in strong shadow,
Saw the slow-wheeling circles and the gradual edging toward the south,
Saw the reflection of the summer sky in the water,
Had my eyes dazzled by the shimmering track of beams,

Look'd at the fine centrifugal spokes of light round the shape of my head in the sunlit water,
Look'd on the haze on the hills southward and south-westward,
Look'd on the vapor as it flew in fleeces tinged with violet,
Look'd toward the lower bay to notice the vessels arriving,
Saw their approach, saw aboard those that were near me,
Saw the white sails of schooners and sloops, saw the ships at anchor,
The sailors at work in the rigging or out astride the spars,
The round masts, the swinging motion of the hulls, the slender serpentine pennants,
The large and small steamers in motion, the pilots in their pilot-houses,
The white wake left by the passage, the quick tremulous whirl of the wheels,
The flags of all nations, the falling of them at sunset,
The scallop-edged waves in the twilight, the ladled cups, the frolicsome crests and glistening,
The stretch afar growing dimmer and dimmer, the gray walls of the granite storehouses by the docks,
On the river the shadowy group, the big steam-tug closely flank'd on each side by the barges, the hay-boat, the belated lighter,
On the neighboring shore the fires from the foundry chimneys burning high and glaringly into the night,
Casting their flicker of black contrasted with wild red and yellow light over the tops of houses, and down into the clefts of streets.

4

These and all else were to me the same as they are to you,
I loved well those cities, loved well the stately and rapid river,
The men and women I saw were all near to me,
Others the same—others who look back on me because I look'd forward to them,
(The time will come, though I stop here to-day and to-night.)

5

What is it then between us?
What is the count of the scores or hundreds of years between us?

Whatever it is, it avails not—distance avails not, and place avails not,
I too lived, Brooklyn of ample hills was mine,

I too walk'd the streets of Manhattan island, and bathed in the waters around it,
I too felt the curious abrupt questionings stir within me,
In the day among crowds of people sometimes they came upon me,
In my walks home late at night or as I lay in my bed they came upon me,
I too had been struck from the float forever held in solution,
I too had receiv'd identity by my body,
That I was I knew was of my body, and what I should be I knew I should be of my body.

6

It is not upon you alone the dark patches fall,
The dark threw its patches down upon me also,
The best I had done seem'd to me blank and suspicious,
My great thoughts as I supposed them, were they not in reality meagre?
Nor is it you alone who know what it is to be evil,
I am he who knew what it was to be evil,
I too knitted the old knot of contrariety,
Blabb'd, blush'd, resented, lied, stole, grudg'd,
Had guile, anger, lust, hot wishes I dared not speak,
Was wayward, vain, greedy, shallow, sly, cowardly, malignant,
The wolf, the snake, the hog, not wanting in me,
The cheating look, the frivolous word, the adulterous wish, not wanting,
Refusals, hates, postponements, meanness, laziness, none of these wanting,
Was one with the rest, the days and haps of the rest,
Was call'd by my nighest name by clear loud voices of young men as they saw me approaching or passing,
Felt their arms on my neck as I stood, or the negligent leaning of their flesh against me as I sat,
Saw many I loved in the street or ferry-boat or public assembly, yet never told them a word,
Lived the same life with the rest, the same old laughing, gnawing, sleeping,
Play'd the part that still looks back on the actor or actress,
The same old role, the role that is what we make it, as great as we like,
Or as small as we like, or both great and small.

7

Closer yet I approach you,
What thought you have of me now, I had as much of you—I laid in my stores in advance,
I consider'd long and seriously of you before you were born.

Who was to know what should come home to me?
Who knows but I am enjoying this?
Who knows, for all the distance, but I am as good as looking at you now, for all you cannot see me?

8

Ah, what can ever be more stately and admirable to me than mast-hemm'd Manhattan?
River and sunset and scallop-edg'd waves of flood-tide?
The sea-gulls oscillating their bodies, the hay-boat in the twilight, and the belated lighter?
What gods can exceed these that clasp me by the hand, and with voices I love call me promptly and loudly by my nighest name as I approach?
What is more subtle than this which ties me to the woman or man that looks in my face?
Which fuses me into you now, and pours my meaning into you?

We understand men do we not?
What I promis'd without mentioning it, have you not accepted?
What the study could not teach—what the preaching could not accomplish is accomplish'd, is it not?

9

Flow on, river! flow with the flood-tide, and ebb with the ebb-tide!
Frolic on, crested and scallop-edg'd waves!
Gorgeous clouds of the sunset! drench with your splendor me, or the men and women generations after me!
Cross from shore to shore, countless crowds of passengers!
Stand up, tall masts of Mannahatta! stand up, beautiful hills of Brooklyn!
Throb, baffled and curious brain! throw out questions and answers!
Suspend here and everywhere, eternal float of solution!
Gaze, loving and thirsting eyes, in the house or street or public assembly!

Sound out, voices of young men! loudly and musically call me by my nighest name!
Live, old life! play the part that looks back on the actor or actress!
Play the old role, the role that is great or small according as one makes it!
Consider, you who peruse me, whether I may not in unknown ways be looking upon you;
Be firm, rail over the river, to support those who lean idly, yet haste with the hasting current;
Fly on, sea-birds! fly sideways, or wheel in large circles high in the air;
Receive the summer sky, you water, and faithfully hold it till all downcast eyes have time to take it from you!
Diverge, fine spokes of light, from the shape of my head, or any one's head, in the sunlit water!
Come on, ships from the lower bay! pass up or down, white-sail'd schooners, sloops, lighters!
Flaunt away, flags of all nations! be duly lower'd at sunset!
Burn high your fires, foundry chimneys! cast black shadows at nightfall! cast red and yellow light over the tops of the houses!
Appearances, now or henceforth, indicate what you are,
You necessary film, continue to envelop the soul,
About my body for me, and your body for you, be hung our divinest aromas,
Thrive, cities—bring your freight, bring your shows, ample and sufficient rivers,
Expand, being than which none else is perhaps more spiritual,
Keep your places, objects than which none else is more lasting.

You have waited, you always wait, you dumb, beautiful ministers,
We receive you with free sense at last, and are insatiate henceforward,
Not you any more shall be able to foil us, or withhold yourselves from us,
We use you, and do not cast you aside—we plant you permanently within us,
We fathom you not—we love you—there is perfection in you also,
You furnish your parts toward eternity,
Great or small, you furnish your parts toward the soul.

As I Ebb'd with the Ocean of Life

1

As I ebb'd with the ocean of life,
As I wended the shores I know,
As I walk'd where the ripples continually wash you Paumanok,
Where they rustle up hoarse and sibilant,
Where the fierce old mother endlessly cries for her castaways,
I musing late in the autumn day, gazing off southward,
Held by this electric self out of the pride of which I utter poems,
Was seiz'd by the spirit that trails in the lines underfoot,
The rim, the sediment that stands for all the water and all the land of the globe.

Fascinated, my eyes reverting from the south, dropt, to follow those slender windrows,
Chaff, straw, splinters of wood, weeds, and the sea-gluten,
Scum, scales from shining rocks, leaves of salt-lettuce, left by the tide,
Miles walking, the sound of breaking waves the other side of me,
Paumanok there and then as I thought the old thought of likenesses,
These you presented to me you fish-shaped island,
As I wended the shores I know,
As I walk'd with that electric self seeking types.

2

As I wend to the shores I know not,
As I list to the dirge, the voices of men and women wreck'd,
As I inhale the impalpable breezes that set in upon me,
As the ocean so mysterious rolls toward me closer and closer,
I too but signify at the utmost a little wash'd-up drift,
A few sands and dead leaves to gather,
Gather, and merge myself as part of the sands and drift.

O baffled, balk'd, bent to the very earth,
Oppress'd with myself that I have dared to open my mouth,
Aware now that amid all that blab whose echoes recoil upon me I have not once had the least idea who or what I am,

But that before all my arrogant poems the real Me stands yet untouch'd, untold, altogether unreach'd,
Withdrawn far, mocking me with mock-congratulatory signs and bows,
With peals of distant ironical laughter at every word I have written,
Pointing in silence to these songs, and then to the sand beneath.

I perceive I have not really understood any thing, not a single object, and that no man ever can,
Nature here in sight of the sea taking advantage of me to dart upon me and sting me,
Because I have dared to open my mouth to sing at all.

3

You oceans both, I close with you,
We murmur alike reproachfully rolling sands and drift, knowing not why,
These little shreds indeed standing for you and me and all.

You friable shore with trails of debris,
You fish-shaped island, I take what is underfoot,
What is yours is mine my father.
I too Paumanok,
I too have bubbled up, floated the measureless float, and been wash'd on your shores,
I too am but a trail of drift and debris,
I too leave little wrecks upon you, you fish-shaped island.

I throw myself upon your breast my father,
I cling to you so that you cannot unloose me,
I hold you so firm till you answer me something.

Kiss me my father,
Touch me with your lips as I touch those I love,
Breathe to me while I hold you close the secret of the murmuring I envy.

4

Ebb, ocean of life, (the flow will return,)
Cease not your moaning you fierce old mother,

Endlessly cry for your castaways, but fear not, deny not me,
Rustle not up so hoarse and angry against my feet as I touch you or gather from you.
I mean tenderly by you and all,
I gather for myself and for this phantom looking down where we lead, and following me and mine.

Me and mine, loose windrows, little corpses,
Froth, snowy white, and bubbles,
(See, from my dead lips the ooze excluding at last,
See, the prismatic colors glistening and rolling,)
Tufts or straw, sands, fragments,
Buoy'd hither from many moods, one contradicting another,
From the storm, the long calm, the darkness, the swell,
Musing, pondering, a breath, a briny tear, a dab of liquid or soil,
Up just as much out of fathomless workings fermented and thrown,
A limp blossom or two, torn, just as much over waves floating, drifted at random,
Just as much for us that sobbing dirge of Nature,
Just as much whence we come that blare of the cloud-trumpets,
We, capricious, brought hither we know not whence, spread out before you,
You up there walking or sitting,
Whoever you are, we too lie in drifts at your feet.

There Was a Child Went Forth

There was a child went forth every day,
And the first object he look'd upon, that object he became,
And that object became part of him for the day or a certain part of the day,
Or for many years or stretching cycles of years.
The early lilacs became part of this child,
And grass and white and red morning-glories, and white and red clover, and the song of the phœbe-bird,
And the Third-month lambs and the sow's pink-faint litter, and the mare's foal and the cow's calf,

And the noisy brood of the barnyard or by the mire of the pond-side,
And the fish suspending themselves so curiously below there, and the beautiful curious liquid,
And the water-plants with their graceful flat heads, all became part of him.

The field-sprouts of Fourth-month and Fifth-month became part of him,
Winter-grain sprouts and those of the light-yellow corn, and the esculent roots of the garden,
And the apple-trees cover'd with blossoms and the fruit afterward, and wood-berries, and the commonest weeds by the road,
And the old drunkard staggering home from the outhouse of the tavern whence he had lately risen,
And the schoolmistress that pass'd on her way to the school,
And the friendly boys that pass'd, and the quarrelsome boys,
And the tidy and fresh-cheek'd girls, and the barefoot negro boy and girl,
And all the changes of city and country wherever he went.

His own parents, he that had father'd him and she that had conceiv'd him in her womb and birth'd him,
They gave this child more of themselves than that,
They gave him afterward every day, they became part of him.

The mother at home quietly placing the dishes on the supper-table,
The mother with mild words, clean her cap and gown, a wholesome odor falling off her person and clothes as she walks by,
The father, strong, self-sufficient, manly, mean, anger'd, unjust,
The blow, the quick loud word, the tight bargain, the crafty lure,
The family usages, the language, the company, the furniture, the yearning and swelling heart,
Affection that will not be gainsay'd, the sense of what is real, the thought if after all it should prove unreal,
The doubts of day-time and the doubts of night-time, the curious whether and how,
Whether that which appears so is so, or is it all flashes and specks?
Men and women crowding fast in the streets, if they are not flashes and specks what are they?

The streets themselves and the façades of houses, and goods in the windows,
Vehicles, teams, the heavy-plank'd wharves, the huge crossing at the ferries,
The village on the highland seen from afar at sunset, the river between,
Shadows, aureola and mist, the light falling on roofs and gables of white or brown two miles off,
The schooner near by sleepily dropping down the tide, the little boat slack-tow'd astern,
The hurrying tumbling waves, quick-broken crests, slapping,
The strata of color'd clouds, the long bar of maroon-tint away solitary by itself, the spread of purity it lies motionless in,
The horizon's edge, the flying sea-crow, the fragrance of salt marsh and shore mud,
These became part of that child who went forth every day, and who now goes, and will always go forth every day.

A SAMPLER OF HYMNS, SPIRITUALS AND SONGS

We Raise de Wheat

We raise de wheat,
Dey gib us de corn:
We bake de bread,
Dey gib us de crust;
We sif de meal,
Dey gib us de huss;
We peel de meat,
Dey gib us de skin;
And dat's de way
Dey take us in;
We skim de pot,
Dey gib us de liquor,
And say dat's good enough for nigger.

Black Soldier's Civil War Chant

Ole Abe (God bless 'is ole soul!)
Got a plenty good victuals, an' a plenty good clo'es.
Got powder, an' shot, an' lead,
To bust in Adam's liddle Confed'
In dese hard times.

Oh, once dere wus union, an' den dere wus peace;
De slave, in de cornfield, bare up to his knees.
But de Rebel's in gray, an' Sesesh's in de way,
An' de slave'll be free
In dese hard times.

Raise a "Rucus" To-night

Two liddle Niggers all dressed in white, (Raise a rucus to-night.)
Want to go to Heaben on de tail of a kite. (Raise a rucus to-night.)
De kite string broke; dem Niggers fell; (Raise a rucus to-night.)
Whar dem Niggers go, I hain't gwineter tell. (Raise a rucus to-night.)

A Nigger an' a w'ite man a playin' seben up; (Raise a rucus to-night.)
De Nigger beat de w'ite man, but 'e's skeered to pick it up. (Raise a rucus to-night.)
Dat Nigger grabbed de money, an' de w'ite man fell. (Raise a rucus to-night.)
How de Nigger run, I'se not gwineter tell. (Raise a rucus to-night.)

Look here, Nigger! Let me tell you a naked fac': (Raise a rucus to-night.)
You mought a been cullud widout bein' dat black; (Raise a rucus to-night.)
Dem 'ar feet look lak youse sho' walkin' back; (Raise a rucus to-night.)
An' yo' ha'r, it look lak a chyarpet tack. (Raise a rucus to-night.)

Oh come 'long, chilluns, come 'long,
W'ile dat moon are shinin' bright.
Let's git on board, an' float down de river,
An' raise dat rucus to-night.

from a Slave Marriage Ceremony

Dark an' stormy may come de wedder;
I jines dis he-male an' dis she-male togedder.
Let none, but Him dat makes de thunder,
Put dis he-male an' dis she-male asunder.
I darfore 'nounce you bofe de same.
Be good, go 'long, an' keep up yo' name.
De broomstick's jumped, de worl's not wide.
She's now yo' own. Salute yo' bride!

I Thank God I'm Free at Las'

Free at las', free at las',
I thank God I'm free at las'.
Free at las', free at las',
I thank God I'm free at las'.

Way down yonder in de graveyard walk,
I thank God I'm free at las'.
Me an' my Jesus gwineter meet an' talk,
I thank God I'm free at las'.

On-a my knees when de light pass by,
I thank God I'm free at las'.
Thought my soul would arise and fly,
I thank God I'm free at las'.

Some o' dese mornin's bright and fair,
I thank God I'm free at las',
Gwineter meet my Jesus in de middle of de air,
I thank God I'm free at las'.

Crucifixion

They crucified my Lord, an' He never said a mumbalin' word;
They crucified my Lord, an' He never said a mumbalin' word.
Not a word, not a word, not a word.

They nailed Him to the tree, an' He never said a mumbalin' word;
They nailed Him to the tree, an' He never said a mumbalin' word.
Not a word, not a word, not a word.

They pierced Him in the side, an' He never said a mumbalin' word,
They pierced Him in the side, an' He never said a mumbalin' word.
Not a word, not a word, not a word.

The blood came twinklin' down, an' He never said a mumbalin' word,
The blood came twinklin' down, an' He never said a mumbalin' word.
Not a word, not a word, not a word.

He bowed His head an' died, an' He never said a mumbalin' word,
He bowed His head an' died, an' He never said a mumbalin' word.
Not a word, not a word, not a word.

Joshua Fit de Battle of Jericho

Joshua fit de battle of Jericho,
Jericho, Jericho,
Joshua fit de battle of Jericho,
And de walls come tumbling down.

You may talk about yo' king of Gideon
Talk about yo' man of Saul,
Dere's none like good old Joshua
At de battle of Jericho.

Up to de walls of Jericho,
He marched with spear in hand;
"Go blow dem ram horns," Joshua cried,
"Kase de battle am in my hand."

Den de lamb ram sheep horns begin to blow,
Trumpets begin to sound,
Joshua commanded de chillen to shout,
And de walls come tumbling down.

Joshua fit de battle of Jericho,
Jericho, Jericho,
Joshua fit de battle of Jericho,
And de walls come tumbling down.

Deep River

Deep river, my home is over Jordan,
Deep river, Lord; I want to cross over into camp ground.

O children, O, don't you want to go to that gospel feast,
That promised land, that land, where all is peace?

Deep river, my home is over Jordan,
Deep river, Lord; I want to cross over into camp ground.

The Star-Spangled Banner

Oh, say, can you see, by the dawn's early light,
  What so proudly we hailed at the twilight's last gleaming,
Whose broad stripes and bright stars through the perilous fight,
  O'er the ramparts we watched were so gallantly streaming?
And the rockets' red glare, the bombs bursting in air,
Gave proof thro' the night that our flag was still there.
Oh, say, does that star-spangled banner yet wave
O'er the land of the free, and the home of the brave!

On the shore, dimly seen thro' the mists of the deep,
  Where the foe's haughty host in dread silence reposes,
What is that which the breeze o'er the towering steep,
  As it fitfully blows, half conceals, half discloses?
Now it catches the gleam of the morning's first beam,
In full glory reflected, now shines on the stream.
'Tis the star-spangled banner; oh, long may it wave
O'er the land of the free, and the home of the brave!

And where is that band who so vauntingly swore
  That the havoc of war and the battle's confusion
A home and a country should leave us no more?
  Their blood has washed out their foul footsteps' pollution.
No refuge could save the hireling and slave
From the terror of flight, or the gloom of the grave:
And the star-spangled banner in triumph doth wave
O'er the land of the free, and the home of the brave!

Oh, thus be it ever when freemen shall stand
  Between their loved homes and the war's desolation;
Blest with victory and peace, may the heaven-rescued land
  Praise the power that hath made and preserved us a nation!
Then conquer we must, when our cause it is just,
And this be our motto: "In God is our trust!"
And the star-spangled banner in triumph doth wave,
O'er the land of the free, and the home of the brave!

FRANCIS SCOTT KEY

Battle Hymn of the Republic

Mine eyes have seen the glory of the coming of the Lord:
He is trampling out the vintage where the grapes of wrath are stored;
He hath loosed the fateful lightning of his terrible swift sword:
  His truth is marching on.

I have seen him in the watch-fires of a hundred circling camps;
They have builded him an altar in the evening dews and damps;
I can read his righteous sentence by the dim and flaring lamps:
  His day is marching on.

I have read a fiery gospel, writ in burnished rows of steel:
"As ye deal with my contemners, so with you my grace shall deal;
Let the Hero, born of woman, crush the serpent with his heel,
  Since God is marching on."

He has sounded forth the trumpet that shall never call retreat;
He is sifting out the hearts of men before his judgment-seat:
O, be swift, my soul, to answer him! be jubilant, my feet!
  Our God is marching on.

In the beauty of the lilies Christ was born across the sea,
With a glory in his bosom that transfigures you and me;
As he died to make men holy, let us die to make men free,
  While God is marching on.

JULIA WARD HOWE

America the Beautiful

O beautiful for spacious skies,
  For amber waves of grain,
For purple mountain majesties
  Above the fruited plain!

America! America!
  God shed His grace on thee
And crown thy good with brotherhood
  From sea to shining sea!

O beautiful for pilgrim feet,
  Whose stern, impassioned stress
A thoroughfare for freedom beat
  Across the wilderness!
America! America!
  God mend thine every flaw,
Confirm thy soul in self-control,
  Thy liberty in law!

O beautiful for heroes proved
  In liberating strife,
Who more than self their country loved,
  And mercy more than life!
America! America!
  May God thy gold refine,
Till all success be nobleness
  And every gain divine!

O beautiful for patriot dream
  That sees beyond the years
Thine alabaster cities gleam
  Undimmed by human tears!
America! America!
  God shed His grace on thee,
And crown thy good with brotherhood
  From sea to shining sea!

KATHARINE LEE BATES

FREDERICK GODDARD TUCKERMAN
(1821–1873)

And Change with Hurried Hand Has Swept These Scenes

And change with hurried hand has swept these scenes:
The woods have fallen, across the meadow-lot
The hunter's trail and trap-path is forgot,
And fire has drunk the swamps of evergreens;
Yet for a moment let my fancy plant
These autumn hills again: the wild dove's haunt,
The wild deer's walk. In golden umbrage shut,
The Indian river runs, Quonecktacut!
Here, but a lifetime back, where falls tonight
Behind the curtained pane a sheltered light
On buds of rose or vase of violet
Aloft upon the marble mantel set,
Here in the forest-heart, hung blackening
The wolfbait on the bush beside the spring.

Under the Mountain, as When First I Knew

Under the mountain, as when first I knew
Its low dark roof and chimney creeper-twined,
The red house stands; and yet my footsteps find,
Vague in the walks, waste balm and feverfew.
But they are gone: no soft-eyed sisters trip
Across the porch or lintels; where, behind,
The mother sat, sat knitting with pursed lip.

The house stands vacant in its green recess,
Absent of beauty as a broken heart.
The wild rain enters, and the sunset wind
Sighs in the chambers of their loveliness
Or shakes the pane—and in the silent noons
The glass falls from the window, part by part,
And ringeth faintly in the grassy stones.

Thin Little Leaves of Wood Fern, Ribbed and Toothed

Thin little leaves of wood fern, ribbed and toothed,
Long curved sail needles of the green pitch pine,
With common sandgrass, skirt the horizon line,
And over these the incorruptible blue!
Here let me gently lie and softly view
All world asperities, lightly touched and smoothed
As by his gracious hand, the great Bestower.
What though the year be late? some colors run
Yet through the dry, some links of melody.
Still let me be, by such, assuaged and soothed
And happier made, as when, our schoolday done,
We hunted on from flower to frosty flower,
Tattered and dim, the last red butterfly,
Or the old grasshopper molasses-mouthed.

An Upper Chamber in a Darkened House

An upper chamber in a darkened house,
Where, ere his footsteps reached ripe manhood's brink,
Terror and anguish were his lot to drink;
I cannot rid the thought nor hold it close
But dimly dream upon that man alone:
Now through autumn clouds most softly pass,
The cricket chides beneath the doorstep stone
And greener than the season grows the grass.

Nor can I drop my lids nor shade my brows,
But there he stands beside the lifted sash;
And with a swooning of the heart, I think
Where the black shingles slope to meet the boughs
And, shattered on the roof like smallest snows,
The tiny petals of the mountain ash.

Here, Where the Red Man Swept the Leaves Away

Here, where the red man swept the leaves away
To dig for cordial bark or cooling root,
The wayside apple drops its surly fruit.
Right through the deep heart of his midmost wood,
Through range and river and swampy solitude,
The common highway landward runs today,
The train booms by with long derisive hoot
And, following fast, rise factory, school, and forge.
I heed them not; but where yon alders shoot,
Searching strange plants to medicine my mood—
With a quick savage sense I stop, or stray
Through the brush pines and up the mountain gorge:
With patient eye, and with as safe a foot,
As though I walked the wood with sagamore George.

HENRY TIMROD
(1828–1867)

Ode

Sung at the Occasion of Decorating the Graves of the Confederate Dead, at Magnolia Cemetery, Charleston, S.C., June 16, 1866

Sleep sweetly in your humble graves,
    Sleep, martyrs of a fallen cause;
Though yet no marble column craves
    The pilgrim here to pause.

In seeds of laurel in the earth
    The blossom of your fame is blown,
And somewhere, waiting for its birth,
    The shaft is in the stone!

Meanwhile, behalf the tardy years
    Which keep in trust your storied tombs,
Behold! your sisters bring their tears.
    And these memorial blooms.

Small tributes! but your shades will smile
    More proudly on these wreaths today,
Than when some cannon-molded pile
    Shall overlook this bay.

Stoop, angels, hither from the skies!
    There is no holier spot of ground
Than where defeated valor lies,
    By mourning beauty crowned!

Charleston

Calm as that second summer which precedes
  The first fall of the snow,
In the broad sunlight of heroic deeds,
  The City bides the foe.

As yet, behind their ramparts stern and proud,
  Her bolted thunders sleep—
Dark Sumter, like a battlemented cloud,
  Looms o'er the solemn deep.

No Calpe frowns from lofty cliff or scar
  To guard the holy strand;
But Moultrie holds in leash her dogs of war
  Above the level sand.

And down the dunes a thousand guns lie couched,
  Unseen, beside the flood—
Like tigers in some Orient jungle crouched
  That wait and watch for blood.

Meanwhile, through streets still echoing with trade,
  Walk grave and thoughtful men,
Whose hands may one day wield the patriot's blade
  As lightly as the pen.

And maidens, with such eyes as would grow dim
  Over a bleeding hound,
Seem each one to have caught the strength of him
  Whose sword she sadly bound.

Thus girt without and garrisoned at home,
  Day patient following day,
Old Charleston looks from roof, and spire, and dome,
  Across her tranquil bay.

Ships, through a hundred foes, from Saxon lands
  And spicy Indian ports
Bring Saxon steel and iron to her hands,
  And Summer to her courts.

But still, along yon dim Atlantic line,
  The only hostile smoke
Creeps like a harmless mist above the brine,
  From some frail, floating oak.

Shall the Spring dawn, and she still clad in smiles,
  And with an unscathed brow,
Rest in the strong arms of her palm-crowned isles,
  As fair and free as now?

We know not; in the temple of the Fates
  God has inscribed her doom;
And, all untroubled in her faith, she waits
  The triumph or the tomb.

EMILY DICKINSON

(1830–1886)

49

I never lost as much but twice,
And that was in the sod.
Twice have I stood a beggar
Before the door of God!

Angels—twice descending
Reimbursed my store—
Burglar! Banker—Father!
I am poor once more!

67

Success is counted sweetest
By those who ne'er succeed.
To comprehend a nectar
Requires sorest need.

Not one of all the purple Host
Who took the Flag today
Can tell the definition
So clear of Victory

As he defeated—dying—
On whose forbidden ear
The distant strains of triumph
Burst agonized and clear!

80

Our lives are Swiss—
So still—so Cool—
Till some odd afternoon
The Alps neglect their Curtains
And we look farther on!

Italy stands the other side!
While like a guard between—
The solemn Alps—
The siren Alps
Forever intervene!

92

My friend must be a Bird—
Because it flies!
Mortal, my friend must be,
Because it dies!
Barbs has it, like a Bee!
Ah, curious friend!
Thou puzzlest me!

108

Surgeons must be very careful
When they take the knife!
Underneath their fine incisions
Stirs the Culprit—*Life!*

165

A *Wounded* Deer—leaps highest—
I've heard the Hunter tell—
'Tis but the Ecstasy of *death*—
And then the Brake is still!

The *Smitten* Rock that gushes!
The *trampled* Steel that springs!
A Cheek is always redder
Just where the Hectic stings!

Mirth is the Mail of Anguish—
In which it Cautious Arm,
Lest anybody spy the blood
And "you're hurt" exclaim!

173

A fuzzy fellow, without feet,
Yet doth exceeding run!
Of velvet, is his Countenance,
And his Complexion, dun!

Sometimes, he dwelleth in the grass!
Sometime, upon a bough,
From which he doth descend in plush
Upon the Passer-by!

All this in summer.
But when winds alarm the Forest Folk,
He taketh *Damask* Residence—
And struts in sewing silk!

Then, finer than a Lady,
Emerges in the spring!
A Feather on each shoulder!
You'd scarce recognize him!

By Men, yclept Caterpillar!
By me! But who am I,
To tell the pretty secret
Of the Butterfly!

185

"Faith" is a fine invention
When Gentlemen can *see*—
But *Microscopes* are prudent
In an Emergency.

214

I taste a liquor never brewed—
From Tankards scooped in Pearl—
Not all the Vats upon the Rhine
Yield such an Alcohol!

Inebriate of Air—am I—
And Debauchee of Dew—
Reeling—thro endless summer days—
From inns of Molten Blue—

When "Landlords" turn the drunken Bee
Out of the Foxglove's door—
When Butterflies—renounce their "drams"—
I shall but drink the more!

Till Seraphs swing their snowy Hats—
And Saints—to windows run—
To see the little Tippler
Leaning against the—Sun—

241

I like a look of Agony,
Because I know it's true—
Men do not sham Convulsion,
Nor simulate, a Throe—

The Eyes glaze once—and that is Death—
Impossible to feign
The beads upon the Forehead
By homely Anguish strung.

249

Wild Nights—Wild Nights!
Were I with thee
Wild Nights should be
Our luxury!

Futile—the Winds—
To a Heart in port—
Done with the Compass—
Done with the Chart!

Rowing in Eden—
Ah, the Sea!
Might I but moor—Tonight—
In Thee!

254

"Hope" is the thing with feathers—
That perches in the soul—
And sings the tune without the words—
And never stops—at all—

And sweetest—in the Gale—is heard—
And sore must be the storm—
That could abash the little Bird
That keeps so many warm—

I've heard it in the chillest land—
And on the strangest Sea—
Yet, never, in Extremity,
It asked a crumb—of Me.

280

I felt a Funeral, in my Brain,
And Mourners to and fro
Kept treading—treading—till it seemed
That Sense was breaking through—

And when they all were seated,
A Service, like a Drum—
Kept beating—beating—till I thought
My Mind was going numb—

And then I heard them lift a Box
And creak across my Soul
With those same Boots of Lead, again,
Then Space—began to toll,

As all the Heavens were a Bell,
And Being, but an Ear,
And I, and Silence, some strange Race
Wrecked, solitary, here—

And then a Plank in Reason, broke,
And I dropped down, and down—
And hit a World, at every plunge,
And Finished knowing—then—

288

I'm Nobody! Who are you?
Are you—Nobody—Too?
Then there's a pair of us?
Don't tell! they'd advertise—you know!

How dreary—to be—Somebody!
How public—like a Frog—
To tell one's name—the livelong June—
To an admiring Bog!

301

I reason, Earth is short—
And Anguish—absolute—
And many hurt,
But, what of that?

I reason, we could die—
The best Vitality
Cannot excel Decay,
But, what of that?

I reason, that in Heaven—
Somehow, it will be even—
Some new Equation, given—
But, what of that?

303

The Soul selects her own Society—
Then—shuts the Door—
To her divine Majority—
Present no more—

Unmoved—she notes the Chariots—pausing—
At her low Gate—
Unmoved—an Emperor be kneeling
Upon her Mat—

I've known her—from an ample nation—
Choose One—
Then—close the Valves of her attention—
Like Stone—

318

I'll tell you how the Sun rose—
A Ribbon at a time—
The Steeples swam in Amethyst—
The news, like Squirrels, ran—
The Hills untied their Bonnets—
The Bobolinks—begun—
Then I said softly to myself—
"That must have been the Sun"!
But how he set—I know not—
There seemed a purple stile
That little Yellow boys and girls
Were climbing all the while—
Till when they reached the other side,
A Dominie in Gray—
Put gently up the evening Bars—
And led the flock away—

341

After great pain, a formal feeling comes—
The Nerves sit ceremonious, like Tombs—
The stiff Heart questions was it He, that bore,
And Yesterday, or Centuries before?

The Feet, mechanical, go round—
Of Ground, or Air, or Ought—
A Wooden way
Regardless grown,
A Quartz contentment, like a stone—

This is the Hour of Lead—
Remembered, if outlived,
As Freezing persons, recollect the Snow—
First—Chill—then Stupor—then the letting go—

441

This is my letter to the World
That never wrote to Me—
The simple News that Nature told—
With tender Majesty

Her Message is committed
To Hands I cannot see—
For love of Her—Sweet—countrymen—
Judge tenderly—of Me

465

I heard a Fly buzz—when I died—
The Stillness in the Room
Was like the Stillness in the Air—
Between the Heaves of Storm—

The Eyes around—had wrung them dry—
And Breaths were gathering firm
For that last Onset—when the King
Be witnessed—in the Room—

I willed my Keepsakes—Signed away
What portions of me be
Assignable—and then it was
There interposed a Fly—

With Blue—uncertain stumbling Buzz—
Between the light—and me—
And then the Windows failed—and then
I could not see to see—

516

Beauty—be not caused—It Is—
Chase it, and it ceases—
Chase it not, and it abides—

Overtake the Creases

In the Meadow—when the Wind
Runs his fingers thro' it—
Deity will see to it
That You never do it—

697

I could bring You Jewels—had I a mind to—
But You have enough—of those—
I could bring You Odors from St. Domingo—
Colors—from Vera Cruz—

Berries of the Bahamas—have I—
But this little Blaze
Flickering to itself—in the Meadow—
Suits Me—more than those—

Never a Fellow matched this Topaz—
And his Emerald Swing—
Dower itself—for Bobadilo—
Better—Could I bring?

712

Because I could not stop for Death—
He kindly stopped for me—
The Carriage held but just Ourselves—
And Immortality.

We slowly drove—He knew no haste
And I had put away
My labor and my leisure too,
For His Civility—

We passed the School, where Children strove
At Recess—in the Ring—
We passed the Fields of Gazing Grain—
We passed the Setting Sun—

Or rather—He passed Us—
The Dews drew quivering and chill—
For only Gossamer, my Gown—
My Tippet—only Tulle—

We paused before a House that seemed
A Swelling of the Ground—
The Roof was scarcely visible—
The Cornice—in the Ground—

Since then—'tis Centuries—and yet
Feels shorter than the Day
I first surmised the Horses' Heads
Were toward Eternity—

844

Spring is the Period
Express from God.
Among the other seasons
Himself abide,

But during March and April
None stir abroad
Without a cordial interview
With God.

970

Color—Caste—Denomination—
These—are Time's Affair—
Death's diviner Classifying
Does not know they are—

As in sleep—All Hue forgotten—
Tenets—put behind—
Death's large—Democratic fingers
Rub away the Brand—

If Circassian—He is careless—
If He put away
Chrysalis of Blonde—or Umber—
Equal Butterfly—

They emerge from His Obscuring—
What Death—knows so well—
Our minuter intuitions—
Deem unplausible—

986

A narrow Fellow in the Grass
Occasionally rides—
You may have met Him—did you not
His notice sudden is—

The Grass divides as with a Comb—
A spotted shaft is seen—
And then it closes at your feet
And opens further on—

He likes a Boggy Acre
A Floor too cool for Corn—
Yet when A Boy, and Barefoot—
I more than once at Noon
Have passed, I thought, a Whip lash
Unbraiding in the Sun
When stooping to secure it
It wrinkled, and was gone—

Several of Nature's People
I know, and they know me—
I feel for them a transport
Of cordiality—

But never met this Fellow
Attended, or alone
Without a tighter breathing
And Zero at the Bone—

1052

I never saw a Moor—
I never saw the Sea—
Yet know I how the Heather looks
And what a Billow be.

I never spoke with God
Nor visited in Heaven—
Yet certain am I of the spot
As if the Checks were given—

1129

Tell all the Truth but tell it slant—
Success in Circuit lies
Too bright for our infirm Delight
The Truth's superb surprise

As Lightning to the Children eased
With explanation kind
The Truth must dazzle gradually
Or every man be blind—

1263

There is no Frigate like a Book
To take us Lands away
Nor any Coursers like a Page
Of prancing Poetry—
This Traverse may the poorest take
Without oppress of Toll—
How frugal is the Chariot
That bears the Human soul.

1274

The Bone that has no Marrow,
What Ultimate for that?
It is not fit for Table
For Beggar or for Cat.

A Bone has obligations—
A Being has the same—
A Marrowless Assembly
Is culpabler than shame.

But how shall finished Creatures
A function fresh obtain?
Old Nicodemus' Phantom
Confronting us again!

1333

A little Madness in the Spring
Is wholesome even for the King,
But God be with the Clown—
Who ponders this tremendous scene—
This whole Experiment of Green—
As if it were his own!

1659

Fame is a fickle food
Upon a shifting plate
Whose table once a
Guest but not
The second time is set.

Whose crumbs the crows inspect
And with ironic caw
Flap past it to the Farmer's Corn—
Men eat of it and die.

EDGAR LEE MASTERS

(1868–1950)

From *Spoon River Anthology*

The Hill

Where are Elmer, Herman, Bert, Tom and Charley,
The weak of will, the strong of arm, the clown, the boozer, the fighter?
All, all, are sleeping on the hill.

One passed in a fever,
One was burned in a mine,
One was killed in a brawl,
One died in a jail,
One fell from a bridge toiling for children and wife—
All, all are sleeping, sleeping, sleeping on the hill.

Where are Ella, Kate, Mag, Lizzie and Edith,
The tender heart, the simple soul, the loud, the proud, the happy one?—
All, all, are sleeping on the hill.

One died in shameful child-birth,
One of a thwarted love,
One at the hands of a brute in a brothel,
One of a broken pride, in the search for heart's desire,
One after life in far-away London and Paris
Was brought to her little space by Ella and Kate and Mag—
All, all are sleeping, sleeping, sleeping on the hill.

Where are Uncle Isaac and Aunt Emily,
And old Towny Kincaid and Sevigne Houghton,
And Major Walker who had talked
With venerable men of the revolution?—
All, all, are sleeping on the hill.

They brought them dead sons from the war,
And daughters whom life had crushed,
And their children fatherless, crying—
All, all are sleeping, sleeping, sleeping on the hill.

Where is Old Fiddler Jones
Who played with life all his ninety years,
Braving the sleet with bared breast,
Drinking, rioting, thinking neither of wife nor kin,
Nor gold, nor love, nor heaven?
Lo! he babbles of the fish-frys of long ago,
Of the horse-races of long ago at Clary's Grove,
Of what Abe Lincoln said
One time at Springfield.

Fiddler Jones

The earth keeps some vibration going
There in your heart, and that is you.
And if the people find you can fiddle,
Why, fiddle you must, for all your life.
What do you see, a harvest of clover?
Or a meadow to walk through to the river?
The wind's in the corn; you rub your hands
For beeves hereafter ready for market;
Or else you hear the rustle of skirts
Like the girls when dancing at Little Grove.
To Cooney Potter a pillar of dust
Or whirling leaves meant ruinous drouth;
They looked to me like Red-Head Sammy
Stepping it off, to "Toor-a-Loor."

How could I till my forty acres
Not to speak of getting more,
With a medley of horns, bassoons and piccolos
Stirred in my brain by crows and robins
And the creak of a wind-mill—only these?
And I never started to plow in my life
That some one did not stop in the road
And take me away to a dance or picnic.
I ended up with forty acres;
I ended up with a broken fiddle—
And a broken laugh, and a thousand memories,
And not a single regret.

Petit, the Poet

Seeds in a dry pod, tick, tick, tick,
Tick, tick, tick, like mites in a quarrel—
Faint iambics that the full breeze wakens—
But the pine tree makes a symphony thereof.
Triolets, villanelles, rondels, rondeaus,
Ballades by the score with the same old thought:
The snows and the roses of yesterday are vanished;
And what is love but a rose that fades?
Life all around me here in the village:
Tragedy, comedy, valor and truth,
Courage, constancy, heroism, failure—
All in the loom, and oh what patterns!
Woodlands, meadows, streams and rivers—
Blind to all of it all my life long.
Triolets, villanelles, rondels, rondeaus,
Seeds in a dry pod, tick, tick, tick,
Tick, tick, tick, what little iambics,
While Homer and Whitman roared in the pines?

From *The New Spoon River*

Marx the Sign Painter

When Spoon River became a ganglion
For the monster brain Chicago
These were the signs I painted, which showed
What ruled America:
Vote for Patrick Kelly and save taxes;
I am for men, and this is the cigar;
This generation shall not see death,
Hear Pastor Valentine;
Eat Healthina and live;
Chew Floss's gum and keep your teeth;
Twenty-five dollars for a complete funeral;
Insure your life;
Three per cent. for your money;
Come to the automat.
And if there is any evidence
Of a civilization better,
I'd like to see the signs.

Unknown Soldiers

Stranger! Tell the people of Spoon River two things:
First that we lie here, obeying their words;
And next that had we known what was back of their words
We should not be lying here!

EDWIN ARLINGTON ROBINSON
(1869–1935)

Richard Cory

Whenever Richard Cory went downtown,
  We people on the pavement looked at him:
He was a gentleman from sole to crown,
  Clean favored, and imperially slim.

And he was always quietly arrayed,
  And he was always human when he talked;
But still he fluttered pulses when he said,
  "Good morning," and he glittered when he walked.

And he was rich—yes, richer than a king,
  And admirably schooled in every grace:
In fine, we thought that he was everything
  To make us wish that we were in his place.

So on we worked, and waited for the light,
  And went without the meat, and cursed the bread;
And Richard Cory, one calm summer night,
  Went home and put a bullet through his head.

Miniver Cheevy

Miniver Cheevy, child of scorn,
  Grew lean while he assailed the seasons;
He wept that he was ever born,
  And he had reasons.

Miniver loved the days of old
  When swords were bright and steeds were prancing;
The vision of a warrior bold
  Would set him dancing.

Miniver sighed for what was not,
  And dreamed, and rested from his labors;
He dreamed of Thebes and Camelot,
  And Priam's neighbors.

Miniver mourned the ripe renown
  That made so many a name so fragrant;
He mourned Romance, now on the town,
  And Art, a vagrant.

Miniver loved the Medici,
  Albeit he had never seen one;
He would have sinned incessantly
  Could he have been one.

Miniver cursed the commonplace
  And eyed a khaki suit with loathing;
He missed the mediaeval grace
  Of iron clothing.

Miniver scorned the gold he sought,
  But sore annoyed was he without it;
Miniver thought, and thought, and thought,
  And thought about it.

Miniver Cheevy, born too late,
  Scratched his head and kept on thinking;
Miniver coughed, and called it fate,
  And kept on drinking.

Reuben Bright

Because he was a butcher and thereby
Did earn an honest living (and did right),
I would not have you think that Reuben Bright
Was any more a brute than you or I;
For when they told him that his wife must die,
He stared at them, and shook with grief and fright,
And cried like a great baby half the night,
And made the women cry to see him cry.

And after she was dead, and he had paid
The singers and the sexton and the rest,
He packed a lot of things that she had made
Most mournfully away in an old chest
Of hers, and put some chopped-up cedar boughs
In with them, and tore down the slaughterhouse.

George Crabbe

Give him the darkest inch your shelf allows,
Hide him in lonely garrets, if you will,—
But his hard, human pulse is throbbing still
With the sure strength that fearless truth endows.
In spite of all fine science disavows,
Of his plain excellence and stubborn skill
There yet remains what fashion cannot kill,
Though years have thinned the laurel from his brows.

Whether or not we read him, we can feel
From time to time the vigor of his name
Against us like a finger for the shame
And emptiness of what our souls reveal
In books that are as altars where we kneel
To consecrate the flicker, not the flame.

Credo

I cannot find my way: there is no star
In all the shrouded heavens anywhere;
And there is not a whisper in the air
Of any living voice but one so far
That I can hear it only as a bar
Of lost, imperial music, played when fair
And angel fingers wove, and unaware,
Dead leaves to garlands where no roses are.

No, there is not a glimmer, nor a call,
For one that welcomes, welcomes when he fears,
The black and awful chaos of the night;
For through it all—above, beyond it all—
I know the far-sent message of the years,
I feel the coming glory of the Light.

Mr. Flood's Party

Old Eben Flood, climbing alone one night
Over the hill between the town below
And the forsaken upland hermitage
That held as much as he should ever know
On earth again of home, paused warily.
The road was his with not a native near;
And Eben, having leisure, said aloud,
For no man else in Tilbury Town to hear:

"Well, Mr. Flood, we have the harvest moon
Again, and we may not have many more;
The bird is on the wing, the poet says,
And you and I have said it here before.

Drink to the bird." He raised up to the light
The jug that he had gone so far to fill,
And answered huskily: "Well, Mr. Flood,
Since you propose it, I believe I will."

Alone, as if enduring to the end
A valiant armor of sacred hopes outworn,
He stood there in the middle of the road
Like Roland's ghost winding a silent horn.
Below him, in the town among the trees,
Where friends of other days had honored him,
A phantom salutation of the dead
Rang thinly till old Eben's eyes were dim.

Then, as a mother lays her sleeping child
Down tenderly, fearing it may awake,
He set the jug down slowly at his feet
With trembling care, knowing that most things break;
And only when assured that on firm earth
It stood, as the uncertain lives of men
Assuredly did not, he paced away,
And with his hand extended paused again:

"Well, Mr, Flood, we have not met like this
In a long time; and many a change has come
To both of us, I fear, since last it was
We had a drop together. Welcome home!"
Convivially returning with himself,
Again he raised the jug up to the light;
And with an acquiescent quaver said:
"Well, Mr. Flood, if you insist, I might.

"Only a very little, Mr. Flood—
For auld lang syne. No more, sir; that will do."
So, for the time, apparently it did,
And Eben evidently thought so too;
For soon amid the silver loneliness
Of night he lifted up his voice and sang,
Secure, with only two moons listening,
Until the whole harmonious landscape rang—

"For auld lang syne." The weary throat gave out,
The last word wavered; and the song being done,
He raised again the jug regretfully
And shook his head, and was again alone.
There was not much that was ahead of him,
And there was nothing in the town below—
Where strangers would have shut the many doors
That many friends had opened long ago.

Eros Turannos

She fears him, and will always ask
  What fated her to choose him;
She meets in his engaging mask
  All reasons to refuse him;
But what she meets and what she fears
Are less than are the downward years,
Drawn slowly to the foamless weirs
  Of age, were she to lose him.

Between a blurred sagacity
  That once had power to sound him,
And Love, that will not let him be
  The Judas that she found him,
Her pride assuages her almost,
As if it were alone the cost.—
He sees that he will not be lost,
  And waits and looks around him.

A sense of ocean and old trees
  Envelops and allures him;
Tradition, touching all he sees,
  Beguiles and reassures him;
And all her doubts of what he says
Are dimmed with what she knows of days—
Till even prejudice delays
  And fades, and she secures him.

The falling leaf inaugurates
  The reign of her confusion;
The pounding wave reverberates
  The dirge of her illusion;
And home, where passion lived and died,
Becomes a place where she can hide,
While all the town and harbor side
  Vibrate with her seclusion.

We tell you, tapping on our brows,
  The story as it should be,—
As if the story of a house
  Were told, or ever could be;
We'll have no kindly veil between
Her visions and those we have seen,—
As if we guessed what hers have been,
  Or what they are or would be.

Meanwhile we do no harm; for they
  That with a god have striven,
Not hearing much of what we say,
  Take what the god has given;
Though like waves breaking it may be
Or like a changed familiar tree,
Or like a stairway to the sea
  Where down the blind are driven.

Charles Carville's Eyes

A melancholy face Charles Carville had,
But not so melancholy as it seemed,
When once you knew him, for his mouth redeemed
His insufficient eyes, forever sad:
In them there was no life-glimpse, good or bad,
Nor joy nor passion in them ever gleamed;
His mouth was all of him that ever beamed,
His eyes were sorry, but his mouth was glad.

He never was a fellow that said much,
And half of what he did say was not heard
By many of us: we were out of touch
With all his whims and all his theories
Till he was dead, so those blank eyes of his
Might speak them. Then we heard them, every word.

The Sheaves

Where long the shadows of the wind had rolled,
Green wheat was yielding to the change assigned;
And as by some vast magic undivined
The world was turning slowly into gold.
Like nothing that was ever bought or sold
It waited there, the body and the mind:
And with a mighty meaning of a kind
That tells the more the more it is not told.

So in a land where all days are not fair,
Fair days went on till on another day
A thousand golden sheaves were lying there,
Shining and still, but not for long to stay—
As if a thousand girls with golden hair
Might rise from where they slept and go away.

The Miller's Wife

The miller's wife had waited long,
  The tea was cold, the fire was dead;
And there might yet be nothing wrong
  In how he went and what he said:
"There are no millers any more,"
  Was all that she had heard him say;
And he had lingered at the door
  So long that it seemed yesterday.

Sick with a fear that had no form
  She knew that she was there at last;
And in the mill there was a warm
  And mealy fragrance of the past.
What else there was would only seem
  To say again what he had meant;
And what was hanging from a beam
  Would not have heeded where she went.

And if she thought it followed her,
  She may have reasoned in the dark
That one way of the few there were
  Would hide her and would leave no mark:
Black water, smooth above the weir
  Like starry velvet in the night,
Though ruffled once, would soon appear
  The same as ever to the sight.

New England

Here where the wind is always north-northeast
And children learn to walk on frozen toes,
Wonder begets an envy of all those
Who boil elsewhere with such a lyric yeast
Of love that you will hear them at a feast
Where demons would appeal for some repose,
Still clamoring where the chalice overflows
And crying wildest who have drunk the least.

Passion is here a soilure of the wits,
We're told, and Love a cross for them to bear;
Joy shivers in the corner where she knits
And Conscience always has the rocking chair,
Cheerful as when she tortured into fits
The first cat that was ever killed by Care.

STEPHEN CRANE
(1871–1900)

A God in Wrath

A god in wrath
Was beating a man;
He cuffed him loudly
With thunderous blows
That rang and rolled over the earth.
All people came running.
The man screamed and struggled,
And bit madly at the feet of the god.
The people cried,
"Ah, what a wicked man!"
And—
"Ah, what a redoubtable god!"

In the Desert

In the desert
I saw a creature, naked, bestial,
Who, squatting upon the ground,
Held his heart in his hands,
And ate of it.
I said, "Is it good, friend?"
"It is bitter—bitter," he answered,
"But I like it
Because it is bitter,
And because it is my heart."

Many Workmen

Many workmen
Built a huge ball of masonry
Upon a mountaintop.
Then they went to the valley below,
And turned to behold their work.
"It is grand," they said;
They loved the thing.

Of a sudden, it moved:
It came upon them swiftly;
It crushed them all to blood.
But some had opportunity to squeal.

Behold, the Grave

Behold, the grave of a wicked man,
And near it, a stern spirit.

There came a drooping maid with violets,
But the spirit grasped her arm.
"No flowers for him," he said.
The maid wept:
"Ah, I loved him."
But the spirit, grim and frowning:
"No flowers for him."

Now, this is it—
If the spirit was just,
Why did the maid weep?

Black Riders Came from the Sea

Black riders came from the sea.
There was clang and clang of spear and shield,
And clash and clash of hoof and heel,
Wild shouts and the wave of hair
In the rush upon the wind:
Thus the ride of Sin.

A Man Said to the Universe

A man said to the universe:
"Sir, I exist!"
"However," replied the universe,
"The fact has not created in me
A sense of obligation."

Many Red Devils

Many red devils ran from my heart
And out upon the page.
They were so tiny
The pen could mash them.
And many struggled in the ink.
It was strange
To write in this red muck
Of things from my heart.

War Is Kind

Do not weep, maiden, for war is kind.
Because your lover threw wild hands toward the sky
And the affrighted steed ran on alone,
Do not weep.
War is kind.

Hoarse, booming drums of the regiment,
Little souls who thirst for fight,
These men were born to drill and die.
The unexplained glory flies above them,
Great is the battle god, great, and his kingdom—
A field where a thousand corpses lie.

Do not weep, babe, for war is kind.
Because your father tumbled in the yellow trenches,
Raged at his breast, gulped and died,
Do not weep.
War is kind.

Swift blazing flag of the regiment,
Eagle with crest of red and gold,
These men were born to drill and die.
Point for them the virtue of slaughter,
Make plain to them the excellence of killing
And a field where a thousand corpses lie.

Mother whose heart hung humble as a button
On the bright splendid shroud of your son,
Do not weep.
War is kind.

ROBERT FROST
(1874–1963)

The Road Not Taken

Two roads diverged in a yellow wood,
And sorry I could not travel both
And be one traveler, long I stood
And looked down one as far as I could
To where it bent in the undergrowth;

Then took the other, as just as fair,
And having perhaps the better claim,
Because it was grassy and wanted wear;
Though as for that the passing there
Had worn them really about the same,

And both that morning equally lay
In leaves no step had trodden black.
Oh, I kept the first for another day!
Yet knowing how way leads on to way,
I doubted if I should ever come back.

I shall be telling this with a sigh
Somewhere ages and ages hence:
Two roads diverged in a wood, and I—
I took the one less traveled by,
And that has made all the difference.

Mending Wall

Something there is that doesn't love a wall,
That sends the frozen-ground-swell under it,
And spills the upper boulders in the sun,
And makes gaps even two can pass abreast.
The work of hunters is another thing:
I have come after them and made repair
Where they have left not one stone on a stone,
But they would have the rabbit out of hiding,
To please the yelping dogs. The gaps I mean,
No one has seen them made or heard them made,
But at spring mending-time we find them there.
I let my neighbor know beyond the hill;
And on a day we meet to walk the line
And set the wall between us once again.
We keep the wall between us as we go.
To each the boulders that have fallen to each.
And some are loaves and some so nearly balls
We have to use a spell to make them balance:
"Stay where you are until our backs are turned!"
We wear our fingers rough with handling them.
Oh, just another kind of outdoor game,
One on a side. It comes to little more:
There where it is we do not need the wall:
He is all pine and I am apple orchard.
My apple trees will never get across
And eat the cones under his pines, I tell him.
He only says, "Good fences make good neighbors."
Spring is the mischief in me, and I wonder
If I could put a notion in his head:
"*Why* do they make good neighbors? Isn't it
Where there are cows? But here there are no cows.
Before I built a wall I'd ask to know
What I was walling in or walling out,
And to whom I was like to give offense.
Something there is that doesn't love a wall,

That wants it down." I could say "Elves" to him,
But it's not elves exactly, and I'd rather
He said it for himself. I see him there
Bringing a stone grasped firmly by the top
In each hand, like an old-stone savage armed.
He moves in darkness as it seems to me,
Not of woods only and the shade of trees.
He will not go behind his father's saying,
And he likes having thought of it so well
He says again, "Good fences make good neighbors."

After Apple Picking

My long two-pointed ladder's sticking through a tree
Toward heaven still,
And there's a barrel that I didn't fill
Beside it, and there may be two or three
Apples I didn't pick upon some bough.
But I am done with apple picking now.
Essence of winter sleep is on the night,
The scent of apples: I am drowsing off.
I cannot rub the strangeness from my sight
I got from looking through a pane of glass
I skimmed this morning from the drinking trough
And held against the world of hoary grass.
It melted, and I let it fall and break.
But I was well
Upon my way to sleep before it fell,
And I could tell
What form my dreaming was about to take.
Magnified apples appear and disappear
Stem end and blossom end,
And every fleck of russet showing clear.
My instep arch not only keeps the ache,
It keeps the pressure of a ladder round.
I feel the ladder sway as the boughs bend.
And I keep hearing from the cellar bin
The rumbling sound
Of load on load of apples coming in.

For I have had too much
Of apple picking: I am overtired
Of the great harvest I myself desired.
There were ten thousand thousand fruit to touch,
Cherish in hand, lift down, and not let fall.
For all
That struck the earth,
No matter if not bruised or spiked with stubble,
Went surely to the cider-apple heap
As of no worth.
One can see what will trouble
This sleep of mine, whatever sleep it is.
Were he not gone,
The woodchuck could say whether it's like his
Long sleep, as I describe its coming on,
Or just some human sleep.

Birches

When I see birches bend to left and right
Across the lines of straighter darker trees,
I like to think some boy's been swinging them.
But swinging doesn't bend them down to stay
As ice storms do. Often you must have seen them
Loaded with ice a sunny winter morning
After a rain. They click upon themselves
As the breeze rises, and turn many-colored
As the stir cracks and crazes their enamel.
Soon the sun's warmth makes them shed crystal shells
Shattering and avalanching on the snow crust—
Such heaps of broken glass to sweep away
You'd think the inner dome of heaven had fallen.
They are dragged to the withered bracken by the load,
And they seem not to break; though once they are bowed
So low for long, they never right themselves:
You may see their trunks arching in the woods
Years afterwards, trailing their leaves on the ground
Like girls on hands and knees that throw their hair
Before them over their heads to dry in the sun.

But I was going to say when Truth broke in
With all her matter of fact about the ice storm,
I should prefer to have some boy bend them
As he went out and in to fetch the cows—
Some boy too far from town to learn baseball,
Whose only play was what he found himself,
Summer or winter, and could play alone.
One by one he subdued his father's trees
By riding them down over and over again
Until he took the stiffness out of them,
And not one but hung limp, not one was left
For him to conquer. He learned all there was
To learn about not launching out too soon
And so not carrying the tree away
Clear to the ground. He always kept his poise
To the top branches, climbing carefully
With the same pains you use to fill a cup
Up to the brim, and even above the brim.
Then he flung outward, feet first, with a swish,
Kicking his way down through the air to the ground.
So was I once myself a swinger of birches.
And so I dream of going back to be.
It's when I'm weary of considerations,
And life is too much like a pathless wood
Where your face burns and tickles with the cobwebs
Broken across it, and one eye is weeping
From a twig's having lashed across it open.
I'd like to get away from earth awhile
And then come back to it and begin over.
May no fate willfully misunderstand me
And half grant what I wish and snatch me away
Not to return. Earth's the right place for love:
I don't know where it's likely to go better.
I'd like to go by climbing a birch tree,
And climb black branches up a snow-white trunk
Toward heaven, till the tree could bear no more,
But dipped its top and set me down again.
That would be good both going and coming back.
One could do worse than be a swinger of birches.

Home Burial

He saw her from the bottom of the stairs
Before she saw him. She was starting down,
Looking back over her shoulder at some fear.
She took a doubtful step and then undid it
To raise herself and look again. He spoke
Advancing toward her: "What is it you see
From up there always?—for I want to know."
She turned and sank upon her skirts at that,
And her face changed from terrified to dull.
He said to gain time: "What is it you see?"
Mounting until she cowered under him.
"I will find out now—you must tell me, dear."
She, in her place, refused him any help,
With the least stiffening of her neck and silence.
She let him look, sure that he wouldn't see,
Blind creature; and awhile he didn't see.
But at last he murmured, "Oh," and again, "Oh."

"What is it—what?" she said.

"Just that I see."

"You don't," she challenged. "Tell me what it is."

"The wonder is I didn't see at once.
I never noticed it from here before.
I must be wonted to it—that's the reason.
The little graveyard where my people are!
So small the window frames the whole of it.
Not so much larger than a bedroom, is it?
There are three stones of slate and one of marble,
Broad-shouldered little slabs there in the sunlight
On the sidehill. We haven't to mind *those.*

But I understand: it is not the stones,
But the child's mound——"

"Don't, don't, don't, don't," she cried.

She withdrew, shrinking from beneath his arm
That rested on the banister, and slid downstairs;
And turned on him with such a daunting look,
He said twice over before he knew himself:
"Can't a man speak of his own child he's lost?"

"Not you!—Oh, where's my hat? Oh, I don't need it!
I must get out of here. I must get air.—
I don't know rightly whether any man can."

"Amy! Don't go to someone else this time.
Listen to me. I won't come down the stairs."
He sat and fixed his chin between his fists.
"There's something I should like to ask you, dear."

"You don't know how to ask it."

"Help me, then."

Her fingers moved the latch for all reply.

"My words are nearly always an offense.
I don't know how to speak of anything
So as to please you. But I might be taught,
I should suppose. I can't say I see how.
A man must partly give up being a man
With womenfolk. We could have some arrangement
By which I'd bind myself to keep hands off
Anything special you're a-mind to name.
Though I don't like such things 'twixt those that love.
Two that don't love can't live together without them.
But two that do can't live together with them."
She moved the latch a little. "Don't—don't go.
Don't carry it to someone else this time.
Tell me about it if it's something human.

Let me into your grief. I'm not so much
Unlike other folks as your standing there
Apart would make me out. Give me my chance.
I do think, though, you overdo it a little.
What was it brought you up to think it the thing
To take your mother-loss of a first child
So inconsolably—in the face of love.
You'd think his memory might be satisfied——"

"There you go sneering now!"

"I'm not, I'm not!
You make me angry. I'll come down to you.
God, what a woman! And it's come to this,
A man can't speak of his own child that's dead."

"You can't because you don't know how to speak.
If you had any feelings, you that dug
With your own hand—how could you?—his little grave;
I saw you from that very window there,
Making the gravel leap and leap in air,
Leap up, like that, like that, and land so lightly
And roll back down the mound beside the hole.
I thought, Who is that man? I didn't know you.
And I crept down the stairs and up the stairs
To look again, and still your spade kept lifting.
Then you came in. I heard your rumbling voice
Out in the kitchen, and I don't know why,
But I went near to see with my own eyes.
You could sit there with the stains on your shoes
Of the fresh earth from your own baby's grave
And talk about your everyday concerns.
You had stood the spade up against the wall
Outside there in the entry, for I saw it."

"I shall laugh the worst laugh I ever laughed.
I'm cursed. God, if I don't believe I'm cursed."

"I can repeat the very words you were saying:
'Three foggy mornings and one rainy day
Will rot the best birch fence a man can build.'

Think of it, talk like that at such a time!
What had how long it takes a birch to rot
To do with what was in the darkened parlor?
You *couldn't* care! The nearest friends can go
With anyone to death, comes so far short
They might as well not try to go at all.
No, from the time when one is sick to death,
One is alone, and he dies more alone.
Friends make pretense of following to the grave,
But before one is in it, their minds are turned
And making the best of their way back to life
And living people, and things they understand.
But the world's evil. I won't have grief so
If I can change it. Oh, I won't, I won't!"

"There, you have said it all and you feel better.
You won't go now. You're crying. Close the door.
The heart's gone out of it: why keep it up?
Amy! There's someone coming down the road!"

"*You*—oh, you think the talk is all. I must go—
Somewhere out of this house. How can I make you——"

"If—you—do!" She was opening the door wider.
"Where do you mean to go? First tell me that.
I'll follow and bring you back by force. I *will!*—"

Dust of Snow

The way a crow
Shook down on me
The dust of snow
From a hemlock tree

Has given my heart
A change of mood
And saved some part
Of a day I had rued.

The Silken Tent

She is as in a field a silken tent
At midday when a sunny summer breeze
Has dried the dew and all its ropes relent,
So that in guys it gently sways at ease,
And its supporting central cedar pole,
That is its pinnacle to heavenward
And signifies the sureness of the soul,
Seems to owe naught to any single cord,
But strictly held by none, is loosely bound
By countless silken ties of love and thought
To everything on earth the compass round,
And only by one's going slightly taut
In the capriciousness of summer air
Is of the slightest bondage made aware.

To Earthward

Love at the lips was touch
As sweet as I could bear;
And once that seemed too much;
I lived on air

That crossed me from sweet things,
The flow of—was it musk
From hidden grapevine springs
Downhill at dusk?

I had the swirl and ache
From sprays of honeysuckle
That when they're gathered shake
Dew on the knuckle.

I craved strong sweets, but those
Seemed strong when I was young;
The petal of the rose
It was that stung.

Now no joy but lacks salt
That is not dashed with pain
And weariness and fault;
I crave the stain

Of tears, the aftermark
Of almost too much love,
The sweet of bitter bark
And burning clove.

When stiff and sore and scarred
I take away my hand
From leaning on it hard
In grass and sand,

The hurt is not enough:
I long for weight and strength
To feel the earth as rough
To all my length.

Design

I found a dimpled spider, fat and white,
On a white heal-all, holding up a moth
Like a white piece of rigid satin cloth—
Assorted characters of death and blight
Mixed ready to begin the morning right,
Like the ingredients of a witches' broth—
A snow-drop spider, a flower like a froth,
And dead wings carried like a paper kite.

What had that flower to do with being white,
The wayside blue and innocent heal-all?
What brought the kindred spider to that height,
Then steered the white moth thither in the night?
What but design of darkness to appall?—
If design govern in a thing so small.

Neither Out Far nor In Deep

The people along the sand
All turn and look one way.
They turn their back on the land.
They look at the sea all day.

As long as it takes to pass
A ship keeps raising its hull;
The wetter ground like glass
Reflects a standing gull.

The land may vary more;
But wherever the truth may be—
The water comes ashore,
And the people look at the sea.

They cannot look out far.
They cannot look in deep.
But when was that ever a bar
To any watch they keep?

The Oven Bird

There is a singer everyone has heard,
Loud, a mid-summer and a mid-wood bird,
Who makes the solid tree trunks sound again.
He says that leaves are old and that for flowers
Mid-summer is to spring as one to ten.
He says the early petal-fall is past,
When pear and cherry bloom went down in showers
On sunny days a moment overcast;
And comes that other fall we name the fall.
He says the highway dust is over all.
The bird would cease and be as other birds
But that he knows in singing not to sing.
The question that he frames in all but words
Is what to make of a diminished thing.

Tree at My Window

Tree at my window, window tree,
My sash is lowered when night comes on;
But let there never be curtain drawn
Between you and me.

Vague dream head lifted out of the ground,
And thing next most diffuse to cloud,
Not all your light tongues talking aloud
Could be profound.

But tree, I have seen you taken and tossed,
And if you have seen me when I slept,
You have seen me when I was taken and swept
And all but lost.

That day she put our heads together,
Fate had her imagination about her,
Your head so much concerned with outer,
Mine with inner, weather.

Stopping by Woods on a Snowy Evening

Whose woods these are I think I know.
His house is in the village, though;
He will not see me stopping here
To watch his woods fill up with snow.

My little horse must think it queer
To stop without a farmhouse near
Between the woods and frozen lake
The darkest evening of the year.

He gives his harness bells a shake
To ask if there is some mistake.
The only other sound's the sweep
Of easy wind and downy flake.

The woods are lovely, dark, and deep,
But I have promises to keep,
And miles to go before I sleep,
And miles to go before I sleep.

Acquainted with the Night

I have been one acquainted with the night.
I have walked out in rain—and back in rain.
I have outwalked the furthest city light.

I have looked down the saddest city lane.
I have passed by the watchman on his beat
And dropped my eyes, unwilling to explain.

I have stood still and stopped the sound of feet
When far away an interrupted cry
Came over houses from another street,

But not to call me back or say good-by;
And further still at an unearthly height
One luminary clock against the sky

Proclaimed the time was neither wrong nor right.
I have been one acquainted with the night.

Desert Places

Snow falling and night falling fast, oh, fast
In a field I looked into going past,
And the ground almost covered smooth in snow,
But a few weeds and stubble showing last.

The woods around it have it—it is theirs.
All animals are smothered in their lairs.
I am too absent-spirited to count;
The loneliness includes me unawares.

And lonely as it is, that loneliness
Will be more lonely ere it will be less—
A blanker whiteness of benighted snow
With no expression, nothing to express.

They cannot scare me with their empty spaces
Between stars—on stars where no human race is.
I have it in me so much nearer home
To scare myself with my own desert places.

Provide, Provide

The witch that came (the withered hag)
To wash the steps with pail and rag
Was once the beauty Abishag,

The picture pride of Hollywood.
Too many fall from great and good
For you to doubt the likelihood.

Die early and avoid the fate.
Or if predestined to die late,
Make up your mind to die in state.

Make the whole stock exchange your own!
If need be occupy a throne,
Where nobody can call *you* crone.

Some have relied on what they knew,
Others on being simply true.
What worked for them might work for you.

No memory of having starred
Atones for later disregard
Or keeps the end from being hard.

Better to go down dignified
With boughten friendship at your side
Than none at all. Provide, provide!

Fire and Ice

Some say the world will end in fire,
Some say in ice.
From what I've tasted of desire
I hold with those who favor fire.
But if it had to perish twice,
I think I know enough of hate
To say that for destruction ice
Is also great
And would suffice.

Nothing Gold Can Stay

Nature's first green is gold,
Her hardest hue to hold.
Her early leaf's a flower;
But only so an hour.
Then leaf subsides to leaf.
So Eden sank to grief,
So dawn goes down to day.
Nothing gold can stay.

GERTRUDE STEIN
(1874–1946)

Susie Asado

Sweet sweet sweet sweet sweet tea.
    Susie Asado.
Sweet sweet sweet sweet sweet tea.
    Susie Asado.
Susie Asado which is a told tray sure.
A lean on the shoe this means slips slips hers.
When the ancient light grey is clean it is yellow, it is a silver seller.
This is a please this is a please there are the saids to jelly.
These are the wets these say the sets to leave a crown to Incy.
Incy is short for incubus.
A pot. A pot is a beginning of a rare bit of trees. Trees tremble, the old vats are in bobbles, bobbles which shade and shove and render clean, render clean must.
    Drink pups.
Drink pups drink pups lease a sash hold, see it shine and a bobolink has pins. It shows a nail.
What is a nail. A nail is unison.
Sweet sweet sweet sweet sweet tea.

Cézanne

The Irish lady can say, that to-day is every day. Caesar can say that every day is to-day and they say that every day is as they say.

In this way we have a place to stay and he was not met because he was settled to stay. When I said settled I meant settled to stay. When I said settled to stay I meant settled to stay Saturday. In this way a mouth is a mouth. In this way if in as a mouth if in as a mouth where, if in as a mouth where and there. Believe they have water too. Believe they have that water too and blue when you see blue, is all blue precious too, is all that that is precious too is all that and they meant to absolve you. In this way Cézanne nearly did nearly in this way. Cézanne nearly did nearly did and nearly did. And was I surprised. Was I very surprised. Was I surprised. I was surprised and in that patient, are you patient when you find bees. Bees in a garden make a specialty of honey and so does honey. Honey and prayer. Honey and there. There where the grass can grow nearly four times yearly.

from *Four Saints in Three Acts*

Pigeons on the grass alas.

Pigeons on the grass alas.

Short longer grass short longer longer shorter yellow grass. Pigeons large pigeons on the shorter longer yellow grass alas pigeons on the grass.

If they were not pigeons what were they.

If they were not pigeons on the grass alas what were they. He had heard of a third and he asked about it it was a magpie in the sky. If a magpie in the sky on the sky can not cry if the pigeon on the grass alas can alas and to pass the pigeon on the grass alas and the magpie in the sky on the sky and to try and to try alas on the grass alas the pigeon on the grass the pigeon on the grass and alas. They might be very well they might be very well very well they might be.

Let Lucy Lily Lily Lucy Lucy let Lucy Lucy Lily Lily Lily Lily Lily let Lily Lucy Lucy let Lily. Let Lucy Lily.

CARL SANDBURG
(1878–1967)

Fog

The fog comes
on little cat feet.

It sits looking
over harbor and city
on silent haunches
and then moves on.

Cool Tombs

When Abraham Lincoln was shoveled into the tombs, he forgot the copperheads and the assassin . . . in the dust, in the cool tombs.

And Ulysses Grant lost all thought of con men and Wall Street, cash and collateral turned ashes . . . in the dust, in the cool tombs.

Pocahontas' body, lovely as a poplar, sweet as a red haw in November or a pawpaw in May, did she wonder? Does she remember? . . . in the dust, in the cool tombs?

Take any streetful of people buying clothes and groceries, cheering a hero or throwing confetti and blowing tin horns . . . tell me if the lovers are losers . . . tell me if any get more than the lovers . . . in the dust . . . in the cool tombs.

The Harbor

Passing through huddled and ugly walls
By doorways where women
Looked from their hunger-deep eyes,
Haunted with shadows of hunger-hands,
Out from the huddled and ugly walls,
I came sudden, at the city's edge,
On a blue burst of lake,
Long lake waves breaking under the sun
On a spray-flung curve of shore;
And a fluttering storm of gulls,
Masses of great gray wings
And flying white bellies
Veering and wheeling free in the open.

Chicago

Hog Butcher for the World,
Tool Maker, Stacker of Wheat,
Player with Railroads and the Nation's Freight Handler;
Stormy, husky, brawling,
City of the Big Shoulders:

They tell me you are wicked and I believe them, for I have seen your painted women under the gas lamps luring the farm boys.
And they tell me you are crooked and I answer: Yes, it is true I have seen the gunman kill and go free to kill again.
And they tell me you are brutal and my reply is: On the faces of women and children I have seen the marks of wanton hunger.
And having answered so I turn once more to those who sneer at this my city, and I give them back the sneer and say to them:
Come and show me another city with lifted head singing so proud to be alive and coarse and strong and cunning.
Flinging magnetic curses amid the toil of piling job on job, here is a tall bold slugger set vivid against the little soft cities;
Fierce as a dog with tongue lapping for action, cunning as a savage pitted against the wilderness,
Bareheaded,
Shoveling,
Wrecking,
Planning,
Building, breaking, rebuilding,
Under the smoke, dust all over his mouth, laughing with white teeth,
Under the terrible burden of destiny laughing as a young man laughs,
Laughing even as an ignorant fighter laughs who has never lost a battle,
Bragging and laughing that under his wrist is the pulse, and under his ribs the heart of the people,
Laughing!
Laughing the stormy, husky, brawling laughter of Youth, half-naked, sweating, proud to be Hog Butcher, Tool Maker, Stacker of Wheat, Player with Railroads and Freight Handler to the Nation.

I Am the People, the Mob

I am the people—the mob—the crowd—the mass.
Do you know that all the great work of the world is done through me?
I am the workingman, the inventor, the maker of the world's food and clothes.
I am the audience that witnesses history. The Napoleons come from me and the Lincolns. They die. And then I send forth more Napoleons and Lincolns.
I am the seed ground. I am a prairie that will stand for much plowing. Terrible storms pass over me. I forget. The best of me is sucked out and wasted. I forget. Everything but Death comes to me and makes me work and give up what I have. And I forget.
Sometimes I growl, shake myself and spatter a few red drops for history to remember. Then—I forget.
When I, the People, learn to remember, when I, the People, use the lessons of yesterday and no longer forget who robbed me last year, who played me for a fool—then there will be no speaker in all the world say the name: "The People," with any fleck of a sneer in his voice or any far-off smile of derision.
The mob—the crowd—the mass—will arrive then.

VACHEL LINDSAY
(1879–1931)

Simon Legree—A Negro Sermon

(To be read in your own variety of Negro dialect)

Legree's big house was white and green.
His cotton fields were the best to be seen.
He had strong horses and opulent cattle,
And bloodhounds bold, with chains that would rattle.
His garret was full of curious things:
Books of magic, bags of gold,
And rabbits' feet on long twine strings.
But he went down to the Devil.

Legree, he sported a brass-buttoned coat,
A snakeskin necktie, a blood-red shirt.
Legree he had a beard like a goat,
And a thick hairy neck, and eyes like dirt.
His puffed-out cheeks were fish-belly white,
He had great long teeth, and an appetite.
He ate raw meat, 'most every meal,
And rolled his eyes till the cat would squeal.
His fist was an enormous size
To mash poor niggers that told him lies:
He was surely a witchman in disguise.
But he went down to the Devil.

He wore hip boots, and would wade all day
To capture his slaves that had fled away.
But he went down to the Devil.

He beat poor Uncle Tom to death
Who prayed for Legree with his last breath.
Then Uncle Tom to Eva flew,
To the high sanctoriums bright and new;
And Simon Legree stared up beneath,
And cracked his heels, and ground his teeth:
And went down to the Devil.

He crossed the yard in the storm and gloom;
He went into his grand front room.
He said, "I liked him, and I don't care."
He kicked a hound, he gave a swear;
He tightened his belt, he took a lamp,
Went down cellar to the webs and damp.
There in the middle of the moldy floor
He heaved up a slab, he found a door—
And went down to the Devil.

His lamp blew out, but his eyes burned bright.
Simon Legree stepped down all night—
Down, down to the Devil.
Simon Legree he reached the place,
He saw one half of the human race,
He saw the Devil on a wide green throne,
Gnawing the meat from a big ham bone,
And he said to Mister Devil:
"I see that you have much to eat—
A red ham bone is surely sweet.
I see that you have lion's feet;
I see your frame is fat and fine,
I see you drink your poison wine—
Blood and burning turpentine."

And the Devil said to Simon Legree:
"I like your style, so wicked and free.
Come sit and share my throne with me,
And let us bark and revel."
And there they sit and gnash their teeth,
And each one wears a hop-vine wreath.

They are matching pennies and shooting craps,
They are playing poker and taking naps.
And old Legree is fat and fine:
He heats the fire, he drinks the wine—
Blood and burning turpentine—
Down, down with the Devil;
Down, down with the Devil;
Down, down with the Devil.

General William Booth Enters into Heaven

(To be sung to the tune of "The Blood of the Lamb" with indicated instrument.)

(Bass drum beaten loudly)
Booth led boldly with his big bass drum—
(Are you washed in the blood of the Lamb?)
The saints smiled gravely and they said: "He's come."
(Are you washed in the blood of the Lamb?)
Walking lepers followed, rank on rank,
Lurching bravos from the ditches dank,
Drabs from the alleyways and drug fiends pale—
Minds still passion-ridden, soul powers frail:—
Vermin-eaten saints with moldy breath,
Unwashed legions with the ways of death—
(Are you washed in the blood of the Lamb?)

(Banjos)
Every slum had sent its half a score
The round world over. (Booth had groaned for more.)
Every banner that the wide world flies
Bloomed with glory and transcendent dyes.
Big-voiced lasses made their banjos bang;
Tranced, fanatical they shrieked and sang:—
"Are you washed in the blood of the Lamb?"
Hallelujah! It was queer to see
Bull-necked convicts with that land make free.
Loons with trumpets blowed a blare, blare, blare
On, on upward thro' the golden air!
(Are you washed in the blood of the Lamb?)

(Bass drum slower and softer)
Booth died blind and still by faith he trod,
Eyes still dazzled by the ways of God.
Booth led boldly, and he looked the chief,
Eagle countenance in sharp relief,
Beard aflying, air of high command
Unabated in that holy land.

(Sweet flute music)
Jesus came from out the courthouse door,
Stretched his hands above the passing poor.
Booth saw not, but led his queer ones there
Round and round the mighty courthouse square.
Then, in an instant all that blear review
Marched on spotless, clad in raiment new.
The lame were straightened, withered limbs uncurled
And blind eyes opened on a new, sweet world.

(Bass drum louder)
Drabs and vixens in a flash made whole!
Gone was the weasel head, the snout, the jowl!
Sages and sibyls now, and athletes clean,
Rulers of empires, and of forests green!

(Grand chorus of all instruments. Tambourine to the foreground)
The hosts were sandaled, and their wings were fire!
(Are you washed in the blood of the Lamb?)
But their noise played havoc with the angel choir.
(Are you washed in the blood of the Lamb?)
Oh, shout salvation! It was good to see
Kings and princes by the Lamb set free.
The banjos rattled and the tambourines
Jing-jing-jingled in the hands of queens.

(Reverently sung, no instruments)
And when Booth halted by the curb for prayer
He saw his Master thro' the flag-filled air.
Christ came gently with a robe and crown
For Booth the soldier, while the throng knelt down.

He saw King Jesus. They were face to face,
And he knelt aweeping in that holy place.
Are you washed in the blood of the Lamb?

The Congo

A Study of the Negro Race

(Being a memorial to Ray Eldred, a Disciple missionary of the Congo River)

I. THEIR BASIC SAVAGERY

Fat black bucks in a wine-barrel room,
Barrel-house kings, with feet unstable,
A deep, rolling bass. Sagged and reeled and pounded on the table,
Pounded on the table,
Beat an empty barrel with the handle of a broom,
Hard as they were able,
Boom, boom, BOOM,
With a silk umbrella and the handle of a broom,
Boomlay, boomlay, boomlay, BOOM.
THEN I had religion, THEN I had a vision.
I could not turn from their revel in derision.
More deliberate. Solemnly chanted. THEN I SAW THE CONGO, CREEPING THROUGH THE BLACK,
CUTTING THROUGH THE FOREST WITH A GOLDEN TRACK.
Then along that riverbank
A thousand miles
Tattooed cannibals danced in files;
Then I heard the boom of the blood-lust song
A rapidly piling climax of speed and racket And a thigh bone beating on a tin-pan gong.
And "BLOOD" screamed the whistles and the fifes of the warriors,
"BLOOD" screamed the skull-faced, lean witch doctors,
"Whirl ye the deadly voodoo rattle,

Harry the uplands,
Steal all the cattle,
Rattle-rattle, rattle-rattle,
Bing.

With a philosophic pause.

Boomlay, boomlay, boomlay, BOOM,"
A roaring, epic, ragtime tune
From the mouth of the Congo
To the Mountains of the Moon.
Death is an elephant,
Torch-eyed and horrible,
Foam-flanked and terrible.

Shrilly and with a heavily accented meter.

BOOM, steal the pygmies,
BOOM, kill the Arabs,
BOOM, kill the white men,

Like the wind in the chimney.

Hoo, Hoo, Hoo.
Listen to the yell of Leopold's ghost
Burning in hell for his hand-maimed host.
Hear how the demons chuckle and yell
Cutting his hands off, down in hell.
Listen to the creepy proclamation,
Blown through the lairs of the forest nation,
Blown past the white ants' hill of clay,
Blown past the marsh where the butterflies play:—

All the "o" sounds very golden. Heavy accents very heavy. Light accents very light. Last line whispered.

"Be careful what you do,
Or Mumbo-Jumbo, god of the Congo,
And all of the other
Gods of the Congo,
Mumbo-Jumbo will hoo-doo you,
Mumbo-Jumbo will hoo-doo you,
Mumbo-Jumbo will hoo-doo you."

II. THEIR IRREPRESSIBLE HIGH SPIRITS

Rather shrill and high.

Wild crap shooters with a whoop and a call
Danced the juba in their gambling hall
And laughed fit to kill, and shook the town,
And guyed the policemen and laughed them down
With a boomlay, boomlay, boomlay, BOOM.

Read exactly as in first section.

THEN I SAW THE CONGO, CREEPING THROUGH THE BLACK
CUTTING THROUGH THE FOREST WITH A GOLDEN TRACK,

Lay emphasis on the delicate ideas. Keep as light-footed as possible.

A Negro fairyland swung into view,
A minstrel river
Where dreams come true.
The ebony palace soared on high
Through the blossoming trees to the evening sky.
The inlaid porches and casements shone
With gold and ivory and elephant bone.
And the black crowd laughed till their sides were sore
At the baboon butler in the agate door,
And the well-known tunes of the parrot band
That trilled on the bushes of that magic land.

With pomposity.

A troupe of skull-faced witchmen came
Through the agate doorway in suits of flame,
Yea, long-tailed coats with a gold-leaf crust
And hats that were covered with diamond dust.
And the crowd in the court gave a whoop and a call
And danced the juba from wall to wall.
But the witchmen suddenly stilled the throng

With a great deliberation and ghostliness. With overwhelming assurance, good cheer, and pomp.

With a stern cold glare, and a stern old song:—
"Mumbo-Jumbo will hoo-doo you." . . .
Just then from the doorway, as fat as shotes,
Came the cakewalk princes in their long red coats,
Canes with a brilliant lacquer shine,
And tall silk hats that were red as wine.
And they pranced with their butterfly partners there,

With growing speed and sharply marked dance rhythm.

Coal-black maidens with pearls in their hair,
Knee skirts trimmed with the jassamine sweet,
And bells on their ankles and little black feet.
And the couples railed at the chant and the frown
Of the witchmen lean, and laughed them down.
(Oh, rare was the revel, and well worth while,
That made those glowering witchmen smile.)
The cakewalk royalty then began
To walk for a cake that was tall as a man
To the tune of "Boomlay, boomlay, BOOM,"

With a touch of Negro dialect, and as rapidly as possible toward the end.

While the witchmen laughed with a sinister air,
And sang with the scalawags prancing there:—
"Walk with care, walk with care,
Or Mumbo-Jumbo, god of the Congo,

And all of the other gods of the Congo,
Mumbo-Jumbo will hoo-doo you.
Beware, beware, walk with care,
Boomlay, boomlay, boomlay, boom.
Boomlay, boomlay, boomlay, boom.
Boomlay, boomlay, boomlay, boom.
Boomlay, boomlay, boomlay, BOOM."

Slow philosophic calm.

(Oh, rare was the revel, and well worth while
That made those glowering witchmen smile.)

III. THE HOPE OF THEIR RELIGION

Heavy bass. With a literal imitation of camp-meeting racket, and trance.

A good old Negro in the slums of the town
Preached at a sister for her velvet gown.
Howled at a brother for his low-down ways,
His prowling, guzzling, sneak-thief days.
Beat on the Bible till he wore it out
Starting the jubilee revival shout.
And some had visions, as they stood on chairs,
And sang of Jacob, and the golden stairs,
And they all repented, a thousand strong
From their stupor and savagery and sin and wrong
And slammed with their hymnbooks till they shook the room
With "glory, glory, glory."
And "Boom, boom, BOOM."

Exactly as in the first section. Begin with terror and power, end with joy.

THEN I SAW THE CONGO, CREEPING THROUGH THE BLACK,
CUTTING THROUGH THE JUNGLE WITH A GOLDEN TRACK.
And the gray sky opened like a new-rent veil
And showed the apostles with their coats of mail.
In bright white steel they were seated round
And their fire eyes watched where the Congo wound.
And the twelve apostles, from their thrones on high
Thrilled all the forest with their heavenly cry:—

Sung to the tune of "Hark, ten thousand harps and voices."

"Mumbo-Jumbo will die in the jungle;
Never again will he hoo-doo you,
Never again will he hoo-doo you."

	Then along that river, a thousand miles
With growing deliberation and joy.	The vine-snared trees fell down in files. Pioneer angels cleared the way For a Congo paradise, for babes at play, For sacred capitals, for temples clean. Gone were the skull-faced witchmen lean.
In a rather high key—as delicately as possible.	There, where the wild ghost gods had wailed A million boats of the angels sailed With oars of silver, and prows of blue And silken pennants that the sun shone through. 'Twas a land transfigured, 'twas a new creation. Oh, a singing wind swept the Negro nation And on through the backwoods clearing flew:—
To the tune of "Hark, ten thousand harps and voices."	"Mumbo-Jumbo is dead in the jungle. Never again will he hoo-doo you. Never again will he hoo-doo you."
	Redeemed were the forests, the beasts and the men, And only the vulture dared again By the far, lone mountains of the moon To cry, in the silence, the Congo tune:—
Dying down into a penetrating, terrified whisper.	"Mumbo-Jumbo will hoo-doo you, Mumbo-Jumbo will hoo-doo you. Mumbo . . . Jumbo . . . will . . . hoo-doo . . . you."

Abraham Lincoln Walks at Midnight

(*In Springfield, Illinois*)

It is portentous, and a thing of state
That here at midnight, in our little town
A mourning figure walks, and will not rest,
Near the old courthouse pacing up and down,

Or by his homestead, or in shadowed yards
He lingers where his children used to play,
Or through the market, on the well-worn stones
He stalks until the dawn stars burn away.

A bronzed, lank man! His suit of ancient black,
A famous high top hat and plain worn shawl
Make him the quaint great figure that men love,
The prairie lawyer, master of us all.

He cannot sleep upon his hillside now.
He is among us—as in times before!
And we who toss and lie awake for long
Breathe deep, and start, to see him pass the door.

His head is bowed. He thinks on men and kings.
Yea, when the sick world cries, how can he sleep?
Too many peasants fight, they know not why,
Too many homesteads in black terror weep.

The sins of all the war lords burn his heart.
He sees the dreadnaughts scouring every main.
He carries on his shawl-wrapped shoulders now
The bitterness, the folly and the pain.

He cannot rest until a spirit-dawn
Shall come;—the shining hope of Europe free:
The league of sober folk, the Workers' Earth,
Bringing long peace to Cornland, Alp and Sea.

It breaks his heart that kings must murder still,
That all his hours of travail here for men
Seem yet in vain. And who will bring white peace
That he may sleep upon his hill again?

WALLACE STEVENS
(1879–1955)

The Emperor of Ice Cream

Call the roller of big cigars,
The muscular one, and bid him whip
In kitchen cups concupiscent curds.
Let the wenches dawdle in such dress
As they are used to wear, and let the boys
Bring flowers in last month's newspapers.
Let be be finale of seem.
The only emperor is the emperor of ice cream.

Take from the dresser of deal,
Lacking the three glass knobs, that sheet
On which she embroidered fantails once
And spread it so as to cover her face.
If her horny feet protrude, they come
To show how cold she is, and dumb.
Let the lamp affix its beam.
The only emperor is the emperor of ice cream.

The Idea of Order at Key West

She sang beyond the genius of the sea.
The water never formed to mind or voice,
Like a body wholly body, fluttering
Its empty sleeves; and yet its mimic motion
Made constant cry, caused constantly a cry,
That was not ours although we understood,
Inhuman, of the veritable ocean.

The sea was not a mask. No more was she.
The song and water were not medleyed sound
Even if what she sang was what she heard,
Since what she sang was uttered word by word.
It may be that in all her phrases stirred
The grinding water and the gasping wind;
But it was she and not the sea we heard.

For she was the maker of the song she sang.
The ever-hooded, tragic-gestured sea
Was merely a place by which she walked to sing.
Whose spirit is this? we said, because we knew
It was the spirit that we sought and knew
That we should ask this often as she sang.

If it was only the dark voice of the sea
That rose, or even colored by many waves;
If it was only the outer voice of sky
And cloud, of the sunken coral water-walled,
However clear, it would have been deep air,
The heaving speech of air, a summer sound
Repeated in a summer without end
And sound alone. But it was more than that,
More even than her voice, and ours, among
The meaningless plungings of water and the wind,
Theatrical distances, bronze shadows heaped
On high horizons, mountainous atmospheres
Of sky and sea.

It was her voice that made
The sky acutest at its vanishing.
She measured to the hour its solitude.
She was the single artificer of the world
In which she sang. And when she sang, the sea,
Whatever self it had, became the self
That was her song, for she was the maker. Then we,
As we beheld her striding there alone,
Knew that there never was a world for her
Except the one she sang and, singing, made.

Ramon Fernandez, tell me, if you know,
Why, when the singing ended and we turned
Toward the town, tell why the glassy lights,
The lights in the fishing boats at anchor there,
As the night descended, tilting in the air,
Mastered the night and portioned out the sea,
Fixing emblazoned zones and fiery poles,
Arranging, deepening, enchanting night.

Oh! Blessed rage for order, pale Ramon,
The maker's rage to order words of the sea,
Words of the fragrant portals, dimly starred,
And of ourselves and of our origins,
In ghostlier demarcations, keener sounds.

Peter Quince at the Clavier

I

Just as my fingers on these keys
Make music, so the selfsame sounds
On my spirit make a music, too.

Music is feeling, then, not sound;
And thus it is that what I feel,
Here in this room, desiring you,

Thinking of your blue-shadowed silk,
Is music. It is like the strain
Waked in the elders by Susanna.

Of a green evening, clear and warm,
She bathed in her still garden, while
The red-eyed elders watching, felt

The basses of their beings throb
In witching chords, and their thin blood
Pulse pizzicati of Hosanna.

II

In the green water, clear and warm,
Susanna lay.
She searched
The touch of springs,
And found
Concealed imaginings.
She sighed,
For so much melody.

Upon the bank, she stood
In the cool
Of spent emotions.
She felt, among the leaves,
The dew
Of old devotions.

She walked upon the grass,
Still quavering.
The winds were like her maids,
On timid feet,
Fetching her woven scarves,
Yet wavering.

A breath upon her hand
Muted the night.
She turned—
A cymbal crashed,
And roaring horns.

III

Soon, with a noise like tambourines,
Came her attendant Byzantines.

They wondered why Susanna cried
Against the elders by her side;

And as they whispered, the refrain
Was like a willow swept by rain.

Anon, their lamps' uplifted flame
Revealed Susanna and her shame.

And then, the simpering Byzantines
Fled, with a noise like tambourines.

IV

Beauty is momentary in the mind—
The fitful tracing of a portal;
But in the flesh it is immortal.
The body dies; the body's beauty lives.
So evenings die, in their green going,
A wave, interminably flowing.
So gardens die, their meek breath scenting
The cowl of winter, done repenting.
So maidens die, to the auroral
Celebration of a maiden's choral.
Susanna's music touched the bawdy strings
Of those white elders; but, escaping,
Left only Death's ironic scraping.
Now, in its immortality, it plays
On the clear viol of her memory,
And makes a constant sacrament of praise.

Sunday Morning

I

Complacencies of the peignoir, and late
Coffee and oranges in a sunny chair,
And the green freedom of a cockatoo
Upon a rug mingle to dissipate
The holy hush of ancient sacrifice.
She dreams a little, and she feels the dark
Encroachment of that old catastrophe,
As a calm darkens among water lights.
The pungent oranges and bright, green wings
Seem things in some procession of the dead,
Winding across wide water, without sound.

The day is like wide water, without sound,
Stilled for the passing of her dreaming feet
Over the seas, to silent Palestine,
Dominion of the blood and sepulcher.

II

Why should she give her bounty to the dead?
What is divinity if it can come
Only in silent shadows and in dreams?
Shall she not find in comforts of the sun,
In pungent fruit and bright, green wings, or else
In any balm or beauty of the earth,
Things to be cherished like the thought of heaven?
Divinity must live within herself:
Passions of rain, or moods in falling snow;
Grievings in loneliness, or unsubdued
Elations when the forest blooms; gusty
Emotions on wet roads on autumn nights;
All pleasures and all pains, remembering
The bough of summer and the winter branch.
These are the measures destined for her soul.

III

Jove in the clouds had his inhuman birth.
No mother suckled him, no sweet land gave
Large-mannered motions to his mythy mind.
He moved among us, as a muttering king,
Magnificent, would move among his hinds,
Until our blood, commingling, virginal,
With heaven, brought such requital to desire
The very hinds discerned it, in a star.
Shall our blood fail? Or shall it come to be
The blood of paradise? And shall the earth
Seem all of paradise that we shall know?
The sky will be much friendlier then than now,
A part of labor and a part of pain,
And next in glory to enduring love,
Not this dividing and indifferent blue.

IV

She says, "I am content when wakened birds,
Before they fly, test the reality
Of misty fields, by their sweet questionings;
But when the birds are gone, and their warm fields
Return no more, where, then, is paradise?"
There is not any haunt of prophecy,
Nor any old chimera of the grave,
Neither the golden underground, nor isle
Melodious, where spirits gat them home,
Nor visionary south, nor cloudy palm
Remote on heaven's hill, that has endured
As April's green endures; or will endure
Like her remembrance of awakened birds,
Or her desire for June and evening, tipped
By the consummation of the swallow's wings.

V

She says, "But in contentment I still feel
The need of some imperishable bliss."
Death is the mother of beauty; hence from her,
Alone, shall come fulfillment to our dreams
And our desires. Although she strews the leaves
Of sure obliteration on our paths,
The path sick sorrow took, the many paths
Where triumph rang its brassy phrase, or love
Whispered a little out of tenderness,
She makes the willow shiver in the sun
For maidens who were wont to sit and gaze
Upon the grass, relinquished to their feet.
She causes boys to pile new plums and pears
On disregarded plate. The maidens taste
And stray impassioned in the littering leaves.

VI

Is there no change of death in paradise?
Does ripe fruit never fall? Or do the boughs
Hang always heavy in that perfect sky,
Unchanging, yet so like our perishing earth,
With rivers like our own that seek for seas

They never find, the same receding shores
That never touch with inarticulate pang?
Why set the pear upon those riverbanks
Or spice the shores with odors of the plum?
Alas, that they should wear our colors there,
The silken weavings of our afternoons,
And pick the strings of our insipid lutes!
Death is the mother of beauty, mystical,
Within whose burning bosom we devise
Our earthly mothers waiting, sleeplessly.

VII

Supple and turbulent, a ring of men
Shall chant in orgy on a summer morn
Their boisterous devotion to the sun,
Not as a god, but as a god might be,
Naked among them, like a savage source.
Their chant shall be a chant of paradise,
Out of their blood, returning to the sky;
And in their chant shall enter, voice by voice,
The windy lake wherein their lord delights,
The trees, like seraphim, and echoing hills,
That choir among themselves long afterward.
They shall know well the heavenly fellowship
Of men that perish and of summer morn.
And whence they came and whither they shall go
The dew upon their feet shall manifest.

VIII

She hears, upon that water without sound,
A voice that cries, "The tomb in Palestine
Is not the porch of spirits lingering.
It is the grave of Jesus, where he lay."
We live in an old chaos of the sun,
Or old dependency of day and night,
Or island solitude, unsponsored, free,
Of that wide water, inescapable.
Deer walk upon our mountains, and the quail
Whistle about us their spontaneous cries;
Sweet berries ripen in the wilderness;

And, in the isolation of the sky,
At evening, casual flocks of pigeons make
Ambiguous undulations as they sink,
Downward to darkness, on extended wings.

Anecdote of the Jar

I placed a jar in Tennessee,
And round it was, upon a hill.
It made the slovenly wilderness
Surround that hill.

The wilderness rose up to it,
And sprawled around, no longer wild.
The jar was round upon the ground
And tall and of a port in air.

It took dominion everywhere.
The jar was gray and bare.
It did not give of bird or bush,
Like nothing else in Tennessee.

No Possum, No Sop, No Taters

He is not here, the old sun,
As absent as if we were asleep.

The field is frozen. The leaves are dry.
Bad is final in this light.

In this bleak air the broken stalks
Have arms without hands. They have trunks

Without legs or, for that, without heads.
They have heads in which a captive cry

Is merely the moving of a tongue.
Snow sparkles like eyesight falling to earth,

Like seeing fallen brightly away.
The leaves hop, scraping on the ground.

It is deep January. The sky is hard.
The stalks are firmly rooted in ice.

It is in this solitude, a syllable,
Out of these gawky flitterings,

Intones its single emptiness,
The savagest hollow of winter sound.

It is here, in this bad, that we reach
The last purity of the knowledge of good.

The crow looks rusty as he rises up.
Bright is the malice in his eye. . . .

One joins him there for company,
But at a distance, in another tree.

Not Ideas About the Thing but the Thing Itself

At the earliest ending of winter,
In March, a scrawny cry from outside
Seemed like a sound in his mind.

He knew that he heard it,
A bird's cry, at daylight or before,
In the early March wind.

The sun was rising at six,
No longer a battered panache above snow. . . .
It would have been outside.

It was not from the vast ventriloquism
Of sleep's faded papier-mâché. . . .
The sun was coming from outside.

That scrawny cry—it was
A chorister whose C preceded the choir.
It was part of the colossal sun,

Surrounded by its choral rings,
Still far away. It was like
A new knowledge of reality.

The Glass of Water

That the glass would melt in heat,
That the water would freeze in cold,
Shows that this object is merely a state,
One of many, between two poles. So,
In the metaphysical, there are these poles.

Here in the centre stands the glass. Light
Is the lion that comes down to drink. There
And in that state, the glass is a pool.
Ruddy are his eyes and ruddy are his claws
When light comes down to wet his frothy jaws

And in the water winding weeds move round.
And there and in another state—the refractions,
The *metaphysica*, the plastic parts of poems
Crash in the mind—But, fat Jocundus, worrying
About what stands here in the centre, not the glass,

But in the centre of our lives, this time, this day,
It is a state, this spring among the politicians
Playing cards. In a village of the indigenes,
One would have still to discover. Among the dogs and dung.
One would continue to contend with one's ideas.

Thirteen Ways of Looking at a Blackbird

I

Among twenty snowy mountains,
The only moving thing
Was the eye of the blackbird.

II

I was of three minds,
Like a tree
In which there are three blackbirds.

III

The blackbird whirled in the autumn winds.
It was a small part of the pantomime.

IV

A man and a woman
Are one.
A man and a woman and a blackbird
Are one.

V

I do not know which to prefer,
The beauty of inflections,
Or the beauty of innuendoes,
The blackbird whistling
Or just after.

VI

Icicles filled the long window
With barbaric glass.
The shadow of the blackbird
Crossed it, to and fro.
The mood
Traced in the shadow
An indecipherable cause.

VII

O thin men of Haddam,
Why do you imagine golden birds?
Do you not see how the blackbird
Walks around the feet
Of the women about you?

VIII

I know noble accents
And lucid, inescapable rhythms;
But I know, too,
That the blackbird is involved
In what I know.

IX

When the blackbird flew out of sight,
It marked the edge
Of one of many circles.

X

At the sight of blackbirds
Flying in a green light,
Even the bawds of euphony
Would cry out sharply.

XI

He rode over Connecticut
In a glass coach.
Once, a fear pierced him,
In that he mistook
The shadow of his equipage
For blackbirds.

XII

The river is moving.
The blackbird must be flying.

XIII

It was evening all afternoon.
It was snowing
And it was going to snow.
The blackbird sat
In the cedar-limbs.

A High-Toned Old Christian Woman

Poetry is the supreme fiction, madame.
Take the moral law and make a nave of it
And from the nave build haunted heaven. Thus,
The conscience is converted into palms,
Like windy citherns hankering for hymns.
We agree in principle. That's clear. But take
The opposing law and make a peristyle,
And from the peristyle project a masque
Beyond the planets. Thus, our bawdiness,
Unpurged by epitaph, indulged at last,
Is equally converted into palms.
Squiggling like saxophones. And palm for palm,
Madame, we are where we began. Allow,
Therefore, that in the planetary scene
Your disaffected flagellants, well-stuffed,
Smacking their muzzy bellies in parade,
Proud of such novelties of the sublime,
Such tink and tank and tunk-a-tunk-tunk,
May, merely may, madame, whip from themselves
A jovial hullabaloo among the spheres.
This will make widows wince. But fictive things
Wink as they will. Wink most when widows wince.

Men Made Out of Words

What should we be without the sexual myth,
The human reverie or poem of death?

Castratos of moon-mash—Life consists
Of propositions about life. The human

Reverie is a solitude in which
We compose these propositions, torn by dreams,

By the terrible incantations of defeats
And by the fear that defeats and dreams are one.

The whole race is a poet that writes down
The eccentric propositions of its fate.

Of Modern Poetry

The poem of the mind in the act of finding
What will suffice. It has not always had
To find: the scene was set; it repeated what
Was in the script.
                    Then the theatre was changed
To something else. Its past was a souvenir.
It has to be living, to learn the speech of the place.
It has to face the men of the time and to meet
The women of the time. It has to think about war
And it has to find what will suffice. It has
To construct a new stage. It has to be on that stage
And, like an insatiable actor, slowly and
With meditation, speak words that in the ear,
In the delicatest ear of the mind, repeat,
Exactly, that which it wants to hear, at the sound
Of which, an invisible audience listens,
Not to the play, but to itself, expressed
In an emotion as of two people, as of two
Emotions becoming one. The actor is
A metaphysician in the dark, twanging
An instrument, twanging a wiry string that gives
Sounds passing through sudden rightnesses, wholly
Containing the mind, below which it cannot descend,
Beyond which it has no will to rise.
                                        It must
Be the finding of a satisfaction, and may
Be of a man skating, a woman dancing, a woman
Combing. The poem of the act of the mind.

WILLIAM CARLOS WILLIAMS
(1883–1963)

Tract

I will teach you my townspeople
how to perform a funeral
for you have it over a troop
of artists—
unless one should scour the world—
you have the ground sense necessary.

See! the hearse leads.
I begin with a design for a hearse.
For Christ's sake not black—
nor white either—and not polished!
Let it be weathered—like a farm wagon—
with gilt wheels (this could be
applied fresh at small expense)
or no wheels at all:
a rough dray to drag over the ground.

Knock the glass out!
My God—glass, my townspeople!
For what purpose? Is it for the dead
to look out or for us to see
how well he is housed or to see
the flowers or the lack of them—
or what?
To keep the rain and snow from him?
He will have a heavier rain soon:
pebbles and dirt and what not.

Let there be no glass—
and no upholstery, phew!
and no little brass rollers
and small easy wheels on the bottom—
my townspeople what are you thinking of?
A rough plain hearse then
with gilt wheels and no top at all.
On this the coffin lies
by its own weight.

No wreaths please—
especially no hot house flowers.
Some common memento is better,
something he prized and is known by:
his old clothes—a few books perhaps—
God knows what! You realize
how we are about these things
my townspeople—
something will be found—anything
even flowers if he had come to that.
So much for the hearse.

For heaven's sake though see to the driver!
Take off the silk hat; In fact
that's no place at all for him—
up there unceremoniously
dragging our friend out to his own dignity!
Bring him down—bring him down!
Low and inconspicuous! I'd not have him ride
on the wagon at all—damn him—
the undertaker's understrapper!
Let him hold the reins
and walk at the side
and inconspicuously too!

Then briefly as to yourselves:
Walk behind—as they do in France,
seventh class, or if you ride
Hell take curtains! Go with some show
of inconvenience; sit openly—
to the weather as to grief.

Or do you think you can shut grief in?
What—from us? We who have perhaps
nothing to lose? Share with us
share with us—it will be money
in your pockets.
                    Go now
I think you are ready.

The Red Wheelbarrow

so much depends
upon

a red wheel
barrow

glazed with rain
water

beside the white
chickens.

The Young Housewife

At ten A.M. the young housewife
moves about in negligee behind
the wooden walls of her husband's house.
I pass solitary in my car.

Then again she comes to the curb
to call the ice-man, fish-man, and stands
shy, uncorseted, tucking in
stray ends of hair, and I compare her
to a fallen leaf.

The noiseless wheels of my car
rush with a crackling sound over
dried leaves as I bow and pass smiling.

Proletarian Portrait

A big young bareheaded woman
in an apron

Her hair slicked back standing
on the street

One stockinged foot toeing
the sidewalk

Her shoe in her hand. Looking
intently into it

She pulls out the paper insole
to find the nail

That has been hurting her

Flowers by the Sea

When over the flowery, sharp pasture's
edge, unseen, the salt ocean

lifts its form—chicory and daisies
tied, released, seem hardly flowers alone

but color and the movement—or the shape
perhaps—of restlessness, whereas

the sea is circled and sways
peacefully upon its plantlike stem

Nantucket

Flowers through the window
lavender and yellow

changed by white curtains—
Smell of cleanliness—

Sunshine of late afternoon—
On the glass tray

a glass pitcher, the tumbler
turned down, by which

a key is lying—And the
immaculate white bed

Young Sycamore

I must tell you
this young tree
whose round and firm trunk
between the wet

pavement and the gutter
(where water
is trickling) rises
bodily

into the air with
one undulant
thrust half its height—
and then

dividing and waning
sending out
young branches on
all sides—

hung with cocoons
it thins
till nothing is left of it
but two

eccentric knotted
twigs
bending forward
hornlike at the top

Queen-Anne's-Lace

Her body is not so white as
anemone petals nor so smooth—nor
so remote a thing. It is a field
of the wild carrot taking
the field by force; the grass
does not raise above it.
Here is no question of whiteness,
white as can be, with a purple mole
at the center of each flower.
Each flower is a hand's span
of her whiteness. Wherever
his hand has lain there is
a tiny purple blemish. Each part
is a blossom under his touch
to which the fibres of her being
stem one by one, each to its end,
until the whole field is a
white desire, empty, a single stem,
a cluster, flower by flower,
a pious wish to whiteness gone over—
or nothing.

The Widow's Lament in Springtime

Sorrow is my own yard
where the new grass
flames as it has flamed
often before but not
with the cold fire
that closes round me this year.
Thirty-five years
I lived with my husband.
The plumtree is white today
with masses of flowers.
Masses of flowers
load the cherry branches
and color some bushes
yellow and some red
but the grief in my heart
is stronger than they
for though they were my joy
formerly, today I notice them
and turned away forgetting.
Today my son told me
that in the meadows,
at the edge of the heavy woods
in the distance, he saw
trees of white flowers.
I feel that I would like
to go there
and fall into those flowers
and sink into the marsh near them.

The Horse Show

Constantly near you, I never in my entire
sixty-four years knew you so well as yesterday
or half so well. We talked. You were never
so lucid, so disengaged from all exigencies
of place and time. We talked of ourselves,
intimately, a thing never heard of between us.
How long have we waited? almost a hundred years.

You said, Unless there is some spark, some
spirit we keep within ourselves, life, a
continuing life's impossible—and it is all
we have. There is no other life, only the one.
The world of the spirits that comes afterward
is the same as our own, just like you sitting
there they come and talk to me, just the same.

They come to bother us. Why? I said. I don't
know. Perhaps to find out what we are doing.
Jealous, do you think? I don't know. I
don't know why they should want to come back.
I was reading about some men who had been
buried under a mountain, I said to her, and
one of them came back after two months,

digging himself out. It was in Switzerland,
you remember? Of course I remember. The
villagers tho't it was a ghost coming down
to complain. They were frightened. They
do come, she said, what you call
my "visions." I talk to them just as I
am talking to you. I see them plainly.

Oh if I could only read! You don't know
what adjustments I have made. All
I can do is to try to live over again

what I knew when your brother and you
were children—but I can't always succeed.
Tell me about the horse show. I have
been waiting all week to hear about it.

Mother darling, I wasn't able to get away.
Oh that's too bad. It was just a show;
they make the horses walk up and down
to judge them by their form. Oh is that
all? I tho't it was something else. Oh
they jump and run too. I wish you had been
there, I was so interested to hear about it.

Danse Russe

If when my wife is sleeping
and the baby and Kathleen
are sleeping
and the sun is a flame-white disc
in silken mists
above shining trees,—
if I in my north room
dance naked, grotesquely
before my mirror
waving my shirt round my head
and singing softly to myself:
"I am lonely, lonely.
I was born to be lonely,
I am best so!"
If I admire my arms, my face,
my shoulders, flanks, buttocks
against the yellow drawn shades,—

Who shall say I am not
the happy genius of my household?

Spring and All

By the road to the contagious hospital
under the surge of the blue
mottled clouds driven from the
northeast—a cold wind. Beyond, the
waste of broad, muddy fields
brown with dried weeds, standing and fallen

patches of standing water
the scattering of tall trees

All along the road the reddish
purplish, forked, upstanding, twiggy
stuff of bushes and small trees
with dead, brown leaves under them
leafless vines—

Lifeless in appearance, sluggish
dazed spring approaches—

They enter the new world naked,
cold, uncertain of all
save that they enter. All about them
the cold, familiar wind—

Now the grass, tomorrow
the stiff curl of wildcarrot leaf
One by one objects are defined—
It quickens: clarity, outline of leaf

But now the stark dignity of
entrance—Still, the profound change
has come upon them: rooted, they
grip down and begin to awaken

To a Poor Old Woman

munching a plum on
the street a paper bag
of them in her hand

They taste good to her
They taste good
to her. They taste
good to her

You can see it by
the way she gives herself
to the one half
sucked out in her hand

Comforted
a solace of ripe plums
seeming to fill the air
They taste good to her

This Is Just to Say

I have eaten
the plums
that were in
the icebox

and which
you were probably
saving
for breakfast

Forgive me
they were delicious
so sweet
and so cold

Between Walls

the back wings
of the

hospital where
nothing

will grow lie
cinders

in which shine
the broken

pieces of a green
bottle

The Dance

In Breughel's great picture, The Kermess,
the dancers go round, they go round and
around, the squeal and the blare and the
tweedle of bagpipes, a bugle and fiddles
tipping their bellies (round as the thick-
sided glasses whose wash they impound)
their hips and their bellies off balance
to turn them. Kicking and rolling about
the Fair Grounds, swinging their butts, those
shanks must be sound to bear up under such
rollicking measures, prance as they dance
in Breughel's great picture, The Kermess.

On Gay Wallpaper

The green-blue ground
is ruled with silver lines
to say the sun is shining

And on this moral sea
of grass or dreams lie flowers
or baskets of desires

Heaven knows what they are
between cerulean shapes
laid regularly round

Mat roses and tridentate
leaves of gold
threes, threes and threes

Three roses and three stems
the basket floating
standing in the horns of blue

Repeating to the ceiling
to the windows
where the day

Blows in
the scalloped curtains to
the sound of rain

Smell!

Oh strong ridged and deeply hollowed
nose of mine! what will you not be smelling?
What tactless asses we are, you and I, boney nose,
always indiscriminate, always unashamed,
and now it is the souring flowers of the bedraggled
poplars: a festering pulp on the wet earth
beneath them. With what deep thirst
we quicken our desires
to that rank odor of a passing springtime!
Can you not be decent? Can you not reserve your ardors
for something less unlovely? What girl will care
for us, do you think, if we continue in these ways?
Must you taste everything? Must you know everything?
Must you have a part in everything?

A Sort of a Song

Let the snake wait under
his weed
and the writing
be of words, slow and quick, sharp
to strike, quiet to wait,
sleepless.
—through metaphor to reconcile
the people and the stones.
Compose. (No ideas
but in things) Invent!
Saxifrage is my flower that splits
the rocks.

from Book I, *Paterson*

Paterson lies in the valley under the Passaic Falls
its spent waters forming the outline of his back. He
lies on his right side, head near the thunder
of the waters filling his dreams! Eternally asleep,
his dreams walk about the city where he persists
incognito. Butterflies settle on his stone ear.
Immortal he neither moves nor rouses and is seldom
seen, though he breathes and the subtleties of his machinations
drawing their substance from the noise of the pouring river
animate a thousand automatons. Who because they
neither know their sources nor the sills of their
disappointments walk outside their bodies aimlessly
        for the most part,
locked and forgot in their desires—unroused.

    —Say it, no ideas but in things—
    nothing but the blank faces of the houses
    and cylindrical trees
    bent, forked by preconception and accident—
    split, furrowed, creased, mottled, stained—
    secret—into the body of the light!

From above, higher than the spires, higher
even than the office towers, from oozy fields
abandoned to gray beds of dead grass,
black sumac, withered weed-stalks,
mud and thickets cluttered with dead leaves—
the river comes pouring in above the city
and crashes from the edge of the gorge
in a recoil of spray and rainbow mists—

    (What common language to unravel?
    . . . combed into straight lines
    from that rafter of a rock's
    lip.)

A man like a city and a woman like a flower
—who are in love. Two women. Three women.
Innumerable women, each like a flower.

                                                            But
only one man—like a city.

EZRA POUND
(1885–1972)

Salutation

O generation of the thoroughly smug
        and thoroughly uncomfortable,
I have seen fishermen picnicking in the sun,
I have seen them with untidy families,
I have seen their smiles full of teeth
        and heard ungainly laughter.
And I am happier than you are,
And they were happier than I am;
And the fish swim in the lake
        and do not even own clothing.

A Pact

I make a pact with you, Walt Whitman—
I have detested you long enough.
I come to you as a grown child
Who has had a pig-headed father;
I am old enough now to make friends.
It was you that broke the new wood,
Now is a time for carving.
We have one sap and one root—
Let there be commerce between us.

The River-Merchant's Wife: A Letter

While my hair was still cut straight across my forehead
Played I about the front gate, pulling flowers.
You came by on bamboo stilts, playing horse,
You walked about my seat, playing with blue plums.
And we went on living in the village of Chokan:
Two small people, without dislike or suspicion.

At fourteen I married My Lord you.
I never laughed, being bashful.
Lowering my head, I looked at the wall.
Called to, a thousand times, I never looked back.

At fifteen I stopped scowling,
I desired my dust to be mingled with yours
Forever and forever and forever.
Why should I climb the look out?

At sixteen you departed,
You went into far Ku-to-yen, by the river of swirling eddies,
And you have been gone five months.
The monkeys make sorrowful noise overhead.

You dragged your feet when you went out.
By the gate now, the moss is grown, the different mosses,
Too deep to clear them away!
The leaves fall early this autumn, in wind.
The paired butterflies are already yellow with August
Over the grass in the West garden;
They hurt me. I grow older.
If you are coming down through the narrows of the river
    Kiang,
Please let me know beforehand,
And I will come out to meet you
                    As far as Cho-fu-Sa.

In a Station of the Metro

The apparition of these faces in the crowd;
Petals on a wet, black bough.

Portrait d'une Femme

Your mind and you are our Sargasso Sea,
London has swept about you this score years
And bright ships left you this or that in fee:
Ideas, old gossip, oddments of all things,
Strange spars of knowledge and dimmed wares of price.
Great minds have sought you—lacking someone else.
You have been second always. Tragical?
No. You preferred it to the usual thing:
One dull man, dulling and uxorious,
One average mind—with one thought less, each year.
Oh, you are patient. I have seen you sit
Hours, where something might have floated up.
And now you pay one. Yes, you richly pay.
You are a person of some interest, one comes to you
And takes strange gain away:
Trophies fished up; some curious suggestion;
Fact that leads nowhere; and a tale or two,
Pregnant with mandrakes, or with something else
That might prove useful and yet never proves,
That never fits a corner or shows use,
Or finds its hour upon the loom of days:
The tarnished, gaudy, wonderful old work;
Idols and ambergris and rare inlays,
These are your riches, your great store; and yet
For all this sea-hoard of deciduous things,
Strange woods half sodden, and new brighter stuff:

In the slow float of different light and deep,
No! there is nothing! In the whole and all,
Nothing that's quite your own.
                    Yet this is you.

A Virginal

No, no! Go from me. I have left her lately.
I will not spoil my sheath with lesser brightness,
For my surrounding air hath a new lightness;
Slight are her arms, yet they have bound me straitly
And left me cloaked as with a gauze of aether;
As with sweet leaves; as with subtle clearness.
Oh, I have picked up magic in her nearness
To sheathe me half in half the things that sheathe her.
No, no! Go from me. I have still the flavour,
Soft as spring wind that's come from birchen bowers.
Green come the shoots, aye April in the branches,
As winter's wound with her sleight hand she staunches,
Hath of the trees a likeness of the savour:
As white their bark, so white this lady's hours.

Hugh Selwyn Mauberley

E. P. Ode Pour l'Election de Son Sepulchre

For three years, out of key with his time,
He strove to resuscitate the dead art
Of poetry; to maintain "the sublime"
In the old sense. Wrong from the start—

No, hardly, but seeing he had been born
In a half-savage country, out of date;
Bent resolutely on wringing lilies from the acorn;
Capaneus; trout for factitious bait;

Ἴδμεν γάρ τοι πάνθ', ὅσ' ἐνὶ Τροίῃ
Caught in the unstopped ear;
Giving the rocks small lee-way
The chopped seas held him, therefore, that year.

His true Penelope was Flaubert,
He fished by obstinate isles;
Observed the elegance of Circe's hair
Rather than the mottoes on sun-dials.

Unaffected by "the march of events,"
He passed from men's memory in *l'an trentuniesme*
De son eage; the case presents
No adjunct to the Muses' diadem.

II

The age demanded an image
Of its accelerated grimace,
Something for the modern stage,
Not, at any rate, an Attic grace;

Not, not certainly, the obscure reveries
Of the inward gaze;
Better mendacities
Than the classics in paraphrase!

The "age demanded" chiefly a mould in plaster,
Made with no loss of time,
A prose kinema, not, not assuredly, alabaster
Or the "sculpture" of rhyme.

III

The tea-rose tea-gown, etc.
Supplants the mousseline of Cos,
The Pianola "replaces"
Sappho's barbitos.

Christ follows Dionysus,
Phallic and ambrosial
Made way for macerations;
Caliban casts out Ariel.

All things are a flowing,
Sage Heracleitus says;
But a tawdry cheapness
Shall outlast our days.

Even the Christian beauty
Defects—after Samothrace;
We see τὸ καλόν
Decreed in the market place.

Faun's flesh is not to us,
Nor the saint's vision.
We have the press for wafer;
Franchise for circumcision.

All men, in law, are equals.
Free of Pisistratus,
We choose a knave or an eunuch
To rule over us.

O bright Apollo,
τίν' ἄνδρα, τίν' ἥρωα, τίνα θεὸν,
What god, man, or hero
Shall I place a tin wreath upon!

IV

These fought in any case,
and some believing,
                pro domo, in any case . . .

Some quick to arm,
some for adventure,
some from fear of weakness,
some from fear of censure,
some for love of slaughter, in imagination,
learning later . . .
some in fear, learning love of slaughter;
Died some, pro patria,
                non "dulce" non "et decor" . . .
walked eye-deep in hell
believing in old men's lies, then unbelieving

came home, home to a lie,
home to many deceits,
home to old lies and new infamy;
usury age-old and age-thick
and liars in public places.

Daring as never before, wastage as never before.
Young blood and high blood,
fair cheeks, and fine bodies;

fortitude as never before

frankness as never before,
disillusions as never told in the old days,
hysterias, trench confessions,
laughter out of dead bellies.

V

There died a myriad,
And of the best, among them,
For an old bitch gone in the teeth,
For a botched civilization,

Charm, smiling at the good mouth,
Quick eyes gone under earth's lid,

For two gross of broken statues,
For a few thousand battered books.

Yeux Glauques

Gladstone was still respected,
When John Ruskin produced
"King's Treasuries"; Swinburne
And Rossetti still abused.

Fetid Buchanan lifted up his voice
When that faun's head of hers
Became a pastime for
Painters and adulterers.

The Burne-Jones cartons
Have preserved her eyes;
Still, at the Tate, they teach
Cophetua to rhapsodize;

Thin like brook-water,
With a vacant gaze.
The English Rubáiyát was still-born
In those days.

The thin, clear gaze, the same
Still darts out faunlike from the half-ruin'd face,
Questing and passive. . . .
"Ah, poor Jenny's case" . . .

Bewildered that a world
Shows no surprise
At her last maquero's
Adulteries.

"Siena Mi Fe'; Disfecemi Maremma"

Among the pickled fetuses and bottled bones,
Engaged in perfecting the catalogue,
I found the last scion of the
Senatorial families of Strasbourg, Monsieur Verog.

For two hours he talked of Gallifet;
Of Dowson; of the Rhymers' Club;
Told me how Johnson (Lionel) died
By falling from a high stool in a pub . . .

But showed no trace of alcohol
At the autopsy, privately performed—
Tissue preserved—the pure mind
Arose toward Newman as the whiskey warmed.

Dowson found harlots cheaper than hotels;
Headlam for uplift; Image impartially imbued
With raptures for Bacchus, Terpsichore and the Church.
So spoke the author of "The Dorian Mood,"

M. Verog, out of step with the decade,
Detached from his contemporaries,
Neglected by the young,
Because of these reveries.

Brennbaum

The skylike limpid eyes,
The circular infant's face,
The stiffness from spats to collar
Never relaxing into grace;

The heavy memories of Horeb, Sinai and the forty years,
Showed only when the daylight fell
Level across the face
Of Brennbaum "The Impeccable."

Mr. Nixon

In the cream gilded cabin of his steam yacht
Mr. Nixon advised me kindly, to advance with fewer
Dangers of delay. "Consider
"Carefully the reviewer.

"I was as poor as you are;
"When I began I got, of course,
"Advance on royalties, fifty at first," said Mr. Nixon,
"Follow me, and take a column,
"Even if you have to work free.

"Butter reviewers. From fifty to three hundred
"I rose in eighteen months;
"The hardest nut I had to crack
"Was Dr. Dundas.

"I never mentioned a man but with the view
"Of selling my own works.
"The tip's a good one, as for literature
"It gives no man a sinecure.

"And no one knows, at sight, a masterpiece.
"And give up verse, my boy,
"There's nothing in it."

* * * *

Likewise a friend of Bloughram's once advised me:
Don't kick against the pricks,
Accept opinion. The "Nineties" tried your game
And died, there's nothing in it.

X

Beneath the sagging roof
The stylist has taken shelter,
Unpaid, uncelebrated,
At last from the world's welter

Nature receives him;
With a placid and uneducated mistress
He exercises his talents
And the soil meets his distress.

The haven from sophistications and contentions
Leaks through its thatch;
He offers succulent cooking;
The door has a creaking latch.

XI

"Conservatrix of Milésian"
Habits of mind and feeling,
Possibly. But in Ealing
With the most bank-clerkly of Englishmen?

No, "Milésian" is an exaggeration.
No instinct has survived in her
Older than those her grandmother
Told her would fit her station.

XII

"Daphne with her thighs in bark
"Stretches toward me her leafy hands,"—
Subjectively. In the stuffed-satin drawing-room
I await The Lady Valentine's commands,

Knowing my coat has never been
Of precisely the fashion
To stimulate, in her,
A durable passion;

Doubtful, somewhat, of the value
Of well-gowned approbation
Of literary effort,
But never of The Lady Valentine's vocation:

Poetry, her border of ideas,
The edge, uncertain, but a means of blending
With other strata
Where the lower and higher have ending;

A hook to catch the Lady Jane's attention,
A modulation toward the theatre,
Also, in the case of revolution,
A possible friend and comforter.

* * * *

Conduct, on the other hand, the soul
"Which the highest cultures have nourished"
To Fleet St. where
Dr. Johnson flourished;

Beside this thoroughfare
The sale of half-hose has
Long since superseded the cultivation
Of Pierian roses.

Envoi (1919)

Go, dumb-born book,
Tell her that sang me once that song of Lawes:
Hadst thou but song
As thou hast subjects known,
Then were there cause in thee that should condone
Even my faults that heavy upon me lie,
And build her glories their longevity.

Tell her that sheds
Such treasure in the air,
Recking naught else but that her graces give
Life to the moment,
I would bid them live
As roses might, in magic amber laid,
Red overwrought with orange and all made
One substance and one colour
Braving time.

Tell her that goes
With song upon her lips
But sings not out the song, nor knows
The maker of it, some other mouth,
May be as fair as hers,
Might, in new ages, gain her worshippers,
When our two dusts with Waller's shall be laid,
Siftings on siftings in oblivion,
Till change hath broken down
All things save Beauty alone.

Canto III

I sat on the Dogana's steps
For the gondolas cost too much, that year,
And there were not "those girls," there was one face,
And the Buccentoro twenty yards off, howling "Stretti,"
The lit cross-beams, that year, in the Morosini,
And peacocks in Koré's house, or there may have been.
        Gods float in the azure air,
Bright gods and Tuscan, back before dew was shed.
Light: and the first light, before ever dew was fallen.
Panisks, and from the oak, dryas,
And from the apple, maelid,
Through all the wood, and the leaves are full of voices,
A-whisper, and the clouds bowe over the lake,
And there are gods upon them,
And in the water, the almond-white swimmers,

The silvery water glazes the upturned nipple,
        As Poggio has remarked.
Green veins in the turquoise,
Or, the gray steps lead up under the cedars.

My Cid rode up to Burgos,
Up to the studded gate between two towers,
Beat with his lance butt, and the child came out,
Una niña de nueve años,
To the little gallery over the gate, between the towers,
Reading the writ, voce tinnula:
That no man speak to, feed, help Ruy Diaz,
On pain to have his heart out, set on a pike spike
And both his eyes torn out, and all his goods sequestered,
"And here, Myo Cid, are the seals,
The big seal and the writing."
And he came down from Bivar, Myo Cid,
With no hawks left there on their perches,
And no clothes there in the presses,
And left his trunk with Raquel and Vidas,
That big box of sand, with the pawn-brokers,
To get pay for his menie;
Breaking his way to Valencia.
Ignez da Castro murdered, and a wall
Here stripped, here made to stand.
Drear waste, the pigment flakes from the stone,
Or plaster flakes, Mantegna painted the wall.
Silk tatters, "Nec Spe Nec Metu."

H.D.
(HILDA DOOLITTLE)
(1886–1961)

Oread

Whirl up, sea—
whirl your pointed pines,
splash your great pines
on our rocks,
hurl your green over us,
cover us with your pools of fir.

Heat

O wind, rend open the heat,
cut apart the heat,
rend it to tatters.

Fruit cannot drop
through this thick air—
fruit cannot fall into heat
that presses up and blunts
the points of pears
and rounds the grapes.

Cut the heat—
plough through it,
turning it on either side
of your path.

Stars Wheel in Purple

Stars wheel in purple, yours is not so rare
as Hesperus, nor yet so great a star
as bright Aldeboran or Sirius,
nor yet the stained and brilliant one of War;

stars turn in purple, glorious to the sight;
yours is not gracious as the Pleiads are
nor as Orion's sapphires, luminous;

yet disenchanted, cold, imperious face,
when all the others blighted, reel and fall,
your star, steel-set, keeps lone and frigid tryst
to freighted ships, baffled in wind and blast.

Helen

All Greece hates
the still eyes in the white face,
the lustre as of olives
where she stands,
and the white hands.

All Greece reviles
the wan face when she smiles,
hating it deeper still
when it grows wan and white,
remembering past enchantments
and past ills.

Greece sees, unmoved,
God's daughter, born of love,
the beauty of cool feet

and slenderest knees,
could love indeed the maid,
only if she were laid,
white ash amid funereal cypresses.

The Mysteries Remain

The mysteries remain,
I keep the same
cycle of seed-time
and of sun and rain;
Demeter in the grass,
I multiply,
renew and bless
Iacchus in the vine;
I hold the law,
I keep the mysteries true,
the first of these
to name the living, dead;
I am red wine and bread.

I keep the law,
I hold the mysteries true,
I am the vine,
the branches, you
and you.

ROBINSON JEFFERS
(1887–1962)

Hurt Hawks

I

The broken pillar of the wing jags from the clotted shoulder,
The wing trails like a banner in defeat,
No more to use the sky forever but live with famine
And pain a few days: cat nor coyote
Will shorten the week of waiting for death, there is game without
talons.
He stands under the oak-bush and waits
The lame feet of salvation; at night he remembers freedom
And flies in a dream, the dawns ruin it.
He is strong and pain is worse to the strong, incapacity is worse.
The curs of the day come and torment him
At distance, no one but death the redeemer will humble that head,
The intrepid readiness, the terrible eyes.
The wild God of the world is sometimes merciful to those
That ask mercy, not often to the arrogant.
You do not know him, you communal people, or you have forgotten
him;
Intemperate and savage, the hawk remembers him;
Beautiful and wild, the hawks, and men that are dying, remember
him.

II

I'd sooner, except the penalties, kill a man than a hawk; but the
great redtail
Had nothing left but unable misery
From the bone too shattered for mending, the wing that trailed under
his talons when he moved.
We had fed him six weeks, I gave him freedom,

He wandered over the foreland hill and returned in the evening, asking for death.
Not like a beggar, still eyed with the old
Implacable arrogance. I gave him the lead gift in the twilight. What fell was relaxed,
Owl-downy, soft feminine feathers; but what
Soared: the fierce rush: the night-herons by the flooded river cried fear at its rising
Before it was quite unsheathed from reality.

Shine, Perishing Republic

While this America settles in the mould of its vulgarity, heavily thickening to empire,
And protest, only a bubble in the molten mass, pops and sighs out, and the mass hardens,

I sadly smiling remember that the flower fades to make fruit, the fruit rots to make earth.
Out of the mother; and through the spring exultances, ripeness and decadence; and home to the mother.

You making haste haste on decay: not blameworthy; life is good, be it stubbornly long or suddenly
A mortal splendor: meteors are not needed less than mountains: shine, perishing republic.

But for my children, I would have them keep their distance from the thickening center; corruption
Never has been compulsory, when the cities lie at the monster's feet there are left the mountains.

And boys, be in nothing so moderate as in love of man, a clever servant, insufferable master.
There is the trap that catches noblest spirits, that caught—they say —God, when he walked on earth.

But I Am Growing Old and Indolent

I have been warned. It is more than thirty years since I wrote—
Thinking of the narrative poems I made, which always
Ended in blood and pain, though beautiful enough—my pain, my
    blood,
They were my creatures—I understood, and wrote to myself:
"Make sacrifices once a year to magic
Horror away from the house"—for that hangs imminent
Over all men and all houses—"This little house here
You have built over the ocean with your own hands
Beside the standing sea-boulders . . ." So I listened
To my Demon warning me that evil would come
If my work ceased, if I did not make sacrifice
Of storied and imagined lives, Tamar and Cawdor
And Thurso's wife—"imagined victims be our redeemers"—
At that time I was sure of my fates and felt
My poems guarding the house, well-made watchdogs
Ready to bite.
        But time sucks out the juice,
A man grows old and indolent.

MARIANNE MOORE
(1887–1972)

Poetry

I, too, dislike it: there are things that are important beyond
all this fiddle.
Reading it, however, with a perfect contempt for it, one
discovers in
it after all, a place for the genuine.
Hands that can grasp, eyes
that can dilate, hair that can rise
if it must, these things are important not because a

high-sounding interpretation can be put upon them but because they are
useful. When they become so derivative as to become
unintelligible,
the same thing may be said for all of us, that we
do not admire what
we cannot understand: the bat
holding on upside down or in quest of something to

eat, elephants pushing, a wild horse taking a roll, a tireless
wolf under
a tree, the immovable critic twitching his skin like a horse
that feels a flea, the base-
ball fan, the statistician—
nor is it valid
to discriminate against "business documents and

school-books"; all these phenomena are important. One
must make a distinction
however: when dragged into prominence by half poets,
the result is not poetry,

nor till the poets among us can be
"literalists of
the imagination"—above
insolence and triviality and can present

for inspection, "imaginary gardens with real toads in them,"
shall we have
it. In the meantime, if you demand on the one hand,
the raw material of poetry in
all its rawness and
that which is on the other hand
genuine, you are interested in poetry.

A Grave

Man looking into the sea,
taking the view from those who have as much right to it as you have
to it yourself,
it is human nature to stand in the middle of a thing,
but you cannot stand in the middle of this;
the sea has nothing to give but a well-excavated grave.
The firs stand in a procession, each with an emerald turkey-foot at
the top,
reserved as their contours, saying nothing;
repression, however, is not the most obvious characteristic of the sea;
the sea is a collector, quick to return a rapacious look.
There are others besides you who have worn that look—
whose expression is no longer a protest; the fish no longer investigate
them
for their bones have not lasted:
men lower nets, unconscious of the fact that they are desecrating
a grave,
and row quickly away—the blades of the oars
moving together like the feet of water-spiders as if there were no
such thing as death.
The wrinkles progress among themselves in a phalanx—beautiful under networks of foam,
and fade breathlessly while the sea rustles in and out of the seaweed;

the birds swim through the air at top speed, emitting catcalls as
    heretofore—
the tortoise-shell scourges about the feet of the cliffs, in motion be-
    neath them;
and the ocean, under the pulsation of lighthouses and noise of bell-
    buoys,
advances as usual, looking as if it were not that ocean in which
    dropped things are bound to sink—
in which if they turn and twist, it is neither with volition nor con-
    sciousness.

Spenser's Ireland

has not altered;—
  a place as kind as it is green,
  the greenest place I've never seen.
Every name is a tune.
Denunciations do not affect
    the culprit; nor blows, but it
is torture to him to not be spoken to.
They're natural,—
      the coat, like Venus'
mantle lined with stars,
buttoned close at the neck,—the sleeves new from disuse.

If in Ireland
  they play the harp backward at need,
  and gather at midday the seed
of the fern, eluding
their "giants all covered with iron," might
    there be fern seed for unlearn-
ing obduracy and for reinstating
the enchantment?
      Hindered characters
seldom have mothers
in Irish stories, but they all have grandmothers.

It was Irish;
  a match not a marriage was made
  when my great great grandmother'd said
with native genius for
disunion, "although your suitor be
    perfection, one objection
is enough; he is not
Irish." Outwitting
    the fairies, befriending the furies,
whoever again
and again says, "I'll never give in," never sees

that you're not free
  until you've been made captive by
  supreme belief,—credulity
you say? When large dainty
fingers tremblingly divide the wings
   of the fly for mid-July
with a needle and wrap it with peacock-tail,
or tie wool and
    buzzard's wing, their pride,
like the enchanter's
is in care, not madness. Concurring hands divide

flax for damask
  that when bleached by Irish weather
  has the silvered chamois-leather
water-tightness of a
skin. Twisted torcs and gold new-moon-shaped
   lunulae aren't jewelry
like the purple-coral fuchsia-tree's. Eire—
the guillemot
    so neat and the hen
of the heath and the
linnet spinet-sweet—bespeak relentlessness? Then

they are to me
  like enchanted Earl Gerald who
  changed himself into a stag, to
a great green-eyed cat of

the mountain. Discommodity makes
    them invisible; they've dis-
appeared. The Irish say your trouble is their
trouble and your
        joy their joy? I wish
I could believe it;
I am troubled, I'm dissatisfied, I'm Irish.

T. S. ELIOT
(1888–1965)

The Love Song of J. Alfred Prufrock

S'io credessi che mia risposta fosse
a persona che mai tornasse al mondo,
questa fiamma staria senza più scosse.
Ma per ciò che giammai di questo fondo
non tornò vivo alcun, s'i'odo il vero,
senza tema d'infamia ti rispondo.

Let us go then, you and I,
When the evening is spread out against the sky
Like a patient etherised upon a table;
Let us go, through certain half-deserted streets,
The muttering retreats
Of restless nights in one-night cheap hotels
And sawdust restaurants with oyster-shells:
Streets that follow like a tedious argument
Of insidious intent
To lead you to an overwhelming question. . .
Oh, do not ask, 'What is it?'
Let us go and make our visit.

In the room the women come and go
Talking of Michelangelo.

The yellow fog that rubs its back upon the window-panes,
The yellow smoke that rubs its muzzle on the window-panes,
Licked its tongue into the corners of the evening,
Lingered upon the pools that stand in drains,
Let fall upon its back the soot that falls from chimneys,
Slipped by the terrace, made a sudden leap,
And seeing that it was a soft October night,
Curled once about the house, and fell asleep.

And indeed there will be time
For the yellow smoke that slides along the street
Rubbing its back upon the window-panes;
There will be time, there will be time
To prepare a face to meet the faces that you meet;
There will be time to murder and create,
And time for all the works and days of hands
That lift and drop a question on your plate;
Time for you and time for me,
And time yet for a hundred indecisions,
And for a hundred visions and revisions,
Before the taking of a toast and tea.

In the room the women come and go
Talking of Michelangelo.

And indeed there will be time
To wonder, 'Do I dare?' and, 'Do I dare?'
Time to turn back and descend the stair,
With a bald spot in the middle of my hair—
(They will say: 'How his hair is growing thin!')
My morning coat, my collar mounting firmly to the chin,
My necktie rich and modest, but asserted by a simple pin—
(They will say: 'But how his arms and legs are thin!')
Do I dare
Disturb the universe?
In a minute there is time
For decisions and revisions which a minute will reverse.
For I have known them all already, known them all—
Have known the evenings, mornings, afternoons,
I have measured out my life with coffee spoons;
I know the voices dying with a dying fall
Beneath the music from a farther room.
  So how should I presume?

And I have known the eyes already, known them all—
The eyes that fix you in a formulated phrase,
And when I am formulated, sprawling on a pin,
When I am pinned and wriggling on the wall,

Then how should I begin
To spit out all the butt-ends of my days and ways?
  And how should I presume?

And I have known the arms already, known them all—
Arms that are braceleted and white and bare
(But in the lamplight, downed with light brown hair!)
Is it perfume from a dress
That makes me so digress?
Arms that lie along a table, or wrap about a shawl.
  And should I then presume?
  And how should I begin?

. . . . .

Shall I say, I have gone at dusk through narrow streets
And watched the smoke that rises from the pipes
Of lonely men in shirt-sleeves, leaning out of windows? . . .

I should have been a pair of ragged claws
Scuttling across the floors of silent seas.

. . . . .

And the afternoon, the evening, sleeps so peacefully!
Smoothed by long fingers,
Asleep . . . tired . . . or it malingers,
Stretched on the floor, here beside you and me.
Should I, after tea and cakes and ices,
Have the strength to force the moment to its crisis?
But though I have wept and fasted, wept and prayed,
Though I have seen my head (grown slightly bald) brought in upon
    a platter,
I am no prophet—and here's no great matter;
I have seen the moment of my greatness flicker,
And I have seen the eternal Footman hold my coat, and snicker,
And in short, I was afraid.
And would it have been worth it, after all,
After the cups, the marmalade, the tea,
Among the porcelain, among some talk of you and me,
Would it have been worth while,
To have bitten off the matter with a smile,
To have squeezed the universe into a ball
To roll it towards some overwhelming question,
To say: 'I am Lazarus, come from the dead,

Come back to tell you all, I shall tell you all'—
If one, settling a pillow by her head,
  Should say: 'That is not what I meant at all.
  That is not it, at all.'
And would it have been worth it, after all,
Would it have been worth while,
After the sunsets and the dooryards and the sprinkled streets,
After the novels, after the teacups, after the skirts that trail along
    the floor—
And this, and so much more?—
It is impossible to say just what I mean!
But as if a magic lantern threw the nerves in patterns on a screen:
Would it have been worth while
If one, settling a pillow or throwing off a shawl,
And turning toward the window, should say:
  'That is not it at all,
  That is not what I meant, at all.'

. . . . .

No! I am not Prince Hamlet, nor was meant to be;
Am an attendant lord, one that will do
To swell a progress, start a scene or two,
Advise the prince; no doubt, an easy tool,
Deferential, glad to be of use,
Politic, cautious, and meticulous;
Full of high sentence, but a bit obtuse;
At times, indeed, almost ridiculous—
Almost, at times, the Fool.

I grow old . . . I grow old . . .
I shall wear the bottoms of my trousers rolled.

Shall I part my hair behind? Do I dare to eat a peach?
I shall wear white flannel trousers, and walk upon the beach.
I have heard the mermaids singing, each to each.

I do not think that they will sing to me.

I have seen them riding seaward on the waves
Combing the white hair of the waves blown back
When the wind blows the water white and black.

We have lingered in the chambers of the sea
By sea-girls wreathed with seaweed red and brown
Till human voices wake us, and we drown.

Gerontion

Thou has nor youth nor age
But as it were an after dinner sleep
Dreaming of both.

Here I am, an old man in a dry month,
Being read to by a boy, waiting for rain.
I was neither at the hot gates
Nor fought in the warm rain
Nor knee deep in the salt marsh, heaving a cutlass,
Bitten by flies, fought.
My house is a decayed house,
And the Jew squats on the window sill, the owner,
Spawned in some estaminet of Antwerp,
Blistered in Brussels, patched and peeled in London.
The goat coughs at night in the field overhead;
Rocks, moss, stonecrop, iron, merds.
The woman keeps the kitchen, makes tea,
Sneezes at evening, poking the peevish gutter.
I an old man,
A dull head among windy spaces.

Signs are taken for wonders. 'We would see a sign!'
The word within a word, unable to speak a word,
Swaddled with darkness. In the juvescence of the year
Came Christ the tiger

In depraved May, dogwood and chestnut, flowering judas,
To be eaten, to be divided, to be drunk
Among whispers; by Mr. Silvero
With caressing hands, at Limoges
Who walked all night in the next room;
By Hakagawa, bowing among the Titians;
By Madame de Tornquist, in the dark room

Shifting the candles: Fräulein von Kulp
Who turned in the hall, one hand on the door.
    Vacant shuttles
Weave the wind. I have no ghosts,
An old man in a draughty house
Under a windy knob.

After such knowledge, what forgiveness? Think now
History has many cunning passages, contrived corridors
And issues, deceives with whispering ambitions,
Guides us by vanities. Think now
She gives when our attention is distracted
And what she gives, gives with such supple confusions
That the giving famishes the craving. Gives too late
What's not believed in, or is still believed,
In memory only, reconsidered passion. Gives too soon
Into weak hands, what's thought can be dispensed with
Till the refusal propagates a fear. Think
Neither fear nor courage saves us. Unnatural vices
Are fathered by our heroism. Virtues
Are forced upon us by our impudent crimes.
These tears are shaken from the wrath-bearing tree.

The tiger springs in the new year. Us he devours. Think at last
We have not reached conclusion, when I
Stiffen in a rented house. Think at last
I have not made this show purposelessly
And it is not by any concitation
Of the backward devils.
I would meet you upon this honestly.
I that was near your heart was removed therefrom
To lose beauty in terror, terror in inquisition.
I have lost my passion: why should I need to keep it
Since what is kept must be adulterated?
I have lost my sight, smell, hearing, taste and touch:
How should I use them for your closer contact?

These with a thousand small deliberations
Protract the profit of their chilled delirium,
Excite the membrane, when the sense has cooled,
With pungent sauces, multiply variety

In a wilderness of mirrors. What will the spider do,
Suspend its operations, will the weevil
Delay? De Bailhache, Fresca, Mrs. Cammel; whirled
Beyond the circuit of the shuddering Bear
In fractured atoms. Gull against the wind, in the windy straits
Of Belle Isle, or running on the Horn.
White feathers in the snow, the Gulf claims,
And an old man driven by the Trades
To a sleepy corner.

Tenants of the house,
Thoughts of a dry brain in a dry season.

The Waste Land

'Nam Sibyllam quidem Cumis ego ipse oculis meis vidi in ampulla pendere, et cum illi pueri dicerent: Σιβυλλα τί θέλεις; *respondebat illa:* ἀποθανεῖν θέλω.'

For Ezra Pound
il miglior fabbro.

I. THE BURIAL OF THE DEAD

April is the cruellest month, breeding
Lilacs out of the dead land, mixing
Memory and desire, stirring
Dull roots with spring rain.
Winter kept us warm, covering
Earth in forgetful snow, feeding
A little life with dried tubers.
Summer surprised us, coming over the Starnbergersee
With a shower of rain; we stopped in the colonnade,
And went on in sunlight, into the Hofgarten,
And drank coffee, and talked for an hour.
Bin gar keine Russin, stamm' aus Litauen, echt deutsch.
And when we were children, staying at the arch-duke's,
My cousin's, he took me out on a sled,
And I was frightened. He said, Marie,
Marie, hold on tight. And down we went.

In the mountains, there you feel free.
I read, much of the night, and go south in the winter.

What are the roots that clutch, what branches grow
Out of this stony rubbish? Son of man,
You cannot say, or guess, for you know only
A heap of broken images, where the sun beats,
And the dead tree gives no shelter, the cricket no relief,
And the dry stone no sound of water. Only
There is shadow under this red rock,
(Come in under the shadow of this red rock),
And I will show you something different from either
Your shadow at morning striding behind you
Or your shadow at evening rising to meet you;
I will show you fear in a handful of dust.
Frisch weht der Wind
Der Heimat zu
Mein Irisch Kind,
Wo weilest du?
'You gave me hyacinths first a year ago;
'They called me the hyacinth girl.'
—Yet when we came back, late, from the hyacinth garden,
Your arms full, and your hair wet, I could not
Speak, and my eyes failed, I was neither
Living nor dead, and I knew nothing,
Looking into the heart of light, the silence.
Oed' und leer das Meer.

Madame Sosostris, famous clairvoyante,
Had a bad cold, nevertheless
Is known to be the wisest woman in Europe,
With a wicked pack of cards. Here, said she,
Is your card, the drowned Phoenician Sailor,
(Those are pearls that were his eyes. Look!)
Here is Belladonna, the Lady of the Rocks,
The lady of situations.
Here is the man with three staves, and here the Wheel,
And here is the one-eyed merchant, and this card,
Which is blank, is something he carries on his back,
Which I am forbidden to see. I do not find
The Hanged Man. Fear death by water.

I see crowds of people, walking round in a ring.
Thank you. If you see dear Mrs. Equitone,
Tell her I bring the horoscope myself:
One must be so careful these days.

Unreal City,
Under the brown fog of a winter dawn,
A crowd flowed over London Bridge, so many,
I had not thought death had undone so many.
Sighs, short and infrequent, were exhaled,
And each man fixed his eyes before his feet.
Flowed up the hill and down King William Street,
To where Saint Mary Woolnoth kept the hours
With a dead sound on the final stroke of nine.
There I saw one I knew, and stopped him, crying: 'Stetson!
'You who were with me in the ships at Mylae!
'That corpse you planted last year in your garden,
'Has it begun to sprout? Will it bloom this year?
'Or has the sudden frost disturbed its bed?
'O keep the Dog far hence, that's friend to men,
'Or with his nails he'll dig it up again!
'You! hypocrite lecteur!—mon semblable,—mon frère!'

II. A GAME OF CHESS

The Chair she sat in, like a burnished throne,
Glowed on the marble, where the glass
Held up by standards wrought with fruited vines
From which a golden Cupidon peeped out
(Another hid his eyes behind his wing)
Doubled the flames of sevenbranched candelabra
Reflecting light upon the table as
The glitter of her jewels rose to meet it,
From satin cases poured in rich profusion.
In vials of ivory and coloured glass
Unstoppered, lurked her strange synthetic perfumes,
Unguent, powdered, or liquid—troubled, confused
And drowned the sense in odours; stirred by the air
That freshened from the window, these ascended
In fattening the prolonged candle-flames,
Flung their smoke into the laquearia,

Stirring the pattern on the coffered ceiling.
Huge sea-wood fed with copper
Burned green and orange, framed by the coloured stone,
In which sad light a carvèd dolphin swam.
Above the antique mantel was displayed
As though a window gave upon the sylvan scene
The change of Philomel, by the barbarous king
So rudely forced; yet there the nightingale
Filled all the desert with inviolable voice
And still she cried, and still the world pursues,
'Jug Jug' to dirty ears.
And other withered stumps of time
Were told upon the walls; staring forms
Leaned out, leaning, hushing the room enclosed.
Footsteps shuffled on the stair.
Under the firelight, under the brush, her hair
Spread out in fiery points
Glowed into words, then would be savagely still.

'My nerves are bad to-night. Yes, bad. Stay with me.
'Speak to me. Why do you never speak. Speak.
  'What are you thinking of? What thinking? What?
'I never know what you are thinking. Think.'

I think we are in rats' alley
Where the dead men lost their bones.

'What is that noise?'
                    The wind under the door.
'What is that noise now? What is the wind doing?'
                    Nothing again nothing.
                                                  'Do
'You know nothing? Do you see nothing? Do you remember
'Nothing?'

  I remember
Those are pearls that were his eyes.
'Are you alive, or not? Is there nothing in your head?'
                                                  But
O O O O that Shakespeherian Rag—
It's so elegant

So intelligent
'What shall I do now? What shall I do?'
'I shall rush out as I am, and walk the street
'With my hair down, so. What shall we do tomorrow?
'What shall we ever do?'
                                        The hot water at ten.
And if it rains, a closed car at four.
And we shall play a game of chess,
Pressing lidless eyes and waiting for a knock upon the door.

When Lil's husband got demobbed, I said—
I didn't mince my words, I said to her myself,
HURRY UP PLEASE ITS TIME
Now Albert's coming back, make yourself a bit smart.
He'll want to know what you done with that money he gave you
To get yourself some teeth. He did, I was there.
You have them all out, Lil, and get a nice set,
He said, I swear, I can't bear to look at you.
And no more can't I, I said, and think of poor Albert,
He's been in the army four years, he wants a good time,
And if you don't give it him, there's others will, I said.
Oh is there, she said. Something o' that, I said.
Then I'll know who to thank, she said, and give me a straight look.
HURRY UP PLEASE ITS TIME
If you don't like it you can get on with it, I said.
Others can pick and choose if you can't.
But if Albert makes off, it won't be for lack of telling.
You ought to be ashamed, I said, to look so antique.
(And her only thirty-one.)
I can't help it, she said, pulling a long face,
It's them pills I took, to bring it off, she said.
(She's had five already, and nearly died of young George.)
The chemist said it would be all right, but I've never been the same.
You *are* a proper fool, I said.
Well, if Albert won't leave you alone, there it is, I said,
What you get married for if you don't want children?
HURRY UP PLEASE ITS TIME
Well, that Sunday Albert was home, they had a hot gammon,
And they asked me in to dinner, to get the beauty of it hot—
HURRY UP PLEASE ITS TIME
HURRY UP PLEASE ITS TIME

Goonight Bill. Goonight Lou. Goonight May. Goonight.
Ta ta. Goonight. Goonight
Good night, ladies, good night, sweet ladies, good night, good night.

III. THE FIRE SERMON

The river's tent is broken; the last fingers of leaf
Clutch and sink into the wet bank. The wind
Crosses the brown land, unheard. The nymphs are departed.
Sweet Thames, run softly, till I end my song.
The river bears no empty bottles, sandwich papers,
Silk handkerchiefs, cardboard boxes, cigarette ends
Or other testimony of summer nights. The nymphs are departed.
And their friends, the loitering heirs of City directors;
Departed, have left no addresses.
By the waters of Leman I sat down and wept . . .
Sweet Thames, run softly till I end my song,
Sweet Thames, run softly, for I speak not loud or long.
But at my back in a cold blast I hear
The rattle of the bones, and chuckle spread from ear to ear.

A rat crept softly through the vegetation
Dragging its slimy belly on the bank
While I was fishing in the dull canal
On a winter evening round behind the gashouse
Musing upon the king my brother's wreck
And on the king my father's death before him.
White bodies naked on the low damp ground
And bones cast in a little low dry garret,
Rattled by the rat's foot only, year to year.
But at my back from time to time I hear
The sound of horns and motors, which shall bring
Sweeney to Mrs. Porter in the spring.
O the moon shone bright on Mrs. Porter
And on her daughter
They wash their feet in soda water
Et O ces voix d'enfants, chantant dans la coupole!
Twit twit twit
Jug jug jug jug jug jug
So rudely forc'd.
Tereu

Unreal City
Under the brown fog of a winter noon
Mr. Eugenides, the Smyrna merchant
Unshaven, with a pocket full of currants
C.i.f. London: documents at sight,
Asked me in demotic French
To luncheon at the Cannon Street Hotel
Followed by a weekend at the Metropole.

At the violet hour, when the eyes and back
Turn upward from the desk, when the human engine waits
Like a taxi throbbing waiting,
I Tiresias, though blind, throbbing between two lives,
Old man with wrinkled female breasts, can see
At the violet hour, the evening hour that strives
Homeward, and brings the sailor home from sea,
The typist home at teatime, clears her breakfast, lights
Her stove, and lays out food in tins.
Out of the window perilously spread
Her drying combinations touched by the sun's last rays,
On the divan are piled (at night her bed)
Stockings, slippers, camisoles, and stays.
I Tiresias, old man with wrinkled dugs
Perceived the scene, and foretold the rest—
I too awaited the expected guest.
He, the young man carbuncular, arrives,
A small house agent's clerk, with one bold stare,
One of the low on whom assurance sits
As a silk hat on a Bradford millionaire.
The time is now propitious, as he guesses,
The meal is ended, she is bored and tired,
Endeavours to engage her in caresses
Which still are unreproved, if undesired.
Flushed and decided, he assaults at once;
Exploring hands encounter no defence;
His vanity requires no response,
And makes a welcome of indifference.
(And I Tiresias have foresuffered all
Enacted on this same divan or bed;
I who have sat by Thebes below the wall
And walked among the lowest of the dead.)

Bestows one final patronising kiss,
And gropes his way, finding the stairs unlit . . .

She turns and looks a moment in the glass,
Hardly aware of her departed lover;
Her brain allows one half-formed thought to pass:
'Well now that's done: and I'm glad it's over.'
When lovely woman stoops to folly and
Paces about her room again, alone,
She smoothes her hair with automatic hand,
And puts a record on the gramophone.

'This music crept by me upon the waters'
And along the Strand, up Queen Victoria Street.
O City city, I can sometimes hear
Beside a public bar in Lower Thames Street,
The pleasant whining of a mandoline
And a clatter and a chatter from within
Where fishmen lounge at noon: where the walls
Of Magnus Martyr hold
Inexplicable splendour of Ionian white and gold.

The river sweats
Oil and tar
The barges drift
With the turning tide
Red sails
Wide
To leeward, swing on the heavy spar.
The barges wash
Drifting logs
Down Greenwich reach
Past the Isle of Dogs.
Weialala leia
Wallala leialala

Elizabeth and Leicester
Beating oars
The stern was formed
A gilded shell
Red and gold

The brisk swell
Rippled both shores
Southwest wind
Carried down stream
The peal of bells
White towers
                    Weialala leia
                    Wallala leialala

'Trams and dusty trees.
Highbury bore me. Richmond and Kew
Undid me. By Richmond I raised my knees
Supine on the floor of a narrow canoe.'

'My feet are at Moorgate, and my heart
Under my feet. After the event
He wept. He promised "a new start."
I made no comment. What should I resent?'

'On Margate Sands.
I can connect
Nothing with nothing.
The broken fingernails of dirty hands.
My people humble people who expect
Nothing.'
                    la la

To Carthage then I came

Burning burning burning burning
O Lord Thou pluckest me out
O Lord Thou pluckest

burning

IV. DEATH BY WATER

Phlebas the Phoenician, a fortnight dead,
Forgot the cry of gulls, and the deep sea swell
And the profit and loss.

A current under sea
Picked his bones in whispers. As he rose and fell
He passed the stages of his age and youth
Entering the whirlpool.
Gentile or Jew
O you who turn the wheel and look to windward,
Consider Phlebas, who was once handsome and tall as you.

V. WHAT THE THUNDER SAID

After the torchlight red on sweaty faces
After the frosty silence in the gardens
After the agony in stony places
The shouting and the crying
Prison and palace and reverberation
Of thunder of spring over distant mountains
He who was living is now dead
We who were living are now dying
With a little patience

Here is no water but only rock
Rock and no water and the sandy road
The road winding above among the mountains
Which are mountains of rock without water
If there were water we should stop and drink
Amongst the rock one cannot stop or think
Sweat is dry and feet are in the sand
If there were only water amongst the rock
Dead mountain mouth of carious teeth that cannot spit
Here one can neither stand nor lie nor sit
There is not even silence in the mountains
But dry sterile thunder without rain
There is not even solitude in the mountains
But red sullen faces sneer and snarl
From doors of mudcracked houses
If there were water

And no rock
If there were rock
And also water
And water
A spring

A pool among the rock
If there were the sound of water only
Not the cicada
And dry grass singing
But sound of water over a rock
Where the hermit-thrush sings in the pine trees
Drip drop drip drop drop drop drop
But there is no water

Who is the third who walks always beside you?
When I count, there are only you and I together
But when I look ahead up the white road
There is always another one walking beside you
Gliding wrapt in a brown mantle, hooded
I do not know whether a man or a woman
—But who is that on the other side of you?
What is that sound high in the air
Murmur of maternal lamentation
Who are those hooded hordes swarming
Over endless plains, stumbling in cracked earth
Ringed by the flat horizon only
What is the city over the mountains
Cracks and reforms and bursts in the violet air
Falling towers
Jerusalem Athens Alexandria
Vienna London
Unreal

A woman drew her long black hair out tight
And fiddled whisper music on those strings
And bats with baby faces in the violet light
Whistled, and beat their wings
And crawled head downward down a blackened wall
And upside down in air were towers
Tolling reminiscent bells, that kept the hours
And voices singing out of empty cisterns and exhausted wells

In this decayed hole among the mountains
In the faint moonlight, the grass is singing
Over the tumbled graves, about the chapel
There is the empty chapel, only the wind's home.

It has no windows, and the door swings,
Dry bones can harm no one.
Only a cock stood on the rooftree
Co co rico co co rico
In a flash of lightning. Then a damp gust
Bringing rain

Ganga was sunken, and the limp leaves
Waited for rain, while the black clouds
Gathered far distant, over Himavant.
The jungle crouched, humped in silence.
Then spoke the thunder
DA
Datta: what have we given?
My friend, blood shaking my heart
The awful daring of a moment's surrender
Which an age of prudence can never retract
By this, and this only, we have existed
Which is not to be found in our obituaries
Or in memories draped by the beneficent spider
Or under seals broken by the lean solicitor
In our empty rooms
DA
Dayadhvam: I have heard the key
Turn in the door once and turn once only
We think of the key, each in his prison
Thinking of the key, each confirms a prison
Only at nightfall, aethereal rumours
Revive for a moment a broken Coriolanus
DA
Damyata: The boat responded
Gaily, to the hand expert with sail and oar
The sea was calm, your heart would have responded
Gaily, when invited, beating obedient
To controlling hands

I sat upon the shore
Fishing, with the arid plain behind me
Shall I at least set my lands in order?
London Bridge is falling down falling down falling down
Poi s'ascose nel foco che gli affina

Quando fiam uti chelidon—O swallow swallow
Le Prince d'Aquitaine à la tour abolie
These fragments I have shored against my ruins
Why then Ile fit you. Hieronymo's mad againe.

Datta. Dayadhvam. Damyata.
Shantih shantih shantih

Journey of the Magi

'A cold coming we had of it,
Just the worst time of the year
For a journey, and such a long journey:
The ways deep and the weather sharp,
The very dead of winter.'
And the camels galled, sore-footed, refractory,
Lying down in the melting snow.
There were times we regretted
The summer palaces on slopes, the terraces,
And the silken girls bringing sherbet.
Then the camel men cursing and grumbling
And running away, and wanting their liquor and women,
And the night-fires going out, and the lack of shelters,
And the cities hostile and the towns unfriendly
And the villages dirty and charging high prices:
A hard time we had of it.
At the end we preferred to travel all night,
Sleeping in snatches,
With the voices singing in our ears, saying
That this was all folly.

Then at dawn we came down to a temperate valley,
Wet, below the snow line, smelling of vegetation,
With a running stream and a water-mill beating the darkness,
And three trees on the low sky.
And an old white horse galloped away in the meadow.
Then we came to a tavern with vine-leaves over the lintel,
Six hands at an open door dicing for pieces of silver,

And feet kicking the empty wine-skins.
But there was no information, and so we continued
And arrived at evening, not a moment too soon
Finding the place; it was (you may say) satisfactory.

All this was a long time ago, I remember.
And I would do it again, but set down
This set down
This: were we led all that way for
Birth or Death? There was a Birth, certainly,
We had evidence and no doubt. I had seen birth and death,
But had thought they were different; this Birth was
Hard and bitter agony for us, like Death, our death.
We returned to our places, these Kingdoms,
But no longer at ease here, in the old dispensation,
With an alien people clutching their gods.
I should be glad of another death.

Little Gidding

(the fourth of the *Four Quartets*)

I

Midwinter spring is its own season
Sempiternal though sodden towards sundown,
Suspended in time, between pole and tropic.
When the short day is brightest, with frost and fire,
The brief sun flames the ice, on pond and ditches,
In windless cold that is the heart's heat,
Reflecting in a watery mirror
A glare that is blindness in the early afternoon.
And glow more intense than blaze of branch, or brazier,
Stirs the dumb spirit: no wind, but pentecostal fire
In the dark time of the year. Between melting and freezing
The soul's sap quivers. There is no earth smell
Or smell of living thing. This is the spring time
But not in time's covenant. Now the hedgerow
Is blanched for an hour with transitory blossom

Of snow, a bloom more sudden
Than that of summer, neither budding nor fading,
Not in the scheme of generation.
Where is the summer, the unimaginable
Zero summer?

                    If you came this way,
Taking the route you would be likely to take
From the place you would be likely to come from,
If you came this way in may time, you would find the hedges
White again, in May, with voluptuary sweetness.
It would be the same at the end of the journey,
If you came at night like a broken king,
If you came by day not knowing what you came for,
It would be the same, when you leave the rough road
And turn behind the pig-sty to the dull façade
And the tombstone. And what you thought you came for
Is only a shell, a husk of meaning
From which the purpose breaks only when it is fulfilled
If at all. Either you had no purpose
Or the purpose is beyond the end you figured
And is altered in fulfilment. There are other places
Which also are the world's end, some at the sea jaws,
Or over a dark lake, in a desert or a city—
But this is the nearest, in place and time,
Now and in England.
                    If you came this way,
Taking any route, starting from anywhere,
At any time or at any season,
It would always be the same: you would have to put off
Sense and notion. You are not here to verify,
Instruct yourself, or inform curiosity
Or carry report. You are here to kneel
Where prayer has been valid. And prayer is more
Than an order of words, the conscious occupation
Of the praying mind, or the sound of the voice praying.
And what the dead had no speech for, when living,
They can tell you, being dead: the communication
Of the dead is tongued with fire beyond the language of the living.
Here, the intersection of the timeless moment
Is England and nowhere. Never and always.

II

Ash on an old man's sleeve
Is all the ash the burnt roses leave.
Dust in the air suspended
Marks the place where a story ended.
Dust inbreathed was a house—
The wall, the wainscot and the mouse.
The death of hope and despair,
    This is the death of air.

There are flood and drouth
Over the eyes and in the mouth,
Dead water and dead sand
Contending for the upper hand.
The parched eviscerate soil
Gapes at the vanity of toil,
Laughs without mirth.
    This is the death of earth.
Water and fire succeed
The town, the pasture and the weed.
Water and fire deride
The sacrifice that we denied.
Water and fire shall rot
The marred foundations we forgot,
Of sanctuary and choir.
    This is the death of water and fire.
In the uncertain hour before the morning
  Near the ending of interminable night
  At the recurrent end of the unending
After the dark dove with the flickering tongue
  Had passed below the horizon of his homing
  While the dead leaves still rattled on like tin
Over the asphalt where no other sound was
  Between three districts whence the smoke arose
  I met one walking, loitering and hurried
As if blown towards me like the metal leaves
  Before the urban dawn wind unresisting.
  And as I fixed upon the down-turned face
That pointed scrutiny with which we challenge
  The first-met stranger in the waning dusk
  I caught the sudden look of some dead master

Whom I had known, forgotten, half recalled
  Both one and many; in the brown baked features
  The eyes of a familiar compound ghost
Both intimate and unidentifiable.
  So I assumed a double part, and cried
  And heard another's voice cry: 'What! are *you* here?'
Although we were not. I was still the same,
  Knowing myself yet being someone other—
  And he a face still forming; yet the words sufficed
To compel the recognition they preceded.
  And so, compliant to the common wind,
  Too strange to each other for misunderstanding.
In concord at this intersection time
  Of meeting nowhere, no before and after,
  We trod the pavement in a dead patrol.
I said: 'The wonder that I feel is easy,
  Yet ease is cause of wonder. Therefore speak:
  I may not comprehend, may not remember.'
And he: 'I am not eager to rehearse
  My thought and theory which you have forgotten.
  These things have served their purpose: let them be.
So with your own, and pray they be forgiven
  By others, as I pray you to forgive
  Both bad and good. Last season's fruit is eaten
And the fullfed beast shall kick the empty pail.
  For last year's words belong to last year's language
  And next year's words await another voice.
But, as the passage now presents no hindrance
  To the spirit unappeased and peregrine
  Between two worlds become much like each other,
So I find words I never thought to speak
  In streets I never thought I should revisit
  When I left my body on a distant shore.
Since our concern was speech, and speech impelled us
  To purify the dialect of the tribe
  And urge the mind to aftersight and foresight,
Let me disclose the gifts reserved for age
  To set a crown upon your lifetime's effort.
  First, the cold friction of expiring sense

Without enchantment, offering no promise
  But bitter tastelessness of shadow fruit
  As body and soul begin to fall asunder.
Second, the conscious impotence of rage
  At human folly, and the laceration
  Of laughter at what ceases to amuse.
And last, the rending pain of re-enactment
  Of all that you have done, and been; the shame
  Of motives late revealed, and the awareness
Of things ill done and done to others' harm
  Which once you took for exercise of virtue.
  Then fools' approval stings, and honour stains.
From wrong to wrong the exasperated spirit
  Proceeds, unless restored by that refining fire
  Where you must move in measure, like a dancer.'
The day was breaking. In the disfigured street
  He left me, with a kind of valediction,
  And faded on the blowing of the horn.

III

There are three conditions which often look alike
Yet differ completely, flourish in the same hedgerow:
Attachment to self and to things and to persons, detachment
From self and from things and from persons; and, growing between them, indifference
Which resembles the others as death resembles life,
Being between two lives—unflowering, between
The live and the dead nettle. This is the use of memory:
For liberation—not less of love but expanding
Of love beyond desire, and so liberation
From the future as well as the past. Thus, love of a country
Begins as attachment to our own field of action
And comes to find that action of little importance
Though never indifferent. History may be servitude,
History may be freedom. See, now they vanish,
The faces and places, with the self which, as it could, loved them,
To become renewed, transfigured, in another pattern.
Sin is Behovely, but
All shall be well, and
All manner of thing shall be well.

If I think, again, of this place,
And of people, not wholly commendable,
Of no immediate kin or kindness,
But some of peculiar genius,
All touched by a common genius,
United in the strife which divided them;
If I think of a king at nightfall,
Of three men, and more, on the scaffold
And a few who died forgotten
In other places, here and abroad,
And of one who died blind and quiet
Why should we celebrate
These dead men more than the dying?
It is not to ring the bell backward
Nor is it an incantation
To summon the spectre of a Rose.
We cannot revive old factions
We cannot restore old policies
Or follow an antique drum.
These men, and those who opposed them
And those whom they opposed
Accept the constitution of silence
And are folded in a single party.
Whatever we inherit from the fortunate
We have taken from the defeated
What they had to leave us—a symbol:
A symbol perfected in death.
And all shall be well and
All manner of thing shall be well
By the purification of the motive
In the ground of our beseeching.

IV

The dove descending breaks the air
With flame of incandescent terror
Of which the tongues declare
The one discharge from sin and error.
The only hope, or else despair
  Lies in the choice of pyre or pyre—
  To be redeemed from fire by fire.

Who then devised the torment? Love.
Love is the unfamiliar Name
Behind the hands that wove
The intolerable shirt of flame
Which human power cannot remove.
  We only live, only suspire
  Consumed by either fire or fire.

V

What we call the beginning is often the end
And to make an end is to make a beginning.
The end is where we start from. And every phrase
And sentence that is right (where every word is at home,
Taking its place to support the others,
The word neither diffident nor ostentatious,
An easy commerce of the old and the new,
The common word exact without vulgarity,
The formal word precise but not pedantic,
The complete consort dancing together)
Every phrase and every sentence is an end and a beginning,
Every poem an epitaph. And any action
Is a step to the block, to the fire, down the sea's throat
Or to an illegible stone: and that is where we start.
We die with the dying:
See, they depart, and we go with them.
We are born with the dead:
See, they return, and bring us with them.
The moment of the rose and the moment of the yew-tree
Are of equal duration. A people without history
Is not redeemed from time, for history is a pattern
Of timeless moments. So, while the light fails
On a winter's afternoon, in a secluded chapel
History is now and England.

  With the drawing of this Love and the voice of this Calling

We shall not cease from exploration
And the end of all our exploring
Will be to arrive where we started
And know the place for the first time.
Through the unknown, remembered gate

When the last of earth left to discover
Is that which was the beginning;
At the source of the longest river
The voice of the hidden waterfall
And the children in the apple-tree
Not known, because not looked for
But heard, half-heard, in the stillness
Between two waves of the sea.
Quick now, here, now, always—
A condition of complete simplicity
(Costing not less than everything)
And all shall be well and
All manner of thing shall be well
When the tongues of flame are in-folded
Into the crowned knot of fire
And the fire and the rose are one.

JOHN CROWE RANSOM
(1888–1974)

Bells for John Whiteside's Daughter

There was such speed in her little body,
And such lightness in her footfall,
It is no wonder her brown study
Astonishes us all.

Her wars were bruited in our high window.
We looked among orchard trees and beyond
Where she took arms against her shadow,
Or harried unto the pond

The lazy geese, like a snow cloud
Dripping their snow on the green grass,
Tricking and stopping, sleepy and proud,
Who cried in goose, Alas,

For the tireless heart within the little
Lady with rod that made them rise
From their noon apple-dreams and scuttle
Goose-fashion under the skies!

But now go the bells, and we are ready,
In one house we are sternly stopped
To say we are vexed at her brown study,
Lying so primly propped.

Piazza Piece

—I am a gentleman in a dust coat trying
To make you hear. Your ears are soft and small
And listen to an old man not at all,
They want the young men's whispering and sighing.
But see the roses on your trellis dying
And hear the spectral singing of the moon;
For I must have my lovely lady soon,
I am a gentleman in a dust coat trying.

—I am a lady young in beauty waiting
Until my truelove comes, and then we kiss.
But what gray man among the vines is this
Whose words are dry and faint as in a dream?
Back from my trellis, sir, before I scream!
I am a lady young in beauty waiting.

Here Lies a Lady

Here lies a lady of beauty and high degree.
Of chills and fever she died, of fever and chills,
The delight of her husband, her aunt, an infant of three,
And of medicos marveling sweetly on her ills.

For either she burned, and her confident eyes would blaze,
And her fingers fly in a manner to puzzle their heads—
What was she making? Why, nothing; she sat in a maze
Of old scraps of laces, snipped into curious shreds—

Or this would pass, and the light of her fire decline
Till she lay discouraged and cold, like a thin stalk white and
  blown,
And would not open her eyes, to kisses, to wine;
The sixth of these states was her last; the cold settled down.

Sweet ladies, long may ye bloom, and toughly I hope ye may
  thole,
But was she not lucky? In flowers and lace and mourning,
In love and great honor we bade God rest her soul
After six little spaces of chill, and six of burning.

Blue Girls

Twirling your blue skirts, traveling the sward
Under the towers of your seminary,
Go listen to your teachers old and contrary
Without believing a word.

Tie the white fillets then about your hair
And think no more of what will come to pass
Than bluebirds that go walking on the grass
And chattering on the air.

Practice your beauty, blue girls, before it fail;
And I will cry with my loud lips and publish
Beauty which all our power shall never establish,
It is so frail.

For I could tell you a story which is true;
I know a lady with a terrible tongue,
Blear eyes fallen from blue,
All her perfections tarnished—yet it is not long
Since she was lovelier than any of you.

Janet Waking

Beautifully Janet slept
Till it was deeply morning. She woke then
And thought about her dainty-feathered hen,
To see how it had kept.

One kiss she gave her mother.
Only a small one gave she to her daddy
Who would have kissed each curl of his shining baby;
No kiss at all for her brother.

"Old Chucky, old Chucky!" she cried,
Running across the world upon the grass
To Chucky's house, and listening. But alas,
Her Chucky had died.

It was a transmogrifying bee
Came droning down on Chucky's old bald head
And sat and put the poison. It scarcely bled,
But how exceedingly

And purply did the knot
Swell with the venom and communicate
Its rigor! Now the poor comb stood up straight
But Chucky did not.

So there was Janet
Kneeling on the wet grass, crying her brown hen
(Translated far beyond the daughters of men)
To rise and walk upon it.

And weeping fast as she had breath
Janet implored us, "Wake her from her sleep!"
And would not be instructed in how deep
Was the forgetful kingdom of death.

Survey of Literature

In all the good Greek of Plato
I lack my roast beef and potato.

A better man was Aristotle,
Pulling steady on the bottle.

I dip my hat to Chaucer,
Swilling soup from his saucer,

And to Master Shakespeare
Who wrote big on small beer.

The abstemious Wordsworth
Subsisted on a curd's-worth,

But a slick one was Tennyson,
Putting gravy on his venison.

What these men had to eat and drink
Is what we say and what we think.

The influence of Milton
Came wry out of Stilton.

Sing a song for Percy Shelley,
Drowned in pale lemon jelly,

And for precious John Keats,
Dripping blood of pickled beets.

Then there was poor Willie Blake,
He foundered on sweet cake.

God have mercy on the sinner
Who must write with no dinner,

No gravy and no grub,
No pewter and no pub,

No belly and no bowels,
Only consonants and vowels.

The Equilibrists

Full of her long white arms and milky skin
He had a thousand times remembered sin.
Alone in the press of people traveled he,
Minding her jacinth, and myrrh, and ivory.

Mouth he remembered: the quaint orifice
From which came heat that flamed upon the kiss,
Till cold words came down spiral from the head.
Gray doves from the officious tower ill sped.

Body: it was a white field ready for love.
On her body's field, with the gaunt tower above,
The lilies grew, beseeching him to take,
If he would pluck and wear them, bruise and break.

Eyes talking: Never mind the cruel words,
Embrace my flowers, but not embrace the swords.
But what they said, the doves came straightway flying
And unsaid: Honor, Honor, they came crying.

Importunate her doves. Too pure, too wise,
Clambering on his shoulder, saying, Arise,
Leave me now, and never let us meet,
Eternal distance now command thy feet.

Predicament indeed, which thus discovers
Honor among thieves, Honor between lovers.
O such a little word is Honor, they feel!
But the gray word is between them cold as steel.

At length I saw these lovers fully were come
Into their torture of equilibrium;
Dreadfully had forsworn each other, and yet
They were bound each to each, and they did not forget.

And rigid as two painful stars, and twirled
About the clustered night their prison world,
They burned with fierce love always to come near,
But honor beat them back and kept them clear.

Ah, the strict lovers, they are ruined now!
I cried in anger. But with puddled brow
Devising for those gibbeted and brave
Came I descanting: Man, what would you have?

For spin your period out, and draw your breath,
A kinder saeculum begins with Death.
Would you ascend to Heaven and bodiless dwell?
Or take your bodies honorless to Hell?

In Heaven you have heard no marriage is,
No white flesh tinder to your lecheries,
Your male and female tissue sweetly shaped
Sublimed away, and furious blood escaped.

Great lovers lie in Hell, the stubborn ones
Infatuate of the flesh upon the bones;
Stuprate, they rend each other when they kiss,
The pieces kiss again, no end to this.

But still I watched them spinning, orbited nice.
Their flames were not more radiant than their ice.
I dug in the quiet earth and wrought the tomb
And made these lines to memorize their doom:—

Epitaph

Equilibrists lie here; stranger, tread light;
Close, but untouching in each other's sight;
Moldered the lips and ashy the tall skull.
Let them lie perilous and beautiful.

CONRAD AIKEN
(1889–1973)

Hatteras Calling

Southeast, and storm, and every weathervane
shivers and moans upon its dripping pin,
ragged on chimneys the cloud whips, the rain
howls at the flues and windows to get in,

the golden rooster claps his golden wings
and from the Baptist Chapel shrieks no more,
the golden arrow into the southeast sings
and hears on the roof the Atlantic Ocean roar.

Waves among wires, sea scudding over poles,
down every alley the magnificence of rain,
dead gutters live once more, the deep manholes
hollo in triumph a passage to the main.

Umbrellas, and in the Gardens one old man
hurries away along a dancing path,
listens to music on a watering-can,
observes among the tulips the sudden wrath,

pale willows thrashing to the needled lake,
and dinghies filled with water; while the sky
smashes the lilacs, swoops to shake and break,
till shattered branches shriek and railings cry.

Speak, Hatteras, your language of the sea:
scour with kelp and spindrift the stale street:
that man in terror may learn once more to be
child of that hour when rock and ocean meet.

Herman Melville

'My towers at last!'—
                                        What meant the words
from what acknowledged circuit sprung
and in the heart and on the tongue
at sight of few familiar birds
when seaward his last sail unfurled
to leeward from the wheel once more
bloomed the pale crags of haunted shore
that once-more-visited notch of world:
and straight he knew as known before
the Logos in Leviathan's roar
he deepest sounding with his lead
who all had fathomed all had said.

Much-loving hero—towers indeed
were those that overhung your log
with entries of typhoon and fog
and thunderstone for Adam's breed:
man's warm Sargasso Sea of faith
dislimned in light by luck or fate
you for mankind set sail by hate
and weathered it, and with it death.
And now at world's end coasting late
in dolphined calms beyond the gate
which Hercules flung down, you come
to the grim rocks that nod you home.

Depth below depth this love of man:
among unnumbered and unknown
to mark and make his cryptic own
one landfall of all time began:
of all life's hurts to treasure one
and hug it to the wounded breast,
in this to dedicate the rest,
all injuries received or done.

Your towers again but towers now blest
your haven in a shoreless west
O mariner of the human soul
who in the landmark notched the Pole
and in the Item loved the Whole.

The Wedding

At noon, Tithonus, withered by his singing,
Climbing the oatstalk with his hairy legs,
Met grey Arachne, poisoned and shrunk down
By her own beauty; pride had shrivelled both.
In the white web—where seven flies hung wrapped—
She heard his footsteps; hurried to him; bound him;
Enshrouded him in silk; then poisoned him.
Twice shrieked Tithonus, feebly; then was still.
Arachne loved him. Did he love Arachne?
She watched him with red eyes, venomous sparks,
And the furred claws outspread . . . 'O sweet Tithonus!
Darling! Be kind, and sing that song again!
Are you much poisoned? sleeping? do you dream?
Shake the bright web again with that deep fiddling!
Darling Tithonus!'

And Tithonus, weakly
Moving one hairy shin against the other
Within the silken sack, contrived to fiddle
A little tune, half-hearted: 'Shrewd Arachne!
Whom pride in beauty withered to this shape
As pride in singing shrivelled me to mine—
Unwrap me, let me go—and let me limp,
With what poor strength your venom leaves me, down
This oatstalk, and away.'

Arachne, angry,
Stung him again, twirling him with rough paws,
The red eyes keen. 'What! You would dare to leave me?
Unkind Tithonus! Sooner I'll kill and eat you
Than let you go. But sing that tune again—
So plaintive was it!'

And Tithonus faintly
Moved the poor fiddles, which were growing cold,
And sang: 'Arachne, goddess envied of gods,
Beauty's eclipse eclipsed by angry beauty,
Have pity, do not ask the withered heart
To sing too long for you! My strength goes out,
Too late we meet for love. O be content
With friendship, which the noon sun once may kindle
To give one flash of passion, like a dewdrop,
Before it goes! . . . Be reasonable,—Arachne!'

Arachne heard the song grow weaker, dwindle
To first a rustle, and then half a rustle,
And last a tick, so small no ear could hear it
Save hers, a spider's ear. And her small heart,
(Rusted away, like his, to a pinch of dust,)
Gleamed once, like his, and died. She clasped him tightly
And sunk her fangs in him. Tithonus dead,
She slept awhile, her last sensation gone;
Woke from the nap, forgetting him; and ate him.

CLAUDE McKAY
(1890–1948)

America

Although she feeds me bread of bitterness,
And sinks into my throat her tiger's tooth,
Stealing my breath of life, I will confess
I love this cultured hell that tests my youth!
Her vigor flows like tides into my blood,
Giving me strength erect against her hate.
Her bigness sweeps my being like a flood.
Yet as a rebel fronts a king in state,
I stand within her walls with not a shred
Of terror, malice, not a word of jeer.
Darkly I gaze into the days ahead,
And see her might and granite wonders there,
Beneath the touch of Time's unerring hand,
Like priceless treasures sinking in the sand.

The Harlem Dancer

Applauding youths laughed with young prostitutes
And watched her perfect, half-clothed body sway;
Her voice was like the sound of blended flutes
Blown by black players upon a picnic day.
She sang and danced on gracefully and calm,
The light gauze hanging loose about her form;
To me she seemed a proudly-swaying palm
Grown lovelier for passing through a storm.
Upon her swarthy neck black shiny curls

Luxuriant fell; and tossing coins in praise,
The wine-flushed, bold-eyed boys, and even the girls,
Devoured her shape with eager, passionate gaze;
But looking at her falsely-smiling face,
I knew her self was not in that strange place.

The White City

I will not toy with it nor bend an inch.
Deep in the secret chambers of my heart
I muse my life-long hate, and without flinch
I bear it nobly as I live my part.
My being would be a skeleton, a shell,
If this dark Passion that fills my every mood,
And makes my heaven in the white world's hell,
Did not forever feed me vital blood.
I see the mighty city through a mist—
The strident trains that speed the goaded mass,
The poles and spires and towers vapor-kissed,
The fortressed port through which the great ships pass,
The tides, the wharves, the dens I contemplate,
Are sweet like wanton loves because I hate.

ARCHIBALD MacLEISH

(1892–   )

You Also, Gaius Valerius Catullus

Fat-kneed god! Feeder of mangy leopards!
You who brought me into that one's bed
Whose breath is sweeter than a grass-fed heifer—
If *you* had not willed it, *I* had not willed it—
You who dumped me like a sack of milt
Limp in her eager taking arms as though
Her breast were no more than a bench to lie on,
Listen! Muncher of the pale-pipped apples!
Keeper of paunchy house-cats! Boozy god!
Dump me where you please, but not hereafter
Where the dawn has that *particular* laughter.

Ars Poetica

A poem should be palpable and mute
As a globed fruit,

Dumb
As old medallions to the thumb,

Silent as the sleeve-worn stone
Of casement ledges where the moss has grown—

A poem should be wordless
As the flight of birds.

A poem should be motionless in time
As the moon climbs,

Leaving, as the moon releases
Twig by twig the night-entangled trees,

Leaving, as the moon behind the winter leaves,
Memory by memory the mind—

A poem should be motionless in time
As the moon climbs.

A poem should be equal to:
Not true.

For all the history of grief
An empty doorway and a maple leaf.

For love
The leaning grasses and two lights above the sea—

A poem should not mean
But be.

The End of the World

Quite unexpectedly as Vasserot
The armless ambidextrian was lighting
A match between his great and second toe
And Ralph the lion was engaged in biting
The neck of Madame Sossman while the drum
Pointed, and Teeny was about to cough
In waltz time swinging Jocko by the thumb—
Quite unexpectedly the top blew off:

And there, there overhead, there, there, hung over
Those thousands of white faces, those dazed eyes,
There in the starless dark the poise, the hover,
There with vast wings across the canceled skies,
There in the sudden blackness the black pall
Of nothing, nothing, nothing—nothing at all.

EDNA ST. VINCENT MILLAY

(1892–1950)

Recuerdo

We were very tired, we were very merry—
We had gone back and forth all night on the ferry.
It was bare and bright, and smelled like a stable—
But we looked into a fire, we leaned across a table,
We lay on a hilltop underneath the moon;
And the whistles kept blowing, and the dawn came soon.

We were very tired, we were very merry—
We had gone back and forth all night on the ferry;
And you ate an apple, and I ate a pear,
From a dozen of each we had bought somewhere;
And the sky went wan, and the wind came cold,
And the sun rose dripping, a bucketful of gold.

We were very tired, we were very merry,
We had gone back and forth all night on the ferry.
We hailed, "Good morrow, mother!" to a shawl-covered head,
And bought a morning paper, which neither of us read;
And she wept, "God bless you!" for the apples and pears,
And we gave her all our money but our subway fares.

Love Is Not All: It Is Not Meat nor Drink

Love is not all: it is not meat nor drink
Nor slumber nor a roof against the rain;
Nor yet a floating spar to men that sink
And rise and sink and rise and sink again;
Love cannot fill the thickened lung with breath,
Nor clean the blood, nor set the fractured bone;
Yet many a man is making friends with death
Even as I speak, for lack of love alone.
It well may be that in a difficult hour,
Pinned down by pain and moaning for release,
Or nagged by want past resolution's power,
I might be driven to sell your love for peace,
Or trade the memory of this night for food.
It well may be. I do not think I would.

Euclid Alone Has Looked on Beauty Bare

Euclid alone has looked on Beauty bare.
Let all who prate of Beauty hold their peace,
And lay them prone upon the earth and cease
To ponder on themselves, the while they stare
At nothing, intricately drawn nowhere
In shapes of shifting lineage; let geese
Gabble and hiss, but heroes seek release
From dusty bondage into luminous air.

O blinding hour, O holy, terrible day,
When first the shaft into his vision shone
Of light anatomized! Euclid alone
Has looked on Beauty bare. Fortunate they
Who, though once only and then but far away,
Have heard her massive sandal set on stone.

What Lips My Lips Have Kissed, and Where, and Why

What lips my lips have kissed, and where, and why,
I have forgotten, and what arms have lain
Under my head till morning; but the rain
Is full of ghosts tonight, that tap and sigh
Upon the glass and listen for reply,
And in my heart there stirs a quiet pain
For unremembered lads that not again
Will turn to me at midnight with a cry.
Thus in the winter stands the lonely tree,
Nor knows what birds have vanished one by one,
Yet knows its boughs more silent than before:
I cannot say what loves have come and gone,
I only know that summer sang in me
A little while, that in me sings no more.

And You As Well Must Die, Beloved Dust

And you as well must die, belovèd dust,
And all your beauty stand you in no stead;
This flawless, vital hand, this perfect head,
This body of flame and steel, before the gust
Of Death, or under his autumnal frost,
Shall be as any leaf, be no less dead
Than the first leaf that fell,—this wonder fled,
Altered, estranged, disintegrated, lost.

Nor shall my love avail you in your hour.
In spite of all my love, you will arise
Upon that day and wander down the air
Obscurely as the unattended flower,
It mattering not how beautiful you were,
Or how belovèd above all else that dies.

I Shall Forget You Presently, My Dear

I shall forget you presently, my dear,
So make the most of this, your little day,
Your little month, your little half a year,
Ere I forget, or die, or move away,
And we are done forever; by and by
I shall forget you, as I said, but now,
If you entreat me with your loveliest lie
I will protest you with my favorite vow.

I would indeed that love were longer-lived,
And oaths were not so brittle as they are,
But so it is, and nature has contrived
To struggle on without a break thus far,—
Whether or not we find what we are seeking
Is idle, biologically speaking.

First Fig

My candle burns at both ends;
  It will not last the night;
But ah, my foes, and oh, my friends—
  It gives a lovely light!

E. E. CUMMINGS
(1894–1962)

my father moved through dooms of love

my father moved through dooms of love
through sames of am through haves of give,
singing each morning out of each night
my father moved through depths of height

this motionless forgetful where
turned at his glance to shining here;
that if(so timid air is firm)
under his eyes would stir and squirm

newly as from unburied which
floats the first who,his april touch
drove sleeping selves to swarm their fates
woke dreamers to their ghostly roots

and should some why completely weep
my father's fingers brought her sleep:
vainly no smallest voice might cry
for he could feel the mountains grow.

Lifting the valleys of the sea
my father moved through griefs of joy;
praising a forehead called the moon
singing desire into begin

joy was his song and joy so pure
a heart of star by him could steer
and pure so now and now so yes
the wrists of twilight would rejoice

keen as midsummer's keen beyond
conceiving mind of sun will stand,
so strictly(over utmost him
so hugely)stood my father's dream

his flesh was flesh his blood was blood:
no hungry man but wished him food;
no cripple wouldn't creep one mile
uphill to only see him smile.

Scorning the pomp of must and shall
my father moved through dooms of feel;
his anger was as right as rain
his pity was as green as grain

septembering arms of year extend
less humbly wealth to foe and friend
than he to foolish and to wise
offered immeasurable is

proudly and(by octobering flame
beckoned)as earth will downward climb,
so naked for immortal work
his shoulders marched against the dark

his sorrow was as true as bread:
no liar looked him in the head;
if every friend became his foe
he'd laugh and build a world with snow.

My father moved through theys of we,
singing each new leaf out of each tree
(and every child was sure that spring
danced when she heard my father sing)

then let men kill which cannot share,
let blood and flesh be mud and mire,
scheming imagine,passion willed,
freedom a drug that's bought and sold

giving to steal and cruel kind,
a heart to fear,to doubt a mind,
to differ a disease of same,
conform the pinnacle of am

though dull were all we taste as bright,
bitter all utterly things sweet,
maggoty minus and dumb death
all we inherit,all bequeath

and nothing quite so least as truth
—i say though hate were why men breathe—
because my father lived his soul
love is the whole and more than all

Spring is like a perhaps hand

Spring is like a perhaps hand
(which comes carefully
out of Nowhere)arranging
a window,into which people look(while
people stare
arranging and changing placing
carefully there a strange
thing and a known thing here)and

changing everything carefully

spring is like a perhaps
Hand in a window
(carefully to
and fro moving New and
Old things,while
people stare carefully
moving a perhaps
fraction of flower here placing
an inch of air there)and

without breaking anything.

i thank You God for most this amazing

i thank You God for most this amazing
day:for the leaping greenly spirits of trees
and a blue true dream of sky;and for everything
which is natural which is infinite which is yes

(i who have died am alive again today,
and this is the sun's birthday;this is the birth
day of life and of love and wings:and of the gay
great happening illimitably earth)

how should tasting touching hearing seeing
breathing any—lifted from the no
of all nothing—human merely being
doubt unimaginable You?

(now the ears of my ears awake and
now the eyes of my eyes are opened)

i carry your heart with me(i carry it in

i carry your heart with me(i carry it in
my heart)i am never without it(anywhere
i go you go,my dear;and whatever is done
by only me is your doing, my darling)
                                                      i fear
no fate(for you are my fate,my sweet)i want
no world(for beautiful you are my world,my true)
and it's you are whatever a moon has always meant
and whatever a sun will always sing is you

here is the deepest secret nobody knows
(here is the root of the root and the bud of the bud
and the sky of the sky of a tree called life;which grows
higher than soul can hope or mind can hide)
and this is the wonder that's keeping the stars apart

i carry your heart(i carry it in my heart)

a man who had fallen among thieves

a man who had fallen among thieves
lay by the roadside on his back
dressed in fifteenthrate ideas
wearing a round jeer for a hat

fate per a somewhat more than less
emancipated evening
had in return for consciousness
endowed him with a changeless grin

whereon a dozen staunch and leal
citizens did graze at pause
then fired by hypercivic zeal
sought newer pastures or because

swaddled with a frozen brook
of pinkest vomit out of eyes
which noticed nobody he looked
as if he did not care to rise

one hand did nothing on the vest
its wideflung friend clenched weakly dirt
while the mute trouserfly confessed
a button solemnly inert.

Brushing from whom the stiffened puke
i put him all into my arms
and staggered banged with terror through
a million billion trillion stars

"next to of course god america i

"next to of course god america i
love you land of the pilgrims' and so forth oh
say can you see by the dawn's early my
country 'tis of centuries come and go
and are no more what of it we should worry
in every language even deafanddumb
thy sons acclaim your glorious name by gorry
by jingo by gee by gosh by gum
why talk of beauty what could be more beautiful than these heroic happy dead
who rushed like lions to the roaring slaughter
they did not stop to think they died instead
then shall the voice of liberty be mute?"

He spoke. And drank rapidly a glass of water

anyone lived in a pretty how town

anyone lived in a pretty how town
(with up so floating many bells down)
spring summer autumn winter
he sang his didn't he danced his did.

Women and men(both little and small)
cared for anyone not at all
they sowed their isn't they reaped their same
sun moon stars rain

children guessed(but only a few
and down they forgot as up they grew
autumn winter spring summer)
that noone loved him more by more

when by now and tree by leaf
she laughed his joy she cried his grief
bird by snow and stir by still
anyone's any was all to her

someones married their everyones
laughed their cryings and did their dance
(sleep wake hope and then)they
said their nevers they slept their dream

stars rain sun moon
(and only the snow can begin to explain
how children are apt to forget to remember
with up so floating many bells down)

one day anyone died i guess
(and noone stooped to kiss his face)
busy folk buried them side by side
little by little and was by was

all by all and deep by deep
and more by more they dream their sleep
noone and anyone earth by april
wish by spirit and if by yes.

Women and men(both dong and ding)
summer autumn winter spring
reaped their sowing and went their came
sun moon stars rain

pity this busy monster,manunkind,

pity this busy monster,manunkind,

not. Progress is a comfortable disease:
your victim(death and life safely beyond)

plays with the bigness of his littleness
—electrons deify one razorblade
into a mountainrange;lenses extend

unwish through curving wherewhen till unwish
returns on its unself.
                                        A world of made
is not a world of born—pity poor flesh

and trees,poor stars and stones,but never this
fine specimen of hypermagical

ultraomnipotence. We doctors know

a hopeless case if—listen:there's a hell
of a good universe next door;let's go

Buffalo Bill's

Buffalo Bill's
defunct
        who used to
        ride a watersmooth-silver
                                        stallion
and break onetwothreefourfive pigeonsjustlikethat
                                                        Jesus
he was a handsome man
                                        and what i want to know is
how do you like your blueeyed boy
Mister Death

the Cambridge ladies who live in furnished souls

the Cambridge ladies who live in furnished souls
are unbeautiful and have comfortable minds
(also, with the church's protestant blessings
daughters, unscented shapeless spirited)
they believe in Christ and Longfellow, both dead,
are invariably interested in so many things—
at the present writing one still finds
delighted fingers knitting for the is it Poles?
perhaps. While permanent faces coyly bandy
scandal of Mrs. N and Professor D
. . . . the Cambridge ladies do not care, above
Cambridge if sometimes in its box of
sky lavender and cornerless, the
moon rattles like a fragment of angry candy

as freedom is a breakfastfood

as freedom is a breakfastfood
or truth can live with right and wrong
or molehills are from mountains made
—long enough and just so long
will being pay the rent of seem
and genius please the talentgang
and water most encourage flame

as hatracks into peachtrees grow
or hopes dance best on bald men's hair
and every finger is a toe
and any courage is a fear
—long enough and just so long
will the impure think all things pure
and hornets wail by children stung

or as the seeing are the blind
and robins never welcome spring
nor flatfolk prove their world is round
nor dingsters die at break of dong
and common's rare and millstones float
—long enough and just so long
tomorrow will not be too late

worms are the words but joy's the voice
down shall go which and up come who
breasts will be breasts thighs will be thighs
deeds cannot dream what dreams can do
—time is a tree(this life one leaf)
but love is the sky and i am for you
just so long and long enough

HART CRANE
(1899–1932)

Black Tambourine

The interests of a black man in a cellar
Mark tardy judgment on the world's closed door.
Gnats toss in the shadow of a bottle,
And a roach spans a crevice in the floor.

Aesop, driven to pondering, found
Heaven with the tortoise and the hare;
Fox brush and sow ear top his grave
And mingling incantations on the air.

The black man, forlorn in the cellar,
Wanders in some mid-kingdom, dark, that lies,
Between his tambourine, stuck on the wall,
And, in Africa, a carcass quick with flies.

from *The Bridge*

From going to and fro in the earth,
and from walking up and down in it
THE BOOK OF JOB

Proem: To Brooklyn Bridge

How many dawns, chill from his rippling rest
The seagull's wings shall dip and pivot him,
Shedding white rings of tumult, building high
Over the chained bay waters Liberty—

Then, with inviolate curve, forsake our eyes
As apparitional as sails that cross
Some page of figures to be filed away;
—Till elevators drop us from our day. . . .

I think of cinemas, panoramic sleights
With multitudes bent toward some flashing scene
Never disclosed, but hastened to again,
Foretold to other eyes on the same screen;

And Thee, across the harbor, silver-paced
As though the sun took step of thee, yet left
Some motion ever unspent in thy stride,—
Implicitly thy freedom staying thee!

Out of some subway scuttle, cell or loft
A bedlamite speeds to thy parapets,
Tilting there momently, shrill shirt ballooning,
A jest falls from the speechless caravan.

Down Wall, from girder into street noon leaks,
A rip-tooth of the sky's acetylene;
All afternoon the cloud-flown derricks turn. . . .
Thy cables breathe the North Atlantic still.

And obscure as that heaven of the Jews,
Thy guerdon. . . . Accolade thou dost bestow
Of anonymity time cannot raise:
Vibrant reprieve and pardon thou dost show.

O harp and altar, of the fury fused,
(How could mere toil align thy choiring strings!)
Terrific threshold of the prophet's pledge,
Prayer of pariah, and the lover's cry,—

Again the traffic lights that skim thy swift
Unfractioned idiom, immaculate sigh of stars,
Beading thy path—condense eternity:
And we have seen night lifted in thine arms.

Under thy shadow by the piers I waited;
Only in darkness is thy shadow clear.
The City's fiery parcels all undone,
Already snow submerges an iron year. . . .

O Sleepless as the river under thee,
Vaulting the sea, the prairies' dreaming sod,
Unto us lowliest sometimes sweep, descend
And of the curveship lend a myth to God.

Voyages

I

Above the fresh ruffles of the surf
Bright striped urchins flay each other with sand.
They have contrived a conquest for shell shucks,
And their fingers crumble fragments of baked weed
Gaily digging and scattering.

And in answer to their treble interjections
The sun beats lightning on the waves,
The waves fold thunder on the sand;
And could they hear me I would tell them:

O brilliant kids, frisk with your dog,
Fondle your shells and sticks, bleached
By time and the elements; but there is a line
You must not cross nor ever trust beyond it
Spry cordage of your bodies to caresses
Too lichen-faithful from too wide a breast.
The bottom of the sea is cruel.

II

And yet this great wink of eternity,
Of rimless floods, unfettered leewardings,
Samite sheeted and processioned where
Her undinal vast belly moonward bends,
Laughing the wrapt inflections of our love;

Take this Sea, whose diapason knells
On scrolls of silver snowy sentences,
The sceptered terror of whose sessions rends
As her demeanors motion well or ill,
All but the pieties of lovers' hands.

And onward, as bells off San Salvador
Salute the crocus lusters of the stars,
In these poinsettia meadows of her tides,—
Adagios of islands, O my Prodigal,
Complete the dark confessions her veins spell.

Mark how her turning shoulders wind the hours,
And hasten while her penniless rich palms
Pass superscription of bent foam and wave,—
Hasten, while they are true,—sleep, death, desire,
Close round one instant in one floating flower.

Bind us in time, O Seasons clear, and awe.
O minstrel galleons of Carib fire,
Bequeath us to no earthly shore until
Is answered in the vortex of our grave
The seal's wide spindrift gaze toward paradise.

III

Infinite consanguinity it bears—
This tendered theme of you that light
Retrieves from sea plains where the sky
Resigns a breast that every wave enthrones;
While ribboned water lanes I wind
Are laved and scattered with no stroke
Wide from your side, whereto this hour
The sea lifts, also, reliquary hands.

And so, admitted through black swollen gates
That must arrest all distance otherwise,—
Past whirling pillars and lithe pediments,
Light wrestling there incessantly with light,
Star kissing star through wave on wave unto

Your body rocking!

and where death, if shed,
Presumes no carnage, but this single change,—
Upon the steep floor flung from dawn to dawn
The silken skilled transmemberment of song;

Permit me voyage, love, into your hands. . . .

IV

Whose counted smile of hours and days, suppose
I know as spectrum of the sea and pledge
Vastly now parting gulf on gulf of wings
Whose circles bridge, I know (from palms to the severe
Chilled albatross's white immutability)
No stream of greater love advancing now
Than, singing, this mortality alone
Through clay aflow immortally to you.

All fragrance irrefragably, and claim
Madly meeting logically in this hour
And region that is ours to wreathe again,
Portending eyes and lips and making told
The chancel port and portion of our June—

Shall they not stem and close in our own steps
Bright staves of flowers and quills today as I
Must first be lost in fatal tides to tell?
In signature of the incarnate word
The harbor shoulders to resign in mingling
Mutual blood, transpiring as foreknown
And widening noon within your breast for gathering
All bright insinuations that my years have caught
For islands where must lead inviolably
Blue latitudes and levels of your eyes,—

In this expectant, still exclaim receive
The secret oar and petals of all love.

V

Meticulous, past midnight in clear rime,
Infrangible and lonely, smooth as though cast
Together in one merciless white blade—
The bay estuaries fleck the hard sky limits.

—As if too brittle or too clear to touch!
The cables of our sleep so swiftly filed,
Already hang, shred ends from remembered stars.
One frozen trackless smile. . . . What words
Can strangle this deaf moonlight? For we

Are overtaken. Now no cry, no sword
Can fasten or deflect this tidal wedge,
Slow tyranny of moonlight, moonlight loved
And changed. . . . "There's

Nothing like this in the world," you say,
Knowing I cannot touch your hand and look
Too, into that godless cleft of sky
Where nothing turns but dead sands flashing.

"—And never to quite understand!" No,
In all the argosy of your bright hair I dreamed
Nothing so flagless as this piracy.
                                        But now
Draw in your head, alone and too tall here.
Your eyes already in the slant of drifting foam;
Your breath sealed by the ghosts I do not know:
Draw in your head and sleep the long way home.

VI

Where icy and bright dungeons lift
Of swimmers their lost morning eyes,
And ocean rivers, churning, shift
Green borders under stranger skies,

Steadily as a shell secretes
Its beating leagues of monotone,
Or as many waters trough the sun's
Red kelson past the cape's wet stone;

O rivers mingling toward the sky
And harbor of the phoenix's breast—
My eyes pressed black against the prow,
—Thy derelict and blinded guest

Waiting, afire, what name, unspoke,
I cannot claim: let thy waves rear
More savage than the death of kings,
Some splintered garland for the seer.

Beyond siroccos harvesting
The solstice thunders, crept away,
Like a cliff swinging or a sail
Flung into April's inmost day—

Creation's blithe and petaled word
To the lounged goddess when she rose
Conceding dialogue with eyes
That smile unsearchable repose—

Still fervid covenant, Belle Isle,
—Unfolded floating dais before
Which rainbows twine continual hair—
Belle Isle, white echo of the oar!

The imaged Word, it is, that holds
Hushed willows anchored in its glow.
It is the unbetrayable reply
Whose accent no farewell can know.

At Melville's Tomb

Often beneath the wave, wide from this ledge
The dice of drowned men's bones he saw bequeath
An embassy. Their numbers as he watched,
Beat on the dusty shore and were obscured.

And wrecks passed without sound of bells,
The calyx of death's bounty giving back
A scattered chapter, livid hieroglyph,
The portent wound in corridors of shells.

Then in the circuit calm of one vast coil,
Its lashings charmed and malice reconciled,
Frosted eyes there were that lifted altars;
And silent answers crept across the stars.

Compass, quadrant and sextant contrive
No farther tides . . . High in the azure steeps
Monody shall not wake the mariner.
This fabulous shadow only the sea keeps.

To Emily Dickinson

You who desired so much—in vain to ask—
Yet fed your hunger like an endless task,
Dared dignify the labor, bless the quest—
Achieved that stillness ultimately best,

Being, of all, least sought for: Emily, hear!
O sweet, dead Silencer, most suddenly clear
When singing that Eternity possessed
And plundered momently in every breast;

—Truly no flower yet withers in your hand,
The harvest you descried and understand
Needs more than wit to gather, love to bind.
Some reconcilement of remotest mind—

Leaves Ormus rubyless, and Ophir chill.
Else tears heap all within one clay-cold hill.

ALLEN TATE
(1899–   )

Ode to the Confederate Dead

Row after row with strict impunity
The headstones yield their names to the element,
The wind whirrs without recollection;
In the river troughs the splayed leaves
Pile up, of nature the casual sacrament
To the seasonal eternity of death;
Then driven by the fierce scrutiny
Of heaven to their election in the vast breath,
They sough the rumour of mortality.

Autumn is desolation in the plot
Of a thousand acres where these memories grow
From the inexhaustible bodies that are not
Dead, but feed the grass row after rich row.
Think of the autumns that have come and gone!—
Ambitious November with the humors of the year,
With a particular zeal for every slab,
Staining the uncomfortable angels that rot
On the slabs, a wing chipped here, an arm there:
The brute curiosity of an angel's stare
Turns you, like them, to stone,
Transforms the heaving air
Till plunged to a heavier world below
You shift your sea-space blindly
Heaving, turning like the blind crab.

Dazed by the wind, only the wind
The leaves flying, plunge

You know who have waited by the wall
The twilight certainty of an animal,
Those midnight restitutions of the blood
You know—the immitigable pines, the smoky frieze
Of the sky, the sudden call: you know the rage,
The cold pool left by the mounting flood,
Of muted Zeno and Parmenides.
You who have waited for the angry resolution
Of those desires that should be yours tomorrow,
You know the unimportant shrift of death
And praise the vision
And praise the arrogant circumstance
Of those who fall
Rank upon rank, hurried beyond decision—
Here by the sagging gate, stopped by the wall.

Seeing, seeing only the leaves
Flying, plunge and expire

Turn your eyes to the immoderate past,
Turn to the inscrutable infantry rising
Demons out of the earth—they will not last.
Stonewall, Stonewall, and the sunken fields of hemp,
Shiloh, Antietam, Malvern Hill, Bull Run.
Lost in that orient of the thick-and-fast
You will curse the setting sun.

Cursing only the leaves crying
Like an old man in a storm

You hear the shout, the crazy hemlocks point
With troubled fingers to the silence which
Smothers you, a mummy, in time.

The hound bitch
Toothless and dying, in a musty cellar
Hears the wind only.

Now that the salt of their blood
Stiffens the saltier oblivion of the sea,
Seals the malignant purity of the flood,

What shall we who count our days and bow
Our heads with a commemorial woe
In the ribboned coats of grim felicity,
What shall we say of the bones, unclean,
Whose verdurous anonymity will grow?
The ragged arms, the ragged heads and eyes
Lost in these acres of the insane green?
The gray lean spiders come, they come and go;
In a tangle of willows without light
The singular screech-owl's tight
Invisible lyric seeds the mind
With the furious murmur of their chivalry.

We shall say only the leaves
Flying, plunge and expire

We shall say only the leaves whispering
In the improbable mist of nightfall
That flies on multiple wing;
Night is the beginning and the end
And in between the ends of distraction
Waits mute speculation, the patient curse
That stones the eyes, or like the jaguar leaps
For his own image in a jungle pool, his victim.

What shall we say who have knowledge
Carried to the heart? Shall we take the act
To the grave? Shall we, more hopeful, set up the grave
In the house? The ravenous grave?

Leave now
The shut gate and the decomposing wall:
The gentle serpent, green in the mulberry bush,
Riots with his tongue through the hush—
Sentinel of the grave who counts us all!

LANGSTON HUGHES

(1902–1967)

Cross

My old man's a white old man
And my old mother's black.
If ever I cursed my white old man
I take my curses back.

If ever I cursed my black old mother
And wished she were in hell,
I'm sorry for that evil wish
And now I wish her well.

My old man died in a fine big house.
My ma died in a shack.
I wonder where I'm gonna die,
Being neither white nor black?

The Negro Speaks of Rivers

I've known rivers:
I've known rivers ancient as the world and
older than the flow of human blood in
human veins.

My soul has grown deep like the rivers.

I bathed in the Euphrates when dawns
were young.
I built my hut near the Congo and it lulled
me to sleep.
I looked upon the Nile and raised the
pyramids above it.
I heard the singing of the Mississippi when
Abe Lincoln went down to New Orleans,
and I've seen its muddy bosom turn all
golden in the sunset.
I've known rivers:
Ancient, dusky rivers.

My soul has grown deep like the rivers.

OGDEN NASH

(1902–1971)

The Turtle

The turtle lives 'twixt plated decks
Which practically conceal its sex.
I think it clever of the turtle
In such a fix to be so fertile.

The Terrible People

People who have what they want are very fond of telling people who
haven't what they want that they really don't want it,
And I wish I could afford to gather all such people into a gloomy
castle on the Danube and hire half a dozen capable Draculas
to haunt it.
I don't mind their having a lot of money, and I don't care how they
employ it,
But I do think that they damn well ought to admit they enjoy it.
But no, they insist on being stealthy
About the pleasures of being wealthy,
And the possession of a handsome annuity
Makes them think that to say how hard it is to make both ends
meet is their bounden duity.
You cannot conceive of an occasion
Which will find them without some suitable evasion.
Yes indeed, with arguments they are very fecund;
Their first point is that money isn't everything, and that they have
no money anyhow is their second.

Some people's money is merited,
And other people's is inherited,
But wherever it comes from,
They talk about it as if it were something you got pink gums from.
This may well be,
But if so, why do they not relieve themselves of the burden by transferring it to the deserving poor or to me?
Perhaps indeed the possession of wealth is constantly distressing,
But I should be quite willing to assume every curse of wealth if I could at the same time assume every blessing.
The only incurable troubles of the rich are the troubles that money can't cure,
Which is a kind of trouble that is even more troublesome if you are poor.
Certainly there are lots of things in life that money won't buy, but it's very funny—
Have you ever tried to buy them without money?

The Anatomy of Happiness

Lots of truisms don't have to be repeated but there is one that has got to be,
Which is that it is much nicer to be happy than it is not to be,
And I shall even add to it by stating unequivocally and without restraint
That you are much happier when you are happy than when you ain't.
Some people are just naturally Pollyanna,
While others call for sugar and cream and strawberries on their manna.
Now, I think we all ought to say a fig for the happiness that comes of thinking helpful thoughts and searching your soul,
The most exciting happiness is the happiness generated by forces beyond your control,
Because if you just depend on your helpful thoughts for your happiness and would just as soon drink butter-

milk as champagne, and if mink is no better than lapin to you,
Why you don't even deserve to have anything nice and exciting happen to you.
If you are really Master of your Fate,
It shouldn't make any difference to you whether Cleopatra or the Bearded Lady is your mate,
So I hold no brief for the kind of happiness or the kind of unhappiness that some people constantly carry around in their breast,
Because that kind of happiness simply consists of being resigned to the worst just as that kind of unhappiness consists of being resentful of the best.
No, there is only one kind of happiness that I take the stump for,
Which is the kind that comes when something so wonderful falls in your lap that joy is what you jump for,
Something not of your own doing,
When the blue sky opens and out pops a refund from the Government or an invitation to a terrapin dinner or an unhoped-for Yes from the lovely creature you have been disconsolately wooing.
And obviously such miracles don't happen every day,
But here's hoping they may,
Because then everybody would be happy except the people who pride themselves on creating their own happiness who as soon as they saw everybody who didn't create their own happiness happy they would probably grieve over sharing their own heretofore private sublimity,
A condition which I could face with equanimity.

COUNTEE CULLEN
(1903–1946)

Yet Do I Marvel

I doubt not God is good, well-meaning, kind,
And did He stoop to quibble could tell why
The little buried mole continues blind,
Why flesh that mirrors Him must some day die,
Make plain the reason tortured Tantalus
Is baited by the fickle fruit, declare
If merely brute caprice dooms Sisyphus
To struggle up a never-ending stair.
Inscrutable His ways are, and immune
To catechism by a mind too strewn
With petty cares to slightly understand
What awful brain compels His awful hand.
Yet do I marvel at this curious thing:
To make a poet black, and bid him sing!

For a Lady I Know

She even thinks that up in heaven
  Her class lies late and snores,
While poor black cherubs rise at seven
  To do celestial chores.

A Brown Girl Dead

With two white roses on her breasts,
White candles at head and feet,
Dark Madonna of the grave she rests;
Lord Death has found her sweet.

Her mother pawned her wedding ring
To lay her out in white;
She'd be so proud she'd dance and sing
To see herself tonight.

CARL RAKOSI

(1903–)

Woman

steps out
from a lily

into the clear,
bearing a quince,

creator
calling

the ships out,
radiant

in cloth
and water

like a daisy
in the hand.

She lifts
her skirt

and speaks.
The ships

are radiant.
Man rises

from the kiss
and answers Yes.

Florida

of bright cities
and citrus,
Florida of coral
and sawgrass pointing
straight north
and hotels full
of ocean air
and little garment manufacturers
with retired eyes
and broads and bartenders
(on the make)
soaking in your orange clef,
of Negro cabins
with the cotton picker's
deep slave voice
imploding
into warm hosannahs,
the other Florida
of patient Africanus.

In a Warm Bath

Buddha is not more strange
and impersonal
Than you, o belly
waiting for the doctor's probe,
or you, phallus
wrinkled as an old crocodile
in a salt marsh. Horn of schlemiel!
Uxorious! Imperative! Boaster! Father!
Outside the order of imagination
and the public interest.

Father! In what way father? Too old. Can't tell him though.
Nor he me. Too much pain in the eyes.
His black obsidian gaze is closed to me.
May be just light refracted.
                                        Why closed?
He can be fond and amiable. Dangerous to press for more.

Engage in argument. God help me!
Like an owl zeroing in on a mouse
aware too late of its exposure
he breaks from ambush with transfixing logic.
Yet he is sympathetic. The clarity I taught him
he has turned against me, and I am satisfied.
I say a man has integrity. For this he cares.
And I. Looks at me long and deep,
a straight beam unavoidable. And I to him.
I was made father for this.
Eyes clasped,
                        down we go into a mine
without a guide or map, and damn the pinched face
of the Puritan who holds us back.
Be careful though in table talk.
Hold in the thought, When I am gone,
though all I mean is fact faceless.
Can't bear to see him laid low.
Careful not to give him pain,
I swear it as a father,
until the time when he and I
must put the figurative prayer shawl
on together and join Abraham.

Inventor of the wheel,
                                    save us from cancer!

Bless this water.
                              I must bathe more often.

RICHARD EBERHART
(1904–   )

The Fury of Aerial Bombardment

You would think the fury of aerial
  bombardment
Would rouse God to relent; the infinite
  spaces
Are still silent. He looks on shock-pried
  faces.
History, even, does not know what is
  meant.

You would feel that after so many
  centuries
God would give man to repent; yet he
  can kill
As Cain could, but with multitudinous will.
No farther advanced than in his ancient
  furies.

Was man made stupid to see his own
  stupidity?
Is God by definition indifferent, beyond us
  all?
Is the eternal truth man's fighting soul
Wherein the Beast ravens in its own
  avidity?

Of Van Wettering I speak, and Averill,
Names on a list, whose faces I do not recall

But they are gone to early death, who late in school
Distinguished the belt feed lever from the belt holding pawl.

The Groundhog

In June, amid the golden fields,
I saw a groundhog lying dead.
Dead lay he; my senses shook,
And mind outshot our naked frailty.
There lowly in the vigorous summer
His form began its senseless change,
And made my senses waver dim
Seeing nature ferocious in him.
Inspecting close his maggots' might
And seething cauldron of his being,
Half with loathing, half with a strange love,
I poked him with an angry stick.
The fever arose, became a flame
And Vigour circumscribed the skies,
Immense energy in the sun,
And through my frame a sunless trembling.
My stick had done nor good nor harm.
Then stood I silent in the day
Watching the object, as before;
And kept my reverence for knowledge
Trying for control, to be still,
To quell the passion of the blood;
Until I had bent down on my knees
Praying for joy in the sight of decay.
And so I left; and I returned
In Autumn strict of eye, to see
The sap gone out of the groundhog,
But the bony sodden hulk remained.
But the year had lost its meaning,
And in intellectual chains
I lost both love and loathing,

Mured up in the wall of wisdom.
Another summer took the fields again
Massive and burning, full of life,
But when I chanced upon the spot
There was only a little hair left,
And bones bleaching in the sunlight
Beautiful as architecture;
I watched them like a geometer,
And cut a walking stick from a birch.
It has been three years, now.
There is no sign of the groundhog.
I stood there in the whirling summer,
My hand capped a withered heart,
And thought of China and of Greece,
Of Alexander in his tent;
Of Montaigne in his tower,
Of Saint Theresa in her wild lament.

STANLEY KUNITZ

(1905–)

The Illumination

In that hotel my life
rolled in its socket
twisting my strings.
All my mistakes,
from my earliest
bedtimes,
rose against me:
the parent I denied,
the friends I failed,
the hearts I spoiled,
including at least
my own left ventricle—
a history of shame.
"Dante!" I cried
to the apparition
entering from the hall,
laureled and gaunt,
in a cone of light.

"Out of mercy you came
to be my Master
and my guide!"
To which he replied:
"I know neither the time
nor the way
nor the number on the door . . .
but this must be my room,

I was here before."
And he held up in his hand
the key,
which blinded me.

After the Last Dynasty

Reading in Li Po
how "the peach blossom follows the water"
I keep thinking of you
because you were so much like
Chairman Mao,
naturally with the sex
transposed
and the figure slighter.
Loving you was a kind
of Chinese guerrilla war.
Thanks to your lightfoot genius
no Eighth Route Army
kept its lines more fluid,
traveled with less baggage,
so nibbled the advantage.
Even with your small bad heart
you made a dance of departures.
In the cold spring rains
when last you failed me
I had nothing left to spend
but a red crayon language
on the character of the enemy
to break appointments,
to fight us not
with his strength
but with his weakness,
to kill us
not with his health
but with his sickness.

Pet, spitfire, blue-eyed pony,
here is a new note
I want to pin on your door,
though I am ten years late
and you are nowhere:
Tell me,
are you still mistress of the valley,
what trophies drift downriver,
why did you keep me waiting?

KENNETH REXROTH

(1905–   )

Song for a Dancer

I dream my love goes riding out
Upon a coal black mare.
A cloud of dark all about
Her—her floating hair.

She wears a short green velvet coat.
Her blouse is of red silk,
Open to her swan like throat,
Her breasts white as milk.

Her skirt is of green velvet, too,
And shows her silken thigh,
Purple leather for her shoe,
Dark as her blue eye.

From her saddle grows a rose.
She rides in scented shade.
Silver birds sing as she goes
This song that she made:

"My father was a nightingale,
My mother a mermaid.
Honeyed notes that never fail
Upon my lips they laid."

Lute Music

The earth will be going on a long time
Before it finally freezes;
Men will be on it; they will take names,
Give their deeds reasons.
We will be here only
As chemical constituents—
A small franchise indeed.
Right now we have lives,
Corpuscles, ambitions, caresses,
Like everybody had once—
All the bright neige d'antan people,
"Blithe Helen, white Iope, and the rest,"
All the uneasy, remembered dead.

Here at the year's end, at the feast
Of birth, let us bring to each other
The gifts brought once west through deserts—
The precious metal of our mingled hair,
The frankincense of enraptured arms and legs,
The myrrh of desperate, invincible kisses—
Let us celebrate the daily
Recurrent nativity of love,
The endless epiphany of our fluent selves,
While the earth rolls away under us
Into unknown snows and summers,
Into untraveled spaces of the stars.

Further Advantages of Learning

One day in the Library,
Puzzled and distracted,
Leafing through a dull book,
I came on a picture
Of the vase containing
Buddha's relics. A chill
Passed over me. I was
Haunted by the touch of
A calm I cannot know,
The opening into that
Busy place of a better world.

Fifty

Rainy skies, misty mountains,
The old year ended in storms.
The new year starts the same way.
All day, from far out at sea,
Long winged birds soared in the
Rushing sky. Midnight breaks with
Driving clouds and plunging moon,
Rare vasts of endless stars.
My fiftieth year has come.

Only Years

I come back to the cottage in
Santa Monica Canyon where
Andree and I were poor and
Happy together. Sometimes we
Were hungry and stole vegetables
From the neighbors' gardens.
Sometimes we went out and gathered
Cigarette butts by flashlight.
But we went swimming every day,
All year round. We had a dog
Called Proclus, a vast yellow
Mongrel, and a white cat named
Cyprian. We had our first
Joint art show, and they began
To publish my poems in Paris.
We worked under the low umbrella
Of the acacia in the dooryard.
Now I get out of the car
And stand before the house in the dusk.
The acacia blossoms powder the walk
With little pills of gold wool.
The odor is drowsy and thick
In the early evening.
The tree has grown twice as high
As the roof. Inside, an old man
And woman sit in the lamplight.
I go back and drive away
To Malibu Beach and sit
With a grey haired childhood friend and
Watch the full moon rise over the
Long rollers wrinkling the dark bay.

ROBERT PENN WARREN
(1905–   )

Bearded Oaks

The oaks, how subtle and marine,
Bearded, and all the layered light
Above them swims; and thus the scene,
Recessed, awaits the positive night.

So, waiting, we in the grass now lie
Beneath the languorous tread of light:
The grasses, kelp-like, satisfy
The nameless motions of the air.

Upon the floor of light, and time,
Unmurmuring, of polyp made,
We rest; we are, as light withdraws,
Twin atolls on a shelf of shade.

Ages to our construction went,
Dim architecture, hour by hour:
And violence, forgot now, lent
The present stillness all its power.

The storm of noon above us rolled,
Of light the fury, furious gold,
The long drag troubling us, the depth:
Dark is unrocking, unrippling, still.

Passion and slaughter, ruth, decay
Descend, minutely whispering down,
Silted down swaying streams, to lay
Foundation for our voicelessness.

All our debate is voiceless here,
As all our rage, the rage of stone;
If hope is hopeless, then fearless is fear,
And history is thus undone.

Our feet once wrought the hollow street
With echo when the lamps were dead
At windows, once our headlight glare
Disturbed the doe that, leaping, fled.

I do not love you less that now
The caged heart makes iron stroke,
Or less that all that light once gave
The graduate dark should now revoke.

We live in time so little time
And we learn all so painfully,
That we may spare this hour's term
To practice for eternity.

Original Sin: A Short Story

Nodding, its great head rattling like a gourd,
And locks like seaweed strung on the stinking stone,
The nightmare stumbles past, and you have heard
It fumble your door before it whimpers and is gone:
It acts like the old hound that used to snuffle your door and moan.

You thought you had lost it when you left Omaha,
For it seemed connected then with your grandpa, who
Had a wen on his forehead and sat on the veranda
To finger the precious protuberance, as was his habit to do,
Which glinted in sun like rough garnet or the rich old brain bulging
through.

But you met it in Harvard Yard as the historic steeple
Was confirming the midnight with its hideous racket,
And you wondered how it had come, for it stood so imbecile,
With empty hands, humble, and surely nothing in pocket:
Riding the rods, perhaps—or Grandpa's will paid the ticket.

You were almost kindly then, in your first homesickness,
As it tortured its stiff face to speak, but scarcely mewed.
Since then you have outlived all your homesickness,
But have met it in many another distempered latitude:
Oh, nothing is lost, ever lost! at last you understood.

It never came in the quantum glare of sun
To shame you before your friends, and had nothing to do
With your public experience or private reformation:
But it thought no bed too narrow—it stood with lips askew
And shook its great head sadly like the abstract Jew.

Never met you in the lyric arsenical meadows
When children call and your heart goes stone in the bosom—
At the orchard anguish never, nor ovoid horror,
Which is furred like a peach or avid like the delicious plum.
It takes no part in your classic prudence or fondled axiom.

Not there when you exclaimed: "Hope is betrayed by
Disastrous glory of sea-capes, sun-torment of whitecaps
—There must be a new innocence for us to be stayed by."
But there it stood, after all the timetables, all the maps,
In the crepuscular clutter of *always, always,* or *perhaps.*

You have moved often and rarely left an address,
And hear of the deaths of friends with a sly pleasure,
A sense of cleansing and hope which blooms from distress;
But it has not died, it comes, its hand childish, unsure,
Clutching the bribe of chocolate or a toy you used to treasure.

It tries the lock. You hear, but simply drowse:
There is nothing remarkable in that sound at the door.
Later you may hear it wander the dark house
Like a mother who rises at night to seek a childhood picture;
Or it goes to the backyard and stands like an old horse cold in the
pasture.

THEODORE ROETHKE
(1908–1963)

Frau Bauman, Frau Schmidt, and Frau Schwartze

Gone the three ancient ladies
Who creaked on the greenhouse ladders,
Reaching up white strings
To wind, to wind
The sweet-pea tendrils, the smilax,
Nasturtiums, the climbing
Roses, to straighten
Carnations, red
Chrysanthemums; the stiff
Stems, jointed like corn,
They tied and tucked,—
These nurses of nobody else.
Quicker than birds, they dipped
Up and sifted the dirt;
They sprinkled and shook;
They stood astride pipes,
Their skirts billowing out wide into tents,
Their hands twinkling with wet;
Like witches they flew along rows
Keeping creation at ease;
With a tendril for needle
They sewed up the air with a stem;
They teased out the seed that the cold kept asleep,—
All the coils, loops, and whorls.
They trellised the sun; they plotted for more than themselves.

I remember how they picked me up, a spindly kid,
Pinching and poking my thin ribs
Till I lay in their laps, laughing,

Weak as a whiffet;
Now, when I'm alone and cold in my bed,
They still hover over me,
These ancient leathery crones,
With their bandannas stiffened with sweat,
And their thorn-bitten wrists,
And their snuff-laden breath blowing lightly over me in my first sleep.

Cuttings

Sticks-in-a-drowse droop over sugary loam,
Their intricate stem-fur dries;
But still the delicate slips keep coaxing up water;
The small cells bulge;

One nub of growth
Nudges a sand-crumb loose,
Pokes through a musty sheath
Its pale tendrilous horn.

Cuttings

(*later*)

This urge, wrestle, resurrection of dry sticks,
Cut stems struggling to put down feet,
What saint strained so much,
Rose on such lopped limbs to a new life?

I can hear, underground, that sucking and sobbing,
In my veins, in my bones I feel it,—
The small waters seeping upward,
The tight grains parting at last.
When sprouts break out,
Slippery as fish,
I quail, lean to beginnings, sheath-wet.

In Evening Air

1
A dark theme keeps me here,
Though summer blazes in the vireo's eye.
Who would be half possessed
By his own nakedness?
Waking's my care—
I'll make a broken music, or I'll die.

2
Ye littles, lie more close!
Make me, O Lord, a last, a simple thing
Time cannot overwhelm.
Once I transcended time:
A bud broke to a rose,
And I rose from a last diminishing.

3
I look down the far light
And I behold the dark side of a tree
Far down a billowing plain,
And when I look again,
It's lost upon the night—
Night I embrace, a dear proximity.

4
I stand by a low fire
Counting the wisps of flame, and I watch how
Light shifts upon the wall.
I bid stillness be still.
I see, in evening air,
How slowly dark comes down on what we do.

Elegy for Jane

My Student, Thrown by a Horse

I remember the neckcurls, limp and damp as tendrils;
And her quick look, a sidelong pickerel smile;
And how, once startled into talk, the light syllables leaped for her,
And she balanced in the delight of her thought,
A wren, happy, tail into the wind,
Her song trembling the twigs and small branches.
The shade sang with her;
The leaves, their whispers turned to kissing;
And the mold sang in the bleached valleys under the rose.

Oh, when she was sad, she cast herself down into such a pure depth,
Even a father could not find her:
Scraping her cheek against straw;
Stirring the clearest water.

My sparrow, you are not here,
Waiting like a fern, making a spiny shadow.
The sides of wet stones cannot console me,
Nor the moss, wound with the last light.

If only I could nudge you from this sleep,
My maimed darling, my skittery pigeon.
Over this damp grave I speak the words of my love:
I, with no rights in this matter,
Neither father nor lover.

My Papa's Waltz

The whiskey on your breath
Could make a small boy dizzy;
But I hung on like death:
Such waltzing was not easy.

We romped until the pans
Slid from the kitchen shelf;
My mother's countenance
Could not unfrown itself.

The hand that held my wrist
Was battered on one knuckle;
At every step you missed
My right ear scraped a buckle.

You beat time on my head
With a palm caked hard by dirt,
Then waltzed me off to bed
Still clinging to your shirt.

Wish for a Young Wife

My lizard, my lively writher,
May your limbs never wither,
May the eyes in your face
Survive the green ice
Of envy's mean gaze;
May you live out your life
Without hate, without grief,
And your hair ever blaze,
In the sun, in the sun,
When I am undone,
When I am no one.

The Waking

I wake to sleep, and take my waking slow.
I feel my fate in what I cannot fear.
I learn by going where I have to go.

We think by feeling. What is there to know?
I hear my being dance from ear to ear.
I wake to sleep, and take my waking slow.

Of those so close beside me, which are you?
God bless the Ground! I shall walk softly there,
And learn by going where I have to go.

Light takes the Tree; but who can tell us how?
The lowly worm climbs up a winding stair;
I wake to sleep, and take my waking slow.

Great Nature has another thing to do
To you and me; so take the lively air,
And, lovely, learn by going where to go.

This shaking keeps me steady. I should know.
What falls away is always. And is near.
I wake to sleep, and take my waking slow.
I learn by going where I have to go.

I Knew a Woman

I knew a woman, lovely in her bones,
When small birds sighed, she would sigh back at them;
Ah, when she moved, she moved more ways than one:
The shapes a bright container can contain!
Of her choice virtues only gods should speak,
Or English poets who grew up on Greek
(I'd have them sing in chorus, cheek to cheek).

How well her wishes went! She stroked my chin,
She taught me Turn, and Counter-turn, and Stand;
She taught me Touch, that undulant white skin;
I nibbled meekly from her proffered hand;
She was the sickle; I, poor I, the rake,
Coming behind her for her pretty sake
(But what prodigious mowing we did make).

Love likes a gander, and adores a goose:
Her full lips pursed, the errant note to seize;
She played it quick, she played it light and loose;
My eyes, they dazzled at her flowing knees;
Her several parts could keep a pure repose,
Or one hip quiver with a mobile nose
(She moved in circles, and those circles moved).

Let seed be grass, and grass turn into hay:
I'm martyr to a motion not my own;
What's freedom for? To know eternity.
I swear she cast a shadow white as stone.
But who would count eternity in days?
These old bones live to learn her wanton ways:
(I measure time by how a body sways).

In a Dark Time

In a dark time, the eye begins to see,
I meet my shadow in the deepening shade;
I hear my echo in the echoing wood—
A lord of nature weeping to a tree.
I live between the heron and the wren,
Beasts of the hill and serpents of the den.

What's madness but nobility of soul
At odds with circumstance? The day's on fire!
I know the purity of pure despair,
My shadow pinned against a sweating wall.
That place among the rocks—is it a cave,
Or winding path? The edge is what I have.

A steady storm of correspondences!
A night flowing with birds, a ragged moon,
And in broad day the midnight come again!
A man goes far to find out what he is—
Death of the self in a long, tearless night,
All natural shapes blazing unnatural light.

Dark, dark my light, and darker my desire.
My soul, like some heat-maddened summer fly,
Keeps buzzing at the sill. Which I is *I?*
A fallen man, I climb out of my fear.
The mind enters itself, and God the mind,
And one is One, free in the tearing wind.

JOSEPHINE JACOBSEN

(1908–)

The Shade-seller

(For A. R. Ammons)

"Sombra?"
he asked us from his little booth. And shade
we bought to leave our car in.

By noon
the sand was a mealy fire; we crossed by planks
to the Revolcadero sea.

One day
we were later and hotter and he peered out
and "No hay sombra!" he told us.

That day
when we came back to our metal box, frightened
we breathed for a terrible instant

the air
fiery and loud of the hooked fish.
Quick! Quick! Our silver key!

Sometimes
now I dream of the shade-seller; from his dark
he leans, and "sombra . . ." I tell him.

There is
candescent sand and a great noise of heat
and it is I who speak that word

heavy
and wide and green. O may he never
answer my one with three.

The Matadors

The dirty money and the sleazy hearts
swell the *fiesta brava;*
in cheap *sol,* dear *sombra,* sit the greedy
strong-armed with expendable Cokes and cushions—
missile-rebukes of buyers to the bought:

pig-eyed, big-assed, the princes of peseta,
tycoon of horses, tycoon of *billetes,*
knowers of the greasy ropes, the skid;
aficionados of the tide that turns:

the bloodshock of the trumpets,
the celestial suit, the very sand
under the sole of the slipper
crying, what is sold a man
if he lose his profit?

Yet it is silly to say
that their blood and their wrists have not spoken,
the fighters with names like lights:
El Espartaro, Manolete, Josalito.
They speak to us.

The bulls were always there;
in the moonlight pastures,
moving through the shadows
the blacker shadows.

They speak,
the matadors. To us.
Right-thinking cannot hush
them, nor the crowds, their enemy;
nor the gentle wish.

They will speak and we will answer.
Unless someone is born
who has not set himself
before the dark horned shape

alone,
set his feet in sand
calling softly, hoarsely,
Toro, toro! Venga!

When the Five Prominent Poets

gathered in inter-admiration
in a small hotel room, to listen
to each other, like Mme. Verdurin
made ill by ecstasy,
they dropped the Muse's name.
Who came.

It was awful.
The door in shivers and a path
plowed like a twister through everything.
Eyeballs and fingers littered that room.
When the floor exploded the ceiling
parted
and the Muse went on and up; and not a sound
came from the savage carpet.

Rainy Night at the Writers' Colony

Dead poets stalk the air,
stride through tall rain and peer
through wet panes where
we sleep, or do not, here.

I know the names of some
and can say what they said.
What do we say worth the while
of the ears of the dead?

I know who shook marred
fruit of difficult bough
and from the rank discard
salvaged enough.

The rain stops; at two
the moon comes clear.
What they did, we know.
It is we who are here.

Naked under their eye,
we—honest, grave, greedy,
pedant, fool—lie
with what we make of need.

It Is the Season

when we learn
or do not learn
to say goodbye.

The crone leaves that as green
virgins opened themselves
to sun, creak at our feet

and all farewells return
to crowd the air:
say, Chinese lovers by a bridge,

with crows, and a waterfall;
He will cross
the bridge, the crows fly;

children who told each other
secrets, and will not speak
next summer;

Some speech of parting
mentions God, as in
à Dieu, Adios,

commending what cannot
be kept
to permanence.

There is nothing of north
unknown, as the dark
comes earlier. The birds

take their lives in their wings
for the cruel trip;
all farewells are rehearsals.

Darling, the sun rose
later today.
Summer, summer

is what we had.
Say nothing yet.
Prepare.

ELIZABETH BISHOP
(1911–)

House Guest

The sad seamstress
who stays with us this month
is small and thin and bitter.
No one can cheer her up.
Give her a dress, a drink,
roast chicken, or fried fish
it's all the same to her.

She sits and watches TV.
No, she watches zigzags.
"Can you adjust the TV?"
"No," she says. No hope.
She watches on and on,
without hope, without air.

Her own clothes give us pause,
but she's not a poor orphan.
She has a father, a mother,
and all that, and she's earning
quite well, and we're stuffing
her with fattening foods.

We invite her to use the binoculars.
We say, "Come see the jets!"
We say, "Come see the baby!"
Or the knife grinder who cleverly
plays the National Anthem
on his wheel so shrilly.
Nothing helps.

She speaks: "I need a little
money to buy buttons."
She seems to think it's useless
to ask. Heavens, buy buttons,
if they'll do any good,
the biggest in the world—
by the dozen, by the gross!
Buy yourself an ice cream,
a comic book, a car!

Her face is closed as a nut,
closed as a careful snail
or a thousand-year-old seed.
Does she dream of marriage?
Of getting rich? Her sewing
is decidedly mediocre.

Please! Take our money! Smile!
What on earth have we done?
What has everyone done
and when did it all begin?
Then one day she confides
that she wanted to be a nun
and her family opposed her.

Perhaps we should let her go,
or deliver her straight off
to the nearest convent—and wasn't
her month up last week, anyway?
Can it be that we nourish
one of the Fates in our bosoms?
Clotho, sewing our lives
with a bony little foot
on a borrowed sewing machine,
and our fates will be like hers,
and our hems crooked forever?

The Armadillo

for Robert Lowell

This is the time of year
when almost every night
the frail, illegal fire balloons appear.
Climbing the mountain height,

rising toward a saint
still honored in these parts,
the paper chambers flush and fill with light
that comes and goes, like hearts.

Once up against the sky it's hard
to tell them from the stars—
planets, that is—the tinted ones:
Venus going down, or Mars,

or the pale green one. With a wind,
they flare and falter, wobble and toss;
but if it's still they steer between
the kite sticks of the Southern Cross,

receding, dwindling, solemnly
and steadily forsaking us,
or, in the downdraft from a peak,
suddenly turning dangerous.

Last night another big one fell.
It splattered like an egg of fire
against the cliff behind the house.
The flame ran down. We saw the pair

of owls who nest there flying up
and up, their whirling black-and-white
stained bright pink underneath, until
they shrieked up out of sight.

The ancient owls' nest must have burned.
Hastily, all alone,
a glistening armadillo left the scene,
rose-flecked, head down, tail down,

and then a baby rabbit jumped out,
short-eared, to our surprise.
So soft!—a handful of intangible ash
with fixed, ignited eyes.

Too pretty, dreamlike mimicry!
O falling fire and piercing cry
and panic, and a weak mailed fist
clenched ignorant against the sky!

JOSEPHINE MILES
(1911–   )

Reason

Said, Pull her up a bit will you, Mac, I want to unload there.
Said, Pull her up my rear end, first come first serve.
Said, Give her the gun, Bud, he needs a taste of his own bumper.
Then the usher came out and got into the act:

Said, Pull her up, pull her up a bit, we need this space, sir.
Said, For God's sake, is this still a free country or what?
You go back and take care of Gary Cooper's horse
And leave me handle my own car.

Saw them unloading the lame old lady,
Ducked out under the wheel and gave her an elbow,
Said, All you needed to do was just explain;
Reason, Reason is my middle name.

Belief

Mother said to call her if the H bomb exploded
And I said I would, and it about did
When Louis my brother robbed a service station
And lay cursing on the oily cement in handcuffs.

But by that time it was too late to tell Mother,
She was too sick to worry the life out of her
Over *why why*. Causation is sequence
And everything is one thing after another.

Besides, my other brother, Eddie, had got to be President,
And you can't ask too much of one family.
The chances were as good for a good future
As bad for a bad one.

Therefore it was surprising that, as we kept the newspapers from Mother,
She died feeling responsible for a disaster unverified,
Murmuring, in her sleep as it seemed, the ancient slogan
Noblesse oblige.

Merchant Marine

Where is the world? not about.
The world is in the heart
And the heart is clogged in the sea lanes out of port.

Not in the work or the west,
Not in the will or the wriest
Task is the world. It is all seaward.

Chart is the world, a sheet
In the hand and a paper page,
A rendable tissue of sea lanes, there is the heart.

JEAN GARRIGUE

(1912–1972)

Bleecker Street

Two infants vis-à-vis
Laughing, striking softly out
At one another in their carriage,
The American flag set out in bulbs—
The crookt stars and tawdry stripes,
Aren't they bizarre
To advertise a church bazaar
By backs of Spanish melons?
That child in the butcher shop
With lids so fine-cut over such a blue—
Inviolate—
Out of where?
O pure and neat, severe
Sentinel angel!
Life! Sister! A kitten sleeping
Ready to paw out if I scratch behind his ear!
I'm laden with your bread, your milk,
I'm thinking of you just the way
I'd think of lips, hair . . .
I'd sense like a kiss upon the cheek
The way you seem to be upon the air
Like one come from far
To favor us with careless smiles and blinks
Inscrutable!
But where the lamb hangs in his wool
I meet the waiter taking dinner
To my blind old neighbor,
Sick, blind, alone.

Yes, but we're disabled
To meet the many that you are,
You'd stifle us in backrooms of the soul!
There's no strutting we can do
Like my neighbor's pigeons who've brought down
Some straw of snatched-up sunlight in their beaks.
Nothing that you do not contradict,
Our gentle, murderous Enigma!
And night comes round the corner after you . . .

Epitaph for My Cat

And now my pampered beast
Who hated to be wet,
The rain falls all night
And you are under it.
Who liked to be warm,
Are cold as any stone,
Who kept so clean and neat,
Cast down in the dirt
Of death's filthy sport.

Shore

Running through the thick wiry grasses to the pond where the wild swans nest, by the broad low spit of sand, by the stream pulsing from it, a narrow thing that goes to the sea, by the mossed flanks of the rocks, by the dunes of the pure bright grass, a Holland green.

Running in the soft swift wind, enough to belly out every sail, that rifts the shallow stream with fast lapping waves and drives the cry of a bird against us, one of those stilt-legged, striped-of-wing birds, sanderling or sandpiper, dipping and veering sideways and windward.

Running in the cry of the bird as we come to the pond, agitated too, veined down the middle, ribbed and splintered by the wind's soft blowing. Black the pond, soot black the claws of the firs and roofs and chimney stacks bulky and hairy with vines, all furred black, lampblack, inkwork black, etched and pressed against this western sky of the hue of geranium, a clear still storm of it as the sandpiper soars up shortly to veer and glide over and some troubled other gives cry and counter cry to the first lamentings.

In this light and this like-weeping as we run on now, over the sand that in wet places keeps the reflection of the new hung moon, over the tusked camel hump of the brindled rock whose ridged sides slope to the sea, by pockets of the sea rose, pickets of grass, soft kerchiefs of the grass-sown sand to the wrinkled prairie of waves caught now in the single chord of burning.

Amsterdam

In this city how many masters are clouds. Just over the roofs—how many portals! How many perspectives endlessly receding down the long aisles closed in an instant by ponderable armies, palpable shadows, shadings of white on white, shelled convolutions through which the sun tilts with a lancing of light as through shutters or, imperceptibly altered, falls, strong and white as that fountain's body whose second flower, fierce as a lily, fitfully plays, blown by the wind that rises to throw it down, to leap to embrace it or to flow, flowering around it, the arc of the jet only just sustained that air with its tensions makes new offsprings of. Nor is it gauze or tulle as painters have had it. What can be seized! In the immersion of splendors, how many changings, progressions from key to key, transformings not ending—for even as I write this there was a moment not to be spoken of when those armadas of the opaqueness of pearl, marbled like snow, their masts as of fume, give way in dissolvings, in effortless partings to let in the great ensign of blue. Gone every watery weight. How the slight ageratums blaze. Roofs by the slate mansards meet the rosebrick angles. Far off now lies the storm-bold barrier low-lying and massive, that yet after but small delay, in the instant eluding, troops back, new pavilions now, new habitations. Intervals then, only intervals when the clair of the pane looked through, not ever ascendant against those batallions, platoons of the voyaging flocks, rain-carrying cargaisons, nacreous kin to the sea-branched foam, spirit of night-massed marches.

Country Villa

What was it like, that country house? You never knew at all. Long and yellow with a faded coat of arms. . . . A road under ilex led up to it but this was only walked now, never driven. The ilex was old, the trunks richly mossed and twisting, perfect for a child to climb and there were many children, and many did, the boughs permitted to meet and tangle overhead so that you walked under an almost tightly woven roof of leaves that gave out scent, an indefinable, dusky scent, somewhat bitter, somewhat tonic, mixed as it was with the scent of the brooding family of cypresses toward which the longly shaded pathway led. It was steeply uphill and small stones rolled under your feet. On a hot late afternoon you were inclined to go slowly. Nevertheless it was delicious to be toiling under those shadows through which the sunlight broke, into which the free winds rarely penetrated, so dense the leaf enclosure. You might be in a latticed tunnel and when you looked down from the house itself the road appeared to be no more than a square-cut aperture, a low stooped door that gave onto the road through much sweet cluster. Yet close-set as the twisted and moss-painted low trunks were, you might at times break through and there lay the outside world of a big field gone over to the blue flowered lucerne. Fields folded into fields, all sloping down to the road where fields on the other side rode up, planted with rows of vines that in the early spring looked like rows of green seams or with haystacks set in what seemed to be mathematically calculated distances.

Coming out of the shaded pathway you met a haystack here also, a broad low cushioned thing not unlike an excessively large divan. The children had put small Siennese banners in its prickly sides and the colors drooped on the windless afternoon like dispirited signals from a battlement.

Movie Actors Scribbling Letters Very Fast in Crucial Scenes

The velocity with which they write—
Don't you know it? It's from the heart!
They are acting the whole part out.
Love! has taken them up—
Like writing to god in the night.
Meet me! I'm dying! Come at once!
The crisis is on them, the shock
Drives from the nerve to the pen,
Pours from the blood into ink.

Song for "Buvez les Vins du Postillon"—Advt.

In the Rue Monsieur le Prince
That Stephen once walked in hunger and toothache
We drank the wines of the postilion.
O I had a broken tooth myself,
I had broken my glasses as well,
And you, you had lost half your time
In the crooked streets of Spain,
But we drank the wines of the postilion
And lovely at the buvette
When a man came by in a blue smock
With a mandolin he did not play,
Yet the lilacs shook in the wake
Of the possibilities of sentiment
Of this marvelous-bodied instrument
Hung with ribbons—so svelte!
O it was lovely at the buvette
Not to think of the Hotel du Depart
Nor weep for lost causes nor why
First you must go, then I,
And O lovely to stay
In the time of the lilac and cherry
And be drunk on the wines of the postilion.

DELMORE SCHWARTZ
(1913–1966)

The Mind Is an Ancient and Famous Capital

The mind is a city like London,
Smoky and populous: it is a capital
Like Rome, ruined and eternal,
Marked by the monuments which no one
Now remembers. For the mind, like Rome, contains
Catacombs, aqueducts, amphitheatres, palaces,
Churches and equestrian statues, fallen, broken or soiled.
The mind possesses and is possessed by all the ruins
Of every haunted, hunted generation's celebration.

"Call us what you will: we are made such by love."
We are such studs as dreams are made on, and
Our little lives are ruled by the gods, by Pan,
Piping of all, seeking to grasp or grasping
All of the grapes; and by the bow-and-arrow god,
Cupid, piercing the heart through, suddenly and forever.

Dusk we are, to dusk returning, after the burbing,
After the gold fall, the fallen ash, the bronze,
Scattered and rotten, after the white null statues which
Are winter, sleep, and nothingness: when
Will the houselights of the universe
Light up and blaze?
                                        For it is not the sea
Which murmurs in a shell,
And it is not only heart, at harp o'clock,
It is the dread terror of the uncontrollable
Horses of the apocalypse, running in wild dread
Toward Arcturus—and returning as suddenly . . .

"The Heavy Bear Who Goes with Me"

"the withness of the body"

WHITEHEAD.

The heavy bear who goes with me,
A manifold honey to smear his face,
Clumsy and lumbering here and there,
The central ton of every place,
The hungry beating brutish one
In love with candy, anger, and sleep,
Crazy factotum, dishevelling all,
Climbs the building, kicks the football,
Boxes his brother in the hate-ridden city.

Breathing at my side, that heavy animal,
That heavy bear who sleeps with me,
Howls in his sleep for a world of sugar,
A sweetness intimate as the water's clasp,
Howls in his sleep because the tight-rope
Trembles and shows the darkness beneath.
—The strutting show-off is terrified,
Dressed in his dress-suit, bulging his pants,
Trembles to think that his quivering meat
Must finally wince to nothing at all.

That inescapable animal walks with me,
Has followed me since the black womb held,
Moves where I move, distorting my gesture,
A caricature, a swollen shadow,
A stupid clown of the spirit's motive,
Perplexes and affronts with his own darkness,
The secret life of belly and bone,
Opaque, too near, my private, yet unknown,
Stretches to embrace the very dear
With whom I would walk without him near,
Touches her grossly, although a word

Would bare my heart and make me clear,
Stumbles, flounders, and strives to be fed
Dragging me with him in his mouthing care,
Amid the hundred million of his kind,
The scrimmage of appetite everywhere.

I Am a Book I Neither Wrote nor Read

I am a book I neither wrote nor read,
A comic, tragic play in which new masquerades
Astonishing as guns crackle like raids
Newly each time, whatever one is prepared
To come upon, suddenly dismayed and afraid,
As in the dreams which make the fear of sleep
The terror of love, the depth one cannot leap.

How the false truths of the years of youth have passed!
Have passed at full speed like trains which never stopped
There where I stood and waited, hardly aware,
How little I knew, or which of them was the one
To mount and ride to hope or where true hope arrives.

I no more wrote than read that book which is
The self I am, half-hidden as it is
From one and all who see within a kiss
The lounging formless blackness of an abyss.

How could I think the brief years were enough
To prove the reality of endless love?

JOHN BERRYMAN
(1914–1972)

from *The Dream Songs*

14

Life, friends, is boring. We must not say so.
After all, the sky flashes, the great sea yearns,
we ourselves flash and yearn,
and moreover my mother told me as a boy
(repeatingly) 'Ever to confess you're bored
means you have no

Inner Resources.' I conclude now I have no
inner resources, because I am heavy bored.
Peoples bore me,
literature bores me, especially great literature,
Henry bores me, with his plights & gripes
as bad as achilles,

who loves people and valiant art, which bores me.
And the tranquil hills, & gin, look like a drag
and somehow a dog
has taken itself & its tail considerably away
into mountains or sea or sky, leaving
behind: me, wag.

94

Ill lay he long, upon this last return,
unvisited. The doctors put everything in the hospital
into reluctant Henry
and the nurses took it out & put it back,
smiling like fiends, with their eternal 'we.'
Henry did a slow burn,

collapsing his dialogue to their white ears
& shiny on the flanges. Sanka he drank
until his memories blurred
& Valerie was coming, lower he sank
and lovely. Teddy on his handlebars
perched, her. One word he heard

insistent: 'on.' He railed a stale abuse
upon his broad shortcomings, then lay still.
That middle-sized wild man was ill.
A hospital is where it all has a use,
so is a makar. . So is substantial God,
tuning in from abroad.

100

How this woman came   by the courage, how she got
the courage, Henry bemused himself in a frantic hot
night of the eight of July,
where it came from, did once the Lord frown down
upon her ancient cradle thinking "This one
will do before she die

for two and seventy years of chipped indignities
at least,' and with his thunder clapped a promise?
In that far away town
who lookt upon my mother with shame & rage
that any should endure such pilgrimage,
growled Henry sweating, grown

but not grown used to the goodness of this woman
in her great strength, in her hope superhuman,
no, no, not used at all.
I declare a mystery, he mumbled to himself,
of love, and took the bourbon from the shelf
and drank her a tall one, tall.

104

Welcome, grinned Henry, welcome, fifty-one!
I never cared for fifty, when nothing got done.
The hospitals were fun
in certain ways, and an honour or so,
but on the whole fifty was a mess as though
heavy clubs from below

and from—God save the bloody mark—above
were loosed upon his skull & soles. O love,
what was you loafing of
that fifty put you off, out & away,
leaving the pounding, horrid sleep by day,
nights naught but fits. I pray

the opening decade contravene its promise
to be as bad as all the others. Is
there something Henry miss
in the jungle of the gods whom Henry's prayer to?
Empty temples—a decade of dark-blue
sins, son, worse than you.

172

Your face broods from my table, Suicide.
Your force came on like a torrent toward the end
of agony and wrath.
You were christened in the beginning Sylvia Plath
and changed that name for Mrs Hughes and bred
and went on round the bend

till the oven seemed the proper place for you.
I brood upon your face, the geography of grief,
hooded, till I allow
again your resignation from us now
though the screams of orphaned children fix me anew.
Your torment here was brief,

long falls your exit all repeatingly,
a poor exemplum, one more suicide
to stack upon the others
till stricken Henry with his sisters & brothers
suddenly gone pauses to wonder why he
alone breasts the wronging tide.

262

You couldn't bear to grow old, but we grow old.
Our differences accumulate. Our skin
tightens or droops: it alters.
Take courage, things are not what they have been
and they will never again. Hot hearts grow cold,
the rush to the surface falters,

secretive grows the disappearing soul
learned & uncertain, young again
but not in the same way:
Heraclitus had a wise word here to say,
which I forget. We wake & blunder on,
wiser, on the whole,

but not more accurate. Leave that to the young,
grope forward, toward where no one else has been
which is our privilege.
Besides, you gave up early in our age
which is your privilege, from Chatterton
to the bitter & present scene.

299

The Irish have the thickest ankles in the world
& the best complexions. Unnerved by both,
Henry reserved his vote.
A dreadful dream, me stranded on a red rock slope
unable to go up, or down, or sideways:
shout for the Fire Department?

Your first day in Dublin is always your worst.
I just found my fly open: panic! A depressing
& badly written letter, very long,
from northern California enclosing a bad poem.
Fear of proving unworthy to my self-imposed task.
Fear.

And how will his last day in Dublin be,
away so many labours?—Offer up prayers,
Mr Bones. Down on your knees.
Life comes against   not all at once but in layers.
—You offers me this hope. Now I thank you,
depressed, down on my knees.

RANDALL JARRELL

(1914–1965)

Losses

It was not dying: everybody died.
It was not dying: we had died before
In the routine crashes—and our fields
Called up the papers, wrote home to our folks,
And the rates rose, all because of us.
We died on the wrong page of the almanac,
Scattered on mountains fifty miles away;
Diving on haystacks, fighting with a friend,
We blazed up on the lines we never saw.
We died like aunts or pets or foreigners.
(When we left high school nothing else had died
For us to figure we had died like.)

In our new planes, with our new crews, we bombed
The ranges by the desert or the shore,
Fired at towed targets, waited for our scores—
And turned into replacements and woke up
One morning, over England, operational.
It wasn't different: but if we died
It was not an accident but a mistake
(But an easy one for anyone to make).
We read our mail and counted up our missions—
In bombers named for girls, we burned
The cities we had learned about in school—
Till our lives wore out; our bodies lay among
The people we had killed and never seen.
When we lasted long enough they gave us medals;
When we died they said, "Our casualties were low."
They said, "Here are the maps": we burned the cities.

It was not dying—no, not ever dying;
But the night I died I dreamed that I was dead,
And the cities said to me: "Why are you dying?
We are satisfied, if you are; but why did I die?"

The Death of the Ball Turret Gunner

From my mother's sleep I fell into the State,
And I hunched in its belly till my wet fur froze.
Six miles from earth, loosed from its dream of life,
I woke to black flak and the nightmare fighters.
When I died they washed me out of the turret with a hose.

90 North

At home, in my flannel gown, like a bear to its floe,
I clambered to bed; up the globe's impossible sides
I sailed all night—till at last, with my black beard,
My furs and my dogs, I stood at the northern pole.

There in the childish night my companions lay frozen,
The stiff furs knocked at my starveling throat,
And I gave my great sigh: the flakes came huddling,
Were they really my end? In the darkness I turned to my rest.

—Here, the flag snaps in the glare and silence
Of the unbroken ice. I stand here,
The dogs bark, my beard is black, and I stare
At the North Pole . . .
And now what? Why, go back.

Turn as I please, my step is to the south.
The world—my world spins on this final point
Of cold and wretchedness: all lines, all winds
End in this whirlpool I at last discover.

And it is meaningless. In the child's bed
After the night's voyage, in that warm world
Where people work and suffer for the end
That crowns the pain—in that Cloud-Cuckoo-Land

I reached my North and it had meaning.
Here at the actual pole of my existence,
Where all that I have done is meaningless,
Where I die or live by accident alone—

Where, living or dying, I am still alone;
Here where North, the night, the berg of death
Crowd me out of the ignorant darkness,
I see at last that all the knowledge

I wrung from the darkness—that the darkness flung me—
Is worthless as ignorance: nothing comes from nothing,
The darkness from the darkness. Pain comes from the darkness
And we call it wisdom. It is pain.

The Woman at the Washington Zoo

The saris go by me from the embassies.

Cloth from the moon. Cloth from another planet.
They look back at the leopard like the leopard.

And I. . . .
this print of mine, that has kept its color
Alive through so many cleanings; this dull null
Navy I wear to work, and wear from work, and so
To my bed, so to my grave, with no
Complaints, no comment: neither from my chief,
The Deputy Chief Assistant, nor his chief—
Only I complain. . . . this serviceable
Body that no sunlight dyes, no hand suffuses
But, dome-shadowed, withering among columns,
Wavy beneath fountains—small, far-off, shining

In the eyes of animals, these beings trapped
As I am trapped but not, themselves, the trap,
Aging, but without knowledge of their age,
Kept safe here, knowing not of death, for death—
Oh, bars of my own body, open, open!

The world goes by my cage and never sees me.
And there come not to me, as come to these,
The wild beasts, sparrows pecking the llamas' grain,
Pigeons settling on the bears' bread, buzzards
Tearing the meat the flies have clouded. . . .
Vulture,
When you come for the white rat that the foxes left,
Take off the red helmet of your head, the black
Wings that have shadowed me, and step to me as man:
The wild brothers at whose feet the white wolves fawn,
To whose hand of power the great lioness
Stalks, purring. . . .
You know what I was,
You see what I am: change me, change me!

The Lost Children

Two little girls, one fair, one dark,
One alive, one dead, are running hand in hand
Through a sunny house. The two are dressed
In red and white gingham, with puffed sleeves and sashes.
They run away from me . . . But I am happy;
When I wake I feel no sadness, only delight.
I've seen them again, and I am comforted
That, somewhere, they still are.

It is strange
To carry inside you someone else's body;
To know it before it's born;
To see at last that it's a boy or girl, and perfect;
To bathe it and dress it; to watch it

Nurse at your breast, till you almost know it
Better than you know yourself—better than it knows itself.
You own it as you made it.
You are the authority upon it.

But as the child learns
To take care of herself, you know her less.
Her accidents, adventures are her own,
You lose track of them. Still, you know more
About her than anyone *except* her.

Little by little the child in her dies.
You say, "I have lost a child, but gained a friend."
You feel yourself gradually discarded.
She argues with you or ignores you
Or is kind to you. She who begged to follow you
Anywhere, just so long as it was you,
Finds follow the leader no more fun.
She makes few demands; you are grateful for the few.

The young person who writes once a week
Is the authority upon herself.
She sits in my living room and shows her husband
My albums of her as a child. He enjoys them
And makes fun of them. I look too
And I realize the girl in the matching blue
Mother-and-daughter dress, the fair one carrying
The tin lunch box with the half-pint thermos bottle
Or training her pet duck to go down the slide
Is lost just as the dark one, who is dead, is lost.
But the world in which the two wear their flared coats
And the hats that match, exists so uncannily
That, after I've seen its pictures for an hour,
I believe in it: the bandage coming loose
One has in the picture of the other's birthday,
The castles they are building, at the beach for asthma.

I look at them and all the old sure knowledge
Floods over me, when I put the album down
I keep saying inside: "I *did* know those children.
I braided those braids. I was driving the car

The day that she stepped in the can of grease
We were taking to the butcher for our ration points.
I *know* those children. I know all about them.
Where are they?"

I stare at her and try to see some sign
Of the child she was. I can't believe there isn't any.
I tell her foolishly, pointing at the picture,
That I keep wondering where she is.
She tells me, "Here I am."
                                        Yes, and the other
Isn't dead, but has everlasting life . . .

The girl from next door, the borrowed child,
Said to me the other day, "You like children so much,
Don't you want to have some of your own?"
I couldn't believe that she could say it.
I thought: "Surely you can look at me and see them."

When I see them in my dreams I feel such joy.
If I could dream of them every night!

When I think of my dream of the little girls
It's as if we were playing hide-and-seek.
The dark one
Looks at me longingly, and disappears;
The fair one stays in sight, just out of reach
No matter where I reach. I am tired
As a mother who's played all day, some rainy day.
I don't want to play it any more, I don't want to,
But the child keeps on playing, so I play.

DUDLEY RANDALL
(1914–   )

The Profile on the Pillow

After our fierce loving
in the brief time we found to be together,
you lay in the half light
exhausted, rich,
with your face turned sideways on the pillow,
and I traced the exquisite
line of your profile, dark against the white,
delicate and lovely as a child's.

Perhaps
you will cease to love me,
or we may be consumed in the holocaust,
but I keep, against the ice and the fire,
the memory of your profile on the pillow.

A *Different Image*

The age
requires this task:
create
a different image;
re-animate
the mask.

Shatter the icons of slavery and fear.
Replace
the leer
of the minstrel's burnt-cork face
with a proud, serene
and classic bronze of Benin.

Roses and Revolutions

Musing on roses and revolutions,
I saw night close down on the earth like a great dark wing,
and the lighted cities were like tapers in the night,
and I heard the lamentations of a million hearts
regretting life and crying for the grave,
and I saw the Negro lying in the swamp with his face blown off,
and in northern cities with his manhood maligned and felt the writhing
of his viscera like that of the hare hunted down or the bear at bay,
and I saw men working and taking no joy in their work
and embracing the hard-eyed whore with joyless excitement
and lying with wives and virgins in impotence.

And as I groped in darkness
and felt the pain of millions,
gradually, like day driving night across the continent,
I saw dawn upon them like the sun a vision
of a time when all men walk proudly through the earth
and the bombs and missiles lie at the bottom of the ocean
like the bones of dinosaurs buried under the shale of eras,
and men strive with each other not for power or the accumulation of paper
but in joy create for others the house, the poem, the game of athletic beauty.

Then washed in the brightness of this vision,
I saw how in its radiance would grow and be nourished and suddenly
burst into terrible and splendid bloom
the blood-red flower of revolution.

JOHN MALCOLM BRINNIN
(1916–   )

Skin Diving in the Virgins
(For Tram Combs)

Alfonso was his name: his sad cantina
leaned against a palm. Over my head,
he scanned a coastline only he could see
and took my order in cuneiform.

My water gear, like loose connections
from some mild machine, dripped on the table. What
a good morning! The wreck I'd shimmied through—
a sunken vessel, like Alfonso, some-
what Spanish in the stern—still weighed its gold,

while angelfish and sunfish still made mouths
to tell me nothing. That kind of poetry
one is, in principle, against. But what
sweet swarms of language to be silent in!
I tasted salt, half dreaming back and down.

All of a sudden came the pelicans:
crazy old men in baseball caps, who flew
like jackknives and collapsed like fans . . .
They'd zeroed in, Alfonso said, on fish
that shark or barracuda'd chased inshore.
Hitting the water, bull's-eye on bull's-eye,
they'd sit there rocking, naked in their smiles.

Those birds ate well.
Was there some new conclusion to be drawn
from such vast hunger without appetite?
In the next rising wave,
I saw a barracuda standing on its tail,
clear as a sea horse in a paperweight.

Alfonso, listing, brought me canned corned beef
and a cool wet Amstel winking in the bottle.
Beware of irony, I thought, and swigged my beer,
seek depths where irony cannot descend.
The bald sun rolled in the bland sky. One clown,
cartwheeling pell-mell to the kill, just missed
another floating off, his big pouch full.

Letter from an Island

(For C.W.W.)

Sweet heart,
A morning, climbing in its brass,
and I—half-naked, pushing fifty, sprawled
on a bone-white gallery—observe again
how day comes on like a coincidence
not asking even to be understood.
Arrived at dawn, the little gull-gray sloops
from down the archipelago—decks high
with limes and goats and Pepsi-Cola bottles—
sit nuzzling the long quay.
Displays of fish
on barbarous Maypole strings are hung about,
the yellow warehouse doors swing open (Scotch,
Thai silk, and singing clocks from Switzerland)
and, flapping for attention from afar,
the paling flags of the sad consulates.
I take it in, as it takes me, and think:
What was the hour of that chill equinox
when, traveling out, I knew that I moved back

toward destinations somehow I had missed?
—the port that winked along the water's edge
—that station deep in the interior.
You must know what I mean
(Enough of this.)

You'd like the way this island seems to sail.
I think you'd like its blowzy innocence:
the mornings full of notices, the nights
striated by steel bands, and the sort of scratch
cantatas in which roosters and wild dogs
make their concordances.
(The other day,
I met a man who studies octopi.
He drops them in a tank, some five or six,
then watches them, it seems, for any sign
that they might bear their own society.
Invariably, he says, the small ones die.
Eyes open, tentacles unfurled—without
a warning and without a wound—they float
like lilies to the top. *What, then,* I said,
do they die of? And he said, *Of despair.*)
Sweet heart, why don't you hop a jet and come?
God knows, one needs a partner in this waltz
d'un certain age, someone who knows the steps.
How many deaths have we endured this year?
How many parties where a whisper spelled
the one guest unavoidably detained?
Come flying—I've been sleeping in the sun—
descend through clouds proclaiming that I am
prince of a kingdom that shall be restored.
(A cry from Clementine—one of those girls
who sit like lotuses along the bar:
My last three lovers were enthusiastic.
Still I despair.)
Come for the hell of it . . .
when the white cruise ships arrive it's holiday
as grim as it's instructive. You should know
those gay old Gorgons in blue rinse, tight pants,
fox-trotting from the vasts of the Midwest,
old boys, old Elmers, jazzy in grass hats,

their shirts awash with mermaids and hibiscus—
dead ringers for the shapes we shall assume.
Pack up at once . . . we'll keep our laughter dry.
And though, this year and next year, our fond sight
be blurred again, and violent declensions
shrink us to the wrinkles on our hands,
how long can one stay totally appalled?
Come . . . it's not much later than we think.
Top down, I'll drive you out to Bluebeard's Beach
and high into these rain-blue panoramas.
I'll snap some Kodachromes—you in those wild
Italian stripes under a sea-grape tree—
you, à la Dietrich, leggy in the sand.

Come soon . . . we'll hit the bars, we'll bamboushay,
as they say here, from Poppa Daddy's Place
to the Fallen Angel and Calypso Joe's . . .
and which of our sweet ghosts would not approve?
Come. Come Saturday.
                                        In my knee pants,
a tall rum swizzle in each hand, I'll meet
your plane and—every mortal inch as brave
as you—read in a moment, face to face,
all that we know, all that we do not know.
I've never been more serious.
                                        Love, J.

Roethke Plain

Light on his pins,
                              upright on his hind legs,
sometimes he'd polka
                              like a dreaming bear.
                                                  Sometimes,
squared off like a Wop heavyweight,
                                        he'd jab the air,
cut down bad shadows with the old
                                        one-two.

In nifty chalk stripes,
Borsalino,
buffing his nails
on a 4-button sleeve,
he'd swank it
like the biggest bootlegger
this side of Cicero.
Poet of love,
he called himself,
poet of praise—
I'm thinking of that morning
at Back Bay:
half-drowned
in the dim sea-light
of a roomette
(its mangy mohair
rank with Cutty Sark,
its window smudged where,
nosing the plate glass,
he'd mooned
on the wild silences
of Buffalo & Utica)
he waited,
a loose bundle of wet wash,
to be
picked up.
I shook his big right hand;
he threw
me a left hook.
"What say, dad? What's the pitch?
This tank town ready for the act?"

5 p.m. to M.I.T.:
an echo chamber echoing
indifference,
14 T-squares
lopsided
in zip jackets & sweat shirts,
pale & agnostic,
waiting to be bored.

Wound up,
life-sized,
he took that empty stage on his own terms:
"I like
to build a charge
& blast away right off—
gags and palaver without books."
After his papa's waltz,
he moved in deep . . . the big house of glass,
the salt
Pacific rose,
the monologues meant for a Galway ghost.
Ordnung! Ordnung!
Stalled of a sudden,
in a web-
foot metaphor,
what made him
search the skylight,
lose the thread,
investigate his ankles as if
he'd been
nipped by a dog?
("I fear those shadows most,"
he wrote,
"That start from my own feet.")
Now,
sotto voce,
to himself he said,
"Nice footwork, Maestro,"
& running scared,
came to his wow finish
sweating ice.
He'd kept a promise:
cold turkey
& straight jazz.
The only echo he lost out to
was his own.

Next afternoon,
still stalking praise,
still sick
for love,
he climbed into a Boston & Albany
club car;
nursing a double bourbon-on-the-rocks
he headed west
. . . & one day my old dancing bear
was dead,
gone to his cave,
holed up for good
in the long snow.
I've kept the first
green letter that came back:
"The people here
are nice . . .
but I get lonesome.
Yours
for heart-throbs.
Theodore.
P.S. My major worry's this:
did I,
at your place,
leave some bedroom shoes?
I need
them bad—
they look like bunny shoes.
Love,
T."

THEODORE WEISS
(1916–)

The Fire at Alexandria

Imagine it, a Sophocles complete,
the lost epic of Homer, including no doubt
his notes, his journals, and his observations
on blindness. But what occupies me most,
with the greatest hurt of grandeur, are those
magnificent authors, kept in scholarly rows,
whose names we have no passing record of:
scrolls unrolling Aphrodite like Cleopatra
bundled in a rug, the spoils of love.

Crated masterpieces on the wharf,
and never opened, somehow started first.
And then, as though by imitation, the library
took. One book seemed to inspire another,
to remind it of the flame enclosed
within its papyrus like a drowsy torch.
The fire, roused perhaps by what it read,
its reedy song, raged Dionysian, a band
of Corybantes, down the halls now headlong.

The scribes, despite the volumes wept
unable to douse the witty conflagration—
spicy too as Sappho, coiling, melted
with her girls: the Nile no less, reflecting,
burned—saw splendor fled, a day consummate
in twilit ardencies. Troy at its climax
(towers finally topless) could not have been
more awesome, not though the aromatic house
of Priam mortised the passionate moment.

Now whenever I look into a flame,
I try to catch a single countenance:
Cleopatra, winking out from every joint;
Tiresias eye to eye; a magnitude, long lost,
restored to the sky and the stars he once
struck unsuspected parts of into words.
Fire, and I see them resurrected,
madly crackling perfect birds, the world
lit up as by a golden school, the flashings
of the fathoms of set eyes.

An Egyptian Passage

Beside me she sat, hand hooked and hovering, nose sharp under black-lacquered hair,
and body, skinny, curving over a brownish big
thick book.
                I glanced past her hand to pages
she checked; there, beside strange symbols,
curious hawk-beaked little birds at attention,
gawky beasts, stiff plants, some more than strange,
set next to words which I, despite the rail-
yard shuttling shadows and the battering light
at the end of the tunnels, gradually made out
as items in a German-Egyptian lexicon.

Then red- and black-brick tenements; billboards;
excavations; three boys with mattocks, digging
by a squat, half-finished, bushy hut;
tumbled-together shacks, drifting in the way
of winter; near the bank, its wharf rotted
through in several places, a gutted house
like something done by fire, slowly floating
(so it seemed) out on the river; smoke stacks;

and the dumps, one burning in three spots,
lurid like old passion among heavy piled-
up boxes and black banged-in pots, and birds
floating above like ashes.

Birds too
on the Hudson: ducks in strict formation,
gulls—like lungs—working their great wings
or perched like dirty, jagged lumps of ice
on the ice caking the shoreward waters,
till another dump, a vast flattened white,
for the train's racing flapped into the air.

And all fashion of ice, from shoots in spray
to zigzag rows, waves at their climbing's apex
trapped, frizzled work, to tesselation.

Along the shore a shaggy red-brown brush,
so thick partridges must be crouching in it,
as in the Hudson, under an icy lid,
a brood of clouds. And heavy-headed, long,
thin, flaggy things like the stuff we think of
growing beside the Nile.
The trees bare,
through them the early light already deepened,
purpling. And rocks rode through, by speed
light as the distant hills, the clouds, crumbling,
fitful, round them.
Like the little crate-
white houses across the river, quiet enough,
but indoors, I knew, no bush for its morning
birds busier.
Still her eyes never left
the ibises that fluttered under her fingers.
Deeper and deeper she went, like the sun
unfolding fields, forsaken spots, and towns,
the dirty sharp details of, always more
and always clearer—like the river itself,
the roads agog with golden high-legged going,
song-sparrows swept from their nests, their wings
praising the sun—the steeples, broken houses
and smoky streets, kids dashing in and out
of hide-and-seek, the billowy wash on lines.

And I thought of sitting on a polar star
a million miles away, looking down at this earth
surrounded by its tiny nimbus of a day.
And I saw the days—each hour a speck, twelve
motes combined—like waves like sparks like bushes
burning, lined up one by one, for its intricate
strokes each a kind of word.
"Poughkeepsie,"
the conductor said as he took her ticket
from the seat. Several times he tapped her
on the shoulder before she looked up, fumbled
for her coat and bag, and lurched out.

"Yes, But . . ."

for WCW again

There he was—having spent
the night with us, the first
time away from home alone,
terribly frail for another stroke,
his dreams still shaking him—
his fame steadily leaping ahead,

and he complaining to me,
struggling just to be somebody,
expecting me to comfort him!

Manfully, if with a bitter sense
of injustice, I did my best:
"Why, Bill, you've left a good
green swath of writing behind you."

And he, in a low voice,
most mournfully, "Yes, but
is it poetry?"
That years ago.
Only now I begin to understand
the doubts necessary to one

always open, always desperate
(his work's honesty, spontaneity—
work nothing, life—depended
on it),
          one too so given
over to the moment, so lover-
faithfully serving it,
he could remember or believe
in little else.

                    (Some months
later Frost would visit,
older, sturdy as an ancient oak,
unlike Williams, who could not read
to the end of a verse,
                         intoning
his poems well over an hour
with tremendous relish, then
standing on his solid stumps
another hour batting it out
with students,
                    no doubts shaking
him and few new leaves breaking
out of him.)
                    And only now,
the years, the doubts accumulating,
can I be grateful to Bill
for his uncertainty,
                         can I lean
on it, lean more than on all
his accomplishments, those greeny
asphodel triumphs.

Barracks Apt. 14

          All must be used:
this clay whisky jug, bearing
a lamp-shade; the four brown pears,
lying ruggedly among each other

in the wicker basket; the cactus
in its pot; and the orange berries,
old now as they dangle from their twigs
as though badly hung there.

These as well as the silence,
the young woman reading Aristotle
with difficulty, and the little girl
in the next room, voluble in bed:
"I'm talking in my sleep . . . laughing
in my sleep . . . waking in my sleep"

all are parts hopeful, possible,
expecting their place in the song;
more appealing because parts
that must harmonize into something
that rewards them for being, rewards
with what they are.

Do this and do,
till suddenly the scampering field
you would catch, the shiny crows
just out of reach, the pears
through which a brown tide breaks,
and the cactus you cannot cling to
long like that thorny Aristotle
suddenly, turning, turn on you

as meaning, the ultimate greenness
they have all the time been seeking
in the very flight they held
before you. No matter what you do,
at last you will be overwhelmed,
the distance will be broken,

the music will confound you.

Off to Patagonia

for Pili

Say it's an important event like this:
a famous foreign dignitary about to arrive
or the government planning an excursion,
a messenger announcing it or a newspaper
dispatch (by now a rumor should do,
a clouding over of the day), and those
under suspicion without a sigh pack a bag,
kiss the family goodbye and for the duration
take themselves off to prison.

It has become a way of life.
But that is the way life is in Spain.
And no doubt countless other lands as well.
When you were a schoolgirl you had this mad
highschool Latin professor who, arranging
the class in two straight rows, kept
the rear section of the classroom clear.
And if anyone of you failed to answer
as he liked, pointing imperiously

to that demarked, empty zone,
he said: "Off to Patagonia with you!"
The Latin you had learned? Forget it!
But you did master something: grammar,
punctuation, syntax of a basic sort that,
whether you realize it or not, now stands
you in good stead. The time, standard
Spanish time, comes when it comes,
and then—for less than a word,

an imperceptible lurch in the day,
you and your life suddenly grown thin—
it says: "Off to Patagonia with you!"

And you, packing a bag, kiss the family
goodbye and for the duration disappear
into that prison, promptly clanking
shut. And there you wait patiently,
stern as the treatment is, doing your best
to remember that, so far, you have returned.

As You Like It

An old master yourself now, Auden,
like that much admired Cavafy and those
older still, in this you were wrong.
                                                            People
are not indifferent, let alone oblivious,
to the momentary, great scene.
                                                    No,
like Mrs. Gudgeon, the smart little char
come with our London flat,
                                            listening
to the wireless, a most impressive array
of "the best minds"
                                    engaged in difficult,
arduous talk, and she intent on it,
to her husband's
                                    "What're you listening for?
You don't understand a word they say,"
rejoining,
            "O I enjoy it, just the sound
of it, so musical. And anyway I take
from it whatever I like,
                                        then make of it,
in my own mind, whatever I will,"
like Mrs. Gudgeon
                                    most of us, watching
the moment, some spectacular event,
whether it be Icarus,

Cleopatra consorting
with the streets, or the astronauts
cavorting on the moon,
bear off those bits
that we can use. This is the greatness
of each creature,
the mouse at the Feast
of the Gods, one crumb doing for it
what heaped-up platters cannot do for Them.

GWENDOLYN BROOKS
(1917–   )

Sadie and Maud

Maud went to college.
Sadie stayed at home.
Sadie scraped life
With a fine-tooth comb.

She didn't leave a tangle in.
Her comb found every strand.
Sadie was one of the livingest chits
In all the land.

Sadie bore two babies
Under her maiden name.
Maud and Ma and Papa
Nearly died of shame.

When Sadie said her last so-long
Her girls struck out from home.
(Sadie had left as heritage
Her fine-tooth comb.)

Maud, who went to college,
Is a thin brown mouse.
She is living all alone
In this old house.

The Bean Eaters

They eat beans mostly, this old yellow pair.
Dinner is a casual affair.
Plain chipware on a plain and creaking
  wood,
Tin flatware.

Two who are Mostly Good.
Two who have lived their day,
But keep on putting on their clothes
And putting things away.

And remembering . . .
Remembering, with twinklings and
  twinges,
As they lean over the beans in their
  rented back room that is full of beads and
  receipts and dolls and cloths, tobacco
  crumbs, vases and fringes.

We Real Cool

The Pool Players.
Seven at the Golden Shovel.

We real cool. We
Left school. We

Lurk late. We
Strike straight. We

Sing sin. We
Thin gin. We

Jazz June. We
Die soon.

Riot

A riot is the language of the unheard.
Martin Luther King

John Cabot, out of Wilma, once a Wycliffe,
all whitebluerose below his golden hair,
wrapped richly in right linen and right wool,
almost forgot his Jaguar and Lake Bluff;
almost forgot Grandtully (which is The
Best Thing That Ever Happened To Scotch); almost
forgot the sculpture at the Richard Gray
and Distelheim; the kidney pie at Maxim's,
the Grenadine de Boeuf at Maison Henri.

Because the Negroes were coming down the street.

Because the Poor were sweaty and unpretty
(not like Two Dainty Negroes in Winnetka)
and they were coming toward him in rough ranks.
In seas. In windsweep. They were black and loud.
And not detainable. And not discreet.

Gross. Gross: "*Que tu es grossier!*" John Cabot
itched instantly beneath the nourished white
that told his story of glory to the World.
"Don't let It touch me! the blackness! Lord!" he whispered
to any handy angel in the sky.

But, in a thrilling announcement, on It drove
and breathed on him: and touched him. In that breath
the fume of pig foot, chitterling and cheap chili,
malign, mocked John. And, in terrific touch, old
averted doubt jerked forward decently,
cried "Cabot! John! You are a desperate man,
and the desperate die expensively today."

John Cabot went down in the smoke and fire
and broken glass and blood, and he cried "Lord!
Forgive these nigguhs that know not what they do."

An Aspect of Love,
Alive in the Ice and Fire

LaBohem Brown

It is the morning of our love.

In a package of minutes there is this We.
How beautiful.
Merry foreigners in our morning,
we laugh, we touch each other,
are responsible props and posts.

A physical light is in the room.

Because the world is at the window
we cannot wonder very long.

You rise. Although
genial, you are in yourself again.
I observe
your direct and respectable stride.
You are direct and self-accepting as a lion
in African velvet. You are level, lean,
remote.

There is a moment in Camaraderie
when interruption is not to be understood.
I cannot bear an interruption.
This is the shining joy;
the time of not-to-end.

On the street we smile.
We go
in different directions
down the imperturbable street.

PAULINE HANSON

(1917–   )

So Beautiful Is the Tree of Night

When I see how high it is,
when I see how its great branches arch across the sky
and how from there, all of a blackness,
its branches bend over and down
until down to the world that must lie in its shadows—
when I see this,
so beautiful is the tree of night,
in country and in country
I am whoever watches it.

And when in their long flight to somewhere,
small and shining birds
begin to come into its darkness;
when its great branches are heavy with them—
heavy with the ones who find their quiet sleep,
heavy with the others who in their dreams of flying
shake their silver feathers—
when I see this,
so beautiful is the tree of night,
before the day fades it
I watch from century and from century.

And I Am Old to Know

No place seemed farther than your death
but when I went there—gone from there,
it was from your love you spoke
and it was to your love I moved.

And as you speak it—you, my own:
in the days, in the nights of your voice,
always the word of love opens,
opens into all its meaning.

And as I longer move to you,
as you wait and as you take me,
not like a lover but like love
you tell me and I am old to know:

love is to the farthest place—
love is to so far a place
from always its greatest distances,
to see where death was, I look back.

From Creature to Ghost

Across the night
until beside me,
the wild dogs crouch
and the hunted, the hurt thing,
cries its anguish,
begs its life.
But night is a country
of dying and dead
and when night voices howl
somewhere and how
the body is torn—
shuddering out of it

what small thing is this
so slant, so uncertain,
the moon will not show
nor darkness describe
the slow way it moves
from creature to ghost
and now from the home of
its body is lost.

Is lost, is alone,
yet so great this anguish
of dying and dead,
I think the small ones
of all the earth
sometime are met in it.

Or time is always
of once and now.
And in any night
when the wind is black
and the wild dogs leap—
hunted and tormented
and torn from the body,
like the animal ones
of all the earth
I come to everywhere,
everywhere this darkness.
And shuddering into it

if once I was only
the one who listened
listening has made me
the one who cries.
Until in this place
of dying and dead:
from creature to ghost
the way is so strange—
I die, I live,
in the anguish of both.

ROBERT LOWELL
(1917–1977)

Sailing Home from Rapallo
(*February 1954*)

Your nurse could only speak Italian,
but after twenty minutes I could imagine your final week,
and tears ran down my cheeks. . . .
When I embarked from Italy with my Mother's body,
the whole shoreline of the *Golfo di Genova*
was breaking into fiery flower.
The crazy yellow and azure sea-sleds
blasting like jack-hammers across
the *spumante*-bubbling wake of our liner,
recalled the clashing colors of my Ford.
Mother travelled first-class in the hold;
her *Risorgimento* black and gold casket
was like Napoleon's at the *Invalides*. . . .

While the passengers were tanning
on the Mediterranean in deck-chairs,
our family cemetery in Dunbarton
lay under the White Mountains
in the sub-zero weather.
The graveyard's soil was changing to stone—
so many of its deaths had been midwinter.
Dour and dark against the blinding snowdrifts,
its black brook and fir trunks were as smooth as masts.
A fence of iron spear-hafts
black-bordered its mostly Colonial grave-slates.
The only "unhistoric" soul to come here
was Father, now buried beneath his recent
unweathered pink-veined slice of marble.

Even the Latin of his Lowell motto:
Occasionem cognosce,
seemed too businesslike and pushing here,
where the burning cold illuminated
the hewn inscriptions of Mother's relatives:
twenty or thirty Winslows and Starks.
Frost had given their names a diamond edge. . . .

In the grandiloquent lettering on Mother's coffin,
Lowell had been misspelled *LOVEL.*
The corpse
was wrapped like *panetone* in Italian tinfoil.

The Quaker Graveyard in Nantucket

(For Warren Winslow, Dead at Sea)

Let man have dominion over the fishes of the sea and the fowls of the air and the beasts and the whole earth, and every creeping creature that moveth upon the earth.

I

A brackish reach of shoal off Madaket,—
The sea was still breaking violently and night
Had steamed into our North Atlantic Fleet,
When the drowned sailor clutched the drag-net. Light
Flashed from his matted head and marble feet.
He grappled at the net
With the coiled, hurdling muscles of his thighs:
The corpse was bloodless, a botch of reds and whites,
Its open, staring eyes
Were lustreless dead-lights
Or cabin-windows on a stranded hulk
Heavy with sand. We weight the body, close
Its eyes and heave it seaward whence it came,
Where the heel-headed dogfish barks its nose
On Ahab's void and forehead; and the name
Is blocked in yellow chalk.

Sailors, who pitch this portent at the sea
Where dreadnaughts shall confess
Its hell-bent deity,
When you are powerless
To sand-bag this Atlantic bulwark, faced
By the earth-shaker, green, unwearied, chaste
In his steel scales: ask for no Orphean lute
To pluck life back. The guns of the steeled fleet
Recoil and then repeat
The hoarse salute.

II

Whenever winds are moving and their breath
Heaves at the roped-in bulwarks of this pier,
The terns and sea-gulls tremble at your death
In these home waters. Sailor, can you hear
The Pequod's sea wings, beating landward, fall
Headlong and break on our Atlantic wall
Off 'Sconset, where the yawing S-boats splash
The bellbuoy, with ballooning spinnakers,
As the entangled, screeching mainsheet clears
The blocks: off Madaket, where lubbers lash
The heavy surf and throw their long lead squids
For blue-fish? Sea-gulls blink their heavy lids
Seaward. The winds' wings beat upon the stones,
Cousin, and scream for you and the claws rush
At the sea's throat and wring it in the slush
Of this old Quaker graveyard where the bones
Cry out in the long night for the hurt beast
Bobbing by Ahab's whaleboats in the East.

III

All you recovered from Poseidon died
With you, my cousin, and the harrowed brine
Is fruitless on the blue beard of the god,
Stretching beyond us to the castles in Spain,
Nantucket's westward haven. To Cape Cod
Guns, cradled on the tide,

Blast the eelgrass about a waterclock
Of bilge and backwash, roil the salt and sand
Lashing earth's scaffold, rock
Our warships in the hand
Of the great God, where time's contrition blues
Whatever it was these Quaker sailors lost
In the mad scramble of their lives. They died
When time was open-eyed,
Wooden and childish; only bones abide
There, in the nowhere, where their boats were tossed
Sky-high, where mariners had fabled news
Of IS, the whited monster. What it cost
Them is their secret. In the sperm-whale's slick
I see the Quakers drown and hear their cry:
"If God himself had not been on our side,
If God himself had not been on our side,
When the Atlantic rose against us, why,
Then it had swallowed us up quick."

IV

This is the end of the whaleroad and the whale
Who spewed Nantucket bones on the thrashed swell
And stirred the troubled waters to whirlpools
To send the Pequod packing off to hell:
This is the end of them, three-quarters fools,
Snatching at straws to sail
Seaward and seaward on the turntail whale,
Spouting out blood and water as it rolls,
Sick as a dog to these Atlantic shoals:
Clamavimus, O depths. Let the sea-gulls wail

For water, for the deep where the high tide
Mutters to its hurt self, mutters and ebbs.
Waves wallow in their wash, go out and out,
Leave only the death-rattle of the crabs,
The beach increasing, its enormous snout
Sucking the ocean's side.
This is the end of running on the waves;
We are poured out like water. Who will dance
The mast-lashed master of Leviathans
Up from this field of Quakers in their unstoned graves?

V

When the whale's viscera go and the roll
Of its corruption overruns this world
Beyond tree-swept Nantucket and Wood's Hole
And Martha's Vineyard, Sailor, will your sword
Whistle and fall and sink into the fat?
In the great ash-pit of Jehoshaphat
The bones cry for the blood of the white whale,
The fat flukes arch and whack about its ears,
The death-lance churns into the sanctuary, tears
The gun-blue swingle, heaving like a flail,
And hacks the coiling life out: it works and drags
And rips the sperm-whale's midriff into rags,
Gobbets of blubber spill to wind and weather,
Sailor, and gulls go round the stoven timbers
Where the morning stars sing out together
And thunder shakes the white surf and dismembers
The red flag hammered in the mast-head. Hide,
Our steel, Jonas Messias, in Thy side.

VI

OUR LADY OF WALSINGHAM

There once the penitents took off their shoes
And then walked barefoot the remaining mile;
And the small trees, a stream and hedgerows file
Slowly along the munching English lane,
Like cows to the old shrine, until you lose
Track of your dragging pain.
The stream flows down under the druid tree,
Shiloah's whirlpools gurgle and make glad
The castle of God. Sailor, you were glad
And whistled Sion by that stream. But see:
Our Lady, too small for her canopy,
Sits near the altar. There's no comeliness
At all or charm in that expressionless
Face with its heavy eyelids. As before,
This face, for centuries a memory,
Non est species, neque decor,

Expressionless, expresses God: it goes
Past castled Sion. She knows what God knows,
Not Calvary's Cross nor crib at Bethlehem
Now, and the world shall come to Walsingham.

VII

The empty winds are creaking and the oak
Splatters and splatters on the cenotaph,
The boughs are trembling and a gaff
Bobs on the untimely stroke
Of the greased wash exploding on a shoal-bell
In the old mouth of the Atlantic. It's well;
Atlantic, you are fouled with the blue sailors,
Sea-monsters, upward angel, downward fish:
Unmarried and corroding, spare of flesh
Mart once of supercilious, wing'd clippers,
Atlantic, where your bell-trap guts its spoil
You could cut the brackish winds with a knife
Here in Nantucket, and cast up the time
When the Lord God formed man from the sea's slime
And breathed into his face the breath of life,
And blue-lung'd combers lumbered to the kill.
The Lord survives the rainbow of His will.

Skunk Hour

(For Elizabeth Bishop)

Nautilus Island's hermit
heiress still lives through winter in her Spartan cottage;
her sheep still graze above the sea.
Her son's a bishop. Her farmer
is first selectman in our village;
she's in her dotage.

Thirsting for
the hierarchic privacy
of Queen Victoria's century,
she buys up all
the eyesores facing her shore,
and lets them fall.

The season's ill—
we've lost our summer millionaire,
who seemed to leap from an L. L. Bean
catalogue. His nine-knot yawl
was auctioned off to lobstermen.
A red fox stain covers Blue Hill.

And now our fairy
decorator brightens his shop for fall;
his fishnet's filled with orange cork,
orange, his cobbler's bench and awl;
there is no money in his work,
he'd rather marry.

One dark night,
my Tudor Ford climbed the hill's skull;
I watched for love-cars. Lights turned down,
they lay together, hull to hull,
where the graveyard shelves on the town. . . .
My mind's not right.

A car radio bleats,
"Love, O careless Love. . . ." I hear
my ill-spirit sob in each blood cell,
as if my hand were at its throat. . . .
I myself am hell;
nobody's here—

only skunks, that search
in the moonlight for a bite to eat.
They march on their soles up Main Street:
white stripes, moonstruck eyes' red fire
under the chalk-dry and spar spire
of the Trinitarian Church.

I stand on top
of our back steps and breathe the rich air—
a mother skunk with her column of kittens swills the garbage pail.
She jabs her wedge-head in a cup
of sour cream, drops her ostrich tail,
and will not scare.

The Public Garden

Burnished, burned-out, still burning as the year
you lead me to our stamping ground.
The city and its cruising cars surround
the Public Garden. All's alive—
the children crowding home from school at five,
punting a football in the bricky air,
the sailors and their pick-ups under trees
with Latin labels. And the jaded flock
of swanboats paddles to its dock.
The park is drying.
Dead leaves thicken to a ball
inside the basin of a fountain, where
the heads of four stone lions stare
and suck on empty fawcets. Night
deepens. From the arched bridge, we see
the shedding park-bound mallards, how they keep
circling and diving in the lanternlight,
searching for something hidden in the muck.
And now the moon, earth's friend, that cared so much
for us, and cared so little, comes again—
always a stranger! As we walk,
it lies like chalk
over the waters. Everything's aground.
Remember summer? Bubbles filled
the fountain, and we splashed. We drowned
in Eden, while Jehovah's grass-green lyre
was rustling all about us in the leaves
that gurgled by us, turning upside down . . .
The fountain's failing waters flash around
the garden. Nothing catches fire.

Night-Sweat

Work-table, litter, books and standing lamp,
plain things, my stalled equipment, the old broom—
but I am living in a tidied room,
for ten nights now I've felt the creeping damp
float over my pajamas' wilted white . . .
Sweet salt embalms me and my head is wet,
everything streams and tells me this is right;
my life's fever is soaking in night sweat—
one life, one writing! But the downward glide
and bias of existing wrings us dry—
always inside me is the child who died,
always inside me is his will to die—
one universe, one body . . . in this urn
the animal night sweats of the spirit burn.
Behind me! You! Again I feel the light
lighten my leaded eyelids, while the gray
skulled horses whinny for the soot of night.
I dabble in the dapple of the day,
a heap of wet clothes, seamy, shivering,
I see my flesh and bedding washed with light,
my child exploding into dynamite,
my wife . . . your lightness alters everything,
and tears the black web from the spider's sack,
as your heart hops and flutters like a hare.
Poor turtle, tortoise, if I cannot clear
the surface of these troubled waters here,
absolve me, help me, Dear Heart, as you bear
this world's dead weight and cycle on your back.

History

History has to live with what was here,
clutching and close to fumbling all we had—
it is so dull and gruesome how we die,
unlike writing, life never finishes.
Abel was finished; death is not remote,
a flash-in-the-pan electrifies the skeptic,
his cows crowding like skulls against high-voltage wire,
his baby crying all night like a new machine.
As in our Bibles, white-faced, predatory,
the beautiful, mist-drunken hunter's moon ascends—
a child could give it a face: two holes, two holes,
my eyes, my mouth, between them a skull's no-nose—
O there's a terrifying innocence in my face
drenched with the silver salvage of the mornfrost.

Reading Myself

Like thousands, I took just pride and more than just,
struck matches that brought my blood to a boil;
I memorized the tricks to set the river on fire—
somehow never wrote something to go back to.
Can I suppose I am finished with wax flowers
and have earned my grass on the minor slopes of Parnassus . . .
No honeycomb is built without a bee
adding circle to circle, cell to cell,
the wax and honey of a mausoleum—
this round dome proves its maker is alive;
the corpse of the insect lives embalmed in honey,
prays that its perishable work live long
enough for the sweet-tooth bear to desecrate—
this open book . . . my open coffin.

LAWRENCE FERLINGHETTI
(1919?–   )

Constantly Risking Absurdity

Constantly risking absurdity
and death
whenever he performs
above the heads
of his audience
the poet like an acrobat
climbs on rime
to a high wire of his own making
and balancing on eyebeams
above a sea of faces
paces his way
to the other side of day
performing entrechats
and sleight-of-foot tricks
and other high theatrics
and all without mistaking
any thing
for what it may not be

For he's the super realist
who must perforce perceive
taut truth
before the taking of each stance or step
in his supposed advance
toward that still higher perch
where Beauty stands and waits
with gravity
to start her death-defying leap

And he
a little charleychaplin man
who may or may not catch
her fair eternal form
spreadeagled in the empty air
of existence

The Pennycandystore Beyond the El

The pennycandystore beyond the El
is where I first
fell in love
with unreality
Jellybeans glowed in the semi-gloom
of that september afternoon
A cat upon the counter moved among
the licorice sticks
and tootsie rolls
and Oh Boy Gum

Outside the leaves were falling as they died

A wind had blown away the sun
A girl ran in
Her hair was rainy
Her breasts were breathless in the little room

Outside the leaves were falling
and they cried
Too soon! too soon!

Frightened

Frightened
by the sound of my own voice
and by the sound of birds
singing on hot wires
in sunday sleep I see myself
slaying sundry sinners and turkeys
loud dogs with sharp dead dugs
and black knights in iron suits
With Brooks labels
and Yale locks upon the pants
Yes
and with penis erectus for spear
I slay all old ladies
making them young again
with a touch of my sweet swaying sword
retrouving them their maiden
hoods and heads
ah yes
in flattering falsehoods of sleep

we come we conquer all
but all the while
real standard time ticks on
and new bottled babies with real teeth
devour our fantastic
fictioned future

In Goya's Greatest Scenes We Seem to See

In Goya's greatest scenes we seem to see
the people of the world
exactly at the moment when
they first attained the title of
'suffering humanity'

They writhe upon the page
in a veritable rage
of adversity
Heaped up
groaning with babies and bayonets
under cement skies
in an abstract landscape of blasted trees
bent statues bats wings and beaks
slippery gibbets
cadavers and carnivorous cocks
and all the final hollering monsters
of the
'imagination of disaster'
they are so bloody real
it is as if they really still existed

And they do

Only the landscape is changed

They still are ranged along the roads
plagued by legionaires
false windmills and demented roosters

They are the same people
only further from home
on freeways fifty lanes wide
on a concrete continent
spaced with bland billboards
illustrating imbecile illusions of happiness

The scene shows fewer tumbrils
but more maimed citizens
in painted cars
and they have strange license plates
and engines
that devour America

EDWIN HONIG
(1919–   )

Through You

Glass I've wanted to live
through you
to be returned to me so

I'd drink the light I see
where you live
in a time you'll always be

without knowing I am
watching me
appear there in you when

wishing not to be ends
with your silent
Now walk through me

Who

It is your last day and hour and you are alone
You have nothing to say even to yourself
Your mind is almost blank
A fly is buzzing in the room
You can kill the fly but you don't Your thoughts will not move you Without color or depth they skim across your mind Before you can read them they disappear
Now after ten minutes or thirty you begin to hear the sound of words spoken words

You think Who speaks You are greedy for another sound another presence
Who speaks Who is speaking
It is a half-friendly Who Like your mother when you were a child Soft round voice with the querulous edge
The words fade The voice goes over the edge and disappears
You look around the room It is bare but things are in it your mind will not name
You look around the room twisting your neck turning your shoulder
You stoop you kneel you lie down
You get up quickly
The voice with the words opens up again
Who you ask
Be still
Who
Be still be still
A silence grows breaking into the voice slowly speaking as you listen word quickening faster more lively
Who
You think It is like my father
No
You think It is like him
Him
Him the other one
No
You think It is like myself in him
Yes
It is coming faster turning the room turning you on your knees again The ceiling moves down
Words pour out faster clearer fresh full of feeling never before spoken words never heard before out of you
You they say You they say You they say You
You YouYou YouYouYouYou Breaking loose they surge out of your chest you pushing to join them till you are all at once all of them in a long water flowing widening flooding an ocean sea world all water without earth or sky a water all over water gone over forever

Being Somebody

He had need of a way
to be himself
without being himself.

He had so little need
of those who said
they had need of him,

He wanted never to see
any of them again,
though he wouldn't say so.

He couldn't say any
of this to them
or to anyone else.

For once in his life
he was satisfied
simply to be.

To be nobody,
nobody but himself,
himself without himself.

He felt empty and full,
not one or the other
but both at once.

He felt chafed like a child
full of flouting wishes,
floating elations.

He felt vague and puffy
like clouds cut up
anywhichway.

But drained of hankerings
like a glass of water
a thirsty man just drank.

He considered someone odd
though familiar may have come
to live inside of him.

Being an egotist,
all this appalled
but gladdened him too.

Because it meant
he was sheltering someone
who needed a home.

He himself had no home,
flitting from friend
to cousin to stranger

As the occasion demanded,
or urged by the heart,
which he often misread.

He lived everywhere
but at home, where sometimes
he stayed overnight.

The city he'd spent
many years in and where
he was certainly known,

Drew him back
like a smelly old coat
he forgot to have cleaned.

Because it had worn
so badly on him,
he couldn't give it away.

Anywhere he slept
he was at home,
if he didn't overstay.

The city he wished most
to live in was nearby
but quite far away.

Near enough to visit
or be visited by
old friends and children.

Far enough off
to forget them all
in a week or a year.

He wanted to live alone
in a den-like apartment,
working nights on his thoughts,

Or in a big rambling house
without tenants and close
to the hub of the city.

He would like also not
to live there but still
to call it his home,

Where he could drop in,
surprising himself hard
at work in his study,

Or, having been called away,
finding the place
shrieking his absence.

He'd like to live there
and in the country as well,
unknown except for

The gas-meter reader
who could recognize him
from that time he allowed

Himself to be home
on the reader's first
bimonthly visit.

He once wrote a letter he thought
he'd only half written himself,
which ended limply:

"How many empties like me
are there left to pick up
before I die?"

Now he believed the letter
was written completely
by somebody else.

Of course he was wrong—
but what if he was
completely somebody else?

W
A
L
WHITMAN

Prophet of the body's
roving magnitude, he still
commands a hope elusive as the Jewish
savior—not dying, not yet born, but always
imminent: coming in a blaze one sunny afternoon
defying winter, to everyone's distinct advantage, then going on
to Eden, half sham, half hearsay, like California or Miami golden.
All his life was squandered
in his poverty when he became
the body's prime revisionist, bankrupt
exploiter, from early middle age, of the nation's
largest unexploited enterprise—baggy, queer,
a Johnny Appleseed freely planting selves the future mashes
into commonplaces, lops off as flourishes, an unweaned appetite.

Yet who can shape his mouth's
beard-brimming bubble, that violent honey
sound? Afterwards, they just blew hard,
Tarzans hamming through the swampy lots.
His patent, never filed, was being man quixotically
alive against the hoax of sin & dying. Paradise is now.
America, whose greatest war was civil, must be born from Abel's wound
& Cain be welcomed home
by Adam—Father Abraham
opening his blood to continents,
all armies, lovers, tramps. A time for heroes but
the captains, shot or dowdy, died. (Had old Abe really smiled
& tipped his hat or had he merely grimaced?) Ulysses,finished,promptly
sighed & chomped cigars & toured the capitals. The people yea'd & shambled
to the greatest fortunes
made, while he conveyed the lippy
cop, the whistling streetcar man, the ferry
pilot billowing upon the apron of his praise.
Nakedly at last he flailed his own paralysis
with mud & flesh-brush. A man, all men himself alone, a rugged blue-
eyed testament, his looks in Brady's lens are calm with after-rages.
"The real war
will never get
in the books."
Below the ragged
line he signed
his chummy name.

WILLIAM MEREDITH

(1919–)

Winter Verse for His Sister

Moonlight washes the west side of the house
As clean as bone, it carpets like a lawn
The stubbled field tilting eastward
Where there is no sign yet of dawn.
The moon is an angel with a bright light sent
To surprise me once before I die
With the real aspect of things.
It holds the light steady and makes no comment.

Practicing for death I have lately gone
To that other house
Where our parents did most of their dying,
Embracing and not embracing their conditions.
Our father built bookcases and little by little stopped reading,
Our mother cooked proud meals for common mouths.
Kindly, they raised two children. We raked their leaves
And cut their grass, we ate and drank with them.
Reconciliation was our long work, not all of it joyful.

Now outside my own house at a cold hour
I watch the noncommittal angel lower
The steady lantern that's worn these clapboards thin
In a wash of moonlight, while men slept within,
Accepting and not accepting their conditions,
And the fingers of trees plied a deep carpet of decay
On the gravel web underneath the field,
And the field tilting always toward day.

The Open Sea

We say the sea is lonely; better say
Our selves are lonesome creatures whom the sea
Gives neither yes nor no for company.

Oh, there are people, all right, settled in the sea—
It is as populous as Maine today—
But no one who will give you the time of day.

A Man who asks there of his family
Or a friend or teacher gets a cold reply
Or finds him dead against that vast majority.

Nor does it signify, that people who stay
Very long, bereaved or not, at the edge of the sea
Hear the drowned folk call: that is mere fancy.

They are speechless. And the famous noise of sea,
Which a poet has beautifully told us in our day,
Is hardly a sound to speak comfort to the lonely.

Although not yet a man given to prayer, I pray
For each creature lost since the start at sea,
And give thanks it was not I, nor yet one close to me.

Wholesome

Hazard's friend Elliot is homosexual. Prodigious
feats of understanding on both sides. It strikes
Hazard as making a complicated matter
more complicated. Very straightforward
on the contrary, Elliot says, who is forever
kissing Hazard's wife hello and goodbye.

In the gallery at the opening almond-
eyed young men materialize. They look at the pictures
as though they were mirrors. Elliot is better known
than Hazard, perhaps a little fashionable.
He administers cocktails, he drinks wisely.

In all fairness, Hazard tells himself
and, *nothing human is alien to me*
and, *the truth is, a great mind must be androgynous,*
(*Coleridge*). But it doesn't bear dwelling on.

His Plans for Old Age

He disagrees with Simone de Beauvoir
in her civilized Gallic gloom, may she be loved
and beautiful without wrinkles until it takes
carbon dating to determine her age.

He's with Yeats, for adult education—
hand-clapping lessons for the soul,
compulsory singing lessons for the soul,
in his case, tone-deaf.
He agrees with Auden, old people can show
'what grace of spirit can create,'
modeling the flesh when it's no longer flashy.
That's the kind of lift he wants for his jowls,
let grace of spirit tuck up the flesh
under his ears and chin with a bare scalpel,
no anesthetic or anything, let grace of spirit
shape up his skull for afterwards.

Man and artist, he is working on his ways
so that when he becomes set in them
as old people must, for all that their souls
clap hands, for all that their spirits dance,
his ways will have grace, his pictures will have class.

He is founding a sect for the radical old,
freaks you may call them but you're wrong,
who persist in being at home in the world,
who must naturally feel it's a good bind to be in,
let the young feel as uncanny as they like.
Oldbodies, he calls them affectionately
as he towels his own in the morning
in front of the mirror, not getting any flashier.
He thinks about Titian and Renoir a lot
in this connection. Nothing is unseemly
that takes its rise in love. If only his energy lasts.

MAY SWENSON
(1919–)

The Shape of Death

What does love look like? We know
the shape of death. Death is a cloud
immense and awesome. At first a lid
is lifted from the eye of light:
there is a clap of sound, a white blossom

belches from the jaw of fright,
a pillared cloud churns from white to gray
like a monstrous brain that bursts and burns,
then turns sickly black, spilling away,
filling the whole sky with ashes of dread;

thickly it wraps, between the clean sea
and the moon, the earth's green head.
Trapped in its cocoon, its choking breath
we know the shape of death:
Death is a cloud.

What does love look like?
Is it a particle, a star—
invisible entirely, beyond the microscope and Palomar?
A dimension unimagined, past the length of hope?
Is it a climate far and fair that we shall never dare

discover? What is its color, and its alchemy?
Is it a jewel in the earth—can it be dug?
Or dredged from the sea? Can it be bought?
Can it be sown and harvested?
Is it a shy beast to be caught?

Death is a cloud,
immense, a clap of sound.
Love is little and not loud.
It nests within each cell, and it
cannot be split.

It is a ray, a seed, a note, a word,
a secret motion of our air and blood.
It is not alien, it is near—
our very skin—
a sheath to keep us pure of fear.

Landing on the Moon

When in the mask of night there shone that cut,
we were riddled. A probe reached down
and stroked some nerve in us,
as if the glint from a wizard's eye, of silver,
slanted out of the mask of the unknown—
pit of riddles, the scratch-marked sky.

When, albino bowl on cloth of jet,
it spilled its virile rays,
our eyes enlarged, our blood reared with the waves.
We craved its secret, but unreachable
it held away from us, chilly and frail.
Distance kept it magnate. Enigma made it white.

When we learned to read it with our rod,
reflected light revealed
a lead mirror, a bruised shield
seamed with scars and shadow-soiled.
A half-faced sycophant, its glitter borrowed,
rode around our throne.

On the moon there shines earth light
as moonlight shines upon the earth . . .
If on its obsidian we set our weightless foot,
and sniff no wind, and lick no rain
and feel no gauze between us and the Fire,
will we trot its grassless skull, sick for the homelike shade?

Naked to the earth-beam we will be,
who have arrived to map an apparition,
who walk upon the forehead of a myth.
Can flesh rub with symbol? If our ball
be iron, and not light, our earliest wish
eclipses. Dare we land upon a dream?

F
I
R
E
ISLAND

The Milky Way
above, the milky
waves beside,
when the sand is night
the sea is galaxy.
The unseparate stars
mark a twining coast
with phosphorescent
surf
in the black sky's trough.
Perhaps we walk on black
star ash, and watch
the milks of light foam forward, swish and spill
while other watchers, out
walking in their white
great
swerve,
gather
our
low
spark,
our little Way
the dark
glitter
in
their
s
i
g
h
t
.

REED WHITTEMORE
(1919–   )

The Departure

The artist must leave these woods now.
He must put his books and files back in the car,
And stuff his bags with shirts and shorts and sweaters,
And clean his room and take a load to the dump, wherever the dump
  is,
And go the rounds and say goodbye to the artists—goodbye—
And the trees—goodbye—
And cash a check and fill up with gas and set out
For the world again, the world, to talk up art.

The world likes that.
It likes to get news of the spirit fresh from the woods,
What birds are saying, and frogs. It sits in its cities,
Thirsty. The artist will fix that.
He will bring in a carload of essences quick on the thruway,
Mists for everyone's parlor, sunsets, done up nice.
Cities want their essences done up nice.

So the artist must leave these woods now. For that.
He takes a last walk in the woods: what is the news, woods?
And the woods reply in their woodsy way that the news
Is woods, woods,
And he hears the news, notes it down and walks back
To his shirts and sweaters, while out of the sky
Art in its arty way keeps saying: goodbye.

Clamming

I go digging for clams once every two or three years
Just to keep my hand in (I usually cut it),
And I'm sure that whenever I do so I tell the
  same story
Of how, at the age of four, I was trapped by the tide
As I clammed a sandbar. It's no story at all,
But I tell it and tell it. It serves my small lust
To be thought of as someone who's lived.
I've a war too to fall back on, and some years of flying,
As well as a high quota of drunken parties,
A wife and children; but somehow the clamming thing
Gives me an image of me that soothes my psyche
Like none of the louder events: me helpless,
Alone with my sandpail,
As fate in the form of soupy Long Island Sound
Comes stalking me.

I've a son now at that age.
He's spoiled. He's been sickly.
He's handsome and bright, affectionate and demanding.
I think of the tides when I look at him.
I'd have him alone and sea-girt, poor little boy.

The self, what a brute it is. It wants, wants.
It will not let go of its even most fictional grandeur,
But must grope, grope down in the muck of its past
For some little squirting life and bring it up tenderly
To the lo and behold of death, that it may weep
And pass on the weeping, keep the thing going.

                    Son, when you clam,
Watch out for the tides and take care of yourself,
Yet no great care,
Lest you care too much and talk of the caring
And bore your best friends and inhibit your children and sicken
At last into opera on somebody's sandbar. Son, when you clam,
Clam.

Thinking of Tents

I am thinking of tents and tentage, tents through the ages.
I had half a tent in the army and rolled it religiously,
But Supply stole it back at war's end, leaving me tentless.
And tentless I thankfully still am, a house man at heart,
Thinking of tents as one who has passed quite beyond tents,
Passed the stakes and the flaps, mosquitoes and mildew,
And come to the ultimate tent, archetypal, platonic,
With one cot in it, and one man curled on the cot
Drinking, cooling small angers, smelling death in the distance—
War's end—
World's end—
Sullen Achilles.

HOWARD NEMEROV
(1920–)

Fugue

You see them vanish in their speeding cars,
The many people hastening through the world,
And wonder what they would have done before
This time of time speed distance, random streams
Of molecules hastened by what rising heat?
Was there never a world where people just sat still?

Yet they might be all of them contemplatives
Of a timeless now, drivers and passengers
In the moving cars all facing to the front
Which is the future, which is destiny,
Which is desire and desire's end—
What are they doing but just sitting still?

And still at speed they fly away, as still
As the road paid out beneath them as it flows
Moment by moment into the mirrored past;
They spread in their wake the parading fields of food,
The windowless works where who is making what,
The grey towns where the wishes and the fears are done.

The Western Approaches

As long as we look forward, all seems free,
Uncertain, subject to the Laws of Chance,
Though strange that chance should lie subject to laws,
But looking back on life it is as if
Our Book of Changes never let us change.

Stories already told a time ago
Were waiting for us down the road, our lives
But filled them out; and dreams about the past
Show us the world is post meridian
With little future left to dream about.

Old stories none but scholars seem to tell
Among us any more, they hide the ways,
Old tales less comprehensible than life
Whence nonetheless we know the things we do
And do the things they say the fathers did.

When I was young I flew past Skerryvore
Where the Nine Maidens still grind Hamlet's meal,
The salt and granite grain of bitter earth,
But knew it not for twenty years and more.
My chances past their changes now, I know

How a long life grows ghostly towards the close
As any man dissolves in Everyman
Of whom the story, as it always did, begins
In a far country, once upon a time,
There lived a certain man and he had three sons . . .

Speculation

Prepare for death. But how can you prepare
For death? Suppose it isn't an exam,
But more like the Tavern Scene in Henry IV,
Or that big drunk, the Symposium?

Remember, everybody will be there,
Sooner or later at first, then all at once.
Maybe the soul at death becomes a star.
Maybe the galaxies are one great dance,

Maybe. For as earth's population grows,
So does the number of the unfixed stars,
Exploding from the sempiternal stars,
Exploding from the sempiternal Rose
Into the void of an expanding universe.

If it be so, it doesn't speak well for
The social life hereafter: faster than light
The souls avoid each other, as each star
Speeds outward, goes out, or goes out of sight.

JAMES SCHEVILL

(1920–)

London Pavement Artist

His place is before, not in, the National Gallery,
On the sidewalk, down on hands and knees,
Grey hair a massive flag of identity,
Hands like hooks grappling with stone,
Savage beard a porcupine defense
Against the jeers of passersby.
Draw to eat. Simple motivation,
But what eats him is the pavement,
Devouring his images of chalk;
That rain-washed, fog-lost, wind-whipped cement
On which he draws flowers and faces,
Simple subjects to elicit simple coins,
Penny and ha'-penny thudding in his cap.
Is it art? Stupid question.
The images of chalk fade in the rain . . .
Art is the pavement that eats you.

Green Frog at Roadstead, Wisconsin

It is the way of a pleasant path
To walk through white birch, fir,
And spruce on a limestone trail
Through the quiet, complacent time
Of summer when, suddenly, the frog jumps
And you jump after him, laughing,
Hopping, frog and woman, to show

The stationary world its flat ways.
Love is a Frog, I grin that greenly
To your green eyes and they leap
At me. Up, I will enter the Frog World
With you and try the leaping ways
Of the heart that we do not fail to find
The sunlit air full of leaping chances.

Freud: Dying in London, He Recalls the Smoke of His Cigar Beginning to Sing

"Double flesh,
Double way;
  Love is a bed
Where angel-devils
Lash and play.

"Double warmth,
Double flame,
  Love is the fury
To love and find
A single name."

In the smoke of my cigars, twenty a day,
I searched the roots of man's desire;
To bed at one in the morning
Until the smoke began to sing.
I enjoyed my food, my meat,
In a city whose name I have forgotten.
Rooted in one house for forty-seven years,
I analyzed and wrote and watched six children
Until the Nazis marched and the booted Commissar
Asked me to sign a statement of gentle handling.
I insisted on adding the sentence:
"I can heartily recommend the Gestapo to anyone."

The cancer grows in my jaw like a separate life.
Krebs, meaning cancer and crabs; strange that I
Who am fond of crabs should suffer from cancer.

A broadcast says: *This is the last war.*
Anyhow, it is my last war. The radium begins
To eat in and my world is what it was before—
An island of pain floating on a sea of indifference.
The stench . . . when my chow is brought to visit me,
She shrinks into a corner of the room.
I spend my hours lying near my study window
Gazing at my flowers in the garden,
My superb almond tree, its pink blossoms
Pouring beauty into the darkening world.
I never believed in a supernatural life;
This world of nature embraces everything.
Why, then, do I dream of religion,
And write of Moses in my final hours?
Man's helplessness remains, his father-longing.
The gods retain their three-fold task:
To exorcise the terrors of nature;
To reconcile the cruelty of death;
To make amends for all suffering and hate
The communal life of culture imposes on man.
In early centuries, men projected the Devil;
Today, their guilt turns in to physical pain.

Jews write to beg me not to tear from Moses,
In time of need, the legend of a Jewish hero;
But the truth must be sought. Moses blazes
In my imagination more than any other leader.
For three lonely September weeks in 1913,
I stood every day by Michelangelo's statue,
Studying it, measuring it, sketching it,
Until I captured the understanding for it:
Moses, angry at the dance of lust,
The sexual fury around the Golden Calf,
But mastering his passion for his cause,
Protecting the Tables of the Law.
It is so logical. Moses was an Egyptian Prince,
Not a Jew; Moses was the God who chose the Jews,
Desiring to make them equal to Egyptians,
To give them one God of purity and power;
And so he marked them with the rite of circumcision
And led them out into a land of freedom.

In the end, he was murdered in rebellion
And that murder bred the hope for a Messiah
Of retribution. Christianity, the son-religion,
Replaced the ancient, Mosaic, father-religion.
The little, Egyptian statues on my desk begin to speak:
God, the Father, always walks on earth
Until his sons unite to slay him.
What was it that surrealist artist said?
My cranium is reminiscent of a snail . . .
I crawled slowly through the years
Until the smoke of my cigar began to sing.
It is useless to go on . . . Burn me,
Place my ashes in a Grecian urn . . .

"Double-flesh,
Double-way;
  Love is a bed
Where angel-devils
Lash and play.

"Double-warmth,
Double-flame,
  Love is the fury
To love and find
A single name."

Huck Finn at Ninety, Dying in a Chicago Boarding House Room

To give up everything . . .
Float away under the sun . . . .
The bliss of a bastard
Cut off from everyone . . .

To feel the Moms and Aunts
Pop their corsets like balloons
And the breasts of love
Soar out in white moons . . .

I sink back, a whiskey case,
Fondling the button I found—
"Make Love—Not War"—
In the park on the ground . . .

I've got the button, button . . .
Let me sleep in the gleam
Of that old raft floating down river
Through the frontier dream . . .

A *Screamer Discusses Methods of Screaming*

We all scream, most of us inside.
Outside is another world.
A neighbor fills her television dinner
With too much pepper and screams.
One woman stabs her door with a sword.
Another, overweight, steps in the shower
And screams, "Fat! Fat! *Fat!*"
A man who takes flying lessons
Soars high in the clouds to scream.
Another dives to the bottom of his pool
Where he screams underwater.
A friend cleans his gun, screaming "Assassin!"
I like an interior, smiling scream.
When you walk past me on the street
I nod my head to you and, smiling, scream.
You never hear me through the smile.
The inside scream has no echo.

JANE MAYHALL

(1921–)

City Sparrow

The city sparrow is the color of a dirty tree;
and noisy, noisy, but not obvious. The sparrow
is not bad poetry, or like our stupid human imi-
tations. He flies like the inevitable stroke
of individuality, up, sideways, and darts unusual
as sunlight sparrow's gold. The upheaval of street
lies in cracked macadam, mingling fossils and stone
waterfalls. Every speck of reality is different
because the sparrow leaps ironically alive.
As people try to deny their hidden joys.

The Human Animal

To make me do the thing I will, I won't.
Facing front, it's back I turn
to scorn the right intent.
The worse I am, the better do. Against
my own impulse I plot; and overthrown
rise up to govern all I have undone.

To live my life, I've lost it. Or reversed,
the greatest loss was living most;
the best I did was least.
By counter causes, grown then capable,
I've come to some short pass. And passing still
go on to learn what's gone; and what I will.

The Marshes

All that running water outside;
the running faces, the rocks of blood,
the melting waste that tangles the bushes;
a strong wind blows, and I will not
                    subvert course.
Blocks of people with hysterical blotches
are rushing past, whirling on their big
television teeth gutturals and maxims.
I knew them before, they were numbers and
mewling crowds, that tangled up
                    our thoughts
among the weeds.

For every clear idea, the marsh is
                    sucking through;
glutted human thrall, majorities
                    and gurgles.
Oily bubbles wrangle out their wars.
How can I keep my course?
                    Chekov, Mozart,
imagining in your mind
lives of discipline and drain,
through whose filaments
the marshes run.

For the Market

It is true, modern life is complicated.
The feedback echoes before it speaks;
the machine, lumping redress, cannot
                    be directed.
Additions radiate into the meaningless,
                    and nothing.

What is left over, but the will to work?
To weave, like an old peasant on a
                    dusty summer day,
rugs of intelligence, berry-dyed lucidities,
to sell to exploiters, and the restless rich.

RICHARD WILBUR

(1921–   )

Love Calls Us to the Things of This World

The eyes open to a cry of pulleys,
And spirited from sleep, the astounded soul
Hangs for a moment bodiless and simple
As false dawn.
Outside the open window
The morning air is all awash with angels.

Some are in bed-sheets, some are in blouses,
Some are in smocks: but truly there they are.
Now they are rising together in calm swells
Of halcyon feeling, filling whatever they wear
With the deep joy of their impersonal breathing;

Now they are flying in place, conveying
The terrible speed of their omnipresence, moving
And staying like white water; and now of a sudden
They swoon down into so rapt a quiet
That nobody seems to be there.
The soul shrinks

From all that it is about to remember,
From the punctual rape of every blessed day,
And cries,
"Oh, let there be nothing on earth but laundry,
Nothing but rosy hands in the rising steam
And clear dances done in the sight of heaven."

Yet, as the sun acknowledges
With a warm look the world's hunks and colors,
The soul descends once more in bitter love
To accept the waking body, saying now
In a changed voice as the man yawns and rises,

"Bring them down from their ruddy gallows,
Let there be clean linen for the backs of thieves;
Let lovers go fresh and sweet to be undone,
And the heaviest nuns walk in a pure floating
Of dark habits,
keeping their difficult balance."

Juggler

A ball will bounce, but less and less. It's not
A light-hearted thing, resents its own resilience.
Falling is what it loves, and the earth falls
So in our hearts from brilliance,
Settles and is forgot.
It takes a sky-blue juggler with five red balls

To shake our gravity up. Whee, in the air
The balls roll round, wheel on his wheeling hands,
Learning the ways of lightness, alter to spheres
Grazing his finger ends,
Cling to their courses there,
Swinging a small heaven about his ears.

But a heaven is easier made of nothing at all
Than the earth regained, and still and sole within
The spin of worlds, with a gesture sure and noble
He reels that heaven in,
Landing it ball by ball,
And trades it all for a broom, a plate, a table.

Oh, on his toe the table is turning, the broom's
Balancing up on his nose, and the plate whirls
On the tip of the broom! Damn, what a show, we cry:
The boys stamp, and the girls
Shriek, and the drum booms
And all comes down, and he bows and says good-bye.

If the juggler is tired now, if the broom stands
In the dust again, if the table starts to drop
Through the daily dark again, and though the plate
Lies flat on the table top,
For him we batter our hands
Who has won for once over the world's weight.

Museum Piece

The good gray guardians of art
Patrol the halls on spongy shoes,
Impartially protective, though
Perhaps suspicious of Toulouse.

Here dozes one against the wall,
Disposed upon a funeral chair.
A Degas dancer pirouettes
Upon the parting of his hair.

See how she spins! The grace is there,
But strain as well is plain to see.
Degas loved the two together:
Beauty joined to energy.

Edgar Degas purchased once
A fine El Greco, which he kept
Against the wall beside his bed
To hang his pants on while he slept.

HOWARD MOSS
(1922–   )

King Midas

My food was pallid till I heard it ring
Against fine china. Every blessed thing
I touch becomes a work of art that baits
Its goldsmith's appetite: My bread's too rich,
My butter much too golden, and my meat
A nugget on my plate, as cold as ice;
Fresh water in my throat turns precious there,
Where every drop becomes a millionaire.

My hands leak gold into the flower's mouth,
Whose lips in tiers of rigid foliage
Make false what flowers are supposed to be.
I did not know I loved their warring thorns
Until they flowered into spikes so hard
My blood made obdurate the rose's stem.
My God was generous. But when I bleed,
It clogs the rosebed and cements the seed.

My dog was truly witty while he breathed.
I saw the tiny hairs upon his skin
Grow like a lion's into golden down.
I plucked them by the handfuls off of him,
And, now he is pure profit, my sculpturing
Might make a King go mad, for it was I
Who made those lively muscles stiffly pose—
This jaundice is relentless, and it grows.

I hate the glint of stars, the shine of wheat,
And when I walk, the tracings of my feet
Are affluent and litter where I go
With money that I sweat. I bank the slow
Gold-leaf of everything and, in my park,
A darkness shimmers that is not the dark,
A daylight glitters that is not the day—
All things are much less darling gilt this way.

Princess, come no closer; my tempered kiss,
Though it is royal still, will make you this
Or that kind of a statue. And my Queen,
Be armed against this gold paralysis,
Or you will starve and thinly bed alone,
And when you dream, a gold mine in your brain
Will have both eyes release their golden ore
And cry for tears they could not cry before.

I would be nothing but the dirt made loud,
A clay that ripples with the worm, decay
In ripeness of the weeds, a timid sun,
Or oppositely be entirely cloud,
Absolved of matter, dissolving in the rain.
Before gold kills me as it kills all men,
Dear Dionysus, give me back again
Ten fingertips that leave the world alone.

The Hand

I have watched your fingers drum
Against each other: thumb against
The fore- and middle-finger. When
Tension leaves your hand alone,
Your face slides back its screen, I see
Such streams begin, such gardens grow
That you must hide more than you hide,
And I must know more than I know.

JAMES DICKEY
(1923–   )

The Heaven of Animals

Here they are. The soft eyes open.
If they have lived in a wood
It is a wood.
If they have lived on plains
It is grass rolling
Under their feet forever.

Having no souls, they have come,
Anyway, beyond their knowing.
Their instincts wholly bloom
And they rise.
The soft eyes open.

To match them, the landscape flowers,
Outdoing, desperately
Outdoing what is required:
The richest wood,
The deepest field.

For some of these,
It could not be the place
It is, without blood.
These hunt, as they have done,
But with claws and teeth grown perfect,

More deadly than they can believe.
They stalk more silently,
And crouch on the limbs of trees,
And their descent
Upon the bright backs of their prey

May take years
In a sovereign floating of joy.
And those that are hunted
Know this as their life,
Their reward: to walk

Under such trees in full knowledge
Of what is in glory above them,
And to feel no fear,
But acceptance, compliance.
Fulfilling themselves without pain

At the cycle's center,
They tremble, they walk
Under the tree,
They fall, they are torn,
They rise, they walk again.

Adultery

We have all been in rooms
We cannot die in, and they are odd places, and sad.
Often Indians are standing eagle-armed on hills

In the sunrise   open wide to the Great Spirit
Or gliding in canoes   or cattle are browsing on the walls
Far away   gazing down with the eyes of our children

Not far away   or there are men driving
The last railspike, which has turned
Gold in their hands. Gigantic forepleasure lives

Among such scenes, and we are alone with it
At last. There is always some weeping
Between us   and someone is always checking

A wrist watch by the bed to see how much
Longer we have left. Nothing can come
Of this   nothing can come

Of us: of me with my grim techniques
Or you who have sealed your womb
With a ring of convulsive rubber:

Although we come together,
Nothing will come of us. But we would not give
It up, for death is beaten

By praying Indians   by distant cows   historical
Hammers   by hazardous meetings that bridge
A continent. One could never die here

Never die   never die
While crying. My lover, my dear one
I will see you next week

When I'm in town. I will call you
If I can. Please get hold of   Please don't
Oh God, Please don't any more I can't bear . . . Listen:

We have done it again   we are
Still living. Sit up and smile,
God bless you. Guilt is magical.

The Sheep Child

Farm boys wild to couple
With anything   with soft-wooded trees
With mounds of earth   mounds
Of pinestraw   will keep themselves off
Animals by legends of their own:
In the hay-tunnel dark
And dung of barns, they will
Say   I have heard tell

That in a museum in Atlanta
Way back in a corner somewhere
There's this thing that's only half

Sheep like a woolly baby
Pickled in alcohol because
Those things can't live his eyes
Are open but you can't stand to look
I heard from somebody who . . .

But this is now almost all
Gone. The boys have taken
Their own true wives in the city,
The sheep are safe in the west hill
Pasture but we who were born there
Still are not sure. Are we,
Because we remember, remembered
In the terrible dust of museums?

Merely with his eyes, the sheep-child may

Be saying saying

I am here, in my father's house.
I who am half of your world, came deeply
To my mother in the long grass
Of the west pasture, where she stood like moonlight
Listening for foxes. It was something like love
From another world that seized her
From behind, and she gave, not lifting her head
Out of dew, without ever looking, her best
Self to that great need. Turned loose, she dipped her face
Farther into the chill of the earth, and in a sound
Of sobbing of something stumbling
Away, began, as she must do,
To carry me. I woke, dying,
In the summer sun of the hillside, with my eyes
Far more than human. I saw for a blazing moment
The great grassy world from both sides,
Man and beast in the round of their need,
And the hill wind stirred in my wool,
My hoof and my hand clasped each other,
I ate my one meal
Of milk, and died
Staring. From dark grass I came straight

To my father's house, whose dust
Whirls up in the halls for no reason
When no one comes   piling deep in a hellish mild corner,
And, through my immortal waters,
I meet the sun's grains eye
To eye, and they fail at my closet of glass.
Dead, I am most surely living
In the minds of farm boys: I am he who drives
Them like wolves from the hound bitch and calf
And from the chaste ewe in the wind.
They go into woods   into bean fields   they go
Deep into their known right hands. Dreaming of me,
They groan   they wait   they suffer
Themselves, they marry, they raise their kind.

from *The Zodiac*

X

Tenderness, ache on me, and lay your neck
On the slight shoulder-breathing of my arm . . .
There's nobody to be tender with—
This man has given up
On anything stronger than he is.

He's traveled everywhere
But no place has ever done any good.
What does his soul matter, saved like a Caesar-headed goldpiece,
When the world's dying?

He goes to the window,
Hating everything, worn out, looking into the shook heart
Of the city.

Yet the stairwell hammers lightly
Alive: a young step, nimble as foxfire,
And the vital shimmer of a real face
Backs-off the white of the room.
He closes his eyes, for the voice.
"My head is paralyzed with longing—"

He is quiet, but his arm is with her   around
        Her belly and tailbone.
His heart broods: he knows that nothing,
 Even love, can kill off his lonesomeness.

        Twilight passes, then night.

Their bodies are found by the dawn, their souls
    Fallen from them, left in the night
Of patterns   the night that's just finished
    Overwhelming the earth.

        Fading fading faded . . .

  They lie like the expanding universe.

        Too much light. Too much love.

ARTHUR GREGOR
(1923–   )

History

What do we know of what is behind us?
The old town we drove through yesterday
is as remote from us now
as the century it was built,
water covering all our yesterdays equally.

What do we know of what lies ahead?
We see the old inns coming toward us,
white irregular walls, windows spaced unevenly,
women and children waiting at corners to cross.
We see the end of a town and the fields and forests
beyond it,
but also hear the water waiting to cover them as we pass.

And what do we know
of what we do not see,
of what neither moves toward us
nor falls into watery wastes as we pass?

Lyric

The embodiment of what
lies at the core of dreams,
in limbs that move as in
a dance; the thrust at the heart
of eyes that pour

deep violet on one's lap,
the music that follows,
the throb at the top of the head:
what are these
but indices
to what can never be attained!
Some warriors died thus
the sun flashing in their eyes,
and others in wet sand
not able to withstand
the drag of watervoices and
the treachery in ears!

Two Shapes

Entwined on the bed in the dark
I am convinced that
two shapes hover above us—
one above each—
which, though of a substance that
escapes the eye, indistinguishable as air,
wait to be fed, for increase in
vitality, a strengthening
so as to rise as sparks
to fire in a wind.

Unlike the whale that by himself
finds what he must eat
and surfacing sings, they
that wait invisibly depend
on us entirely. Do we assume
it is only for the body
that we lie together here
(as others seeing us might guess),
the shapes are as flecks of ash
adrift in an unnecessary waste.

Enough

Enough! Let this season end,
this summer of unnatural heat,
of untimely storms,
of water subject to winds,
of land subject to
nature's whims, aridity of
human imprint: phantoms
whose eyes speak of
wasted lives, journeys left,
loves not had, lusts

not tried; phantoms
in place of flesh
and passion in the night. Enough!
Enough of nature's wiles
and torments of
the solitary mind.
Give me the human touch and need . . .
Give me the great structures in the mist . . .
the hand held out,
the far-off lines that feed and feed.

DENISE LEVERTOV
(1923–   )

O Taste and See

The world is
not with us enough.
O taste and see

the subway Bible poster said,
meaning *The Lord*, meaning
if anything all that lives
to the imagination's tongue,

grief, mercy, language,
tangerine, weather, to
breathe them, bite,
savor, chew, swallow, transform

into our flesh our
deaths, crossing the street, plum, quince,
living in the orchard and being

hungry, and plucking
the fruit.

Mad Song

My madness is dear to me.
I who was almost always the sanest among my friends,
one to whom others came for comfort,

now at my breasts (that look timid and ignorant,
            that don't look as if milk had flowed from them,
            years gone by)
cherish a viper.
                  Hail, little serpent of useless longing
that may destroy me,
that bites me with such idle
needle teeth.

I who am loved by those who love me
for honesty,
to whom life was an honest breath
                  taken in good faith,
I've forgotten how to tell joy from bitterness.

Dear to me, dear to me,
blue poison, green pain in the mind's veins.
How am I to be cured against my will?

The Ache of Marriage

The ache of marriage:

thigh and tongue, beloved,
are heavy with it,
it throbs in the teeth

We look for communion
and are turned away, beloved,
each and each

It is leviathan and we
in its belly
looking for joy, some joy
not to be known outside it

two by two in the ark of
the ache of it.

LOUIS SIMPSON

(1923–)

American Poetry

Whatever it is, it must have
A stomach that can digest
Rubber, coal, uranium, moons, poems.

Like the shark, it contains a shoe.
It must swim for miles through the desert
Uttering cries that are almost human.

The Man Who Married Magdalene

The man who married Magdalene
Had not forgiven her.
God might pardon every sin . . .
Love is no pardoner.

Her hands were hollow, pale and blue,
Her mouth like watered wine.
He watched to see if she were true
And waited for a sign.

It was old harlotry, he guessed,
That drained her strength away,
So gladly for the dark she dressed,
So sadly for the day.

Their quarrels made her dull and weak
And soon a man might fit
A penny in the hollow cheek
And never notice it.

At last, as they exhausted slept,
Death granted the divorce,
And nakedly the woman leapt
Upon that narrow horse.

But when he woke and woke alone
He wept and would deny
The loose behavior of the bone
And the immodest thigh.

To the Western World

A siren sang, and Europe turned away
From the high castle and the shepherd's crook.
Three caravels went sailing to Cathay
On the strange ocean, and the captains shook
Their banners out across the Mexique Bay.

And in our early days we did the same.
Remembering our fathers in their wreck
We crossed the sea from Palos where they came
And saw, enormous to the little deck,
A shore in silence waiting for a name.

The treasures of Cathay were never found.
In this America, this wilderness
Where the axe echoes with a lonely sound,
The generations labor to possess
And grave by grave we civilize the ground.

A Story About Chicken Soup

In my grandmother's house there was always chicken soup
And talk of the old country—mud and boards,
Poverty,
The snow falling down the necks of lovers.

Now and then, out of her savings
She sent them a dowry. Imagine
The rice-powdered faces!
And the smell of the bride, like chicken soup.

But the Germans killed them.
I know it's in bad taste to say it,
But it's true. The Germans killed them all.

. . .

In the ruins of Berchtesgaden
A child with yellow hair
Ran out of a doorway.

A German girl-child—
Cuckoo, all skin and bones—
Not even enough to make chicken soup.
She sat by the stream and smiled.

Then as we splashed in the sun
She laughed at us.
We had killed her mechanical brothers,
So we forgave her.

. . .

The sun is shining.
The shadows of the lovers have disappeared.
They are all eyes; they have some demand on me—
They want me to be more serious than I want to be.

They want me to stick in their mudhole
Where no one is elegant.
They want me to wear old clothes,
They want me to be poor, to sleep in a room with many others—

Not to walk in the painted sunshine
To a summer house,
But to live in the tragic world forever.

My Father in the Night Commanding No

My father in the night commanding No
Has work to do. Smoke issues from his lips;
    He reads in silence.
The frogs are croaking and the streetlamps glow.

And then my mother winds the gramophone;
The Bride of Lammermoor begins to shriek—
    Or reads a story
About a prince, a castle, and a dragon.

The moon is glittering above the hill.
I stand before the gateposts of the King—
    So runs the story—
Of Thule, at midnight when the mice are still.

And I have been in Thule! It has come true—
The journey and the danger of the world,
    All that there is
To bear and to enjoy, endure and do.

Landscapes, seascapes . . . where have I been led?
The names of cities—Paris, Venice, Rome—
    Held out their arms.
A feathered god, seductive, went ahead.

Here is my house. Under a red rose tree
A child is swinging; another gravely plays.
    They are not surprised
That I am here; they were expecting me.

And yet my father sits and reads in silence,
My mother sheds a tear, the moon is still,
    And the dark wind
Is murmuring that nothing ever happens.

Beyond his jurisdiction as I move
Do I not prove him wrong? And yet, it's true
    They will not change
There, on the stage of terror and of love.

The actors in that playhouse always sit
In fixed positions—father, mother, child
    With painted eyes.
How sad it is to be a little puppet!

Their heads are wooden. And you once pretended
To understand them! Shake them as you will,
    They cannot speak.
Do what you will, the comedy is ended.

Father, why did you work? Why did you weep,
Mother? Was the story so important?
    "*Listen!*" the wind
Said to the children, and they fell asleep.

JANE COOPER
(1924–   )

A Circle, A Square, A Triangle and A Ripple of Water

Sex floated like a moon
over the composition. Home
was transpierced, ego
thrust out of line and
shaded. But sex floated
over the unconscious, pulling it
up like a sea in points to
where she dreamed, rolling
on and on, immaculate, a full moon
or a breast full of milk.
Seemingly untouched she
was the stone at the center of
the pool whose circles
shuddered off around her.

Waiting

My body knows it will never bear children.
What can I say to my body now,
this used violin?
Every night it cries out desolately
from its secret cave.

Old body, old friend,
why are you so unforgiving?

Why are you so stiff and resistant
clenched around empty space?
An instrument is not a box.

But suppose you are an empty box?
Suppose you are like that famous wooden music hall in Troy,
  New York,
waiting to be torn down
where the orchestras love to play?

Let compassion breathe in and out of you
filling you with poems.

Rent

If you want my apartment, sleep in it
but let's have a clear understanding:
the books are still free agents.

If the rocking chair's arms surround you
they can also let you go,
they can shape the air like a body.

I don't want your rent, I want
a radiance of attention
like the candle's flame when we eat,

I mean a kind of awe
attending the spaces between us.
Not a roof but a field of stars.

Childhood in Jacksonville, Florida

What is happening to me now that loved faces
are beginning to float free of their names
like a tide of balloons, while a dark street
wide enough only for carriages, in a familiar city
loses itself
to become South America?

Oh I am the last member of the nineteenth century!
And my excitement about sex, which was not of today,
is diffusing itself in generosity of mind.

For my mind is relaxing its grip, and a fume
of antique telephones, keys, fountain pens, torn roadmaps,
old stories of the way Nan Powell died
poor girl, rises in the air
detached but accurate—
almost as accurate
as if I'd invented them.

Welcome then poverty!
flights of strings above the orange trees!

Praise

But I love this poor earth, because
I have not seen another. . . .
—Osip Mandelstam

Between five and fifty
most people construct a little lifetime:
they fall in love, make heirs, they suffer
and pitch the usual tents of understanding.
But I have built a few unexpected bridges.
Out of inert stone, with its longing to embrace inert stone,
I have sent a few vaults into untouched air.
Is this enough—when I love our poor sister earth?
Sister earth, I kneel and ask pardon.
A clod of turf is no less than inert stone.
Nothing is enough.
In this field set free for our play
who could have foretold
I would live to write at fifty?

MAXINE KUMIN
(1925–)

After Love

Afterwards, the compromise.
Bodies resume their boundaries.

These legs, for instance, mine.
Your arms take you back in.

Spoons of our fingers, lips
admit their ownership.

The bedding yawns, a door
blows aimlessly ajar

and overhead, a plane
singsongs coming down.

Nothing is changed, except
there was a moment when

the wolf, the mongering wolf
who stands outside the self

lay lightly down, and slept.

A Family Man

We are talking in bed. You show me snapshots.
Your wallet opens like a salesman's case
on a dog, a frame house hung with shutters
and your eyes reset in a child's face.
Here is your mother standing in full sun
on the veranda back home. She is wearing
what we used to call a washdress. Geraniums
flank her as pious in their bearing
as the soap and water she called down on your head.
We carry around our mothers. But mine is dead.

Out of the celluloid album, cleverly as a shill
you pull an old snap of yourself squatting beside
a stag you shot early in the war in the Black Hills.
The dog tags dangle on your naked chest.
The rifle, broken, lies across your knees.
What do I say to the killer you love best,
that boy-man full of his summer expertise?
I with no place in the file will
wake on dark mornings alone with him in my head.
This is what comes of snapshots. Of talking in bed.

At the End of the Affair

That it should end in an Albert Pick hotel
with the air conditioner gasping like a carp
and the bathroom tap plucking its one-string harp
and the sourmash bond half gone in the open bottle,

that it should end in this stubborn disarray
of stockings and car keys and suitcases,
all the unfoldings that came forth yesterday
now crammed back to overflow their spaces,

considering the hairsbreadth accident of touch
the nightcap leads to—how it protracts
the burst of colors, the sweetgrass of two tongues,
then turns the lock in Hilton or in Sheraton,
in Marriott or Holiday Inn for such
a man and woman—bearing in mind these facts,

better to break glass, sop with towels, tear
snapshots up, pour whiskey down the drain
than reach and tangle in the same old snare
saying the little lies again.

A. R. AMMONS

(1926–   )

The Confirmers

The saints are gathering at the real
places, trying tough skin on sharp
  conscience,
endurance in the hot spots—
searching out to define, come up
against, mouth
the bitterest bit:
you can hear them yelping
down in the dark greeny groves of
  condemnation:
their lips slice back
with jittery suctions, cold
insweeps of conjured grief:
if they, footloose, wham up the
precise damnation,
  consolation
may be more than us trudging
down from paunchy dinners,
swatting hallelujah arms at
dusk bugs and telling them pure
terror has obviously made them
earnest of mind and of motion lithe.

Clarity

After the event the rockslide
realized,
in a still diversity of completion,
grain and fissure,
declivity
&
force of upheaval,
whether rain slippage,
ice crawl, root
explosion or
stream erosive undercut:

well I said it is a pity:
one swath of sight will never
be the same: nonetheless,
this
shambles has
relieved a bind, a taut of twist,
revealing streaks &
scores of knowledge
now obvious and quiet.

Cut the Grass

The wonderful workings of the world: wonderful,
wonderful: I'm surprised half the time:
ground up fine, I puff if a pebble stirs:

I'm nervous: my morality's intricate: if
a squash blossom dies, I feel withered as a stained
zucchini and blame my nature: and

when grassblades flop to the little red-ant
queens burring around trying to get aloft, I blame
my not keeping the grass short, stubble

firm: well, I learn a lot of useless stuff, meant
to be ignored: like when the sun sinking in the
west glares a plane invisible, I think how much

revelation concealment necessitates: and then I
think of the ocean, multiple to a blinding
oneness and realize that only total expression

expresses hiding: I'll have to say everything
to take on the roundness and withdrawal of the deep dark:
less than total is a bucketful of radiant toys.

Viable

Motion's the dead giveaway,
eye catcher, the revealing risk:
the caterpillar sulls on the hot macadam

but then, risking, ripples to the bush:
the cricket, startled, leaps the
quickest arc: the earthworm, casting,

nudges a grassblade, and the sharp robin
strikes: sound's the other
announcement: the redbird lands in

an elm branch and tests the air with
cheeps for an answering, reassuring
cheep, for a motion already cleared:

survival organizes these means down to
tension, to enwrapped, twisting suasions:
every act or non-act enceinte with risk or

prize: why must the revelations be
sound and motion, the poet, too, moving and
saying through the scary opposites to death.

ROBERT CREELEY
(1926–   )

The Warning

For love—I would
split open your head and put
a candle in
behind the eyes.

Love is dead in us
if we forget
the virtues of an amulet
and quick surprise.

The Language

Locate *I*
love you some-
where in

teeth and
eyes, bite
it but

take care not
to hurt, you
want so

much so
little. Words
say everything,

I
love you
again,

then what
is emptiness
for. To

fill, fill.
I heard words
and words full

of holes
aching. Speech
is a mouth.

The Window

Position is where you
put it, where it is,
did you, for example, that

large tank there, silvered,
with the white church along-
side, lift

all that, to what
purpose? How
heavy the slow

world is with
everything put
in place. Some

man walks by, a
car beside him on
the dropped

road, a leaf of
yellow color is
going to

fall. It
all drops into
place. My

face is heavy
with the sight. I can
feel my eye breaking.

ALLEN GINSBERG
(1926–   )

from *Howl*
(For Carl Solomon)

I

I saw the best minds of my generation destroyed by madness, starving hysterical naked,
dragging themselves through the negro streets at dawn looking for an angry fix,
angelheaded hipsters burning for the ancient heavenly connection to the starry dynamo in the machinery of night,
who poverty and tatters and hollow-eyed and high sat up smoking in the supernatural darkness of cold-water flats floating across the tops of cities contemplating jazz,
who bared their brains to Heaven under the El and saw Mohammedan angels staggering on tenement roofs illuminated,
who passed through universities with radiant cool eyes hallucinating Arkansas and Blake-light tragedy among the scholars of war,
who were expelled from the academies for crazy & publishing obscene odes on the windows of the skull,
who cowered in unshaven rooms in underwear, burning their money in wastebaskets and listening to the Terror through the wall,
who got busted in their pubic beards returning through Laredo with a belt of marijuana for New York,
who ate fire in paint hotels or drank turpentine in Paradise Alley, death, or purgatoried their torsos night after night

with dreams, with drugs, with waking nightmares, alcohol
and cock and endless balls,
incomparable blind streets of shuddering cloud and lightning in the mind leaping toward poles of Canada & Paterson, illuminating all the motionless world of Time between,
Peyote solidities of halls, backyard green tree cemetery dawns, wine drunkenness over the rooftops, storefront boroughs of teahead joyride neon blinking traffic light, sun and moon and tree vibrations in the roaring winter dusks of Brooklyn, ashcan rantings and kind king light of mind,
who chained themselves to subways for the endless ride from Battery to holy Bronx on benzedrine until the noise of wheels and children brought them down shuddering mouth-wracked and battered bleak of brain all drained of brilliance in the drear light of Zoo,
who sank all night in submarine light of Bickford's floated out and sat through the stale beer afternoon in desolate Fugazzi's, listening to the crack of doom on the hydrogen jukebox,
who talked continuously seventy hours from park to pad to bar to Bellevue to museum to the Brooklyn Bridge,
a lost battalion of platonic conversationalists jumping down the stoops off fire escapes off windowsills off Empire State out of the moon,
yacketayakking screaming vomiting whispering facts and memories and anecdotes and eyeball kicks and shocks of hospitals and jails and wars,
whole intellects disgorged in total recall for seven days and nights with brilliant eyes, meat for the Synagogue cast on the pavement,
who vanished into nowhere Zen New Jersey leaving a trail of ambiguous picture postcards of Atlantic City Hall,
suffering Eastern sweats and Tangerian bone-grindings and migraines of China under junk-withdrawal in Newark's bleak furnished room,
who wandered around and around at midnight in the railroad yard wondering where to go, and went, leaving no broken hearts,

who lit cigarettes in boxcars boxcars boxcars racketing through snow toward lonesome farms in grandfather night, ...
who studied Plotinus Poe St. John of the Cross telepathy and bop kaballa because the cosmos instinctively vibrated at their feet in Kansas,
who loned it through the streets of Idaho seeking visionary indian angels who were visionary indian angels,
who thought they were only mad when Baltimore gleamed in supernatural ecstasy,
who jumped in limousines with the Chinaman of Oklahoma on the impulse of winter midnight streetlight smalltown rain,
who lounged hungry and lonesome through Houston seeking jazz or sex or soup, and followed the brilliant Spaniard to converse about America and Eternity, a hopeless task, and so took ship to Africa,
who disappeared into the volcanoes of Mexico leaving behind nothing but the shadow of dungarees and the lava and ash of poetry scattered in fireplace Chicago,
who reappeared on the West Coast investigating the F.B.I. in beards and shorts with big pacifist eyes sexy in their dark skin passing out incomprehensible leaflets,
who burned cigarette holes in their arms protesting the narcotic tobacco haze of Capitalism,
who distributed Supercommunist pamphlets in Union Square weeping and undressing while the sirens of Los Alamos wailed them down, and wailed down Wall, and the Staten Island ferry also wailed,
who broke down crying in white gymnasiums naked and trembling before the machinery of other skeletons,
who bit detectives in the neck and shrieked with delight in policecars for committing no crime but their own wild cooking pederasty and intoxication,
who howled on their knees in the subway and were dragged off the roof waving genitals and manuscripts,
who let themselves be fucked in the ass by saintly motorcyclists, and screamed with joy,
who blew and were blown by those human seraphim, the sailors, caresses of Atlantic and Caribbean love,

who balled in the morning in the evenings in rosegardens
and the grass of public parks and cemeteries scattering their semen freely to whomever come who may,
who hiccupped endlessly trying to giggle but wound up with
a sob behind a partition in a Turkish Bath when the blonde & naked angel came to pierce them with a sword,
who lost their loveboys to the three old shrews of fate the
one eyed shrew of the heterosexual dollar the one eyed shrew that winks out of the womb and the one eyed shrew that does nothing but sit on her ass and snip the intellectual golden threads of the craftsman's loom,
who copulated ecstatic and insatiate with a bottle of beer a
sweetheart a package of cigarettes a candle and fell off the bed, and continued along the floor and down the hall and ended fainting on the wall with a vision of ultimate cunt and come eluding the last gyzym of consciousness,
who sweetened the snatches of a million girls trembling in
the sunset, and were red eyed in the morning but prepared to sweeten the snatch of the sunrise, flashing buttocks under barns and naked in the lake,
who went out whoring through Colorado in myriad stolen
night-cars, N.C., secret hero of these poems, cocksman and Adonis of Denver—joy to the memory of his innumerable lays of girls in empty lots & diner backyards, moviehouses' rickety rows, on mountaintops in caves or with gaunt waitresses in familiar roadside lonely petticoat upliftings & especially secret gas-station solipsisms of johns, & hometown alleys too,
who faded out in vast sordid movies, were shifted in dreams,
woke on a sudden Manhattan, and picked themselves up out of basements hungover with heartless Tokay and horrors of Third Avenue iron dreams & stumbled to unemployment offices,
who walked all night with their shoes full of blood on the
snowbank docks waiting for a door in the East River to open to a room full of steamheat and opium,

who created great suicidal dramas on the apartment cliff-banks of the Hudson under the wartime blue flood-light of the moon & their heads shall be crowned with laurel in oblivion,
who ate the lamb stew of the imagination or digested the crab at the muddy bottom of the rivers of Bowery,
who wept at the romance of the streets with their pushcarts full of onions and bad music,
who sat in boxes breathing in the darkness under the bridge, and rose up to build harpsichords in their lofts,
who coughed on the sixth floor of Harlem crowned with flame under the tubercular sky surrounded by orange crates of theology,
who scribbled all night rocking and rolling over lofty incantations which in the yellow morning were stanzas of gibberish,
who cooked rotten animals lung heart feet tail borscht & tortillas dreaming of the pure vegetable kingdom,
who plunged themselves under meat trucks looking for an egg,
who threw their watches off the roof to cast their ballot for Eternity outside of Time, & alarm clocks fell on their heads every day for the next decade,
who cut their wrists three times successively unsuccessfully, gave up and were forced to open antique stores where they thought they were growing old and cried,
who were burned alive in their innocent flannel suits on Madison Avenue amid blasts of leaden verse & the tanked-up clatter of the iron regiments of fashion & the nitroglycerine shrieks of the fairies of advertising & the mustard gas of sinister intelligent editors, or were run down by the drunken taxicabs of Absolute Reality,
who jumped off the Brooklyn Bridge this actually happened and walked away unknown and forgotten into the ghostly daze of Chinatown soup alleyways & fire-trucks, not even one free beer,
who sang out of their windows in despair, fell out of the subway window, jumped in the filthy Passaic, leaped on negroes, cried all over the street, danced on

broken wineglasses barefoot smashed phonograph records of nostalgic European 1930's German jazz finished the whiskey and threw up groaning into the bloody toilet, moans in their ears and the blast of colossal steamwhistles,
who barreled down the highways of the past journeying to each other's hotrod-Golgotha jail-solitude watch or Birmingham jazz incarnation,
who drove crosscountry seventytwo hours to find out if I had a vision or you had a vision or he had a vision to find out Eternity,
who journeyed to Denver, who died in Denver, who came back to Denver & waited in vain, who watched over Denver & brooded & loned in Denver and finally went away to find out the Time, & now Denver is lonesome for her heroes,
who fell on their knees in hopeless cathedrals praying for each other's salvation and light and breasts, until the soul illuminated its hair for a second,
who crashed through their minds in jail waiting for impossible criminals with golden heads and the charm of reality in their hearts who sang sweet blues to Alcatraz,
who retired to Mexico to cultivate a habit, or Rocky Mount to tender Buddha or Tangiers to boys or Southern Pacific to the black locomotive or Harvard to Narcissus to Woodlawn to the daisychain or grave,
who demanded sanity trials accusing the radio of hypnotism & were left with their insanity & their hands & a hung jury,
who threw potato salad at CCNY lecturers on Dadaism and subsequently presented themselves on the granite steps of the madhouse with shaven heads and harlequin speech of suicide, demanding instantaneous lobotomy,
and who were given instead the concrete void of insulin metrasol electricity hydrotherapy psychotherapy occupational therapy pingpong & amnesia,
who in humorless protest overturned only one symbolic pingpong table, resting briefly in catatonia,

returning years later truly bald except for a wig of blood, and tears and fingers, to the visible madman doom of the wards of the madtowns of the East,
Pilgrim State's Rockland's and Greystone's foetid halls, bickering with the echoes of the soul, rocking and rolling in the midnight solitude-bench dolmen-realms of love, dream of life a nightmare, bodies turned to stone as heavy as the moon,
with mother finally ******, and the last fantastic book flung out of the tenement window, and the last door closed at 4 AM and the last telephone slammed at the wall in reply and the last furnished room emptied down to the last piece of mental furniture, a yellow paper rose twisted on a wire hanger in the closet, and even that imaginary, nothing but a hopeful little bit of hallucination—
ah, Carl, while you are not safe I am not safe, and now you're really in the total animal soup of time—
and who therefore ran through the icy streets obsessed with a sudden flash of the alchemy of the use of the ellipse the catalog the meter & the vibrating plane,
who dreamt and made incarnate gaps in Time & Space through images juxtaposed, and trapped the archangel of the soul between 2 visual images and joined the elemental verbs and set the noun and dash of consciousness together jumping with sensation of Pater Omnipotens Aeterna Deus
to recreate the syntax and measure of poor human prose and stand before you speechless and intelligent and shaking with shame, rejected yet confessing out the soul to conform to the rhythm of thought in his naked and endless head,
the madman bum and angel beat in Time, unknown, yet putting down here what might be left to say in time come after death,
and rose reincarnate in the ghostly clothes of jazz in the goldhorn shadow of the band and blew the suffering of America's naked mind for love into an eli eli lamma lamma sabacthani saxophone cry that shivered the cities down to the last radio

with the absolute heart of the poem of life butchered out
of their own bodies good to eat a thousand years.

II

What sphinx of cement and aluminum bashed open their
skulls and ate up their brains and imagination?
Moloch! Solitude! Filth! Ugliness! Ashcans and unobtainable
dollars! Children screaming under the stairways!
Boys sobbing in armies! Old men weeping in the
parks!
Moloch! Moloch! Nightmare of Moloch! Moloch the loveless!
Mental Moloch! Moloch the heavy judger of
men!
Moloch the incomprehensible prison! Moloch the crossbone
soulless jailhouse and Congress of sorrows! Moloch
whose buildings are judgement! Moloch the vast
stone of war! Moloch the stunned governments!
Moloch whose mind is pure machinery! Moloch whose
blood is running money! Moloch whose fingers are
ten armies! Moloch whose breast is a cannibal dynamo!
Moloch whose ear is a smoking tomb!
Moloch whose eyes are a thousand blind windows! Moloch
whose skyscrapers stand in the long streets like endless
Jehovahs! Moloch whose factories dream and
croak in the fog! Moloch whose smokestacks and
antennae crown the cities!
Moloch whose love is endless oil and stone! Moloch whose
soul is electricity and banks! Moloch whose poverty
is the specter of genius! Moloch whose fate is a cloud
of sexless hydrogen! Moloch whose name is the
Mind!
Moloch in whom I sit lonely! Moloch in whom I dream
Angels! Crazy in Moloch! Cocksucker in Moloch!
Lacklove and manless in Moloch!
Moloch who entered my soul early! Moloch in whom *I* am a
consciousness without a body! Moloch who frightened
me out of my natural ecstasy! Moloch whom
I abandon! Wake up in Moloch! Light streaming out
of the sky!

Moloch! Moloch! Robot apartments! invisible suburbs! skeleton treasuries! blind capitals! demonic industries! spectral nations! invincible madhouses! granite cocks! monstrous bombs!
They broke their backs lifting Moloch to Heaven! Pavements, trees, radios, tons! lifting the city to Heaven which exists and is everywhere about us!
Visions! omens! hallucinations! miracles! ecstasies! gone down the American river!
Dreams! adorations! illuminations! religions! the whole boatload of sensitive bullshit!
Breakthroughs! over the river! flips and crucifixions! gone down the flood! Highs! Epiphanies! Despairs! Ten years' animal screams and suicides! Minds! New loves! Mad generation! down on the rocks of Time!
Real holy laughter in the river! They saw it all! the wild eyes! the holy yells! They bade farewell! They jumped off the roof! to solitude! waving! carrying flowers! Down to the river! into the street!

A Supermarket in California

What thoughts I have of you tonight, Walt Whitman, for I walked down the sidestreets under the trees with a headache self-conscious looking at the full moon.

In my hungry fatigue, and shopping for images, I went into the neon fruit supermarket, dreaming of your enumerations!

What peaches and what penumbras! Whole families shopping at night! Aisles full of husbands! Wives in the avocados, babies in the tomatoes!—and you, Garcia Lorca, what were you doing down by the watermelons?

I saw you, Walt Whitman, childless, lonely old grubber, poking among the meats in the refrigerator and eyeing the grocery boys.

I heard you asking questions of each: Who killed the pork chops? What price bananas? Are you my Angel?

I wandered in and out of the brilliant stacks of cans following you, and followed in my imagination by the store detective.

We strode down the open corridors together in our solitary fancy tasting artichokes, possessing every frozen delicacy, and never passing the cashier.

Where are we going, Walt Whitman? The doors close in an hour. Which way does your beard point tonight?

(I touch your book and dream of our odyssey in the supermarket and feel absurd.)

Will we walk all night through solitary streets? The trees add shade to shade, lights out in the houses, we'll both be lonely.

Will we stroll dreaming of the lost America of love past blue automobiles in driveways, home to our silent cottage?

Ah, dear father, graybeard, lonely old courage-teacher, what America did you have when Charon quit poling his ferry and you got out on a smoking bank and stood watching the boat disappear on the black waters of Lethe?

A Prophecy

O Future bards
chant from skull to heart to ass
as long as language lasts
Vocalize all chords
zap all consciousness
I sing out of mind jail
in New York State
without electricity
rain on the mountain
thought fills cities
I'll leave my body
in a thin motel
my self escapes
through unborn ears
Not my language
but a voice
chanting in patterns
survives on earth
not history's bones
but vocal tones
Dear breaths and eyes
shine in the skies
where rockets rise
to take me home

JAMES MERRILL

(1926–)

The Mad Scene

Again last night I dreamed the dream called Laundry.
In it, the sheets and towels of a life we were going to share,
The milk-stiff bibs, the shroud, each rag to be ever
Trampled or soiled, bled on or groped for blindly,
Came swooning out of an enormous willow hamper
Onto moon-marbly boards. We had just met. I watched
From outer darkness. I had dressed myself in clothes
Of a new fiber that never stains or wrinkles, never
Wears thin. The opera house sparkled with tiers
And tiers of eyes, like mine enlarged by belladonna,
Trained inward. There I saw the cloud-clot, gust by gust,
Form, and the lightning bite, and the roan mane unloosen.
Fingers were running in panic over the flute's nine gates.
Why did I flinch? I loved you. And in the downpour laughed
To have us wrung white, gnarled together, one
Topmost mordent of wisteria,
As the lean tree burst into grief.

The Grand Canyon

It is early, yet
Clear waves of heat,
Eye-watering, dilute
What powers drive
The warped pine to the brink.
You, too, must conquer

Involuntary nausea
Before you look. Far under-
foot are your wept-over
Sunsets, your every year
Deepened perspectives, layer
On monstrous layer of mouse,
Marigold, madder—
All petrifying, not
To be approached without
Propitiatory oohs.
By all means undertake
A descent on gargoyle-faced ass-back
To the degrading yellow
River. This first mistake
Made by your country is also
The most sublime.
Now let its convulsions
Mimic your heart's
And you will guess the source.
Be strong then. Find no fault
With the white-wigged, the quartz-
Pated up there, wrapped
In whipping vestments, neither
Man can corrupt
Nor heaven wholly melt.
They have sat a long time
In one of our highest courts.

Manos Karastefanís

Death took my father.
The same year (I was twelve)
Thanási's mother taught me
Heaven and hell.

None of my army buddies
Called me by name—
Just "Styles" or "Fashion Plate."
One friend I had, my body,

And, evenings at the gym
Contending with another,
Used it to isolate
Myself from him.

The doctor saved my knee.
You came to the clinic
Bringing *War and Peace,*
Better than any movie.

Why are you smiling?
I fought fair, I fought well,
Not hurting my opponent,
To win this black belt.

Why are you silent?
I've brought you a white cheese
From my island, and the sea's
Voice in a shell.

Last Words

My life, your light green eyes
Have lit on me with joy.
There's nothing I don't know
Or shall not know again,
Over and over again.
It's noon, it's dawn, it's night,
I am the dog that dies
In the deep street of Troy
Tomorrow, long ago—
Part of me dims with pain,
Becomes the stinging flies,
The bent head of the boy.
Part looks into your light
And lives to tell you so.

FRANK O'HARA
(1926–1966)

Homosexuality

So we are taking off our masks, are we, and keeping
our mouths shut? as if we'd been pierced by a glance!

The song of an old cow is not more full of judgment
than the vapors which escape one's soul when one is sick;

so I pull the shadows around me like a puff
and crinkle my eyes as if at the most exquisite moment

of a very long opera, and then we are off!
without reproach and without hope that our delicate feet

will touch the earth again, let alone "very soon."
It is the law of my own voice I shall investigate.

I start like ice, my finger to my ear, my ear
to my heart, that proud cur at the garbage can

in the rain. It's wonderful to admire oneself
with complete candor, tallying up the merits of each

of the latrines. 14th Street is drunken and credulous,
53rd tries to tremble but is too at rest. The good

love a park and the inept a railway station,
and there are the divine ones who drag themselves up

and down the lengthening shadow of an Abyssinian head
in the dust, trailing their long elegant heels of hot air

crying to confuse the brave "It's a summer day,
and I want to be wanted more than anything else in the world."

An Abortion

Do not bathe her in blood,
the little one whose sex is
undermined, she drops leafy
across the belly of black
sky and her abyss has not
that sweetness of the March
wind. Her conception ached
with the perversity of nursery
rhymes, she was a shad a
snake a sparrow and a girl's
closed eye. At the supper, weeping,
they said let's have her and
at breakfast: no.

Don't bathe
her in tears, guileless, beguiled
in her peripheral warmth, more
monster than murdered, safe
in all silences. From our tree
dropped, that she not wither,
autumn in our terrible breath.

Meditations in an Emergency

Am I to become profligate as if I were a blonde? Or religious as if I were French?

Each time my heart is broken it makes me feel more adventurous (and how the same names keep recurring on that interminable list!), but one of these days there'll be nothing left with which to venture forth.

Why should I share you? Why don't you get rid of someone else for a change?

I am the least difficult of men. All I want is boundless love.

Even trees understand me! Good heavens, I lie under them, too, don't I? I'm just like a pile of leaves.

However, I have never clogged myself with the praises of pastoral life, nor with nostalgia for an innocent past of perverted acts in pastures. No. One need never leave the confines of New York to get all the greenery one wishes—I can't even enjoy a blade of grass unless I know there's a subway handy, or a record store or some other sign that people do not totally *regret* life. It is more important to affirm the least sincere; the clouds get enough attention as it is and even they continue to pass. Do they know what they're missing? Uh huh.

My eyes are vague blue, like the sky, and change all the time; they are indiscriminate but fleeting, entirely specific and disloyal, so that no one trusts me. I am always looking away. Or again at something after it has given me up. It makes me restless and that makes me unhappy, but I cannot keep them still. If only I had grey, green, black, brown, yellow eyes; I would stay at home and do something. It's not that I'm curious. On the contrary, I am bored but it's my duty to be attentive, I am needed by things as the sky must be above the earth. And lately, so great has *their* anxiety become, I can spare myself little sleep.

Now there is only one man I love to kiss when he is unshaven. Heterosexuality! you are inexorably approaching. (How discourage her?)

St. Serapion, I wrap myself in the robes of your whiteness which is like midnight in Dostoevsky. How am I to become a legend, my dear? I've tried love, but that hides you in the bosom of another and I am always springing forth from it like the lotus—the ecstasy of always bursting forth! (but one must not be distracted by it!) or like a hyacinth, "to keep the filth of life away," yes, there, even in the heart, where the filth is pumped in and slanders and pollutes and determines. I will my will, though I may become famous for a mysterious vacancy in that department, that greenhouse.

Destroy yourself, if you don't know!

It is easy to be beautiful; it is difficult to appear so. I admire you, beloved, for the trap you've set. It's like a final chapter no one reads because the plot is over.

"Fanny Brown is run away—scampered off with a Cornet of Horse; I do love that little Minx, & hope She may be happy, tho' She has vexed me by this Exploit a little too.—Poor silly Cecchina! or F: B: as we used to call her. —I wish She had a good Whipping and 10,000 pounds." —Mrs. Thrale.

I've got to get out of here. I choose a piece of shawl and my dirtiest suntans. I'll be back, I'll re-emerge, defeated, from the valley; you don't want me to go where you go, so I go where you don't want me to. It's only afternoon, there's a lot ahead. There won't be any mail downstairs. Turning, I spit in the lock and the knob turns.

W. D. SNODGRASS
(1926–   )

The Operation

From stainless steel basins of water
They brought warm cloths and they washed me,
From spun aluminum bowls, cold Zephiran sponges, fuming;
Gripped in the dead yellow glove, a bright straight razor
Inched on my stomach, down my groin,
Paring the brown hair off. They left me
White as a child, not frightened. I was not
Ashamed. They clothed me, then,
In the thin, loose, light, white garments,
The delicate sandals of poor Pierrot,
A schoolgirl first offering her sacrament.

I was drifting, inexorably, on toward sleep.
In skullcaps, masked, in blue-green gowns, attendants
Towed my cart, afloat in its white cloths,
The body with its tributary poisons borne
Down corridors of the diseased, thronging:
The scrofulous faces, contagious grim boys,
The huddled families, weeping, a staring woman
Arched to her gnarled stick,—a child was somewhere
Screaming, screaming—then, blind silence, the elevator rising
To the arena, humming, vast with lights; blank hero,
Shackled and spellbound, to enact my deed.

Into flowers, into women, I have awakened.
Too weak to think of strength, I have thought all day,
Or dozed among standing friends. I lie in night, now,
A small mound under linen like the drifted snow.

Only by nurses visited, in radiance, saying, Rest.
Opposite, ranked office windows glare; headlamps, below,
Trace out our highways; their cargoes under dark tarpaulins,
Trucks climb, thundering, and sirens may
Wail for the fugitive. It is very still. In my brandy bowl
Of sweet peas at the window, the crystal world
Is inverted, slow and gay.

April Inventory

The green catalpa tree has turned
All white; the cherry blooms once more.
In one whole year I haven't learned
A blessed thing they pay you for.
The blossoms snow down in my hair;
The trees and I will soon be bare.

The trees have more than I to spare.
The sleek, expensive girls I teach,
Younger and pinker every year,
Bloom gradually out of reach.
The pear tree lets its petals drop
Like dandruff on a tabletop.

The girls have grown so young by now
I have to nudge myself to stare.
This year they smile and mind me how
My teeth are falling with my hair.
In thirty years I may not get
Younger, shrewder, or out of debt.

The tenth time, just a year ago,
I made myself a little list
Of all the things I'd ought to know,
Then told my parents, analyst,
And everyone who's trusted me
I'd be substantial, presently.

I haven't read one book about
A book or memorized one plot.
Or found a mind I did not doubt.
I learned one date. And then forgot.
And one by one the solid scholars
Get the degrees, the jobs, the dollars.

And smile above their starchy collars.
I taught my classes Whitehead's notions;
One lovely girl, a song of Mahler's.
Lacking a source-book or promotions,
I showed one child the colors of
A luna moth and how to love.

I taught myself to name my name,
To bark back, loosen love and crying;
To ease my woman so she came,
To ease an old man who was dying.
I have not learned how often I
Can win, can love, but choose to die.

I have not learned there is a lie
Love shall be blonder, slimmer, younger;
That my equivocating eye
Loves only by my body's hunger;
That I have forces, true to feel,
Or that the lovely world is real.

While scholars speak authority
And wear their ulcers on their sleeves,
My eyes in spectacles shall see
These trees procure and spend their leaves.
There is a value underneath
The gold and silver in my teeth.

Though trees turn bare and girls turn wives,
We shall afford our costly seasons;
There is a gentleness survives
That will outspeak and has its reasons.
There is a loveliness exists,
Preserves us, not for specialists.

The Campus on the Hill

Up the reputable walks of old established trees
They stalk, children of the *nouveaux riches;* chimes
Of the tall Clock Tower drench their heads in blessing:
"I don't wanna play at your house;
I don't like you anymore."
My house stands opposite, on the other hill,
Among meadows, with the orchard fences down and
falling;
Deer come almost to the door.
You cannot see it, even in this clearest morning.
White birds hang in the air between
Over the garbage landfill and those homes thereto
adjacent,
Hovering slowly, turning, settling down
Like the flakes sifting imperceptibly onto the little town
In a waterball of glass.
And yet, this morning, beyond this quiet scene,
The floating birds, the backyards of the poor,
Beyond the shopping plaza, the dead canal, the hillside
lying tilted in the air,
Tomorrow has broken out today:
Riot in Algeria, in Cyprus, in Alabama;
Aged in wrong, the empires are declining,
And China gathers, soundlessly, like evidence.
What shall I say to the young on such a morning?—
Mind is the one salvation?—also grammar?—
No; my little ones lean not toward revolt. They
Are the Whites, the vaguely furiously driven, who resist
Their souls with such passivity
As would make Quakers swear. All day, dear Lord, all day
They wear their godhead lightly.
They look out from their hill and say,
To themselves, "We have nowhere to go but down;
The great destination is to stay."

Surely the nations will be reasonable;
They look at the world—don't they?—the world's way?
The clock just now has nothing more to say.

"After Experience Taught Me . . ."

After experience taught me that all the ordinary
Surroundings of social life are futile and vain;

I'm going to show you something very
Ugly: someday, it might save your life.

Seeing that none of the things I feared contain
In themselves anything either good or bad

What if you get caught without a knife;
Nothing—even a loop of piano wire;

Excepting only in the effect they had
Upon my mind, I resolved to inquire

Take the first two fingers of this hand;
Fork them out—kind of a "V for Victory"—

Whether there might be something whose discovery
Would grant me supreme, unending happiness.

And jam them into the eyes of your enemy.
You have to do this hard. Very hard. Then press

No virtue can be thought to have priority
Over this endeavor to preserve one's being.

Both fingers down around the cheekbone
And setting your foot high into the chest

No man can desire to act rightly, to be blessed,
To live rightly, without simultaneously

You must call up every strength you own
And you can rip off the whole facial mask.

Wishing to be, to act, to live. He must ask
First, in other words, to actually exist.

And you, whiner, who wastes your time
Dawdling over the remorseless earth,
What evil, what unspeakable crime
Have you made your life worth?

Lobsters in the Window

First, you think they are dead.
Then you are almost sure
One is beginning to stir.
Out of the crushed ice, slow
As the hands of a schoolroom clock,
He lifts his one great claw
And holds it over his head;
Now, he is trying to walk.

But like a run-down toy;
Like the backward crabs we boys
Splashed after in the creek,
Trapped in jars or a net,
And then took home to keep.
Overgrown, retarded, weak,
He is fumbling yet
From the deep chill of his sleep

As if, in a glacial thaw,
Some ancient thing might wake
Sore and cold and stiff
Struggling to raise one claw
Like a defiant fist;
Yet wavering, as if
Starting to swell and ache
With that thick peg in the wrist.

I should wave back, I guess.
But still in his permanent clench
He's fallen back with the mass
Heaped in their common trench
Who stir, but do not look out
Through the rainstreaming glass,
Hear what the newsboys shout,
Or see the raincoats pass.

JOHN ASHBERY
(1927–)

White Roses

The worst side of it all—
The white sunlight on the polished floor—
Pressed into service,
And then the window closed
And the night ends and begins again.
Her face goes green, her eyes are green;
In the dark corner playing "The Stars and Stripes
Forever." I try to describe for you,
But you will not listen, you are like the swan.

No stars are there,
No stripes,
But a blind man's cane poking, however clumsily, into
the inmost corners of the house.
Nothing can be harmed! Night and day are beginning again!
So put away the book,
The flowers you were keeping to give someone:
Only the white, tremendous foam of the street has any
importance,
The new white flowers that are beginning to shoot up
around now.

The Tennis Court Oath

What had you been thinking about
the face studiously bloodied
heaven blotted region
I go on loving you like water but
there is a terrible breath in the way all of this
You were not elected president, yet won the race
All the way through fog and drizzle
When you read it was sincere the coasts
stammered with unintentional villages the
horse strains fatigued I guess . . . the calls . . .
I worry

the water beetle head
why of course reflecting all
then you redid you were breathing
I thought going down to mail this
of the kettle you jabbered as easily in the yard
you come through but
are incomparable the lovely tent
mystery you don't want surrounded the real
you dance
in the spring there was clouds

The mulatress approached in the hall—the
lettering easily visible along the edge of the *Times*
in a moment the bell would ring but there was time
for the carnation laughed here are a couple of "other"

to one in yon house

The doctor and Philip had come over the road
Turning in toward the corner of the wall his hat on
reading it carelessly as if to tell you your fears were justified
the blood shifted you know those walls
wind off the earth had made him shrink

undeniably an oboe now the young
were there there was candy
to decide the sharp edge of the garment
like a particular cry not intervening called the dog "he's coming! he's
coming" with an emotion felt it sink into peace

there was no turning back but the end was in sight
he chose this moment to ask her in detail about her family and the
others
The person pleaded—"have more of these
not stripes on the tunic—or the porch chairs
will teach you about men—what it means"
to be one in a million pink stripe
and now could go away the three approached the doghouse
the reef. Your daughter's
dream of my son understand prejudice
darkness in the hole
the patient finished
They could all go home now the hole was dark
lilacs blowing across his face glad he brought you

Thoughts of a Young Girl

"It is such a beautiful day I had to write you a letter
From the tower, and to show I'm not mad:
I only slipped on the cake of soap of the air
And drowned in the bathtub of the world.
You were too good to cry much over me.
And now I let you go. Signed, The Dwarf."

I passed by late in the afternoon
And the smile still played about her lips
As it has for centuries. She always knows
How to be utterly delightful. Oh my daughter,
My sweetheart, daughter of my late employer, princess,
May you not be long on the way!

Fear of Death

What is it now with me
And is it as I have become?
Is there no state free from the boundary lines
Of before and after? The window is open today

And the air pours in with piano notes
In its skirts, as though to say, "Look, John,
I've brought these and these"—that is,
A few Beethovens, some Brahmses,

A few choice Poulenc notes. . . . Yes,
It is being free again, the air, it has to keep coming back
Because that's all it's good for.
I want to stay with it out of fear

That keeps me from walking up certain steps,
Knocking at certain doors, fear of growing old
Alone, and of finding no one at the evening end
Of the path except another myself

Nodding a curt greeting: "Well, you've been awhile
But now we're back together, which is what counts."
Air in my path, you could shorten this,
But the breeze has dropped, and silence is the last word.

GALWAY KINNELL
(1927–   )

Night in the Forest

1

A woman
sleeps next to me on the earth. A strand
of hair flows
from her cocoon sleeping bag, touching
the ground hesitantly, as if thinking
to take root.

2

I can hear
a mountain brook
and somewhere blood winding
down its ancient labyrinths. And
a few feet away
charred stick-ends surround
a bit of ashes, where burnt-out, vanished
  flames
absently
waver, absently leap.

The Bear

1

In the late winter
I sometimes glimpse bits of steam
coming up from
some fault in the old snow
and bend close and see it is lung-colored
and put down my nose
and know
the chilly, enduring odor of bear.

2

I take a wolf's rib and whittle
it sharp at both ends
and coil it up
and freeze it in blubber and place it out
on the fairway of the bears.

And when it has vanished
I move out on the bear tracks,
roaming in circles
until I come to the first, tentative, dark
splash on the earth.

And I set out
running, following the splashes
of blood wandering over the world.
At the cut, gashed resting places
I stop and rest,
at the crawl-marks
where he lay out on his belly
to overpass some stretch of bauchy ice
I lie out
dragging myself forward with bear-knives in
  my fists.

3

On the third day I begin to starve,
at nightfall I bend down as I knew I would
at a turd sopped in blood,
and hesitate, and pick it up,
and thrust it in my mouth, and gnash it
   down,
and rise
and go on running.

4

On the seventh day,
living by now on bear blood alone,
I can see his upturned carcass far out
   ahead, a scraggled,
steamy hulk,
the heavy fur riffling in the wind.

I come up to him
and stare at the narrow-spaced, petty eyes,
the dismayed
face laid back on the shoulder, the nostrils
flared, catching
perhaps the first taint of me as he
died.

I hack
a ravine in his thigh, and eat and drink,
and tear him down his whole length
and open him and climb in
and close him up after me, against the wind,
and sleep.

5

And dream
of lumbering flatfooted
over the tundra,
stabbed twice from within,

splattering a trail behind me,
splattering it out no matter which way I
  lurch,
no matter which parabola of bear-
  transcendence,
which dance of solitude I attempt,
which gravity-clutched leap,
which trudge, which groan.

6

Until one day I totter and fall—
fall on this
stomach that has tried so hard to keep up,
to digest the blood as it leaked in,
to break up
and digest the bone itself: and now the
  breeze
blows over me, blows off
the hideous belches of ill-digested bear
  blood
and rotted stomach
and the ordinary, wretched odor of bear,

blows across
my sore, lolled tongue a song
or screech, until I think I must rise up
and dance. And I lie still.

7

I awaken I think. Marshlights
reappear, geese
come trailing again up the flyway.
In her ravine under old snow the dam-bear
lies, licking
lumps of smeared fur
and drizzly eyes into shapes
with her tongue. And one
hairy-soled trudge stuck out before me,

the next groaned out,
the next,
the next,
the rest of my days I spend
wandering: wondering
what, anyway,
was that sticky infusion, that rank flavor of
  blood, that poetry, by which I lived?

The Correspondence School Instructor Says Goodbye to His Poetry Students

Goodbye, lady in Bangor, who sent me
snapshots of yourself, after definitely hinting
you were beautiful; goodbye,
Miami Beach urologist, who enclosed plain
brown envelopes for the return of your *very*
"Clinical Sonnets"; goodbye, manufacturer
of brassieres on the Coast, whose eclogues
give the fullest treatment in literature yet
to the sagging breast motif; goodbye, you in San Quentin,
who wrote, "Being German my hero is Hitler,"
instead of "Sincerely yours," at the end of long,
neat-scripted letters demolishing
the pre-Raphaelites:

I swear to you, it was just my way
of cheering myself up, as I licked
the stamped, self-addressed envelopes,
the game I had
of trying to guess which one of you, this time,
had poisoned his glue. I did care.
I did read each poem entire.
I did say what I thought was the truth
in the mildest words I knew. And now,
in this poem, or chopped prose, not any better,
I realize, than those troubled lines
I kept sending back to you,
I have to say I am relieved it is over:

at the end I could feel only pity
for that urge toward more life
your poems kept smothering in words, the smell
of which, days later, would tingle
in your nostrils as new, God-given impulses
to write.

Goodbye,
you who are, for me, the postmarks again
of shattered towns—Xenia, Burnt Cabins, Hornell—
their loneliness
given away in poems, only their solitude kept.

PAUL PETRIE

(1927–   )

The Dream

I dreamed you were my child, and I had come
to tell you you must die. Your back was bowed,
and brittle as the wings of a dead moth
which let the light shine through. Through the late window
we watched the sun spreading in meres of haze
over the crisp September fields that crumbled,
dissolving in our glances, into gold
and then the dark words came, and with them, tears
rolling down my cheeks, and you were the one
to comfort me—your arm about my shoulders—
and childhood's fears were all charmed away—
the kitchen floor quaking beneath black boots,
the leather strap descending (that hurt you more
than me), the tears I hid to make you sad—
and hunched together there we watched the shadows
come flocking from beneath the eaves—great bats
whose interwoven dartings blocked the sun
and brought night down.

                                        Let dreams invade the night
that holds you now, Father—dark voices tell you
how after many nightmares we are friends.

The Phases of Darkness

1

Climbing the rutted path, the lights of town
left far beneath, curled in the mist; below,
the blind mutterings of the sea; upon the right
black mountains rising with their massive shade;
and overhead—emptied of moon or star—
like an inverted pit—the sky, I found the night;
and found again what I had always known—
that when the light goes all shadows go,
and on the walls of this internal cave
the moving pictures blend and disappear.

2

I used to watch the crack under the door
for hours, curled fetus-like in bed,
the covers rising and falling with my heart,
and glimpse out of the corners of my eyes
the black closet's mouth with all its rows
of hanging men, the window glazed with dark,
fingers of trees tap-tapping across the floor—
until the light failed and into my head
night flooded, tricked in the weird disguise
of dreams, old shadows wearing borrowed clothes.

3

Before the first Word, there was the Dark—
self-shrouding in its ministerial folds
all landscapes of the sun, fashioned to be
the imageless imago of one face,
the world's names all hidden in one name,
under one mask—all anonymity.
And still behind each sunlit thing it lurks,
waiting till the limbs tire in the rigid molds
to lift them down from crosses where they waste
back to the arms from which all being came.

4

Like jewels, against the velvet of the box
in which they lie, all objects come alive
and shine with a borrowed light, taking forms
from murky backgrounds, and in translucent depths
burning the night like coal. The good know
that darkness gathered lamb-like in their arms
is their defining grace, and wise men fix
their scrutiny on worlds beyond their eyes.
It bleaches the wings of swans, and makes their steps
shine on the air, although they melt like snow.

5

Letting the music roam through the darkened rooms
and rocking there, half-hidden from the gaze
of things that know me best—unfeatured, freed
from the lean mirror's silver-chiseled stare,
I grow to like it, willing more and more
propinquity with this retiring shade
that gives the outside world to me: warm homes
glowing across dark fields; lamp-fashioned trees;
and those black spaces in between that peer
so strangely at me through half-opened doors.

Not Seeing Is Believing

From across the stream, on the side of the opposite hill,
I see a woman in a blue, wool coat who is walking her dog.
Her hair is as white as snow, and her dog snow-white.
They are walking through the plum-brown, silvery branches of trees.

Step after step she moves,
leaning on each foot as the old do.
She is walking her dog and thinking.

Under the nest of her hair is another world—
are many other worlds—present, past, future—
but none of this shows.

She is walking her dog and thinking, and the dog too
is thinking—Bushes are telling damp, excited tales
of an earlier sun, of a darkness before this sun—

and the trees around them are thinking—slow, wooden thoughts
that stretch over centuries, and the earth in which the trees
root down also is pondering—deep, stone thoughts—
but none of this shows.

I see a woman in a blue, wool coat
who is walking a small, white dog
through the plum-brown, silvery trees.

The Old Pro's Lament

Each year the court expands,
the net moves back, the ball
hums by—with more spin.

I use my second serve,
lob deeper, slice more,
stay away from the net, and fail
to win.

As any fool can tell
it is time
to play the game purely
for the game's sake—to applaud
the puff of white chalk,
shake hands
and grin.

Others retire
into the warm corners of memory,
invent new rules, new games
and win.

Under the hot lances
of the shower, I play each point over,
and over,
and over
again.

Wisdom is the natural business
of old men—
to let the body go,
the rafters, moth-eaten and decayed,
cave in.

But nightly in dreams I see
an old man
playing in an empty court
under the dim floodlights
of the moon
with a racket gone in the strings—
no net, no ball, no game—
and still playing
to win.

JAMES WRIGHT
(1927–)

Complaint

She's gone. She was my love, my moon or more.
She chased the chickens out and swept the floor,
Emptied the bones and nut-shells after feasts,
And smacked the kids for leaping up like beasts.
Now morbid boys have grown past awkwardness;
The girls let stitches out, dress after dress,
To free some swinging body's riding space
And form the new child's unimagined face.
Yet, while vague nephews, spitting on their curls,
Amble to pester winds and blowsy girls,
What arm will sweep the room, what hand will hold
New snow against the milk to keep it cold?
And who will dump the garbage, feed the hogs,
And pitch the chickens' heads to hungry dogs?
Not my lost hag who dumbly bore such pain:
Childbirth and midnight sassafras and rain.
New snow against her face and hands she bore,
And now lies down, who was my moon or more.

A Poem About Breasts

Already she seems bone thin
When her clothes are on.
The lightest wind blows
Her dress toward the doorways.
Everybody thinks he can see

Her body longing to follow
Helpless and miserable,
Dreaming itself
Into an apparition of loneliness,
A spirit of vine wondering
At a grape here and there,
As the September spider,
The master, ascends
Her long spine.

Already she weighs more, yet
She still bows down slightly,
As I stand in her doorway.
It's not hunching, it's only
That children have been reaching
Upward for years to gather
Sweetness of her face.
They are innocent and passionate
Thieves of the secret hillsides.
Now she rises, tall, round, round,
And round again, and, again, round.

Speak

To speak in a flat voice
Is all that I can do.
I have gone every place
Asking for you.
Wondering where to turn
And how the search would end
And the last streetlight spin
Above me blind.

Then I returned rebuffed
And saw under the sun
The race not to the swift
Nor the battle won.

Liston dives in the tank,
Lord, in Lewiston, Maine,
And Ernie Doty's drunk
In hell again.

And Jenny, oh my Jenny
Whom I love, rhyme be damned,
Has broken her spare beauty
In a whorehouse old.
She left her new baby
In a bus-station can,
And sprightly danced away
Through Jacksontown.

Which is a place I know,
One where I got picked up
A few shrunk years ago
By a good cop.
Believe it, Lord, or not.
Don't ask me who he was.
I speak of flat defeat
In a flat voice.

I have gone forward with
Some, a few lonely some.
They have fallen to death.
I die with them.
Lord, I have loved Thy cursed,
The beauty of Thy house:
Come down. Come down. Why dost
Thou hide thy face?

DONALD HALL
(1928–   )

White Apples

when my father had been dead a week
I woke
with his voice in my ear
                                I sat up in bed
and held my breath
and stared at the pale closed door

white apples and the taste of stone

if he called again
I would put on my coat and galoshes

The Town of Hill

Back of the dam, under
a flat pad

of water, church
bells ring

in the ears of lilies,
a child's swing

curls in the current
of a yard, horned

pout sleep
in a green

mailbox, and
a boy walks

from a screened
porch beneath

the man-shaped
leaves of an oak

down the street looking
at the town

of Hill that water
covered forty

years ago,
and the screen

door shuts
under dream water.

The Raisin

I drank cool water from the fountain
in the undertaker's parlor
near the body of a ninety-two-year-old man.

Harry loved horses and work.
He curried the flanks of his Morgan,
he loaded crates twelve hours—to fill in
when his foreman got drunk—
never kicking a horse,
never kind to a son.

He sobbed on the sofa ten years ago,
when Sally died.
We heard of him dancing
with widows in Florida, cheek
to cheek, and of scented
letters that came to Connecticut
all summer.

When he was old he made up for the weeping
he failed to do earlier—
grandchildren, zinnias,
Morgans, great-grandchildren—
he wept over everything. His only
advice. 'Keep your health.'
He told old stories, laughing slowly.
He sang old songs.

Forty years ago his son
who was parked making love in the country
noticed Harry parked making love
in a car up ahead.

When he was ninety he wanted to die.
He couldn't ride or grow flowers
or dance
or tend the plots in the graveyard
that he had kept up
faithfully, since Sally died.

This morning I looked into the pale
raisin of Harry's face.

The Brain Cells

Inside the brain they are holding a mass funeral for the dead brain cells.

Survivors stand like poplars at the side of *l'avenue George Cinq.* Gray rain. The brain cells carry umbrellas which are also gray. The funeral cortège is eighty miles long. All day, from ten in the morning until seven in the evening, the procession hauls its body along the avenue.

It is June first, 1972. On the night of May thirty-first, the dikes burst, strangling and dragging away the citizens.

Muted drums beat slowly.

Black horses wearing black plumes draw black carriages and caissons past the viewing stand draped with mourning where the President, the Prime Minister, members of the Cabinet, and leading Senators stand all day in their black suits with black armbands, hands over their hearts.

Trumpets play death music. Newspapers bordered with black announce:

MASS DISASTER FIVE BILLION DEAD

and newsboys walk slowly on the edge of the crowd.

As the long day slopes into night the last brain cell is buried. The brain cells, weary of marching, grave-digging, and standing in the rain all day, walk homeward slowly to their gray apartments off Battleship Potemkin Square. They switch on their hot plates and make themselves bouillon.

Then they sit back on their tatty sofas, turn on the TV, and watch the replays, in black and white, over and over.

PHILIP LEVINE
(1928–)

Animals Are Passing from Our Lives

It's wonderful how I jog
on four honed-down ivory toes
my massive buttocks slipping
like oiled parts with each light step.

I'm to market. I can smell
the sour, grooved block, I can smell
the blade that opens the hole
and the pudgy white fingers

that shake out the intestines
like a hankie. In my dreams
the snouts drool on the marble,
suffering children, suffering flies,

suffering the consumers
who won't meet their steady eyes
for fear they could see. The boy
who drives me along believes

that any moment I'll fall
on my side and drum my toes
like a typewriter or squeal
and shit like a new housewife

discovering television,
or that I'll turn like a beast
cleverly to hook his teeth
with my teeth. No. Not this pig.

Salami

Stomach of goat, crushed
sheep balls, soft full
pearls of pig eyes,
snout gristle, fresh earth,
worn iron of trotter, slate
of Zaragoza, dried cat heart,
cock claws. She grinds
them with one hand and
with the other fists
mountain thyme, basil,
paprika, and knobs of garlic.
And if a tooth of stink thistle
pulls blood from the round
blue marbled hand
all the better for
this ruby of Pamplona,
this bright jewel of Vich,
this stained crown
of Solsona, this
salami.

The daughter
of mismatched eyes,
36 year old infant smelling
of milk. Mama, she cries, mama,
but mama is gone,
and the old stone cutter
must wipe the drool
from her jumper. His puffed fingers
unbutton and point her
to toilet. Ten, twelve hours
a day, as long as the winter sun
holds up he rebuilds
the unvisited church
of San Martin. Cheep cheep

of the hammer high above
the town, sparrow cries
lost in the wind or lost
in the mind. At dusk he leans
to the coal dull wooden Virgin
and asks for blessings on
the slow one and peace
on his grizzled head, asks
finally and each night
for the forbidden, for
the knowledge of every
mysterious stone, and
the words go out on
the overwhelming incense
of salami.

A single crow
passed high over the house,
I wakened out of nightmare.
The winds had changed,
the Tremontana was tearing
out of the Holy Mountains
to meet the sea winds
in my yard, burning and
scaring the young pines.
The single poplar wailed
in terror. With salt,
with guilt, with the need
to die, the vestments
of my life flared, I
was on fire, a stranger
staggering through my house
butting walls and falling
over furniture, looking
for a way out. In the last room
where moonlight slanted
through a broken shutter
I found my smallest son
asleep or dead, floating
on a bed of colorless light.

When I leaned closer
I could smell the small breaths
going and coming, and each
bore its prayer for me,
the true and earthy prayer
of salami.

On the Edge

My name is Edgar Poe and I was born
In 1928 in Michigan.
Nobody gave a damn. The gruel I ate
Kept me alive, nothing kept me warm,
But I grew up, almost to five foot ten,
And nothing in the world can change my weight.

I have been watching you these many years,
There in the office, pencil poised and ready,
Or on the highway when you went ahead.
I did not write; I watched you watch the stars
Believing that the wheel of fate was steady;
I saw you rise from love and go to bed;

I heard you lie, even to your daughter.
I did not write, for I am Edgar Poe,
Edgar the mad one, silly, drunk, unwise,
But Edgar waiting on the edge of laughter,
And there is nothing that he does not know
Whose page is blanker than the raining skies.

To a Child Trapped in a Barber Shop

You've gotten in through the transom
    and you can't get out
till Monday morning or, worse,
    till the cops come.

That six-year-old red face
    calling for mama
is yours; it won't help you
    because your case

is closed forever, hopeless.
    So don't drink
the Lucky Tiger, don't
    fill up on grease

because that makes it a lot worse,
    that makes it a crime
against property and the state
    and that costs time.

We've all been here before,
    we took our turn
under the electric storm
    of the vibrator

and stiffened our wills to meet
    the close clippers
and heard the true blade mowing
    back and forth

on a strip of dead skin,
    and we stopped crying.
You think your life is over?
    It's just begun.

ANNE SEXTON
(1928–1974)

Ringing the Bells

And this is the way they ring
the bells in Bedlam
and this is the bell-lady
who comes each Tuesday morning
to give us a music lesson
and because the attendants make you go
and because we mind by instinct,
like bees caught in the wrong hive,
we are the circle of the crazy ladies
who sit in the lounge of the mental house
and smile at the smiling woman
who passes us each a bell,
who points at my hand
that holds my bell, E flat,
and this is the gray dress next to me
who grumbles as if it were special
to be old, to be old,
and this is the small hunched squirrel girl
on the other side of me
who picks at the hairs over her lip,
who picks at the hairs over her lip all day,
and this is how the bells really sound,
as untroubled and clean
as a workable kitchen,
and this is always my bell responding
to my hand that responds to the lady
who points at me, E flat;
and although we are no better for it,
they tell you to go. And you do.

Her Kind

I have gone out, a possessed witch,
haunting the black air, braver at night;
dreaming evil, I have done my hitch
over the plain houses, light by light:
lonely thing, twelve-fingered, out of mind.
A woman like that is not a woman, quite.
I have been her kind.

I have found the warm caves in the woods,
filled them with skillets, carvings, shelves,
closets, silks, innumerable goods;
fixed the suppers for the worms and the elves:
whining, rearranging the disaligned.
A woman like that is misunderstood.
I have been her kind.

I have ridden in your cart, driver,
waved my nude arms at villages going by,
learning the last bright routes, survivor
where your flames still bite my thigh
and my ribs crack where your wheels wind.
A woman like that is not ashamed to die.
I have been her kind.

The Truth the Dead Know

FOR MY MOTHER, BORN MARCH 1902, DIED MARCH 1959
AND MY FATHER, BORN FEBRUARY 1900, DIED JUNE 1959

Gone, I say and walk from church,
refusing the stiff procession to the grave,
letting the dead ride alone in the hearse.
It is June. I am tired of being brave.

We drive to the Cape. I cultivate
myself where the sun gutters from the sky,
where the sea swings in like an iron gate
and we touch. In another country people die.

My darling, the wind falls in like stones
from the whitehearted water and when we touch
we enter touch entirely. No one's alone.
Men kill for this, or for as much.

And what of the dead? They lie without shoes
in their stone boats. They are more like stone

Wanting to Die

Since you ask, most days I cannot remember.
I walk in my clothing, unmarked by that voyage.
Then the almost unnameable lust returns.

Even then I have nothing against life.
I know well the grass blades you mention,
the furniture you have placed under the sun.

But suicides have a special language.
Like carpenters they want to know *which tools.*
They never ask *why build.*

Twice I have so simply declared myself,
have possessed the enemy, eaten the enemy,
have taken on his craft, his magic.

In this way, heavy and thoughtful,
warmer than oil or water,
I have rested, drooling at the mouth-hole.

I did not think of my body at needle point.
Even the cornea and the leftover urine were gone.
Suicides have already betrayed the body.

Still-born, they don't always die,
but dazzled, they can't forget a drug so sweet
that even children would look on and smile.

To thrust all that life under your tongue!—
that, all by itself, becomes a passion.
Death's a sad bone; bruised, you'd say,

and yet she waits for me, year after year,
to so delicately undo an old wound,
to empty my breath from its bad prison.

Balanced there, suicides sometimes meet,
raging at the fruit, a pumped-up moon,
leaving the bread they mistook for a kiss,

leaving the page of the book carelessly open,
something unsaid, the phone off the hook
and the love, whatever it was, an infection.

RICHARD HOWARD
(1929–   )

209 *Canal*

Not hell but a street, not
Death but a fruit-stand, not
Devils just hungry devils
Simply standing around the stoops, the stoops.

We find our way, wind up
The night, wound uppermost,
In four suits, a funny pack
From which to pick ourselves a card, any card:

Clubs for beating up, spades
For hard labor, diamonds
For buying up rough diamonds,
And hearts, face-up, face-down, for facing hearts.

Dummies in a rum game
We count the tricks that count
Waiting hours for the dim bar
Like a mouth to open wider After Hours.

Natural History

What since August, when the sound
Of bees filled the lindens
And broke like a hot
Berry rotten

In ripeness
Where we
Lay,
What
After
Late motions
Of the sun, what
Grief on the hills, what
Chill stiffening the stream
Changes our love thus to our loss?

We have outgrown the weather;
The months have made only
Diminishing days.
Questioning, we
Were eager,
And grave,
But
Now,
Given
Our wan tact
And the wasting
Of fevers, who could
Hope to print Hell's lavish
Product on a face of snow?

I do not know how we fell,
Having once embellished
Every bud with bloom;
Yet if sap runs
At the root
Of time,
Down
Where
The dark
And warm life
Hides away, then
May we grow again,
Re-according by light
The heart of our green season.

Recipe for an Ocean in the Absence of the Sea

You have the ingredients on hand.
    Get to the edge of something,
    yourself best of all, and take
yourself in hand. Take, I mean, your hand,
    trace out the blue menaces
    released and lapsing there,
watch closely around the wrist: they will
    remind you what you must do.
    They are what you must do. Be
them, until there is nothing but them,
    then you are ready. Now take
    time, all there is in the house—
it does not have to be yours. Take time
    and never for a moment
    losing track of what changes
back into yourself, bitter enough
    so that you will need almost
    no salt, mix well and then leap
over the edge. Wait there. When you can
    wait no longer, it is done.
    Serve at once. It does not keep.

On Arrival

Waiting is the poem of waiting.
    Tomorrow you will be here
and I can leave off the anthology,
    heroic couplets, haiku,
projective verse—it is all making
    do, and it has done for me
whatever making can: a coming
    to terms with nothing, until
something is on those terms, my poems.
    By tomorrow this waiting
will be over and done with, it will
    be my best poem ever,
and it will never have been written.

ADRIENNE RICH
(1929–   )

Living in Sin

She had thought the studio would keep itself;
no dust upon the furniture of love.
Half heresy, to wish the taps less vocal,
the panes relieved of grime. A plate of pears,
a piano with a Persian shawl, a cat
stalking the picturesque amusing mouse
had risen at his urging.
Not that at five each separate stair would writhe
under the milkman's tramp; that morning light
so coldly would delineate the scraps
of last night's cheese and three sepulchral bottles;
that on the kitchen shelf among the saucers
a pair of beetle-eyes would fix her own—
envoy from some village in the moldings . . .
Meanwhile, he, with a yawn,
sounded a dozen notes upon the keyboard,
declared it out of tune, shrugged at the mirror,
rubbed at his beard, went out for cigarettes;
while she, jeered by the minor demons,
pulled back the sheets and made the bed and found
a towel to dust the table-top,
and let the coffee-pot boil over on the stove.
By evening she was back in love again,
though not so wholly but throughout the night
she woke sometimes to feel the daylight coming
like a relentless milkman up the stairs.

Attention

The ice age is here.
I sit burning cigarettes,
burning my brain.
A micro-Tibet,
deadly, frivolous, complete,
blinds the four panes.
Veils of dumb air
unwind like bandages
from my lips
half-parted, steady as the mouths
of antique statues.

Peeling Onions

Only to have a grief
equal to all these tears!

There's not a sob in my chest.
Dry-hearted as Peer Gynt
I pare away, no hero,
merely a cook.

Crying was labor, once
when I'd good cause.
Walking, I felt my eyes like wounds
raw in my head,
so postal-clerks, I thought, must stare.
A dog's look, a cat's, burnt to my brain—
yet all that stayed
stuffed in my lungs like smog.

These old tears in the chopping-bowl.

Two Songs

1

Sex, as they harshly call it,
I fell into this morning
at ten o'clock, a drizzling hour
of traffic and wet newspapers.
I thought of him who yesterday
clearly didn't
turn me to a hot field
ready for plowing,
and longing for that young man
pierced me to the roots
bathing every vein, etc.
All day he appears to me
touchingly desirable,
a prize one could wreck one's peace for.
I'd call it love if love
didn't take so many years
but lust too is a jewel
a sweet flower and what
pure happiness to know
all our high-toned questions
breed in a lively animal.

2

That "old last act"!
And yet sometimes
all seems post coitum triste
and I a mere bystander.
Somebody else is going off,
getting shot to the moon.
Or, a moon-race!
Split seconds after
my opposite number lands
I make it—

we lie fainting together
at a crater-edge
heavy as mercury in our moonsuits
till he speaks—
in a different language
yet one I've picked up
through cultural exchanges . . .
we murmur the first moonwords:
Spasibo. Thanks. O.K.

Dialogue

She sits with one hand poised against her head, the
other turning an old ring to the light
for hours our talk has beaten
like rain against the screens
a sense of August and heat-lightning
I get up, go to make tea, come back
we look at each other
then she says (and this is what I live through
over and over)—she says: *I do not know*
if sex is an illusion

I do not know
who I was when I did those things
or who I said I was
or whether I willed to feel
what I had read about
or who in fact was there with me
or whether I knew, even then
that there was doubt about these things

The Ninth Symphony of Beethoven Understood at Last as a Sexual Message

A man in terror of impotence
or infertility, not knowing the difference
a man trying to tell something
howling from the climacteric
music of the entirely
isolated soul
yelling at Joy from the tunnel of the ego
music without the ghost
of another person in it, music
I begin to see that woman
doing things: stirring rice
ironing a skirt
typing a manuscript till dawn

trying to make a call
from a phonebooth

The phone rings unanswered
in a man's bedroom
she hears him telling someone else
Never mind. She'll get tired—
hears him telling her story to her sister

who becomes her enemy
and will in her own time
light her own way to sorrow

ignorant of the fact this way of grief
is shared, unnecessary
and political

Re-forming the Crystal

I am trying to imagine
how it feels to you
to want a woman

trying to hallucinate
desire
centered in a cock
focused like a burning-glass

desire without discrimination:
to want a woman like a fix

Desire: yes: the sudden knowledge, like coming out of 'flu, that the body is sexual. Walking in the streets with that knowledge. That evening in the plane from Pittsburgh, fantasizing going to meet you. Walking through the airport blazing with energy and joy. But knowing all along that you were not the source of that energy and joy; you were a man, a stranger, a name, a voice on the telephone, a friend; this desire was mine, this energy my energy; it could be used a hundred ways, and going to meet you could be one of them.

Tonight is a different kind of night.
I sit in the car, racing the engine,
calculating the thinness of the ice.
In my head I am already threading the beltways
that rim this city,
all the old roads that used to wander the country
having been lost.

Tonight I understand
my photo on the license is not me,
my
name on the marriage-contract was not mine.
If I remind you of my father's favorite daughter,
look again. The woman
I needed to call my mother
was silenced before I was born.

Tonight if the battery charges I want to take the car out on sheet ice; I want to understand my fear both of the machine and of the accidents of nature. My desire for you is not trivial; I can compare it with the greatest of those accidents. But the energy it draws on might lead to racing a cold engine, cracking the frozen spiderweb parachuting into the field of a poem wired with danger, or to a trip through gorges and canyons, into the cratered night of female memory, where delicately and with intense care the chieftainess inscribes upon the ribs of the volcano the name of the one she has chosen.

Power

Living   in the earth-deposits   of our history

Today a backhoe divulged   out of a crumbling flank of earth
one bottle   amber   perfect   a hundred-year-old
cure for fever   or melancholy   a tonic
for living on this earth   in the winters of this climate

Today I was reading about Marie Curie:
she must have known she suffered   from radiation sickness
her body bombarded for years   by the element
she had purified
It seems she denied to the end
the source of the cataracts on her eyes
the cracked and suppurating skin   of her finger-ends
till she could no longer hold   a test-tube or a pencil

She died   a famous woman   denying
her wounds
denying
her wounds   came   from the same source as her power

NANCY SULLIVAN
(1929–)

Telling It

To speak out clean.
Let the words be
not wonderful but the plainest
nouns, the skinniest verbs
that are themselves
the poem, not merely holding
it together.
The shape of poetry:
the shape of words, the words their own shapes,
the shape of many words together.
All right.
Poetry is the soup,
not the can or kettle
wrapped around it.
Telling it, telling it clean
is the meat.
Today the words are right.
They are right here.
I find what I mean
to tell myself the truth.

Eclipses

eclipse 1—*what happened*

A scapular of birds hung fast
on the shoulders of the world
crowing and complaining
because the sun was out
behind the rindless moon.
There was darkness at quarter of two
though the world had not yet ended.
It was Saturday afternoon.
It was like the end of the world,
the sallow color of an ending
and the hush of light was like a sound.

Often back in the Garden,
another garden, a kindergarten
they had said the world was ending
when thunder hollered on East 84th Street
and the alley of street darkened
and lightning wrote its spooky script
in the sky.

The world is always ending:
day succumbs to stingy night.
Sleep travels in a pill.
Vietnam splinters in the East.
Bathwater cools, stomachs sag.
The ears harbor static.
The eye hoards cataract.
Who denies the essential flaw?
Every poem fails.

eclipse 2—*call it ecology*

It all has to do with the last going out. With death.
The salmon sinks, in its mouth the waste of centuries.
The ponderosa pine sags, its needles blunted by smog.
Tomatoes burst, gorgeous with chemicals,
as ruddypretty as the fabled apple.

Commerce tints the orange orange making it more *real.*
Mere signs of the first blight,
the initial discharge, our first going out,
the initiation into death.

In Eden the grass entangled and choked;
the fruits, the flowers, and assorted vegetables
withered after the betrayal, the fall into the state of death.
So it began. Who claims corruption as a cause?
It is a *momento mori.*
Death began. Acceleration is its footman.
The going down is hard.

See my father dead, his face
made puppet-live by his boyhood friend—
his body drained, tidied, plugged.
He has trickled out of himself to where he has gone.
Is it to the Eden land? O no.
The humps of rock in St. Columba's cemetery say
that stone is the final fruit of man's husbandry.

eclipse 3—*old men on the porch*

Done ding-donging
their limp tassels
dangle like raped bananas
inside the heart-high pants,
the flies grounded
by longing zippers
whose teeth grip each other.

They sit on the porch
in Saratoga Springs.

69 69
AL WEISS
(Palace)
Furnished Rooms
Open
Year Round
69 69

Nearby, Mother Goldsmith's
Restaurant and the Executive
Delicatessen where they never go.
Why go? They've been. Some have
wives who boil chickens, weak tea,
wives with bad feet and balding wigs.

This porch is an open coffin.
Make me know, old men, how it happens.
What takes us out when we're done?
Do you, please, sometimes meander through
that old movie, your lives, while
mumbling here in the sun?

To My Body

I am in the tub with my body.
I look down at it from inside my face.

'Body,' I say, 'you're a foreign person.
We've been together all this time
and still, in very serious ways,
we are strangers.'

The body smiles on the water.

'You're not all lean and bone
as you are in my head.
You bulge in the tub.
There are bubbles clinging
to this wedge of curling moss.
These breasts are cantaloupe.
I don't understand, given the chance,
how you could reproduce,
how you could get me out of yourself
to make room for another.

(There are many problems we'd have to work out.)
In a sense, you've had me,
and I'm glad I have you.
We're enough trouble to each other.'

His Necessary Darkness

From the frantic weather into his creaking tomb,
we discover the color of God.
He is the background,
the weight that surrounds him,
the thick and furry air, all bursting
in the roundness of his crescent world.
He is not the golden Man another man has made
to shimmer so that all the lightning threads should
enter into us as he on that cross
crosses over to glitter in his necessary darkness.

The whirling black, the color of God:
dense, dry like the prattle of parrots,
heady as smoke, bleak as wet furnaces to fire.
He is dangerous Coal
waiting the spastic match that can ignite
only as it grates the flint of his own dark pitch.
He is coal, dangerous and waiting.

We concede nothing
and walk as toward some banquet.
If he must, skin to skin, inform us
may we find in his conversation another spectrum,
and if he ignites, let our black ashes
celebrate his necessary darkness.

GREGORY CORSO
(1930–   )

Marriage

Should I get married? Should I be good?
Astound the girl next door with my velvet suit and faustus hood?
Don't take her to movies but to cemeteries
tell all about werewolf bathtubs and forked clarinets
then desire her and kiss her and all the preliminaries
and she going just so far and I understanding why
not getting angry saying You must feel! It's beautiful to feel!
Instead take her in my arms lean against an old crooked tombstone
and woo her the entire night the constellations in the sky—

When she introduces me to her parents
back straightened, hair finally combed, strangled by a tie,
should I sit knees together on their 3rd degree sofa
and not ask Where's the bathroom?
How else to feel other than I am,
often thinking Flash Gordon soap—
O how terrible it must be for a young man
seated before a family and the family thinking
We never saw him before! He wants our Mary Lou!
After tea and homemade cookies they ask What do you do for a living?
Should I tell them? Would they like me then?
Say All right get married, we're losing a daughter
but we're gaining a son—
And should I then ask Where's the bathroom?

O God, and the wedding! All her family and her friends
and only a handful of mine all scroungy and bearded
just wait to get at the drinks and food—

And the priest! he looking at me as if I masturbated
asking me Do you take this woman for your lawful wedded wife?
And I trembling what to say say Pie Glue!
I kiss the bride all those corny men slapping me on the back
She's all yours, boy! Ha-ha-ha!
And in their eyes you could see some obscene honeymoon going on—
Then all that absurd rice and clanky cans and shoes
Niagara Falls! Hordes of us! Husbands! Wives! Flowers! Chocolates!
All streaming into cozy hotels
All going to do the same thing tonight
The indifferent clerk he knowing what was going to happen
The lobby zombies they knowing what
The whistling elevator man he knowing
The winking bellboy knowing
Everybody knowing! I'd be almost inclined not to do anything!
Stay up all night! Stare that hotel clerk in the eye!
Screaming: I deny honeymoon! I deny honeymoon!
running rampant into those almost climactic suites
yelling Radio belly! Cat shovel!
O I'd live in Niagara forever! in a dark cave beneath the Falls
I'd sit there the Mad Honeymooner
devising ways to break marriages, a scourge of bigamy
a saint of divorce—

But I should get married I should be good
How nice it'd be to come home to her
and sit by the fireplace and she in the kitchen
aproned young and lovely wanting my baby
and so happy about me she burns the roast beef
and comes crying to me and I get up from my big papa chair
saying Christmas teeth! Radiant brains! Apple deaf!
God what a husband I'd make! Yes, I should get married!
So much to do! like sneaking into Mr Jones' house late at night
and cover his golf clubs with 1920 Norwegian books
Like hanging a picture of Rimbaud on the lawnmower
like pasting Tannu Tuva postage stamps all over the picket fence
like when Mrs Kindhead comes to collect for the Community Chest
grab her and tell her There are unfavorable omens in the sky!
And when the mayor comes to get my vote tell him
When are you going to stop people killing whales!
And when the milkman comes leave him a note in the bottle
Penguin dust, bring me penguin dust, I want penguin dust—

Yet if I should get married and it's Connecticut and snow
and she gives birth to a child and I am sleepless, worn,
up for nights, head bowed against a quiet window, the past behind
me,
finding myself in the most common of situations a trembling man
knowledged with responsibility not twig-smear nor Roman coin
soup—
O what would that be like!
Surely I'd give it for a nipple a rubber Tacitus
For a rattle a bag of broken Bach records
Tack Della Francesca all over its crib
Sew the Greek alphabet on its bib
And build for its playpen a roofless Parthenon
No, I doubt I'd be that kind of father
not rural not snow no quiet window
but hot smelly tight New York City
seven flights up, roaches and rats in the walls
a fat Reichian wife screeching over potatoes Get a job!
And five nose running brats in love with Batman
and the neighbors all toothless and dry haired
like those hag masses of the 18th century
all wanting to come in and watch TV
The landlord wants his rent
Grocery store Blue Cross Gas & Electric Knights of Columbus
Impossible to lie back and dream Telephone snow, ghost parking—
No! I should not get married I should never get married!
But—imagine If I were married to a beautiful sophisticated woman
tall and pale wearing an elegant black dress and long black gloves
holding a cigarette holder in one hand and a highball in the other
and we lived high up in a penthouse with a huge window
from which we could see all of New York and ever farther on
clearer days
No, can't imagine myself married to that pleasant prison dream—

O but what about love! I forget love
not that I am incapable of love
it's just that I see love as odd as wearing shoes—
I never wanted to marry a girl who was like my mother
And Ingrid Bergman was always impossible
And there's maybe a girl now but she's already married
And I don't like men and—

but there's got to be somebody!
Because what if I'm 60 years old and not married,
all alone in a furnished room with pee stains on my underwear
and everybody else is married! All the universe married but me!

Ah, yet well I know that were a woman possible as I am possible
then marriage would be possible—
Like SHE in her lonely alien gaud waiting her Egyptian lover
so I wait—bereft of 2,000 years and the bath of life.

GARY SNYDER
(1930–)

Things to Do Around a Lookout

Wrap up in a blanket in cold weather and just read.
Practise writing Chinese characters with a brush
Paint pictures of the mountains
Put out salt for deer
Bake coffee cake and biscuit in the iron oven,
Hours off hunting twisty firewood, packing it all back up and chopping.
Rice out for the ptarmigan and the conies
Mark well sunrise and sunset—drink lapsang soochong.
Rolling smokes
The Flower book and the Bird book and the Star book
Old Reader's Digests left behind
Bullshitting on the radio with a distant pinnacle, like you, hid in clouds;
Drawing little sexy sketches of bare girls.
Reading maps, checking on the weather, airing out musty Forest Service sleeping bags and blankets
Oil the saws, sharpen axes,
Learn the names of all the peaks you see
          and which is highest
Learn by heart the drainages between.
Go find a shallow pool of snowmelt on a good day, bathe in the lukewarm water.
Take off in foggy weather and go climbing all alone
The Rock book,—strata, dip, and strike
Get ready for the snow, get ready
To go down.

The Bath

Washing Kai in the sauna,
The kerosene lantern set on a box
  outside the ground-level window,
Lights up the edge of the iron stove and the
  washtub down on the slab
Steaming air and crackle of waterdrops
  brushed by on the pile of rocks on top
He stands in warm water
Soap all over the smooth of his thigh and stomach
  "Gary don't soap my hair!"
  —his eye-sting fear—
  the soapy hand feeling
  through and around the globes and curves of his body,
  up in the crotch,
And washing-tickling out the scrotum, little anus,
  his penis curving up and getting hard
  as I pull back skin and try to wash it
Laughing and jumping, flinging arms around,
  I squat all naked too,

is this our body?

Sweating and panting in the stove-steam hot-stone
  cedar-planking wooden bucket water-splashing
  kerosene lantern-flicker wind-in-the-pines-out
  sierra forest ridges night—
Masa comes in, letting fresh cool air
  sweep down from the door
  a deep sweet breath
And she tips him over gripping neatly, one knee down
  her hair falling hiding one whole side of
  shoulder, breast, and belly,
Washes deftly Kai's head-hair
  as he gets mad and yells—
The body of my lady, the winding valley spine,
  the space between the thighs I reach through,

cup her curving vulva arch and hold it from behind,
a soapy tickle   a hand of grail
The gates of Awe
That open back a turning double-mirror world of
wombs in wombs, in rings,
that start in music,
is this our body?

The hidden place of seed
The veins net flow across the ribs, that gathers
milk and peaks up in a nipple—fits
our mouth—
The sucking milk from this our body sends through
jolts of light; the son, the father,
sharing mother's joy
That brings a softness to the flower of the awesome
open curling lotus gate I cup and kiss
As Kai laughs at his mother's breast he now is weaned
from, we
wash each other,
this our body

Kai's little scrotum up close to his groin,
the seed still tucked away, that moved from us to him
In flows that lifted with the same joys forces
as his nursing Masa later,
playing with her breast,
Or me within her,
Or him emerging,
this is our body:

Clean, and rinsed, and sweating more, we stretch
out on the redwood benches hearts all beating
Quiet to the simmer of the stove,
the scent of cedar
And then turn over,
murmuring gossip of the grasses,
talking firewood,
Wondering how Gen's napping, how to bring him in
soon wash him too—

These boys who love their mother
  who loves men, who passes on
  her sons to other women;
The cloud across the sky. The windy pines.
  The trickle gurgle in the swampy meadow
  this is our body.

Fire inside and boiling water on the stove
We sigh and slide ourselves down from the benches
  wrap the babies, step outside,

black night & all the stars.

Pour cold water on the back and thighs
Go in the house—stand steaming by the center fire
Kai scampers on the sheepskin
Gen standing hanging on and shouting,

"Bao! bao! bao! bao! bao!

This is our body. Drawn up crosslegged by the flames
  drinking icy water
  hugging babies, kissing bellies,

Laughing on the Great Earth

Come out from the bath.

Meeting the Mountains

He crawls to the edge of the foaming creek
He backs up the slab ledge
He puts a finger in the water
He turns to a trapped pool
Puts both hands in the water
Puts one foot in the pool
Drops pebbles in the pool

He slaps the water surface with both hands
He cries out, rises up and stands
Facing toward the torrent and the mountain
Raises up both hands and shouts three times!

Mid-August at Sourdough Mountain Lookout

Down valley a smoke haze
Three days heat, after five days rain
Pitch glows on the fir-cones
Across rocks and meadows
Swarms of new flies.

I cannot remember things I once read
A few friends, but they are in cities.
Drinking cold snow-water from a tin cup
Looking down for miles
Through high still air.

PATRICIA GOEDICKE

(1931–   )

On the Night in Question

Under a sky studded with asterisks
And the fat cipher of the moon

First came the upper and lower cases of the cobblestones,
The hyphenated shadows,

Next came the last faint questions of the birds,
The italics of goodbye . . .

Finally the unintelligible exclamations
And loud interjections of the drunks

Past all the living rooms, so late at night
And then silence

Down the long sentences of the streets

The semi-colon of a parked car
The horizontal howls of the dogs

To the dim brackets of a house,
The dark period of a door.

After the Second Operation

A little nearer, this time
Fragile as clear glass but singing

It is like being your own target
Balanced on a tightrope, trembling

It is the shape of something
Without shape: joy

Coming and going like heat lightning,
Flashing across the sky.

Leaving the hospital, for a while
The whole landscape erupts

Into pure ecstasy: cliffs, crags
Sheer drops of delight,
Sudden peaks of pain . . .

I tell you it is ridiculous
Standing here on one foot

Half the time off balance,
Most of the time blinded
By tears like diamonds in the eyes

But after the long flatness, the plains
And deserts of daily life

It is as if the soul
Were stretching itself, and flying

For now nothing is ordinary: each step
Newness pierces the heart,

The tender horizon of the body tilts
Up one side of the mountain and down the other

For now everything is as it should be, everyday
Danger brandishes its spear
So beautifully, along the way

All around you you can feel it
Glancing off you like the light
That hovers but will not stay.

The Serious Merriment of Women

There is a kind of lace laid over the City, a lightness
The airiness of those in love
Not with each other but with their work.

I see it and am moved by it,
The serious merriment of women who laugh
Not with self-deprecation but with pride,

Slow stalking, leaders with round limbs
Moving easily, at last

Among the black pipestems,
The piston whips of anger

They have their own necessities, and follow them
Like gliders in the sky, with such clarity

When they have caressed a problem
Just long enough to control it they take off,

Over the perpendicular forests of the City I see them
In all their beautiful calm, stretched out
The superior lift of their wings lifts the heart.

Daily the Ocean Between Us
(Psalm for My 43rd)

After the first shallows have dropped away
Leaving us gasping for breath

Suddenly the air is much thicker,
I swim in it, almost choking
Except for you

It is as if we had fallen into a blood pudding.

Wave upon wave it rises,
Slowly the hot heaviness settles . . .

After 43 years I'm still struggling to get through
These sodden labyrinths that have sprung up

Everywhere around us:
Roots, water snakes, lilies . . .

Surely it is a kind of pleasure, this pain.

In the tender suck of the bayou
Mangroves caress our knees

But also there is this slow,
Powerful, deep pull:

In between rages, red-faced
Here we are, holding hands

Under water there is this current
Flowing like lava between us:

Teaching each other how to breathe
Gradually we move out to the center:

Wrestling together in the dark
At least, for a while, we don't drown,
We fight side by side,

Each of us embraces the other
With fists or kisses, no matter:

Whenever you shift, I shift
From one stroke to the other,

Daily the ocean between us
Grows deeper but not wider.

SYLVIA PLATH
(1932–1963)

The Colossus

I shall never get you put together entirely,
Pieced, glued, and properly jointed.
Mule-bray, pig-grunt and bawdy cackles
Proceed from your great lips.
It's worse than a barnyard.

Perhaps you consider yourself an oracle,
Mouthpiece of the dead, or of some god or other.
Thirty years now I have labored
To dredge the silt from your throat.
I am none the wiser.

Scaling little ladders with gluepots and pails of lysol
I crawl like an ant in mourning
Over the weedy acres of your brow
To mend the immense skull plates and clear
The bald, white tumuli of your eyes.

A blue sky out of the Oresteia
Arches above us. O father, all by yourself
You are pithy and historical as the Roman Forum.
I open my lunch on a hill of black cypress.
Your fluted bones and acanthine hair are littered

In their old anarchy to the horizon-line.
It would take more than a lightning-stroke
To create such a ruin.
Nights, I squat in the cornucopia
Of your left ear, out of the wind,

Counting the red stars and those of plum-color.
The sun rises under the pillar of your tongue.
My hours are married to shadow.
No longer do I listen for the scrape of a keel
On the blank stones of the landing.

Cut

For Susan O'Neill Roe

What a thrill—
My thumb instead of an onion.
The top quite gone
Except for a sort of a hinge

Of skin,
A flap like a hat,
Dead white.
Then that red plush.

Little pilgrim,
The Indian's axed your scalp.
Your turkey wattle
Carpet rolls

Straight from the heart.
I step on it,
Clutching my bottle
Of pink fizz.

A celebration, this is.
Out of a gap
A million soldiers run,
Redcoats, every one.

Whose side are they on?
O my
Homunculus, I am ill.
I have taken a pill to kill

The thin
Papery feeling.
Saboteur,
Kamikaze man—

The stain on your
Gauze Ku Klux Klan
Babushka
Darkens and tarnishes and when

The balled
Pulp of your heart
Confronts its small
Mill of silence

How you jump—
Trepanned veteran,
Dirty girl,
Thumb stump.

Lady Lazarus

I have done it again.
One year in every ten
I manage it——

A sort of walking miracle, my skin
Bright as a Nazi lampshade,
My right foot

A paperweight,
My face a featureless, fine
Jew linen.

Peel off the napkin
O my enemy.
Do I terrify?——

The nose, the eye pits, the full set of teeth?
The sour breath
Will vanish in a day.

Soon, soon the flesh
The grave cave ate will be
At home on me

And I a smiling woman.
I am only thirty.
And like the cat I have nine times to die.

This is Number Three.
What a trash
To annihilate each decade.

What a million filaments.
The peanut-crunching crowd
Shoves in to see

Them unwrap me hand and foot——
The big strip tease.
Gentleman, ladies,

These are my hands,
My knees.
I may be skin and bone,

Nevertheless, I am the same, identical woman.
The first time it happened I was ten.
It was an accident.

The second time I meant
To last it out and not come back at all.
I rocked shut

As a seashell.
They had to call and call
And pick the worms off me like sticky pearls.

Dying
Is an art, like everything else.
I do it exceptionally well.

I do it so it feels like hell.
I do it so it feels real.
I guess you could say I've a call.

It's easy enough to do it in a cell.
It's easy enough to do it and stay put.
It's the theatrical

Comeback in broad day
To the same place, the same face, the same brute
Amused shout:

"A miracle!"
That knocks me out.
There is a charge

For the eyeing of my scars, there is a charge
For the hearing of my heart——
It really goes.

And there is a charge, a very large charge,
For a word or a touch
Or a bit of blood

Or a piece of my hair or my clothes.
So, so, Herr Doktor.
So, Herr Enemy.

I am your opus,
I am your valuable,
The pure gold baby

That melts to a shriek.
I turn and burn.
Do not think I underestimate your great concern.

Ash, ash—
You poke and stir.
Flesh, bone, there is nothing there——

A cake of soap,
A wedding ring,
A gold filling.

Herr God, Herr Lucifer,
Beware
Beware.

Out of the ash
I rise with my red hair
And I eat men like air.

Edge

The woman is perfected.
Her dead

Body wears the smile of accomplishment,
The illusion of a Greek necessity

Flows in the scrolls of her toga,
Her bare

Feet seem to be saying:
We have come so far, it is over.

Each dead child coiled, a white serpent,
One at each little

Pitcher of milk, now empty.
She has folded

Them back into her body as petals
Of a rose close when the garden

Stiffens and odors bleed
From the sweet, deep throats of the night flower.

The moon has nothing to be sad about,
Staring from her hood of bone.

She is used to this sort of thing.
Her blacks crackle and drag.

ETHERIDGE KNIGHT
(1933–   )

Hard Rock Returns to Prison from the Hospital for the Criminal Insane

Hard Rock was "known not to take no shit
From nobody," and he had the scars to prove it:
Split purple lips, lumped ears, welts above
His yellow eyes, and one long scar that cut
Across his temple and plowed through a thick
Canopy of kinky hair.

The WORD was that Hard Rock wasn't a mean nigger
Anymore, that the doctors had bored a hole in his head,
Cut out part of his brain, and shot electricity
Through the rest. When they brought Hard Rock back,
Handcuffed and chained, he was turned loose,
Like a freshly gelded stallion, to try his new status.
And we all waited and watched, like indians at a corral,
To see if the WORD was true.

As we waited we wrapped ourselves in the cloak
Of his exploits: "Man, the last time, it took eight
Screws to put him in the Hole." "Yeah, remember when he
Smacked the captain with his dinner tray?" "He set
The record for time in the Hole—67 straight days!"
"Ol Hard Rock! man, that's one crazy nigger."
And then the jewel of a myth that Hard Rock had once bit
A screw on the thumb and poisoned him with syphilitic spit.

The testing came, to see if Hard Rock was really tame.
A hillbilly called him a black son of a bitch
And didn't lose his teeth, a screw who knew Hard Rock

From before shook him down and barked in his face.
And Hard Rock did *nothing*. Just grinned and looked silly,
His eyes empty like knot holes in a fence.

And even after we discovered that it took Hard Rock
Exactly 3 minutes to tell you his first name,
We told ourselves that he had just wised up,
Was being cool; but we could not fool ourselves for long,
And we turned away, our eyes on the ground. Crushed.
He had been our Destroyer, the doer of things
We dreamed of doing but could not bring ourselves to do,
The fears of years, like a biting whip,
Had cut grooves too deeply across our backs.

Haiku

1

Eastern guard tower
Glints in sunset; convicts rest
Like lizards on rocks.

2

The piano man
Is sting at 3 am
His songs drop like plum.

3

Morning sun slants cell.
Drunks stagger like cripple flies
On Jailhouse floor.

4

To write a blues song
Is to regiment riots
And pluck gems from graves.

5

A bare pecan tree
Slips a pencil shadow down
A moonlit snow slope.

6

The falling snow flakes
Can not blunt the hard aches nor
Match the steel stillness.

7

Under moon shadows
A tall boy flashes knife and
Slices star bright ice.

8

In the August grass
Struck by the last rays of sun
The cracked teacup screams.

9

Making jazz swing in
Seventeen syllables AIN'T
No square poet's job.

IMAMU AMIRI BARAKA
(LeRoi Jones)
(1934–)

Biography

Hangs.
whipped
blood
striped
meat pulled
clothes ripped
slobber
feet dangled
pointing
noised
noise
churns
face
black sky
and moon
leather night
red
bleeds
drips
ground
sucks
blood
hangs
life wetting
sticky
mud

laughs
bonnets
wolfmoon
crazyteeth

hangs

hangs

granddaddy
graddady, they tore

his
neck

Poem for Half-White College Students

Who are you, listening to me, who are you
listening to yourself? Are you white or
black, or does that have anything to do
with it? Can you pop your fingers to no
music, except those wild monkies go on
in your head, can you jerk, to no melody,
except finger poppers get it together
when you turn from starchecking to checking
yourself. How do you sound, your words, are they
yours? The ghost you see in the mirror, is it really
you, can you swear you are not an imitation greyboy,
can you look right next to you in that chair, and swear,
that the sister you have your hand on is not really
so full of Elizabeth Taylor, Richard Burton is
coming out of her ears. You may even have to be Richard
with a white shirt and face, and four million negroes
think you cute, you may have to be Elizabeth Taylor, old lady,
if you want to sit up in your crazy spot dreaming about dresses,
and the sway of certain porters' hips. Check yourself, learn who it is
speaking, when you make some ultrasophisticated point, check
yourself

when you find yourself gesturing like Steve McQueen, check it out,
ask
in your black heart who it is you are, and is that image black or
white,

you might be surprised right out the window, whistling dixie on the
way

Ka 'Ba

A closed window looks down
on a dirty courtyard, and black people
call across or scream across or walk across
defying physics in the stream of their will

Our world is full of sound
Our world is more lovely than anyone's
tho we suffer, and kill each other
and sometimes fail to walk the air

We are beautiful people
with african imaginations
full of masks and dances and swelling chants

with african eyes, and noses, and arms,
though we sprawl in grey chains in a place
full of winters, when what we want is sun.

We have been captured,
brothers. And we labor
to make our getaway, into
the ancient image, into a new

correspondence with ourselves
and our black family. We need magic
now we need the spells, to raise up
return, destroy, and create. What will be

the sacred words?

MARK STRAND
(1934–   )

Keeping Things Whole

In a field
I am the absence
of field.
This is
always the case.
Wherever I am
I am what is missing.

When I walk
I part the air
and always
the air moves in
to fill the spaces
where my body's been.

We all have reasons
for moving.
I move
to keep things whole.

Eating Poetry

Ink runs from the corners of my mouth.
There is no happiness like mine.
I have been eating poetry.

The librarian does not believe what she sees.
Her eyes are sad
and she walks with her hands in her dress.

The poems are gone.
The light is dim.
The dogs are on the basement stairs and
  coming up.

Their eyeballs roll,
their blond legs burn like brush.
The poor librarian begins to stamp her feet
  and weep.

She does not understand.
When I get on my knees and lick her hand,
she screams.

I am a new man.
I snarl at her and bark.
I romp with joy in the bookish dark.

JEAN VALENTINE
(1934–)

Pilgrims

For S. & R.F.

Standing there they began to grow skins
dappled as trees, alone in the flare
of their own selves: the fire
died down in the open ground

and they made a place for themselves.
It wasn't much good,
they'd fall, and freeze,

some of them said
Well, it was all they could,

some said it was beautiful, some days,
the way the little ones took to the water,
and some lay smoking, smoking,

and some burned up for good,
and some waited,
lasting, staring
over each other's merciful shoulders,
listening:
                    only high in a sudden January thaw
or safe a second in some unsmiling eyes
they'd known always

whispering
Why are we in this life.

April

Suppose we are standing together a minute
on the wire floor of a *gaswagen:*
suppose we are in the dark.

It's warm and dry.
We have food.
We aren't in hiding waiting, mostly
we're sitting in our own light rooms.

Come over, bring things: bring
milk, peanut butter,
your pills, your woollens, crayons.

Nuns pray.
Snow. It's dark.
Pray for our friends who died
last year and the year
before and who will die this year.

Let's speak,
as the bees do.

He said,

"When I found where we had crashed, in the snow, the two of us, alone, I made a plan. It takes all my energy to like it.
The trees keep thinning, and the small animals.
She swims over me every night like warmth, like my whole life going past my eyes. She is the sleep they talk about, and some days all I can want is sleep."

Anaesthesia

Right after her birth they crowded in,
into the white room, huge tall masks
of women's faces

brick-red lips, chalked-in triangular eyes
gazed at us: nothing; said:
nothing; not-women they were suicides, trees, soft,
pale, freckled branches bending over her—
I knew them as my own, their cries
took on the family whiskey voice, refusal,
need,—their human need peeled down, tore,
scratched for her life—
I hacked and hacked them apart—

then who knows
when you murder things like that
who comes in and takes over

LUCILLE CLIFTON
(1936–   )

For deLawd

people say they have a hard time
understanding how I
go on about my business
playing my Ray Charles
hollering at the kids—
seem like my Afro
cut off in some old image
would show I got a long memory
and I come from a line
of black and going on women
who got used to making it through murdered sons
and who grief kept on pushing
who fried chicken
ironed
swept off the back steps
who grief kept
for their still alive sons
for their sons coming
for their sons gone
just pushing

Good Times

My Daddy has paid the rent
and the insurance man is gone
and the lights is back on
and my uncle Brud has hit

for one dollar straight
and they is good times
good times
good times

My Mama has made bread
and Grampaw has come
and everybody is drunk
and dancing in the kitchen
and singing in the kitchen
Oh these is good times
good times
good times

oh children think about the
good times

JUNE JORDAN
(1936–   )

Poem to My Sister, Ethel Ennis, Who Sang "The Star-spangled Banner" at the Second Inauguration of Richard Milhous Nixon, January 20, 1973

gave proof through the night
that our flag was still there

on this 47th inauguration of the killer king
my sister
what is this song
you have chosen to sing?

and the rockets' red glare
the bombs bursting in air
my sister
what is your song to a flag?

to the twelve days of Christmas
bombing when the homicidal holiday shit tore forth
pouring from the B-52 bowels loose over Hanoi and the skin
and the agonized the blown limbs and blinded eyes the
silence of the children dead on the street and the
incinerated homes and Bach Mai Hospital blasted and
drowned by the military the American shit vomit
dropping down death and burying the lives the people
of the new burial ground
under the flag

for the second coronation of the killer king
what is this song
you have chosen to sing?

my sister
when will it come finally clear
in the rockets' red glare
            choking
smoke to celebrate murder
will it be clear
in that red that bloody red glare
my sister
that glare of murder and atrocity/atrocities
of power
strangling every program
to protect and feed and educate and heal and house
the people

(talking about *us*/you and me talking
about *us*)
when will it be clear to you

which night will curse out the stars with the blood
of the flag
for you
for enough of us

by the rockets' red glare
when will it be clear
that the flag that this flag is still there is still
here and will smother you smother your songs

can you see
my sister
in the night
and the red glaring blood clear at last
say

can you see
my sister

say you can see
my sister

and sing no more of war

Getting Down to Get Over
(dedicated to my mother)

MOMMA MOMMA MOMMA
momma momma
mammy
nanny
granny
woman
mistress
sista

luv

blackgirl
slavegirl

gal

honeychile
sweetstuff
sugar
sweetheart
baby
Baby Baby
MOMMA MOMMA
Black Momma
Black bitch
Black pussy
piecea tail
nice piecea ass

hey daddy! hey
bro!
we walk together (an)
talk together (an)
dance and *do*
(together)
dance and do hey!

daddy!
bro!
hey!
nina nikki nonni nommo nommo
momma Black
Momma

Black Woman
Black
Female Head of Household
Black Matriarchal Matriarchy
Black Statistical
Lowlife Lowlevel Lowdown
Lowdown and *up*
to be Low-down
Black Statistical
Low Factor
Factotem
Factitious Fictitious
Figment Figuring in Lowdown Lyin
Annual Reports
Black Woman Black
Hallelujah Saintly
patient
smilin
humble
givin thanks
for
Annual Reports and
Monthly Dole
and
Friday night
and
(*good* God!)
Monday mornin: Black and Female
martyr masochist
(A BIG WHITE LIE)
Momma Momma

What does Mothafuckin mean?
WHO'S THE MOTHAFUCKA
FUCKED MY MOMMA
messed yours over
and right now
be trippin on my starveblack
female soul
a macktruck
mothafuck
the first primordial
the paradig digmatic
dogmatistic mothafucka who
is he?
hey!
momma momma

dryeyes on the
shy dark hidden cryin Black
face
of the loneliness
the rape
the brokeup mailbox
an' no western union roses
come inside the kitchen
and no poem
take you through the whole night
and no big
Black
burly
hand
be holdin yours
to have to hold onto
no
big Black burly hand
no nommo
no Black prince
come riding from the darkness
on a beautiful black horse
no bro
no daddy

"I was sixteen when I met my father.
In a bar.
In Baltimore.
He told me who he was
and what he does.
Paid for the drinks.
I looked.
I listened.
And I left him.
It was civil
perfectly
and absolute bull
shit.
The drinks was leakin waterweak
and never got down to my knees."

hey daddy
what they been and done to you
and what you been and done
to me
to momma
momma momma
hey
sugar daddy
big daddy
sweet daddy
Black Daddy
The Original Father Divine
the everlovin
deep
tall
bad
buck
jive
cold
strut
bop
split
tight
loose
close

hot
hot
hot
sweet SWEET DADDY
WHERE YOU BEEN AND
WHEN YOU COMIN BACK TO ME
HEY
WHEN YOU COMIN BACK
TO MOMMA
momma momma

AND SUPPOSE HE FINALLY SAY
"LOOK. BABY.
I LOVES ME SOME
EVERYTHING ABOUT YOU.
LET ME BE YOUR MAN."
That reach around the hurtin
like a dream.
And I ain never wakin up
from that one.
momma momma
momma momma

II
Consider the Queen

hand on her hip
sweat restin from
the corn/bean/greens' field
steamy under the pale/sly
suffocatin sun

Consider the Queen

she fix the cufflinks
on his Sunday shirt
and fry some chicken
bake some cake
and tell the family

"Never mind about the bossman
don' know how a human
bein spozed to act. Jus'
never mind about him.
Wash your face.
Sit down. And let
the good Lord bless this table."

Consider the Queen

her babies pullin at the nipples
pullin at the momma milk

the infant fingers gingerly
approach caress the
soft/Black/swollen/momma breast

and there
inside the mommasoft
life-spillin treasure chest
the heart
breaks
rage by grief by sorrow
weary weary
breaks
breaks quiet
silently
the weary sorrow
quiet now the furious
the adamant the broken
busted beaten down and beaten up
the beaten beaten beaten
weary heart beats
tender-steady
and the babies suck/
the seed of blood
and love glows at the
soft/Black/swollen/momma breast

Consider the Queen

she works when she works
in the laundry *in jail*
in the school house *in jail*
in the office *in jail*
on the soap box *in jail*
on the desk
on the floor
on the street
on the line
at the door
lookin fine
at the head of the line
steppin sharp from behind
in the light
with a song
wearing boots
or a belt
and a gun
drinkin wine when it's time
when the long week is done
but she works when she works
in the laundry in jail
she works when she works

Consider the Queen

she sleeps when she sleeps
with the king in the kingdom
she
sleeps when she sleeps
with the wall
with whatever it is who happens
to call
with me and with you
(to survive you make
do/you explore more and more)
so she sleeps when she sleeps
a really deep sleep

Consider the Queen

a full/Black/glorious/a purple rose
aroused by the tiger breathin
beside her
a shell with the moanin
of ages inside her
a hungry one feedin the folk
what they need

Consider the Queen.

III

Blackman
let that white girl go.
She know what you ought to know.
(By now.)

IV

MOMMA MOMMA
momma momma
family face
face of the family alive
momma
mammy
momma
woman
sista
baby
luv
the house on fire
poison waters/
earthquake/
and the air a nightmare/
turn
turn
turn around the
national gross product
growin
really gross/turn
turn

turn the pestilence away
the miserable killers
and Canarsie
Alabama
people beggin to be people
warfare on the welfare
of the folk/
hey
turn
turn away
the trickbag university/the
trickbag propaganda/
trickbag
tricklins of prosperity/of
pseudo-"status"
lynchtree necklace
on the strong
round
neck of you
my momma
momma momma
turn away
the f.b.i./the state police/the cops/
the/everyone of the
infest/incestuous investigators
into you
and Daddy/into us
hey
turn
my mother
turn
the face of history
to your own
and please be smilin
if you can
be smilin
at the family
momma momma

let the funky forecast
be the last
one we will ever
want to listen to

And Daddy see
the stars fall down
and burn a light
into the singing
darkness of your eyes
my Daddy
my Blackman
you take my body in
your arms/you use
the oil of coconuts/of trees and
flowers/fish and new fruits
from the new world
to enflame me in this otherwise
cold place
please

meanwhile
momma
momma momma
teach me how to kiss
the king within the kingdom
teach me how to t.c.b./to make do
and be
like you
teach me to survive my
momma
teach me how to hold a new life
momma
help me
turn the face of history
to your face.

Queen Anne's Lace

Unseemly as a marvellous and astral renegade
now luminous and startling (rakish)
at the top of its thin/ordinary stem
the flower overpowers or outstares me
as I walk by thinking *weeds* and *poison*
ivy, bush and *fern* or *runaway grass:*
You (where are you, really?) never leave me
to my boredom: numb as I might like to be.
Repeatedly
you do revive
arouse alive

a suffering.

MARGE PIERCY
(1936–   )

We Become New

How it feels to be touching
you: an Io moth, orange
and yellow as pollen,
wings through the night
miles to mate,
could crumble in the hand.

Yet our meaning together
is hardy as an onion
and layered.
Goes into the blood like garlic.
Sour as rose hips.
Gritty as whole grain.
Fragrant as thyme honey.

When I am turning slowly
in the woven hammocks of our talk,
when I am chocolate melting into you,
I taste everything new
in your mouth.

You are not my old friend.
How did I used to sit
and look at you? Now
though I seem to be standing still
I am flying flying flying
in the trees of your eyes.

Apron Strings

So hard for women to believe each other.
Mama said she loved me
then screamed for years
to give me away.
I learned early to lie about boys.

Any breast masks the maternal.
Any dress
can rustle her loose.
Brush of hair, perfume,
wet body smells, blood
touch that first pain.

I am not mothering you,
I am not putting you
inside me for keeps,
I am not going to be afraid
you will swallow me
or break me to mewling child.

I am not doing much yet
that is real
except trying
to see you with me.

The Spring Offensive of the Snail

Living someplace else is wrong
in Jerusalem the golden
floating over New England smog,
above paper company forests,
deserted brick textile mills

square brooders on the rotten rivers,
developer-chewed mountains.

Living out of time is wrong.
The future drained us thin as paper.
We were tools scraping.
After the revolution
we would be good, love one another
and bake fruitcakes.
In the meantime eat your ulcer.

Living upside down is wrong,
roots in the air
mouths filled with sand.
Only what might be sang.
I cannot live crackling
with electric rage always.
The journey is too long
to run, cursing those
who can't keep up.

Give me your hand.
Talk quietly to everyone you meet.
It is going on.
We are moving again
with our houses on our backs.
This time we have to remember
to sing and make soup.

Pack the *Kapital* and the vitamin E,
the basil plant for the sill,
Apache tears you
picked up in the desert.

But remember to bury
all old quarrels
behind the garage for compost.
Forgive who insulted you.
Forgive your self for being wrong.
You will do it again
for nothing living

resembles a straight line,
certainly not this journey
to and fro, zigzagging
you there and me here
making our own road onward
as the snail does.

Yes, for some time we might contemplate
not the tiger, not the eagle or grizzly
but the snail who always remembers
that wherever you find yourself eating
is home, the center
where you must make your love,
and wherever you wake up
is here, the right place to be
where we start again.

JUDITH JOHNSON SHERWIN
(1936–)

Rhyme for the Child as a Wet Dog

The hands that eased my mother's labor drew
Me out of a sure thing,
Cut the dream through, knotted it, then threw me
Onto a day of straw.

And the days I run yapping and hungry, ears
Flapping under the sky
That gives no orders, are happy;
The nights are one long

Run on a lawn where the rabbits' ears and the birds'
Beaks spring up like grass;
And in no hole, under no tree, chained up in no
yard, around no daybreak
Corner lurks the big black

Half-wolf to worry my heels with bite of his night-
Call, or howl out how
Tonight I'll hold down the big job, take the long
run on command, tomorrow let fall
The rabbits' ears, the birds' beaks/
on call.

The Light Woman's Song

love me with the left hand
leave me with the right
love me at height of day
leave before night

let no scurrying pulse tell
sunken in the vein
what the rough hounds bell
when they give tongue

what cunning the fox gnaws
panting in covert
what every beast knows
hide from your heart

left-handed lovers know
what I cast to know
what shall I hunger for
and not let go

Just

yesterday, sitting
with you, eating
grapefruit, a word i'd stuck
too hard or at the wrong angle squirted
tart into my eye.

talk of love, always, yes, like that,
your bristles up, the hairs on your neck
stiff, sharp as your voice, what is it
makes you take love so hard?

DIANE WAKOSKI

(1937–   )

The Night a Sailor Came to Me in a Dream

At the point of shining feathers,
that moment when dawn
ran her finger along the knife edge sky;
at the point when chickens come out of the living room rug
to peck for corn and the grains like
old yellow eyes
roll as marbles across the floor;
at that sweet sprouting point when the seed of day
rests on your tongue,
and you haven't swallowed reality yet. Then,
then, yes, at that instant of shimmering new pine needles
came a dream, a blister from a new burn,
and you walked in,
old times,
no player piano or beer,
reality held my toes,
the silver ball of sleep was on my stomach,
the structure of dream,
like a harness
lowered over my head, around me,
and I cannot remember what you said, though the harbor was foggy,
and your pea coat seemed to drip with moisture.

Thirty years of travelling this ocean.

Perhaps you told me
you were not
dead.

The Father of My Country

All fathers in Western civilization must have
a military origin. The
ruler,
governor,
yes,
he is
was the
general at one time or other.
And George Washington
won the hearts
of his country—the rough military man
with awkward
sincere
drawing-room manners.

My father;
have you ever heard me speak of him? I seldom
do. But I had a father,
and he had military origins—or my origins from
him
are military,
militant. That is, I remember him only in uniform. But of the navy,
30 years a chief petty officer,
Always away from home.

It is rough/hard for me to
speak now.
I'm not used to talking
about him.
Not used to
naming his objects/
objects
that never surrounded me.

A woodpecker with fresh bloody crest
knocks
at my mouth. Father, for the first
time I say
your name. Name rolled in thick Polish parchment scrolls,
name of Roman candle drippings when I sit at my table
alone, each night,
name of naval uniforms and name of
telegrams, name of
coming home from your aircraft carrier,
name of shiny shoes,
name of Hawaiian dolls, name
of mess spoons, name of greasy machinery, and name of
stencilled names.
Is it your blood I carry in a test tube,
my arm,
to let fall, crack, and spill on the sidewalk
in front of the men
I know,
I love,
I know, and
want? So you left my house when I was under two,
being replaced by other machinery, and
I didn't believe you left me.

This scene: the trunk yielding treasures of
a green fountain pen, heart-shaped mirror,
amber beads, old letters with brown ink, and
the gopher snake stretched across the palm tree
in the front yard with woody trunk like monkey skins,
and a sunset through the skinny persimmon trees. You
came walking, not even a telegram or post card from
Tahiti. Love, love, through my heart like ink in
the thickest nubbed pen, black and flowing into words.
You came to me, and I at least six. Six doilies
of lace, six battleship cannon, six old beerbottles,
six thick steaks, six love letters, six clocks running
backwards, six watermelons, and six baby teeth, a six
cornered hat on six men's heads, six lovers at once
or one lover at sixes and sevens; how I confuse

all this with my
dream
walking the tightrope bridge
with gold knots
over
the mouth of an anemone/ tissue spiral lips
and holding on so that the ropes burned
as if my wrists had been tied

If George Washington
had not
been the Father
of my Country,
it is doubtful that I would ever have
found
a father. Father in my mouth, on my lips, in my
tongue, out of all my womanly fire,
Father I have left in my steel filing cabinet as a name on my birth
certificate, Father, I have left in the teeth pulled out at
dentists' offices and thrown into their garbage cans,
Father living in my wide cheekbones and short feet,
Father in my Polish tantrums and my American speech, Father, not a
holy name, not a name I cherish but the name I bear, the name
that makes me one of a kind in any phone book because
you changed it, and nobody
but us
has it,
Father who makes me dream in the dead of night of the falling cherry
blossoms, Father who makes me know all men will leave me
if I love them,
Father who made me a maverick,
a writer
a namer,
name/father, sun/father, moon/father, bloody mars/father,

other children said, "My father is a doctor,"
or
"My father gave me this camera,"
or
"My father took me to
the movies,"

or
"My father and I went swimming,"
but
my father is coming in a letter
once a month
for a while,
and my father
sometimes came in a telegram
but
mostly
my father came to me
in sleep, my father because I dreamed in one night that I dug through the ash heap in back of the pepper tree and found a diamond shaped like a dog and my father called the dog and it came leaping over to him and he walked away out of the yard down the road with the dog jumping and yipping at his heels,

my father was not in the telephone book
in my city;
my father was not sleeping with my mother
at home;
my father did not care if I studied the
piano;
my father did not care what
I did;
and I thought my father was handsome and I loved him and I wondered why
he left me alone so much,
so many years
in fact, but
my father
made me what I am
a lonely woman
without a purpose, just as I was
a lonely child
without any father. I walked with words, words, and names,
names. Father was not
one of my words.
Father was not
one of my names. But now I say, George you have become my father,

in his 20th century naval uniform. George Washington, I need your
love; George, I want to call you Father, Father, my Father,
Father of my country,
that is
me. And I say the name to chant it. To sing it. To lace it around me
like weaving cloth. Like a happy child on that shining afternoon in
the palmtree sunset with her mother's trunk yielding treasures,
I cry and
cry,
Father,
Father,
Father,
have you really come home?

An Apology

Past exchanges have left orbits of rain around my face,
Words used-up as the empty shell of the beetle.
        I did not mean to insult you,
        but perhaps wanted to scorch you with that steamy teakettle
        of my 2700 years,
        to tell you youth shouldn't be humble as the tablecloth,
        but arrogant and fierce/
        we get toothless with age;
        should bite hard when we're young.
        To tell you not to follow masters whose egos are sponges,
        To tell you not that you had nothing to say
        but that you need to pour it out at you own speed,
        in an empty space where it will knock against you.
        I saw the dream of the tongue floating in a bowl of water
        as a desperate sacrifice. You,
        giving up your own words,
        You, giving up identity to float safely on display in
        another man's ocean;
        I saw everything that made me weep spools of rotten thread
        for my own disconnected life—
        drop cement trowels from my knees and
        broken clocks from my elbows.

Wanting to discard the past; renege my own life, the pain
of recognition and hate mingles with the identity.
I apologize for lack of grace—
not passing you with a zen stance.
Elders should be lacquered in their place.
And women commit their words
to the dream code; toads & shooting stars in the blood,
icy milk pails,
snow,
oranges,
diamonds, eyes to the ground. Women should be
silently riding their zebras.

Walking Past Paul Blackburn's Apt. on 7th St.

I wanted to take a walk
and think of the city
whose only remaining beauty
is that you wrote about it.

I bought an ounce
of Carpathian mushrooms from the mountains
of the Ukraine
in the store beneath your old
apartment
            Paul, for you,
            these gestures:

I walked into the store,
seeing in the window a string/ many strings
of powdery white mushroom caps,
brown-gilled underneath, among the amber
and big crocks of honey, nestled next
to embroidered ribbons of purple green red
yellow and blue, simple
puffed blouses and thick books with gold letters.

"How much for a string of mushrooms?" I
innocently asked.

Wonder. Awe.
"A string?" A pause.
"We sell them by the ounce,
and they are light as a feather. But a string—
$30 maybe?"
"I'd like an ounce then," and he put them in
a tiny paper bag which might have also held a
child's glove
or a marshmallow.

He smiled and told me how delicious they were;
how they would swell up and fill a soup,
how choice they were—only the caps

Paul, I walked out
thinking how you have taught all of us
to dwell in this city and
to make friends with our neighborhoods.

Hello, Paul, I hope you have
found the ultimate
city.
Or maybe you have wisely moved to the country
in your old age?

GARY GILDNER
(1938–   )

Nails

My father, his mouth full of nails,
is building my mother's dream house.

My mother is listing the grief
it cost her, & pointing out how smooth

the woodwork is. To her brothers:
well, the blacks are taking over—

& her cousins passing through from Santa Monica
swear the church is kissing ass. Ah,

a dream house draws the line on many
fronts. (St. Monica, if I remember, wed thou thee

a pagan, no? & brought him in the fold.
& when he died thou set

to work on sonny boy, old dissolute Augustine, right?
Any food in there for thought?)

Meanwhile, time to pour
the basement floor,

& the Ready Mix man plops
his concrete through the future

rec room window, *Lord*
it isn't wet enough to spread!

Just lays there like a load some giant chicken
dropped. My father, mixing figures,

says all hell will hit the fan
if our fannies do not *move*

& sets my little brother on it with the hose
while we grab hoes & shovels, Lord

I liked that part & afterwards
the lump all smooth

we drank our beer & pop
& mopped our sweat,

& talked about What Next.
The future meant:

cut the lumber square,
make the nails go straight

& things will hold.
I loved that logic, saw him prove it—

then he said we're done
& covered up the last nail's head

with wood paste;
everything was smooth.

I moved around a lot
when I left home, making stories up.

In one blockbuster there's a lady says:
"You taste like roofing nails, father."

And: "You're growing shorter!"
Terrific dialogue but not much plot.

Like building dream houses—
no one knows what you mean.

The House on Buder Street

My father found it after the war—
five rooms and two long rows of purple grapes
beside the picket fence in back
—which Eddie Hill, holding his jewels, leaped
the night we peppered a township
cruiser with bird-shot cut
from shotgun shells and stuffed in our BB rifles.

Every summer my mother made grape jelly
and Eddie, who had it down pat, polished my curve ball.
Up in his attic we gagged on rum-soaked Crooks;
he described taking a flashlight to bed
and crawling under the sheets
the nights he slept with his older half-sister.
Our houses were back to back.

The Buder Street brain was Jerry Skellinger.
He had a wing like a chicken
but could figure a Tiger's average without a stick or paper.
Once throwing darts I got him in the shoulder.
His father taught math and after school put peacocks
and roses in blocks of clear plastic.
They had a black cocker named Silly.

The night my brother was born
my father and I slept in the basement—
on Grandma's brass bed hauled down from the farm.
I was afraid of spiders
and clung to his back.
My aunt Sophie came from Detroit and steamed bottles
and made my sister and me eat everything.

I thought I'd be a doctor.
I took a kitchen knife and cut the cry
thing from my sister's doll. She screamed.

My aunt sighed Be constructive.
I filled a can with polliwogs from Miller's Pond.
I watched Shirley Fox bite her warts.
Shirley came from Arkansas; her parents hated Catholics.

When my brother could toddle he climbed
a ladder and fell on his liver.
Then he picked up hepatitis.
When he got on his feet we lit sparklers
and buried hot stones to bake potatoes.
Shirley's warts were gone, too.
She'd lifted a robin's egg and rubbed on bloody bird.

Now we needed a bigger house.
Bigger also meant better.
My mother hated the dusty unpaved street,
the soot from the coal-burning furnace;
and her fruit cellar was packed!—
she couldn't can another pickle.
Some nights my father slept in our room.

The fall my mother insisted I still needed
long underwear, I threw them at her.
My father knocked me down,
then grabbed a long-handled hammer
and began to hit the house.
The rest of us cleaned up the chips.
By winter we had a new bedroom.

In the spring Shirley's breasts appeared.
Eddie worked on my slider and Miller's Pond
was filled in to build what my father called cracker boxes;
they were painted orange and lime and raspberry sherbet.
Some of Shirley's kin from Arkansas moved in one.
They went to work for Fisher Body, like her father,
and called each other shop rats.

My sister and I attended the Catholic school—
everyone else went to public. Eddie reported
that Shirley crossed her legs in Algebra; he figured
to make All-County and carried Trojans in his wallet.

My mother counted the Baptists on the street.
My father called it harping.
Sunday drives meant looking for a lot.

The Runner

Show the runner coming through the shadows,
show him falling into a speckled rhythm,
and then show the full expression of light,
there, where the trees quit and the road
goes on alone, marked by the moon-glazed gravel

Show the runner trying to disappear
where sky and road meet far in the distance,
show him always a step too late,
show a train going by hauling a long silence,
and show the runner leaving the road
where the killdeer starts from a charred stump

Show the runner saying the names of streams
as if he were working off days in Purgatory,
show the Chocolay, the Rifle, the Fox,
the Laughing Whitefish, the Escanaba,
show the runner's pocketful of worms
and show the runner's father
sitting alone by a hole in the ice

Show the runner stopping at farm after farm
until a woman appears who is wearing a child's
pink kimono over her shoulders,
show her feet in hunting socks,
a kitchen arranged in cream and linoleum,
show that the wind has toasted her cheeks,
show that she doesn't know what he wants

Show the runner's old room, the crucifix
he tied fresh palms around each year,
the five nice birch his father planted,

the two blue spruce, the silver maple,
the cherry from the nursery that was going broke,
the man who said take it for a buck,
the hail storm that knocked them over

Show the runner setting out all spruced up,
show the sun, poached, above a grove of leggy birch,
show the runner cruising down a cowpath
trying to catch his breath,
and show the slim white limbs dividing
letting him in

Show the runner peeling bark
and scratching messages with sticks,
then show him diving into a drift,
nosing like a mole out of season,
rolling over and over
and yipping for luck or in pain

Show the runner approach the only light
in Little Lake, there, over the grocer's
fading pack of Camels,
show the grocer chewing Red Man,
listen to him play his pocket change
and resurrect the dead,
listen to him spit them back

Show the runner running on,
show the moon, then show it stalking him
across the road into the second growth,
show the runner's father in his garden
blue and out of breath and looking hard
at something nothing can distract him from,
show the lake all frozen over,
show the mound of snow

MICHAEL S. HARPER

(1938–)

Poetry Concert

We remember you
calling America
on the phone:
frontal friends from college
who worked in animal ecstasy,
hypos in the animal hotel;
the drenched finger of syrup
you took up in a high,
that high gone
in the papers of the factory
in its oily cones,
'Detroit, please'
and our fingers dialing:
you called it primal,
the code your scream,
and on the assembly line
of Cadillac I heard you sigh.

Grandfather

In 1915 my grandfather's
neighbors surrounded his house
near the dayline he ran
on the Hudson
in Catskill, NY
and thought they'd burn
his family out

in a movie they'd just seen
and be rid of his kind:
the death of a lone black
family is *the Birth*
of a Nation,
or so they thought.
His 5′4″ waiter gait
quenched the white jacket smile
he'd brought back from watered
polish of my father
on the turning seats,
and he asked his neighbors
up on his thatched porch
for the first blossom of fire
that would burn him down.

They went away, his nation,
spittooning their torched necks
in the shadows of the riverboat
they'd seen, posse decomposing;
and I see him Sutter
with white bag from your
restaurant, challenged by his first
grandson to a foot-race
he will win in white clothes.

I see him as he buys galoshes
for his railed yard near Mineo's
metal shop, where roses jump
as the el circles his house
toward Brooklyn, where his rain fell;
and I see cigar smoke in his eyes,
chocolate Madison Square Garden chews
he breaks on his set teeth,
stitched up after cancer,
the great white nation immovable
as his weight wilts
and he is on a porch
that won't hold my arms,
or the legs of the race run
forwards, or the film
played backwards on his grandson's eyes.

Nightmare Begins Responsibility

I place these numbed wrists to the pane
watching white uniforms whisk over
him in the tube-kept
prison
fear what they will do in experiment
watch my gloved stickshifting gasolined hands
breathe *boxcar-information-please* infirmary tubes
distrusting white-pink mending paperthin
silkened end hairs, distrusting tubes
shrunk in his *trunk-skincapped*
shaven head, in thighs
distrusting-white-hands-picking-baboon-light
on this son who will not make his second night
of this wardstrewn intensive airpocket
where his father's asthmatic
hymns of *night-train,* train done gone
his mother can only know that he has flown
up into essential calm unseen corridor
going boxscarred home, *mamaborn, sweetsonchild*
gonedowntown into *researchtestingwarehousebatteryacid*
mama-son-done-gone/ me telling her 'nother
train tonight, no music, no breathstroked
heartbeat in my infinite distrust of them:

and of my distrusting self
white-doctor-who-breathed-for-him-all-night
say it for two sons gone,
say nightmare, say it loud
panebreaking heartmadness:
nightmare begins responsibility.

RICHARD KOSTELANETZ
(1940–)

Tribute to Henry Ford

TRIBUTE TO HENRY FORD 1

T T T
T T T
T T T
T T
T T T
T T
T T
T T T
T T T

TRIBUTE TO HENRY FORD 2

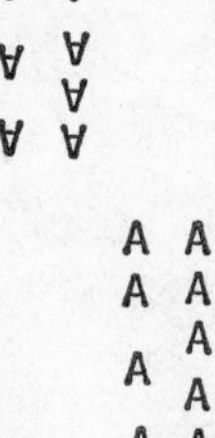

TRIBUTE TO HENRY FORD 3

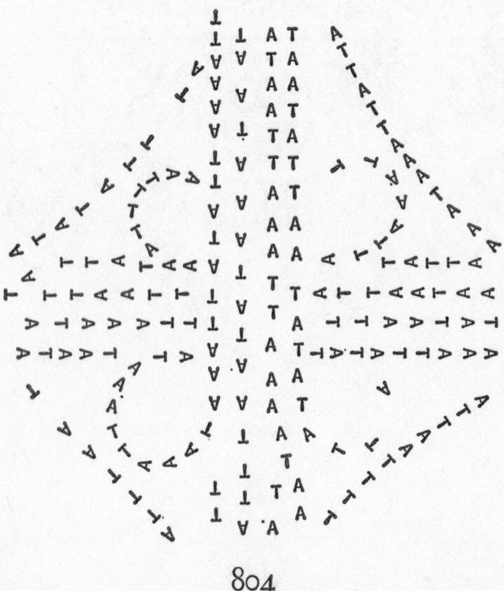

ERICA JONG
(1942–   )

The Woman Who Loved to Cook

Looking for love, she read cookbooks,
She read recipes for *tartelettes,*
terrines de boeuf, timbales,
& Ratatouille.
She read cheese fondue
& Croque Monsieur,
& Hash High Brownies
& Lo Mein.

If no man appeared who would love her
(her face moist with cooking,
her breasts full of apple juice
or wine),
she would whip one up:
of gingerbread,
with baking powder
to make him rise.

Even her poems
were recipes.
"Hunger," she would write, "hunger."
The magic word to make it go away.
But nothing filled her up
or stopped that thump.
Her stomach thought it was a heart.

Then one day she met a man,
his cheeks brown as gingerbread,
his tongue a slashed pink ham

upon a platter.
She wanted to eat him whole
& save his eyes.
Her friends predicted he'd eat her.

How does the story end?
    You know it well.

    She's getting fatter
    & she drinks too much.

    Her shrink has read her book
    & heard her tale.

    "Oral," he says,
    & coughs
    & puffs his pipe.

    "Oral,"
    he says,
    & now
    "time's up."

HAKI R. MADHUBUTI (Don L. Lee)
(1942–   )

Judy-One

she's the camera's
subject:
the sun for colored film.

her smile is like
clear light bouncing off
the darkness of the
mediterranean at nighttime.

we all know it,
her smile.
when it's working,
moves like sea water—
always going somewhere

strongly.

Mixed Sketches

u feel that way sometimes
wondering:
as a nine year old sister
with burned out hair oddly
smiles at you and sweetly calls you
brother.

u feel that way sometimes
wondering:
as a blackwoman & her 6 children
are burned out of their apartment with no place
to go & a nappy-headed nigger comes running thru
our neighborhood with a match in his hand crying
revolution.

u feel that way sometimes
wondering:
seeing sisters in two hundred dollar wigs & suits
fastmoving in black clubs in late surroundings talking
about late thoughts in late language waiting for late men
that come in with, "i don't want to hear bout nothing black tonight."

u feel that way sometimes
wondering:
while eating on newspaper tablecloths
& sleeping on clean bed sheets that couldn't
stop bed bugs as black children watch their
mothers leave the special buses returning from
special neighborhoods
to clean their "own" unspecial homes.
u feel that way sometimes
wondering:
wondering, how did we survive?

Change Is Not Always Progress
(For Africa & Africans)

Africa.

don't let them
steal
your face   or
take your circles
and make them squares.

don't let them
steel
your body   as to put
100 stories of concrete on you
so that you
                    arrogantly
scrape
the

sky.

NIKKI GIOVANNI
(1943–   )

Nikki-Rosa

childhood rememberances are always a drag
if you're Black
you always remember things like living in Woodlawn
with no inside toilet
and if you become famous or something
they never talk about how happy you were to have your mother
all to yourself and
how good the water felt when you got your bath from one of those
big tubs that folk in chicago barbecue in
and somehow when you talk about home
it never gets across how much you
understood their feelings
as the whole family attended meetings about Hollydale
and even though you remember
your biographers never understand
your father's pain as he sells his stock
and another dream goes
and though you're poor it isn't poverty that
concerns you
and though they fought a lot
it isn't your father's drinking that makes any difference
but only that everybody is together and you
and your sister have happy birthdays and very good christmasses
and I really hope no white person ever has cause to write about me
because they never understand Black love is Black wealth and they'll
probably talk about my hard childhood and never understand that
all the while I was quite happy

Kidnap Poem

ever been kidnapped
by a poet
if i were a poet
i'd kidnap you
put you in my phrases and meter
you to jones beach
or maybe coney island
or maybe just to my house
lyric you in lilacs
dash you in the rain
blend into the beach
to complement my see
play the lyre for you
ode you with my love song
anything to win you
wrap you in the red Black green
show you off to mama
yeah if i were a poet i'd kid
nap you

AUTHOR INDEX

Aiken, Conrad (Potter) (1889–1973), 464
Ammons, A. R. (1926–), 656
Ashbery, John (1927–), 686
Baraka, Imamu Amiri (LeRoi Jones) (1934–), 757
Barlow, Joel (1754–1812), 39
Berryman, John (1914–1972), 549
Bishop, Elizabeth (1911–), 535
Bradstreet, Anne (1612–1672), 1
Brinnin, John Malcolm (1916–), 562
Brooks, Gwendolyn (1917–), 578
Bryant, William Cullen (1794–1878), 53
Clifton, Lucille (1936–), 765
Cooper, Jane (1924–), 649
Corso, Gregory (1930–), 733
Crane, Hart (Harold) (1899–1932), 487
Crane, Stephen (1871–1900), 337
Creeley, Robert (1926–), 659
Cullen, Countee (1903–1946), 504
Cummings, E. E. (Edward Estlin) (1894–1962), 477
Dickey, James (1923–), 633
Dickinson, Emily (1830–1886), 307
Eberhart, Richard (1904–), 509
Eliot, T. S. (Thomas Stearns) (1888–1965), 430
Emerson, Ralph Waldo (1803–1882), 74
Ferlinghetti, Lawrence (1919?–), 595
Freneau, Philip (1752–1832), 18
Frost, Robert (1874–1963), 341
Garrigue, Jean (1912–1972), 541
Gildner, Gary (1938–), 794
Ginsberg, Allen (1926–), 662
Giovanni, Nikki (1943–), 810
Goedicke, Patricia (1931–), 742
Gregor, Arthur (1923–), 639
H.D. (Hilda Doolittle) (1886–1961), 419
Hall, Donald (1928–), 704
Hanson, Pauline (1917–), 582
Harper, Michael S. (1938–), 800
Holmes, Oliver Wendell (1809–1894), 141
Honig, Edwin (1919–), 599
Howard, Richard (1929–), 717
Hughes, Langston (1902–1967), 499
Jacobsen, Josephine (1908–), 530
Jarrell, Randall (1914–1965), 554
Jeffers, Robinson (1887–1962), 422
Jong, Erica (1942–), 805
Jordan, June (1936–), 767
Kinnell, Galway (1927–), 690
Knight, Etheridge (1933–), 754
Kostelanetz, Richard (1940–), 803
Kumin, Maxine (1925–), 653
Kunitz, Stanley (1905–), 512

Levertov, Denise (1923–   ), 642
Levine, Philip (1928–   ), 708
Lindsay, Vachel (1879–1931), 364
Longfellow, Henry Wadsworth (1807–1882), 93
Lowell, James Russell (1819–1891), 180
Lowell, Robert (1917–1977), 585
MacLeish, Archibald (1892–   ), 470
Madhubuti, Haki R. (Don L. Lee) (1942–   ), 807
Masters, Edgar Lee (1868–1950), 323
Mayhall, Jane (1921–   ), 625
McKay, Claude (1890–1948), 468
Melville, Herman (1819–1891), 192
Meredith, William (1919–   ), 606
Merrill, James (1926–   ), 672
Miles, Josephine (1911–   ), 539
Millay, Edna St. Vincent (1892–1950), 473
Moore, Marianne (1887–1972), 425
Moss, Howard (1922–   ), 631
Nash, Ogden (1902–1971), 501
Nemerov, Howard (1920–   ), 617
O'Hara, Frank (1926–1966), 675
Petrie, Paul (1927–   ), 696
Piercy, Marge (1936–   ), 780
Plath, Sylvia (1932–1963), 747
Poe, Edgar Allan (1809–1849), 147
Pound, Erza (1885–1972), 406
Rakosi, Carl (1903–   ), 506
Randall, Dudley (1914–   ), 560
Ransom, John Crowe (1888–1974), 457
Rexroth, Kenneth (1905–   ), 515
Rich, Adrienne (1929–   ), 721
Robinson, Edwin Arlington (1869–1935), 327
Roethke, Theodore (1908–1963), 522
Sandburg, Carl (1878–1967), 360
Schevill, James (1920–   ), 620
Schwartz, Delmore (1913–1966), 546
Sexton, Anne (1928–1974), 713
Sherwin, Judith Johnson (1936–   ), 784
Simpson, Louis (1923–   ), 644
Snodgrass, W. D. (1926–   ), 679
Snyder, Gary (1930–   ), 737
Stein, Gertrude (1874–1946), 358
Stevens, Wallace (1879–1955), 374
Strand, Mark (1934–   ), 760
Sullivan, Nancy (1929–   ), 728
Swenson, May (1919–   ), 610
Tate, Allen (1899–   ), 496
Taylor, Edward (1645?–1729), 12
Thoreau, Henry David (1817–1862), 177
Timrod, Henry (1828–1867), 304
Tuckerman, Frederick Goddard (1821–1873), 301
Tyler, Royall (1757–1826), 50
Valentine, Jean (1934–   ), 762
Very, Jones (1813–1880), 171
Wakoski, Diane (1937–   ), 786
Warren, Robert Penn (1905–   ), 519
Weiss, Theodore (1916–   ), 569
Wheatley, Phillis (Phillis Peters) (1753?–1784), 34
Whitman, Walt (Walter) (1819–1892), 200
Whittemore, Reed (1919–   ), 614
Whittier, John Greenleaf (1807–1892), 112
Wilbur, Richard (1921–   ), 628
Williams, William Carlos (1883–1963), 390
Wright, James (1927–   ), 701

INDEX OF TITLES

(Asterisk denotes excerpt from Poem)

Abortion, An, 676
Abraham Lincoln Walks at Midnight, 372
Ache of Marriage, The, 643
Acquainted with the Night, 354
Adultery, 634
After Apple Picking, 343
"After Experience Taught Me . . .", 683
After great pain, a formal feeling comes– (341), 315
After Love, 653
Aftermath, 111
After the Last Dynasty, 513
After the Second Operation, 743
America, 468
American Poetry, 644
American Soldier, The, 28
America the Beautiful, 299
Amsterdam, 543
Anaesthesia, 764
Anatomy of Happiness, The, 502
And Change with Hurried Hand Has Swept These Scenes, 301
And I Am Old to Know, 583
And You As Well Must Die, Belovèd Dust, 475
Anecdote of the Jar, 382
Animals Are Passing from Our Lives, 708
Annabel Lee, 168
anyone lived in a pretty how town, 482
Apology, An, 791
April, 763
April Inventory, 680
Apron Strings, 781
Armadillo, The, 537
Ars Poetica, 471
as freedom is a breakfastfood, 485
As I Ebb'd with the Ocean of Life, 288
Aspect of Love, Alive in the Ice and Fire, An, 581
As You Like It, 576
At Melville's Tomb, 494
Attention, 722
At the End of the Affair, 654
Auspex, 189
Author to Her Book, The, 11

Barracks Apt. 14, 573
Bath, The, 738
Battle Hymn of the Republic, 299
Bean Eaters, The, 579
Bear, The, 691
Bearded Oaks, 519
Beauty–be not caused–It Is– (516), 316
Because I could not stop for Death– (712), 317
Behold, the Grave, 338
Being Somebody, 601
Belief, 539
Bells, The, 161
Bells for John Whiteside's Daughter, 457
Berg, The, 195
Between Walls, 401
Biography, 757

Birches, 344
Black Riders Came from the Sea, 339
Black Soldier's Civil War Chant, 293
Black Tambourine, 487
Bleecker Street, 541
Blue Girls, 459
Bone that has no Marrow, The (1274), 321
Book I, *Paterson,** 404
Brahma, 74
Brain Cells, The, 707
Bridge, The, Proem: To Brooklyn Bridge,* 487
Brown Girl Dead, A, 505
Buffalo Bill's, 484
But I Am Growing Old and Indolent, 424

Cambridge ladies who live in furnished souls, the, 485
Campus on the Hill, The, 682
Canto III, 417
Cavalry Crossing a Ford, 277
Cézanne, 358
Change Is Not Always Progress, 809
Charles Carville's Eyes, 334
Charleston, 305
Chaucer, 100
Chicago, 362
Childhood in Jacksonville, Florida, 651
Circle, A Square, A Triangle and A Ripple of Water, A, 649
City in the Sea, The, 150
City Sparrow, 625
Clamming, 615
Clarity, 657
Color–Caste–Denomination–(970), 318
Colossus, The, 747
Compensation, 84
Complaint, 701
Concentric, 803
Concord Hymn, 74
Confirmers, The, 656
Congo, The, 368
Constantly Risking Absurdity, 595
Cool Tombs, 360
Correspondence School Instructor Says Goodbye to His Poetry Students, The, 694
Country Villa, 544
Credo, 330
Cross, 499
Crossing Brooklyn Ferry, 282
Cross of Snow, The, 110
Crucifixion, 296
Cut, 748
Cut the Grass, 657
Cuttings, 523
Cuttings (later), 523

Daily the Ocean Between Us, 745
Dalliance of the Eagles, The, 277
Dance, The, 401
Danse Russe, 398
Days, 81
Deacon's Masterpiece or, The Wonderful "One-Hoss Shay", The, 143
Dead, The, 174
Death of Lincoln, The, 73
Death of the Ball Turret Gunner, The, 555
Deep River, 297
Deliverance from a Fit of Fainting, 7
Departure, The, 614
Desert Places, 355
Design, 351
Dialogue, 724
Different Image, A, 560
Divina Commedia, 98
Dream, The, 696
Dreamland, 155
Dreams, 147
Dream Songs, The,* 549
Dream Within a Dream, A, 148
Dust of Snow, 349

Each and All, 76
Eagles, The, 172

Earth Song, 82
Eating Poetry, 761
Eclipses, 729
Edge, 753
Egyptian Passage, An, 570
Eldorado, 167
Elegy for Jane, 525
Emperor of Ice Cream, The, 374
End of the World, The, 472
Enough, 641
Epitaph for My Cat, 542
Equilibrists, The, 462
Eros Turannos, 332
Euclid Alone Has Looked on Beauty Bare, 474
Experience, 83

*Fable for Critics, A,** 180–189
Emerson, 182
Bryant, 183
Hawthorne, 185
Cooper, 186
Poe, 187
Irving, 188
Lowell, 188
Facing West from California's Shores, 275
"Faith" is a fine invention (185), 310
Fame is a fickle food (1659), 322
Family Man, A, 654
Father of My Country, The, 787
Fear of Death, 689
Fifty, 517
Fire and Ice, 357
Fire at Alexandria, The, 569
Fire Island, 613
Fire of Drift-wood, The, 106
First Fig, 476
First Snowfall, The, 190
Flesh and the Spirit, The, 4
Florida, 507
Flowers by the Sea, 393
Fog, 360
For a Lady I Know, 504
Forbearance, 84
For deLawd, 765
Forest Hymn, A, 58
"Formerly a Slave", 197
For the Market, 627
Four Saints in Three Acts: "Pigeons on the grass alas",* 359
Frau Bauman, Frau Schmidt, and Frau Schwartze, 522
Freud: Dying in London, He Recalls the Smoke of His Cigar Beginning to Sing, 621
Frightened, 597
from a Slave Marriage Ceremony, 295
From Creature to Ghost, 583
Fugitive Slaves, The, 175
Fugue, 617
Further Advantages of Learning, 517
Fury of Aerial Bombardment, The, 509
fuzzy fellow, without feet, A (173), 309

Gambling, 50
Garden, The, 173
General William Booth Enters into Heaven, 366
George Crabbe, 329
Gerontion, 434
Getting Down to Get Over, 769
Give All to Love, 89
Glass of Water, The, 384
God in Wrath, A, 337
Good-bye, 92
Good-bye My Fancy! 273
Good Times, 765
Grand Canyon, The, 672
Grandfather, 800
Grave, A, 426
Green Frog at Roadstead, Wisconsin, 620
Groundhog, The, 510

Haiku, 755
Hamatreya, 81

Hand, The, 632
Hand and Foot, The, 172
Harbor, The, 361
Hard Rock Returns to Prison from the Hospital for the Criminal Insane, 754
Harlem Dancer, The, 468
Hasty Pudding, The, 39
Hatteras Calling, 464
Haunted Palace, The, 153
Heat, 419
Heaven of Animals, The, 633
Heavy Bear Who Goes with Me", "The, 547
Helen, 420
Here Lies a Lady, 458
Here, Where the Red Man Swept the Leaves Away, 303
Her Kind, 714
Herman Melville, 465
He said, 763
High-Toned Old Christian Woman, A, 387
His Necessary Darkness, 732
His Plans for Old Age, 608
History, 594
History, 639
Home Burial, 346
Homosexuality, 675
"Hope" is the thing with feathers— (254), 312
Horse Show, The, 397
House Guest, 535
House on Buder Street, The, 796
Howl, parts I & II,* 662
How this woman came by the courage, how she got (100), 550
Huck Finn at Ninety, Dying in a Chicago Boarding House Room, 623
Hugh Selwyn Mauberley, 409
Human Animal, The, 625
Hurricane, The, 22
Hurt Hawks, 422
Huswifery, 12
Hymn to the Morning, An, 37
Hymn to the Night, 93

I Am a Book I Neither Wrote nor Read, 548
I Am a Parcel of Vain Strivings Tied, 178
I Am the People, the Mob, 363
i carry your heart with me(i carry it in, 480
Ichabod, 114
I could bring You Jewels—had I a mind to— (697), 317
Idea of Order at Key West, The, 374
I felt a Funeral, in my Brain, (280), 312
I heard a Fly buzz—when I died— (465), 316
I Knew a Woman, 528
I like a look of Agony, (241), 311
Ill lay he long, upon this last return, (94), 549
I'll tell you how the Sun rose— (318), 314
Illumination, The, 512
I'm Nobody! Who are you? (288), 313
In a Dark Time, 529
In a Station of the Metro, 408
In a Warm Bath, 507
Indian Burying Ground, The, 32
Indian Convert, The, 31
In Evening Air, 524
I never lost as much but twice, (49), 307
I never saw a Moor— (1052), 320
In Goya's Greatest Scenes We Seem to See, 597
In Reference to Her Children, 23 June 1659, 1
Inscription for the Entrance to a Wood, 56
In the Churchyard at Cambridge, 102
In the Desert, 337

In the Prison Pen, 196
I reason, Earth is short— (301), 313
Irish have the thickest ankles in the world, The (299), 552
I Shall Forget You Presently, My Dear, 476
I Sit and Look Out, 263
Israfel, 169
I taste a liquor never brewed— (214), 310
I Thank God I'm Free at Las', 295
i thank You God for most this amazing, 480
It Is the Season, 533

Janet Waking, 459
Jewish Cemetery at Newport, The, 103
Joshua Fit de Battle of Jericho, 297
Journey of the Magi, 448
Joy, Shipmate, Joy! 273
Judy-One, 807
Juggler, 629
Just, 785

Ka 'Ba, 759
Keats, 101
Keeping Things Whole, 760
Kidnap Poem, 811
King Midas, 631

Lady Lazarus, 749
Landing on the Moon, 611
Language, The, 659
Last Words, 674
Letter from an Island, 563
Life, friends, is boring. We must not say so. (14), 549
Light-winged Smoke, Icarian Bird, 177
Light Woman's Song, The, 785
Literary Importation, 27
Little Gidding, 449
little Madness in the Spring, A (1333), 322
Living in Sin, 721
Lobsters in the Window, 684
London Pavement Artist, 620
Losses, 554
Lost Children, The, 557
Love Calls Us to the Things of This World, 628
Love Is Not All: It Is Not Meat nor Drink, 474
Love Song, A, 52
Love Song of J. Alfred Prufrock, The, 430
Lute Music, 516
Lyric, 639

Mad Scene, The, 672
Mad Song, 642
Maldive Shark, The, 192
Malvern Hill, 194
Manos Karastefanís, 673
Man Said to the Universe, A, 339
man who had fallen among thieves, a, 481
Man Who Married Magdalene, The, 644
Many Red Devils, 339
Many Workmen, 338
March into Virginia, The, 193
Marriage, 733
Marshes, The, 626
Martyr, The, 198
Matadors, The, 531
Maud Muller, 115
Meditation. Canticles 2:1. I am . . . the Lily of the Valleys (6), 13
Meditation. Isaiah 25:6. A Feast of Fat Things (11), 15
Meditation. John 6:51. I am the Living Bread (8), 13
Meditation on Rhode Island Coal, A, 62
Meditations in an Emergency, 676
Meeting the Mountains, 740
Mending Wall, 342
Men Made Out of Words, 388

Merchant Marine, 540
Mezzo Cammin, 105
Mid-August at Sourdough Mountain Lookout, 741
Miller's Wife, The, 335
Milton, 101
Mind Is an Ancient and Famous Capital, The, 546
Miniver Cheevy, 328
Mixed Sketches, 807
Movie Actors Scribbling Letters Very Fast in Crucial Scene, 545
Mr. Flood's Party, 330
Museum Piece, 630
My Aunt, 142
My Father in the Night Commanding No, 647
my father moved through dooms of love, 477
My friend must be a Bird (92), 308
My Lost Youth, 95
My Papa's Waltz, 526
Mysteries Remain, The, 421

Nails, 794
Nantucket, 394
narrow Fellow in the Grass, A (986), 319
Natural History, 717
Nature, 105
Negro Speaks of Rivers, The, 500
Neither Out Far nor In Deep, 352
New England, 336
*New Spoon River, The,** 326
  Marx the Sign Painter, 326
  Unknown Soldiers, 326
"next to of course god america i, 482
Night a Sailor Came to Me in a Dream, The, 786
Night in the Forest, 690
Nightmare Begins Responsibility, 802
Night-Sweat, 593
Nikki-Rosa, 810
90 North, 555
Ninth Symphony of Beethoven Understood at Last as a Sexual Message, The, 725
Noiseless Patient Spider, A, 275
No Possum, No Sop, No Taters, 382
Nothing Gold Can Stay, 357
Not Ideas About the Thing but the Thing Itself, 383
Not Seeing Is Believing, 698

O Captain! My Captain!, 272
Ode, 304
Ode Inscribed to W. H. Channing, 86
Ode to the Confederate Dead, 496
Off to Patagonia, 575
Of Modern Poetry, 389
"Oh Fairest of the Rural Maids", 71
Old Age in His Ailing, 199
Old Ironsides, 141
Old Pro's Lament, The, 699
On a Honey Bee, 19
On Arrival, 720
On Being Brought from Africa to America, 36
On Gay Wallpaper, 402
Only Years, 518
On the Beach at Night Alone, 276
On the Completion of the Pacific Telegraph, 176
On the Edge, 711
On the Emigration to America and Peopling the Western Country, 25
On the Night in Question, 742
On Virtue, 38
On Visiting the Graves of Hawthorne and Thoreau, 173
Open Sea, The, 607
Operation, The, 679
Oread, 419
Original Sin: A Short Story, 520
O Taste and See, 642
Our lives are Swiss (80), 308
Out of the Cradle Endlessly Rocking, 257
Oven Bird, The, 353

Pact, A, 406
Past, The, 85
Peeling Onions, 722
Pennycandystore Beyond the El, The, 596
Peter Quince at the Clavier, 376
Phases of Darkness, The, 697
Piazza Piece, 458
Pilgrims, 762
pity this busy monster,manunkind, 483
Poem About Breasts, A, 701
Poem For Half-White College Students, 758
Poem to My Sister, Ethel Ennis, Who Sang "The Star-Spangled Banner" at the Second Inauguration of Richard Milhous Nixon, January 20, 1973, 767
Poet, The, 69
Poetry, 425
Poetry Concert, 800
Portent, The, 192
Portrait d'une Femme, 408
Power, 727
Prairies, The, 65
Praise, 652
Problem, The, 77
Proem, 139
Profile on the Pillow, The, 560
Proletarian Portrait, 393
Prologue, The, 9
Prophecy, A, 671
Provide, Provide, 356
Psalm of Life, A, 94
Public Garden, The, 592

Quaker Graveyard in Nantucket, The, 586
Queen-Anne's-Lace, 395
Queen Anne's Lace, 779

Rainy Night at the Writers' Colony, 532
Raise a "Rucus" To-night, 294
Raisin, The, 705
Raven, The, 156
Reading Myself, 594
Reason, 539
Recipe for an Ocean in the Absence of the Sea, 719
Recuerdo, 473
Red Wheelbarrow, The, 392
Re-forming the Crystal, 726
Rent, 650
Reuben Bright, 329
Rhodora, The, 75
Rhyme for the Child as a Wet Dog, 784
Richard Cory, 327
Ringing the Bells, 713
Riot, 580
River-Merchant's Wife: A Letter, The, 407
Road Not Taken, The, 341
Roethke Plain, 565
Roses and Revolutions, 561
Runner, The, 798

Sadie and Maud, 578
Sailing Home from Rapallo, 585
Salami, 709
Salutation, 406
Screamer Discusses Methods of Screaming, A, 624
Seaweed, 108
Serious Merriment of Women, The, 744
Shade-seller, The, 530
Shape of Death, The, 610
Sheaves, The, 334
Sheep Child, The, 635
Shine, Perishing Republic, 423
Shore, 542
Sight in Camp in the Daybreak Gray and Dim, A, 278
Silken Tent, The, 350
Simon Legree–A Negro Sermon, 364
Skin Diving in the Virgins, 562
Skunk Hour, 590
Slave, The, 175

Sleeper, The, 151
Smell!, 403
Snow-bound, 119
Snow-flakes, 106
Snowstorm, The, 80
So Beautiful Is the Tree of Night, 582
Some Verses upon the Burning of Our House, July 10, 1666, 7
Song for a Dancer, 515
Song for "Buvez Les Vins du Postillon" –Advt., 545
Song of Myself, 200
Sonnet–To Science, 149
Sort of a Song, A, 403
Soul selects her own Society–, The (303), 314
Speak, 702
Speculation, 619
Spenser's Ireland, 427
*Spoon River Anthology,** 323–325
  Hill, The, 323
  Fiddler Jones, 324
  Petit, The Poet, 325
Spring and All, 399
Spring is like a perhaps hand, 479
Spring is the Period (844), 318
Spring Offensive of the Snail, The, 781
Star-Spangled Banner, The, 298
Stars Wheel in Purple, 420
Stopping by Woods on a Snowy Evening, 354
Story About Chicken Soup, A, 646
Success is counted sweetest (67), 307
Sunday Morning, 378
Supermarket in California, A, 670
Surgeons must be very careful (108), 308
Survey of Literature, 460
Susie Asado, 358

Tell all the Truth but tell it slant– (1129), 320
Telling It, 728
Telling the Bees, 112
Tennis Court Oath, The, 687
Terminus, 90
Terrible People, The, 501
Thanatopsis, 53
There is no Frigate like a Book (1263), 321
There Was a Child Went Forth, 290
Things to Do Around a Lookout, 737
Thinking of Tents, 616
Thin Little Leaves of Wood Fern, Ribbed and Toothed, 302
Thirteen Ways of Looking at a Blackbird, 385
This Is Just to Say, 400
This is my letter to the World (441), 315
Thoughts of a Young Girl, 688
Through You, 599
Thy Brother's Blood, 174
Tide Rises, the Tide Falls, The, 110
Tides, The, 72
To a Caty-did, 20
To a Child Trapped in a Barber Shop, 712
To a Lady on the Death of Her Husband, 35
To a Locomotive in Winter, 274
To a Noisy Politician, 30
To a Poor Old Woman, 400
To a Waterfowl, 57
Tobacco, 30
To Cole, the Painter, Departing for Europe, 70
Today, 171
To Earthward, 350
To Emily Dickinson, 495
To Helen, 149
To My Body, 731
To My Dear and Loving Husband, 1
To One in Paradise, 160
To Sir Toby, 23
To the Fringed Gentian, 65

To the King's Most Excellent Majesty, 35
To the University of Cambridge in New England, 34
To the Western World, 645
Town of Hill, The, 704
Tract, 390
Tree at My Window, 353
Tribute to Henry Ford, 804
Truth the Dead Know, The, 714
Turtle, The, 501
209 Canal, 717
Two Shapes, 640
Two Songs, 723

Ulalume–A Ballad, 164
Under the Mountain, as When First I Knew, 301
Upon a Spider Catching a Fly, 16
Upper Chamber in a Darkened House, An, 302

Viable, 658
Vigil Strange I Kept on the Field One Night, 281
Virginal, A, 409
Voyages, 489

Waiting, 649
Waking, The, 527
Walking Past Paul Blackburn's Apt. on 7th St., 792
Walt Whitman, 604
Wanting to Die, 715
War Is Kind, 340
Warning, The, 659
Warning to America, A, 29
Waste Land, The, 436
We Become New, 780
Wedding, The, 466
Welcome, grinned Henry, welcome, fifty-one! (104), 551
We Raise de Wheat, 293
We Real Cool, 579
Western Approaches, The, 618
What Lips My Lips Have Kissed, and Where, and Why, 475
What's the Railroad to Me, 177
When I Heard the Learn'd Astronomer, 276
When Lilacs Last in the Dooryard Bloomed, 263
When the Five Prominent Poets, 532
White Apples, 704
White City, The, 469
White Roses, 686
Who, 599
Wholesome, 607
Widow's Lament in Springtime, The, 396
Wild Honey Suckle, The, 18
Wild Nights–Wild Nights! (249), 311
Window, The, 660
Winter Verse for His Sister, 606
Wish for a Young Wife, 526
Woman, 506
Woman at the Washington Zoo, The, 556
Woman Who Loved to Cook, The, 805
Woodnotes, 79
Woof of the Sun, Ethereal Gauze, 178
Wound-dresser, The, 278
Wounded Deer–leaps highest–, A (165), 309

Yellow Violet, The, 55
"Yes, But . . .", 572
Yet Do I Marvel, 504
You Also, Gaius Valerius Catullus, 470
You couldn't bear to grow old, but we grow old. (262), 552
Young Housewife, The, 392
Young Sycamore, 394
Your face broods from my table, Suicide. (172), 551

Zodiac, The, X "Tenderness, ache on me, and lay your neck", 637

INDEX OF FIRST LINES

(Asterisk denotes excerpt from Poem)

A ball will bounce, but less and less. It's not, 629
A big young bareheaded woman, 393
About the Shark, phlegmatical one, 192
Above the fresh ruffles of the surf, 489
A brackish reach of shoal off Madaket,–, 586
A closed window looks down, 759
'A cold coming we had of it, 448
Across the night/until beside me, 583
A dark theme keeps me here, 524
A Deity of Love Incorporate, 15
Africa./don't let them, 809
After experience taught me that all the ordinary, 683
After great pain, a formal feeling comes–, 315
After our fierce loving, 560
After the event the rockslide, 657
After the first shallows have dropped away, 745
Afterwards, the compromise. 653
A fuzzy fellow, without feet, 309
Again last night I dreamed the dream called Laundry. 672
A god in wrath/Was beating a man; 337
Alfonso was his name: his sad cantina, 562
A line in long array where they wind betwixt green islands, 277
A little Madness in the Spring, 322
A little nearer, this time, 743
All fathers in Western civilization must have, 787
All Greece hates/the still eyes in the white face, 420
All must be used:/this clay whisky jug, bearing, 573
All that running water outside; 626
Already she seems bone thin, 701
Although she feeds me bread of bitterness, 468
A man in terror of impotence, 725
A man said to the universe: 339
a man who had fallen among thieves, 481
A melancholy face Charles Carville had, 334

Am I thy Gold? Or Purse, Lord, for thy Wealth; 13
Am I to become profligate as if I were a blonde? 676
Among twenty snowy mountains, 385
A narrow Fellow in the Grass, 319
And change with hurried hand has swept these scenes: 301
And now my pampered beast, 542
And this is the way they ring, 713
And you as well must die, belovèd dust, 475
An Indian, who lived at *Muskingum*, remote, 31
Announced by all the trumpets of the sky, 80
A noiseless patient spider, 275
An old man bending I come among new faces, 278
An old man in a lodge within a park; 100
An old master yourself now, Auden, 576
An upper chamber in a darkened house, 302
anyone lived in a pretty how town, 482
A poem should be palpable and mute, 471
Applauding youths laughed with young prostitutes, 468
April is the cruellest month, breeding, 436
As a fond mother, when the day is o'er, 105
A scapular of birds hung fast, 729
as freedom is a breakfastfood, 485
As I ebb'd with the ocean of life, 288
A sight in camp in the daybreak gray and dim, 278
A siren sang, and Europe turned away, 645
As long as we look forward, all seems free, 618
At home, in my flannel gown, like a bear to its floe, 555
At midnight, in the month of June, 151
At noon, Tithonus, withered by his singing, 466
At ten A.M. the young housewife, 392
Attend my lays, ye ever honour'd nine, 37
At the earliest ending of winter, 383
At the point of shining feathers, 786
A woman/sleeps next to me on the earth. A strand, 690
A *Wounded* Deer–leaps highest–, 309
Ay, tear her tattered ensign down! 141

Back of the dam, under/a flat pad, 704
Beautifully Janet slept, 459
Beauty–be not caused–It Is–, 316
Because he was a butcher and thereby, 329
Because I could not stop for Death–, 317
Behold, the grave of a wicked man, 338
Beneath these shades, beside yon winding stream, 173
Beside me she sat, hand hooked and hover-, 570

Between five and fifty, 652
Black riders came from the sea. 339
Booth led boldly with his big bass drum—, 366
Buddha is not more strange, 507
Buffalo Bill's/defunct, 484
Bulkeley, Hunt, Willard, Hosmer, Meriam, Flint, 81
Burnished, burned-out, still burning as the year, 592
By a route obscure and lonely, 155
By the fierce flames of Love I'm in a sad taking, 52
By the road to the contagious hospital, 399
By the rude bridge that arched the flood, 74

Call the roller of big cigars, 374
Calm as that second summer which precedes, 305
childhood rememberances are always a drag, 810
Climbing the rutted path, the lights of town, 697
Color—Caste—Denomination—, 318
Complacencies of the peignoir, and late, 378
CONCENTRIC, 803
Constantly near you, I never in my entire, 397
Constantly risking absurdity/and death, 595

Dark an' stormy may come de wedder; 295
Daughters of Time, the hypocritic Days, 81
Dead poets stalk the air, 532
Death took my father. 673
Deep in a vale, a stranger now to arms, 28
Deep river, my home is over Jordan, 297
Did all the lets and bars appear, 193
Do not bathe her in blood, 676
Do not weep, maiden, for war is kind. 340
"Double flesh,/Double way; 621
Down valley a smoke haze, 741

Each year the court expands, 699
Eastern guard tower/glints in sunset; convicts rest, 755
Enough! Let this season end, 641
Entwined on the bed in the dark, 640
Euclid alone has looked on Beauty bare. 474
ever been kidnapped/by a poet, 811

Facing west from California's shores, 275
Fair flower, that dost so comely grow, 18
"Faith" is a fine invention, 310
Fame is a fickle food, 322

Farm boys wild to couple, 635
Fat black bucks in a wine-barrel room, 368
Fat-kneed god! Feeder of mangy leopards! 470
First, you think they are dead. 684
Flood-tide below me! I see you face to face! 282
Flowers through the window, 394
For love—I would/split open your head and put, 659
For three years, out of key with his time, 409
Free at las', free at las', 295
Frightened/by the sound of my own voice, 597
From across the stream, on the side of the opposite hill, 698
From my mother's sleep I fell into the State, 555
From stainless steel basins of water, 679
From the frantic weather into his creaking tomb, 732
Full of her long white arms and milky skin, 462

Gaily bedight,/A gallant knight, 167
gathered in inter-admiration, 532
gave proof through the night, 767
Give all to love;/Obey thy heart; 89
Give him the darkest inch your shelf allows, 329
Glass I've wanted to live, 599
Gone, I say and walk from church, 714
Gone the three ancient ladies, 522
Goodbye, lady in Bangor, who sent me, 694
Good-bye my Fancy! 273
Good-bye, proud world! I'm going home: 92
Good Friday was the day, 198
Grim monarch! see, deprived of vital breath, 35

Half of my life is gone, and I have let, 105
Hanging from the beam, 192
Hangs./whipped/blood/striped, 757
Happy the man who, safe on shore, 22
Hard Rock was "known not to take no shit, 754
has not altered;—/a place as kind as it is green, 427
Hast thou named all the birds without a gun? 84
Have you heard of the wonderful one-hoss shay, 143
Hazard's friend Elliot is homosexual. Prodigious, 607
Hear the sledges with the bells—, 161
He crawls to the edge of the foaming creek, 740
He disagrees with Simone de Beauvoir, 608
He had need of a way, 601
He is not here, the old sun, 382
Helen, thy beauty is to me, 149

Her body is not so white as, 395
Here I am, an old man in a dry month, 434
Here is the place; right over the hill, 112
Here lies a lady of beauty and high degree. 458
"Here's Cooper, who's written six volumes to show,* (Cooper), 186
Here they are. The soft eyes open. 633
Here, where the red man swept the leaves away, 303
Here where the wind is always north-northeast, 336
He saw her from the bottom of the stairs, 346
His place is before, not in, the National Gallery, 620
History has to live with what was here, 594
Hog Butcher for the World, 362
"Hope" is the thing with feathers–, 312
However we wrangled with Britain awhile, 27
How it feels to be touching, 780
How many dawns, chill from his rippling rest, 487
How strange it seems! These Hebrews in their graves, 103
How this woman came by the courage, how she got, 550

I am a book I neither wrote nor read, 548
–I am a gentleman in a dust coat trying, 458
I am a parcel of vain strivings tied, 178
I am in the tub with my body. 731
I am the people–the mob–the crowd–the mass. 363
I am thinking of tents and tentage, tents through the ages. 616
I am trying to imagine, 726
I cannot find my way: there is no star, 330
i carry your heart with me(i carry it in, 480
I celebrate myself, and sing myself, 200
I come back to the cottage in, 518
I could bring You Jewels–had I a mind to–, 317
I doubt not God is good, well-meaning, kind, 504
I drank cool water from the fountain, 705
I dreamed you were my child, and I had come, 696
I dream my love goes riding out, 515
I felt a Funeral, in my Brain, 312
If ever two were one, then surely we. 1
I found a dimpled spider, fat and white, 351
If the red slayer think he slays, 74
If there exists a hell–the case is clear–, 23
If when my wife is sleeping, 398
If you want my apartment, sleep in it, 650
I go digging for clams once every two or three years, 615
I had eight birds hatched in one nest, 1
I have been one acquainted with the night. 354

I have been warned. It is more than thirty years since I wrote–, 424
I have done it again./One year in every ten, 749
I have eaten/the plums, 400
I have gone out, a possessed witch, 714
I have no brother. They who meet me now, 174
I have watched your fingers drum, 632
I heard a Fly buzz–when I died–, 316
I heard the trailing garments of the Night, 93
I kening through Astronomy Divine, 13
I knew a woman, lovely in her bones, 528
I like a church; I like a cowl; 77
I like a look of Agony, 311
I live but in the present,–where art thou? 171
Ill lay he long, upon this last return, 549
I'll tell you how the Sun rose–, 314
I love the old melodious lays, 139
Imagine it, a Sophocles complete, 569
I make a pact with you, Walt Whitman–, 406
I'm Nobody! Who are you? 313
I must tell you/this young tree, 394
In a branch of a willow hid, 20
In a dark time, the eye begins to see, 529
In a field/I am the absence, 760
In all the good Greek of Plato, 460
In Breughel's great picture, The Kermess, 401
I never lost as much but twice, 307
I never saw a Moor–, 320
In Goya's greatest scenes we seem to see, 597
In Heaven a spirit doth dwell, 169
In June, amid the golden fields, 510
Ink runs from the corners of my mouth. 761
In May, when sea winds pierced our solitudes, 75
In my grandmother's house there was always chicken soup, 646
In 1915 my grandfather's, 800
In secret place where once I stood, 4
Inside the brain they are holding a mass funeral for the, 707
In silent night when rest I took, 7
In spite of all the learned have said, 32
In that hotel my life, 512
In the desert/I saw a creature, naked, bestial, 337
In the greenest of our valleys, 153
In the late winter/I sometimes glimpse bits of steam, 691
In the long, sleepless watches of the night, 110
In the Rue Monsieur le Prince, 545
In the village churchyard she lies, 102

In this city how many masters are clouds. Just over the roofs–, 543
In unplowed Maine he sought the lumberers' gang, 79
I pace the sounding sea-beach and behold, 101
I placed a jar in Tennessee, 382
I place these numbed wrists to the pane, 802
I reason, Earth is short–, 313
I remember the neckcurls, limp and damp as tendrils; 525
I sat beside the glowing grate, fresh heaped, 62
I sat on the Dogana's steps, 417
I saw a ship of martial build, 195
I saw him forging link by link his chain, 175
I saw the best minds of my generation destroyed by madness, 662
I saw the spot where our first parents dwelt; 173
I see them,—crowd on crowd they walk the earth, 174
I shall forget you presently, my dear, 476
I shall never get you put together entirely, 747
I sit and look out upon all the sorrows of the world, and upon, 263
I taste a liquor never brewed–, 310
i thank You God for most this amazing, 480
It is early, yet/Clear waves of heat, 672
It is portentous, and a thing of state, 372
"It is such a beautiful day I had to write you a letter, 688
It is the morning of our love. 581
It is the way of a pleasant path, 620
It is time to be old, 90
It is true, modern life is complicated. 627
It is your last day and hour and you are alone, 599
I, too, dislike it: there are things that are important beyond, 425
It's wonderful how I jog, 708
It was many and many a year ago, 168
It was not dying: everybody died, 554
I've known rivers:/I've known rivers ancient as the world and, 500
I wake to sleep, and take my waking slow. 527
I wanted to take a walk, 792
I will not toy with it nor bend an inch. 469
I will teach you my townspeople, 390

John Cabot, out of Wilma, once a Wycliffe, 580
Joshua fit de battle of Jericho, 297
Joy, shipmate, joy! 273
Just as my fingers on these keys, 376

Legree's big house was white and green. 364
Let the snake wait under, 403
Let us go then, you and I, 430

Life, friends, is boring. We must not say so. 549
Light on his pins,/upright on his hind legs, 565
Light-winged Smoke, Icarian bird, 177
Like thousands, I took just pride and more than just, 594
Listless he eyes the palisades, 196
Little thinks, in the field, yon red-cloaked clown, 76
Living in the earth-deposits of our history, 727
Living someplace else is wrong, 781
Locate *I/love you* some-/where in, 659
Lo! Death has reared himself a throne, 150
Looking for love, she read cookbooks, 805
Lots of truisms don't have to be repeated but there is, 502
Love at the lips was touch, 350
Love is not all: it is not meat nor drink, 474
love me with the left hand, 785

Make me, O Lord, thy Spining Wheele compleate. 12
Man looking into the sea, 426
Many red devils ran from my heart, 339
Many workmen/Built a huge ball of masonry, 338
Maud Muller on a summer's day, 115
Maud went to college, 578
Midwinter spring is its own season, 449
"Mine and yours;/Mine, not yours. 82
Mine eyes have seen the glory of the coming of the Lord: 299
Miniver Cheevy, child of scorn, 328
MOMMA MOMMA MOMMA/momma momma, 769
Moonlight washes the west side of the house, 606
Mother said to call her if the H bomb exploded, 539
Motion's the dead give away, 658
munching a plum on/the street a paper bag, 400
Musing on roses and revolutions, 561
My aunt! my dear unmarried aunt! 142
My body knows it will never bear children. 649
My candle burns at both ends; 476
My Daddy has paid the rent, 765
My father found it after the war—, 796
My father, his mouth full of nails, 794
My father in the night commanding No, 647
my father moved through dooms of love, 477
My food was pallid till I heard it ring, 631
My friend must be a Bird—, 308
My heart, I cannot still it, 189
My life, your light green eyes, 674
My lizard, my lively writher, 526

My long two-pointed ladder's sticking through a tree, 343
My madness is dear to me. 642
My name is Edgar Poe and I was born, 711
My old man's a white old man, 499
'My towers at last!'—/What meant the words, 465

Nature's first green is gold, 357
Nautilus Island's hermit, 590
"next to of course god america i, 482
Nodding, its great head rattling like a gourd, 520
No, no! Go from me. I have left her lately. 409
No place seemed farther than your death, 583
Not hell but a street, not, 717

O beautiful for spacious skies, 299
O Captain! my Captain! our fearful trip is done, 272
of bright cities/and citrus, 507
Of every vice pursued by those, 50
Often beneath the wave, wide from this ledge, 494
Often I think of the beautiful town, 95
Oft have I seen at some cathedral door, 98
O Future bards/chant from skull to heart to ass, 671
O generation of the thoroughly smug, 406
Oh fairest of the rural maids! 71
Oh, say, can you see, by the dawn's early light, 298
Oh, slow to smite and swift to spare, 73
Oh strong ridged and deeply hollowed, 403
Oh! that my young life were a lasting dream! 147
Old Age in his ailing, 199
Old Eben Flood, climbing alone one night, 330
Ole Abe (God bless 'is ole soul!), 293
Once upon a midnight dreary, while I pondered, weak and weary, 156
One day in the Library, 517
Only to have a grief, 722
On the beach at night alone, 276
O Thou bright jewel in my aim I strive, 38
Our lives are Swiss—, 308
Out of the bosom of the Air, 106
Out of the cradle endlessly rocking, 257
O wind, rend open the heat, 419

Passing through huddled and ugly walls, 361
Past exchanges have left orbits of rain around my face, 791
Paterson lies in the valley under the Passaic Falls, 404
people say they have a hard time, 765

People who have what they want are very fond of telling people, 501
Pigeons on the grass alas. 359
pity this busy monster,manunkind, 483
Poetry is the supreme fiction, madame, 387
Position is where you, 660
Prepare for death. But how can you prepare, 619
Prophet of the body's, 604

Quite unexpectedly as Vasserot, 472

Rainy skies, misty mountains, 517
Reading in Li Po/how "the peach blossom follows the water", 513
Removed from Europe's feuds, a hateful scene, 29
Right after her birth they crowded in, 764
Row after row with strict impunity, 496
Running through the thick wiry grasses to the pond where the, 542

Said, Pull her up a bit will you, Mac, I want to unload there. 539
Say it's an important event like this: 575
Science! true daughter of old Time thou art! 149
Seeds in a dry pod, tick, tick, tick, 325
Sex, as they harshly call it, 723
Sex floated like a moon, 649
She even thinks that up in heaven, 504
She fears him, and will always ask, 332
She had thought the studio would keep itself; 721
She is as in a field a silken tent, 350
She sang beyond the genius of the sea. 374
She's gone. She was my love, my moon or more. 701
She sits with one hand poised against her head, the, 724
she's the camera's/subject: 807
Should I get married? Should I be good? 733
Show the runner coming through the shadows, 798
Since *Shylock's* book has walk'd the circles *here*, 30
Since you ask, most days I cannot remember. 715
Skirting the river road, (my forenoon walk, my rest,), 277
Sleep sweetly in your humble graves, 304
Snow falling and night falling fast, oh, fast, 355
So fallen! so lost! the light withdrawn, 114
So hard for women to believe each other. 781
"Sombra?"/he asked us from his little booth. And shade, 530
Some say the world will end in fire, 357
Something there is that doesn't love a wall, 342
so much depends/upon, 392
Sorrow is my own yard, 396

Southeast, and storm, and every weathervane, 464
So we are taking off our masks, are we, and keeping, 675
Spring is like a perhaps hand, 479
Spring is the Period, 318
Standing there they began to grow skins, 762
Stars wheel in purple, yours is not so rare, 420
steps out/from a lily, 506
Sticks-in-a-drowse droop over sugary loam, 523
Stomach of goat, crushed, 709
Stranger, if thou hast learned a truth which needs, 56
Stranger! Tell the people of Spoon River two things: 326
Success is counted sweetest, 307
Suppose we are standing together a minute, 763
Surgeons must be very careful, 308
Sweet heart,/A morning, climbing in its brass, 563
Sweet sweet sweet sweet sweet tea. 358
Swift to the western bounds of this wide land, 176

Take this kiss upon the brow! 148
Tell all the Truth but tell it slant–, 320
Tell me not, in mournful numbers, 94
Tenderness, ache on me, and lay your neck, 637
That it should end in an Albert Pick hotel, 654
That the glass would melt in heat, 384
The ache of marriage: 643
The age/requires this task: 560
The apparition of these faces in the crowd; 408
The artist must leave these woods now. 614
the back wings/of the, 401
The Bone that has no Marrow, 321
The broken pillar of the wing jags from the clotted shoulder, 422
the Cambridge ladies who live in furnished souls, 485
The city sparrow is the color of a dirty tree; 625
The debt is paid,/The verdict said, 85
The dirty money and the sleazy hearts, 531
The eagles gather on the place of death, 172
The earth keeps some vibration going, 324
The earth will be going on a long time, 516
Thee for my recitative, 274
The embodiment of what, 639
The eyes open to a cry of pulleys, 628
The fog comes/on little cat feet. 360
The good gray guardians of art, 630
The green-blue ground, 402
The green catalpa tree has turned, 680

The groves were God's first temples. Ere man learned, 58
The hand and foot that stir not, they shall find, 172
The hands that eased my mother's labor drew, 784
The heavy bear who goes with me, 547
The ice age is here. 722
The interests of a black man in a cellar, 487
The Irish have the thickest ankles in the world, 552
The Irish lady can say, that to-day is every day. 358
The lords of life, the lords of life,–, 83
The man who married Magdalene, 644
The Milky Way/above, the milky, 613
The miller's wife had waited long, 335
The mind is a city like London, 546
The moon is at her full, and, riding high, 72
The mysteries remain,/I keep the same, 421
The oaks, how subtle and marine, 519
The pennycandystore beyond the El, 596
The people along the sand, 352
The poem of the mind in the act of finding, 389
The Pool Players. 579
"There comes Emerson first, whose rich words, every one,* (Emerson), 182
"There comes Poe, with his raven, like Barnaby Rudge,* (Poe), 187
There he was–having spent, 572
There is a kind of lace laid over the City, a lightness, 744
There is a singer everyone has heard, 353
"There is Bryant, as quiet, as cool, and as dignified,* (Bryant), 183
"There is Hawthorne, with genius so shrinking and rare,* (Hawthorne), 185
"There is Lowell, who's striving Parnassus to climb,* (Lowell), 188
There is no Frigate like a Book, 321
There was a child went forth every day, 290
There was such speed in her little body, 457
The sad seamstress/who stays with us this month, 535
The saints are gathering at the real, 656
The saris go by me from the embassies. 556
These are the gardens of the Desert, these, 65
The skies they were ashen and sober; 164
The snow had begun in the gloaming, 190
The Soul selects her own Society–, 314
The sufferance of her race is shown, 197
The sun that brief December day, 119
The tide rises, the tide falls, 110
The turtle lives 'twixt plated decks, 501
The velocity with which they write–, 545
The way a crow/Shook down on me, 349

The whiskey on your breath, 526
The witch that came (the withered hag), 356
The woman is perfected. 753
The wonderful workings of the world: wonderful, 657
The world is/not with us enough. 642
The worst side of it all–, 686
They crucified my Lord, an' He never said a mumbalin' word; 296
They eat beans mostly, this old yellow pair. 579
The young Endymion sleeps Endymion's sleep; 101
Thine eyes shall see the light of distant skies; 70
Thin little leaves of wood fern, ribbed and toothed, 302
This *Indian weed*, that once did grow, 30
This is my letter to the World, 315
This is the time of year, 537
This urge, wrestle, resurrection of dry sticks, 523
Thou blossom bright with autumn dew, 65
Thou, born to sip the lake or spring, 19
Though loath to grieve, 86
Thou ill-formed offspring of my feeble brain, 11
Thou sorrow, venom elf; 16
Thou wast that all to me, love, 160
Thou, who wouldst wear the name, 69
To give up everything . . . , 623
To him who in the love of Nature holds, 53
To make me do the thing I will, I won't. 625
To sing of wars, of captains, and of kings, 9
To speak in a flat voice, 702
To speak out clean./Let the words be, 728
To western woods, and lonely plains, 25
Tree at my window, window tree. 353
Tribute to Henry Ford, 804
'Twas mercy brought me from my *Pagan* land, 36
Twirling your blue skirts, traveling the sward, 459
Two infants vis-à-vis, 541
Two liddle Niggers all dressed in white, (Raise a rucus, 294
Two little girls, one fair, one dark, 557
Two roads diverged in a yellow wood, 341

u feel that way sometimes, 807
Under a sky studded with asterisks, 742
Under the mountain, as when first I knew, 301
Unseemly as a marvellous an astral renegade, 779
Up the reputable walks of old established trees, 682

Vigil strange I kept on the field one night; 281

Waiting is the poem of waiting. 720
Washing Kai in the sauna, 738
We all scream, most of us inside. 624
We are talking in bed. You show me snapshots. 654
We have all been in rooms, 634
Welcome, grinned Henry, welcome, fifty-one! 551
We raise de wheat, 293
We remember you/calling America, 800
We sat within the farm-house old, 106
We say the sea is lonely; better say, 607
We were very tired, we were very merry—, 473
What a thrill—/My thumb instead of an onion. 748
What does love look like? We know, 610
What do we know of what is behind us? 639
Whatever it is, it must have, 644
What had you been thinking about, 687
"What! Irving? thrice welcome, warm heart and fine brain,* (Irving), 188
What is happening to me now that loved faces, 651
What is it now with me, 689
What lips my lips have kissed, and where, and why, 475
What should we be without the sexual myth, 388
What since August, when the sound, 717
What's the railroad to me? 177
What thoughts I have of you tonight, Walt Whitman, for, 670
What was it like, that country house? You never knew at all. 544
When Abraham Lincoln was shoveled into the tombs, he forgot the, 360
When beechen buds begin to swell, 55
When descends on the Atlantic, 108
Whenever Richard Cory went downtown, 327
"When I found where we had crashed, in the snow, the two of us, 763
When I heard the learn'd astronomer, 276
When in the mask of night there shone that cut, 611
When I see birches bend to left and right, 344
When I see how high it is, 582
When lilacs last in the dooryard bloomed, 263
when my father had been dead a week, 704
When over the flowery, sharp pasture's, 393
When Spoon River became a ganglion, 326
When the summer fields are mown, 111
when we learn/or do not learn, 533
Where are Elmer, Herman, Bert, Tom and Charley, 323
Where is the world? not about. 540
Where long the shadows of the wind had rolled, 334
While an intrinsic ardor prompts to write, 34
While my hair was still cut straight across my forehead, 407

While this America settles in the mould of its vulgarity, heavily, 423
Whirl up, sea—/whirl your pointed pines, 419
Whither, midst falling dew, 57
Who are you, listening to me, who are you, 758
Whose woods these are I think I know. 354
Why should I keep holiday, 84
Wild Nights—Wild Nights! 311
With two white roses on her breasts, 505
Woof of the sun, ethereal gauze, 178
Work-table, litter, books and standing lamp, 593
Worthy art Thou, O Lord, of praise, 7
Wrap up in a blanket in cold weather and just read. 737

Ye Alps audacious, through the heavens that rise, 40
Ye elms that wave on Malvern Hill, 194
Ye sorrowing people! who from bondage fly, 175
yesterday, sitting/with you, eating, 785
You couldn't bear to grow old, but we grow old. 552
You have the ingredients on hand. 719
Your face broods from my table, Suicide. 551
Your mind and you are our Sargasso Sea, 408
Your nurse could only speak Italian, 585
Your subjects hope, dread Sire—, 35
You see them vanish in their speeding cars, 617
You've gotten in through the transom, 712
You who desired so much—in vain to ask—, 495
You would think the fury of aerial, 509